Lecture Notes in Computer Science   10799

Commenced Publication in 1973
Founding and Former Series Editors:
Gerhard Goos, Juris Hartmanis, and Jan van Leeuwen

More information about this series at http://www.springer.com/series/7412

Shin'ichi Satoh (Ed.)

Image and Video Technology

PSIVT 2017 International Workshops
Wuhan, China, November 20–24, 2017
Revised Selected Papers

 Springer

Editor
Shin'ichi Satoh
National Institute of Informatics
Tokyo
Japan

ISSN 0302-9743   ISSN 1611-3349 (electronic)
Lecture Notes in Computer Science
ISBN 978-3-319-92752-7   ISBN 978-3-319-92753-4 (eBook)
https://doi.org/10.1007/978-3-319-92753-4

Library of Congress Control Number: 2018944410

LNCS Sublibrary: SL6 – Image Processing, Computer Vision, Pattern Recognition, and Graphics

Cover illustration: Yellow Crane Pagoda, Wuhan. Photo by Reinhard Klette, Auckland, New Zealand

Printed on acid-free paper

This Springer imprint is published by the registered company Springer International Publishing AG
part of Springer Nature
The registered company address is: Gewerbestrasse 11, 6330 Cham, Switzerland

Preface

The 8th Pacific Rim Symposium on Image and Video Technology (PSIVT 2017), held in Wuhan, China, during November 20–24, 2017, was accompanied by a series of five high-quality workshops covering the full range of state-of-the-art research topics in image and video technology.

The workshops consisted of two full-day workshops and three half-day workshops and took place on November 21. Their topics ranged from well-established areas to novel current trends: human behavior analysis; educational cloud and image- and video-enriched cloud services; vision meets graphics; passive and active electro-optical sensors for aerial and space imaging; and computer vision and modern vehicles.

The workshops received 103 paper submissions (including dual submissions with the main conference) and 36 presentations were selected by the individual workshop committee, yielding an overall acceptance rate of 35%. The PSIVT 2017 workshop proceedings comprise a short introduction to each workshop and all workshop contributions arranged by each of the workshop organizers. We thank everyone involved in the remarkable programs, i.e., committees, reviewers, and authors, for their distinguished contributions. We hope that you will enjoy reading these contributions, which may inspire your research.

November 2017   Shin'ichi Satoh

Contents

Vision Meets Graphics

Passive and Active Electro-Optical Sensors for Areal and Space Imaging

Computer Vision and Modern Vehicles

Human Behaviour Analysis

Workshop on Human Behavior Analysis

With the rapid development of image and video technologies, it became possible to analyze human behavior via nonintrusive sensors. This endows computers with a capacity to understand what people are doing, the things they are interested in, their preference and personality in a nonintrusive manner. Human behavior analysis has long been a critical issue in developing human-centered multimedia interaction systems including affect-sensitive systems with educational goals, intelligent surveillance, gesture interaction system, and smart tutoring, etc.

This workshop received 18 submissions about using image and video technologies for human behavior analysis, including action and activity recognition, affect and attention analysis, social signal processing, face analysis, gestures interaction, intelligent surveillance, and smart tutoring. After a rigorous peer reviewing, this workshop accepted six submissions. The workshop was held on November 21, 2017, and all the accepted papers were presented.

Organization

Workshop Committee

Jingying Chen (Co-chair)	China Central Normal University, China
Dan Chen (Co-chair)	Wuhan University, China
Bernard Tiddeman	Aberystwyth University, UK
Suya You	University of Southern California, USA
Liyuan Li	Institute for Infocomm Research, Singapore
Joanna Kolodziej	University of Bielsko-Biała, Poland
Rajiv Ranjan	Newcastle University, UK
Xun Xu	National University of Singapore, Singapore
Jiayi Ma	Wuhan University, China
Changxin Gao	Huazhong University of Science and Technology, China
Quan Zhou	Nanjing University of Posts and Telecommunications, China
Jingang Yu	South China University of Technology, China
Bin Sun	University of Electronic Science and Technology of China, China
Leyuan Liu	China Central Normal University, China
Kun Zhang	China Central Normal University, China

Deep Transfer Feature
Based Convolutional Neural Forests
for Head Pose Estimation

Yuanyuan Liu, Zhong Xie, Xi Gong$^{(\boxtimes)}$, and Fang Fang

Faculty of Information Engineering, China University of Geosciences,
Wuhan 430074, China
gongxi_cug@126.com

Abstract. In real-world applications, factors such as illumination, occlusion, and poor image quality, etc. make robust head pose estimation much more challenging. In this paper, a novel deep transfer feature based on convolutional neural forest method (D-CNF) is proposed for head pose estimation. Deep transfer features are extracted from facial patches by a transfer network model, firstly. Then, a D-CNF is devised to integrate random trees with the representation learning from deep convolutional neural networks for robust head pose estimation. In the learning process, we introduce a neurally connected split function (NCSF) as the node splitting strategy in a convolutional neural tree. Experiments were conducted using public Pointing'04, BU3D-HP and CCNU-HP facial datasets. Compared to the state-of-the-art methods, the proposed method achieved much improved performance and great robustness with an average accuracy of 98.99% on BU3D-HP dataset, 95.7% on Pointing'04 and 82.46% on CCNU-HP dataset. In addition, in contrast to deep neural networks which require large-scale training data, our method performs well even when there are only a small amount of training data.

Keywords: Convolutional neural network · Random forest
Transfer network · Head pose estimation

1 Introduction

Head pose estimation is the key step in many computer vision applications, such as human computer interaction, intelligent robotics, face recognition, and recognition of visual focus of attention [14,28]. The existing techniques achieve satisfactory results in well-designed environments. In real-world applications, however, factors, such as illumination variation, occlusion, poor image quality, etc., make head pose estimation much more challenging [19,22]. Hence, we propose a deep transfer feature based convolutional neural forest (D-CNF) method to estimate head pose estimation in unconstrained environment.

© Springer International Publishing AG, part of Springer Nature 2018
S. Satoh (Ed.): PSIVT 2017, LNCS 10799, pp. 5 16, 2018.
https://doi.org/10.1007/978-3-319-92753-4_1

A general head pose estimation framework appeared in most of previous works can be divided into two major steps, one is the feature extraction and the other is classifier construction [13]. Extracting robust facial features and designing effective classifier are the two key factors in unconstrained head pose estimation. For feature extraction, based on different features, several methods for the problem can be briefly divided into two categories, facial local feature and facial global feature based methods. The former methods usually require high image resolution for facial local feature identification, such as eyes, eyebrows, nose or lips [13,27], etc. These methods can provide accurate recognition results relying on accurate detection of facial feature points and high quality images. The latter methods based on facial global feature usually use texture features from an entire face to estimate head poses [1,4,17], etc. It may be good for dealing with low resolution image but not robust to occlusion and illumination. In the real-life scene, the various illumination occlusion, low image resolution and wide scene make facial local feature extraction difficult. In order to extract robust high-level features for head pose estimation, we address the problem based on globe deep transfer feature representation.

For the head pose classifier construction, most of the traditional classifiers, such as Support vector machine (SVM), Random forest (RF), Bays classifier and convolutional neural network (CNN), together with some unsupervised learning techniques are employed in the head pose estimation [17,21,25]. Recent years, CNN and RF become popular learning algorithms for head pose estimation in some real-life applications. CNN has an ability to automatically learn high-level feature representations from raw image data [11,16,20,24,30]. CNN achieves huge success in face recognition [23] and object multi-classification [26]. However, a limit for CNN is that the learning procedure needs a large amount of datasets and GPUs [6,9,15]. RF is a popular method given their capability to handle large training datasets, high generalization power and speed, and easy implementation [2,3,5,7]. In this paper, we are interested in constructing an effective head pose classifier using a limited amount of image data with a hybrid deep convolution networks enhanced decision forest. Our method aims at improving both accuracy and efficiency. The pipeline of our proposed D-CNF is depicted in Fig. 1. The deep transfer feature is extracted by transfer CNN model to suppress the influence of illumination, occlusion, and low image resolution, firstly. Then, head poses are estimated by the trained D-CNF model.

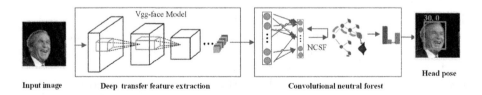

Input image   Deep transfer feature extraction   Convolutional neutral forest

Fig. 1. The pipeline of D-CNF for head pose estimation

Our contributions include the following:

1. We propose a deep transfer feature based convolutional neural forest method (D-CNF) for head pose estimation in unconstrained environment, which unifies classification trees with the representation learning from deep convolution networks, by training them in an end-to-end way.
2. We introduce a neurally connected split function (NCSF) as new split node learning in a D-CNF tree. The D-CNF method can achieve fast and accurate recognized results in the limited amount of image data, rather than a large amount of data by CNN.
3. We propose a robust deep transfer feature representation based on a pre-trained CNN model.

The rest of this paper is organized as follows: Sect. 2 presents our D-CNF method in details. Section 3 discusses the experimental results using publicly available datasets. Section 4 concludes this paper with a summary of our method.

2   Deep Transfer Feature Based Convolution Neural Forests for Head Pose Estimation

In this section, we address the D-CNF approach for head pose estimation in unconstrained environment. First, we present robust deep feature representation based on facial patches, which can reduce the influence of various noises, such as over-fitting, illumination, low image resolution, etc. Then, we describe the framework of D-CNF training procedure for head pose estimation in details. Finally, we give the D-CNF prediction for head pose estimation in unconstrained environment.

2.1   Deep Transfer Feature Representation

We extract deep transfer feature from facial patches with a pre-trained CNN model, i.e., Vgg-face [23]. We employ the Vgg-face architecture that is pre-trained with the LFW and YTF face datasets [23] to derive deep high-level feature representation, as shown in Fig. 2. The model includes 13 convolution layers, 5 max-pooling layers, and 3 fully connected layers. The deep transfer feature is described as:

$$y^j = \max(0, \sum_i x^i w^{i,j} + b^j), \tag{1}$$

where y^j is the jth output feature value of the first fully connected layer, x^i is the ith feature map of the last convolution layer, $w^{i,j}$ indicates the weight between the ith feature map and the jth output feature value, and b^j donates the bias of the jth output feature value. The deep transfer feature is used to train a two-layer network through back propagation, which can transfer the original Vgg-face feature to the pose feature.

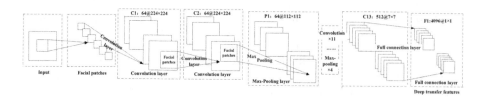

Fig. 2. The structure of pre-trained CNN network for deep feature representation. The trained network model includes 13 convolution layers, 5 max-pooling layers, and 3 full connection layers. In our work, we extract deep features from facial patches on the first connection layer.

2.2   D-CNF Training

In this paper, we propose a fast and efficient D-CNF method for robust head pose estimation on limit training sets, which is unifies classification trees with the representation learning from deep convolution networks, by training them in end-to-end way. The training of a traditional decision tree of a random forest (RF) consists in a recursive procedure, which starts from the root and iteratively builds the tree by splitting nodes [2]. The proposed D-CNF is also an ensemble of convolution neural trees, where split nodes are computed by the proposed neural connected split function (NCSF). The proposed NCSF can improve the learning capability of splitting node by deep neural learning representation, thus to improve the discrimination and efficiency of a tree. The detail training procedure is given as below.

Learning Splitting Nodes by NCSF. For facial patches, we extract a set of deep transfer features P, $P = \{P_i\}$ and $P_i = \{y^j\}$. We propose a NCSF-f_n to reinforce the learning capability of a splitting node by deep neural learning representation. Each output of f_n is brought in correspondence with a splitting node $d_n(P_i; Y)$,

$$d_n(P; Y) = \sigma(f_n(P; Y)), \tag{2}$$

where $\sigma(x) = (1 + e^{-x})^{-1}$ is the sigmoid function and Y is the decision node parametrization.

We employ a Stochastic Gradient Descent (SGD) approach to minimize the risk with respect to Y:

$$Y^{(t+1)} = Y^{(t)} - \frac{\eta}{|B|} \sum_{(P,\pi) \in B} \frac{\partial L}{\partial Y}(Y^{(t)}, \pi; P), \tag{3}$$

where $\eta > 0$ is the learning rate, π is facial expression label and B is a random subset (a.k.a. mini-batch) of samples. The gradient with respect to Y is obtained by chain rule as follows:

$$\frac{\partial L(Y, \pi; P)}{\partial Y} = \sum_{n \in N} \frac{\partial L(Y, \pi; P)}{\partial f_n(P; Y)} \cdot \frac{\partial f_n(P; Y)}{\partial Y}. \tag{4}$$

Hence, the gradient term that depends on the neutral decision tree is

$$\frac{\partial L(Y, \pi; P)}{\partial f_n(P; Y)} = -(d_n^{N_r}(P; Y) + d_n^{N_l}(P; Y)), \tag{5}$$

where given a node N in a tree and N_r and N_l denote its right and left child, respectively.

To split a node, Information Gain (IG) is maximized:

$$\tilde{\varphi} = \arg\max_{\varphi}(H(d_n) - \sum_{S \in \{N_r, N_l\}} \frac{|d_n^S|}{|d_n|}(H(d_n))), \tag{6}$$

where $\frac{|d_n^S|}{|d_n|}, s \in \{N_r, N_l\}$ is the ratio between the number of samples in $d_n^{N_l}$ (arriving at the left child node), set $d_n^{N_r}$ (arriving at the right child node), and $H(d_n)$ is the entropy of d_n.

Learning Leaf Nodes. Create a leaf l when IG is below a predefined threshold or when a maximum depth is reached. Otherwise continue recursively for the two child nodes $d_n^{N_l}$ and $d_n^{N_r}$ at the splitting node step. For a leaf node in a conditional D-CNF tree, it stores the conditional multi-probability $p(\pi|\theta, y)$. Therefore, we simplify the distribution over head poses by a multivariate Gaussian Mixture Model (GMM) [17] as in:

$$p(\theta, l) = N(\theta; \overline{\theta}, \Sigma_l^{\theta}), \tag{7}$$

where $\overline{\theta}$ and Σ_l^{θ} are the mean and covariance of leaves' head pose probabilities, respectively.

2.3 D-CNF for Head Pose Estimation

This section provides the prediction procedure of the D-CNF for head pose estimation. Deep transfer feature patches pass through the trees in a trained D-CNF. All feature patches end in a set of leaves of the forest. In the leaves of a D-CNF forest, there are muti-probabilistic models of head poses. We simplify the distributions over multi-probabilities by adopting multivariate GMM as:

$$p(\theta|l) = N(\theta; \overline{\theta}, \Sigma_l^{\theta}), \tag{8}$$

where $\overline{\theta}$ and Σ_l^{θ} are the mean and covariance of leaves' head pose probabilities, respectively.

While Eq. 8 models the probability for a feature patch p_i ending in the leaf l of a single tree, the probability of the forest is obtained by averaging over all trees:

$$p(\theta|P) = \frac{1}{T} \sum_t p(\theta|l_t(P)) \tag{9}$$

where l_t is the corresponding leaf for the tree T_t, T is the number of trees in D-CNF.

3   Experimental Results

3.1   Datasets and Settings

To evaluate our approach, three challenging face datasets were used: Pointing'04 dataset [10], BU3D-HP dataset [31], and CCNU-HP dataset in the wide classroom [17]. These datasets were chosen since they contained unconstrained face images with poses ranging from $-90°$ to $+90°$. The Pointing'04 head pose dataset is a benchmark of 2790 monocular face images of 15 people with variations of yaw and pitch angles from $-90°$ to $+90°$. For every person, 2 series of 93 images (93 different poses) are available. The CCNU dataset was collected included an annotated set of 38 people with 75 different head poses from an overhead camera in the wide scene. It contains head poses spanning from $-90°$ to $90°$ in horizontal direction, and $-45°$ to $90°$ in vertical direction. The multi-view BU3D-HP database contains 100 people of different ethnicities, including 56 females and 44 males with variations of yaw angles from $-90°$ to $+90°$.

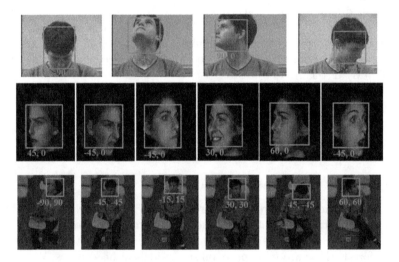

Fig. 3. The examples of head pose estimation on Pointing'04, BU3D-HP and CCNU-HP datasets. Top row: results of Pointing'04. Middle row: results of the BU3D-HP dataset. Bottom row: results of CCNU-HP dataset.

The examples of head pose estimation on Pointing'04, BU3D-HP and CCNU-HP datasets are shown in Fig. 3. The D-CNF method can achieve fast and accurate recognized results in limited amount of image data, rather than a large amount of data by CNN. Our method was trained with 2000 images from Pointing'04 dataset, 15498 images from BU3D-HP dataset and 2121 images from CCNU-HP dataset. In evaluation, we used 870 images from Pointing'04 dataset, 5166 images from BU3D-HP dataset and 707 images from CCNU-HP dataset. The experiments were conducted in a PC with Intel(R) Core(TM) i7-6700 CPU@

4.00 GHz, RAM 32 GB, NVIDIA GeForce GTX 1080 (2). We use the Caffe framework [12] for the transfer CNN and deep feature representation.

3.2   Experiments on Pointing'04 Datasets

Figure 4 shows the head poses estimation results on Pointing'04 datasets in yaw and pitch rotations, respectively. The average accuracy on 9 yaw head poses and 9 pitch head poses is 95.6%. As it is shown, the highest accuracy is 98.4% of 90° in the yaw rotation. The lowest accuracy is 92.6% of −45° in the pitch rotation, due to more occlusion in a face area.

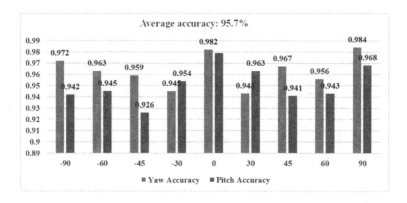

Fig. 4. Head pose estimation on Pointing'04 datasets in the yaw and pitch rotations

In comparison with the state-of-the-art head pose estimation methods, we conducted experiments using the MSHF [18], Multivariates label distribution (MLD-wj) [29], CNN(6convs+2fc) [15], multi-class SVM (M-SVM) [22] and HF [8] on Pointing'04 head pose dataset. The same training and testing datasets were used, and we employed a 4-fold cross-validation. Table 1 lists the average accuracy and error across using these methods. MLD-wj [29], CNN [15] and HF [8] yielded comparable results with an accuracy of approximately 70% in yaw and pitch rotations. MLD-wj [29] proposed to associate a multivariate label distribution to each image for head pose estimation in yaw and pitch rotations. MSHF [18] proposed a hybrid structure hough forest to 25 class head pose estimation and achieved the second highest accuracy of 84%. HF [8] improved random forests with Hough voting for real-time head pose estimation. M-SVM [22] produced similar accuracy in the range of 60%. Our proposed D-CNF exhibited the best performance with the accuracy of 95.7% in yaw and pitch rotations. In addition, the standard deviation of D-CNF indicates that D-CNF achieved the greatest consistency with a smallest STD. It is evidential that our D-CNF improved the head pose estimation with great robustness.

Table 1. Accuracy (%) and average error (in degrees) using different methods on Pointing'04 dataset.

Methods	Yaw	Pitch	Yaw + Pitch	STD
MSHF [18]	92.3	90.7	84.0	3.5
MLD-wj [29]	84.30	86.24	72.3	4.9
CNN [15]	83.52	86.94	71.83	5.5
HF [8]	82.3	84.86	70.54	5.2
SVM [22]	80.6	82.5	60.46	5.7
D-CNF	99.05	94.36	95.7	0.8

3.3 Experiments on Multi-view BU3D-HP Dataset

Each image in the BU3D-HP dataset is automatically annotated with one out of the nine head pose labels ($\{-90°, -60°, -45°, -30°, 0°, +30°, +60°, +75°, 90°\}$). We train a D-CNF of 50 neural trees using 15498 head pose images. Figure 5 shows the confusion matrix of head pose estimation on BU3D-HP dataset. The D-CNF estimated 9 head pose classes in the horizontal direction and achieved the average accuracy of 98.99%. Examples of the estimated head pose are shown in Fig. 3.

	-90	-60	-45	-30	0	30	45	60	90
-90	1	0		0	0	0	0	0	0
-60	0.0087	0.9878	0.0174	0	0	0	0	0	0.0017
-45	0	0.0157	0.9808	0.0017	0	0.0017	0	0	0
-30	0.0017	0	0.0052	0.993	0	0	0	0	0
0	0	0	0	0	0.9965	0.0017	0	0	0.0017
30	0	0	0	0	0	0.9913	0.007	0.0174	0
45	0	0	0	0	0	0.0105	0.9774	0.0122	0
60	0	0	0	0	0	0	0.0139	0.9843	0.0017
90	0	0	0	0	0	0	0	0.0017	0.9983

Fig. 5. Confusion matrix of head pose estimation on BU3D-HP dataset.

The average accuracy of our D-CNF method is compared with that of CNN, Zheng GSRRR [33], and SIFT + CNN [32] in Table 2. The CNN in this experiment contains three convolution layers followed by three max-pooling layers and two fully connected layers. Each filter is of size 5×5 and there are 32, 64, and 128 such filters in the first three layers, respectively. The input images are rescaled to 224 by 224.

The accuracy of the CNN on BU3D-HP dataset is 69.61% as presented in Table 2. The accuracies achieved with SIFT using algorithms proposed in [32, 33] are 87.36% and 92.26%, respectively. Our method achieves 98.99% which is

Table 2. Accuracy (%) and STD using different methods on multi-view BU3D-HP dataset.

Methods	Features	Poses	Accuracy	STD.
CNN	Image	9	69.61	0.9
Zheng GSRRR [33]	Sparse SIFT	9	87.36	0.8
SIFT + CNN [32]	SIFT	9	92.26	0.7
D-CNF	Deep transfer feature	9	98.99	0.5

competitive to the methods above. The lowest STD. of 0.5% using our method also proved the robustness of the proposed D-CNF.

3.4   Experiments on CCNU-HP Dataset in the Wide Scene

In this case, we evaluated the proposed D-CNF on CCNU-HP dataset in the wide scene. For evaluation, a 4-fold cross-validation was conducted. In our experiments, we annotate the dataset into 5 classes in the yaw rotation as Fig. 6(a) and 4 classes in the pitch rotation as Fig. 6(b). The final classified classes are 20 categories in the wide scene dataset.

(a) The annotation categories of the yaw angels. The first row are the yaw angles in
      the dataset and the second row are the annotation class,

(b) The annotation categories of the pitch angels. The first row are the pitch angles
      in the dataset and the second row are the annotation class.

Fig. 6. The annotation categories of the yaw and pitch angels in the experiments. (a) The annotation classes in the yaw rotation, (b) The annotation classes in the yaw rotation.

Figure 7 shows the confusion matrixs of head pose estimation on CCNU-HP dataset in the yaw and pitch rotations, respectively. The D-CNF achieved the average accuracy of 88.54% in the yaw rotation and 76.38% in the more challenging pitch rotation. Examples of the estimated head pose are shown in Fig. 3.

Table 3 lists the average accuracy and error across on more challenging CCNU-HP datasets using four state-of-the-art methods. The average accuracy of the CNN on CCNU-HP dataset is 59.52% as presented in Table 3. The second highest accuracy is achieved 77.9% with combined features using D-RF method. Our method achieves 82.46% which is competitive to the methods above.

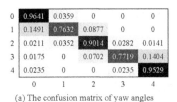

(a) The confusion matrix of yaw angles   (b) The confusion matrix of pitch angles

Fig. 7. Confusion matrixs of head pose estimation on CCNU-HP dataset. (a) The matrix of yaw angles, (b) The matrix of pitch angles.

Table 3. Accuracy (%) using different methods on CCNU-HP dataset.

Methods	Features	Yaw	Pitch	Yaw + Pitch
CNN	Image	65.25	53.79	59.52
Gabor + RF	Gabor	75.42	67.57	71.5
D-RF [17]	Combined features	85.6	70.19	77.90
D-CNF	Deep transfer feature	88.54	76.38	82.46

4   Conclusion

This paper described a novel deep transfer feature based convolutional neural enhanced forests (D-CNF) method for head pose estimation in unconstrained environment. In this method, robust deep transfer features are extracted from facial patches using transfer CNN model, firstly. Then, the D-CNF integrates random trees with the representation learning from deep convolutional neural networks for head pose estimation. Besides, a neural connected split function (NCSF) is introduced to D-CNF to split node learning. Finally, a prediction procedure of the trained D-CNF can classify head pose in unconstrained environment. Our method can perform well in limit number of datasets owing to transferring pre-trained CNN to fast decision node splitting in a Random Forest. The experiments demonstrate that our method has remarkable robustness and efficiency.

Experiments were conducted using public Pointing'04, BU3D-HP and CCNU-HP datasets. Our results demonstrated that the proposed deep feature outperformed the other popular image features. Compared to the state-of-the-art methods, the proposed D-CNF achieved improved performance and great robustness with an average accuracy of 98.99% on BU3D-HP dataset, 95.7% on Pointing'04 dataset, and 82.46% on CCNU-HP dataset. The average time for performing a head pose estimation is about 113 ms.

Compared to CNN method from popular deep learning, our method achieved the greatest performance on limited number of datasets. In future, we plan to investigate on-line learning methods to achieve real-time estimation by integrating head movement tracking.

Acknowledgments. This work was supported by the National Natural Science Foundation of China (No. 61602429), China Postdoctoral Science Foundation (No. 2016M592406), and Research Funds of CUG from the Colleges Basic Research and Operation of MOE (No. 26420160055).

References

1. Ahn, B., Park, J., Kweon, I.S.: Real-time head orientation from a monocular camera using deep neural network. In: Cremers, D., Reid, I., Saito, H., Yang, M.-H. (eds.) ACCV 2014. LNCS, vol. 9005, pp. 82–96. Springer, Cham (2015). https://doi.org/10.1007/978-3-319-16811-1_6
2. Breiman, L.: Random forests. Mach. Learn. **45**(1), 5–32 (2001)
3. Bulo, S.R., Kontschieder, P.: Neural decision forests for semantic image labeling. In: IEEE Conference on Computer Vision and Pattern Recognition, pp. 81–88 (2014)
4. Chu, X., Ouyang, W., Li, H., Wang, X.: Structured feature learning for pose estimation. In: Proceedings of the IEEE Conference on Computer Vision and Pattern Recognition, pp. 4715–4723 (2016)
5. Dantone, M., Gall, J., Fanelli, G., Van Gool, L.: Real-time facial feature detection using conditional regression forests. In: 2012 IEEE Conference on Computer Vision and Pattern Recognition (CVPR), pp. 2578–2585. IEEE (2012)
6. Donahue, J., Jia, Y., Vinyals, O., Hoffman, J., Zhang, N., Tzeng, E., Darrell, T.: Decaf: a deep convolutional activation feature for generic visual recognition. In: ICML, vol. 32, 647–655 (2014)
7. Fanelli, G., Yao, A., Noel, P.-L., Gall, J., Van Gool, L.: Hough forest-based facial expression recognition from video sequences. In: Kutulakos, K.N. (ed.) ECCV 2010. LNCS, vol. 6553, pp. 195–206. Springer, Heidelberg (2012). https://doi.org/10.1007/978-3-642-35749-7_15
8. García-Montero, M., Redondo-Cabrera, C., López-Sastre, R., Tuytelaars, T.: Fast head pose estimation for human-computer interaction. In: Paredes, R., Cardoso, J.S., Pardo, X.M. (eds.) IbPRIA 2015. LNCS, vol. 9117, pp. 101–110. Springer, Cham (2015). https://doi.org/10.1007/978-3-319-19390-8_12
9. Girshick, R.: Fast r-cnn. In: Proceedings of the IEEE International Conference on Computer Vision, pp. 1440–1448 (2015)
10. Gourier, N., Hall, D., Crowley, J.: Estimating face orientation from robust detection of salient facial features in pointing. In: International Conference on Pattern Recognition Workshop on Visual Observation of Deictic Gestures, pp. 1379–1382 (2004)
11. Insafutdinov, E., Pishchulin, L., Andres, B., Andriluka, M., Schiele, B.: DeeperCut: a deeper, stronger, and faster multi-person pose estimation model. In: Leibe, B., Matas, J., Sebe, N., Welling, M. (eds.) ECCV 2016. LNCS, vol. 9910, pp. 34–50. Springer, Cham (2016). https://doi.org/10.1007/978-3-319-46466-4_3
12. Jia, Y., Shelhamer, E., Donahue, J., Karayev, S., Long, J., Girshick, R., Guadarrama, S., Darrell, T.: Proceedings of the 22nd ACM International Conference on Multimedia
13. Wu, J., Trivedi, M.M.: A two-stage head pose estimation framework and evaluation. Pattern Recogn. **41**, 1138–1158 (2008)
14. Kim, H., Sohn, M., Kim, D., Lee, S.: Kernel locality-constrained sparse coding for head pose estimation. IET Comput. Vis. **10**(8), 828–835 (2016)

15. Krizhevsky, A., Sutskever, I., Hinton, G.E.: ImageNet classification with deep convolutional neural networks. In: Advances in Neural Information Processing Systems, pp. 1097–1105 (2012)
16. Liu, X., Liang, W., Wang, Y., Li, S., Pei, M.: 3D head pose estimation with convolutional neural network trained on synthetic images. In: 2016 IEEE International Conference on Image Processing (ICIP), pp. 1289–1293. IEEE (2016)
17. Liu, Y., Chen, J., Shu, Z., Luo, Z., Liu, L., Zhang, K.: Robust head pose estimation using dirichlet-tree distribution enhanced random forests. Neurocomputing **173**, 42–53 (2016)
18. Liu, Y., Xie, Z., Yuan, X., Chen, J., Song, W.: Multi-level structured hybrid forest for joint head detection and pose estimation. Neurocomputing **266**, 206–215 (2017)
19. Ma, B., Li, A., Chai, X., Shan, S.: CovGa: a novel descriptor based on symmetry of regions for head pose estimation. Neurocomputing **143**, 97–108 (2014)
20. Mukherjee, S.S., Robertson, N.M.: Deep head pose: gaze-direction estimation in multimodal video. IEEE Trans. Multimedia **17**(11), 2094–2107 (2015)
21. Murphy-Chutorian, E., Trivedi, M.M.: Head pose estimation in computer vision: a survey. IEEE Trans. Pattern Anal. Mach. Intell. **31**(4), 607–626 (2009)
22. Orozco, J., Gong, S., Xiang, T.: Head pose classification in crowded scenes. In: British Machine Vision Conference, London, UK, pp. 1–3, 7–10 September 2009
23. Parkhi, O.M., Vedaldi, A., Zisserman, A.: Deep face recognition. In: BMVC, vol. 1, p. 6 (2015)
24. Patacchiola, M., Cangelosi, A.: Head pose estimation in the wild using convolutional neural networks and adaptive gradient methods. Pattern Recogn. **71**, 132–143 (2017)
25. Ranjan, R., Patel, V.M., Chellappa, R.: Hyperface: a deep multi-task learning framework for face detection, landmark localization, pose estimation, and gender recognition. arXiv preprint arXiv:1603.01249 (2016)
26. Rastegari, M., Ordonez, V., Redmon, J., Farhadi, A.: XNOR-Net: imagenet classification using binary convolutional neural networks. In: Leibe, B., Matas, J., Sebe, N., Welling, M. (eds.) ECCV 2016. LNCS, vol. 9908, pp. 525–542. Springer, Cham (2016). https://doi.org/10.1007/978-3-319-46493-0_32
27. Schwarz, A., Lin, Z., Stiefelhagen, R.: HeHOP: highly efficient head orientation and position estimation. In: 2016 IEEE Winter Conference on Applications of Computer Vision (WACV), pp. 1–8. IEEE (2016)
28. Wu, S., Kan, M., He, Z., Shan, S., Chen, X.: Funnel-structured cascade for multi-view face detection with alignment-awareness. Neurocomputing **221**, 138–145 (2017)
29. Xin, G., Xia, Y.: Head pose estimation based on multivariate label distribution. In: IEEE Conference on Computer Vision and Pattern Recognition, Ohio, USA, pp. 1837–1842, 24–27 June 2014
30. Xu, X., Kakadiaris, I.A.: Joint head pose estimation and face alignment framework using global and local CNN features. In: Proceedings of the 12th IEEE Conference on Automatic Face and Gesture Recognition, Washington, DC, vol. 2 (2017)
31. Yin, L., Wei, X., Sun, Y., Wang, J., Rosato, M.J.: A 3D facial expression database for facial behavior research. In: 2006 7th International Conference on Automatic Face and Gesture Recognition, FGR 2006, pp. 211–216. IEEE (2006)
32. Zhang, T., Zheng, W., Cui, Z., Zong, Y., Yan, J., Yan, K.: A deep neural network-driven feature learning method for multi-view facial expression recognition. IEEE Trans. Multimedia **18**(12), 2528–2536 (2016)
33. Zheng, W.: Multi-view facial expression recognition based on group sparse reduced-rank regression. IEEE Trans. Affect. Comput. **5**(1), 71–85 (2014)

Biometric System Based on Registration of Dorsal Hand Vein Configurations

Szidónia Lefkovits[1](✉), Simina Emerich[2], and László Szilágyi[3]

[1] Department of Computer Science,
"Petru Maior" University of Tîrgu-Mureş, Tîrgu-Mureş, Romania
szidonia.lefkovits@science.upm.ro
[2] Department of Communication,
Technical University of Cluj-Napoca, Cluj-Napoca, Romania
[3] Department of Electrical Engineering, Sapientia University of Tîrgu-Mureş,
Tîrgu-Mureş, Romania

Abstract. In this paper we present a biometric system based on dorsal hand vein recognition. The preprocessing steps are tuned for image similar or captured with the same scanner as used for the creation of NCUT database. Image quality was improved according to the segmentation method applied. A coarse segmentation technique based on ordinal image encoding has been proposed to determine the significant parts of the vein skeleton. The vein skeleton obtained is the basis of an accurate image registration. The current work shall prove that the geometric attributes of the segmented vascular network are a solid basis for the dorsal hand vein registration process. The designed authentication system is based on the similarity of registered images applying the k-NN classification. A novel and promising similarity method capable of measuring the distance between two point sets, which have comparable visual aspects, has been introduced. The system was evaluated on the NCUT database. The experimental approach shows that the geometric attributes proposed can reach high performances (near 100% accuracy on the considered database).

1 Introduction

Nowadays biometric authentication systems are becoming more and more important. There are several biometrics-based identification methods, such as face, iris, vein, fingerprint [18] and DNA recognition [11]. In this article we place emphasis on vein-based biometric systems. These systems can be considered more secure because they assume a living human being in whom the vascular system is unique and stable. Technically, the dorsal hand vein is the easiest compared to finger vein, palm vein or other vein pattern acquisitions. It is usually done via Near Infrared (NIR) or Far Infrared (FIR) cameras which do not highlight the vein part from the skin and produce low-quality and low-contrast greyscale images. Vein-based approaches can be classified into three categories: geometry-based methods, holistic methods and local aspect-based methods. Geometry-based methods use the vascular structure information, extracting line or curve

© Springer International Publishing AG, part of Springer Nature 2018
S. Satoh (Ed.): PSIVT 2017, LNCS 10799, pp. 17–29, 2018.
https://doi.org/10.1007/978-3-319-92753-4_2

features and measuring different types of distances or angles like Hausdorff distance [9] or Line Segment Hausdorff distance [2]. In case of vessel detection, the vein is approximated by multiple segments of lines that are detected with Hough transform. The disadvantage of these methods is the need of registered images.

Holistic methods consider the dorsal part of the hand as a whole. These are Principal Component Analysis (PCA) [14], Fisher Linear Discriminant [5] and Independent Component Analysis (ICA) [19]. The region of interest in a hand is resized, registered and aligned. The registration is based on local invariant features. In this sense the most used interest points are SIFT (Scale Invariant Feature Transform) [6], SURF (Speed-Up Robust Features) [10] and Hessian-Laplace interest points [7].

Local aspect methods are based on descriptors like LBP (Locally Binary Pattern) [16], HOG (Histogram of Oriented Gradients) [21], Gabor wavelets [20], OGM (Oriented Gradient Maps) [3] etc.

Our approach may be included in geometry-based methods. It begins with a course hand vein segmentation based on a fast ordinal image encoding which allows an easy image registration. The proposed similarity distance combined with the k-NN (k-Nearest Neighbour) classification accomplishes a highly accurate biometric identification.

This paper is organized as follows: after a short introduction of similar systems in the literature, the database employed in the experimental setup is presented (Sect. 2), followed by the detailed description of the proposed biometric system (Sect. 3). In this section we shall place emphasis on inhomogeneity correction Sect. 3.1, image registration Sect. 3.4 and similarity evaluation Sect. 3.6. Finally, our experiments and results are presented in Sect. 4, followed by the conclusion and future work.

2   The Database

The proposed approach is evaluated on the North China University of Technology (NCUT) Part A [15] dorsal hand vein dataset. It is considered to be the largest publicly available database used for validating dorsal hand vein image recognition systems. The NCUT database contains 2040 NIR images of dorsal hand veins from the left and right hands of 102 individuals (10 samples for each hand). Due to the low-cost acquisition equipment this database contains low-quality images with a high noise level. All photos were taken by the same dorsal hand scanner, resulting in roughly aligned images. There are only small changes in rotation, translation and illumination. We can observe more significant changes in viewpoint variation because of the hand rotation around the handle of the scanner considered to be the Ox axis of the images. The NIR intensity is stable, but there is a circular variation in illumination from the centre to the margins. Thus, some veins near the margins are difficult to distinguish and vein pixel intensities are sometimes similar to skin pixels intensities. The acquisition equipment through the NIR camera determined the low contrast with a resolution of 640×480 pixels on an 8-bit greyscale image. Moreover the dorsal hand occupies only about half of the available area and there are only 80 integer intensity values in the range of $[101, 180]$.

3   The Proposed System

An IR dorsal hand vein-based authentication system is presented in this section. The proposed system is worked out on the previously described NCUT database, Part A. It consists of the following six stages: (1) inhomogeneity correction, (2) preprocessing, (3) vein extraction, (4) vein registration, (5) similarity evaluation and (6) classification (Fig. 1).

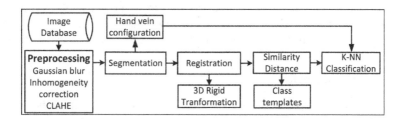

Fig. 1. Block diagram of the proposed approach

3.1   Inhomogeneity Correction

By analysing the database images, we can notice a variation in intensity on the captured hand surface. The central part of the hands is much more illuminated compared to the margins. The illumination varies smoothly across the image in such a manner that the intensities of the veins are very similar to the intensities of the skin, and thus some veins can be difficult to distinguish from the background. This non-uniform intensity is due to poor IR illumination and the short distance between hand and camera. In such cases, the performance of automatic segmentation is significantly weakened. To obtain accurate vein segmentation we must reduce the effect of non-uniform illumination. The variation in illumination can be modelled by a smooth multiplicative field. Consider the multiplicative model

$$u(x) = v(x) \cdot f(x) + n(x), \tag{1}$$

where $u(x)$ is the captured pixel intensity at location x, $v(x)$ is the real pixel intensity, $f(x)$ is an unknown smoothly varying intensities, called bias field (intensities around 1) and $n(x)$ is white Gaussian noise assumed to be independent of $f(x)$. The problem of compensating for varying illuminations is the task of estimating $f(x)$. This problem has several solutions; we adopted the N3 inhomogeneity correction algorithm, which is one of the most efficient ways of correcting these kinds of artefacts [13].

3.2   Preprocessing

Inhomogeneity correction is followed by preprocessing. First, Gaussian blur was used to filter the discrete intensity values to smooth continuous real intensity values. The role of this filter is smoothing of the sharp edges and eliminating noise of high frequency. The next step is the local contrast enhancement of the image. Due to the low-quality images and the restricted intensity range of grey levels, the application of a contrast enhancement technique is indispensable. The adaptive or local histogram equalization changes the intensity of every pixel by considering the surrounding region of a given size $(N \times N)$, and computes the *pdf* (probability density function) and *cdf* (cumulative distribution function) based on N^2 pixels [22]. The contrast limitation reduces the drastic increase of the *pdf* and *cdf* functions. Cutting down the histogram at a certain value will amplify only values lower than a given limit (L). Contrast-limiting parameter $(N \times N, L)$ should be experimentally determined to obtain good contrast correction.

3.3   Vein Segmentation

The vascular pattern extraction represents a crucial stage and is further used in order to obtain segmented and labelled binary images (where the background is black and the extracted veins are white). The extraction procedure consists of two phases: the extraction of the vein profiles and their thinning, which gives us the medial axis of the vein. In order to extract veins of various width and intensity levels, our method examines the cross-sectional profile of the dorsal hand vein in a horizontal direction. Obviously, the veins are darker than the surrounding area of the hand and represent the local minima in a given region of interest. The cross-sectional profile of the veins consists of concave curves with large curvatures. A method similar to ours which considers the curvature maximums of the cross-sectional profile $(Pr_y(x))$ of finger veins is presented in [8]. The curvatures have to be computed where the derivate of profiles is 0 $(Pr_y'(x) = 0)$. The numerical definition of the derivate is

$$Pr_y'(x) = [Pr_y(x + h) - Pr_y(x - h)] / 2h, \tag{2}$$

where $h = 1$ pixel in discrete domain.

We considered the decreasing slope (Eq. 3a) and the increasing slope (Eq. 3b) to be the ordinal measure of the intensity variation. The decreasing slope is denoted by 0, the increasing slope by 255 and 128 otherwise (none of the Eqs. (3) are true). The values 128 represents the veins zones. The T threshold is fine-tuned to determine the real vein width.

$$Pr_y(x + h) - Pr_y(x) > T \quad \text{(3a)} \qquad Pr_y(x - h) - Pr_y(x) > T \quad \text{(3b) (3)}$$

To obtain the vein configuration in the entire image we compute the local minima for every sectional slice in the horizontal direction. The local minima is a section between a decreasing and increasing slope. The medial axis of the veins is obtained based on vein thinning using the morphological skeleton operation.

3.4   Vein Registration

We identified three important constraints in the registration: the inappropriate cropping of hand contours by cutting down the top and bottom margins of the hand produces an inadequate contour for the registration process; the low quality of the images makes it more difficult to determine the matching keypoints in the image pair required for good registration; the high level of image similarity keeps us from using correlation measures necessary for the determination of corresponding points. The goal of image registration is to align the input image to the existing templates by applying rigid spatial transformation of the input image onto the given template. The first image is the one analysed and the second is considered to be the template or reference image. In our system we have defined a template image for each person. The dorsal hand images from the NCUT database were recorded with the same NIR scanner, resulting in only slight changes regarding the rotation and translation in plane, but the spatial rotation of the hand around the Ox axis is much more important. With this in mind, we had to apply a 3D rigid transformation in order to register the hand images. The best-known methods for the block-matching of corresponding points, such as SIFT (Scale Invariant Feature Transform) or MSOP (Multi-Scale Oriented Patches), need higher pixel resolution and some distinguishable patches in order to obtain good image registration [17]. These methods can be very slow and the accuracy obtained is not good enough for our purposes. The main part of our system is a fast and accurate registration process which considers hand vein configuration. We used an automatic registration system of binary images representing the segmented veins of the dorsal hand.

We have only defined 3D rigid transformations in a limited range, according to the variation of the database. The rotation angles are evaluated in the frequency domain of log-polar images by using the Fourier shift theorem [12]. Likewise, the FFT (Fast Fourier Transform) of the registered images is used for fast calculation of the translation vectors based on the evaluation of the correlation. The goal of automatic registration is to maximize the correlation between the target and template images; therefore, almost all computations are made in the frequency domain, and we define an image set for each subject consisting of one template binary image corresponding to the hand vein configuration, its Fourier transform and its log-polar transform.

3.5   Similarity Evaluation

The segmented hand vein images for the same subject are very similar, whereas for different subjects or different hands, the vein structure differs. Shape similarity is easily observable for the human eye; this identification method is similar to character recognition. Biometric identification systems require a similarity function that compares two segmented hand vein images. To be more specific, after the registration process of the vein images we must classify the test image into one of the known classes, or in case of considerable discrepancy, reject it.

This type of similarity measure leads to the problem of curve fitting and similarity or point set matching. The similarity measurements of two point sets representing certain curves in two co-registered images can be evaluated by distance matching, such as the Jaccard, Hausdorf or Frechet distance or the area between curves [1]. These distances measure the similarity between two curves. If a set of curves have to be compared to another set of curves the correspondence between pairs of curves have to be determined in order to apply the mentioned distances. This is a difficult task because our segmented images contain a lot of curves. We had to define a distance measure taking into account only corresponding points of similar shaped configurations. We have to use an averaged Euclidean distance between corresponding points. The similarity from target to template is evaluated by a distance determined in the following way: we determine a correspondence from each point of the target set (B) to the closest point in the template set (A). Some points are eliminated from the target set (B), keeping only one corresponding point for each template point, and considering only the minimum distance to it. Mathematically, the function that defines the correspondence must be injective. The points which have analogues in the other set are considered inliers $(a2 - b1, a3 - b2, a4 - b4, a6 - b8, a8 - b11)$, while the others are outliers (Fig. 2). Only the inliers from both sets are considered in the final computation of the average pairwise distance. For a valid similarity we experimentally determined that the outlier points from each set must be less than 25% of the total points and the average distance below 10 pixels.

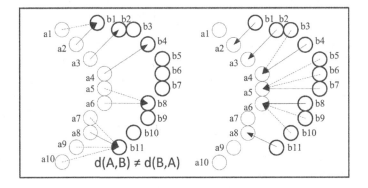

Fig. 2. The proposed similarity measure

3.6   Classification

In the recognition system created we used the k-NN classification algorithm with the previously proposed distance measure based on the minimum distances between point pairs in the two point sets. All the computational complexity is given by the number of comparisons and the distance measure applied in the test phase.

In our case we defined for 102 subjects one or two templates in the training database. The problem was to determine the template of every subject. In fact, each of them could be chosen as template. Nevertheless, we determined the best fit: the image that had the average minimum distance to all the other images of the same subject, surely considering the training set only (Sects. 3.4 and 3.5). Of course, the images were pair-wise registered beforehand, and this is how we selected the template for every class.

4   Results and Experiments

In this section we describe the experimental settings of preprocessing, the creation of template images and the classification process. The inhomogeneity correction, preprocessing and image segmentation steps are the same for every image to be processed. All these steps were fine-tuned and carried out on the NCUT Part A dorsal hand image database [15] described in Sect. 2 (Fig. 3(a)). Correct preprocessing requires a mask in order to differentiate the background and the hand region of the image. This last one is considered to be the ROI (region of interest). All pixels with an intensity value of less than 16 are converted to 0. The 0-intensity background is not taken into consideration in any of the steps applied. Therefore, we created a mask with an intensity value of 1 (Fig. 3(b)) that covers the ROI of the image. Before further processing, a separate mask is applied onto every image in order to eliminate the background. The binary representation of the pixel intensity domain is converted from an 8-bit short integer to a 32-bit real number to facilitate smooth pixel intensity transitions. We applied a 3×3-pixel-wide 2D Gaussian kernel over the image with a standard deviation of $\sigma = 0.5$ and a mean of $\mu = 0$ that reduces the noise and provides a continuous, mathematically smooth domain for further processing (Fig. 3(c)). The inhomogeneity correction tries to uniformise the illumination across the ROI. The correction is given in the multiplicative bias fields whose intensity values are in the interval

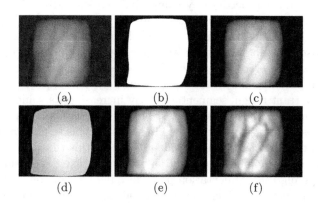

(a)   (b)   (c)

(d)   (e)   (f)

Fig. 3. (a) Original image; (b) Mask image; (c) Noise-filtered image; (d) Bias field; (e) Inhomogeneity-filtered; (f) CLAHE

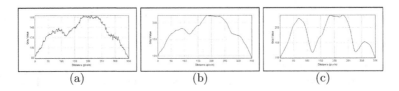

(a)   (b)   (c)

Fig. 4. Profiles of (a) original; (b) noise-filtered; (c) inhomogeneity and CLAHE

Fig. 5. Coded images with ordinal measure

$[0.7, 1.3]$, with the mean at about 1 (Fig. 3(d)). In the illumination-corrected images (Fig. 3(e)) certain thin or lateral veins become more notable, facilitating the subsequent segmentation process. Another important step is the contrast-limited adaptive histogram enhancement (CLAHE) (Fig. 3(f)) that ensures the image quality required for segmentation (Sect. 3.2). The parameters used in our application are $N = 127$ for the block size and 7 for the contrast-limiting threshold. In Fig. 4, the profiles along a horizontal line of Figs. 3(a), (c), (f) are given by considering a horizontal section at the position of the auxiliary line. The profiles show the image quality progress obtained through preprocessing. It is obvious that the first profile is noisy with only one minimum (Fig. 4(a)). The second profile obtained after illumination correction and noise filtering is more stable, but the minima corresponding to veins are still ambiguous (Fig. 4(b)). The third profile corresponding to the preprocessed images shows three minima clearly corresponding to vein centres (Fig. 4(c)). These images are segmented according to theoretical cues. In order to facilitate fast processing, we proposed an ordinal based image encoding procedure by comparing the successive pixel intensities along a horizontal line. Pixels with decreasing intensities are coded black (value 0), pixels with increasing intensities are coded with white (value 255) and pixels with almost constant intensities are coded grey (value 128) (Fig. 5). The threshold (T) which determines increasing, decreasing or constant behaviour is a parameter imposed by the width of the veins detected (Eq. (3)). This threshold has an important role in segmentation. By increasing its value, the number of pixels belonging to the vein increases, but false detection rises at the same time. This threshold must be determined in such a way as to maximize the ratio between true and false detections. A value of 0.5 for this threshold and a minimum region around the minimum point larger than 4 pixels is considered a vein centre. By applying this segmentation procedure in only horizontal direction we obtained vein segmentation adequate for further processing. Figure 6 shows our segmentation results for one subject on the left hand alone. In this figure, an auxiliary cross line is shown in order to see the differences between different vein configurations, while knowing that the auxiliary cross is always in the same position. The skeleton of the vein configuration is not suitable for the registration of image pairs. A morphologic dilation of 5 pixels significantly aids the correct registration of binary images. The dilation is necessary because the registration process uses the correlation function for determining the corresponding parameters of the rigid 3D transformation. The maximum of the correlation between template and target image is the stop criterion for the registration of image pairs. In Fig. 7 we showed 4 registered images to the 1st iamge that was determined to be the template. This image was determined to be the template. Registration performances can be visually evaluated by considering the reference cross line or by observing the corresponding configurations between the target and the template. Figure 8 shows the overlapping target and template configurations on the same image before and after registration. We can observe a few differences due to the segmentation of the veins from different hand positions, but the similarity of the entire configuration is obvious to the human eye. To measure the similarity between configurations we used our previously defined distance between point sets (Sect. 3.5).

Fig. 6. Segmented veins

Fig. 7. Registered veins

Fig. 8. Similarity distance before and after registration (a)–(b), (c)–(d)

Table 1. Classification performances on the NCUT database

Template	p-class Img.	$10 - p$ test Img.	Recognition rate %	False acceptance	False rejection
1	1	9	91.3	1.35	7.35
1	3	7	97.8	1	2.2
1	5	5	99.5	0	0.5
2	5	5	100	0	0
2	7	3	100	0	0

This distance cannot be used for image registration because it is only suitable for relatively similar objects situated close to each other in the image. The overlap and rotation onto each other is solved by the registration process. The similarity distances measured between registered images are less than 5 pixels.

The average similarity distances between unregistered images or different configurations are far more than 15 pixels. In the similarity distance, we take into account only the inlier points that have a single correspondent in distance evaluation. Taking segmentation errors and imperfect registration into account, we determined via experiment that the distance proposed for the similarity measure is relevant in the case of more than 75% of inlier points from the total number of points in the segmented image. We determined that the percentage of inlier points is less than 75% for hands that were rotated around the Ox axis by more than 30°. In this case the captured image is the projection of the hand on the camera plane. The lower number of inlier points obtained in the similarity distance evaluation is due to the reconstruction of the projection and due to segmentation errors. This error occurs in less than 5% of the images in the database analysed, and can be reduced through hardware by limiting the possible hand rotations around the Ox axis or by software definition of an additional two or even more templates (different rotation angles) for each subject. We implemented a biometric recognition system using the NCUT database by using p images for defining each class and the rest of $10 - p$ images for testing. We determined a template image for each class with the smallest distance to the other images from the training set belonging to the same class. During the testing process the new image is registered to each template. The k-NN classification algorithm is applied only to classes for which a similarity distance of less than 10 pixels. In our experiments the k closest entities were considered to participate in the weighted voting decision. The final decision was made after evaluating the distance of the test image to $l \times m$ other images, l is the number of classes and m are the selected images from each of the l closest classes. Therefore, in the final k-NN-based decision, the evaluated image was compared to $l \times m$ selected samples. The selected class was determined by a weighted voting procedure of the closest k samples. The final recognition rate depends on the number of p images involved in training and $10 - p$ in testing. Table 1 shows the classification results with respect to this parameter. In Table 1 recognition rate means that the subject is correctly identified; false acceptance rate - the subject is misclassified and false rejection rate - the subject is not recognized within a given database. Table 2 displays the comparative results of our system to the state of the art methods for rank one recognition rate on NCUT database. Our method can mostly be compared with the holistic graph model in [20] which assumes a much precise segmentation determining about 30 vertices.

Table 2. Comparison table

Approach	Results acceptance rate %
Multi-level Keypoint + SIFT [3]	98.04
OGMs + SIFT [3]	99.02
LBP + Graph [21]	96.67
Holistic Graph [20]	92.65
Graph + Gabor [20]	99.22
WSM [4]	99.31
Our method	91.3–100

5   Conclusion and Future Work

The contributions of this paper can be summarized as follows: (1) It has been proved that human identification based on the NCUT dorsal hand vein image database can be achieved by considering the vascular network geometry of the individuals. (2) It has been demonstrated that the geometric attributes of the segmented vascular network are a solid basis for the dorsal hand vein registration process. The shapes of the vein configuration are more stable in comparison to other keypoints localized by different image gradients or visual properties. It is illumination, rotation and hand aspect invariant. (3) The proposed image registration and classification, with the adequate similarity distance, is very efficient in dorsal hand vein image matching and biometric identification.

A more complex database is required for the real-life validation of a dorsal hand vein biometric identification system in everyday use. This must contain images from many more subjects acquired by different hand scanners running in real-life environments. In such cases image registration and skeleton similarity evaluation might not be enough for a high recognition and low rejection rate. In this case an improvement of the system is required in the form of extracting additional features from various keypoints. The hand vein geometrical structure segmentation presented can lead to more stable keypoints that can be used for local feature extraction. In future we intend to apply our method in a fusion hand vein-based human identification system relying on the dorsal vein and palm vein structure of both hands.

Acknowledgement. The work of S. Emerich was supported by a grant of the Romanian National Authority for Scientific Research and Innovation, CNCS-UEFISCDI, project number PN-II-RU-TE-2014-4-2080.

The work of L. Szilágyi was supported by the Institute for Research Programs of the Sapientia University.

References

1. Chambers, E.W., Wang, Y.: Measuring similarity between curves on 2-manifolds via homotopy area. In: Proceedings of the Twenty-Ninth Annual Symposium on Computational Geometry, pp. 425–434. ACM (2013)
2. Gao, Y., Leung, M.K.: Line segment hausdorff distance on face matching. Pattern Recogn. **35**(2), 361–371 (2002)
3. Huang, D., Zhang, R., Yin, Y., Wang, Y., Wang, Y.: Local feature approach to dorsal hand vein recognition by centroid-based circular key-point grid and fine-grained matching. Image Vis. Comput. **58**, 266–277 (2017)
4. Li, X., Huang, D., Zhang, R., Wang, Y., Xie, X.: Hand dorsal vein recognition by matching width skeleton models. In: 2016 IEEE International Conference on Image Processing (ICIP), pp. 3146–3150. IEEE (2016)
5. Liu, J., Zhang, Y.: Palm-dorsa vein recognition based on two-dimensional fisher linear discriminant. In: 2011 International Conference on Image Analysis and Signal Processing, pp. 550–552, October 2011
6. Lowe, D.G.: Distinctive image features from scale-invariant keypoints. Int. J. Comput. Vis. **60**(2), 91–110 (2004)
7. Mikolajczyk, K., Schmid, C.: An affine invariant interest point detector. In: Heyden, A., Sparr, G., Nielsen, M., Johansen, P. (eds.) ECCV 2002. LNCS, vol. 2350, pp. 128–142. Springer, Heidelberg (2002). https://doi.org/10.1007/3-540-47969-4_9
8. Miura, N., Nagasaka, A., Miyatake, T.: Extraction of finger-vein patterns using maximum curvature points in image profiles. IEICE Trans. Inf. Syst. **90**(8), 1185–1194 (2007)
9. Pal, M.M., Jasutkar, R.W.: Implementation of hand vein structure authentication based system. In: 2012 International Conference on Communication Systems and Network Technologies, pp. 114–118, May 2012
10. Pan, M., Kang, W.: Palm vein recognition based on three local invariant feature extraction algorithms. In: Sun, Z., Lai, J., Chen, X., Tan, T. (eds.) CCBR 2011. LNCS, vol. 7098, pp. 116–124. Springer, Heidelberg (2011). https://doi.org/10.1007/978-3-642-25449-9_15
11. Prinz, M., Carracedo, A., Mayr, W., Morling, N., Parsons, T., Sajantila, A., Scheithauer, R., Schmitter, H., Schneider, P.M.: DNA commission of the international society for forensic genetics (ISFG): recommendations regarding the role of forensic genetics for disaster victim identification (DVI). Forensic Sci. Int. Genet. **1**(1), 3–12 (2007)
12. Sarvaiya Jignesh, N., Patnaik, S., Kothari, K.: Image registration using log polar transform and phase correlation to recover higher scale. J. Pattern Recogn. Res. JPRR **7**(1), 90–105 (2011)
13. Tustison, N., Avants, B., Cook, P., Zheng, Y., Egan, A., Yushkevich, P., Gee, J.: N4ITK: improved N3 bias correction. IEEE Trans. Med. Imaging **29**(6), 1310–1320 (2010)

14. Wang, L., Leedham, G., Cho, D.S.Y.: Minutiae feature analysis for infrared hand vein pattern biometrics. Pattern Recogn. **41**(3), 920–929 (2008)
15. Wang, Y., Li, K., Cui, J.: Hand-dorsa vein recognition based on partition local binary pattern. In: 2010 IEEE 10th International Conference on Signal Processing (ICSP), pp. 1671–1674. IEEE (2010)
16. Wang, Y., Li, K., Cui, J., Shark, L.-K., Varley, M.: Study of hand-dorsa vein recognition. In: Huang, D.-S., Zhao, Z., Bevilacqua, V., Figueroa, J.C. (eds.) ICIC 2010. LNCS, vol. 6215, pp. 490–498. Springer, Heidelberg (2010). https://doi.org/10.1007/978-3-642-14922-1_61
17. Wyawahare, M.V., Patil, P.M., Abhyankar, H.K., et al.: Image registration techniques: an overview. Int. J. Sig. Process. Image Process. Pattern Recogn. **2**, 11–28 (2009)
18. Xiuyan, L., Changyun, M., Tiegen, L., Chenhu, Y.: Research on personal identity verification based on hand vein iris and fingerprint. In: 2011 International Symposium on Computer Science and Society (ISCCS), pp. 16–19. IEEE (2011)
19. Yuksel, A., Akarun, L., Sankur, B.: Hand vein biometry based on geometry and appearance methods. IET Comput. Vis. **5**(6), 398–406 (2011)
20. Zhang, R., Huang, D., Wang, Y.: Textured detailed graph model for dorsal hand vein recognition: a holistic approach. In: 2016 International Conference on Biometrics (ICB), pp. 1–7. IEEE (2016)
21. Zhu, X., Huang, D., Wang, Y.: Hand dorsal vein recognition based on shape representation of the venous network. In: Huet, B., Ngo, C.-W., Tang, J., Zhou, Z.-H., Hauptmann, A.G., Yan, S. (eds.) PCM 2013. LNCS, vol. 8294, pp. 158–169. Springer, Cham (2013). https://doi.org/10.1007/978-3-319-03731-8_15
22. Zuiderveld, K.: Contrast limited adaptive histogram equalization. In: Graphics Gems IV, pp. 474–485. Academic Press Professional Inc., San Diego (1994)

A Multi-scale Triplet Deep Convolutional Neural Network for Person Re-identification

Mingfu Xiong[1,3], Jun Chen[1,2,3(✉)], Zhongyuan Wang[1,4], Chao Liang[1,2,3], Bohan Lei[5], and Ruimin Hu[1,2,3]

[1] School of Computer, National Engineering Research Center for Multimedia Software, Wuhan University, Wuhan 430072, China
{xmf2013,chenj,cliang,hrm}@whu.edu.cn
[2] Collaborative Innovation Center of Geospatial Technology, Wuhan, China
[3] Hubei Key Laboratory of Multimedia and Network Communication Engineering, Wuhan University, Wuhan 430072, China
[4] Research Institute of Wuhan University, Shenzhen, China
wzy_hope@163.com
[5] School of Computer Science, Wuhan University, Wuhan 430072, China
leibohan@whu.edu.cn

Abstract. Person re-identification, aiming to identify images of the same person from non-overlapping camera views in different places, has attracted a lot of interests in intelligent video surveillance. As one of the newly emerging applications, deep learning has been incorporated into the feature representation of person re-identification. However, the existing deep feature learning methods are difficult to generate the robust and discriminative features since they use a fixed scale training and thus fail to adapt to diversitified scales for the same persons under realistic conditions. In this paper, a multi-scale triplet deep convolutional neural network (MST-CNN) is proposed to produce multi-scale features for person re-identification. The proposed MST-CNN consists of three sub-CNNs with respect to full scale, top scale (top part of persons) and half scale of the person images, respectively. In addition, these complementary scale-specific features are then passed to the l2-normalization layer for feature selection to obtain a more robust person descriptor. Experimental results on two public person re-identification datasets, i.e., CUHK-01 and PRID450s, demonstrate that our proposed MVT-CNN method outperforms most of the existing feature learning algorithms by 8%–10% at rank@1 in term of the cumulative matching curve (CMC) criterion.

Keywords: Intelligent surveillance · Person re-identification
Deep feature learning · Multi-scale

1 Introduction

The task of person re-identification aims to recognize or judge whether two persons obtained from different camera views distributed over non-overlapping

© Springer International Publishing AG, part of Springer Nature 2018
S. Satoh (Ed.): PSIVT 2017, LNCS 10799, pp. 30–41, 2018.
https://doi.org/10.1007/978-3-319-92753-4_3

locations belong to the same one [1,2]. Owing to its significance in tracking the escape route of suspects in video surveillance network, it has been widely used in the criminal investigation and intelligent surveillance, such as person retrieval [3], movement analysis [4], long-term multi-camera tracking [5] and forensic search [6]. Person re-identification can be regarded as a person-based image retrieval problem [7]. Given a query person image taken from one camera view, the algorithm is expected to search images of the same person captured by another camera views. It then generates a ranking list where top results are more likely the same person to the query one. Although image retrieval has made great progress, person re-identification remains a challenging problem because of various adverse factors, such as view switching, lighting variations and image scaling in real-world surveillance conditions.

Previous efforts for the person re-identification problem have been roughly classified into three categories: feature representation (including traditional visual and deep features) [8,9], metric learning [10,11] and deep learning unified framework manner [12,13].

Feature Representation: The feature representation methods aim to construct a set of discriminative and robust visual descriptors which can easily distinguish different persons in non-overlapping cameras views. Suffered from low image resolutions, partial occlusion and view changes could cause significant person appearance variations. Designing or obtaining a discriminative feature is extremely challenging under realistic surveillance conditions [14].

Metric Learning: The metric learning methods are devoted to learn an appropriate distance function for comparing two persons features in one projected space. Unfortunately, the learnt distance functions are usually suitable for the linear transformation of samples, but ignore the nonlinear transformation characteristics of feature vectors [15,16]. In addition, it is difficult to handle the problem of imbalanced samples for the training data, thus yielding insufficient results during testing [17].

Deep Learning: Recently, with the huge success of deep learning, deep network has also been exploited in person re-identification problem [12,16]. Most of these methods train deep neural networks in a hierarchical manner based on layer-by-layer training paradigm. The output of the last layer is their primary concern and may neglect the fact that if the person information is missed in the previous layer, the higher layers of the model will have an increasingly diluted input [20,21].

This paper intends to create a more effective and appropriate deep feature for the person re-identification problem under realistic surveillance conditions. Constructing a discriminative feature plays a fundamental role for this task. Although some previous deep feature extraction algorithms have achieved promising performance for person re-identification [16,21], it is still confronted with many limitations. They have trained the person images into a unified scale which ignored diversified changes of the person views in real conditions [22]. As shown in Fig. 1, a fixed input training scale cannot satisfy the multiple views where persons appear in real surveillance scenes. This results in poor recognition performance, especially for the small person view, like that in the center of Fig. 1.

Fig. 1. In real surveillance images, persons can appear at very different scales, as illustrated by the yellow bounding boxes. A fixed training scale cannot match this variability. (Color figure online)

To boost the performance of deeply learnt features, this work proposes a unified multi-scale triplet deep CNN (MST-CNN) for person re-identification. The MST-CNN consists of three sub-networks, with the first sub-network trained via the full scale person images, the second one of fewer convolutional layers learned via the top scale person images and the third one of fewer convolutional layers trained by the half scale person image, respectively. In computation, all of them are learned via end-to-end manner with the triplet loss. Moreover, feature representation with respect to the three output layers is used to ease the inconsistency between the scales of person images, with each layer corresponding to persons within certain scale ranges (see Fig. 2). Intuitively, lower network layers with smaller receptive fields are matched to small scale person images, while higher layers are suited for the recognition of large scales.

In summary, the major contributions of this paper can be summarized as follows:

- A unified MST-CNN is presented to learn person visual features in different scales via stepwise training manner.
- The proposed MST-CNN has exploited the triplet loss to train the sub-network, which turns out more promising than previous re-identification approaches for feature learning.
- Extensive evaluation and analysis of the experimental results are conducted in three benchmark datasets: CUHK-01 [30] and PRID450s [25].

2   The Proposed MST-CNN Architecture

In this section, we exploit the multi-scale triplet CNN to learn multiple scale deep features for appearances of the person. The network architecture and the triplet loss optimization process are presented, respectively. At last, how to joint learning the multiple scales deep features is stated.

2.1 Formulation

We firstly state the formulations and terminologies associated with our problem. In this study, we present a multi-scale triplet CNN (MST-CNN) based the multiple scale triplet architecture for person re-identification task. For each sub-CNN, the optimization process is implemented by a set of triplet units (x_i, x_j, x_k), where x_i and x_j are from the same class, where x_i and x_k are from different classes. Thus, in terms of the features extracted via different input scales sub-CNN, the truly matched images are closer than the mismatched images by training the model on a set of triplets (x_i, x_j, x_k) as depicted in Fig. 2. Let $W = W_j$ denote the network parameters and $g_W(x)$ denote the deep network output of each scale image x, i.e. feature representation for each input image x. To train the triplet units (x_i, x_j, x_k) for the person re-identification problem, the desired feature should satisfy the following condition under the L_2 norm:

$$||g_W(x_i) - g_W(x_j)|| < ||g_W(x_i) - g_W(x_k)|| \tag{1}$$

and this formulation equals

$$||g_W(x_i) - g_W(x_j)||^2 < ||g_W(x_i) - g_W(x_k)||^2 \tag{2}$$

In this work, we use the squared form to facilitate the partial derivative calculation like in [26]. For a given training set $(X = x_i)$, the triplet constraints

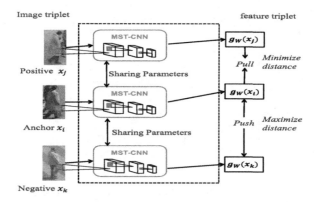

Fig. 2. The overall architecture of the MST-CNN based the triplet loss. The triplet person images (x_i, x_j, x_k) denote the anchor image, positive image and negative image, respectively. The learnt features $(g_W(x_i), g_W(x_j), g_W(x_k))$ make positive pairs closer whereas negative pairs further away from each other in each triplet.

are converted to the minimization problem of the following objective function, i.e. maximizing the distance between the same class and different classes, where N is the number of the training triplets:

$$d(W, X) = \sum_{i=1, j=1}^{N} \max\{||g_W(x_i) - g_W(x_j)||^2 - ||g_W(x_i) - g_W(x_k)||^2, C\} \quad (3)$$

where the C is similar to the technique widely used in hinge-loss functions. And it is used to prevent the overall value of the object function. Like in [26], we set $C = 1$ in this paper.

2.2   The Network Architecture

The detailed network architecture of the proposed MST-CNN is described in Fig. 3. This architecture is composed of three separate sub-CNNs with each sub-CNN embedding images of different triplet scales or different parts. The first sub-CNN takes full scale of size 227×227 and the second sub-CNN takes top scale of size 114×114. These two sub-CNNs can employ different levels of invariance at different scales. The last sub-CNNs take the half scale which the input scale is also as 114×114. By training the deep network for different scale of the person images, the final representation can be more robust to local variations in terms of scale and occlusion. Like in [12,16], the bottom part is not included since two legs capture the least discriminative information.

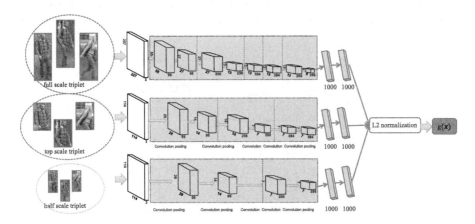

Fig. 3. The detailed architecture of the MST-CNN.

Figure 3 shows the pipeline of the multiple scales triplet training paradigm. Given one person image, we fist derive the full scale, half scale, top scale image from the original images. Then, we could select the positive and negative samples for each scale image. The triplet loss is exploited to train the three sub-CNNs respectively. For the full scale image, there are four convolutional layers for the feature extraction and the top scale image equips with three one. At last, the half scale image is with two convolutional layers. As described above, The intuition is that lower network layers have smaller receptive fields, better matched to recognize small scale person images. Conversely, higher layers, are best suited for the recognition of large scales.

In this work, the proposed network proposal shown in Fig. 4, which is based on the Caffenet [20]. The size of kernel filters for each convolutional layer is 11×11, 5×5, 3×3 respectively. The convolution operation formula is expressed as

$$a_i^{(l)} = relu(b_i^{(l)} + \sum_j k_{ij}^{(l)} \bigotimes a_i^{(l-1)}) \tag{4}$$

where $a_i^{(l)}$ and $a_i^{(l-1)}$ denote the i-th output channel at the l-th layer and the j-th input channel at the $(l-1)$-th layer respectively; $k_{ij}^{(l)}$ is the convolutional kernel between the i-th and j-th feature map; and $b_i^{(l)}$ is the bias of the i-th map. The Rectified Linear Unit (ReLU) is used as the neuron activation function, denoted as relu(x) = max(x, 0). Max-pooling is following in the corresponding convolutional layers, which is formulated as

$$a_{(i,j)}^{(l)} = \max_{\forall (p,q) \in \Psi_{(i,j)}} \{a_{(p,q)}^{(l)}\} \tag{5}$$

where $\Psi_{(i,j)}$ stands for the pooling region with index (i, j). Max-pooling at the first two layer is followed by local response normalization, leading to feature maps that are roust to illumination and contrast variations.

2.3 Triplet Selection

It is crucial to select triplets that violate the constraint given in Eq. (1). This means that, given a anchor scale person image x_i, we want to select an positive sample x_j satisfying $argmax_{x_i} \| x_i - x_j \|_2^2$ while a negative sample R_k satisfying $argmin_{x_k} \| x_i - x_k \|_2^2$. However, it is unrealistic and infeasible to compute the $argmin$ and $argmax$ for the whole training set. Therefore, it requires an efficient way to compute the $argmin$ and $argmax$. There are two methods to be chosen as mentioned in [27,28].

Off-line Triplets Selection. The triplets are generated every few steps, and the most recent network checkpoint is employed to compute the $argmin$ and $argmax$.

On-line Triplets Selection. The selection can be done within a mini-batch. However, in this work, we adopt the on-line triplets selection method in this paper.

2.4 L2 Normalization

To make the network converge faster, the concatenated features are passed to the $L_2 - normalization$ layer as the output of attention components:

$$y = \frac{g}{\sqrt{\sum_{p=1}^{k} g_p^2}} \tag{6}$$

where $g = [g_1, g_2, ..., g_p]$ is the output of the concatenation layer with dimension k. The importance of $l_2 - normalization$ layer is that ensures the distance computed from each triplet can not exceed the margin described in Eq. (1).

3   Experimental Results

In this section, we evaluate our algorithm on three standard person re-identification datasets. We first describe the datasets. Then the evaluation protocol and training strategy are presented. At last we show the experiment results.

3.1   The Datasets

We evaluate our algorithm on two public datasets. et. CUHK01 and PRID450s. Some typical samples of these public datasets can be seen as Fig. 4. The detail information of them are described as below respectively. Then, the baseline algorithm is introduced in the next part.

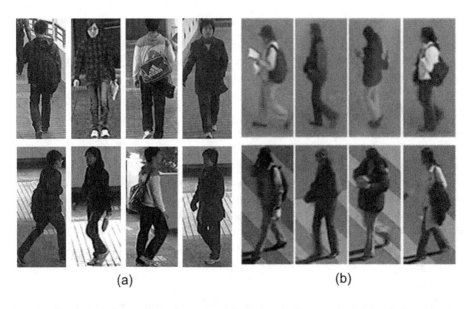

Fig. 4. Some typical samples of three public datasets. Each column shows two images of the same person from two different cameras with significant changes on scales and illumination condition. (a) CUHK01 is similar to VIPeR, but more challenge as it contains more person pairs. (b) PRID450s dataset has significant and consistent lighting changes.

CUHK01 Dataset: The CUHK01 Campus dataset [30] contains 1816 persons and five pairs of camera views (P1-P5, ten camera views). They have 971, 306, 107, 193 and 239 persons respectively. Each person has two images in each camera view. This dataset is used to evaluate the performance when camera views in test are different than those in training. In our experiment, we choose view pair P1 for evaluation. And this view includes 971 subjects, 1942 images. Each subjects has two images from 2 camera views. All images are normalized to 160 × 60. Some examples are shown as Fig. 4(b). Similar to VIPeR, view changes are the most significant cause of appearance change with most of the matched image pairs containing one front or back view and one side-view

PRID450s Dataset: The PRID 450S dataset builds on PRID 2011 [25], however, is arranged according to VIPeR by image pairs and contains more linked samples than PRID 2011. In particular, the dataset contains 450 single-shot image pairs depicting walking humans captured in two spatially disjoint camera views. And the original images with resolution of 720 × 576 pixels, person patches were annotated manually by bounding boxes with a vertical resolution of 100–150 pixels. All images are normalized to 12848 pixels. Some examples are shown as Fig. 4(c).

3.2   The Evaluation Protocol

We adopted the widely used cumulative match curve (CMC) approach [23] for quantitative evaluation. Given an algorithm and a test set of images of people with labels, each image in the test set is compared against the remaining images under the given algorithmic model and the position of the correct match is recorded. The CMC curve indicates for each rank the fraction of test samples which had that rank or better. A perfect CMC curve would reach the value 1 for rank@1.

3.3   Training Strategy

Our implementation is based on the caffe-master [20] linked against the NVIDIA CuDNN libraries to accelerate training, which have removed the final full connection layer for training the person re-identification datasets. As the dataset is so small that cannot be train the deep model effectively. We first pre-train the CNNs on the entire dataset of Market-1501 [29] and CUHK-03 [30], then fine tune them on the 316 training identities to get the final model. And the based learn rating was set 0.001. The gamma was set as 0.1. The maximal iteration and momentum were set as 50000 and 0.9 respectively.

3.4   Experimental Results on CUHK01 Dataset

In the first experiment, we evaluate our algorithm on the CUHK-01 dataset. This dataset includes 971 persons, divided into 486 person pairs for training and 485 for testing. They were also randomly selected.

As this dataset, we compare our method with previous methods. As shown in Table 1, the methods like LMNN [31], LMMN-R [32], KISSME [6], LFDA [33], FPNN [30], DML [12]. From Table 1, the rank@1 matching rate of our method exceeds these methods about 10% is also the best, including the traditional and deep approaches. However, the performance of the proposed method is worse than FPNN when Rank = 10. We have also analyzed the reason that the dimension of the integrated feature are too high and too many connections or associated parameters between the different deep networks. They are difficult to tailor the performance.

Table 1. Experimental results on CUHK-01. From Table 1, it shows that our method gives the best performance for rank@1.

Method	Rank = 1	Rank = 10	Rank = 20
LMNN [31]	21.17	57.53	–
LMNN-R [32]	13.45	42.25	54.11
KISSME [6]	29.40	60.22	–
LFDA [33]	22.08	53.85	64.51
FPNN [30]	27.87	**81.07**	87.01
DML [12]	16.17	45.82	57.56
halfScale	10.06	22.64	28.70
topScale	22.54	47.61	56.12
fullScale	23.48	48.66	58.41
Ours	**40.35**	75.71	**87.60**

3.5 Experimental Results on PRID450s Dataset

In the third experiment, we evaluate our algorithm on the PRID450s dataset. The resolution of PRID450s dataset is different for each person images. We have resized them into 128 × 48 first. Then the person images are split into two parts equally as the previous datasets. We can also get different scales and hierarchical deep features for each person. As this dataset contains 900 outdoor images obtained from two views of 450 persons. We randomly select 225 persons for training and the others are used for testing.

As this dataset, we compare our method with previous methods. As shown in Table 2, the methods like LMNN [31], LMMN-R [32], KISSME [6], LFDA [33], ITML [34], and Ahmed [12]. From Table 2, the rank@1 matching rate of our method exceeds these methods about 10%, including the traditional and deep approaches

3.6 Single Scale Performance for Each Sub-CNN

In this work, we have exploited the Multi-Scale Triplet CNNs for person re-identification. The single sub-CNN scale is also for testing. The performance can be seen as Fig. 5. From the figure, we can see that the more convolutional layers of the networks are, the better performance will be. The full scale has the best recognition accuracy comparing the top and half scales.

Table 2. Experimental results on PRID450s. From Table 2, it shows that our method gives the best performance for rank@1.

Method	Rank = 1	Rank = 10	Rank = 20
LMNN [31]	24.00	62.00	73.00
LMNN-R [32]	28.98	67.64	78.36
KISSME [6]	28	65	76
ITML [34]	24.27	58.67	70.89
LFDA [33]	36.18	72.40	82.67
DML [12]	34.81	76.24	81.90
halfScale	21.69	52.93	62.71
topScale	26.22	57.60	69.16
fullScale	34.89	66.64	74.93
Ours	**47.96**	**80.81**	**87.42**

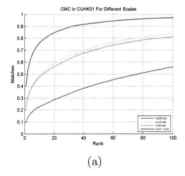
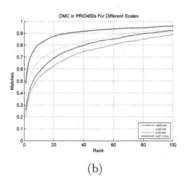

(a)   (b)

Fig. 5. The single scale CMC curves for each dataset: (a) CUHK-01; (b) PRID450s.

4   Conclusion and in Future Work

This study has proposed a multi-scale triplet CNN for person re-identification, which is equipped with three sub-CNNs in different scales respectively. The triplet loss for different scales of the same person is formulated to train the deep networks. We conduct extensive experiments on two public available person re-identification datasets (CUHK01 and PRID450s) to validate our algorithm. Experimental results indicate that the proposed method yields a superior performance over the previous algorithms in terms of recognition accuracy.

Acknowledgments. This work was supported by the National High Technology Research and Development Program of China (No.2015AA016306), the Natural Science Foundation of Jiangsu Province (No. BK20161563), EU-FP7-QUICK project under Grant Agreement (No. PIRSES-GA-2013-612652), National Nature Science Foundation of China (U1611461, 61231015, 61772380, 61671336, 61671332), the Technology Research Program of Ministry of Public Security (No. 2016JSYJA12), Hubei Province

Technological Innovation Major Project (No. 2016AAA015). National Key Research and Development Program of China (No.2016YFB0100901), the Fundamental Research Funds for the Central Universities (2042016gf0033), the Basic Research Program of Shenzhen City (JCYJ20170306171431656).

References

1. Wang, J., Wang, Z., Gao, C., Sang, N., Huang, R.: DeepList: learning deep features with adaptive listwise constraint for person reidentification. IEEE Trans. Circuits Syst. Video Technol. **27**, 513–524 (2017)
2. Wang, Z., Hu, R., Chen, C., Yu, Y., Jiang, J., Liang, C., Satoh, S.: Person reidentification via discrepancy matrix and matrix metric. IEEE Trans. Cybern. (2017). https://doi.org/10.1109/TCYB.2017.2755044
3. Wang, X., Zhang, T., Tretter, D.R., Lin, Q.: Personal clothing retrieval on photo collections by color and attributes. IEEE Trans. Multimedia **15**, 2035–2045 (2013)
4. Wang, J., Wang, Z., Liang, C., Gao, C., Sang, N.: Equidistance constrained metric learning for person re-identification. Pattern Recogn. (2017). https://doi.org/10.1016/j.patcog.2017.09.014
5. Ye, M., Liang, C., Yu, Y., Wang, Z., Leng, Q., Xiao, C., Chen, J., Hu, R.: Person reidentification via ranking aggregation of similarity pulling and dissimilarity pushing. IEEE Trans. Multimedia **13**, 2553–2566 (2016)
6. Vezzani, R., Baltieri, D., Cucchiara, R.: People reidentification in surveillance and forensics: a survey. ACM Comput. Surv. **46**, 1–37 (2013)
7. Ye, M., Andy, M.J., Zheng, L., Li, J.W., Yuen, P.C.: Dynamic label graph matching for unsupervised video re-identification. In: International Conference on Computer Vision, pp. 11–19 (2017)
8. Liang, C., Huang, B., Hu, R.: A unsupervised person re-identification method using model based representation and ranking. In: ACM International Conference on Multimedia, pp. 771–774 (2015)
9. Figueira, D., Bazzani, L., Minh, H.Q.: Semi-supervised multi-feature learning for person re-identification. In: IEEE International Conference on Advanced Video and Signal Based Surveillance, pp. 111–116 (2013)
10. Xiong, M.F., Chen, J., Wang, Z., Wang, Z.Y., Hu, R., Liang, C., Shi, D.: Person re-identification via multiple coarse-to-fine deep metrics. In: IOS Press European Conference on Artificial Intelligence, pp. 355–362 (2016)
11. Dong, Y., Zhen, L., Liao, S.C., Li, S.: Deep metric learning for person re-identification. In: IEEE International Conference Pattern Recognition, pp. 34–39 (2014)
12. Ahmed, E., Jones, M., Marks, T.K.: An improved deep learning architecture for person re-identification. In: IEEE Computer Vision and Pattern Recognition, pp. 3908–3916 (2015)
13. Xiao, T., Li, H., Ouyang, W., Wang, X.: Learning deep feature representations with domain guided dropout for person re-identification, pp. 1249–1258 (2016)
14. Wang, Z., Hu, R., Liang, C., Yu, Y.: Zero-shot person reidentification via cross-view consistency. IEEE Trans. Multimedia **18**, 260–272 (2016)
15. He, Y., Mao, Y., Chen, W., Chen, Y.: Nonlinear metric learning with kernel density estimation. IEEE Trans. Knowl. Data Eng. **27**, 1602–1614 (2015)
16. Wang, J., Sang, N., Wang, Z., Gao, C.: Similarity learning with top-heavy ranking loss for person re-identification. IEEE Sig. Process. Lett. **23**, 1–15 (2015)

17. Gong, S., Cristani, M., Yan, S., Chen, C.L.: Person re-identification. Vis. Anal. Behav. **42**, 301–313 (2013)
18. Gens, R., Domingos, P.: Discriminative learning of sum-product networks. In: MIT Press Advances in Neural Information Processing Systems, pp. 3239–3247 (2012)
19. Hinton, G.E., Salakhutdinov, R.R.: Reducing the dimensionality of data with neural networks. Science **313**, 504–507 (2006)
20. Krizhevsky, A., Sutskever, I., Hinton, G.E.: Imagenet classification with deep convolutional neural networks. In: MIT Press Advances in Neural Information Processing Systems, pp. 1097–1105 (2012)
21. Wu, S., Chen, Y.C., Li, X., Wu, A.C., You, J.J., Zheng, W.S.: An enhanced deep feature representation for person re-identification. In: IEEE Winter Conference on Applications of Computer Vision, pp. 1–8 (2016)
22. Cai, Z., Fan, Q., Feris, R.S., Vasconcelos, N.: A unified multi-scale deep convolutional neural network for fast object detection. In: Leibe, B., Matas, J., Sebe, N., Welling, M. (eds.) ECCV 2016. LNCS, vol. 9908, pp. 354–370. Springer, Cham (2016). https://doi.org/10.1007/978-3-319-46493-0_22
23. Gray, D., Brennan, S., Tao, H.: Evaluating appearance models for recognition, reacquisition, and tracking. In: IEEE International Workshop on Performance Evaluation for Tracking and Surveillance, pp. 309–314 (2007)
24. Li, W., Wang, X.: Locally aligned feature transforms across views. In: IEEE Computer Vision and Pattern Recognition, pp. 3594–3601 (2013)
25. Hirzer, M., Beleznai, C., Roth, P.M., Bischof, H.: Person re-identification by descriptive and discriminative classification. In: Heyden, A., Kahl, F. (eds.) SCIA 2011. LNCS, vol. 6688, pp. 91–102. Springer, Heidelberg (2011). https://doi.org/10.1007/978-3-642-21227-7_9
26. Ding, S., Lin, L., Wang, G.: Deep feature learning with relative distance comparison for person re-identification. Pattern Recogn. **48**, 2993–3003 (2015)
27. Schroff, F., Kalenichenko, D., Philbin, J.: Facenet: a unified embedding for face recognition and clustering. In: IEEE Conference on Computer Vision and Pattern Recognition, pp. 815–823 (2015)
28. Liu, H., Feng, J., Qi, M.: End-to-end comparative attention networks for person re-identification. IEEE Trans. Image Process. **26**, 3492–3506 (2017)
29. Zheng, L., Shen, L., Tian, L., Wang, S., Wang, J., Tian, Q.: Scalable person re-identification: a benchmark. In: IEEE International Conference on Computer Vision, pp. 1116–1124 (2015)
30. Li, W., Zhao, R., Xiao, T., Wang, X.: DeepReID: deep filter pairing neural network for person re-identification. In: IEEE Conference on Computer Vision and Pattern Recognition, pp. 152–159 (2014)
31. Weinberger, K.Q., Saul, L.K.: Distance metric learning for large margin nearest neighbor classification. J. Mach. Learn. Res. **10**, 207–244 (2009)
32. Dikmen, M., Akbas, E., Huang, T.S., Ahuja, N.: Pedestrian recognition with a learned metric. In: Kimmel, R., Klette, R., Sugimoto, A. (eds.) ACCV 2010. LNCS, vol. 6495, pp. 501–512. Springer, Heidelberg (2011). https://doi.org/10.1007/978-3-642-19282-1_40
33. Pedagadi, S., Orwell, J., Velastin, S., Boghossian, B.: Local fisher discriminant analysis for pedestrian re-identification. In: IEEE Conference on Computer Vision and Pattern Recognition, pp. 3318–3325 (2013)
34. Davis, J.V., Kulis, B., Jain, P., Sra, S., Dhillon, I.S.: Information-theoretic metric learning. In: International Conference on Machine Learning, pp. 209–216 (2007)

Facial Expression Recognition Using Cascaded Random Forest Based on Local Features

Mingjian Tuo and Jingying Chen[✉]

National Research Center for E-learning, Central China Normal University,
Luoyu Street, Wuhan, China
89002359@qq.com, chenjy@mail.ccnu.edu.cn

Abstract. Automatic facial expression recognition (FER) is an interesting and challenging topic which has potential applications in natural human-computer interaction. Researches in this field have made great progress. However, continuous efforts should be made to further improve the recognition accuracy for practical use. In this paper, an effective method is proposed for FER using a cascaded random forest based on local features. First, the hybrid features of appearance and geometric features are extracted within the salient facial regions sensitive to different facial expressions; second, a cascaded random forest based on the hybrid local features is developed to classify facial expressions in a coarse-to-fine way. Extensive experiments show that the proposed method provides better performance compared to the state of the art on different datasets.

Keywords: Cascaded random forests · Facial expression recognition
Feature fusion

1 Introduction

Facial expression is one of the most direct and powerful way for human emotion communication. In the field of computer vision, automatic facial expression recognition is crucial to realize the nature human-computer interaction. During the past two decades, many works in the field of FER focus on recognition of six prototypic expressions (i.e. happiness, disgust, fear, anger, surprise and sadness) defined by Ekman and Friesen (1978). Although a lot of progress has been made, continuous efforts should be made to further improve the recognition accuracy for practical use.

Automatic facial expression recognition consists of two main steps, i.e., feature extraction and expression classification. The features representing the facial part changes caused by different facial expressions are usually categorized into geometric feature and appearance feature. Geometric feature uses the location of facial feature points, e.g., (1) the corners of eyes, eyebrows, lips, and nostrils; (2) outer mid-points of the lips and eyes; (3) the tips of the nose and chin.

© Springer International Publishing AG, part of Springer Nature 2018
S. Satoh (Ed.): PSIVT 2017, LNCS 10799, pp. 42–53, 2018.
https://doi.org/10.1007/978-3-319-92753-4_4

Appearance feature uses facial texture from the whole face, or from specific regions. Several efforts (Chen et al. 2012) have also been reported that hybrid features (both geometric and appearance-feature) based approaches achieve a better performance than single features based approaches respectively.

On the other hand, various pattern recognition approaches are developed to classify different facial expressions, e.g. Convolutional Neural Networks (CNN) (Kim et al. 2016), Neural Network Ensemble (NNE) (Ali 2016), SVM (Owusu 2014), Adaboost (Gudipati 2017) and Random Forest (RF) (El Meguid and Levine 2014) etc. Bagga et al. (2015) using LBP images in place of original images, and the proposed approach has obvious promotion in the accuracy of the system. Ali (2016) trained the binary neural networks and combined the predictions of binary neural networks to form NNE. Owusu and Zhan (2014) fed selected Gabor features into a support vector machines (SVM) classifier and obtain an average recognition rate of 97.57%.

Some attempts using 3D face models for identity and expression analysis have been made, Soyel and Demirel (2007) applied neural network classifier with five typical facial distance features on BU-3DFE dataset, the average facial expression recognition rate of the proposed system reaches up to 91.3%. Tang and Huang (2008) proposed a 3D facial expression recognition method based on properties of the line segments connecting certain facial feature points. They used normalized distances and slopes of these line segments as features with a multi-class SVM classifier to recognize six universal facial expressions, and they claimed that an average rate of recognition 87.1% is achieved on the BU-3DFE dataset. Due to the limitations of the special 3D image capture device and different application environment, high resolution 3D image information is not always available.

The Random Forest (RF) based methods have been studied extensively, because the method shows its excellent robustness and good accuracy in solving computer vision problems (El Meguid and Levine 2014). To further improve the efficiency and accuracy of the traditional RF, a cascaded random forest algorithm based on local features is proposed for FER in this paper. First, the hybrid features of appearance and geometric features are extracted within the salient facial regions sensitive to different facial expressions, the salient regions are the areas of facial features changing obviously caused by the movements of facial muscles according the description of Facial Action Coding System (FACS) (Ekman 1978); second, a cascaded random forest based on hybrid local features is developed to classify facial expressions in a coarse-to-fine way. The experiment results show that the proposed method provide better performance compared to the state of the art on different datasets.

The remainder of this paper is organized as follows: The proposed method is presented in Sect. 2. Section 3 gives the experimental results while Sect. 4 presents the conclusions.

2   Cascaded RF Based on Local Features

In this section, we describe the proposed method in details. First, the hybrid features of appearance and geometric features are extracted within the salient facial regions sensitive to different facial expressions; second, a cascaded random forest based on the hybrid local features is developed to classify facial expressions in a coarse-to-fine way (Fig. 1).

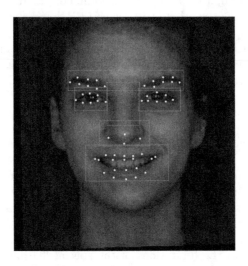

Fig. 1. Examples of local salient region

2.1   Feature Extraction Based on Local Salient Region

Facial Action Coding System (FACS) (Ekman 1978) is a widely used method for manual labeling of facial expressions, which studied the distribution of muscle groups that cause facial deformation, and described different facial movements. FACS also associates different facial expressions with actions of the muscle groups. It defines 9 different action units (AUs) in the upper face, 18 in the lower face, and the other AUs that cannot be classified as belonging to either the upper or the lower face. Different facial expressions can be represented using different combination of AUs (Valstar 2012). Although the facial action units describe the expressions effectively, locating the action unit precisely is still a challenging problem in practical use, hence we propose to extract the hybrid features of appearance and geometric features within local salient regions based on different AUs. In this paper, 6 salient regions are chosen, including eyebrow area, eyes area, nose area and mouth area. The examples of regions are shown in the follow (Figs. 2, 3, 4, 5 and 6).

Hybrid features are extracted within these salient regions, Gabor features are used as the texture features (see Fig. 7) while the locations of feature points are

Fig. 2. The brows region

Fig. 3. The nasion region

Fig. 4. The nose region

Fig. 5. The eyes region.

Fig. 6. The mouth region.

Fig. 7. The Gabor features from the mouth region.

Fig. 8. The geometrical features from the mouth region.

used as geometric features (see Fig. 8). These two kinds of features complement to each other, texture features are good to describe nose wrinkle, nasolabial furrow and so on, feature points are suitable to represent brow raise, eyes open and so on, the facial feature points are detected using the extended Active Shape Model (ASM) (Milborrow and Nicolls 2008).

2.2 Random Forest Algorithm

The Random Forest algorithm is an ensemble learning algorithm composed of multiple decision trees, whose basic idea is to integrate multiple weak classifiers into a strong classifier $\{h(x, \theta_k)\}$, $k = \{1, \ldots, L\}$, where $\{\theta_k\}$ are independent and identically distributed random vectors and each tree $h(x, \theta_k)$ casts a unit vote for the most popular class at input x.

The traditional RF algorithm, called Breiman's RF in the following, has been introduced by Breiman (2001). It used two randomization principles: bagging and random feature selection (RFS). By bagging, the training samples of each decision tree $h(x, \theta_k)$ are randomly selected from the total set, the output of the random forest is the result of all decision tree classification results voting. And RFS introduces randomization of the splitting test designed for each node of the tree. This choice is usually based on an impurity measure to determine the best feature for the partition of the current node into several child nodes. The Information Gain (IG) is employed in our method, which is defined as:

$$IG = argmax(H(P|a_j) - (\omega_L H(P_L|a_j) + \omega_R H(P_R|a_j))) \tag{1}$$

where ω_L, ω_R are the ratio between the number of samples in set P_L (arriving to left subset using the binary tests), set P_R (arriving to right subset using the binary tests) and set P (total node samples). $H(P|a_j)$ is the defined class uncertainty measure and the entropy of the continuous image labels.

Breiman's RF has a very good recognition rate for binary classification, but when it comes to multi-classification, e.g. facial expressions classification, the drawback of Breiman's RF becomes obvious. To improve the recognition rate of the expressions, we propose the cascaded Random Forest with the hybrid features.

2.3 Cascaded Random Forest

Because of the cascaded random forest's high accuracy and efficiency, it is introduced into the random forests framework to classify the expressions in the paper. As shown in Fig. 9, the proposed model includes 4 layers:

- The first layer constructs a RF trained using the texture features from the nose region and the geometric features of eyebrow region as well as mouth region. The RF of this layer distinguishes the "surprise" expression from the other facial expressions;

- The second layer constructs a RF trained using the texture features from the mouth regions and the geometric features of the mouth region. The RF of this layer distinguishes the "happiness" expression from the other facial expressions;
- The third layer constructs a RF trained using the texture features from the nose and the mouth regions and the geometric features of the eyebrow region as well as mouth region. The sub-RF classifies the rest four facial expressions into two groups: "anger", "disgust" and "fear", "sadness";
- The last layer constructs two RFs corresponding to the two groups at the previous layer. One RF is trained using the texture features from the nose region and the geometric features of mouth region as well as eyes region to distinguish "anger" from "disgust", the other RF is trained using the texture features from the mouth region and the geometric features of mouth as well as eyebrow to distinguish "fear" from "sadness".

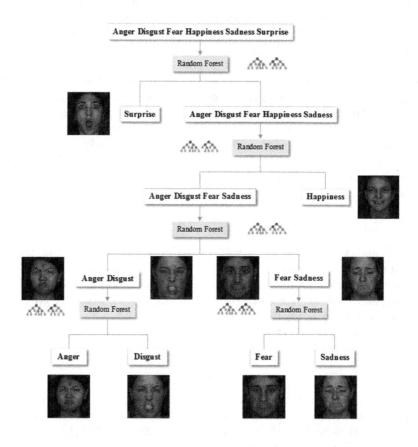

Fig. 9. Cascaded random forest model.

From the tree-structure model, it is noted that each child layer in the forest is related to his parent. Is. Hence the cascaded random forest only computes the probability of the trees in child layer instead of all trees' probabilities in all layers of the model. While the original random forest classifies the facial expressions using leaves' probabilities of all training trees to vote. Therefore, the Cascaded Random Forest can provide high accuracy and efficiency.

Due to the classification of each layer is different, the image can be defined as $P_i = \{I_i, C_i\}$. Where I_i represents the appearance and C_i represents the set of six prototypic expressions. In this case, we extract a multiple channels local features $I_i = \{I_i^1, I_i^2\}$. Where I_i^1 represents the geometrical characteristic of mouth, nose, eyes and eyebrows regions; and I_i^2 represents the texture features of several local regions such as mouth corners, third eye area and bridge of nose, which is extracted with Gabor filter. The set of $C_i^n = (c_i^1, (c_i^2|c_i^1), (c_i^3|c_i^2, c_i^1), (c_i^4|c_i^3, c_i^2, c_i^1))$ contains the expressions classification in different layers of the tree-structure model, where c_i^1 are 2 classifications including surprise in the first layer of the cascaded random forest, $(c_i^2|c_i^1)$ are 2 classifications including happiness in the second layer, $(c_i^3|c_i^2, c_i^1)$ are 2 classifications in the third layer, $(c_i^4|c_i^3, c_i^2, c_i^1)$ are 4 expressions including anger, disgust, fear and sadness, in the fourth layer.

For a given expression image, we initially extract multiple channel features I_i based on the local area defined in Sect. 2.1, the multiple channel feature set I_i is then fed into the trees in the cascaded random forest. At each node of a tree, the image is evaluated according to the stored binary test and passed either to the right or left child until a leaf node is reached. By passing the feature sets down all the trees in the cascaded random forest for expression recognition, each image P_n ends in a set of leaves L of the different sub-forest of cascaded random forest. In each leaf l, there are classification probabilities of expressions classification, and the distributions of the continuous expression parameter by a multivariate Gaussian:

$$p(C^m|l) = N(C^m; \overline{C_l^m}, \textstyle\sum_l^m) \tag{2}$$

where $\overline{C_l^m}$ and $\sum_l^m$ are the mean and covariance matrix of the estimations of the m-th class.

In cascaded random forest, each layer of decision-making is determined by a sub-forest, and generates the corresponding classification probability $p(C_j^m|P_j)$, which can be defined as Eq. (3):

$$p(C_j^m|P_j) = \frac{1}{T_0} \sum_{k=1}^{T_0} p_k(C_j^m|P_j) \tag{3}$$

where C_j^m is the expression classifications of j-th layer, P_j is the sample of the j-th layer in the cascaded random forest. T_0 denotes the number of decision trees that make up the sub-forest in the current layer, and $p_k(C_j^m|P_j)$ indicates the classification probability of the leaf node.

Because the distribution probability of each sub-forest is only related to its parent, the cascaded random forest outputs the probability that the sample P belongs to the class $C^m (m \in 1, \ldots, N)$ can be described in Eq. (4).

$$p(C^m|P) = \prod_{j}^{N} p(C_j^m|P_j)$$ (4)

Based on Eqs. (3) and (4), the classification probability can be defined as:

$$p(C^m|P) = \prod_{j=1}^{N} \left(\frac{1}{T_0} \sum_{k=1}^{T_0} p_k(C_j^m|P_j) \right)$$ (5)

3   Experiments

In this section, the proposed approach is evaluated on two public datasets: Cohn-Kanade+ dataset (Kanade 2000), Binghamton University 3D Facial Expression (BU-3DFE) Dataset (Yin 2006). To further demonstrate the generalization of the proposed approach, a new dataset named CCNU-FE is collected for cross-dataset experiments. The CK+ database (Kanade 2000) contains 486 sequences across 97 subjects. Each of the sequences contains images from neutral to peak expression. Six prototypic expressions have been labelled to peak expression by visual inspection from emotion researchers. BU3D-FE database contains 100 subjects (56% female, 44% male), ranging age from 18 years to 70 years old, with a variety of ethnic/racial ancestries, including White, Black, East-Asian, Middle-east Asian, Indian, and Hispanic Latino. CCNU-FE database consists of 2881 images from 20 subjects from our laboratory (50% female, 50% male), and all images are labelled by visual inspection from emotion researchers. The details of these three datasets are listed in Table 1, and some exemplar expression images are presented in Fig. 10

Table 1. Details of the CK+, BU3D-FE, and CCNU-FE datasets

Dataset	Subjects	Gender(F/M)	Age	Ethnicity	Glasses
CK+	97	63:34	18–30	Multiethnic	N
BU3D-FE	100	56:44	18–70	Multiethnic	N
CCNU-FE	20	10:10	20–35	Asian	Y

3.1   Settings

All face images are normalized in size of 250×250 pixels before training, the dimensions of local Gabor features based PCA of salient regions is 35×12. We use the extended Active Shape Model to mark 56 facial characteristic points, which are divided into 3 sets: eyebrows, eyes and mouth with the dimension as 32, 32 and 40. Each feature channel is given a weight to reduce the effect of

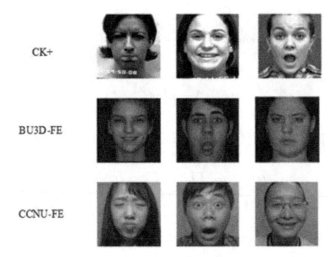

CK+

BU3D-FE

CCNU-FE

Fig. 10. Exemplar expression images in the CK+, BU-3DFE, and CCNU-FE datasets.

differences in dimensions. For training the RF, we fixed some parameters on the basis of empirical observations. The trees have a maximum depth of 15 and at each node we randomly generate 2000 splitting candidates and 32 thresholds.

In the experiment, we used the five-fold method for cross-validation: divide all the images into five groups, each group contains the same number of expressions of all class, of which 4 groups are used for training, the rest group is used for testing. The samples for testing include 60 images from CK dataset, 500 images from BU3D-FE dataset and 2881 images from CCNU-FE dataset. The parameters in the test procedure are fixed exactly the same as the training process.

3.2 Comparison with State of the Art

On CK+ dataset, we compared the proposed cascaded random forest with other state of the art algorithms, the kernel discriminant isomap (KDIsomap) (Zhao and Zhang 2011), which use LBP features of local facial regions and produce low-dimensional discriminant embedded data representations with striking performances improvement on facial expression recognition. And RF and SVM are also tested on the same dataset as contrast test. The experiment results are shown in Table 2.

As shown in Table 2, the average accuracy of the Cascaded random forest and KDIsomap are 95.48% and 94.88% respectively. The results show that cascaded random forest provides higher average accuracy than KDIsomap and traditional methods.

On BU3D-FE dataset, we compared the performance of cascaded random forest with LDA (Wang et al. 2006), which also used 3D facial geometric shapes and associated texture features to recognize facial expressions. In order to test

Table 2. Comparison of results using different methods on CK+ dataset.

Expressions	SVM	KDIsomap (Zhao and Zhang 2011)	Traditional RF	Cascaded RF
Anger	0.400	0.9760	0.8027	0.9404
Disgust	0.960	0.9421	0.9126	0.9398
Fear	0.560	0.9962	0.7998	0.9500
Happiness	0.960	0.9553	0.9960	0.9627
Sadness	0.840	0.8984	0.7555	0.9598
Surprise	0.840	0.9718	0.9434	0.9762
Average	0.76	0.9488	0.8683	0.9548

the influence of feature points on recognition rate, the same cascaded random forest experiment was processed on 3DBU-FE dataset without feature points. The experiments results are shown in Table 3.

Table 3. Comparison of cascaded random forest and LDA on BU3D-FE dataset

Expressions	Proposed method	Cascaded RF (without feature points)	Cascaded RF (without texture features)	LDA (Wang et al. 2006)
Anger	0.827	0.600	0.735	0.800
Disgust	0.850	0.551	0.712	0.804
Fear	0.783	0.331	0.694	0.750
Happiness	0.984	0.922	0.911	0.950
Sadness	0.828	0.463	0.707	0.804
Surprise	0.955	0.753	0.833	0.908
Average	0.871	0.603	0.765	0.836

From Table 3 one can see that the recognition rate of our proposed method outperforms LDA method proposed in (Wang et al. 2006). And the average recognition rate of the proposed method with feature points are 87.1% while the recognition rate is only 60.3% without feature points. It means that the proposed cascaded random forest model based on hybrid features helps to improve the accuracy, and the feature points are good in describing the shape-features in various conditions.

3.3 Cross-Dataset Performance

To test the generalization of the proposed method, a cross-dataset experiment is conducted between BU3D-FE and CCNU-FE datasets. In this experiment, the FER models are trained by 2000 labelled peak sequence of expression images selected from BU3D-FE dataset, and then test on the CCNU-FE dataset. The experiments results are shown in Table 4. The proposed method achieves an average recognition accuracy of 88.9%.

Table 4. Results of Lab dataset

Expressions	Proposed method
Anger	0.8127
Disgust	0.8194
Fear	0.8442
Happiness	0.9905
Sadness	0.8800
Surprise	0.9851
Average	0.8886

4   Conclusions

In this paper, we propose a facial expression recognition method using a cascaded random forest model based on different local regions. The facial expression is represented by the fusion of local texture features (i.e. Gabor features) and facial feature points. Then a cascaded model consisting of a set of RFs based on salient regions from FACS is introduced to classify six basic expressions in a coarse-to-fine way. Extensive experiments show that the proposed method provides better performance compared to the state of the art on CK+ and BU3D-FE datasets.

Acknowledgements. This work was supported by the National Social Science Foundation of China (Grant no. 16BSH107).

References

Chen, J., Chen, D., Gong, Y., Yu, M., Zhang, K., Wang, L.: Facial expression recognition using geometric and appearance features. In: International Conference on Internet Multimedia Computing and Service, pp. 29–33. ACM (2012)

Gudipati, K., Barman, O.R., Gaffoor, M., Abuzneid, A.: Efficient facial expression recognition using adaboost and haar cascade classifiers. In: Industrial Electronics, Technology and Automation (2017)

Kim, B.K., Roh, J., Dong, S.Y., Lee, S.Y.: Hierarchical committee of deep convolutional neural networks for robust facial expression recognition. J. Multimodal User Interfaces **10**(2), 1–17 (2016)

Valstar, M.F., Pantic, M.: Fully automatic recognition of the temporal phases of facial actions. IEEE Trans. Syst. Man Cybern. Part B (Cybern.) **42**(1), 28–43 (2012)

Bagga, S., Jain, S., Hablani, R., Choudhari, N., Tanwani, S.: Facial expression representation and classification using LBP, 2DPCA and their combination. In: It in Business, Industry and Government, pp. 1–5 (2015)

Ali, G., Iqbal, M.A., Choi, T.S.: Boosted NNE collections for multicultural facial expression recognition. Pattern Recogn. **55**, 14–27 (2016)

Owusu, E., Zhan, Y., Mao, Q.R.: An SVM-AdaBoost facial expression recognition system. Appl. Intell. **40**(3), 536–545 (2014)

El Meguid, M.K.A., Levine, M.D.: Fully automated recognition of spontaneous facial expressions in videos using random forest classifiers. IEEE Trans. Affect. Comput. **5**(2), 141–154 (2014)

Soyel, H., Demirel, H.: Facial expression recognition using 3D facial feature distances. In: Kamel, M., Campilho, A. (eds.) ICIAR 2007. LNCS, vol. 4633, pp. 831–838. Springer, Heidelberg (2007). https://doi.org/10.1007/978-3-540-74260-9_74

Tang, H., Huang, T.S.: 3D facial expression recognition based on properties of line segments connecting facial feature points. In: IEEE International Conference on Automatic Face and Gesture Recognition (FG 2008), Amsterdam (2008)

Breiman, L.: Random forests. Mach. Learn. **45**(1), 5–32 (2001)

Yin, L., Wei, X., Sun, Y., Wang, J., Rosato, M.J.: A 3D facial expression database for facial behavior research. In: 7th International Conference on Automatic Face and Gesture Recognition, 10–12 April 2006, pp. 211–216 (2006)

Zhao, X., Zhang, S.: Facial expression recognition based on local binary patterns and kernel discriminant Isomap. Sensors **11**, 9573–9588 (2011)

Wang, J., Yin, L., Wei, X., Sun, Y.: 3D facial expression recognition based on primitive surface feature distribution. In: CVPR (2006)

Milborrow, S., Nicolls, F.: Locating facial features with an extended active shape model. DBLP **5305**, 504–513 (2008)

Ekman, P., Friesen, W.V.: Facial action coding system (FACS): a technique for the the measurement of facial actions. Rivista Di Psichiatria **47**(2), 126–38 (1978)

Lucey, P., Cohn, J.F., Kanade, T., et al.: The Extended Cohn-Kanade Dataset (CK+): acomplete dataset for action unit and emotion-specified expression. ComputerVision and Pattern Recognition Workshops, pp. 94–101. IEEE (2010)

Detection of Salient Regions in Crowded Scenes Based on Weighted Networks Approach

Juan Zheng[1]([⊠]) and Xuguang Zhang[2]

[1] Yanshan University, Qinhuangdao 066004, Hebei, China
soniadeboke@sina.cn
[2] School of Communication Engineering, Hangzhou Dianzi University,
Hangzhou, China
zhangxuguang78@163.com

Abstract. Crowd behavior analysis is a hot research topic in the field of computer vision. This paper proposes a salient region detection method based on weighted networks approach in crowded scenes. Firstly, crowd velocity field is calculated from video sequences by using Pyramid Lucas-Kanade optical flow algorithm. Secondly, every velocity vector for each point in the 2D velocity field is regarded as a node, and the included angle of two velocity vectors is calculated by a vector dot product formula. After that an angle threshold is set to judge whether there is an edge between these two nodes. Finally, the connection degree between nodes is evaluated by the numerical value of the included angle. The node degree strength can reflect the number of edges and the edge strength between nodes. In this context, the salient regions refer to the areas with high node degree strength in relation to the dominant crowded scenes. In the experiments, several different scenarios are used to evaluate the performance of the proposed method, and the results show that the proposed method can detect salient regions in crowded scenes effectively.

Keywords: Weighted networks · Crowd saliency detection
Crowd velocity field · Vector dot product formula · Node strength

1 Introduction

Video surveillance is a very important research field in computer vision. There are many research field about video surveillance, such as target tracking, object detection and crowd analysis. As for crowd analysis, one of the advantage for analyzing crowd video information automatically is to improve working efficiency and save resources. There is no doubt that crowd behavior analysis becomes a hot topic in the field of computer vision research. Anomalous activity or behavior in a crowd scene can be very subtle and imperceptible to human operator [1]. The intelligent monitoring system can help monitoring personnel to focus on salient regions in crowded scenes, and it can raise the alarm earlier when abnormal behavior happens in crowded scenes.

The definition of interesting region in crowd has been causing much debates in the literature due to the subjective nature and complexity of the human behaviors. Some researchers consider any deviation from the ordinary observed events as anomaly,

© Springer International Publishing AG, part of Springer Nature 2018
S. Satoh (Ed.): PSIVT 2017, LNCS 10799, pp. 54–62, 2018.
https://doi.org/10.1007/978-3-319-92753-4_5

whereas others consider rare or outstanding event as interesting [2]. Most existing saliency detection methods are devoted to static images [3–5]. Methods for motion saliency detection have been proposed in [6, 7], but most of them need to be further developed and perfected. Hou and Zhang in [3] proposed a popular spectral residual approach, based on this method, Loy et al. in [8] showed how to detect global anomalous motion flows in a video by analyzing spectral singularities in the motion space. Boiman and Irani in [6] proposed a graphical inference algorithm to detect abnormal behaviors in videos. Although their methods work well in detecting the irregularities in both the images and the videos, large-scale crowd saliency detection is still an open question [9].

In this paper, a salient detection in crowded scenes based on weighted networks approach is proposed. The weighted network is built based on the crowd velocity field which is obtained from the Pyramid Lucas-Kanade optical flow algorithm. We can detect and analyze the moving object in image on the basis of velocity vector characteristics at the position of every pixel. The complex networks can reflect the global topology of the complex system, and due to the fact that complex networks represent the topological skeleton of complex systems there are many dynamical processes that can take place on the nodes and links of these network [10]. Typical example is the pulse coupled neural network [11], which has been widely applied in image segmentation, fusion and thinning [12]. However, only recently the network topology has been considered in the application of crowd behavior analysis. In this paper, we detect the salient region in a crowd using complex network based method. Firstly, we get the crowd velocity field via Pyramid Lucas-Kanade optical flow algorithm. Secondly, each velocity vector is considered as a node, and the included angle of two nodes is calculated by the vector dot product formula, than an angle threshold is set to estimate whether there is an edge between these two nodes. Finally, the numerical value of included angle is regarded as the correlative extent between these two nodes. We can therefore consider the possibility of salient region occurring, when the motion dynamics of individuals differs from the dominant crowd flows. Node strength reflects the status of nodes in whole topological structure, in relation to the dominant crowd flows, it is observed that the nodes in salient region obviously have higher node strength degree.

2   Crowd Weighted Network

2.1   Calculating Crowd Velocity Field

Putting the video converted into current and previous frames, and every pixel in each image is endowed with a velocity vector via optical flow algorithm, then a motion vector field is built. In our paper, we adopt an improved algorithm that is Pyramid optical flow algorithm [13] based on Lucas-Kanade optical flow algorithm [14].

The pre-conditions of Lucas-Kanade optical flow algorithm are the lower velocity, and that the brightness does not change after a period time. When the object moves faster, these conditions are not satisfied in the actual situation and there will be a lot of catastrophic errors in the follow-up work. But Pyramid optical flow algorithm can make up these deficiencies. In addition, the original crowd velocity field is scaled down, then we can get the final crowd velocity field Q. And we make all velocity values on x-axis direction and y-axis direction round to the integer, thus, we can get an orderly crowd velocity vector field as shown as Fig. 1.

Fig. 1. The crowd velocity field (red) of sampled frames. (Color figure online)

2.2   Representation of Crowd Network

Regarding each element inside the system unit as a node, regarding relationship between elements as connection, thus the system can be represent as a network. Emphasizing the internal structure of the system and analyzing system function from the perspective of structure are the research approach of complex networks. The topological structure property of nonobjective real networks and its dynamic property are different from previous research networks, there are lots of nodes in networks, so it is called complex networks. The edges are weighted in complex network model, such as the degree to which person know each other [15].

The crowd velocity field loads more information by the cross correlation of velocity vectors than the property of every velocity. The information storing in the cross correlation of velocity vectors cannot be obtained by measuring the property of each individual velocity vector independently.

Establishment of Nodes. The crowd velocity field is a two-dimensional matrix consisted of velocities with M rows and N columns as shown as Fig. 1. In the crowd weighted network model, first of all, velocity vectors and relationships between them are respectively regarded as nodes and edges in the network. Whether there have an edge between nodes depends on the included angle of them, which can be calculated by velocity vector dot product formula, and the numerical value of included angle between velocities is the weight of edge. Weighted undirected network G^w with node set

$V = \{v_1, v_2, \cdots, v_n\}$ will be generated, the n is the total number of nodes. The number of nodes in network is equal to the number of velocity vectors in the crowd velocity field.

Establishment of Edges and Weight. For given crowd velocity field $Q(M, N)$ with M rows and N columns, selecting a velocity vector $\boldsymbol{q}_{xoyo}$ and a two-dimensional neighborhood δ, the size is $(x_0 \pm \varepsilon, y_0 \pm \varepsilon)$. The expression of deciding whether there is or not an edge between central velocity vector $\boldsymbol{q}_{xoyo}$ and any other velocity vector $\boldsymbol{q}_{xy}(x \neq x_0, y \neq y_0)$ is shown as follows:

$$e\left(\boldsymbol{q}_{xoyo}, \boldsymbol{q}_{xy}\right) \begin{cases} \exists, & \theta \geq \theta_T, \boldsymbol{q}_{xy} \in \delta \\ \nexists, & otherwise \end{cases} \tag{1}$$

where θ_T is an angle threshold, and θ is calculated by velocity vector dot product formula:

$$\theta = arccos \frac{\boldsymbol{q}_{x0y0} \cdot \boldsymbol{q}_{xy}}{|\boldsymbol{q}_{x0y0}||\boldsymbol{q}_{xy}|} \tag{2}$$

Then we can get the weight of edge, the value of the edge weight We can be expressed as follows:

$$We = \theta \tag{3}$$

The significance of the weight of edge is different in different network, weight is divided into similar weight and dissimilar weight. In our weighted network model, the greater weight between nodes is, the closer relationship nodes have, so the weight is similar weight.

Finally, traversing every velocity vector by repeating the steps above. Converting two-dimensional crowd velocity field to the weighted undirected network $G^w(V, E, We)$. The node set of corresponding weighted undirected network $G^w(V, E, We)$ is $V = \{v_1, v_2, \cdots, v_n\}$, and the edge set is $E = \{e_1, e_2, \cdots, e_m\}$. The connected relation between nodes and the connection degree on edges in crowd weighted network model can be expressed by adjacency matrix A.

$$A = \begin{bmatrix} \theta_{11} & \theta_{12} \cdots & \theta_{1n} \\ \vdots & \ddots & \vdots \\ \theta_{n1} & \theta_{n2} \cdots & \theta_{nn} \end{bmatrix} \tag{4}$$

3   Feature Extraction of Crowd Weighted Network

3.1   Calculating Node Strength

Many statistical characteristic parameters of networks can be used to express network characteristic, such as node degree, average path length, clustering coefficient and so on. In this paper, we select node strength to describe the characteristic of crowd weighted network. In complex network model, node strength is the generalization of node degree, it integrates the edges with connection strength between nodes [16]. From adjacency matrix A, the degree strength $s(v_i)$ of node v_i can be expressed as follows:

$$s(v_i) = \sum_{j=1}^{n} \theta_{ij} \tag{5}$$

Then we can get the node strength of all nodes. The node strength field $S(M, N)$ is also a two-dimensional matrix with M rows and N columns. And there is a one-to-one correspondence between the node strength field and crowd velocity field.

$$S = \begin{bmatrix} S_{11} & \cdots & S_{1N} \\ \vdots & \ddots & \vdots \\ S_{M1} & \cdots & S_{MN} \end{bmatrix} \tag{6}$$

3.2 Normalization of Node Strength

The numerical value of included angle between every two velocities is the weight on the edges, it is expressed by radian measure, the interval is $[0, \pi]$. For the convenience of subsequent data processing, we take measures to normalize node strength. We take the relative position of the interval to normalize node strength. The degree strength $s(v_i)$ of node v_i normalized as follows:

$$S = \frac{1}{S_{max} - S_{min}} \begin{bmatrix} S_{11} & \cdots & S_{1N} \\ \vdots & \ddots & \vdots \\ S_{M1} & \cdots & S_{MN} \end{bmatrix} \tag{7}$$

S_{max} and S_{min} are the maximum and minimum in all node strength of nodes.

3.3 Smooth Node Strength Field by Mean Filter Template

Two-dimensional node strength field with M rows and N columns is shown as Eq. (7). Smoothing node strength field with mean filter template $\frac{1}{9} \times \begin{bmatrix} 1 & 1 & 1 \\ 1 & 1 & 1 \\ 1 & 1 & 1 \end{bmatrix}$, it can eliminate negatively affect about experimental results due to too high or too low node strength.

In order to describe and observe the value of node strength intuitively, we take color map to visualize the node strength. The pixel value of color map respond to the value of the node strength. In crowd scene, it is obvious that the nodes in salient region show higher pixel value, and lower pixel value in dominant crowd region.

4 Experimental Results

In our experiments, three crowded scenes from [2] and one video sequence in [17] have been test to show the performance of the proposed method. The counter flow and crowd instability region are detected in our experiments respectively. In different crowded scenes, the size of crowd velocity field $Q(M, N)$, the ε of two-dimensional neighborhood and the angle threshold θ_T are shown as Table 1.

4.1 Counter Flow Detection

In many actual public scenarios, as shown as Figs. 2, 3, there will be some people moving against the dominant crowd flow, which is likely to imply a possible security threat. The method in our paper can detect the retrograde motion of person, for instance, in Figs. 2(a), 3(a), one person moves against the dominant crowd flow. In the color map of node degree strength for crowded scenes, the nodes in retrograde region have higher node strength as shown in Figs. 2(b), 3(b). And Figs. 2(c), 3(c) show that the color map of node degree strength overlays on the input frame. The experiment demonstrates that our method can detect the person who moves against dominant crowd flow.

Table 1. An overview of the parameters in my proposed method.

Crowded scenes	Symbol of parameter	The value
Crowd scene in Fig. 2	ε	15
	θ_T	$8\pi/9$
	M × N	90 × 120
Train station scene in Fig. 3	ε	7
	θ_T	$4\pi/9$
	M × N	180 × 240
Marathon scene in Fig. 4	ε	9
	θ_T	$5\pi/6$
	M × N	120 × 160
Pilgrimage scene in Fig. 5	ε	15
	θ_T	$4\pi/9$
	M × N	120 × 160

4.2 Counter Flow Detection

For counter flow detection, two crowd scenes are shown in Figs. 2, 3. In these scenes, some pedestrians move against the dominant crowd flow, which can be regard as abnormal behavior. The method in our paper can detect the retrograde motion of person, for instance, in Figs. 2(a), 3(a), some pedestrians move against the dominant crowd flow. In the color map of node degree strength for crowded scenes, the nodes in retrograde region have higher node strength as shown in Figs. 2(b), 3(b). And Figs. 2(c), 3(c) show that the color map of node degree strength overlays on the input frame.

The experiment demonstrates that our method can detect the person who moves against dominant crowd flow.

4.3 Crowd Instability Detection

We detect instability in extremely crowded scenes, such as the marathon scene and pilgrimage scene depicted in Figs. 4, 5. In Figs. 4(a) and 5(a), some pedestrians moved different with dominant crowd flow, which is regarded as instability region. In this scenes, synthetic instability were inserted into the original videos by flipping and rotating the flow of a random location [8]. And the ground truth of salient regions is marked in red bounding box. The nodes in instability region have higher node strength as shown in Figs. 4(b), 5(b), our method is able to locate the area which is instability. Figures 4(c), 5(c) show that the color map of node degree strength overlays on the input frame. The experiments prove that our method can detect crowd instability in large-scale crowded scenes. We also compare the results of our method with ground truth and the method proposed in [18]. From Figs. 4 and 5 we can see both the proposed complex network based method and the method in [18] can detect the instability regions well. Our approach detects instability regions more structured. Comparing with traditional methods, our method provides a different idea for crowd instability regions detection using the node strength of complex network.

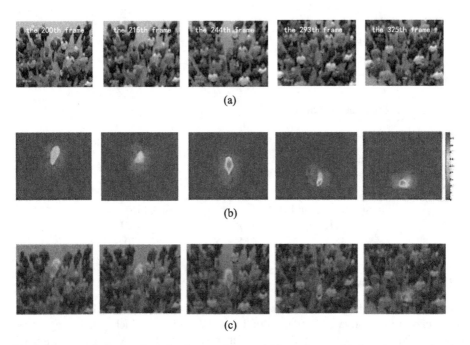

(a)

(b)

(c)

Fig. 2. Retrograde motion detection in crowd scene: (a) input frames (b) the color map of node degree strength (c) saliency map overlaid on the input frame.

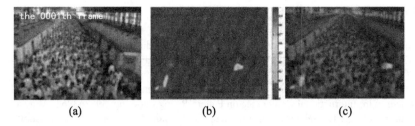

Fig. 3. Retrograde motion detection in train station scene: (a) input frames (b) the color map of node degree strength (c) saliency map overlaid on the input frame.

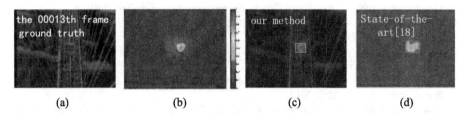

Fig. 4. Crowd instability detection in marathon scene: (a) the ground truth of salient region (as enclosed in red bounding box) (b) the color map of node degree strength (c) saliency map overlaid on the input frame (d) the result of other method. (Color figure online)

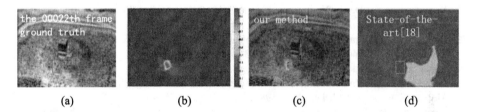

Fig. 5. Crowd instability detection in pilgrimage scene: (a) the ground truth of salient region (as enclosed in red bounding box) (b) the color map of node degree strength (c) saliency map overlaid on the input frame (d) the result of other method. (Color figure online)

5 Conclusion

In this work, a salient region detection method based on crowd weighted network which is constructed from crowd velocity field is proposed. Experimental results show that the proposed method has a good performance both on counter flow detection and crowd instability detection in crowded scenes. In further studies, we will extracted more parameters of complex network to reveal more crowd motion.

Acknowledgments. This research is supported by National Natural Science Foundation of China (No. 61771418, 61271409).

References

1. Challenger, R., Clegg, C.W., Robinson, M.A.: Understanding crowd behaviours: supporting evidence. In: Leigh, M. (ed.): Understanding Crowd Behaviours (Crown, 2009), pp. 1–326 (2009)
2. Lim, M.K., Kok, V.J., Loy, C.C., Chan, C.S.: Crowd saliency detection via global similarity structure. In: International Conference on Pattern Recognition, pp. 3957–3962, August 2014
3. Hou, X., Zhang, L.: Saliency detection: a spectral residual approach. In: IEEE Conference Computer Vision and Pattern Recognition, pp. 1–8 (2007)
4. Itti, L., Koch, C., Niebur, E.: A model of saliency-based visual attention for rapid scene analysis. IEEE Trans. Pattern Anal. Mach. Intell. **20**(11), 1254–1259 (1998)
5. Goferman, S., Zelnik-Manor, L., Tal, A.: Context-aware saliency detection. In: IEEE Conference Computer Vision and Pattern Recognition, pp. 2376–2383 (2010)
6. Boiman, O., Irani, M.: Detecting irregularities in images and in video. Int. J. Comput. Vis. **74**(1), 17–31 (2007)
7. Hung, H.S.W.: From visual saliency to video behavior understanding, Ph.D. thesis, University of London (2007)
8. Loy, C., Xiang, T., Gong, S.: Salient motion detection in crowded scenes. In: ISCCSP, Rome, Italy, pp. 1–4, May 2012
9. Lim, M.K., Chan, C.S., Monekosso, D., Remagnino, P.: Detection of salient regions in crowded scenes. Electron. Lett. **50**(5), 363–365 (2014)
10. Chen, G., Wang, X., Li, X.: Introduction to Complex Networks: Models, Structures and Dynamics. Higher Education Press, Beijing (2012)
11. Johnson, J.L., Padgett, M.L.: Pcnn models and applications. IEEE Trans. Neural Netw. **10** (3), 480–498 (1998)
12. Wu, Z., Lu, X., Deng, Y.: Image edge detection based on local dimension: a complex networks approach. Physica Statis. Mech. Appl. **440**, 9–18 (2015)
13. Bouguet, J.Y.: Pyramidal implementation of the Lucas Kanade feature tracker description of the algorithm. Opencv Documents **22**(2), 363–381 (1999)
14. Lucas, B.D., Kanade, T.: An iterative image registration technique with an application to stereo vision. In: International Joint Conference on Artificial Intelligence, pp. 674–679. Morgan Kaufmann Publishers Inc. (1981)
15. Scientific collaboration networks. I. Network construction and fundamental results. Physical Review E Statistical Nonlinear & Soft Matter Physics, **64**(1 Pt 2), 016131 (2001)
16. Boccaletti, S., Latora, V., Moreno, Y., et al.: Complex networks: structure and dynamics. Phys. Rep. **424**(4–5), 175–308 (2006)
17. Mehran, R., Oyama, A., Shah, M.: Abnormal crowd behavior detection using social force model. In: IEEE Conference on Computer Vision and Pattern Recognition, pp. 935–942 (2009)
18. Ali, S., Shah, M.: A lagrangian particle dynamics approach for crowd flow segmentation and stability analysis. In: CVPR, Minneapolis, MN, USA, pp. 1–6, June 2007

Selecting Salient Features from Facial Components for Face Recognition

A. Gumede, S. Viriri$^{(\boxtimes)}$, and M. V. Gwetu

School of Mathematics, Statistics and Computer Science,
University of KwaZulu-Natal, Pietermaritzburg, South Africa
{211513796,viriris,gwetum}@ukzn.ac.za

Abstract. A robust facial recognition system aims at achieving an optimum accuracy when matching and comparing faces. The system meets an accepted degree of precision when it selects distinctive and salient features from the feature space. This work proposes an approach to select salient features from facial components for identification and verification, disregard of the face configuration. The proposed method employs two local feature descriptors, Scale Invariant Feature Transform (SIFT) and Speed-Up Robust Features (SURF). The descriptors primarily rely on the gradient computation of the facial components to extracts local features from the forehead, eyes, nose, cheeks, mouth and chin. The study evaluates the proposed technique from two face datasets, SCface and CMU-PIE and achieves an excellent performance. The results corroborate that facial components contain rich features and choosing only the prominent features from the feature space can improve the accuracy of facial recognition.

Keywords: Face recognition · Facial components · Shape descriptors
Texture descriptors

1 Introduction

Feature selection is another way of removing redundant features and obtain compact information about the face. Its aim is to select a small subset of features that minimise redundancy and maximise relevance to class labels in facial classification. Very little research is available in feature selection for facial recognition. The paradigm is mainly on face appearance data, template-based algorithms, and their concomitant subspace versions.

Principal Component Analysis (PCA) and Linear Discriminant Analysis (LDA) are the most popular algorithms, and recently Independent Component Analysis (ICA) is employed by numerous studies for face recognition as an alternative subspace method [9]. Although the feature selection criterion used in PCA-based face recognition systems yields to the most compact set of features for the reconstruction, it does not necessarily guarantee optimality from face recognition point of view.

© Springer International Publishing AG, part of Springer Nature 2018
S. Satoh (Ed.): PSIVT 2017, LNCS 10799, pp. 63–75, 2018.
https://doi.org/10.1007/978-3-319-92753-4_6

Similar approaches to PCA such as ICA methods do not have feature selection criterion. Instead, the number of ICA features is pre-determined in the PCA stage of data processing [9,15]. Both feature extraction and feature selection are capable of optimizing the computational complexity of a learning algorithm. This improves the mapping of original features to a new optimum feature space with lower dimensions.

The analysis of new features is problematic since there is no physical meaning for the transformed features obtained from the original feature space. In this regard, feature selection is superior regarding better readability and understanding. This property has its significance in many practical applications such as finding relevant face features to represent the identity of an individual analysis. In this case, feature selection is more reliable to obtain fully representative information of faces.

For the classification problem, feature selection aims to select the subset of highly discriminant features. In other words, it selects elements that are capable of discriminating samples that belong to different classes. For the problem of feature selection for classification, due to the availability of label information, the relevance of features is assessed as the capability of distinguishing various classes.

This work addresses the significance of selecting a subset of salient features to improve the accuracy of facial recognition. The rest of the paper organises as follows: Sect. 2 is the overview of the methodology to the proposed approach, Sect. 3 discusses the experimental results and Sect. 4 concludes and outline the future work.

2 Methods and Techniques

2.1 Preprocessing

The performance of a face recognition technique largely depends on numerous factors, such as noise which comes in all sort of forms. Hence, pre-processing is essential to overcome these factors. A combination of three preprocessing techniques is proposed, i.e. Gamma Correction, Difference of Gaussian (DOG) filter, and Contrast Equalization (CE) [8,10,20]. Gamma correction enhances shadowed regions. The pixel intensities of the input image are scaled from $[0, 255]$ to $[0, 1.0]$. Then the filter (1) is applied to an input image to produce a gamma corrected image.

$$I_{output} = I_{input}^{1/\gamma} \begin{cases} \text{if } G < 1, \text{shift towards dark.} \\ \text{if } G > 1, \text{shift towards light.} \\ \text{if } G = 0, \text{no effect.} \end{cases} \tag{1}$$

The effect of $G < 1$ shift the image towards darker spectrum, while $G > 1$ shift towards lighter and $G = 1$ has no effect. Gamma corrections does not remove all shading effects therefore further preprocessing using the DOG filter overcome this factor. The DOG filter (2) eliminates shadowing effects and suppresses high-frequency spatial information that is present in the image.

$$DOG(x,y) = \frac{1}{2\pi\sigma_1^2}e^{-\frac{(x^2+y^2)}{2\pi\sigma_1^2}} - \frac{1}{2\pi\sigma_2^2}e^{-\frac{(x^2+y^2)}{2\pi\sigma_2^2}}. \tag{2}$$

This filter increases the visibility of edges to make it easier to detect and locate the face and the facial components. However, it reduces the overall contrast of an image, hence the contrast has to be enhanced in subsequent stages, using the Contrast Enhancement(CE). CE adjusts pixel intensities to standardise the overall intensity variations and normalises the histogram of discrete grey values of the image, which is adjusted using Histogram Equalisation (HE) technique defined by (3) and (4).

$$p_n = \frac{n}{n_t} \tag{3}$$

where n is number of pixels with intensity n and n_t is the total number of pixels. The image g with adjusted intensities is defined by

$$g_{(i,j)} = floor((L-1)\sum_{n=0}^{f_{(i,j)}} p_n). \tag{4}$$

where **floor()** rounds down to the nearest integer. HE has simplified the detection and recognition of image in low lighting conditions.

2.2 Component Detection

The face detection algorithm is based on the work from Viola and Jones mainly because of its fast execution speed [19]. However, it is further trained to detect per-component, i.e. Forehead, Cheeks and Chin. Figure 1 show a complete face and component detection. The three other components are presumably considered to be distinct for the facial recognition model of this work.

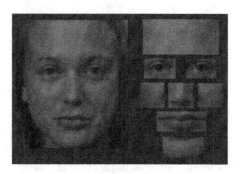

Fig. 1. Face component detection.

2.3   Feature Extraction

Local features are extracted at various levels of sparsity. The idea is to use interest points found at different scales, where scales are implemented as image pyramids. The pyramids consist of levels obtained by the Gaussian filter (smoothing parameter) and image sub-sampling techniques. Scale Invariant Feature Transform (SIFT) and Speeded-Up Robust Features (SURF) have been used to extract local features from the facial components [14].

The former works well in pose and expression invariant, whereas the latter is robust in various illumination changes. These two descriptors offer scale and rotation invariant properties; therefore they are suitable to model the problem of interest of this work. The SIFT descriptor is popular in visual object categorization and baseline matching [1,13]. It is a vector of 128-dimensions that stores the gradients of pixel locations of size 4×4 [3].

It applies in face recognition as a rotation invariant descriptor. However, some studies [1,5,17] reports that in some instances where the face is not in upright view the descriptor results to false matching. To overcome this problem, upright version of this descriptor (U-SIFT) substitutes the normal 128-SIFT. Figure 2 shows the feature scores of the two descriptors extracted from various levels of sparsity from the facial components.

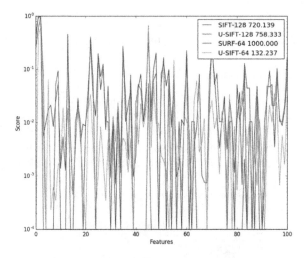

Fig. 2. SIFT and SURF feature scores.

Algorithm 1 is the extraction of features using SIFT and SURF descriptors. The majority of images from the databases utilised in this work have different face poses. Hence, this work employs both the SIFT and U-SIFT descriptors to capture obvious points from the components. Table 1 lists the feature scores of computed by 128-SIFT descriptor for all seven facial components with corresponding total number of features for each component. It can be seen from

---

Algorithm 1. Extract SIFT and SURF descriptors.

    Input   : Set of components as sub-images.
    Output: $F_{descriptors}$.
1 $SIFT_{keypoints} \leftarrow$ Detect
2 $SURF_{keypoints} \leftarrow$ Detect
3 **for** *each component* **do**
4 | $SIFT'_{keypoints} \leftarrow Compute[SIFT_{keypoints}]$
5 | $SURF'_{keypoints} \leftarrow compute[SURF_{keypoints}]$
6 | /** Normalize using Algorithm 3.*/
7 | $SIFT_{descriptors} \leftarrow$ **NORMALIZE**$(SIFT'_{keypoints})$
8 | $SURF_{descriptors} \leftarrow$ **NORMALIZE**$(SURF'_{keypoints})$
9 | $F_{descriptors} \leftarrow (SIFT_{descriptors} + SURF_{descriptors})$
10 **end**
11 **return** $F_{descriptors}$

---

the table below that each component has large number of features and there are susceptible to noise. Similarly, the SURF descriptor is a scale and rotation invariant detector and descriptor to detect key points [12]. Unlike the SIFT, the 64-dimensional SURF focusses on the spatial distribution of gradient information within the interest point neighbourhoods [4]. According to [4], when SURF is applied in face recognition, invariance rotation is often not necessary. Therefore, this work uses the upright version of the SURF descriptor (i.e. U-SURF) to compute distinct interest point features.

Table 1. SIFT total feature scores for all facial components.

Face components	SIFT	Total features
Forehead	$[-0.0081, \ldots, -0.0094]$	395
Eyes	$[-0.0019, \ldots, -0.0065]$	393
Nose	$[-0.0008, \ldots, -0.0100]$	387
Left-Cheek	$[-0.0064, \ldots, -0.0014]$	402
Right-Cheek	$[-0.0035, \ldots, -0.0036]$	386
Mouth	$[-0.0004, \ldots, -0.0121]$	391
Chin	$[-0.0004, \ldots, -0.0121]$	345

SURF that stays more robust to various image perturbations than the more locally operating SIFT descriptor. In [4], they analyse if this effect to observe if the SURF are effective in recognising faces under various illuminations and their analysis was positive in that SURF is effective in facial recognition. This work employs the implementation described [2] to extracts SURF from different facial components. Table 2 lists the feature scores of computed by 64-SURF descriptor for all seven facial components with corresponding total number of features for each component. It can be seen from the table below that each component has large number of features and there are susceptible to noise.

Table 2. SURF total feature scores for all facial components.

Face components	SURF	Total features
Forehead	$[-0.0004, \ldots, -0.0017]$	502
Eyes	$[-0.0013, \ldots, -0.0151]$	483
Nose	$[-0.0018, \ldots, -0.0111]$	378
Left-Cheek	$[-0.1434, \ldots, -0.0139]$	502
Right-Cheek	$[-0.0117, \ldots, -0.0111]$	483
Mouth	$[-0.0004, \ldots, -0.0018]$	401
Chin	$[-0.0004, \ldots, -0.0317]$	435

The scores represent the amount of features from a complete set of the facial components from a single face. This shows the amount of potential features a single face may have and they are susceptible to noise and feature selection is crucial in this case. Figure 3 shows a Receiver Operating Characteristic (ROC) curve measuring the performance of each descriptor with potential features extracted by both descriptors. The SURF descriptor seems to have more features compared to the SIFT descriptor. Algorithm 1 is the extraction of features using SIFT and SURF descriptors.

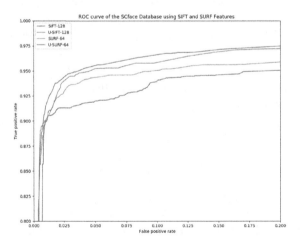

Fig. 3. Comparisons of ROC curve of the SIFT and SURF features..

2.4   Feature Selection

Face recognition systems often encounter a large number of features during feature extraction. The SIFT and SURF have shown positive results in selecting prominent features. Any feature is most likely to be susceptible to noise, which may cause the learning algorithm to over fit. Hence, selecting only relevant features is essential to minimise performance bias. This work employs a wrapper-based approach from Sequential Selection (SSA), i.e. Sequential Forward Selection (SFS) [16].

The model selects salient features from SIFT & SURF key points using a bottom-up search technique which starts with an empty feature set and gradually adds selected features using an evaluation function to minimises the classification error [11]. Algorithm 2, a tuned version of SFS applied to facial components, the original version of the algorithm can be found in [11].

The algorithm takes the SIFT + SURF descriptor feature set as an input and returns a subset of features, i.e. the number of selected features k, where $k < d$, where d is the dimensionality of the descriptors. An additional parameter x^+ is added to the feature subset, to maximize every feature that is associated with the best classifier performance if it is added to X_k. All these are then classified by the Support Vector Machine classifier.

Algorithm 2. Feature Selection on SIFT + SURF.

Input   : $Y \leftarrow \{y_1, y_2, \ldots, y_d\}$.
Output: $X_k \leftarrow \{x_j | j = 1, 2, \ldots, x_j \in Y\}$, where k=(0, 1, 2, 3, ..., d).
1 **initialize:** $X_0 \leftarrow \emptyset, k \leftarrow 0$.
2 **repeat**
3 $\quad$ $x^+ \leftarrow arg_{max} J(x_k + x)$, where $x \in Y - X_k$.
4 $\quad$ $X_k + 1 \leftarrow X_k + x_+$.
5 $\quad$ $k \leftarrow k + 1$
6 **until**;
7 **return** X_k

Figure 4 shows the SIFT and SURF features respectively (represented in black), and after the application of SFS, all the unnecessary features remain in black and only salient features remain dominant (represented in red). The area under each curve indicates the rate at which the features are relevant (feature score). This show that many features remain clustered at the lower level. Also, this implies that the features are not rich as a result they degrade the performance of an algorithm.

2.5   Feature Normalization

The SIFT and SURF descriptors contain heterogeneous features, hence to transform them into a common domain, they need a processing mechanism. This work employs the Min-Max normalisation scheme defined by Eq. (5).

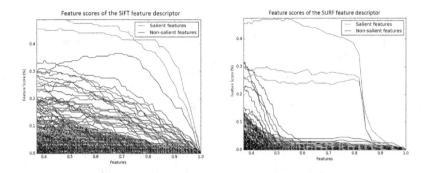

Fig. 4. SIFT and SURF relevant features represented in red. (Color figure online)

$$\bar{x} = \frac{x - \min(F_x)}{\max(F_x) - \min(F_x)} \tag{5}$$

where F_x represent the function that generates x, and $\min(F_x)$ and $\min(F_x)$ represents the minimum and maximum values respectively for all possible x. Algorithm 3 is the Min-max for normalizing a set of feature vector of facial components. The algorithm output a augmented feature vector with homogeneous features vector scaled between [0–1] for each component.

Algorithm 3. Feature vector normalization

---

1 <u>function NORMALIZE (F)</u>;
   Input   : Set of component feature vectors F.
   Output: Augmented feature vector F_a.
2 $F_{min} \leftarrow 0$
3 $F_{size} \leftarrow lenght(F)$
4 **for** $i{=}1$ to F_{size} **do**
5     $x_{norm} \leftarrow []$
6     $x \leftarrow F[i]$
7     $F_{max} \leftarrow lenght(x)$
8   **for** $j{=}1$ to F_{max} **do**
9        $x_{norm}[j] \leftarrow (x[i] - F_{min})/(F_{max} - F_{min})$
10   **end**
11    $F_a \leftarrow x_{norm}$
12 **end**
13 **return** F_a

---

3   Experiment Analysis

3.1   Facial Databases

For a facial recognition system to perform face detection and face recognition (FR) successfully, it requires a facial database. This work uses two state-of-the-art facial recognition databases i.e. SCFace and CMU-PIE. The SCface is a database of static images that were taken in the uncontrolled indoor environment using cameras of various qualities. The database contains 4160 static images of 130 subjects. Images from different quality cameras mimic the real-world conditions and allow facial recognition algorithm testing [6].

CMU-PIE is a database of 41,368 images of 68 subjects, with every person configure under 13 different poses, 43 different illumination conditions, and with four different expressions [18]. This study employs these two state-of-the-art databases because they appear in high frequencies in the literature. As a result, this will enable this work to benchmark the results with those of other studies using the similar database.

3.2   Results and Performance Evaluation

The motivation behind feature selection is to automatically select a subset of features that are most relevant to the problem. Therefore the goal of this work is to improve the computation efficiency and reduce the generalisation error of the model by removing irrelevant features. As a result, this study presents a wrapper approach to select salient features for face recognition. The testing and evaluation of the selected features are done by conducting facial recognition using the identification procedure defined in [7]. The recognition is done on every face from each of the state-of-the-art databases. Table 3 lists the face recognition results using a combination of selected facial features from SIFT and SURF descriptors on the SCFace database.

Table 3. SCface database classifications and recognition results.

Descriptor	Probe View Accuracy (%)		Time (ms)
	Front	Non-frontal	
SURF-64	96.6	94	0.7
U-SURF-64	97	93.5	0.75
SIFT-128	92.5	90	0.33
U-SIFT-128	95.6	94.64	0.88
Combined descriptors	97.57	95.43	0.94

Table 4 lists the face recognition results using a combination of selected facial features from SIFT and SURF descriptors on the SCFace database. In many classification problems, it's hard to learn good classifiers before removing these unwanted features due to the massive size of the data. Reducing the number of redundant features can drastically reduce the running time of the learning algorithms and yields a more general classifier. This can be seen from Tables 3 and 4, that the time taken to execute is significantly less than a one second. This justifies rich features carries a lot of unnecessary information that degrades the quality of component features from the face. Assessing the performance of the proposed method using the two face databases, the recognition results are significant.

Table 4. SCface database classifications and recognition results.

Descriptor	Probe View Accuracy (%)		Time (ms)
	Front	Non-frontal	
SURF-64	93	80	0.3
U-SURF-64	94	85	0.10
SIFT-128	84	80	0.12
U-SIFT-128	91	88	0.10
Combined descriptors	91	83.25	0.45

Table 5 lists the results on the SCFace database with an overall recognition rate is 95.4%, and CMU-PIE is 97.83%, with a fall-out of 4.6% and 2.17% respectively.

Table 5. SCface database classifications and recognition results.

Alarm rate	Accuracy (%)	
	Front	Non-frontal
Sensitivity (TPR)	95.4	97.83
Fall-out (FPR)	4.6	2.17

The performance evaluation of the classification of features of the two descriptors is depicted in Fig. 5. It can be seen that the SURF descriptor can obtain significant features compare to the SIFT. Although, filtering these features is essential for better performance. The objective of this study minimizes the fall-out and maximises the sensitivity, and the results seem to support that this objective has been met by carefully choosing salient features.

3.3 Comparison with the State of the Art Methods

Principal Component Analysis (PCA) and Linear Discriminant Analysis (LDA) are the state of the art algorithms that have been employed by various studies in

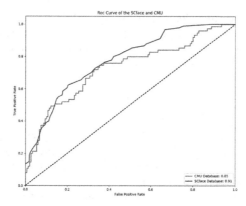

Fig. 5. Performance evaluation the SCface and CMU-PIE face databases.

many applications. Recently, the Independent Component Analysis (ICA) has shown significant improvements as an alternative subspace method [9]. Although the feature selection criterion used in PCA-based face recognition systems yields to the most compact set of features for the reconstruction, it does not necessarily guarantee optimality from face recognition point of view. Also, PCA such as ICA methods do not have feature selection criterion. Instead, the number of ICA features is pre-determined in the PCA stage of data processing [9,15]. Hence, this study proposes a dedicated approach to select salient features for face recognition.

4   Conclusion and Future Work

In this study, we have explored feature selection on two local feature descriptors, SURF and SIFT basis for facial recognition. This study was carried out on two state-of-the-art face databases, CMU-PIE and SCFace. These databases contain both facial expression and illumination variations. Among a family of feature selection algorithms, Sequential Selection Algorithms (SSA) have been used comparatively, and a wrapper approach Sequential Forward Selection (SFS) method was observed to be uniformly effective in all classes, in that the maximum correct classification rate was obtained with its feature subset.

This study concludes with that feature selection applied improves the recognition performance. Also, if features are selected from the augmented pool of both SIFT and SURF features, the performance improvement becomes 97%. In other words, it pays to select feature subset from a larger pool of them, particularly SIFT and SURF rather than deciding a priori for the dimensionality of the final feature subset. Indeed, instead of selecting features on the basis pre-defined feature selection strategies, it is more beneficial to search for the subset resulting in the best possible classification performance from a larger pool.

The discriminatory features from larger pools are observed to be concentrated around fiduciary spatial details of the nose, eyes and the facial contour.

It is important to note that elements from local descriptors benefited from this approach when a subset of them was selected from the of a pool via Sequential Forward Selection (SFS) algorithm instead just choosing the first most energetic ones, as is commonly done in the literature.

References

1. Aly, M.: Face recognition using SIFT features. CNS/Bi/EE report, 186 (2006)
2. Bay, H., Tuytelaars, T., Van Gool, L.: SURF: speeded up robust features. In: Leonardis, A., Bischof, H., Pinz, A. (eds.) ECCV 2006. LNCS, vol. 3951, pp. 404–417. Springer, Heidelberg (2006). https://doi.org/10.1007/11744023_32
3. Lowe, D.G.: Distinctive image features from scale-invariant keypoints. Int. J. Comput. Vis. (IJCV) **60**(2), 91–110 (2004)
4. Dreuw, P., Steingrube, P., Hanselmann, H., Ney, H., Aachen, G.: SURF-face: face recognition under viewpoint consistency constraints. In: BMVC, pp. 1–11, September 2009
5. Geng, C., Jiang, X.: Face recognition using sift features. In: 2009 16th IEEE International Conference on Image Processing (ICIP), pp. 3313–3316. IEEE, November 2009
6. Grgic, M., Delac, K., Grgic, S.: SCface–surveillance cameras face database. Multimed. Tools Appl. **51**(3), 863–879 (2011)
7. Gumede, A., Viriri, S., Gwetu, M.: Hybrid component-based face recognition. In: Conference on Information Communication Technology and Society (ICTAS), pp. 1–6. IEEE, March 2017
8. Guo, H., He, H., Chen, M.: Gamma correction for digital fringe projection profilometry. Appl. Opt. **43**(14), 2906–2914 (2004)
9. Jain, A.K., Li, S.Z.: Handbook of Face Recognition. Springer, New York (2011). https://doi.org/10.1007/978-0-85729-932-1
10. Kim, T.K., Paik, J.K., Kang, B.S.: Contrast enhancement system using spatially adaptive histogram equalization with temporal filtering. IEEE Trans. Consum. Electron. **44**(1), 82–87 (1998)
11. Kittler, J.: Feature selection and extraction. In: Handbook of Pattern Recognition and Image Processing, pp. 59–83 (1986)
12. Lenc, L., Král, P.: A combined SIFT/SURF descriptor for automatic face recognition. In: Sixth International Conference on Machine Vision (ICMV 2013), pp. 90672C–90672C. International Society for Optics and Photonics, December 2013
13. Lowe, D.G.: Distinctive image features from scale-invariant key points. Int. J. Comput. Vis. **60**(2), 91–110 (2004)
14. Mikolajczyk, K., Schmid, C.: A performance evaluation of local descriptors. IEEE Trans. Pattern Anal. Mach. Intell. **27**(10), 1615–1630 (2005)
15. Nina, Z., Wang, L.: Class-dependent feature selection for face recognition. In: Köppen, M., Kasabov, N., Coghill, G. (eds.) ICONIP 2008. LNCS, vol. 5507, pp. 551–558. Springer, Heidelberg (2009). https://doi.org/10.1007/978-3-642-03040-6_67
16. Oh, I.S., Lee, J.S., Moon, B.R.: Hybrid genetic algorithms for feature selection. IEEE Trans. Pattern Anal. Mach. Intell. **26**(11), 1424–1437 (2004)
17. Patnaik, R.: Face Recognition using SIFT features. Symphony of Vision, p. 84 (2004)

18. Sim, T., Baker, S., Bsat, M.: The pose, illumination, and expression (PIE) database. In: International Conference on Automatic Face and Gesture Recognition (2002)
19. Viola, P., Jones, M.: Rapid object detection using a boosted cascade of simple features. In: Proceedings of the 2001 IEEE Computer Society Conference on Computer Vision and Pattern Recognition, CVPR 2001, vol. 1, p. I (2001)
20. Wang, S., Li, W., Wang, Y., Jiang, Y., Jiang, S., Zhao, R.: An improved difference of gaussian filter in face recognition. J. Multimed. **7**(6), 429–433 (2012)

Educational Cloud and Image and Video Enriched Cloud Services

Workshop on Educational Cloud and Image and Video Enriched Cloud Services

The workshop on Educational Cloud and Image and Video Enriched Cloud Services was held in conjunction with the 8th Pacific Rim Symposium on Image and Video Technology (PSIVT 2017), held in Wuhan, China, on November 21, 2017.

The workshop aims to present the most recent works in the area of image/video-enriched services and the educational cloud for innovative education, and to provide researchers with a forum to exchange and discuss recent progress in this area. The educational cloud in the education domain aims to build intelligent educational systems. Promoting the educational cloud service has been a long-term endeavor, and the importance of cloud computing in education has been universally recognized for a long time. Many countries and organizations set up projects to fund research on the education cloud. It is important to facilitate innovative collaboration between education methodology and the educational cloud. The topics of the workshop include image- and video-enriched AI tutoring, Finland–China cooperation on EduCloud, intelligent educational evaluation, corpus construction, learning map, data mining as a service, point cloud modeling, parallel education systems, adaptive English ability assessment, machine vision-based foot modeling, etc.

We would like to thank our authors for their efforts. We would also like to thank the Program Committee members for providing very useful and detailed comments. In addition, we thank the local organizers of PSIVT 2017 for their support.

November 2017

Xiwei Liu
Jiehan Zhou

Organization

Workshop Organizers

Xiwei Liu	Chinese Academy of Science, China
Jiehan Zhou	Jukka Riekki, University of Oulu, Finland
Pengpeng Jian	Central China Normal University, China

Program Committee

Xiwei Liu	Chinese Academy of Science, China
Jiehan Zhou	Jukka Riekki, University of Oulu
Xiaoyan Gong	Chinese Academy of Science, China
Arto Hellas	University of Helsinki, Finland
Petri Ihantola	Tampere University of Technology, Finland
Wei Tang	Beijing Normal University, China
Matti Hämäläinen	DIMECC, Finland
Pengpeng Jian	Central China Normal University, China
Pasi Mattila	Finpeda Oy, Finland

Research on Optimization of Point Cloud Registration ICP Algorithm

Jian Liu[1,3], Xiuqin Shang[2], Shuzhan Yang[1,4], Zhen Shen[5,6],
Xiwei Liu[5], Gang Xiong[2,6(✉)], and Timo R. Nyberg[2,7]

[1] The State Key Laboratory for Management and Control of Complex Systems,
Institute of Automation, Chinese Academy of Sciences, Beijing 100190, China
[2] Cloud Computing Center, Chinese Academy of Sciences,
Dongguan 523808, China
gang.xiong@ia.ac.cn
[3] College of Information Science and Technology, Beijing University
of Chemical Technology, Beijing 100029, China
[4] Department of Mechanics and Engineering Science (MES),
College of Engineering, Peking University, Beijing 100871, China
[5] Institute of Smart Education Systems, Qingdao Academy
of Intelligent Industries, Qingdao 266109, China
[6] Beijing Engineering Research Center of Intelligent Systems and Technology,
Institute of Automation, Chinese Academy of Sciences, Beijing 100190, China
[7] Department of Industrial Engineering and Management, School of Science,
Aalto University, P.O. Box 11000, 00076 Aalto, Finland

Abstract. Point cloud data, as a basis for the three-dimensional data types has attracted more and more attention these years. compared with other types of three-dimensional data, point cloud data can be collected by simple ways, and it contains surface texture, surface color, and other types of features on the surface of the target object. Recently, in the field of cloud data processing, many new point cloud processing methods have been proposed on the basis of existed theory, among which, the most notable one is the newly proposed algorithm in the field of point cloud registration. In this paper, an improved point cloud registration algorithm based on classical ICP algorithm is proposed. In the classical ICP algorithm, the main part which limit the efficiency of the algorithm is the iterative search process of the corresponding point, the new algorithm proposed in this paper uses the 4-point coincidence algorithm to accelerate the corresponding point search process as an improvement to the classical ICP algorithm, and to verify its improvement by experiment.

Keywords: Point cloud data · Point cloud registration · ICP algorithm
4-point consistent algorithm

1 Introduction

With the development of 3D scanning technology and related hardware manufacturing technology, there are a variety of cheap and useful scanning equipment could be used for documenting high-precision 3D data. And the acquired 3D can be applied to many

© Springer International Publishing AG, part of Springer Nature 2018
S. Satoh (Ed.): PSIVT 2017, LNCS 10799, pp. 81–90, 2018.
https://doi.org/10.1007/978-3-319-92753-4_7

areas including digital city, intelligent transportation, game, films [1] and so on. Point cloud data is a basic three-dimensional data type, it could be obtained through a variety of scanning equipment by directly scan, and retain a large number of surface features related to the target object, and thus it applicate in the machine vision, 3D printing, reverse engineering and many other fields [2]. The point cloud data obtained from direct scanning is derived from the massive surface measurement point on the surface of the target object [3]. The surface measurement point can achieve the accurate performance of the surface features of the target objects [4]. In practice, however, the point cloud data about the target object, which is simply obtained by the three-dimensional scanning, is often disturbed by a variety of factors, among them, due to differences in the scanning angle, which caused by the difference between the different points of view and the applicable coordinate system, could have a huge impact on the accuracy and operability of the overall point cloud data. Therefore, it is necessary to register the obtained point cloud data so that the point cloud data which sets at different angles will apply to the same three-dimensional coordinate system.

Point cloud registration refers to the need to deal with the set of points to a series of rotation, translation and other operations to transform the point set to the target perspective [5], that is, transfer point cloud data from different scanning angles to the same three-dimensional coordinates. The study of point cloud registration began in the 1980s and has a breakthrough in the 1990s. In 1992, Besl and Mckay of General Motors Laboratory proposed the Iterative Closest Point (ICP) algorithm [6], the algorithm obtains the transformation parameters of the point set transformation by collecting and analyzing the geometric and geometric distances between the corresponding points between two or several point sets, and further derives the transformation matrix of the point set, transforms the set of points by transform matrix and makes the final result reach the precision requirement. The algorithm is now a classic algorithm in the field of point cloud registration. At present, many new 3D point cloud registration algorithms are actually improved types of ICP algorithm. But with the expansion of point cloud data applications, the classic ICP algorithm has been unable to adapt to the current operational requirements, and gradually exposed many of its design shortcomings [7]. Since the classical ICP algorithm is based on the iterative algorithm, the processing speed can be very high, but the processing efficiency of the algorithm can also be affected by the iterative process, and the requirement of the classical ICP for the initial point cloud dataset is difficult to achieve in the real scene, therefore, the corresponding processing module in the ICP algorithm needs to be improved to accommodate the current point cloud registration processing requirements.

2 ICP Algorithm and the Improved Method

At present, the general-purpose three-dimensional scanner equipment has realized that the surface characteristic of the target object can be collected with high precision and converted into three-dimensional point cloud form [8]. At the same time, considering the various problems that may be encountered on the actual use, such as limited field of view, the surface of the object is complex, ambient light interference, scanners need to go through a number of different angles under the scan to get all the objects surface 3D information [9]. In order to process point cloud data in the same coordinate system, it is necessary to register the point cloud data at different angles [10].

2.1 Classic ICP Algorithm

The specific operation of the point cloud registration is to transform it into a unified three-dimensional coordinate system by rotating the pan-point data at different viewing angles or coordinate systems. The main form of the registration operation is the conversion of the point cloud data coordinate system, and then the fitting operation of several points is completed, so that the scattered point set can be a complete set of point clouds that express the surface features of the target object. In the process of registration operation, the transformation of point set can be divided into Euclidean transformation and rigid transformation.

The main method of 3D point cloud registration operation can be expressed by Eq. 1:

$$P_m = M \cdot P_d + T \tag{1}$$

In Eq. 1, P_m and P_d are denoted by two corresponding points at two different points of view, which can be searched by iterative methods, Where the P_m belongs to the set of target points, P_d belongs to the set of points to be processed, M represents the rotation matrix for the rotation of P_d, and T represents the translation matrix that translates P_d. It can be seen from the Eq. 1, in the point cloud data registration operation, the first thing need to do is quantifying and estimating geometric positional relationship between the two cloud points. And the estimate of the relationship between the corresponding points in the point cloud is the key problem in the point cloud registration operation.

The essence of the Iterative Closest Point (ICP) algorithm is an optimal iterative registration method based on the least squares method. The ICP algorithm performs iterative search and iterative transformation of the corresponding points between the point sets. The key point is the search of the corresponding point and the selection of the rotation translation matrix.

The computational idea of the ICP algorithm can be regarded as a process of minimizing the operation of the objective function as shown in Eq. 2:

$$f(R, T) = \sum_{i=1}^{n} \left\| P_i^k - (RP_i + T) \right\|^2 \tag{2}$$

Where P_i represents the corresponding point to be processed, R represents the rotation matrix, T represents the translation matrix and the offset variables that need to be taken into account in the operation. It can be found from Eq. 2 that the objective function calculates the sum of the Euclidean distances between the corresponding points between several point sets. From the above analysis, it can be seen that the core step of the ICP algorithm lies in the search for the corresponding point P_i and the operation of the corresponding operation matrices R and T, so that the classical ICP algorithm can be completed for the two known points to be registered Its registration operation:

(1) Find the corresponding point: Because the initial state do not know the two points between the corresponding points is punctual. Therefore, in the case of the original point cloud data, we can first set the rotation of the original rotation matrix, and then use the rotation and translation matrix to deal with the point cloud to transform, and then the original matrix transformation results obtained with the target point cloud comparison. If the distance between some points in the two point clouds is less than the set threshold (the threshold setting will be discussed below), these points can be determined as the corresponding points. The decision for the corresponding point is also the origin of the "nearest point" in the ICP (iterative nearest point) algorithm name.

(2) Optimize the R and T matrices: Through the first step of the process, we can use the R (rotation) matrix and T (translation) matrix to extract the corresponding point of the point cloud data to transform. In the classical ICP algorithm, the degree of freedom of the rotation translation matrix is only 6, but the maximum number of corresponding points are treated when the redundancy detection value needs to be considered. The best solution at the present is to use the least squares method and the like method to solve the optimal rotation of the rotation matrix.

Iterative operation: In the second step of the process, we will get the optimized rotation of the translation matrix, however, the use of this step to optimize the matrix after the point cloud rotation shift operation does not necessarily allow the point cloud to be accurately registered to the target point cloud, but because of the step of the operation, the point cloud to be processed changes, at this point, the ICP algorithm needs to return to the second step to re-select the optimal rotation translation matrix, the second step is iterated. The iteration is terminated when the Euclidean distance square sum obtained from the initial objective function 1 is lower than a certain set value, or the change amount of the rotation translation matrix is ultimately below a certain value. And then get the three-dimensional point cloud model after registration.

Based on the above steps, we can get the algorithm flow chart shown in Fig. 1:

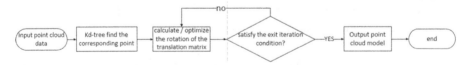

Fig. 1. Classic ICP algorithm flow chart.

2.2 Analysis of ICP Algorithm

For the classical ICP algorithm, the corresponding point search and the rotation translation matrix are optimized by using the nearest neighbor search algorithm to find the optimal pair of points, and make it to rotate the translation matrix to make it modify and Optimization, the entire process iterates until the output value reaches the iteration termination condition. It should be noted that the optimization process for the rotation translation matrix will reduce the Euclidean distance between the corresponding points of the cloud point and the target point cloud, so the rotation translation matrix optimization operation will reduce the initial target of the ICP algorithm Function of the value, which means that the ICP algorithm has convergence.

In the process of algorithm operation, it should be noted that the algorithm need to set two important parameters to ensure that the ICP algorithm can be successfully implemented, the two important parameters are the corresponding point in the search process of the adjacent distance parameters, and the iterative process of the iteration termination parameters. The choice of parameters should be based on the requirements of practical application. For example, if the accuracy of the required model is 1 mm, the point pairs with adjacent neighbors less than 1 mm should be set as corresponding points in the corresponding point search process. Should be terminated when the adjacent distance of each matching point is less than 1 mm.

2.3   Improved ICP Algorithm

Because the main processing steps of ICP algorithm are based on iterative calculation, when the number of points which contained in the point cloud data is too large, it is easy to have a bad effect to the efficiency of ICP algorithm. At the same time, in the actual application, the points data often tends to have many inaccurate and even erroneous points or points after the pretreatment can have an effect on the final result. Also, the ICP algorithm is not able to handle the point cloud where the initial position is too large in many cases correctly. As there are many deficiencies in the traditional algorithm, later researchers get a lot of room for improvement [11]. In this paper, we try to use the 4-point coincidence algorithm to replace the module with the kd-tree method in the traditional ICP algorithm to improve the search efficiency of the corresponding point.

The four-point Congruent (4PC) algorithm's core search strategy is to find four corresponding points [12] in the same plane at the point cloud and target point cloud, as shown in Fig. 2:

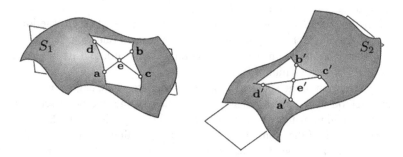

Fig. 2. 4-point coincidence algorithm

In Fig. 2, *S1* and *S2* represent the point cloud surfaces of the point cloud and the target point cloud, respectively, and *a*, *b*, *c*, *d* and *a* ^, *b* ^, *c* ^, *d* ^ Represents the points of the *S1* and *S2* surfaces in the same plane. As shown in the figure, the four coplanar points in the *S1* and *S2* surfaces intersect at the *e* and *e* ^ points, respectively. These common plane points The connection consists of several triangles, and the following relationship can be obtained from a similar triangular theorem:

$$|ae| \, / \, |eb| = |a^1e^1| \, / \, |e^1b^1|, \; |de| \, / \, |ec| = |d^1e^1| \, / \, |e^1c^1| \tag{3}$$

The invariant relationship of the above lines is invariant in the point cloud rigid transformation or affine transformation.

Therefore, in the process of performing the corresponding point retrieval, the search for the midpoint of the common point can be converted into the search for *e* and *e* ^, so that the time complexity of the algorithm in the key search operation is reduced, the time complexity of the consistent algorithm is:

$$o(n^2 + k) \tag{4}$$

In the 4-point coincidence algorithm, the Euclidean distance of the four points of the common plane affects the robustness of the algorithm. Generally speaking, the farther the distance of the four points is, the higher the robustness of the algorithm is, the better the effect of the corresponding point means that the accuracy of the cloud model is higher after the subsequent registration. But it should be noted that, during the operation, the search for four coplanar points receives the effect of point cloud overlap, in addition, the point cloud noise will also affect the effect of the algorithm.

In many cases, the ICP algorithm needs to input a three-dimensional point set and a primary rotation-shift matrix before the operation. If the input initial data is incorrect, the greedy strategy used in the ICP algorithm may lead to an error in the algorithm and the minimum value obtained by the objective function is only adapted to the local optimal point. Therefore, in the case of no significant breakthrough in the current rough registration method, it is possible to try to further optimize the corresponding point search method in ICP algorithm to improve the processing efficiency of ICP algorithm in dealing with large-scale point cloud data.

Before the optimization of the ICP algorithm, it is necessary to set a criterion for the processing effect of the ICP algorithm. At present, the evaluation standard of the commonly used ICP algorithm is the most common standard, and its English abbreviation is LCP (Largest Common Point set).

The main criterion of the standard is based on the size of the degree of overlap, the calculation method of the overlap degree is: for the existing two point sets A and B, given a transformation matrix M, A can be achieved through the M and B registration, After the registration of the point cloud B at any point within a given range, there is a point in the A, then this point is the coincidence point, the point of the number of coincidence points accounted for the number of points is the ratio of the degree of overlap.

In the process of registration, the main factor that determines the overlap degree is the search speed of the corresponding point. Therefore, after introducing the 4-point coincidence algorithm in the classical ICP algorithm, we can improve the efficiency of the corresponding point The effect of the final processing results to enhance the degree of overlap, so as to achieve the purpose of improving the ICP algorithm to enhance the improvement of the flow chart as shown below (Fig. 3):

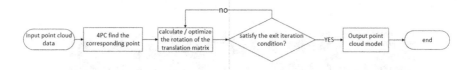

Fig. 3. Improved ICP algorithm flow chart

3   Improved ICP Algorithm Test

The improved ICP algorithm replaces the greedy search strategy in the original algorithm using a 4-point consistent point search strategy, which requires an experiment to verify its improved performance.

The test used in the test three-dimensional point cloud data from the Internet public test data, the provider is the point cloud library (Point Cloud Library). Code running environment for the VisualStudio2015 and PCL-1.8.0 point cloud development environment, the operating system used for the windows10 operating system, computing equipment for the Lenovo G400 laptop.

The specific steps of this test are as follows:

(1) Enter the 3D point cloud data.
(2) The input of the three-dimensional point cloud data preprocessing operation.
(3) The three-dimensional point cloud data subjected to preprocessing operation is processed using the improved ICP algorithm.
(4) Output point cloud registration results, record processing time.

The registration process is as follows, the gray point cloud represents the target point cloud, and the red point cloud represents the point cloud being processed. The algorithm execution process is the registration process of the red point cloud to the black point cloud:

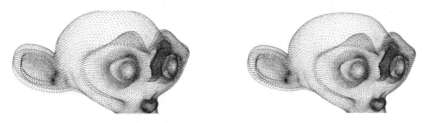

Fig. 4. Classic ICP algorithm registration effect (left) and improved ICP registration effect (right)

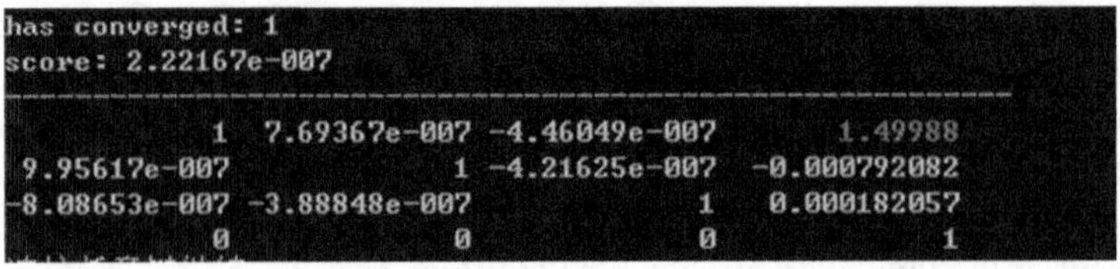

Fig. 5. The distance between the obtained point and the final transformed matrix is obtained by the classic ICP algorithm

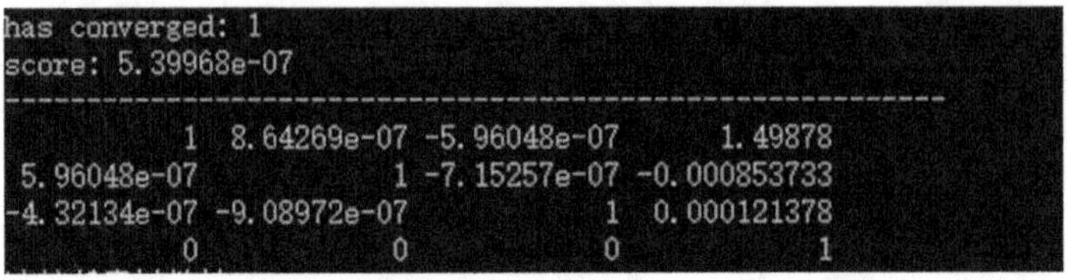

Fig. 6. The distance between the obtained point and the final transformed matrix is obtained by the improved ICP algorithm

In Figs. 5 and 6, the "has converged" indicates whether or not the registration process is completed. When the registration process is completed, the value is 1 and vice versa. "Score" represents the sum of the squares of the points to be operated from the set of points to be set. The bottom of the dashed line shows the final resulting translation of the translation matrix.

As shown in Fig. 4, the improved ICP algorithm is similar to the final effect of the point cloud registration of the classical ICP algorithm. Compared with the comparison between Figs. 5 and 6, compared with the classical ICP algorithm, the improved ICP algorithm has the same position and angle Far away from the point set has a better robustness.

In the course of the experiment, we calculated the running time of the classical ICP algorithm and the improved ICP algorithm, and reduce the accidental error by performing multiple tests and calculating the average time consumed by the two algorithms. At the same time, To the convergence of the value of the statistics, the results shown in Table 1.

Table 1. Comparison of classical ICP algorithm and improved ICP algorithm.

Algorithm	Average time of registration (in seconds)	Average convergence
Classic ICP	289.79	0.011475
Improved ICP	224.93	0.010973

It can be seen from Table 1 that the improved ICP algorithm is faster than the classical ICP algorithm, but the final convergence value of the two algorithms is not obvious.

The experimental results show that under the experimental conditions, the 4-point coincidence algorithm improves the efficiency of the corresponding point processing ICP algorithm in the convergence value of the difference is not the case with the classic ICP algorithm better point cloud registration efficiency.

4 Conclusion

Based on the analysis of ICP algorithm, an improved method of corresponding point search, which based on the 4-point coincidence, is proposed by synthetically applying 4-point coincidence algorithm, stereo geometry analysis method and matrix transformation, and the method is able to enhance the ICP algorithm for point cloud data registration efficiency. This improved method is suitable for point cloud registration in a variety of scenarios and exhibits good handling under experimental conditions. However, the optimization of the point cloud registration algorithm is still a difficult problem in the field of 3D data processing. The optimization route proposed in this paper still has some optimization space, and it is still worthy of further research work.

Acknowledgments. We would like to acknowledge support in part from the National Natural Science Foundation of China under Grants 61233001, 71232006, 61533019, 61773381 and 61773382; Chinese Guangdong's S&T project (2015B010103001, 2016B090910001), Dongguan's Innovation Talents Project (Gang Xiong).

References

1. Wong, S.T.C., Hoo, K.S., Knowlton, R.C., et al.: Issues and applications of digital library technology in biomedical imaging. Int. J. Digital Libr. **1**(3), 209–218 (1997)
2. Liu, J., Xiong, G., Shang, X., Nyberg, T.R., et al.: Social manufacturing development with sino-finnish innovation cooperation. In: IEEE SOLI, July 2016
3. Shang, X., Xiong, G., Nyberg, T.R., Wang, F., Cheng, C., et al.: Social manufacturing cloud for high-end apparel customization. Acta Automatica Sinica **42**(1), 1–12 (2017)
4. Qian, G., Tong, R., Peng, W., Dong, J.: Maintain the characteristic point cloud adaptive network reconstruction. J. Image Graph. **25**(3), 572–582 (2009)
5. Shang, X., Su, B., Liu, X., Xiong, G., You, Z.: Social manufacture cloud mode in high-end apparel, footwear and hats. In: The 11th World Congress on Intelligent Control and Automation Shenyang, China (2014)
6. Besl, P.J., Mckay, N.D.: A method of registration of 3D shapes. IEEE Trans. Pattern Anal. Mach. Intell. **9**(5), 698–700 (1992)
7. Wang, J., Wang, M.: Three-dimensional modeling of shoe lasts based on binocular stereoscopic vision. Comput. Technol. Develop. (2009)
8. Peng, H., Shang, X., Guo, C., Xiong, G., Nyberg, T.R., Shen, Z., Fan, D., Wang, Y.: A survey on big data for human body shape. In: 2016 IEEE International Conference on Service Operations and Logistis, and Informatics, July 2016
9. Shang, X., Liu, X., Cheng, C., Xiong, G.: A new model of social manufacturing for the customization needs of the clothing industry. In: Proceedings of the Eighth Annual meeting of Chinese management (2013)

10. Babak, M., Nelson, M.M., Nyberg, T.R., Xiong, G., Jesse, K.: Contributions of social manufacturing to sustainable apparel industry. In: 2016 IEEE International Conference on Service Operations and Logistics, and Informatics, July 2016
11. Ye, J., Ma, G., Jiang, L., Chen, L., Li, J., Xiong, G., Zhang, X., Tang, M.: A unified cloth untangling framework through discrete collision detection. Comput. Graph. Forum 36(7), 217–228 (2017)
12. Aiger, D., Mitra, N.J., Cohen-Or, D.: 4-Points congruent sets for robust pairwise surface registration. ACM Trans. Graph. 27, 85:1–85:10 (2008)

High School Statistical Graph Classification Using Hierarchical Model for Intelligent Mathematics Problem Solving

Yantao Wei[✉], Yafei Shi, Huang Yao, Gang Zhao, and Qingtang Liu

School of Educational Information Technology, Central China Normal University,
Wuhan 430079, China
yantaowei@mail.ccnu.edu.cn

Abstract. High school statistical graph classification is one of the key steps in intelligent mathematics problem solving system. In this paper, a hierarchial classification method is proposed for high school statistical graph classification. Firstly, the dense Scale-invariant Feature Transform (SIFT) features of the input images are extracted. Secondly, the sparse coding of the SIFT features are obtained. Thirdly, these sparse features are pooled in multiscale. Finally, these pooled features are concatenated and then fed into single-hidden layer feedforward neural network for classification. The effectiveness of the proposed method is demonstrated on the constructed dataset, which contains 400 statistical graphs. In contrast to several state-of-the-art methods, the proposed method achieves better performance in terms of classification accuracy, especially when the size of the training samples is small.

Keywords: Intelligent mathematics problem solving
Hierarchical model · Statistical graph classification
Kernel extreme learning machine

1 Introduction

The development of information technology in education is gradually entering into a new stage. Nowadays, educational information systems need to provide personalized, intelligent adaptive learning models for students, which requires strong supports from intelligent question-answering techniques. In the field of educational information system, mathematics problem solving machine is a challenging research direction [9,14,19,27,28]. Mathematics problem solving machine is to conduct a machine or computer system, in which users can input problems from mathematical textbooks, exercises or exams and get humanoid outputs. In this paper, we focus on the high school mathematics problem solving relate to statistical graphs.

© Springer International Publishing AG, part of Springer Nature 2018
S. Satoh (Ed.): PSIVT 2017, LNCS 10799, pp. 91–101, 2018.
https://doi.org/10.1007/978-3-319-92753-4_8

In general, intelligent mathematics problem solving related to statistical graphs includes: statistical graphs classification, the identification of relevant information in statistical graphs and the solution of the mathematics problem. Consequently, the performance of statistical graph classification directly relates to problem solving. It is easy to find that statistical graph classification is one of the image classification tasks. In the images of statistical graphs, there are different complex backgrounds, texts and numbers (see Fig. 1). This phenomenon makes the statistical graph classification more challenging.

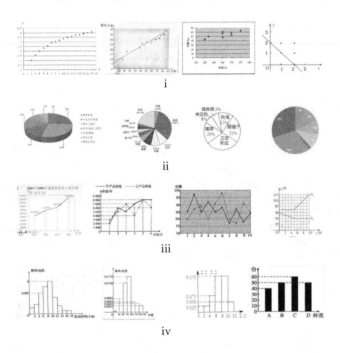

Fig. 1. Sample statistical graphs: (i) scatter charts, (ii) pie charts, (iii) line graphs, and (iv) bar graphs.

Image classification is one of the core problems in computer vision, and has a large variety of practical applications [24]. In order to improve the classification accuracy, scientists have laid path in developing the advanced classification techniques. In general, the image classification mainly includes two stages: image representation and classification [5]. In the stage of representation for images, many algorithm have been designed. Serre et al. proposed a feature extraction algorithm inspired by visual cortex named HMAX [25]. Freeman and Roth introduced the method by employing histograms of local orientation to recognizing hand gestures [6]. Dalal and Bill applied the Histograms of Oriented Gradient (HOG) to human detection [4], which achieved good results. Bosch et al. used Bag of Visual Words (BoW) to represent images [2]. Lowe proposed a feature representation method which is invariant to image scaling, translation, and rotation, called Scale-invariant Feature Transform (SIFT) [21,22]. Lazebnik et al. proposed an enhanced bag-of-features image representation method by introducing spatial information of local image [16]. Yang et al. proposed the Spatial Pyramid Matching using Sparse Coding (ScSPM) [30]. Currently, hierarchical algorithms (e.g., HMAX, Convolutional Neural Network (CNN)) have received more and more attention [17,18,31]. The hierarchical architecture (deep learning architecture) is more flexible than global methods and more selective than local histogram-based methods. These methods combine local features into a global image representation suited to recognition. In particular, the HMAX model strictly follows the organization of human visual cortex and has been used in face recognition [23], scene classification [11], and handwritten-word spotting [34]. Deep learning methods have achieved big success in image classification [13,33]. However, deep learning methods usually need big data. The number of the images of statistical graphs is limited so far. In the stage of classification, Support Vector Machine (SVM) [3], Maximum Entropy [15], Naive Bayesian [12], Adaboost [7] are widely used for a variety of classification problems. Recently, Kernel Extreme Learning Machine (KELM) has been proposed [10]. It is a single-hidden layer feedforward neural network, and comparable in accuracy with SVM and has lower computational complexity [10,35]. However, these algorithms have not been used in the classification of statistical graphs for high school student.

Seen from the above analysis, it is difficult to classify the statistical graphs. Consequently, a hierarchical statistical graph classification method is proposed in this paper. Firstly, the dense Scale-invariant Feature Transform (SIFT) features of the input images are extracted. Secondly, the sparse coding of the SIFT features are obtained. Thirdly, these sparse features are pooled in multiscale. Finally, these pooled features are concatenated and then fed into KELM for classification.

The structure of this paper is as follows: Sect. 2 describes the proposed method in detail. Experimental results and discussions are given in Sect. 3. Section 4 summarizes the conclusions.

2   The Proposed Method

In this section, we propose a new hierarchical method for high school statistical graph classification, as shown in Fig. 2. It is based on ScSPM and KELM. Firstly, the dense SIFT features of the input image are obtained. Secondly, the sparse coding of the SIFT features are obtained. Thirdly, feature pooling operation is carried out on the sparse features. Finally, these pooled features are concatenated and then fed into a single-hidden layer feedforward neural network for classification. We will provide a detailed description of the proposed method as follows.

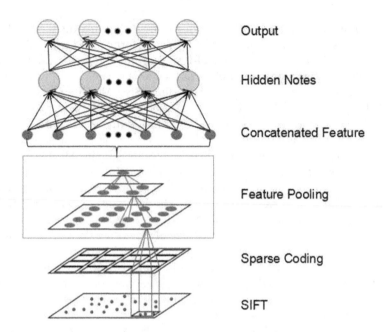

Output

Hidden Notes

Concatenated Feature

Feature Pooling

Sparse Coding

SIFT

Fig. 2. Flowchart of the proposed hierarchical model.

(1) SIFT Feature Extraction

SIFT is a widely used local descriptor to characterize local gradient information [21]. In [21], SIFT descriptor is a sparse feature representation that consists of both feature extraction and detection. In this paper, however, we only use the feature extraction component. That is extracting dense SIFT feature. For the given pixel in an image, we divide its neighborhood (e.g. 16×16) into a 4×4 cell array, quantize the orientation into 8 bins in each cell, and obtain a 128-dimensional vector as the SIFT representation for a pixel. Regular grid spacing of 6 pixels is used in the calculation of SIFT.

(2) Feature Encoding

Recently, sparse representation has been widely used in some challenging tasks such as target tracking [8], image denoising [20], face recognition [29], image classification [1,30] and so on. In this paper, the sparse coding is used to represent the SIFT features.

Let $X = [x_1, x_2, \cdots, x_m]^{\mathrm{T}} \in \mathcal{R}^{m \times d}$ be the SIFT feature set in the d-dimensional feature space, $E = (e_1, e_2, \ldots, e_m)$ be the representation of the input, and $C = (c_1, c_2, \ldots, c_K)$ be dictionary. The feature encoding can be transformed into the optimization of Eq. (1) [30]

$$\min_{E,C} \sum_{i=1}^{m} \parallel x_i - Ce_i \parallel_2^2 + \lambda \parallel e_i \parallel_1 \tag{1}$$

$$s.t. \parallel c_k \parallel_2 \leq 1, \forall k = 1, 2, \ldots, K$$

where $\parallel e_i \parallel_1$ denotes the $L1$-norm of the e_i and λ is the regularization parameter. And the optimization problem of Eq. (1) is essentially a sparse coding problem with L1 regularization constraints. A unit L2-norm constraint on c_k is typically applied to avoid trivial solutions. Compared with the vector quantization using k-means algorithm, sparse representation for images can reduce the error caused by the reconstruction and the description of the image semantics is more distinct [30].

(3) **Feature Pooling**

Feature pooling is an important strategy to achieve high performance in image classification. In this paper, the pooling function is a max pooling function on the absolute sparse codes. For a statistical graph, its sparse representation matrix E can be obtained from Eq. (1). Through the max pooling operation, the local image block of statistical graphs can be represented by a vector L. Consequently, the pooling operation can be given as [30]

$$L_j = \max(|e_{1j}|, |e_{2j}|, \ldots, |e_{mj}|) \tag{2}$$

where e_{mj} denotes the m-th row, j-th column elements of the sparse representation matrix E and m is the number of the local feature point. The maximum pooling operation has been shown to be consistent with biometric characteristics [26] and has been widely used for image classification, such as HMAX [25]. In the proposed method, 2 scales are used. The pooled features from various locations and scales are then concatenated to form a spatial pyramid representation of the image.

(4) **Classification**

Finally, in order to perform classification utilizing the learned features, we feed the learned features to a standard KELM classifier [10]. After feature transformation of the hidden layer, the data structure becomes much simpler. The size of the output-layer is set to be the same as the total number of classes. The labels of the test samples are determined by the maximum value of the output.

The proposed method is a hierarchical model. It can learn more abstract features learning by stacking multiple layers of learning nodes. In this way, the invariant features of the statistical graphs can be learned.

3 Experimental Results and Analysis

In this section, the proposed hierarchical classification method is compared with other widely used methods, such as HMAX, HOG, and BOW. In this paper, 400 statistical graphs (per class 100) containing the line graphs, bar graphs, scatter charts and pie charts are used. Examples of experimental statistical graphs are shown in Fig. 3. For the sake of stability, each experiment is performed 10 times, and the mean results are reported. In this paper, the testing hardware and software conditions are listed as follows: Laptop, Intel-i7 3.6G CPU, 12G DDR3 RAM, Windows 10, MATLAB R2014a.

3.1 Dataset Description

This image dataset collected online contains four types of statistical graphs: line graphs, bar graphs, scatter charts and pie charts. There are 400 graphs in the image dataset in which each category contains 100 graphs. As shown in Figs. 1 and 3, the within class variance is large and between class variance is small (between line graphs and scatter charts) in this dataset. Therefore, this brings a great challenge to classify statistical graphs [32]. In our experiments, the images were converted to grayscale image and resized to be no larger than 300×300 pixels with preserved aspect ratio.

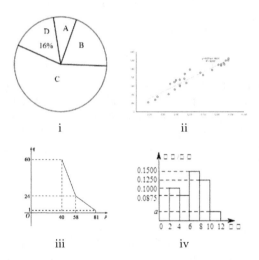

Fig. 3. Samples of the statistical graph: (i) pie chart, (ii) scatter chart, (iii) line graph and (iv) bar graph.

3.2 Experimental Results

Firstly, in order to demonstrate the effectiveness of the proposed method, we randomly selected 10 images from each class to form training set, and the rest as test set. We used the trained dictionary with 1024 bases from Caltech-101, and used 2×2 and 1×1 sub-regions for the proposed method. We compared our result with several existing approaches. Detailed results are shown in Table 1, and it can be seen that our proposed method leads to the better performance. What's more, BOW has the comparable performance to HMAX, and HOG has a poor performance compared with other methods.

Table 1. Classification accuracies of different methods

Method	BOW	HOG	HMAX	Ours
Accuracy(%)	75.89	65.28	74.14	**88.33**

Secondly, Fig. 4 shows that the classification accuracies of all the methods are improved with the increase of the number of training samples. We can also find that the proposed method significantly outperforms other methods when 10% of the samples are chosen as training samples. These results show that the proposed method has low sample complexity. This is very important due to that the labeled training data is often difficult to be collected in practice. Consequently, we can conclude that the proposed method is fit for small sample learning.

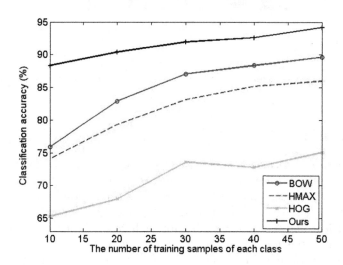

Fig. 4. Classification accuracies of different methods with different numbers of training samples.

Finally, the confusion matrix of the proposed method for this data set is shown in Fig. 5, where the vertical axis represents the ground truth classes and the horizontal axis represents the results for each class. The orders of classes are the same in both axes. The classification accuracies for individual class are listed along with the diagonal. The entry in the ith row and jth column is the percentage of samples from class i that were misidentified as class j. Obviously, confusion usually occurs between scatter charts and line graphs. The reason for this may be that scatter charts are similar with line graphs in some cases (see Fig. 3). We can also find that the most successful class is pie chart.

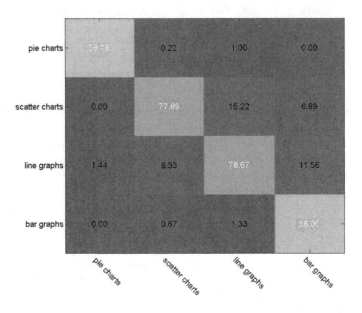

Fig. 5. Confusion matrix generated by the proposed method.

4   Conclusion

In this paper, a hierarchical classification method is proposed for high school statistical graph classification. It can be used in the intelligent mathematics problem solving system. Experimental results on the dataset constructed by us demonstrate that the proposed method can achieve good performance, and the hierarchical learning model is suitable for high school statistical graph classification. The reason for this maybe that the hierarchical learning model can learn high leave features for classification. This work is beneficial to intelligent mathematics problem solving.

Acknowledgments. This work was supported in part by the National Natural Science Foundation of China under Grants 61502195 and 61772012, in part by the National Science & Technology Supporting Program during the Twelfth Five-year Plan Period granted by the Ministry of Science and Technology of China under Grant 2015BAK27B02, in part by the Humanities and Social Science project of Chinese Ministry of Education under Grant 17YJA880104, and in part by the Self-Determined Research Funds of CCNU From the Colleges' Basic Research and Operation of MOE under Grants CCNU16A05022 and CCNU15A02020.

References

1. Bhuvaneswari, N., Sivakumar, V.: A comprehensive review on sparse representation for image classification in remote sensing. In: International Conference on Communication and Electronics Systems (ICCES), pp. 1–4. IEEE (2016)
2. Bosch, A., Zisserman, A., Muñoz, X.: Scene classification using a hybrid generative/discriminative approach. IEEE Trans. Pattern Anal. Mach. Intell. **30**(4), 712–727 (2008)
3. Cortes, C., Vapnik, V.: Support-vector networks. Mach. Learn. **20**(3), 273–297 (1995)
4. Dalal, N., Triggs, B.: Histograms of oriented gradients for human detection. In: IEEE Computer Society Conference on Computer Vision and Pattern Recognition, vol. 1, pp. 886–893. IEEE (2005)
5. Dammak, M., Mejdoub, M., Amar, C.B.: A survey of extended methods to the bag of visual words for image categorization and retrieval. In: 2014 International Conference on Computer Vision Theory and Applications (VISAPP), vol. 2, pp. 676–683. IEEE (2014)
6. Freeman, W.T., Roth, M.: Orientation histograms for hand gesture recognition. In: International Workshop on Automatic Face and Gesture Recognition, vol. 12, pp. 296–301 (1995)
7. Freund, Y., Schapire, R.E., et al.: Experiments with a new boosting algorithm. In: Proceedings of International Conference on Machine Learning, vol. 96, pp. 148–156 (1996)
8. He, Z., Yi, S., Cheung, Y.M., You, X., Tang, Y.Y.: Robust object tracking via key patch sparse representation. IEEE Trans. Cybern. **47**(2), 354–364 (2017)
9. Hosseini, M.J., Hajishirzi, H., Etzioni, O., Kushman, N.: Learning to solve arithmetic word problems with verb categorization. In: EMNLP, pp. 523–533 (2014)
10. Huang, G.B., Zhou, H., Ding, X., Zhang, R.: Extreme learning machine for regression and multiclass classification. IEEE Trans. Syst. Man Cybern. Part B (Cybern.) **42**(2), 513–529 (2012)
11. Huang, K., Tao, D., Yuan, Y., Li, X., Tan, T.: Biologically inspired features for scene classification in video surveillance. IEEE Trans. Syst. Man Cybern. Part B (Cybern.) **41**(1), 307–313 (2011)
12. Jin-hua, T.: Research of vehicle video image recognition technology based on naive bayesian classification model. In: 2010 Third International Conference on Information and Computing (ICIC), vol. 2, pp. 17–20. IEEE (2010)
13. Krizhevsky, A., Sutskever, I., Hinton, G.E.: Imagenet classification with deep convolutional neural networks. In: Advances in Neural Information Processing Systems, pp. 1097–1105 (2012)
14. Kushman, N., Artzi, Y., Zettlemoyer, L., Barzilay, R.: Learning to Automatically Solve Algebra Word Problems. Association for Computational Linguistics (2014)
15. Lazebnik, S., Schmid, C., Ponce, J.: A maximum entropy framework for part-based texture and object recognition. In: Tenth IEEE International Conference on Computer Vision, vol. 1, pp. 832–838. IEEE (2005)
16. Lazebnik, S., Schmid, C., Ponce, J.: Beyond bags of features: spatial pyramid matching for recognizing natural scene categories. In: 2006 IEEE Computer Society Conference on Computer Vision and Pattern Recognition, vol. 2, pp. 2169–2178. IEEE (2006)
17. LeCun, Y., Bengio, Y., Hinton, G.: Deep learning. Nature **521**(7553), 436–444 (2015)

18. Li, H., Wei, Y., Li, L., Chen, C.P.: Hierarchical feature extraction with local neural response for image recognition. IEEE Trans. Cybern. **43**(2), 412–424 (2013)

19. Lin, Y.C., Liang, C.C., Hsu, K.Y., Huang, C.T., Miao, S.Y., Ma, W.Y., Ku, L.W., Liau, C.J., Su, K.Y.: Designing a tag-based statistical math word problem solver with reasoning and explanation. Int. J. Comput. Linguist. Chin. Lang. Process. (IJCLCLP) **20**(2), 1–26 (2015)

20. Liu, L., Chen, L., Chen, C.P., Tang, Y.Y., et al.: Weighted joint sparse representation for removing mixed noise in image. IEEE Trans. Cybern. **47**(3), 600–611 (2017)

21. Lowe, D.G.: Object recognition from local scale-invariant features. In: The Proceedings of the Seventh IEEE International Conference on Computer Vision, vol. 2, pp. 1150–1157. IEEE (1999)

22. Lowe, D.G.: Distinctive image features from scale-invariant keypoints. Int. J. Comput. Vision **60**(2), 91–110 (2004)

23. Meyers, E., Wolf, L.: Using biologically inspired features for face processing. Int. J. Comput. Vision **76**(1), 93–104 (2008)

24. Ren, X.D., Guo, H.N., He, G.C., Xu, X., Di, C., Li, S.H.: Convolutional neural network based on principal component analysis initialization for image classification. In: IEEE International Conference on Data Science in Cyberspace (DSC), pp. 329–334. IEEE (2016)

25. Serre, T., Wolf, L., Bileschi, S., Riesenhuber, M., Poggio, T.: Robust object recognition with cortex-like mechanisms. IEEE Trans. Pattern Anal. Mach. Intell. **29**(3) (2007)

26. Serre, T., Wolf, L., Poggio, T.: Object recognition with features inspired by visual cortex. In: IEEE Computer Society Conference on Computer Vision and Pattern Recognition, vol. 2, pp. 994–1000. IEEE (2005)

27. Shi, S., Wang, Y., Lin, C.Y., Liu, X., Rui, Y.: Automatically solving number word problems by semantic parsing and reasoning. In: EMNLP, pp. 1132–1142 (2015)

28. Upadhyay, S., Chang, M.W., Chang, K.W., Yih, W.T.: Learning from explicit and implicit supervision jointly for algebra word problems. In: Conference on Empirical Methods in Natural Language Processing, pp. 297–306 (2016)

29. Wagner, A., Wright, J., Ganesh, A., Zhou, Z., Mobahi, H., Ma, Y.: Toward a practical face recognition system: robust alignment and illumination by sparse representation. IEEE Trans. Pattern Anal. Mach. Intell. **34**(2), 372–386 (2012)

30. Yang, J., Yu, K., Gong, Y., Huang, T.: Linear spatial pyramid matching using sparse coding for image classification. In: IEEE Conference on Computer Vision and Pattern Recognition, pp. 1794–1801. IEEE (2009)

31. Yu, S., Abraham, Z.: Concept drift detection with hierarchical hypothesis testing. In: Proceedings of the 2017 SIAM International Conference on Data Mining, pp. 768–776. SIAM (2017)

32. Yu, S., Cao, Z., Jiang, X.: Robust linear discriminant analysis with a laplacian assumption on projection distribution. In: IEEE International Conference on Acoustics, Speech and Signal Processing, pp. 2567–2571 (2017)

33. Yu, S., Emigh, M., Santana, E., Príncipe, J.C.: Autoencoders trained with relevant information: blending shannon and wiener's perspectives. In: 2017 IEEE International Conference on Acoustics, Speech and Signal Processing (ICASSP), pp. 6115–6119. IEEE (2017)

34. Van der Zant, T., Schomaker, L., Haak, K.: Handwritten-word spotting using biologically inspired features. IEEE Trans. Pattern Anal. Mach. Intell. **30**(11), 1945–1957 (2008)
35. Zhang, R., Lan, Y., Huang, G.B., Xu, Z.B., Soh, Y.C.: Dynamic extreme learning machine and its approximation capability. IEEE Trans. Cybern. **43**(6), 2054–2065 (2013)

Machine Solving on Hypergeometric Distribution Problems

Chao Sun, Yao Su, and Xinguo Yu$^{(\boxtimes)}$

National Engineering Research Center for E-learning,
Central China Normal University, Wuhan, China
{csun,xgyu}@mail.ccnu.edu.cn

Abstract. Hypergeometric distribution is one of the most important mathematical models in probabilistic subjects, and also an integral part of the intelligent tutoring system based on automatic machine solving. In this paper, we propose a set of solutions to automatically solve the Hypergeometric distribution problems. Our method combines the syntactic and semantic information of the subject, establishes the matching rule between the topic narration and the type template, and implement the problem solving by establishing the solution formula corresponding to the topic, as well as extracting and complementing the corresponding problem data. Experiments conducted on a dataset which collected from the Internet and College Entrance Examination questions over the years demonstrate the feasibility of our method.

1 Introduction

Machine solving on math problems dates back to the 1960s, and receives more and more attentions recently. Most efforts to automatically machine solving focused on arithmetic or geometry problems in primary or junior school mathematics, and have produced many effective algorithms and methods [1,11–13]. However, researches to automatically solve probability problems in high school are rare. Comparing to other math problems in primary or junior school mathematics, probability problems have more complicated lexical structures and varied embedding semantic presentations, which lead to much more difficulties in automatically machine solving.

Among the variety of probability distributions, Hypergeometric Distribution is an important discrete probability distribution model, as it is regarded as the theoretical fundamental of reliability testing technology. It not only occupies an increasingly important position in the probability section of high school, but also has an important position in ecology. An illustration of Hypergeometric distribution problem is shown as Fig. 1. Hypergeometric distribution is often used for various enrichment analyses, which is also the basis for the preparation of Fisher exact test. Meanwhile, we found that the Hypergeometric distribution problems have some explicit types and solving process of the same type problems is almost the same. Hence, the effort to automatically solve Hypergeometric distribution could be a cutting-in point to automatically solve probability problems.

© Springer International Publishing AG, part of Springer Nature 2018
S. Satoh (Ed.): PSIVT 2017, LNCS 10799, pp. 102–115, 2018.
https://doi.org/10.1007/978-3-319-92753-4_9

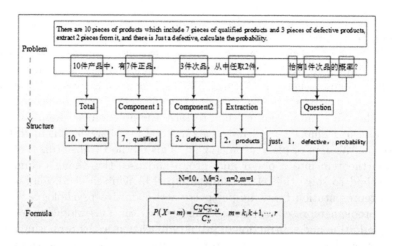

Fig. 1. Illustration of Hypergeometric distribution problem

This paper presents a novel machine solving framework to Hypergeometric distribution problems. We take the machine solution for the problem that satisfies Hypergeometric distribution as the breakthrough point, and divide the process of solving the problem into two parts: judging the type of the problem and solving the problem. The type judgment is realized by processing the data and extracting the feature information of the problem, and the output is the type of the problem with its feature tag. The problem solution process is realized by extracting and supplementing the data needed by the formula. In our method, we flexibly use the combination rules between template primitives and make them automatically combine into complete templates that related to the topic, which lead to higher matching accuracy and flexibility. Our framework combines the syntactic and semantic information of the subject, then has higher tolerance of diversity of syntax of problems.

Our contributions are summarized as follows.

1. We proposed a general machine solving framework which can deal with Hypergeometric distribution problems.
2. In our method, we used a combination rules which lead to much less templates requirement than other existing methods.
3. To the best of our knowledge, our work is the first attempt to machine solving solution on Hypergeometric distribution problems.

2   Related Work

In recent years, solving problems with machine has been a hot topic in the field of artificial intelligence. The earliest intelligent teaching system called STUDENT was developed in 1964. The system translates complex sentences into simple sentences by pre-prepared sentence models, and it can automatically understand or solve some algebraic problems written in English [1]. The second typical system for solving mathematical problems is ARIHTPRO, which solves the problem by finding the type of the given mathematical problem and using the corresponding computing program [3]. Wu et al. established a new method for the proof of theorem of plane geometry problem in 1977, which is called Folin-Wu method. This method transforms the planar geometric theorem into a polynomial group and uses the Wu's elimination method to solve the polynomial group [3]. Zhang et al. established Zhang's problem-solving method in 1992, which is mainly used to prove the theorem of plane geometry [2]. This method transforms the planar geometric theorem into a polynomial group and uses the Zhang's elimination point method to solve the relationship group [14]. Kintsch et al. analyzed the problem representation from the perspective of cognitive psychology, and proposed a problem representation model in 1985 [7,8]. This model answers the first-step addition and subtraction of primary mathematics by proposing a problem framework [7]. Ma et al. extended the knowledge framework of Kintsch and realized the machine solver of multi-step mathematics word problems at primary school level [5]. They set some object slots, and match the processed data with the semantic sentence pattern, then fill the objects in each slot according to the matching result. The SoMaTePs system proposed in 2012 uses the extended semantic web to represent the math topics [10]. The system extracts the objects from the problem and saves them as nodes. The relationship between the nodes is composed of four operations. ARIS system proposed in 2014 take the verb in the problem as the main object [4]. The system makes the machine to learn the verb in the problem and then these verbs are classified as addition or subtraction, and on this basis, mathematical problem is transformed into a state diagram with the verb as the core, and the verb relationship as the mode, but this method is currently only considered the addition and subtraction of one unknown quantity. Kushman et al. established the MIT problem-solving framework which uses machine learning techniques to extract quantitative relationships in the problem and establish linear equations [9]. This method consists of two steps. First, according to the topic, the problem is mapped to an equation. Then, according to the predefined data slot, the corresponding data is extracted from the title and filled, and the solution is solved by solving the equation.

We can conclude from the existing researches that, in order to make the computer to solve the problems and get the correct answer, people have to make the computer to understand the language description of the title, and get the related mathematical relationship or expression from the expression of the problem. To create a complete problem-solving system, we need three steps. First, we should make the computer to understand the language description of the problem (natural language understanding). Second, according to the understanding of the problem, we transform the semantics into expression and mapping of mathematical relations. Third, we get the formula of the problem by the way of mathematical reasoning, and get the answer according to the formula and the relevant data. An undeniable fact is that it is difficult for computer to understand the natural language. This involves not only the expression of various grammatical relations, but also the powerful knowledge base and commonsense knowledge base. From the steps of semantic expression and mathematical reasoning, we can transform the solution of a math problem into a calculation of one or a group of formulas. If we can find the formula corresponding to the problem according to the expression of the problem, and then extract the appropriate variables from the problem and fill into the right formula, the problem will be solved. The process of finding the formula needed to solve the problem and calculating the formula is the solution to the problem.

3   Hypergeometric Distribution Problems

We often encounter such problems, *"There are N pieces of products, which include M pieces of defective and N − M pieces of qualified, taking n pieces from the whole products, which just have m pieces of defective, calculating this probability."* The concept that describes the general rule of this type of sampling test is called Hypergeometric distribution [6]. We define the description of the problem as the model of Hypergeometric distribution. Assume that the probability distribution of the random variable X is:

$$P\left(X = m\right) = \frac{C_M^m C_{N-M}^{n-m}}{C_N^n} m = k, k+1, \cdots, r \qquad (1)$$

In which $k = \max\left(0, n + M - N\right), r = \min\left(n, M\right)$, and $n \leq N, M \leq N$, $n, N, M \in \mathbb{N}$. Then we called the random variable X obeys Hypergeometric distribution with parameters n, N, M, and abbreviate it as $X \sim H\left(n, N, M\right)$. Here C denotes the mathematical operation "Combination", which is an un-ordered collection of distinct elements, usually of a prescribed size and taken from a given set. It is noteworthy that when n equals 1, Hypergeometric distribution becomes Bernoulli distribution and when N is infinite, Hypergeometric distribution can be seen as a Binomial distribution.

Hypergeometric distribution is a very special probability distribution. When a problem is being solved, it is necessary to judge whether it satisfies the model of Hypergeometric distribution. Only when it is satisfied, the problem can be solved according to the probability formula of Hypergeometric distribution [6].

Our goal is to make the machine solve the problem that satisfies Hypergeometric distribution. However, the current problems that can be solved need to have a complete statement *"N pieces of products, M pieces of defective and N−M pieces of qualified, taking n pieces from the whole products, which just have m pieces of defective, calculating this probability"*, and there is no interference. The interference here refers to meaningless quantifiers and nouns, such as the number "201" in the phrase *"classroom 201"*. Our solutions of Hypergeometric distribution problems are as follows: First, we determine whether the problem conforms to the model of the Hypergeometric distribution. Second, we extract the relevant parameters (n, N, M) in the problem. Third, we use the probability formula of Hypergeometric probability to obtain the probability of the relevant variables, and then get the answer. During the process, we need to find out what is equivalent to "qualified products", and what is equivalent to "defective products", and then calculate the problem by combining the corresponding formula of Hypergeometric distribution.

4   Our Method

In this paper, we take the machine solution for Hypergeometric distribution problems as the breakthrough point, and divide the process of solving the problem into two parts: judging the type of the problem and solving the problem. The type judgment is realized by processing the data and extracting the feature information of the problem, and the output is the type of the problem with its feature tag. The type of the problem can determine the corresponding solution formula. The problem solution process is realized by extracting and supplementing the data needed by the formula. We generate alternative answers from the data of the "fixed quantity", and extract answers based on the key information from the *Q&A* section. The process of solving the problems is achieved by extracting and supplementing the data needed to calculate the formula. We combine the key data and the "fixed amount" of the problem to generate an alternative set of answers, and then extract the answers from the key information of the *Q&A* section. The framework of our method is shown as Fig. 2, and we elaborate it as follows.

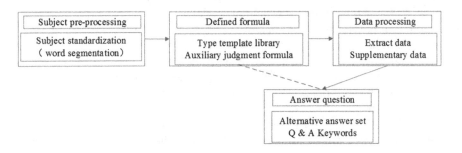

Fig. 2. The framework of our method

4.1   Problem Type Determination

If we can learn the solving formula of a problem, and extract the key information that needed for the solving of the formula from the problem, then the automatic solving of the problem is feasible. Hence, in this paper, we conduct the problem type determination first, that is to determine whether the subject meets the model of Hypergeometric distribution, and get the solving formula. The subject is added with the type label, and the structure information of the topic is more abundant, which provides more reference for the subsequent question answering process.

While determining of the type of problem that satisfies Hypergeometric distribution, we combine the structure information of the problem and the keywords extracted from the problem. The keywords information that often appears in the subject could benefit the judgement of the type. The structure information that is unique to each topic could be treated as type tag.

Determine Type by the Templates. Template matching has a rule: the more generic the templates are, the less the number of templates, the more imprecise the matching; the more detailed the template, the more the number of templates, and the more accurate matching. In this paper, we construct a certain number of template primitives, which are not versatile, but have high matching rate. These template primitives can be combined into a complete template by permutations and combinations. Although the number of generated templates is large, the establishment of them is simple and fast, and the template primitives can be re arranged and assembled in the process of matching, so the versatility is also improved.

The Hypergeometric distribution problem is composed of four important parts: "Total", "Component", "Extraction" and "Question". In the model of Hypergeometric distribution, the "Total" refers to "*N pieces of products*", the "Component" refers to "*M pieces of defective and N-M pieces of qualified*", the "Extraction" refers to "*taking n pieces from the whole products*" and the "Question" refers to "*just have m pieces of defective, calculating this probability*". We define all the possible cases of each part as a set. Then a Hypergeometric distribution problem can be treated as an element of the Cartesian product which consists of four sets. We record "Total" as set A, "Component" as set B, "Extraction" as set C and "Question" as set D. In view of the common problem that satisfies Hypergeometric distribution, we can summary the four important parts as Table 1.

Table 1. Template base pool

Set/Element	A	B	C	D
1	Total	Two components	Take any x	Calculate probability
2	Total missing	One component		Calculate distribution list
3	Multiple	Half component		One-step derivation
4	N/A	Multiple components		Complex problem

The "Half component" represents part of the information of a component is given. In this paper, we assume the "Half component" represents the proportionality information of a component. For example, the expression as "*defective percentage is 4%*" and "*is one-third of the total*", and so on. The "One-step derivation" refers to that the "Question" can be transformed to "Calculate the probability" through one-step calculation or conversion. In fact, "One-step derivation" involves a variety of situations, and in this paper, we acquiesce the "One-step derivation" as "*m pieces of a certain component represent 'Something', and then calculate the probability of 'Something'*" which equals to "*calculate the probability of m pieces of a certain component*". We ignore the elements A_3, B_4, D_4 in the table whose narrative is complex, and their answering involves the knowledge of natural language processing. Define each set as follows:

$$\mathbf{A} = \{A_i \mid i = 1, 2\}; \mathbf{B} = \{B_i \mid i = 1, 2, 3\};$$
$$\mathbf{C} = \{C_i \mid i = 1\}; \mathbf{D} = \{D_i \mid i = 1, 2, 3\} \tag{2}$$

Every element in these sets could be represented as a template primitive, which can be used to form a common template with higher accuracy by permutations and combinations. We define $\mathbf{L}$ as the set of the solvable Hypergeometric distribution problems, where $\mathbf{L} = \mathbf{A} \times \mathbf{B} \times \mathbf{C} \times \mathbf{D}$. That is:

$$\mathbf{L} = \{(x, y, m, n) \mid x \in \mathbf{A}, y \in \mathbf{B}, m \in \mathbf{C}, n \in \mathbf{D}\}$$

Every problem that satisfies Hypergeometric distribution can be regard as an element of $\mathbf{L}$. Practically, there is an interdependent relationship between the "Total" and "Component", and at least one of the two is required to be known. So the elements A_2 and B_2, as well as A_2 and B_3 cannot coexist.

Note that a hierarchical relationship is exist in all types of problems. The simpler of the statement of the type, the outermost layer in the inclusion relation it belongs to; the richer of the information of the type, the inner layer in the inclusion relation it belongs to.

Corresponding to the type of the problems, there is also a hierarchical relationship between the type decision templates. When a problem belongs to several templates, select the type of the innermost template.

Auxiliary Judgement of Problem Type. When judging the type of the problem, we should consider the structural information hidden in the problem and the keywords contained in the problem. Keywords could not be used to directly judge the problem type. Hence we take the information extract from the keywords as auxiliary judgement. Keywords are derived from the common problems set that satisfy Hypergeometric distribution. We treat the keywords as the basis, which consist of the nouns, quantifiers, verbs and total words, and record them as symbol F_n, F_q, F_v and F_0. The auxiliary judgment formula is as follows:

$$F = a_0 + a_1 F_n + a_2 F_q + a_3 F_v + a_4 F_0 \tag{3}$$

in which a_0, a_1, a_2, a_3, a_4 denote the coefficients. We use multiple regression analysis to calculate the coefficients.

4.2 Data Extraction and Processing

After determining the type of problem, we need to extract the data and obtain the values of all variables, then fill into the Hypergeometric distribution formula to calculate the result. Hence, data extraction and values determination of variables are the key points of our method.

Data Extraction. The variables extracted from the problems should contain a noun which represents its character and a quantifier which represents its attribute. In a problem, the attributes of all variables should be consistent. The character of a variable and its value appear in pairs, which are the key information for calculation and hence are defined as a unit. In the process of extracting data from the problem, we put the data extracted from the problem into a data list. All key variables required for the solving of the problem constitute a complete data list. The goal of this paper is to solve the problem that satisfies Hypergeometric distribution with "one 'Total' and two 'Components'". The model of the problem can be expressed as:

$$\mathbf{L} = [\mathbf{A}\,(m_1, n_1), \mathbf{B}\,[(m_2, n_2), (m_3, n_3)], \mathbf{C}\,(m_4, n_4), \mathbf{D}\,(m_5, n_5, n_6, d)] \quad (4)$$

In which the n refers to the noun, m refers to the numeral, and d refers to the adverb.

Analyzing the problem that satisfies Hypergeometric distribution, we can find that there is a certain relationship between data extracted from the problem, such as the number of the "Total" is equal to the sum of the "Components", and the number of the "Extraction" is less than the number of the "Total", etc. According to the definition of each quantity in the complete data list, we get the three relationships: relationships between numerals, relationships between nouns, and relationships between nouns and numerals.

Establish Data List. In Hypergeometric distribution problems, numerals usually appear in pairs with nouns or quantifiers. These nouns represent the character features of numerals, and quantifiers are the attribute characteristics of numerals. Therefore, we should extract not only the numerals, but also the nouns and quantifiers, which constitute a complete conceptual structure for the numerals data.

We define H3 $= \{x, y, z\}$ as three-element structure and H2 $= \{x, y\}$ as two-element structure. The elements in this structure are words extracted from the problem that is to be solved. These words need to meet three conditions when they are extracted. First, the distance between the words is closest in the subject. Second, there is no punctuation between the words. Third, the elements of the structure is disordered. In a Hypergeometric distribution problem, the numerical data related to the solution will have a uniform quantifier attribute. Based on this, we extract the quantifiers in the subject and sort the numbers in order to extract the most quantifier and record it as Q. In data extraction, if the quantifier in the two-element structure H2 $= \{m, q\}$ is not Q, then it will be identified as interference items and the two-element structure will be removed from the subject.

The data extraction process can be summarized as two steps. First, remove the interference items, and then extract and judge the data. Second, remove the data that has been determined and extract data from the left of the problem again. In the process of the extracting of the data, the problem is updated by extracting the data and removing it until there is no extractable data.

Complementary Data. Practically, a problem does not always include all the data needed to solve the problem, which is necessary to complement the data. This paper defines a standard type that contains complete data, compares other problems to this standard type, designs the type conversion route, and complements the data by type conversion.

We assume P as the transformation step (the distance between the problem and the standard problem). $P = 0$ means the transformation is complete and the data related to the solving of the problem has been complemented. The combination of "Total" and "Component" associated with the type of the problem are as follows:

$$\mathbf{X} = \{ (A_1, B_1), (A_1, B_2), (A_1, B_3), (A_2, B_1) \}$$

In which, X is the set of the combination of "Total" and "Component".

There is a progressive relationship between the various parts of the problem, which result in a containment relationship between these types of the problems. Thus, as far as the set is concerned the progressive relationship between its elements is as follows:

$$\begin{cases} (A_1, B_3) \to (A_1, B_2) \to (A_1, B_1) \\ (A_2, B_1) \to (A_1, B_1) \end{cases}$$

Similarly, the "Question" that affects the type of the problem is expressed as:

$$\mathbf{Y} = \{D_3, D_1, D_2\}$$

In which, Y is the set of "Question". Similar to X, there is a progressive relationship between the elements of Y, which is as follows:

$$D_3 \to D_1 \to D_2$$

In our method, the value of P is determined by the derivation process above. When the direction of the derivation is reversed, P is defined as zero, such as that $P(D_2, D_1) = 0$. Adding the above two conversion steps, we can get the steps to the standard type.

4.3 Solution to Hypergeometric Distribution Problem

Mathematically, to solve the Hypergeometric distribution problem is to calculate a certain probability or a few probabilities. Hence, we solve all the possible problems in the subject, and then extract the answer according to the keywords of "Question". In this paper, we expand the "Question" and transform the computational process of the problem into the selection process of results.

We calculate all the possible of "Question" according to "Total", "Component" and "Extraction", and divide the problem into "fixed quantity" and "Question". We calculate all the possible "Question" based on the data in the complete data list and define it as the extended distribution list, which is shown in Table 2.

Table 2. Extended distribution list

Component x	0	1	$\cdots$	M	≥ 1	$\cdots$	$\geq M-1$	< 1	$\cdots$	$< M-1$
Adverb	null	just	$\cdots$	just	no less than	$\cdots$	no less than	less than	$\cdots$	less than
Numeral	0	1		M	1		M-1	1		M
Probability	q_0	q_1		q_M	q_1^{+}		q_{M-1}^{+}	q_1^{-}		q_M^{-}

In which, the calculation formula of each quantity is as Eq. 5.

$$
\begin{cases}
M = \min(m_4, x) \\
q_1^{+} = q_1 + q_2 + \ldots + q_M; q_{M-1}^{+} = q_{M-1} + q_M \\
q_1^{-} = q_0; q_M^{-} = q_1 + q_2 + \ldots + q_{M-1} \\
q_0 = \dfrac{C_{m_3}^{0} C_{m_2}^{m_4}}{C_{m_1}^{m_4}}; q_1 = \dfrac{C_{m_3}^{1} C_{m_2}^{m_4-1}}{C_{m_1}^{m_4}}; \ldots; q_m = \dfrac{C_{m_3}^{m} C_{m_2}^{m_4-m}}{C_{m_1}^{m_4}}, m \leq \min(m_3, m_4)
\end{cases}
$$
$$(5)$$

The m and n in Eq. 5 derived from the complete data list. Adverbs and Numerals extracted from "Question" determine the data to be selected from the extended distribution list. In this way, Noun determines the extended distribution list, Adverb determines the calculation formula, and the Numeral determines the computational complexity.

5 Experiments

5.1 Experimental Data

The experimental dataset was collected from the network, which covers all kinds of Hypergeometric distribution problems. We divide the problems with clear patterns into two categories: One is the problems which satisfy the concept of Hypergeometric distribution with one "Total" and two "Component". Another is Multidimensional Hypergeometric distribution problems (such as card problems, playing cards, par the problem of a plurality of balls, etc.). The topic classification of all collected problems are shown in Fig. 3.

5.2 Experimental Results and Analysis

The recognition accuracy of problem type judgement is shown in Fig. 4.

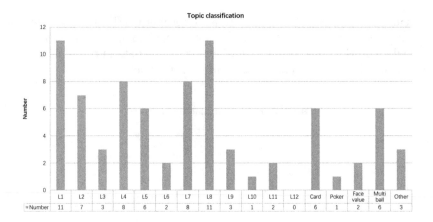

Fig. 3. Topics classification in dataset

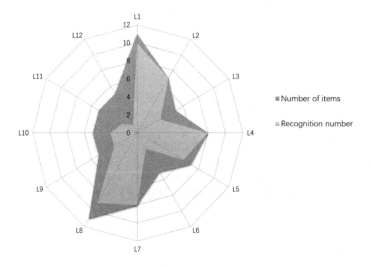

Fig. 4. Recognition results

It can be seen from the Fig. 4 that the recognition accuracy of the templates $L_1, L_2, L_4, L_5, L_7, L_8$ is high and the recognition accuracy of the remaining templates is low, which mainly because the remaining templates involve the derivation of a variable that is related to the complexity of the problem.

Our keyword list contains 14 quantifiers, 26 nouns, 16 verbs and 12 adverbs. Based on the experiment we can get the auxiliary judgment formula as follows:

$$F = 0.408F_n + 0.465F_q + 0.035F_v + 0.276F_0 - 0.103$$

When the result for a problem is greater than 0.6, it is considered that it may be satisfies Hypergeometric distribution, otherwise it is not. When the template matching result is incorrect, the data is saved for subsequent analysis based on the result of auxiliary judgment.

The experimental testing dataset consists of 180 questions from the network, in which 80 are Hypergeometric distributions, 50 are Non-Hypergeometric distributive probabilities, and the remaining 50 is the probability of unrelated college entrance examination. Before the automatic solution, we need to standardize the subject. All of the subjects will be handled as a question form.

Table 3. Accuracy of different types of problems

	Number of questions	Number of answers
Hypergeometric distribution with Clear type	82	60
Multidimensional Hypergeometric distribution	18	1
Non-Hypergeometric	100	0
Accuracy	73.2%	

The experimental results in Table 3 show that the accuracy of our method to some problems with defined types is more than 70%. We can conclude from the experimental results that the closer the description of the problem to the model of Hypergeometric distribution, the higher the accuracy of the type judgement; the fewer the transformation steps of the problem, the higher the accuracy of the solution. When the description of the problem contains the derivation process or the grammar of it is confused, the answer is very difficult, and the accuracy is low. The results demonstrate that our method is feasible to solve Hypergeometric distribution problems.

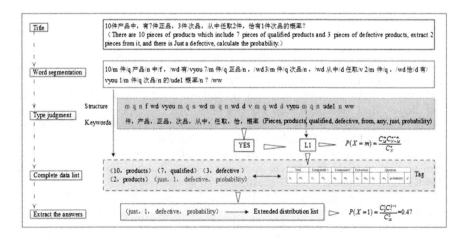

Fig. 5. An illustration using our method to solve the problem

5.3   An Illustration

We give an illustration of using our method to solve the Hypergeometric distribution problems. The first step is to conduct word segmentation, which can enrich the information of the subject. Then extract the structure information of part of speech and the keyword information that based on the segmentation results. The type of the topic is determined by type decision template and auxiliary judgment formula, and the corresponding type label is given at the same time. And then extract the required data from the subject, combined with the type label to modify and supplement the data. Finally, select the correct answers to the questions from the answer candidates (Fig. 5).

6   Conclusion

We proposed in this paper a machine solution to Hypergeometric distribution problems. We obtain the problem solving formula by establishing the matching rules between mathematic expressions and the solution of the corresponding problem description, and solve the problem based on the extraction of relevant quantitative relations. Our method belongs to template-based learning method. However, it can obtain efficient performance while only using very few template. To the best of our knowledge, our work is the first attempt to machine solving solution to Hypergeometric distribution problems. Our empirical evaluations demonstrate that our method is feasible to solve the Hypergeometric distribution problems.

Acknowledgement. This work is supported by the Fundamental Research Funds for the Central Universities (No. 20205170442).

References

1. Bobrow, D.G.: Natural language input for a computer problem solving system (1964)
2. Chou, S.C., Gao, X.S., Zhang, J.Z.: Automated production of traditional proofs for theorems in Euclidean geometry. In: Proceedings of Eigth IEEE Symposium on Login in Computer Science, pp. 48–56 (1993)
3. Dellarosa, D.: A computer simulation of children's arithmetic word-problem solving. Behav. Res. Methods **18**(2), 147–154 (1986)
4. Hosseini, M.J., Hajishirzi, H., Etzioni, O., Kushman, N.: Learning to solve arithmetic word problems with verb categorization. In: EMNLP, pp. 523–533 (2014)
5. Huang, C.-Y., Ren, Q.-L., L.M.: The de-composability and representation of strategies used in auto-solving system of primary school mathematic word problems. Mod. Educ. Technol. **20**, 24–27 (2010)
6. Jianliang, Y.: Hypergeometric distribution and its generalization. J. TaiYuan Normal Univ. **12**, 20–23 (2013)
7. Kintsch, W.: Learning from text. Cognit. Instr. **3**(2), 87–108 (1986)
8. Kintsch, W., Greeno, J.G.: Understanding and solving word arithmetic problems. Psychol. Rev. **92**(1), 109 (1985)

9. Kushman, N., Artzi, Y., Zettlemoyer, L., Barzilay, R.: Learning to Automatically Solve Algebra Word Problems. Association for Computational Linguistics (2014)
10. Liguda, C., Pfeiffer, T.: Modeling math word problems with augmented semantic networks. In: Bouma, G., Ittoo, A., Métais, E., Wortmann, H. (eds.) NLDB 2012. LNCS, vol. 7337, pp. 247–252. Springer, Heidelberg (2012). https://doi.org/10.1007/978-3-642-31178-9_29
11. Ma, Y.H., Tan, K., Shang, X.J.: Research on method of semantic comprehension based on semantic sentence template. Comput. Technol. Dev. **10**, 031 (2012)
12. Tun, W.D.: On the decision problem and the mechanization of theorem-proving in elementary geometry. Sci. Sinica **21**(2), 159–172 (1978)
13. Zhang, J.Z., Chou, S.C., Gao, X.S.: Automated production of traditional proofs for theorems in euclidean geometry i. The hilbert intersection point theorems. Ann. Math. Artif. Intell. **13**(1), 109–137 (1995)
14. Zhang, J.Z., Yang, L., Yang, X.C.: The realization of elementary configurations in euclidean space. Sci. China Ser. A-Math. Phys. Astron. Technol. Sci. **37**(1), 15–26 (1994)

Extracting Algebraic Relations from Circuit Images Using Topology Breaking Down and Shrinking

Bin He, Pengpeng Jian$^{(\boxtimes)}$, Meng Xia, Chao Sun, and Xinguo Yu

National Engineering Research Center for E-Learning,
Central China Normal University, Wuhan, China
{hebin, csun, xgyu}@mail.ccnu.edu.cn,
{jianpengpeng, xiameng}@mails.ccnu.edu.cn

Abstract. Extracting algebraic relations from a given circuit image is still a challenge task due to the complex topology of considered circuit. This paper presents an approach for extracting algebraic relations from circuit images through producing a set of atomic topologies from the complex topology of a given circuit. In which, algebraic relations, in form of a set of equations involving voltage, current and resistance relations from atomic topologies that is obtained by an iteratively operation of transforming a complex series/parallel connection into a series of atomic connection topology breaking down and shrinking. The extracted algebraic relations can be used to solve the exercise problem described by the circuit. Experimental results on 20 exercise problems show that the proposed algorithm can obtain a complete set of algebraic relations that can be used to solve the given problem. Further experiments conducted on a dataset of 200 scanned circuit images from the text books and exam papers demonstrate the proposed algorithm is the robustness and effectiveness.

Keywords: Relations extraction · Components recognition
Topology shrinking · Atomic topology analysis

1 Introduction and Related Work

To extract the complete set of algebraic relations, such as the equations of voltage and current relationship (shorted for VCR) between nodes and branches, from a circuit diagram is a necessary way to automatically solve physics problems [1, 2]. According to our statistics, more than 80% of the algebraic relations needed for problem solving are given by circuit diagram. However, it is a challenge for machine to not only analyze the circuit diagrams but also extract the proper relations for a given circuit problem. This paper proposes a new method to extract algebraic relations from circuit images by using topology breaking down and shrinking.

The task of circuit schematic analysis has received growing interest in recent years [2, 3]. One of the more interesting phenomenon of this research is that it combines visual question answering, web-based learning and intelligent tutoring system [1, 4]. In topology analysis of a linear circuit, symbolic analysis is the backbone of electronic circuits analysis [5]. Typical applications including circuit recognition [6, 7], topology

© Springer International Publishing AG, part of Springer Nature 2018
S. Satoh (Ed.): PSIVT 2017, LNCS 10799, pp. 116–130, 2018.
https://doi.org/10.1007/978-3-319-92753-4_10

representation [8, 9], etc. The symbolic approach is also considered to be most valuable in circuit analysis teaching and instruction [10, 11]. For example, some researchers integrated circuit quantities and equations into electrical circuits to improve circuit analysis learning [1, 3]. A tutoring system is developed for automatically problem solving and solution generation according to the given topology information [12].

Several works have been reported in extracting relations by topology analysis of circuit diagrams. For example, a network function detecting method [2, 13] was introduced to validate a student's problem-solving steps in a circuit analysis tutoring system, in which voltage and current relations are extracted by using node and mesh analysis. Another work reported in [14, 15] made a maiden attempt to identify sub-circuits connected in series and parallel according to the structures of symbols interconnection. However, the performances of all these works do not satisfy the requirement of applications.

The proposed method first separates the circuit diagram from a given image and identifies all components contained in the diagram. Then, a traversing based procedure of topology analysis is employed for series and parallel connection searching. In the end, algebraic relations are extracted by an iterative operation of topology breaking down and shrinking.

2   Algorithm Based on Topology Shrinking

A linear resistance circuit usually consists of a source, loads and connected lines. For convenience, all loads in the circuit, such as lamp, bell and motor, are treated as resistors during analyzing in our process. For any linear resistance circuits, the circuit topology can be constructed by a set of atomic topologies.

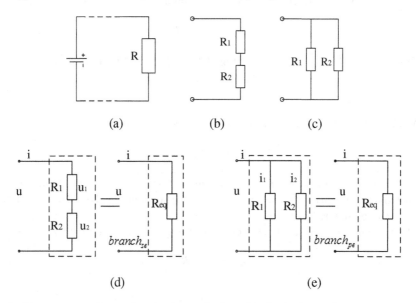

Fig. 1. Three types of atomic circuit topologies. (a) Basic loop. (b) and (c) Atomic series/parallel. (d) Series shrinking. (e) Parallel shrinking.

In our work, three atomic topologies of circuit are defined in Fig. 1(a), (b), (c), whose name are atomic loop, atomic series, and atomic parallel separately. The algebraic equations of current and voltage relationship for each atomic topology can be extracted according to basic circuit laws directly. According to series/parallel analysis theory, elements in series in a complex circuit and branches in parallel can be equivalently converted into a single node as shown in Fig. 1(d) and (e), called topology shrinking, which is presented as follows in this section.

Scope Definition

Linear resistance circuits are considered in our approach because all relations can be described by a set of linear equations by using basic circuit laws and theorems. Two forms of element connection (series and parallel) and three physical qualities (voltage, current and resistance) are considered in our approach. Furthermore, all loads are treated as resistors and there is only one voltage source in the circuit.

Terms Definition

Algebraic relations: Three physical qualities (VCR) are considered in our work: voltage, current and resistance. Kirchhoff's current law (KCL) and Kirchhoff's voltage law (KVL) are used to extract the VCR relations.

Topology Shrinking

Rules 1 (Relations from basic loop). The topology shrinking means to convert a complex circuit into a set of basic topologies as shown in Fig. 1(a) and a set of series/parallel cub-circuit as shown in Fig. 1(b) and (c). Each basic topology can be expressed by a set of algebraic equations by using circuit laws and theorems directly. The detail definitions of relation extraction from basic topologies are described as:

According to KVL and KCL, relations between connected elements in the basic loop in Fig. 1(a) is described as follows by formula

$$V_R = V_{source}, I_R = I_{source} \tag{1.1}$$

Current through series resistors in Fig. 1(b) is described by formula

$$I_{R1} = I_{R2} \tag{1.2}$$

Voltage on parallel resistors in Fig. 1(c) is described by formula

$$V_{R1} = V_{R2} \tag{1.3}$$

Rules 2 (Relations from component shrinking). Components in a series branch can be contracted into an equivalent resistance element as shown in Fig. 1(d). The substitution relations can be defined as follows:

The resistance of new equivalent element in Fig. 1(d) is described by formula

$$R_{eq} = R_1 + R_2 \tag{2.1}$$

Current through the new equivalent element in Fig. 1(d) is described by formula

$$I_{R_{eq}} = I_{R_1} = I_{R_2} = i \tag{2.2}$$

Voltage on the new equivalent element in Fig. 1(d) is described by formula

$$V_{R_{eq}} = u_1 + u_2 \tag{2.3}$$

When existing more than two components, shrinking process will be applied iteratively until only one component left in the branch.

Rules 3 (Relations from branch shrinking). Branches beginning at node n_i and ending at node n_j can be shrunk to an equivalence resistant element as shown in Fig. 1(e). The shrinkage relations can be defined as follows:

The resistance of the new equivalent element in Fig. 1(e) is described by formula

$$R_{eq} = \frac{R_1 * R_2}{R_1 + R_2} \tag{3.1}$$

Current through the new equivalent element in Fig. 1(e) is described by formula

$$I_{R_{eq}} = i_1 + i_2 \tag{3.2}$$

Voltage on the new equivalent element in Fig. 1(e) is described by formula

$$V_{R_{eq}} = V_{R_1} = V_{R_2} \tag{3.3}$$

The proposed approach for topology analysis and relations extraction possesses three main steps: element recognition, structure analysis and equivalent relations extraction, which is described in Algorithm I. The input of our approach is a circuit image containing a set of labels and connected symbols, and the output is the algebraic equations extracted from the circuits.

Circuit Graph Generation: This is the first and basic step of our approach in which OCR technology and SVM classifier are used to recognize labels and symbols in circuit diagrams. Line segments of wires are detected and the gaps on the location of symbols are filled by short lines. A circuit graph composed by a set of line segments is generated in the end of this step.

Topology Analysis: For circuit topology analyzing, a branch analysis method is conducted on circuit graph obtained above to search the main branch and all parallel sub-branches in circuit diagrams. Different with method in [14], the fork nodes are detected and treated as vertexes in circuit graph which can be intuitively used to describe the structure of parallel/series and perform topology shrinking later in relation extraction.

Relations Extraction: This is the final and also the critical step in our approach. Based on the result of topology analysis, a set of algebraic equations of elements

---

Algorithm I: The framework of algebraic relations extraction

Input: circuit image containing labels and symbols.

Output: the equivalent algebraic equations.

Step 1: circuit graph generation from circuit image

    1.1: circuit components recognition;

    1.2: topology construction;

Step 2: topology analysis on circuit graph

    2.1: branch searching;

    2.2: series/parallel analyzing;

Step 3: relations extraction from atomic topologies

    3.1: topology shrinking transform;

    3.2: equations extraction;

(called direct algebraic equation) can be extracted according to KCL and KVL. By using topology shrinking, the original circuit will be converted into a set of atomic topologies, for each atomic topology, algebraic equations of shrinking relations (called indirect algebraic equation) are extracted by circuit laws and theorems.

3   Circuit Graph Generation

Circuit graph provides a basic input for our algorithm, so before topology analyzing, a circuit graph generation method is described based on components recognition and fork nodes analysis in this section. The purpose of our method is to detect and recognize electrical components from a given circuit image. Based on the results of line detection and symbols recognition, a circuit graph, in which fork nodes are denoted as vertexes and the connected lines among fork nodes are denoted as edges, is generated to describe the topology of interconnection of the circuit elements.

Usually, circuit diagrams appear in a digital document which contains textual question stems and circuit figures. Before our recognition, method [16, 17] are used to extract most PDF images and circuit figures automatically from the digital document. Then, a segmentation process [18] is implemented to separate the textual and non-textual components in the image and circuit region is located by a convex bounding operation of non-text classes on the images.

3.1 Components Recognition

Method of components detection and recognition is described in this section. Components in a circuit mainly includes labels, symbols and line segments. Labels are segmented and recognized firstly by using OCR technology and then removed from the circuit. Then line segments are detected by LSD detector and a specific refinement process and a mask image based on gaps between segments is generated for symbols location. After symbols segmented, a SVM classifier is applied for symbols recognition.

Label Recognition. Circuit Labels include these characters and numbers outside of circuit symbols, such as resistance labels "R_1", and inside of circuit symbols which are part of the symbol, such as "V_1" in the voltmeter symbol. In our method, all labels will be located and recognized at first. The recognized labels inside the symbols will be put back and add to the graph figure.

First, characters and numbers are located and recognized using tesseract OCR engine [19]. Only clusters have a structure of "C", "C_n" and "C_{nn}" will be accepted as a valid label, in which "C" stands for character and "n" for number. Record all the candidate labels and their locations in a table named T_{label}.

Second, characters and number belonging to voltmeter, ammeter and motor are pushed back to graph figure, which means the character of "V", "A", "G" and "M" will be drawn back to the circuit diagram, and they still in T_{label} as an accepted label.

To avoid destroying the original image feature of circuit, we do not really redraw these characters to the circuit diagram. Instead, we calculate a bounding rectangle for each of them and copy the pixel value of each rectangle from the source to our diagram.

Connected Line Detection. The main work in this section is to detect the short lines from circuit images. Symbols are connected by vertical and horizontal short lines, while some short lines are part of symbols. In this section, only connected lines are detected. The detecting process is based on LSD [20]. Salient segments are removed and short segments are merged to amend the defects by a set of optimization processes.

There are three possible defects in the lines detected from a diagram by applying LSD algorithm: (1) a visually line segment may be detected as a series of unconnected parallel short ones, (2) a line in the figure is detected as some disconnected short segments, (3) the start or end points of a sub-circuit and the turning points of two connective segments cannot be accurately detected. The following sub steps are used to amend the defects.

To solve these problems, a set of optimization processes is performed. For each segment, we first find out all co-line segments as a segment group, then remove those segments far away from others and finally merge the remained segments into a new longer one. The distance between endpoints of two different segments is used for segments grouping. For example, in stage of grouping, put seed segment l_{vi} selected from L_v into a new group G_{vi}, add all co-line segments l_{vj} into G_{vi} if $dist(l_{vi}, l_{vj}) < \tau_v$, and remove l_{vj} from L_v. Where, τ_v is a pre-specified distance tolerance, $dist(l_{vi}, l_{vj})$ is the Euler distance. In stage of short segments merging, pair (l_{vi}, l_{vj}) is replaced by a new segment l'_{vi} when $co(l_{vi}, l_{vj}) > \delta_v$, Where $co(,)$ is the overlapping ratio on Y axis of (l_{vi}, l_{vj}), δ_v is a pre-specified tolerance. Put l'_{vi} into L'_v. Same strategies are used to merge short segments in L_h into L'_h.

Symbol Recognition. There are more than 9 classes, 12 types of circuit symbols in junior middle school physical courses shown in Fig. 2. So in this part, a classification process is implemented based on SVM [21] for circuit symbols recognition.

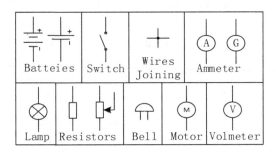

Fig. 2. Symbol classes

In a circuit, symbols are usually presented between two collinear segments. Based on this regularity, the gaps between two collinear segments are collected and the bounding rectangles G are calculated in *Step1.2 of Algorithm 1*. Remove blank rectangles in G which contain no symbols by contours analyzing.

Due to the contour of battery(s) contains two or more separate connective component (Fig. 3(a)), a joint model is used for accurate battery symbols segmentation. In this model, we analyze the connectivity of each set of online segments and generate a default bounding box between two online segments. Then a combination operating is implemented on results of contour segmentation on gaps and all default boxes. The final segmentation results are shown in Fig. 3(c).

The corresponding sub-figure defined by box r in Fig. 3(c) is considered as a candidate circuit symbol and is resized to 32*32. Then the sub-figure is reshaped to a size of 1*1024 row vector which is used as the input of SVM classifier for training and prediction. A recognized sub-figure located by r is defined as a 3-element row vector *symbol* stored in a vector S:

$$symbol = (typeID, label, r)$$

Where, *label* is the corresponding label found in T_{label} according to the position correlation, *TypeID* denotes the symbol type obtained by SVM prediction.

3.2 Graph Node Analysis

Based on the results of components recognition, two types of intersection nodes can be obtained, which are fork nodes and turning nodes. In the circuit topology, fork nodes denote the starting and ending of a parallel connection. Degree analyzing is applied to identify fork nodes from all intersection nodes in this step. Before degree analyzing, circuit will be converted to a connected graph $G_{connected}$ by combination of the position of row symbols vector S and segments clusters L'_v and L'_h.

Degree analyzing is implemented in this section to identify fork nodes and turning nodes. The degree of node $n_i(1 \leq i \leq N)$ is denoted as $D(n_i)$. If degree$(n_i) \geq 3$, then n_i will be marked as a fork node. Figure 4 shows the result of topology reconstruction of the diagram in Fig. 3(a).

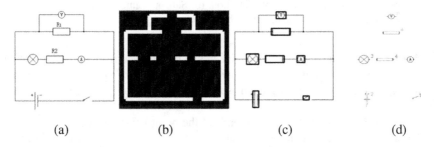

| (a) | (b) | (c) | (d) |

Fig. 3. Symbols location and recognition. (a) Input image (b) overstriking mask for elements location (c) location results (d) results of symbols recognition

The battery of the circuit, which is marked as n_0, is added to the set of fork node and treated as the start and end node of the circuit.

4   Algebraic Relations Extraction

Based on the circuit graph generated in Sect. 3, an atomic topology analysis and topology shrinking operation method is explained for extracting of current and voltage equations. In this section, the extraction of algebraic relations will be presented involving the method of topology breaking down and topology shrinking.

4.1   Topology Breaking Down

As defined in Sect. 2, three types of atomic topologies are mainly included in a circuit graph. Fork nodes are used in our algorithm to search and identify these atomic topologies from a complex circuit graph. A branch traversing method is described to find out all the shunt paths from the graph and a generalized connection analysis is presented to identify each atomic topology.

Branch Searching. A branch traversing method is introduced to search all the shunt paths in the circuit graph, including a main path and a set of sub-paths. The main path is a set of visited nodes starting with n_o and ending with n_0. Different with traditional DFS in graph traversing, several strategies for branch traversing are defined as follows:

Strategy **1.** Each edge will be visited only once and DFS is used for node searching;

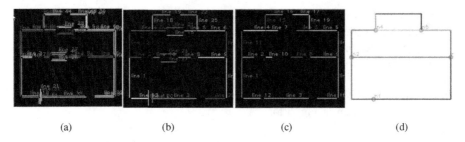

| (a) | (b) | (c) | (d) |

Fig. 4. Graph generation. (a) Segments detection. (b) Salient segments removing. (c) Gaps of elements. (d) After redraw the circuit structure and fork nodes.

Strategy 2. For main path, the intra-node n_i will be removed from the path if there is no path to n_0 under strategy 1 and the traversal will backtrack to n_{i-1};

Strategy 3. Each point in the main path and obtained sub-paths can start a new sub-path traversal;

Strategy 4. Each sub-path traversal ends at the point being visited above;

The process of path searching by branch traversing is described in Procedure I.

Procedure I: Path searching by branch traversing

Input: a connected graph $G_{connected}$ with nodes n_i and edges s_i.

Output: a list of paths, including a main path and several sub-paths.

Step1: Set visited flag of each edge to false;

Step2: Searching paths using strategy1-2, and find the longest as the main path;

Step3: Searching all sub-paths by using strategy 3-4;

The traversal begins at node n_0, it then iteratively transitions to an adjacent, unvisited vertex, until it can no longer find an unexplored node. The traversal then backtracks along previously visited nodes, until it finds a node connected to yet more uncharted territory. Searching stops when the traversal has backtracked past the node n_0. Figure 5 shows an example of the branch searching result of main path and all sub-paths.

Generalized-Connection Analysis. All shunt paths have been found in path list by branch traversing described above and the next work is to classify the paths into

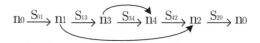

Fig. 5. Branches in the main path

different topology groups, which is called generalized-connection analysis. The topology of generalized-connection is defined as follows:

Generalized-Connection in Parallel. The sub-paths with a same starting node and ending node, are considered to be a generalized-connection in parallel.

Generalized-Connection in Series. Each sub-circuit in the path list is considered to be a generalized-connection in series.

The generalized-connection analysis (G-CA) is described in Procedure II as follows:

Procedure II: Generalized-connection analyzing

Input: path list produced by branch traversing.
Output: structure description of generalized parallel/series connection.

Step1: Finding all paths p_{ij} ($p_{ij} = \{n_i, n_j : (s_{ij})\}$) from path list which contains only two nodes;

Step2: Searching all paths { p_{ij}', $\cdots$ } starting with n_i and end with n_j ;

Step3: Denoting path set $pb_{ij} = \{p_{ij}, p_{ij}', \cdots\}$ as a generalized-connection in parallel;

Step4: Denoting each sub-path of $s_{ij}, s_{ij}', \cdots$ as a generalized-connection in series.

G-CA makes it easier for topology analysis of a circuit graph. However, a generalized-connection produced by Procedure II may be containing another generalized-connection which means it still containing complex topology. To identify an atomic topology connection from a generalized-connection, the length of a path is calculated and the sub-path s_{ij} corresponds to an atomic series only if the length of s_{ij} equals to 2, and P_b corresponds to an atomic parallel while each path in P_b corresponds to an atomic series.

4.2 Topology Shrinking

To transform a generated-connection with a complex topology into a set of atomic topologies, the procedure of topology shrinking is presented in this section. Based on the result of G-CA on the circuit graph, a branch shrinking and a component shrinking operation is implemented, which simplifies an atomic series and an atomic parallel to an equivalent element separately. After topology shrinking, the algebraic relations can be extracted through the formulas defined in Sect. 2.

From procedure II, a set of path pb with generalized-connection in parallel is obtained and assume n_{i-1} is the previous node of n_i and n_{j+1} is the next node of n_j, s_{i-1} is the edge of (n_{i-1}, n_i) and s_{j+1} is the edge of (n_j, n_{j+1}). The topology shrinking process is described in procedure III.

Procedure III: Topology shrinking process

Input: the path set of P_b produced by procedure II.

Output: a basic loop and a set of shrinking descriptions.

Step 1: For the path set P_b, repeat the following operations until the circuit graph is transformed into the basic loop shown in Fig.1 (a);

Step 2: Branch simplification according to Rule 3: For branches $pb_{ij} = \{p_{ij}, p_{ij}', \cdots\}$ in P_b, if pb_{ij} corresponds to an atomic parallel, replace pb_{ij} with R_{ij}, where, R_{ij} is an equivalent resistance element of $pb_{ij} = \{p_{ij}, p_{ij}', \cdots\}$;

Step 3: Component simplification according to Rule 2: For R_{ij} and elements R_{i-1} and R_{j+1} in branch $< s_{i-1}, s_{j+1} >$, replace $< R_{i-1}, R_{ij}, R_{j+1} >$ with R_{i-1j+1}', where, R_{i-1j+1}' is an equivalent resistance element of $< R_{i-1}, R_{ij}, R_{j+1} >$;

Step 4: Update the path lists: remove p_{ij} for path lists, replace

$(n_{i-1}, n_i, n_j, n_{j+1} : s_{i-1}, si_j, s_{j+1})$ with $(n_{i-1}, n_{j+1} : s_{i-1j+1})$;

In each iteration of procedure III, at least one parallel connection is shrunk to a standard series connection as shown in Fig. 1(b). During the shrinking, an equivalent element R_{ij}/R_{i-1j+1}' is created to keep the relationship of the circuit before and after the shrinking.

Relations are generated in each iteration of topology shrinking. For relations in branch shrinking, the VIR relationship between { $p_{ij}, p_{ij}', \cdots$ } and R_{ij} in step 2 of procedure III can be calculated according to formula 3.1–3.3. For relations in component shrinking, the VIR relationship between $< R_{i-1}, R_{ij}, R_{j+1} >$ and R_{ij}' in step 3 of procedure III can be calculated according to formula 2.1–2.3. At last, relations in the basic loop, the VIR relationship between battery and load can be calculated according to formula 1.1.

5   Experimental Results

In this section, we present some experimental results with a preliminary implementation of the approach. It first describes the dataset and the setting for experiments. Then it shows a set of results on topology analysis and relations extraction.

5.1   Dataset Preparation and Experiment Settings

All experiments have been carried out by us on a machine with Intel® core™ Duo CPU i-4590 3.3 GHz and 4 GB Memory. The dataset contains 200 scanned images of circuit diagrams collected from text books and examinations. The algorithm described in Sects. 3 and 4 have been implemented in C++ and OpenCV functions [19] are used in images preprocess. Line segments are detected by using LSD detector [20].

To improve the accuracy of segments and nodes detection, five parameters $\tau_h, \tau_v, \tau_{ep}, \tau_l, \sigma_v, \sigma_h$ are used to specify the tolerances of in our approach for symbols segmentation and structure reconstruction, in which τ_h, τ_v are the distance threshold between two parallel segments, τ_{ep} is the distance tolerance of endpoints between two segments, τ_l is the length tolerance of each segment and σ_v, σ_h are the max size of a valid gap in vertical and horizontal direction separately. We firstly acquire empirical values for these parameters by making experiments on a set of test images. Then, for any given image I of diagram, the tolerance will be automatically adjusted according to the statistics of line segments, such as segment length, distance between parallel segments and endpoints.

5.2   Experiments on Relations Extraction

Take the problem of the diagram in Fig. 3(a) for example, *"resistor R_1 is 50 Ω, R_2 is 20 Ω, the reading of voltmeter is 5 V and the ammeter is 10 mA, $R_{light} = ?$".*

Step-by-step results of topology analysis for a typical image are already shown in Figs. 3 and 4. After branch analyzing, a main path containing 6 nodes and 2 sub paths are found and two parallel sub-circuits of the first level are extracted. The detail results of branch analyzing, circuit shrinking and equations extraction at first level is shown as follows:

Level 1:

Results of branch searching: Results of GPSCA:

Main path: $P_0 \xrightarrow{S_{01}} P_1 \xrightarrow{S_{13}} P_3 \xrightarrow{S_{34}} P_4 \xrightarrow{S_{42}} P_2 \xrightarrow{S_{20}} P_0$

$gpc_1\begin{cases} 3: P_1 \xrightarrow{S_{13}} P_3 \xrightarrow{S_{34}} P_4 \xrightarrow{S_{42}} P_2 \\ 1: P_1 \xrightarrow{S_{12}} P_2 \end{cases}$

Sub path: $1: P_1 \xrightarrow{S_{12}} P_2$

$\qquad\qquad 2: P_3 \xrightarrow{S_{34}} P_4$

$gpc_2\begin{cases} 4: P_3 \xrightarrow{S_{34}} P_4 \\ 2: P_3 \xrightarrow{S_{34}} P_4 \end{cases}$

Results of topology shrinking:

$gpc_2\begin{cases} 4: P_3 \xrightarrow{S_{34}} P_4 \\ 2: P_3 \xrightarrow{S_{34}} P_4 \end{cases} \xrightarrow{\text{branch shrinking}} -[R_{34}] \Rightarrow \begin{cases} V_{s34}=V'_{s34} \\ i_{p34}=i'_{s34}+i_{s34} \\ r_{34}=r'_{s34}*r_{s34}/(r'_{s34}+r_{s34}) \end{cases}$

$gsc: P_1 -[R_{34}] - P_2 \xrightarrow{\text{component shrinking}} P_1 \xrightarrow{S_{12}} P_2 \Rightarrow \begin{cases} V'_{s12}=V_{s13}+V_{s34}+V_{s42} \\ i_{p12}=i_{p34} \\ r'_{12}=r_{s13}+r_{34}+r_{s42} \end{cases}$

To test the generality and practicability of our approach, we have made experiments on the prepared dataset and part of the results are shown in Table 1. N_s denotes the number of symbols recognized; N_f denotes the number of fork node calculated; N_p denotes the number of parallel sub-circuit detected; N_{re} and N_{ru} denote the number of algebraic equations extracted and used in problem solving separately.

Table 1. Part of experiment results

No.	01	02	03	460	3100	3740	3750	3820	3890	3930
N_s	7	6	6	6	6	6	5	6	6	5
N_f	5	2	2	5	5	4	2	2	4	2
N_p	2	1	1	2	2	0	1	1	2	1
N_{re}/N_{ru}	14/4	8/4	8/3	14/2	14/2	5/3	8/2	13/3	14/4	8/2

Table 1 shows a summary of our experimental results[1]. From the table, it is evident that the symbols identification and forks detection are done successfully and branches in parallel are discovered correctly. A further validation experiment on about 20 exercises is conducted to evaluate the completeness of the extracted relations for automatic problem solving. The result shows the equations needed from the circuit diagram for solving the given problem can be entirely extracted by our approach.

It should be noticed that the switch in the circuit should be set to status of close or open before our processing by text understanding. The nodes and edges of the graph in the open sub-circuit will be ignored in our topology analyzing process. For example, there are three switches in image 3740 in Table 1. According to the result of text understanding, only one switch is closed in each case and no sub-circuit connected in parallel is formed. So the value of N_p is zero and 3 equations from components shrinking and 2 equations from basic loop have been extracted in the experiment.

In our test, once the symbols are properly segmented out, the topology and relations can be understood and extracted correctly. Some over-segmentation and also under-segmentation of the symbols may arise due to un-normal distance between two adjacent parallel line segments. One such case is shown in Fig. 6.

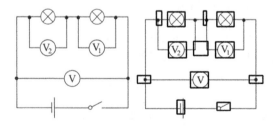

Fig. 6. Over-segmentation. Left: Input image. Right: Segmented symbols, the gap between voltmeter 1 and 2 being over-segmented.

---

[1] More input images and corresponding results are available at: http://pan.baidu.com/s/1kUKwcV9.

6   Conclusions and Future Work

This paper presents an algorithm for extracting algebraic relations from circuit images through producing a set of atomic topologies from a complex topology of a circuit. The group of the extracted algebraic relations for a given circuit can be used to solve the exercise problem described by the circuit. A test result shows that all relations needed from the circuit for the problem solving can be extracted by the proposed algorithm. And further experiments show that a better performance in terms of robustness and effectiveness can be achieved by the proposed algorithm compared with the existing methods [2, 14].

This work can be easily extended to geometrical and chemical diagram understanding and has potential applications in diagram searching and animated tutoring. In our next work, this new method will be applied in automatic problem solving and intelligent tutoring system for circuit course teaching in stage of junior middle school. Furthermore, we plan to improve the proposed approach so that it can be used in circuit understanding of camera and hand-written circuits.

Acknowledgment. This work is supported by the Fundamental Research Funds for the Central Universities (No. 20205170499).

References

1. Reisslein, J., Johnson, A.M., Reisslein, M.: Color coding of circuit quantities in introductory circuit analysis instruction. IEEE Trans. Educ. **58**, 7–14 (2015)
2. Weyten, L., Rombouts, P., Catteau, B., De Bock, M.: Validation of symbolic expressions in circuit analysis e-learning. IEEE Trans. Educ. **54**, 564–568 (2011)
3. Ozogul, G., Johnson, A.M., Moreno, R., Reisslein, M.: Technological literacy learning with cumulative and stepwise integration of equations into electrical circuit diagrams. IEEE Trans. Educ. **55**, 480–487 (2012)
4. Weyten, L., Rombouts, P., Maeyer, J.D.: Web-Based Trainer for Electrical Circuit Analysis. IEEE Press (2009)
5. Huelsman, L.P.: Symbolic analysis-a tool for teaching undergraduate circuit theory. IEEE Trans. Educ. **39**, 243–250 (1996)
6. De, P., Mandal, S., Bhowmick, P.: Recognition of electrical symbols in document images using morphology and geometric analysis. In: International Conference on Image Information Processing, pp. 1–6 (2011)
7. Escalera, S., Fornés, A., Pujol, O., Radeva, P., Sánchez, G., Lladós, J.: Blurred shape model for binary and grey-level symbol recognition. Patt. Recogn. Lett. **30**, 1424–1433 (2009)
8. Sridar, S., Subramanian, K.: Circuit recognition using netlist. In: 2013 IEEE Second International Conference on Image Information Processing, pp. 242–246 (2013)
9. Li, J., Lee, F.C.: New modeling approach and equivalent circuit representation for current-mode control. IEEE Trans. Power Electron. **25**, 1218–1230 (2010)
10. Johnson, A.M., Butcher, K.R., Ozogul, G., Reisslein, M.: Introductory circuit analysis learning from abstract and contextualized circuit representations: effects of diagram labels. IEEE Trans. Educ. **57**, 160–168 (2014)

11. Skromme, B.J., Rayes, P.J., Whitlatch, C.D., Wang, Q., Barrus, A., Quick, J.M., Atkinson, R.K., Frank, T.S.: Computer-aided instruction for introductory linear circuit analysis. In: Frontiers in Education Conference, pp. 314–319 (2013)
12. Skromme, B.J., Rayes, P.J., Mcnamara, B.E., Seetharam, V., Gao, X., Thompson, T., Wang, X., Cheng, B., Huang, Y.F., Robinson, D.H.: Step-based tutoring system for introductory linear circuit analysis. In: IEEE Frontiers in Education Conference, pp. 1–9 (2015)
13. Djordjević, S., Petković, P.: Topology oriented symbolic circuit analysis based on limit variables. In: European Conference on Circuits and Systems for Communications, pp. 63–66 (2010)
14. Mandal, P.D.S., Bhowmick, P., Chanda, B.: Topological simplification of electrical circuits by super-component analysis. In: International Conference on Document Analysis and Recognition, pp. 211–215 (2015)
15. De, P., Mandal, S., Bhowmick, P.: Identification of annotations for circuit symbols in electrical diagrams of document images. In: Fifth International Conference on Signal and Image Processing, pp. 297–302 (2014)
16. Chiu, P., Chen, F., Denoue, L.: Picture detection in document page images. In: ACM Symposium on Document Engineering, Manchester, United Kingdom, pp. 211–214, September 2010
17. Xu, C., Tao, X.: Graphic composite segmentation for PDF documents with complex layouts. In: Proceedings of SPIE - The International Society for Optical Engineering, vol. 8658, p. 27 (2013)
18. Zirari, F., Ennaji, A., Nicolas, S., Mammass, D.: A simple text/graphic separation method for document image segmentation, pp. 1–4 (2013)
19. Smith, R.: An overview of the tesseract OCR engine. In: International Conference on Document Analysis and Recognition, pp. 629–633 (2007)
20. Rafael, G.V.G., Jakubowicz, J., Morel, J.M., Randall, G.: LSD: a fast line segment detector with a false detection control. IEEE Trans. Patt. Anal. Mach. Intell. 32, 722–732 (2010)
21. Chang, C.C., Lin, C.J.: LIBSVM: a library for support vector machines. ACM Trans. Intell. Syst. Technol. 2, 27 (2011)

Parallel Education Systems Under Perspective of System Construction for New IT Era

Xiaoyan Gong[1,2(✉)], Xiwei Liu[1,2], Sifeng Jing[1,2], and Xiao Wang[1,3]

[1] The State Key Laboratory for Management and Control of Complex Systems, Institute of Automation, Chinese Academy of Sciences, Beijing 100190, China
xiaoyan.gong@ia.ac.cn
[2] Institute of Smart Education Systems, Qingdao Academy of Intelligent Industries, Qingdao 266109, China
[3] Department of Computer Science and Technology, Xi'an Jiaotong University, Xi'an 710049, China

Abstract. New IT (Intelligent Technology) era calls for a new generation of lifelong-learning talents with scientific literacy, humanistic literacy and sound personality. Development of intelligent technology has changed organization of knowledge, interactions among new generation of learners and way of learning and living, and even social organization and social structure, which brings big challenges to current educational ideas, methods and models. Constructivism as a popular educational theory, has been applied ever since it was introduced into China. But most focuses more on knowledge construction and less on personality construction, and separate these two constructions from each other. So based on combing development of constructivism, and absorbing achievements of personality psychology, this paper puts forward system construction based on knowledge construction and personality construction. Introducing ACP (Artificial systems, Computational experiments, Parallel execution) approach toward CPSS (Cyber-Physical-Social Systems), this paper proposes parallel education system framework under perspective of system construction to explore feasible way to cultivate new generation of talents.

Keywords: New IT era · Constructivism · System construction
CPSS · ACP · Parallel education systems

1 New IT Era and Challenges in Education

Today, the world has entered a period of rapid development, from the "Old IT" (Industrial Technology) era through the "Current IT" information technology era (Information Technology) to the "New IT" intelligent technology (Intelligent Technology) era [1]. Development of science and technology presents exponential changes, and intelligent devices as "new species" enter every corner of our life, and society presents unprecedented complexity and uncertainty. This poses a huge challenge to survival and development of mankind, future learners and thus our education system.

In the new IT era, huge amount of online and offline learning resources greatly changed organization and access patterns of knowledge, learners' cognitive model and learning habits, which generates a new generation of learners known as "Digital Natives"

[2, 3], who have long been immersed in various types of intelligent devices and are well versed in information and intelligence technologies. They prefer screen-style fragmented reading, game-based teaching, "perception-vision" type of learning and multi-tasking implementing. This requires educational systems to make changes in educational philosophy, technology, methods and models.

New IT era brings diversification of social culture, virtualization of social interactions and even changes in social relations, social structure and social form, which causes psychological development dilemmas to new generation of learners. They are accustomed to computer-based and text-based communication, but inadequate at face-to-face communication. So in context of pluralistic social culture, such social interaction missing and interpersonal online make their personality virtual, lost and closed, exacerbating their personality identity crisis [4].

New IT era requires lifelong learning and innovative talents, just as 《Core Competencies and Values for Chinese Students' Development》, issued by National Ministry of Education, clearly pointed out that new generation of learners needs to have three kinds of core qualities such as scientific literacy, humanistic accomplishment and sound personality [5]. Therefore, it is of great significance to explore new way of teaching for new generation of learners and our society.

Constructivism as a cognitive theory has become a mainstream of international education reform [6]. In 1996, US published 《National Science Education Standards》, the first national science education document, is based on constructivism [7]. Its essence is that knowledge cannot be transmitted and must be constructed initially by learners, which is suitable for today: reorganization of knowledge and "screen reading" learning mode of new generation of learners. Since 1980s, constructivism has been introduced into China, it has become popular in education research and teaching activities, which focuses more on application research, less on theoretical research, more on scientific knowledge construction, but less personality construction, and separate these two constructions from each other.

So based on combing development of constructivism, absorbing results of psychological research, this paper proposes system construction integrating knowledge construction and personality construction, and explores its implementation by introducing ACP-based [19–21] parallel system theory and parallel education system framework.

2   Development of Constructivism

2.1   History

As a cognitive mode or educational practice mode, emerging from contemporary western countries, constructivism is a combination of fragmented and unsystematic complex social science theory ever since it existed. From the ancient Chinese Lao's "Tutors should not enlighten students, until they has turned problems over in their minds and are willing to obtain some thoughts but cannot speak out standard answers" to well-known Socrates "Midwifery Teaching Method", from modern constructivist pioneer, Italian famous philosopher Vico (Giambattista Vico) to contemporary American social psychologist

George Kelley's personal construction, from epistemology of Swiss child psychologist Jean Piaget, to language acquisition theory of Lev Vygotsky, constructivism has gone through series of development process. Education related constructivism includes individual constructivism, radical constructivism and social constructivism [8].

Individual constructivism: It was proposed by American social psychologist Kelly in her book 《The Psychology of Personal Constructs》, which pointed out that individuals build knowledge alone through understanding of repeated events, therefore, knowledge would rather be personal and adaptive, but not objective [9]. In 1972, Jean Piaget proposed individual knowledge construction in 《The Principles of Genetic Epistemology》, pointing out that through assimilation and adaptation, individuals change schema in their minds to achieve construction of objective world ultimately [10]. American LOGO language inventor and education information master, also known as "father of maker", Seymour Papert inherited Piaget's constructivism to constructionism, emphasizing learning by making, computer-based and game-based learning scene, tools, and importance of sharing [11].

Table 1. Individual constructivism, radical constructivism and social constructivism

Type	Conception of knowledge	Conception of learning	Conception of teaching
Individual constructivism	Personal, existence of objective world	Personal constructs	Guiding learners, encouraging sharing and cooperation
Radical constructivism	Personal, existence of objective world	Personal constructs, sharing	Guiding learners, encouraging sharing and cooperation in certain social contexts
Social constructivism	Personal, existence of objective world	Personal constructs, sharing in certain social contexts	Guiding learners, encouraging sharing and cooperation, trying to solve life-related problems

Radical constructivism: It is represented by Italian constructionist E. Von Glasersfeld. He assured existence of objective reality, but individuals cannot get objective knowledge, because human cannot get "God eyes" to truly see the universe [12]. Thus, knowledge is not a real copy of objective world, but a personal construct that seeks to understand society or natural environments.

Social constructivism: Individual constructivism and radical constructivism focus mainly on construction of personal knowledge, but to some degrees, ignoring social factors. As Joan Solomon pointed out, knowledge is personal, but reason of revision of personal knowledge is to achieve recognition from peers and society, which is a social impact and it might be the only reason in learning science and forming a scientific attitude [13].

Therefore, from individual constructivism, radical constructivism to social constructivism, with development of human's cognition of human-mind, nature and society, cognitive and learning theory developed as well. As shown in Table 1, from personal construct, sharing with others, to cooperation and sharing in certain social situations, from personal constructs to personal constructs in certain social contexts, constructivism has gone through a process of gradual integration of more and more cognition and learning-related factors.

2.2   Constructivism from Perspective of Cybernetics

Since Norbert Wiener published 《Cybernetics: Or Control and Communication in the Animal and the Machine》 in 1948, cybernetics, as a science that studies how dynamic systems maintain balanced state or steady state under changing environments, its ideas and methods have penetrated into almost all fields of natural sciences and social sciences [14]. Its essence is that if there is deviation between dynamic systems' current state of and stable state, then dynamic systems will start automatic control process. With deviation as inputs to automatic controller, automatic controller figures out and outputs instructions to change current system state. By observer's obtaining current system state, automatic controller compares it with stable state again, and keeps doing adjusting process until deviation is zero or accepted.

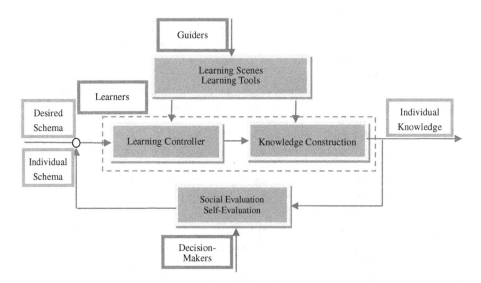

Fig. 1.   Knowledge construction process from view of cybernetics

Based on cybernetics, this paper transforms Piaget's Schema-based [10] constructivism into control schematic shown in Fig. 1. Piaget thought knowledge exists in human's minds as a form called schema (system state), the reason why learners start learning process (automatic control process) is the unaccepted deviation between desired knowledge schema (steady state) and current knowledge schema (current state), which means learners need to learn to grasp knowledge as expected by themselves or society. Then "learning area" or learning controller (automatic controller) in people's brain starts learning process (automatic control process), which is also called personal knowledge constructs. Then examinations or other evaluation methods (observer) obtain how much and how well learners have learned (current system state) or what current schema is in learners' brains. If deviation is accepted then learning process stops, otherwise continues.

For normal learners, they can achieve goals through normal personal knowledge construction and learning processes. But for special learners, they might need special way of learning. Seymour Papert has done a lot in this area, and his famous LOGO language and lovely little turtle have helped many learners find confidence and pleasure in learning mathematics [11].

3 Personality Construction

Personality is relative stable and unique psychological and behavioral patterns formed by interactions between people and acquired environment based on genetic qualities. Personality is both product of social and cultural shaping and result of people's adaptation and selection. Development of personality psychology has been similar to that of cognitive and learning theory. From earliest personal personality construction to personal personality construction among interactions to personal personality construction under social contexts [15].

According to Freud's theory, personality has three parts such as "Self", "Ego" and "Super-ego". Self is primitive desire, pursuit of happiness, and avoidance of pain; "Ego" serves "Self" under certain realistic constraints, "Super-ego" is moral strength as strict restrictions to "Ego". In fierce struggles of personality, "Self", "Ego" and "Super-ego" never stopped suppressing and anti-suppressing [16]. When three parts cannot be effectively coordinated, personality will be imbalanced and lost. Recently, young people's suicide rate' rising is tragedies of imbalanced and lost personalities.

New era has brought personality construction dilemmas under cruel struggles among "Self", "Ego" and "Super-ego". Social and cultural diversities increase desire of "Self", and makes power of "Ego" gradually lost; Online human-computer interactions, rather than face to face communications, cannot meet emotional needs of "Super-ego" to balance "Self" and "Ego", resulting in lost personalities. Therefore, it's important to explore personality construction in new era as required by our society.

Schematic diagram of personality construction from perspective of cybernetics is shown in Fig. 2. Personality constructions are dynamic adjustment processes to achieve dynamic balances. When there is unaccepted deviations between "Self" (desired state) and "Ego" (system state), that is when personal desire and social expectations don't match, as known as psychological imbalance, "Super-ego" initiates adjustment process by active or passive psychological construction/reconstruction to achieve psychological balance; otherwise, long-term psychological imbalance will lead to extreme behaviors and eccentric personalities.

Active psychological construction refers to self-discovery of psychological imbalance by self-reflection, face to face effective communications, playing games, doing sports or other hobbies to achieve dynamic balances again. Passive process refers to process of psychological reconstruction by certain ways through guidance and intervention of psychoanalysts and therapists. After Dora Kalff absorbed analytical psychology from Carl Gustav Jung, "Game Kingdom Technology" from Margaret Lowenfeld and oriental culture, in her book 《Sandplay—The Psychotherapeutic Approach to Spirituality》, she proposed a sandplay game-based psychological therapy theory and methods [17].

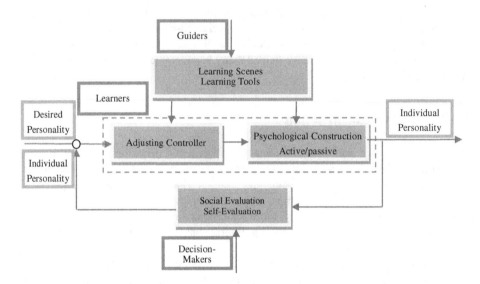

Fig. 2. Psychological/personality construction process from view of cybernetics

4   System Construction Based on Knowledge Construction and Psychological Construction

Education-related research and practices of constructivism has been carried out widely in China, but under current education evaluation system, most focuses on knowledge construction, less on psychological construction, and separate these two construction processes. But knowledge construction and psychological construction are inseparable, instead they complement each other, and should be improved together. Usually, people with strong and well-built psychology more likely learn well because they can face all difficulties in the right way. Knowledge construction provides good chance for people to train their psychology because they will meet different situations during knowledge construction process. In a sense, psychological construction is the base of knowledge construction, and knowledge construction is carriers of psychological construction. This paper proposes a framework of system construction based on knowledge construction and psychological construction shown in Fig. 3.

System construction contains five elements such as guiders, learners, learning tools, learning scenes, social scenarios, which are interrelated and mutually influenced. Guiding and learning processes take place in certain social contexts through learning scenes and learning tools, any changes in each element will affect others. That is, in certain social contexts, based on guiders' understanding of learners' dynamic knowledge schema and "Self", "Ego" and "Super-ego", guiders design learning scenes and choose effective learning tools, to let learners build personal knowledge schema and personality under guidance and achieve personal or social expectations. There are two levels of construction caused by personal evaluation and social evaluation respectively, and sometime they are contradictory. So with help of guiders, learners need to learn to manage these two constructions, that is, unity of individual needs and social needs.

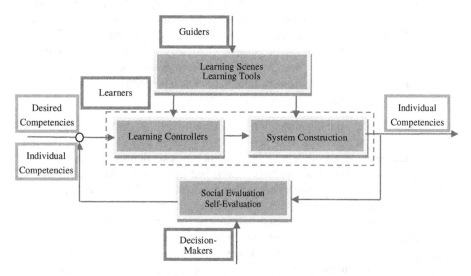

Fig. 3. System construction process from view of cybernetics

Social contexts (mainly include social evaluation system): In the context of globalization, based on current domestic education situation, decision-makers need to develop new national education policy, new core literacy and new evaluation standards toward new IT era to cultivate innovative workforce, and enhance individual and social core competitiveness. Social evaluation is the core since it determines concepts of education, methods and modes.

Guiders: Guiders need to understand connotations of social evaluation and its requirements to talents in knowledge construction and psychological construction. At the same time, accordingly, guiders need to understand learners' dynamic knowledge construction and psychological construction. Then guiders design learning scenes according to learners' current situation and social evaluation. With effective use of teaching tools (such as computers or intelligent equipment), and continuous observation of learners' development, guiders lead learners to complete learning process. Therefore, guiders are the key to success of education since they are bridges between society and learners, communicator and practitioners of educational conceptions.

Learners: learners need to understand their own knowledge construction and psychological construction, requirements from social evaluation, by interactions with guiders, and complete knowledge construction and personality construction. Successful and life-long learners are final goal of entire education systems. Since each learner has a distinctive nature, guiders should conduct guidance based on coordination of social evaluation and learners' situation; learners should never stop exploring their potential and utilize them to the fullest.

Learning Scenes: Learning scenes are links between learners and guiders where guiding process and learning process take place, where guiders and learners understand and interact with each other. Learning scenes should be systematic, interesting and personalized, and they should stimulate learners' desire and interests in learning and exploring. Therefore, learners can actively carry out knowledge and personality construction under proper intervention of guiders. Obviously it is hard to carry out personalized learning scenes in "one for many" collective teaching mode, however, computers and other intelligent learning devices provide a powerful and feasible way to turn "one for many" mode to "one on one" mode.

Learning tools: Today, intelligent learning equipment (such as computers, iPad, VR) have become the first choice for new generation of learners. Since intelligent learning equipment can provide unparalleled, "real" immersed experiences and personalized self-learning environments, learners have established tight relationship with them. So correct understanding of cooperative relationship and role distributions among guiders, learning tools (computers) and learners, becomes an important topic.

But how to make guiders get whole pictures of learner's knowledge schema and psychological patterns? How to implement effective guidance? When to implement psychological construction? When to implement knowledge construction? When to do both? How to design effective and personalized learning scenes? How to deliver personal ideas to learners in "one for many" education mode? How to figure out correct relationship among guiders, intelligent learning equipment and learners? What are learners' roles and tasks? What are guiders' roles and tasks? What are intelligent equipment' roles and tasks? How to achieve effective and comprehensive evaluation of learners? How to achieve personalized guidance and learning in certain social contexts to build their own knowledge and psychology?

Obviously from questions above, we know that five factors are interrelated, affecting one another. So how to adjust all these factors to optimize three processes, including learning process optimization, guiding process optimization, and education policy-making process optimization? In certain social contexts, learning process optimization may not be consistent with guiding process optimization and policy-making optimization. For such a complex system with multi-coupled inputs, multi-coupled outputs, multi-contradicting objective optimization, it is hard to describe, analyze and optimize only through mathematical analysis or experimental methods.

Guiders, learners, learning tools (computers), learning scene, social situation form a typical Cyber-Physical-Social System (CPSS) [18]. Based on Cyber-Physical-Systems (CPS), CPSS extends study scope to social network systems by integrating social information, virtual space and artificial system information. It focuses on integration and coordination of human brain resources, computing resources and physical resources through intelligent human-computer interactions and effective cooperation of human and physical entities. It intends to achieve that human or organizations could manipulate physical entities through cyberspace in a reliable, real-time, safe and collaborative way.

Actually guiders, learners, learning tools (mainly computers), learning scene and social situation (by decision-makers) form a special educational CPSS, where guiders, learners and decision-makers stand for both Physical and Social in CPSS, which also means unity of human's social and natural attributes. By integrating and coordinating human brain resources (learners, mentors, decision-makers), computing resources (computers) and physical resources (learners, mentors, decision-makers), educational CPSS means to achieve learner-centered efficient learning, effective guiding and optimal decision-making and thus cultivate creative learners, innovative guiders and shrew decision-makers for new era. Next section this paper will introduce ACP approach and parallel education systems framework based on system construction.

5 ACP and Parallel Education System Framework from Perspective of System Construction

5.1 ACP Based on Parallel Systems

ACP, including Artificial Systems, Computational Experiments and Parallel Execution, which provides a viable solution to management and control of complex systems [19–21]. It has three steps, A, C, P. A: Artificial Systems is to build one or more corresponding artificial systems based on real systems. Artificial systems don't have to be exactly the same as real systems, and they might be "real copy" or "creative copy" of real systems. C: By conducting variety of feasible solutions or implementing different kinds of computational experiments on artificial systems, it finds out optimal solutions; P: Finally, optimal solutions are applied on real systems and artificial systems at the same time, artificial systems and real systems will learn from each other, develop together by parallel and continuous interactions.

For example, in transportation systems involving engineering complexity and social complexity, there are thousands of parameters to adjusts, so many situations to explore, so many solutions to try and error. And it's impossible to carry out in real transportation systems, since solutions might cause chaos. So based on ACP approach, by building virtual transportation systems in cyber world, all kinds of parameters and solutions could be adjusted and carried out and thus generate optimal solution by computational experiments on virtual systems. Then by conducting optimal solution in real transportations systems, feedback can be used to improve optimal solution on virtual transportations systems and therefore outcome iterated optimal solutions to be carried out on real transportation systems until certain criterions are met both in virtual systems and real systems, which is parallel execution. And real systems and virtual systems are parallel systems.

As to people, we wish we could build such systems too to accompany people's grow up. That is to say, you are not alone ever since you are born, there is another "You" in virtual world. Real you and virtual you will be life-long learning partners to grow up together by learning from each other. But it is too complicated to model people and peoples' grow up environments, so we could only focus on certain fields at first, and later expand to more and more fields. That is the power what parallel systems could bring you, making you grow up faster and stronger since you could always find optimal solutions from virtual you or artificial You. Parallel "Yous" (real you and virtual you) are moving forward together.

5.2   Parallel Education System Framework from Perspective of System Construction

From system construction perspective, ACP-based and learner-centered parallel education system framework is shown in Fig. 4. Upper part, full of Dashed line boxes, means virtual education systems, while bottom part, full of solid lines, mean real education system. In upper part, there are virtual learners, virtual guiders and virtual decision makers and virtual learning environment; in bottom part, there are real

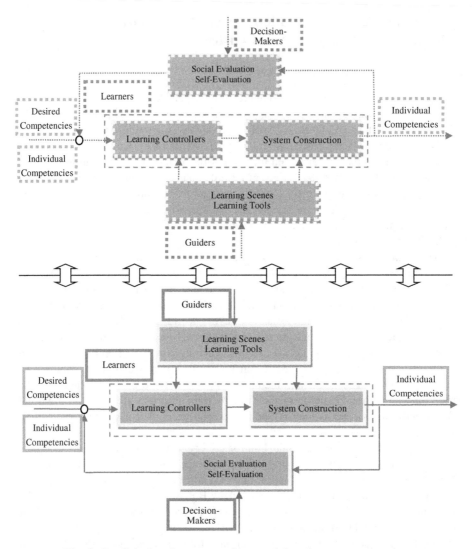

Fig. 4. Parallel education systems framework based system construction

learners, real guiders and real decision makers and real learning environment. Artificial education systems are constructed based on all factors such as teaching scene, social situation, guiders, learners and learning tools in real education systems. According to individual learners, personalized learning scenes will be designed by guiders together with artificial systems' assistance, guiding method and personalized knowledge systems are carried out through human-in-loop computational experiments in artificial systems. Comprehensive evaluation of learning process in artificial education systems is carried out to guide real teaching process optimization.

5.3 Key Technologies

Key technologies of parallel education systems include environmental perception, knowledge modeling, psychological modeling, cognitive modeling, personalized interaction, adaptive learning methods and so on. Teaching and learning process involves cognitive psychological factors such as memory, intelligence, psychological and behavioral patterns, motives and intentions, and macro and micro social environment impacts such as evaluation systems, curriculum, teaching materials, teaching methods, knowledge structure systems, its evolution and so on. Learners-centered personalized teaching and learning, personalized knowledge system, and personalized psychological system should be carried out on the basis of knowledge database construction, cognitive psychological analysis, big data analysis etc.

Parallel education systems should be built on interoperable education information platforms with rich big data resources. From all levels of systems and products, parallel education systems obtain learning scenarios, knowledge systems, learners and guiders' behavioral and psychological characteristics, together with open online big data. Parallel education systems is designed to achieve personalized teaching and learning process and provide real-time, efficient, automated, customized, adaptive, rolling optimal support to promote good educational environment. New generation of artificial intelligence technology will lead to educational methods' revolution and "daily", "entertainment", parallel system-based learning, which will become main part of people's life.

6 Conclusions

This paper put forward parallel education system framework from perspective of system construction, and tried to explore how to cultivate well-trained talents who could meet needs of society and individuals. Parallel education system framework contains many factors, which keep changing along with development of society, so, on the basis of continuous iteration and optimization, there is a long way before it could achieve final goals, which is cultivation of learners, guiders and decision makers for new IT era.

The new IT era provides great opportunities to achieve goals above. Continuous development of intelligent technology and equipment will make cooperation of human-machine-entities, integration of Cyber-Physical-Social systems, coordination of social resources, human brain resources and computer resources become true, thus make learning process, a special process including social and physical factors, visualized, computed, and optimized. Hopefully one day parallel education systems could become a feasible way to completely change patterns of current educational system, optimize human learning process, and dig out human creativity and potential to the fullest, and fun, personalized, fair and lifelong learning will truly become a natural and joyful part of human life.

Acknowledgments. We would like to acknowledge support in part from the National Natural Science Foundation of China under Grants 61233001, 71232006, 61533019.

References

1. Wang, F.-Y., Wang, X., Li, L., Li, L.: Steps toward parallel intelligence. IEEE/CAA J. Automatica Sinica **3**(4), 345–348 (2016)
2. Prensky, M.: Digital natives, digital immigrants Part 1. Horizon **9**(5), 1–6 (2001)
3. Prensky, M.: Digital natives, digital immigrants Part 2, do they really think differently. Horizon **9**(6), 1–6 (2001)
4. Turkle, S.: Alone Together: Why We Expect More from Technology and Less from Each Other. Basic Books, New York (2012)
5. Core Competencies and Values for Chinese Students' Development Officially Released. http://www.jyb.cn/. Accessed 09 Jan 2017
6. Matthews, M.R.: Introductory comments on philosophy and constructivism in science education. Sci. Educ. **6**(1, 2), 5–14 (1997)
7. Ji, S., Jin, Q., Liang, J., Zhang, Z., Cheng, Y., (Transl.): National Science Education Standard. Scientific and Technological Literature Publishing House, Beijing (1999)
8. Ding, B.: Constructivism and the reform of science education facing the 21st Century. Comp. Educ. Rev. **22**(8), 6–10 (2001)
9. Kelly, G.A.: The Psychology of Personal Constructs. Chapman & Hall, London (2001)
10. Piaget, J.: The Principles of Genetic Epistemology. The Commercial Press, Beijing (1970)
11. Seymour, A.: Papert: Mindstorms: Children, Computers and Powerful Ideas. Basic Books, New York (1993)
12. Glaserfeld, E.V. (Ed.): Constructivism in Education. Pergamon Press, Oxford (1989)
13. Solomon, J.: Social influences on the construction of Pupils' understanding of science. Stud. Sci. Educ. **14**(1), 63–82 (1987)
14. Wiener, N.: Cybernetics. Science Press, Beijing (2009). Translated by Hao, J.
15. Burger, J.M.: Personality Psychology. China Light Industry Press, Beijing (2010). Translated by Chen, H.
16. Freud, S.: The Ego and the Id. Createspace, US (2013)
17. Kalff, D.M.: Sandplay-The Psychotherapeutic Approach to Spirituality. Temenos Press, Cloverdale (2003)

18. Wang, F.-Y.: The emergence of intelligent enterprises: from CPS to CPSS. IEEE Intell. Syst. **25**(4), 85–88 (2010)
19. Wang, F.-Y., Lansing, J.S.: From artificial life to artificial societies-new methods for studies of complex systems. Complex Syst. Complex. Sci. **1**(1), 33–41 (2004)
20. Wang, F.-Y.: Parallel system methods for management and control of complex systems. Control Decis. **19**(5), 485–489 (2004)
21. Wang, F.-Y.: Computational experiments for behavior analysis and decision evaluation of complex systems. J. Syst. Simul. **16**(5), 893–897 (2004)

Foot Modeling Based on Machine Vision and Social Manufacturing Research

Hongli Peng[1,2,3], Zhen Shen[2,3], Xiuqin Shang[2,3,5], Xiwei Liu[3,4],
Gang Xiong[2,3,5(✉)], Taozhong Liu[3,6], and Timo R. Nyberg[2,3,7]

[1] The State Key Laboratory for Management and Control of Complex Systems,
Institute of Automation, Chinese Academy of Sciences, Beijing 100190, China
[2] Cloud Computing Center, Chinese Academy of Sciences,
Dongguan 523808, China
gang.xiong@ia.ac.cn
[3] College of Information Science and Technology, Beijing University
of Chemical Technology, Beijing 100190, China
[4] Institute of Smart Education Systems, Qingdao Academy of Intelligent
Industries, Qingdao 266109, China
[5] Beijing Engineering Research Center of Intelligent Systems and Technology,
Institute of Automation, Chinese Academy of Sciences, Qingdao 266109, China
[6] Joint Laboratory of Parallel Management and Control and Business
Intelligence, Hainan Zhongke Flower Ocean,
Cloud Commerce Technology Co. Ltd., Haikou, China
[7] Department of Industrial Engineering and Management, School of Science,
Aalto University, P.O. Box 11000, 00076 Aalto, Finland

Abstract. With the development of productive forces, the manufacturing industry has developed from the "craft manufacturing" of agricultural society to mass production in industrial society, and then to mass customization manufacturing in the information society. In the future, manufacturing will be upgraded to "social manufacturing" in an intelligent society. The Internet of things, cloud computing, social networking, and other related to the most advanced technology will be introduced in the manufacturing process of the whole life cycle of society, aims to make every consumer can participate in the design, manufacture, service and consumption of this product in. In this paper, we discuss the future of highly customized high-end customization in social manufacturing - footwear customization.

On the basis of studying a great deal of related literature, this paper introduces the development of social manufacture of shoes and the socialized production of shoemaking industry, moreover, expounds the working principle of machine vision for 3D model reconstruction and carries out simulation experiments to ensure the correctness of the results.

Keywords: Social manufacturing · 3D modeling rebuilding · Footwear
Machine vision

S. Satoh (Ed.): PSIVT 2017, LNCS 10799, pp. 144–157, 2018.
https://doi.org/10.1007/978-3-319-92753-4_12

1 Introduction

The rapid development of 3D scanning technology and 3D printing technology is changing our world, and its promotion of social manufacturing has also brought about an industrial revolution - relying on the Internet and Canadian manufacturing equipment to form a social manufacturing network. Social people fully participate in the whole life manufacturing process of the product through crowdsourcing, etc. to promote personalized, real-time, economical production and consumption patterns [1]. Footwear customization as a "mass customization" into a "social manufacturing" epitome, which contains information technology of four areas: information collection and transmission, virtual services, intelligent services, collaborative services.

First, use Three-dimensional scanning, RFID, Internet of Things and other technologies in the entire manufacturing process to obtain and share data and information.

Secondly, in the virtual service, use three-dimensional modeling technology and three-dimensional virtual technology to achieve custom information exchange between customer and designer.

Intelligent service is to optimize the intelligent customization process of manufacturing source.

Collaborative service refers to perform customization processes with the collaboration of designers, customers, manufacturers, and suppliers to maximize productivity.

The structure of the paper is as follows:

The first section describes what is the social manufacturing of the footwear industry, tells system structure and its core technology of the whole footwear industry social manufacturing [2].

In the second section, the feasibility of three-dimensional reconstruction method based on machine vision for footwear customization is verified for the increasing demand of high precision model reconstruction.

The third section summarizes the research contents and achievements of the article, and puts forward the possible expectations and prospects for the further research work in this field.

2 Social Manufacturing of the Footwear Industry

With the approach of "industry 4.0" and the development of cloud manufacturing and cloud computing, a model of customized production for customers - the socialized manufacturing model came into being. In social manufacturing, every consumer can participate in all stages of the product's life cycle, including product design, manufacturing and consumption. Use Internet of things, cloud computing and big data technology to form social manufacturing network system. On this basis, social manufacturing is bound to bring about revolutionary changes in the current manufacturing industry, the social manufacturing system in the future will be able to meet all the unique needs of all customers.

2.1 Introduction to Social Manufacturing

Social manufacturing can be defined as a personalized, real-time, intelligent manu-facturing model. In addition to footwear industry, the social manufacturing model is also applicable to the apparel industry, mobile phones, furniture, photography, edu-cation and other personal fashion products. With the increasing demand for person-alized customization, socialize manufacture is becoming more and more widely used and prospects. Among them, everyone can participate in social production and par-ticipate in "personalized needs to capture the entire product life cycle at any stage, personalized product design, personalized product manufacturing, and enjoy person-alized service", through new information technology such as information network, social media, 3D printers and so on. The production model of social production has the following characteristics: [3, 4].

Every detail can be customized in depth, so called "a class of custom". through the personalized needs of customers to collect the full life cycle of the product to explore the potential market, personalized product design, personalized product manufacturing, and enjoy personalized service to improve customers' satisfaction.

The platform should support the full range of services for customers and manu-facturers, as well as other roles in the model to make information flow and material flow unimpeded.

2.2 Social Manufacturing System of Footwear Industry

Social manufacturing is based on mass customization. Social manufacturing is a new business model that takes full advantage of new support technologies and takes full account of customer needs.

System Structure
Footwear industry social manufacturing platform as shown, including the user layer, service layer, tool layer [5, 6].

User Layer
Social manufacturing users include consumers, service providers (including designers), online retailers, shoe dealers and logistics distributors. The user layer provides a platform for human-computer interaction, providing a user interface.

Service Layer
Users can participate in the socialization process of footwear industry. User-supplied requirements information and online retailers recommend appropriate options for users. Users can also choose to fully customize, independent design. The art resources, raw material resources, and plant resources used in the design can be fully shared in the social manufacturing cloud, and users can use them to design styles, provide materials, and process footwear. The production process and the distribution process can also be remotely controlled. For the after-sales service department, the service evaluation module can collect customer feedback information, continuous improvement services (Fig. 1).

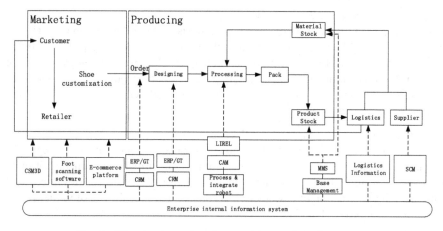

Fig. 1. The structure of modern social manufacturing system

Tool Layer

The tool layer provides technical support for the realization of social manufacturing, including resource allocation and access technology, resource virtualization technology, human-computer interaction technology, network security technology and evaluation technology.

In addition, it also includes some of the actual physical manufacturing class resources, mainly: customer information, factory information, material information, design resources, modern logistics network, modern physical networking.

Core Technology

Footwear social manufacturing system used in the core technology mainly for: information collection technology, information transmission technology, virtualization and service information technology, intelligent technology, collaborative management technology.

Information Collection Technology

Information collection and transmission to the cloud platform is the first step in achieving mass customization. Various manufacturing resources in the footwear production lifecycle include soft manufacturing resources and hard manufacturing resources. The process of collecting information includes customer information and enterprise information. We collect information through 3D scanning technology, RFID technology and sensor technology to facilitate resource management and virtualization.

Material supplier information includes information on global shoe material suppliers such as leather, fabric and sole suppliers, including their business qualification and material costs, material properties, and so on. The social manufacturing system will receive information on all qualified raw material distributors. In addition, the social manufacturing system also needs different styles of footwear designers around the world, footwear manufacturers information. The above information is based on RFID technology, intelligent sensor technology, GPS technology, laser scanner acquisition technology to achieve.

Information Transmission Technology
After collecting the information of all the participants in the footwear supply chain, all the information will be safely transferred to the social manufacturing platform. Information will be added to the cloud, through the Internet of things technology to achieve interconnection, identification, manufacturing resource perception. The main technologies include: communication network, 3G /4G network, GPRS network, broadcast network, NGB wide area network.

Virtualization and Service Information Technology
The information collected through the above information collection technology and information transmission technology will be put into the virtual world, making it more conducive to control the supply chain, make full use of production resources and ensure the full participation of customers. This process requires the use of virtualization and service technology (Fig. 2).

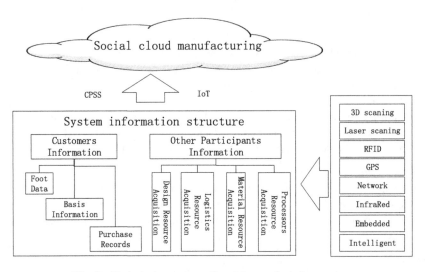

Fig. 2. Technical structure of social manufacturing system

Intelligent Technology
The intelligentization and manufacturing intelligence in the production process will be reflected in the process of description, recommendation, matching, transaction, execution, scheduling, settlement, evaluation and so on in the social manufacturing system. For example, when choosing shoes for raw materials, people only need to enter the relevant information (price, shoe type), the system will recommend the most cost-effective materials, the best suppliers and the approximate price.

Collaborative Management Technology
In the social manufacturing cloud model, the design and processing of a product is no longer a business can be done alone, it requires the global participation of different

enterprises to complete. Collaborative management system is both an efficient and collaborative work platform based on the Internet, and it is also an excellent collaborative management system. It uses advanced computer technology, and then into the collaborative management concept, through the same platform, the same authority of the staff can work together. In the practical application can effectively improve the efficiency of business operations. Mainly include: collaborative products business, product life cycle management, office automation.

3 Machine Vision Technology Used in Footwear Society Manufacturing

Three-dimensional model reconstruction using machine vision is an important technology in computer vision technology. It is also the core of machine vision. It mainly studies how to restore depth information of the object of a collected image by analyzing and deposing one or more images. In the machine vision stereo reconstruction technology, binocular vision based on two images technology is a hot topic in recent years. Binocular stereoscopic vision is imitating the human eye structure, to reproduce the actual process of human stereoscopic perception, calculate different images in the same object pixel position deviation through simple geometric principles, obtain the depth of information of target object. Because such methods do not require a specific instrument, and the instrument cost is low, the expected calculation is not large, the degree of automation is high [7, 8].

Compared with the machine vision modeling under the analogous large scene, this method has the uniqueness for the specialized problem. Because of the high accuracy of footwear customization, a binocular vision modeling with reference is proposed in this method. And because of the particularity of the binocular vision technique, the calibration of the camera also uses a combination of stratified calibration and Tsai two-step calibration, and is expected to improve accuracy.

3.1 The Use of Binocular Vision for the Establishment of Three-Dimensional Model

The advantages of the laser scanning type three-dimensional model described above have high accuracy and good model integrity, but the shortcomings are also obvious, because of its "industrial 4.0" "Made in China 2015" and other manufacturing industry changes in the status quo, The past desktop high-precision scanner has not meet the trend of the times, the future is in urgent need of low cost, high efficiency, everyone can easily achieve high-precision data acquisition technology. The technology of image acquisition, data acquisition and then achieve three-dimensional reconstruction using binocular vision technology just to meet this demand (Fig. 3).

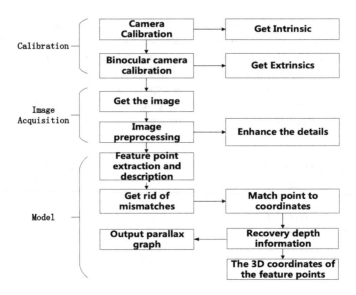

Fig. 3. A flow chart of 3D reconstruction based on machine vision technology

3.2 Camera Calibration

Most of these technologies are currently used for 3D reconstruction of large-sized objects, and there is no systematic application in the social manufacturing system. However, due to the low cost and portability of such methods, such methods are in the trend of global industrial change can be efficient and low-cost for customers required products to achieve data acquisition and three-dimensional model reconstruction.

In the three-dimensional machine stereoscopic vision system, the target object's position, shape, attitude and other physical information are dependent on the camera to take pictures. The camera calibration says that the internal optical geometric characteristics of the camera being used (the internal reference) and the coordinates of the two cameras in the three-dimensional world (the external reference) are checked by a set of information knowed pictures (include the image coordinates and the reference point coordinates). Through the lens, a three-dimensional object in the space will be mapped into an inverted image and be perceived by the sensor.

Ideally, the optical axis of the lens should pass through the middle of the image. However, the actual camera quality and the problem of installation accuracy, there is always error, this error needs to use a set of parameters to correct, this group of parameters is called internal parameters.

In the ideal case, the size of the reduction ratio of the camera in the horizontal axis (x direction) and the vertical axis (y direction) should be the same, but in fact, the lens quality, sensor (CCD or CMOS) quality varies, if the lens is not perfect circles, or pixel-sensitive points on the sensor are not perfectly aligned squares, which can lead to inconsistencies in the reduction of the horizontal and vertical axes. This asymmetry error requires two parameters to correct.

Ideally, we think that the lens strictly follows the principle of projective transformation (that is, the straight line in the three-dimensional space is still a straight line through the lens), but in fact, the lens accuracy is not high enough, cannot be so perfect, after the lens mapping, originally a straight line will have a certain degree of bending, where a set of distortion parameters to correct this deformation.

The above three correction parameters in accordance with certain rules into a matrix called the camera's internal parameters (Fig. 4).

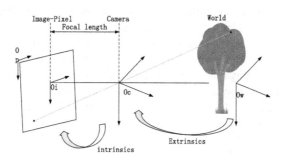

Fig. 4. The meaning of intrinsics and extrinsics

The extrinsic reference obtained by the camera calibration is indeed an exact value, but the acquired camera interior parameter is an approximation of the optical properties of the camera. The calibration of each camera is only an approximation for the cameras in the sampling space. Therefore, in view of the particularity of foot modeling in paper, we choose 20 cm distance to calibrate to obtain higher accuracy.

The calibration of the camera is the study of the imaging transformation. The imaging transformation involves the transformation between different coordinate systems: pixel plane coordinate system (u, v), image physical coordinate system (x, y), camera coordinate system (Xc, Yc, Zc) and world coordinate system (Xw, Yw, Zw) among them, [10, 11].

Pixel plane coordinate system (u, v), also known as the computer frame memory system, which in the computer by a matrix of M rows and N columns describes an image, the value of each element (pixel) in the matrix is the gray value of the image of the location.

The image physical coordinate system (x,y) makes up the defect of the pixel plane coordinate system has no physical unit to represent the pixel position, the actual measurement size of each pixel in the x (u) axis and y (v) axis direction is dx, dy. So, where any of the pixels in the digital image satisfies the following relation in the (u, v) and (x, y) coordinate systems (where dx − 1, dy − 1 is called the scale factor):

$$u = \frac{x}{dx} + u_o$$
$$v = \frac{y}{dy} + v_o$$

(1)

Will be used in homogeneous coordinates in matrix form as:

$$
\begin{bmatrix} u \\ v \\ 1 \end{bmatrix} = \begin{bmatrix} \frac{1}{dx} & 0 & u_0 \\ \frac{1}{dy} & 0 & v_0 \\ 0 & 0 & 1 \end{bmatrix} \begin{bmatrix} x \\ y \\ 1 \end{bmatrix} \quad or \quad \begin{bmatrix} x \\ y \\ 1 \end{bmatrix} = \begin{bmatrix} dx & 0 & -u_0 dx \\ 0 & dy & -v_0 dy \\ 0 & 0 & 1 \end{bmatrix} \begin{bmatrix} u \\ v \\ 1 \end{bmatrix} \tag{2}
$$

Camera coordinate system (Xc, Yc, Zc), the Xc, Yc axis in the coordinate system are parallel to the x, y axis in the image, the Zc axis is the camera axis, perpendicular to the image plane. The intersection of the plane xy is the origin of the image coordinate system [10]. The intersection of the Zc axis and the plane Xc and Yc is the optical center O of the camera. The rectangular coordinate system composed of the point O and the Xc, Yc and Zc axes is called the camera coordinate System.

The world coordinate system (Xw, Yw, Zw), the coordinate system used to describe the location of any object, by the Xw, Yw, Zw axis composition, also known as the absolute coordinate system [11]. The camera coordinate system and the world coordinate system can be described its conversion mode by the rotation matrix R, translation vector T [12, 13].

$$
\begin{bmatrix} X_c \\ Y_c \\ Z_c \\ 1 \end{bmatrix} = \begin{bmatrix} R & t \\ 0^T & 1 \end{bmatrix} \begin{bmatrix} X \\ Y \\ Z \\ 1 \end{bmatrix} = L_W \begin{bmatrix} X \\ Y \\ Z \\ 1 \end{bmatrix} \tag{3}
$$

R is the eye (3); T is the 3-row and 1-column translation vector; $0T = (0,0,0)$ T; LW is a 4×4 reduced matrix.

Camera Model

The relationship between the pixel plane coordinate system (u, v) and the camera coordinate system (Xc, Yc, Zc) can be obtained from the camera model:

$$
\left\{ \begin{array}{c} \frac{x}{f} = \frac{X_c}{Z_c} \\ \frac{y}{f} = \frac{Y_c}{Z_c} \end{array} \right\} \quad or \quad \left\{ \begin{array}{c} Z_c \cdot x = f \cdot X_c \\ Z_c \cdot y = f \cdot Y_c \end{array} \right\} \tag{4}
$$

Will be used in homogeneous coordinates in matrix form as:

$$
Z_c \begin{bmatrix} x \\ y \\ 1 \end{bmatrix} = \begin{bmatrix} f & 0 & 0 & 0 \\ 0 & f & 0 & 0 \\ 0 & 0 & 1 & 0 \end{bmatrix} \begin{bmatrix} X_c \\ Y_c \\ Z_c \\ 1 \end{bmatrix} \tag{5}
$$

The above relationship is:

$$Z_c \begin{bmatrix} u \\ v \\ 1 \end{bmatrix} = \begin{bmatrix} \frac{1}{dx} & 0 & u_o \\ 0 & \frac{1}{dy} & v_o \\ 0 & 0 & 1 \end{bmatrix} \begin{bmatrix} f & 0 & 0 & 0 \\ 0 & f & 0 & 0 \\ 0 & 0 & 1 & 0 \end{bmatrix} \begin{bmatrix} R & t \\ 0^T & 1 \end{bmatrix} \begin{bmatrix} X \\ Y \\ Z \\ 1 \end{bmatrix} = L \begin{bmatrix} X \\ Y \\ Z \\ 1 \end{bmatrix}$$

$$= \begin{bmatrix} l_1 & l_2 & l_2 & l_4 \\ l_5 & l_6 & l_7 & l_8 \\ l_9 & l_9 & l_{11} & l_{12} \end{bmatrix} \begin{bmatrix} X \\ Y \\ Z \\ 1 \end{bmatrix} \qquad (6)$$

Expressed in the form of an equation:

$$\begin{aligned} u &= (l_1 X + l_2 Y + l_3 Z + l_4)/Z_c \\ v &= (l_5 X + l_6 Y + l_7 Z + l_8)/Z_c \\ Z_c &= l_9 X + l_{10} Y + l_{11} Z + l_{12} \end{aligned} \qquad (7)$$

Will Zc into the formula 7:

$$\begin{cases} u = \dfrac{l_1 X + l_2 Y + l_3 Z + l_4}{l_9 X + l_{10} Y + l_{11} Z + l_{12}} \\ v = \dfrac{l_5 X + l_6 Y + l_7 Z + l_8}{l_9 X + l_{10} Y + l_{11} Z + l_{12}} \end{cases} \qquad (8)$$

Where l_1 to l_{11} are 11 coefficients associated with u0, v0, f, Kx, Ky, U, X, J and XS, YS, ZS; they together determine the imaging characteristics of the camera.

X0, y0, f called the camera within the unit; U, X, J and XS, YS, ZS known as the camera outside the bit.

If we know that more than six space points (X i, Y i, Z i) and its coordinates (u i, v i) can be explained L1, L2, ..., L11by the above formula; to get the camera parameters [14]. If you know the parameters of two or more cameras L1, L2,..., L11; according to the spatial point's coordinates (xj, yj) in the camera, from the above formula can be resolved space coordinates (X,Y,Z). The process of determining L1, L2, ..., L11 is called calibration. Known (xj, yj), the process of solving (X, Y, Z) is called reconstruction. Will pass on the above points and points out:

$$\begin{aligned} l_1 X + l_2 Y + l_3 Z + l_4 - l_9 uX - l_{10} uY - l_{11} uZ &= l_{12} u \\ l_5 X + l_6 Y + l_7 Z + l_8 - l_9 uX - l_{10} uY - l_{11} uZ &= l_{12} u \end{aligned} \qquad (9)$$

From the above equation, we can see that there are six or more known points in space and their image coordinates to obtain the L matrix. In the normal calibration work, the feature points on the calibration plate will be far more than six, which makes the number of equations far more than the number of unknowns, we can use the least squares method to filter the data, making the error as much as possible small.

We assume that the known calibration points have N, and we can write 2N equations of the above equation, a matrix of which is expressed as:

$$AL = U \tag{10}$$

Where L is: $[l1, l2, l3, l4, l5, l6, l7, l8, l9, l10, l11, l12]^T$;
A is:

$$\begin{bmatrix} X_1 & Y_1 & Z_1 & 1 & 0 & 0 & 0 & 0 & -u_1X_1 & -u_1Y_1 & -u_1Z_1 \\ 0 & 0 & 0 & 0 & X_1 & Y_1 & Z_1 & 1 & -v_1X_1 & -v_1Y_1 & -v_1Z_1 \\ \cdots & \cdots & \cdots & \cdots & \cdots & \cdots & \cdots & \cdots & \cdots & \cdots & \cdots \\ X_n & Y_n & Z_n & 1 & 0 & 0 & 0 & 0 & -u_nX_n & -u_nY_n & -u_nZ_n \\ 0 & 0 & 0 & 0 & X_n & Y_n & Z_n & 1 & -v_nX_n & -v_nY_n & -v_nZ_n \end{bmatrix} \tag{11}$$

U is: $[u1L12, v1L12, \cdots unL12, vnL12]^T$

In the matrix U, L12 (l12) has no effect on the other values, so that it can be any value, then we make it a value of 1. So that there are only 11 unknowns in the vector L, after solving the L, you can reverse out of the internal and external parameters of the camera through the L [15].

3.3   Experimental Results

The camera used in this test using Sony IMX105PQ sensor, 1/3.2-in. color CMOS, the camera total pixels are 8.1 million pixels, effective pixels are 7990272 pixels. Fixed F2.4 aperture, the lens equivalent focal length is 35 mm [16].

The calibration plate is generated by MATLAB, as shown in the figure, displayed on the LCD screen, this digital calibration plate has high flatness, can clearly obtain the feature points after shooting pictures, eliminating many image processing steps. Figure x is a photograph of 10 secondary calibration plates (Fig. 5).

Fig. 5. Photo to test

The following figure shows the two detected angles (cross) and the grid point (circle) of the re-projection, the arrow in the figure is the existence of corner detection error point and its offset direction (Figs. 6 and 7).

Fig. 6. Angular point calibration

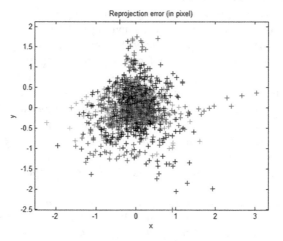

Fig. 7. The calibration of ten pictures

Points of the re-error are also marked out by the cross of different colors in the figure [17].

The following figure shows the world center coordinate system and the camera center coordinate system diagram. The left graph shows the calibration with the origin of the calibration plate; the right graph is the calibration with the origin of the camera (Fig. 8).

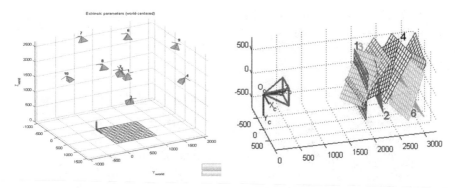

Fig. 8. Calibration result schematic

4   Conclusion

With the "Industrial 4.0" and cloud manufacturing approaching, this paper presents a socialized manufacture mode for the footwear industry customized manufacturing. In social manufacturing, each consumer can participate in all stages of the product life cycle, such as product design, manufacturing and consumption. Through the Internet of Things of manufacturing industry, cloud computing and large data, social manufacturing network system is formed and achieved. With the increasing demand for personalized customization, socialized manufacturing is becoming more and more widely used and prospects. This paper predicts the possible changes in the future manufacturing industry, and puts forward some countermeasures to the reform of the footwear industry in China, and proves the feasibility of a three-dimensional reconstruction method based on machine vision for the customization of footwear. The experiments show that in the footwear social manufacturing process based on the machine vision technology, each of the two related pictures can obtain more than ten information of characteristics matching successfully, this method has great application prospects.

Acknowledgments. We would like to acknowledge support in part from the National Natural Science Foundation of China under Grants 61233001, 71232006, 61533019, 61773381 and 61773382; Chinese Guangdong's S&T project (2015B010103001, 2016B090910001), Dongguan's Innovation Talents Project (Gang Xiong).

References

1. Wang, F.Y.: From social computing to social manufacturing: one coming industrial revolution. Bull. Chin. Acad. Sci. **27**(6), 658–669 (2012)
2. Shang, X., Xiong, G., Nyberg, T.R., Wang, F., Cheng, C., et al.: Social manufacturing cloud for high-end apparel customization. Acta Automatica Sinica, May 2017
3. Peng, H., Shang, X., Guo, C., Xiong, G., Nyberg, T.R., Shen, Z., Fan, D., Wang, Y.: A survey on big data for human body shape. In: 2016 IEEE International Conference on Service Operations and Logistis, and Informatics. 10–12 July 2016, Beijing, China (2016)

4. Xiong, S., Goonetilleke, R.S., Zhao, J., Li, W., Witana, C.P.: Foot deformationsunder different load-bearing conditions and their relationships to statureand body weight. Anthropol. Sci. **117**, 77–88 (2009)
5. Liu, J., Xiong, G., Shang, X., Nyberg, T.R., Wang, Y., Ji, T.: Social manufacturing development with sino-finnish innovative cooperation. In: 2016 IEEE International Conference on Service Operations and Logistics, and Informatics. 10–12 July 2016, Beijing, China (2016)
6. Hobson, J.P.: Development of a combustion chamber cooling ring inspection machine. In: Proceedings of International Conference on Vision and Sensory Control, USA, pp. 359–368. IEEE Press (1990)
7. Mohajeri, B., Nelson, M.M., Nyberg, T.R., Xiong, G., Jesse, K.: Contributions of social manufacturing to sustainable apparel industry. In: 2016 IEEE International Conference on Service Operations and Logistics, and Informatics, 10–12 July 2016, Beijing, China (2016)
8. Hashim, A.A., Clements, P.E.: Computer vision in manufacturing process. Proc. Robots Vis. **12**(4), 417–427 (1994)
9. Lu, R.S.: On-line measurement of the straightness of steel pipes using machine vision technique. Sens. Actuators **6**(94), 95–101 (2001)
10. Chen, M., Chen, C.: Roundness measurement for discontinuous perimeters via machine vision. Comput. Ind. **32**(4), 185–197 (2002)
11. Karjalainen, J., Xiong, G.: Social manufacturing and business model innovation. In: 2016 IEEE International Conference on Service Operations and Logistics, and Informatics, 10–12 July 2016, Beijing, China (2016)
12. Xiong, G., Shang, X.: Intelligent manufacturing for personalized product: upgrade from mass customization to social manufacturing, vol. 9, pp. 28–32 (2016)
13. Shang, X., Liu, X., Xiong, G., Cheng, C., Nyberg, T.R.: Social manufacturing cloud service platform for the mass customization in apparel industry. In: IEEE International Conference on Service Operations and Logistics, and Informatics, pp. 220–224, July 2013
14. Shang, X., Su, B., Liu, X., Xiong, G., You, Z.: Social manufacture cloud mode in high-end apparel, footwear and hats. In: The 11th World Congress on Intelligent Control and Automation Shenyang, 29 June–4 July, China (2014)
15. Mohajeri, B., Nyberg, T., Nelson, M., Shang, X., Xiong, G., Karjalainen, J., Tukiainen, T.: The impact of social manufacturing on the value chain model in the apparel industry. In: 2014 IEEE International Conference on Service Operations and Logistics, and Informatics, 8–10 October 2014, Qingdao, Shandong, China (2014)
16. Shang, X., Liu, X., Cheng, C., Xiong, G.: A new model of social manufacturing for the customization needs of the clothing industry. In: Proceedings of the Eighth Annual Meeting of Chinese Management (2013)
17. Ye, J., Ma, G., Jiang, L., Chen, L., Li, J., Xiong, G., Zhang, X., Tang, M.: A unified cloth untangling framework through discrete collision detection. Comput. Graph. Forum **36**(7), 217–228 (2017)

Computerized Adaptive English Ability Assessment Based on Deep Learning

Xiao Wang[1,2], Yuanyuan Zhang[3], Shengnan Yu[4], Xiwei Liu[1,5(✉)],
and Fei-Yue Wang[1]

[1] The State Key Laboratory of Management and Control for Complex Systems,
Institute of Automation, Chinese Academy of Sciences, Beijing 100080, China
xiwei.liu@ia.ac.cn, feiyue.trans@gmail.com
[2] Department of Computer Science and Technology,
Xi'an Jiaotong University, Xi'an 710049, China
gzzkdx867155@stu.xjtu.edu.cn
[3] College of Computer Science, Sichuan University, Chengdu 610065, China
2014141462362@stu.scu.edu.cn
[4] Department of Computerized Mathematics, The Ocean University of China,
Qingdao 266100, China
shengnanyu_ocu@126.com
[5] Institute of Smart Education Systems, Qingdao Academy of Intelligent Industries,
Qingdao 266109, China

Abstract. In this paper, we propose Computerized Adaptive Testing (CAT) method based on deep learning, which is improved in some aspects. First, training samples used for Model-GRU is generated by monte carlo simulation, as a data-driven method. Second, comparing with time consuming conventional methods, the proposed deep learning based methods can greatly reduce necessary time to evaluate ability after finishing training. Third, our model can notice the embedded relationships among the performances for neighboring items, thus human's memory effect during testing can be considered. In the implementation of CAT, the recently developed Gated Recurrent Unit (GRU) is applied. Testing results have shown that the proposed model can response more quickly and accurately compared with the conventional CAT. The findings offer a new way to study the student's ability through testing.

Keywords: Computerized adaptive Testing
English ability assessment · Monte carlo simulation · Deep learning
Gated Recurrent Unit (GRU) neural networks

1 Introduction

Computerized Adaptive Testing (CAT) plays an important role in ability assessment and online education [1–5]. Now the application of it is not limited in the education field, whose performance is also significant in other fields such as health field [6], assessment field [7]. Now with the rapid development of online

© Springer International Publishing AG, part of Springer Nature 2018
S. Satoh (Ed.): PSIVT 2017, LNCS 10799, pp. 158–171, 2018.
https://doi.org/10.1007/978-3-319-92753-4_13

learning systems, more and more researchers draw attention to the CAT, hoping to judge the students' ability through their performance online.

Although the conventional CAT has been proposed for several years and applied in many fields, there still exist some shortcomings waiting to be optimized.

First, conventional CAT [8–11] mostly based on the Item Response Theory [12–14], which is easy to perform and calculate through the earlier computers. However, it has some disadvantages. For instance, it is based on users and items, so it will calculate the ability and item difficulty when a user enters the system. That will leave a possible danger that some unauthorized user will influence the evaluation in an unexpected way. What's more, when the number of users and items increase, the time for a new update increase in an exponential trend.

Second, some CAT research [15,16] based on decision trees [17] did a good job on predicting the students' performance. Nevertheless, the conventional algorithm of decision trees such as ID3 [17], C4.5 [18] all have their own limits. First of all, how to set the threshold for the decision trees is a problem which needs to be carefully decided, for the threshold will decide how the decision tree will expand. Secondly, how to choose the objective function for the decision trees influences the priority of different factors in the evaluation process. Thirdly, the complexity of the algorithm increases when it comes to big data.

Third, the existing models for CAT do not fully consider the memory effect of students and only consider instantaneously performance to evaluate students. But in fact, performances of every consecutive questions for a student have embedded connections which need to be taken into account, since the memory and state of students accumulated in the testing process leave a hidden influence on his later performance.

To solve these problems and optimize the CAT model, we propose CAT based on deep learning. This model takes the performance of students on 70 questions as input and directly output the English ability evaluation. We adopt this input-output structure for its following benefits:

(1) The whole model is based on the empirical data, in which the inputs of training samples are from the monte carlo simulation based on performance of students in testing, and the outputs of training samples are evaluated abilities calculated from improved conventional Item Response Theory (IRT).
(2) The memory effect of students can be handled in a natural and efficient way. Because embedded relationships of the performance relationship at different time can be discovered through the GRU and without artificial interference.
(3) The deep learning is suitable for the big data times with advent of online learning, especially by the spread of a great number of online learning platforms. Although the training process in the deep learning is time-consuming, the successful networks can offer an accurate evaluation immediately and won't be disturbed by new items. Consequently, the response time of CAT based on deep learning is much shorter than other methods. In addition, the accuracy of evaluation of our model is much higher than previous models since it won't be interrupted by new user's performance which is invalid.

To better present our findings, the rest of this paper is arranged as follows. Section 2 first reviews conventional CAT models and then present the CAT based on deep learning model. Section 3 explains how to set the parameters of the "deep" neural networks and train them. Section 4 provides numerical testing results with different models and compares them. Finally, Sect. 5 concludes the paper and forecast the future development.

2   Different CAT Models

2.1   Conventional CAT Model Based on IRT

Nowadays, the ability assessment is mostly based on the classical Item Response Theory [11,12,14], in which the logistic method proposed by Brinbaum [11]. According to different numbers of parameters, the characteristic function is grouped as 1 parameter logistic model (1PLM), 2 parameters logistic model (2PLM) and 3 parameters logistic model (3PLM). In our model, to calculate the output of the evaluation and to offer comparison of our model, we adopt the most applicable and reliable 3PLM as Model-IRT, whose details will be discussed later.

To introduce Model-IRT, let's first review the basic algorithm of IRT. The basic idea of IRT is to calculate probabilities from collected samples and then obtain the users' abilities based on Maximum likelihood estimation, so that the adaptive recommendation could be accessed later. The formula of accuracy possibility is defined in Eq. (1).

$$P_j(\theta) = c_j + \frac{1 - c_j}{1 + e^{-1.7a_j(\theta - b_j)}} \tag{1}$$

where $P_j(\theta)$ denotes the accuracy possibility of student with ability θ in jth item; θ denotes the ability of student, whose range is [0,1]; a_j denotes the distinction rate of jth item, which means the ability to distinguish students of the item; b_j denotes the difficulty of jth item, which satisfies $P(b_j) = 0.5$; c_j denotes the guess coefficient, whose monotonicity is same as the difficulty of jth item.

Usually, three parameters of each items are calculated by the performance matrix. However, since each question items in our system have been carefully picked up, our parameters (a_j, b_j, c_j) can be given through experts' experience. To be more accurate and reduce the artificial influences by experts, we use a modified way to calculate the parameters combining the conventional logistic model and the parameters offered by experts. That's due to all our testing items are picked up from College entrance examination of China, whose difficulty and extinction are carefully offered by professional experts and are tested by millions of students each year. The detail of our data source will be stated in Sect. 4.1.

First, we will calculate three parameters in IRT through the difficulties offered by experts. The detail will be demonstrated in Eq. (2).

$$\begin{cases} a_{j1} = (level_j * 1.8)/10 \\ b_{j1} = (level_j)/5 \\ c_{j1} = 0.25 + (5 - level_j)/10 \end{cases} \tag{2}$$

where a_{j1}, b_{j1} and c_{j1} denote three important parameters in accuracy possibility defined in Eq. (1), which here is calculated from the difficulty given by experts; $level_j$ denotes the difficulty given by experts for jth item.

Second, based on the 3PLM, we adopt maximum likelihood fitting to calculate the students' performance and the parameters of each items. The classical method exists a shortcoming that each item is independent. Although each item has no connections with each other in common, the performances of a student in each item have unnoticed connections. That's why we need to propose the new model.

In the classical 3PLM, the distribution of possibility of a student with ability for m items is given in Eq. (3).

$$L(u_1, u_2, \cdots, u_m | \theta) = \prod_{j=1}^{m} P_j(\theta)^{u_j} Q_j(\theta)^{1-u_j} \tag{3}$$

where L denotes the possibility of $\vec{u}$ performance in m items of a student with ability θ, which in fact is a likelihood function; u_j denotes the performance of student in jth item, and it has 2 bool values, in which 1 denotes the student choose the right answer for the item while 0 denotes the opposite; $P_j(\theta)$ denotes the accuracy possibility of student with ability θ in jth item, whose detail is shown in Eq. (1), while $Q_j(\theta)$ denotes the error possibility in the same condition.

When it comes to N students, the $\vec{u}$ will turn into a matrix with size $N * m$ instead of a vector. So the likelihood function can be represented as Eq. (4).

$$L(U|\theta, a, b, c) = \prod_{i=1}^{N} \prod_{j=1}^{m} P_{ij}(\theta_i)^{u_{ij}} Q_{ij}(\theta_i)^{1-u_{ij}} \tag{4}$$

where L denotes the likelihood function of the performance U under students with ability θ and items with parameters $\vec{a}$, $\vec{b}$, $\vec{c}$; U denotes the performance matrix whose u_{ij} represents ith student performance in jth item; θ is a vector representing the ability of N students; $\vec{a}$, $\vec{b}$, $\vec{c}$ are vectors of length m showing the parameters of m items; N denotes the number of students while m denotes the number of items; $P_{ij}(\theta_i)$ denotes the accuracy possibility of ith student with ability θ_i in jth item, while $Q_{ij}(\theta_i)$ denotes the error possibility in the same condition.

According to maximum likelihood estimation, to get the most possible P, the likelihood function $L(U|\theta, a, b, c)$ will obtain the maximum value. To simplify the process, we use $\ln(L)$ to replace L. When $\ln(L)$ obtained maximum value, it will satisfy Eq. (5).

$$\begin{cases} \dfrac{\partial \ln L}{\partial \theta_i} = 0, i = 1, 2, \ldots \ldots N \\[2mm] \dfrac{\partial \ln L}{\partial a_j} = 0, j = 1, 2, \ldots \ldots m \\[2mm] \dfrac{\partial \ln L}{\partial b_j} = 0, j = 1, 2, \ldots \ldots m \\[2mm] \dfrac{\partial \ln L}{\partial a_j} = 0, j = 1, 2, \ldots \ldots m \end{cases} \tag{5}$$

Combining Eqs. (1), (4) and (5), we can obtain Eq. (6), which shows the detail of Eq. (5).

$$
\begin{cases}
\displaystyle\sum_{j=1}^{m} \frac{u_{ij} - P_{ij}(\theta_i)}{P_{ij}(\theta_i)(1 - P_{ij}(\theta_i))} \frac{\partial P_{ij}(\theta_i)}{\partial \theta_i} = 0, i = 1, 2, \ldots \ldots N \\[3mm]
\displaystyle\sum_{i=1}^{N} \frac{u_{ij} - P_{ij}(\theta_i)}{P_{ij}(\theta_i)(1 - P_{ij}(\theta_i))} \frac{\partial P_{ij}(\theta_i)}{\partial a_j} = 0, j = 1, 2, \ldots \ldots m \\[3mm]
\displaystyle\sum_{i=1}^{N} \frac{u_{ij} - P_{ij}(\theta_i)}{P_{ij}(\theta_i)(1 - P_{ij}(\theta_i))} \frac{\partial P_{ij}(\theta_i)}{\partial b_j} = 0, j = 1, 2, \ldots \ldots m \\[3mm]
\displaystyle\sum_{i=1}^{N} \frac{u_{ij} - P_{ij}(\theta_i)}{P_{ij}(\theta_i)(1 - P_{ij}(\theta_i))} \frac{\partial P_{ij}(\theta_i)}{\partial c_j} = 0, j = 1, 2, \ldots \ldots m
\end{cases}
\tag{6}
$$

Through the classical Levenberg-Marquardt algorithm [19, 20], Eq. (6) can be solved and the 3 parameters $\vec{a}, \vec{b}, \vec{c}$ for m items can be calculated, which we will refer as a_{j2}, b_{j2}, c_{j2} in following article.

Third, with the parameters given by experts in Eq. (2) and parameters calculated through Eq. (6) with Newton - Raphson Iteration Method, we define Eq. (7) to define the real parameters for m items.

$$
\begin{cases}
a_j = 0.5 \times a_{j1} + 0.5 \times a_{j2} \\
b_j = 0.5 \times c_{j1} + 0.5 \times b_{j2} \\
c_j = 0.5 \times c_{j1} + 0.5 \times c_{j2}
\end{cases}
\tag{7}
$$

Finally, through the newly obtained $\vec{a}, \vec{b}, \vec{c}$ of each item, the ability of any student with ability θ can be calculated with Eq. (8).

$$
\sum_{j=1}^{m} \frac{u_j - P_j(\theta)}{P_j(\theta)(1 - P_j(\theta))} \frac{\partial P_j(\theta)}{\partial \theta} = 0
\tag{8}
$$

With exact $\vec{a}, \vec{b}, \vec{c}$ of each item and Eq. (8), we can calculate the students; ability by his performance in the m items. Consequently, we can provide the performance in m items as input and ability θ as output to train our neural networks. However, we should notice the students' performances in m items will have 2^m possible combinations. It's obvious that we can't offer all possible combinations to calculate θ to train neural networks. To solve the problem, we will use monte carlo simulation [21] to offer input to train the neural networks. The detail of implementation will be stated in Sect. 4.2.

2.2   CAT Based on Deep Learning

To better evaluate the ability of students, we proposed a neural network based on improved CAT which has been demonstrated in Sect. 2.1 which is formulated as in Eq. (9).

$$\theta = f(\vec{u}) \tag{9}$$

where θ denotes the assessment of a student's ability; u denotes the performance of student in m items; $f(\cdot)$ is a special function that will be learned by deep neural network.

Deep learning is the hottest area of machine learning, and plays important roles on different areas [22–24] since it was proposed [25–29]. Comparing with conventional neural networks, deep learning aims to learn the most important features by constructing a network with neutrons in a layer having some connections with each other or connections with neutrons in other layers.

Up to now, a great number of networks [26,27,30] have been proposed to implement deep learning. In this paper, we apply the Gated Recurrent Unit (GRU) neural networks [30]. GRU networks is a type of newly proposed recurrent neural networks (RNN)[26,27]. As shown in Fig. 1, recurrent neural networks have connections among neutrons in the same layer, which allows the memory effect in the network. And compared with conventional feedforward neural networks (FNN), the GRU can deal with more complexed feature capturing.

To make the new concept and working mechanism of GRU, it can be regard as a simpler kind of Long-Short Time Memory [27,31], which is a conventional method of deep learning and makes great differences in the area. Compared with conventional FNN, the output of a neuron at time $(t-1)$ can be taken as input for itself at time t, which is called memory effect. The detail of implementation have been stated in [30].

For our problem, since the three important parameters of m items have been decided, we can take the randomly generated performances of students to calculated the θ to train the neural networks. When the training finishes, any students with performance $\vec{u}$ can get the θ evaluated ability immediately. Compared with the conventional CAT, even if three parameters have been decided, it's very time

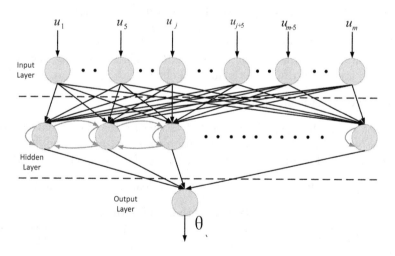

Fig. 1. The simple structure of GRU networks for CAT

consuming to solve m equations. In summary, our model can not only access the underlying relationships among items and is time-saving. In the following passage, our model will be referred as Model-GRU.

3   Settings of Deep Neural Networks for CAT

3.1   Performance Index

As suggested in [32,33], we use the widely adopted Mean Squared Error(MSE) to test the performance of our model. More precisely, the performance index compares the ability evaluated by improved CAT and deep learning to evaluate the performance of CAT. Equation (10) shows the definition of our performance index.

$$\min_{\vec{u} \in \Omega} \quad g(w) = \frac{1}{L} \sum_{j=1}^{L} \left[\theta_j(\vec{u}) - \hat{\theta}_j(\vec{u}) \right]^2 \tag{10}$$

where Ω is solution space of $\vec{u}$; $\vec{u}$ denotes the students' performances in m items; denotes the validation samples for our model; $\theta_j(\vec{u})$ denotes the ability judged by Model-GRU for jth validation sample; $\hat{\theta}_j(\vec{u})$ denotes the ability judged by improved Model-IRT for jth validation sample.

3.2   Decision Variables

To obtain a more accurate model, we analyze three important parameters for our model.

(1) The type of transfer function.

As suggested in classical masterpiece [33], the sigmoid function is chosen as the transfer function for the neurons in the input layer to make sure all the inputs will be normalized into range [0, 1].

For the neurons in the hidden layers of GRU models, as many masterpieces [26,27] suggested, ReLu function is an ideal choice.

(2) The structure of neural networks

There exist no methods to decide the best structure for any neural networks. So, we test several representative combinations of structures to find a relatively better structure. The numerical testing results are presented in Sect. 4.3.

(3) The weight coefficients whose values will be learned from training.

Since the weight coefficients is learned through updating, so the only thing we decided is the initial weight coefficients. As suggested in [32], our initial weight coefficients follows glorot uniform for each layer.

3.3   Training Algorithms of Neural Networks

The training algorithm of neural networks usually needs to solve two problems: how updating weight coefficients in hidden layers and how to validate to avoid the local optimal solution.

For updating weight coefficients, we adopt the classical backpropagation algorithm [34,35] and stochastic gradient descent algorithm [26] together with the adaptive learning rates trick proposed in [36] to train Model-GRU. The learning rate adaption rule follows what suggested in [36].

In order to quickly find global minimum while try to avoid local minimum, it's also very important to set the initial value of learning rate and regularization parameter. Here we choose 0.0001 as learning rate and 10^{-7} as regularization parameter.

Also, to avoid local minimum, cross-validation method [37] is adopted in our model. The method updates the weight coefficients to make sure the error of validation set and training set will both decrease. In our model, we choose validation split as 0.3, which means nearly 30% of the training set is used for validation.

4   Testing Results

In this section, we first introduce the data source of our experiment. And then we demonstrate the detail process of calculating three parameters by improved conventional CAT methods. Farthermore, we will use the mentor carlo method to generate the random input and ideal output calculated by improved CAT. Finally, we test different structures of GRU to obtain the most suitable model which we refer as $Model - GRU_{Best}$. Finally, we compare the performance of improved CAT and $Model - GRU_{Best}$, so it's safe to say $Model - GRU_{Best}$ can be put into practice.

4.1   Testing Data

To obtain the accurate parameters, we pick up the items from the College Entrance Examination in China, which is the most important examination in China. There are nearly tens of millions of high school students taking the examination every year. Therefore, the parameters offered by experts such as difficulty and distinction are very careful considered and examined by the College Entrance Exam.

Considering the English ability for a high school student consists of many aspects, we just choose the fundamental English ability to evaluate students. To be simpler, we concentrate on the performance in multiple-choice questions, which can combine the fundamental knowledge of English and the ability to comprehend English. After clearly study the multiple-choice questions in the examinations for 5 years, we divide the ability tested in the examination into 14 aspects such as grammar, vocabulary and so on. And for every aspect,

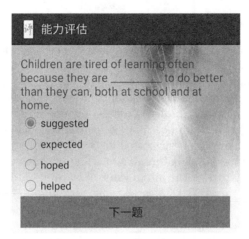

Fig. 2. The interface of our testing systems

we carefully picked up 5 items whose level range from 1 to 5. Finally, we picked up 70 items for us to evaluate students' English abilities in a more comprehensive way.

Moreover, to reassure three parameters for our items, we randomly invited students in different Universities and high schools to take the test. Figure 2 shows the interface of our testing systems. To eliminate unnecessary error, we only choose the student who finish all the items as effective sample. In the end, we picked up 100 valid samples to modify our parameters.

4.2   Improved IRT Testing Results

Based on Eq. (6), considering 70 items and 100 testers, we need to calculate 310 equations with exponential term. So how to solve the equations is a big problem for us. In the beginning, we adopt several algorithm to solve the problem, such as Newton-Raphson Iteration Method [38], Levenberg–Marquardt algorithm [19,20], Trust–Region–Reflective algorithm [39,40]. Finally we adopt the Levenberg–Marquardt algorithm [19,20], for its Mean-Squared Error(MSE) can be smaller.

$$\hat{\beta} = \arg\min_{\beta} \sum_{i=1}^{235} [y_i - f(x_i, \vec{\beta})] \tag{11}$$

where $\hat{\beta}$ denotes the squares of the deviations; y_i denotes the aim result of our equations; $f(\cdot)$ denotes the function that we defined in Eq. (6); $\vec{\beta}$ denotes the parameters that we need to calculate.

Through Matlab help, all the parameters are calculated with 967 iterations. And the mean-squared-error of such parameters is nearly, which is enough for us to carry later research.

Table 1. Different structure settings for GRU

Structure	Hidden Layer		
	1	2	3
1	30	0	0
2	50	0	0
3	100	0	0
4	200	0	0
5	300	0	0
6	10	10	0
7	30	10	0
8	30	30	0
9	10	10	5
10	10	10	10
11	30	10	10

Then we use the obtained $\vec{a_2}, \vec{b_2}, \vec{c_2}$, combining with the conventional $\vec{a_1}, \vec{b_1}, \vec{c_1}$, we obtain the $\vec{a}$, $\vec{b}$, $\vec{c}$, which are all in a proper range.

Consequently, through the newly obtained $\vec{a}$, $\vec{b}$, $\vec{c}$, the ability of any student with ability θ can be calculated with Eqs. (1) and (8), in which $m = 70$. So now we use monte carlo simulation [21] to randomly generate 100,000 possible $\vec{u}$, which denotes the possible performances in 70 items. With Eqs. (1) and (8), we can obtain the estimated θ for every input $\vec{u}$. So now we obtain 100000 input and corresponding output, which will serve as train set and aim set in Sect. 4.3.

4.3   The Appropriate Structure of Model-GRU

It's obvious that the structure of a neural network has a great effect on the performance of the neural network, which also applies to GRU. Therefore, we need to test some empirical structure listed in Table 1 to pick up a more accurate model.

We use the input-output data pair generated in Sect. 4.2 to train networks with different structures. As described in Sect. 3.2, we use cross−validation to avoid over−fitting, in which 30% of training sample will serve as validation set. Moreover, we check the weight coefficients to make sure our model make sense. Based on MSE defined in Eq. (11), Fig. 3 can show the performance of neural networks with different structures.

Figure 3 compares the MSE of different structures, and we can find Model-GRU with structure 11 can obtain the best performance. To be simplify our naming, we can call this model as $Model - GRU_{Best}$, which will be referred to later.

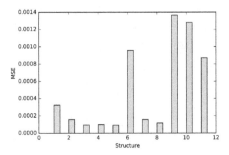

Fig. 3. MSE values of GRU with different structures

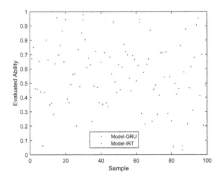

Fig. 4. Evaluated ability comparison of Model-GRU and Model-IRT

4.4   Comparison Between Conventional Improved CAT and Model-GRU

To compare the performance of two models, we consider two different situations to compare the performances.

First, we randomly choose 100 different students' performances to observe the evaluated performance of two models. Figure 4 shows the evaluated ability comparison with the same combination inputs.

Fig. 4 demonstrates evaluated ability of 100 samples with different input combinations. It's clearly revealed that the evaluated abilities with Model-GRU and Model-IRT are mostly similar, which indicates our model has an excellent performance.

Second, we choose the extreme example to test the model. For instance, we list some extreme performances combinations in Table 2 and then test them.

Taking all input combinations listed in Table 2, the evaluated ability can be shown in Table 3. In the vector, as we discussed above, 1 denotes the testor did right in the corresponding question, while 0 denotes the testor gave a wrong answer. Therefore, if a person gets more 1 in the vector, he should get a higher ability score in the evaluation process. As shown in Table 3,

Table 2. Different performance input combinations

Input 1	A vector with all values 1
Input 2	A vector with all values 0
Input 3	A vector with only one value is 0 and others 1
Input 4	A vector with one value is 1 and others 0

Table 3. Evaluated ability with different input

Input 1	Input 2	Input 3	Input 4
1.0563	0.0793	1.0491	0.1190

From Table 3, we can recognize our model works well in evaluating the extreme performances. So now it's safe to say Model-GRU can replace the conventional model with a faster speed. The speed advantage is resulted due to huge calculation amount from solving equation groups by conventional methods. However, proposed method only needs to do a simple neural network calculation with input after training.

5 Conclusion

In this paper, we propose a new CAT implementation based on deep learning, which is first applied in computerized adaptive testing. Through the comparison with improved conventional CAT, we can discover that Model−GRU is more accurate. In addition, compared to the conventional CAT, Model−GRU is time−saving and quick−response. Therefore, our model can be more applicable to Internet education platform, such as MOOC, which can offer a more user−friendly interaction.

Further more, GRU has the ability to extract the feature that the embedded relationships of the performances at different items, which may be closely interlocked. As a result, our model may can notice the relationship and offer a more accurate ability evaluation. However, the detail of the relationship needs to be carefully researched in the near future. For future use, considering push questions dynamically, we need to analyze the hidden relationship of each items and improve our model to work in a more intelligent way. Also, we should point out we lack testing accuracy again on real samples after finishing training, therefore further validation may be necessary for a mature system.

Acknowledgment. We would like to acknowledge support in part from the National Natural Science Foundation of China under Grants 61233001, 71232006, 61533019 and Science and Technology Innovation Program of Chinese Academy of Sciences (CAS).

References

1. Enhancing teaching and learning through educational data mining and learning analytics: an issue brief. In: Proceedings of Conference on Advanced Technology for Education (2012)
2. Bates, A.T.: Technology, E-learning and Distance Education. Routledge, New York (2005)
3. Rosenberg, M.J.: E-learning: Strategies for Delivering Knowledge in the Digital Age. vol. 9. McGraw-Hill, New York (2001)
4. Aroyo, L., Dolog, P., Houben, G.J., Kravcik, M., Naeve, A., Nilsson, M., Wild, F., et al.: Interoperability in personalized adaptive learning. Educ. Technol. Soc. 9(2), 4–18 (2006)
5. Downes, S.: E-learning 2.0. Elearn Mag. 2005(10), 1 (2005)
6. Garrison, D.R.: E-learning in the 21st Century: A Framework for Research and Practice. Taylor & Francis, London (2011)
7. Sun, P.C., Tsai, R.J., Finger, G., Chen, Y.Y., Yeh, D.: What drives a successful e-learning? an empirical investigation of the critical factors influencing learner satisfaction. Comput. Educ. 50(4), 1183–1202 (2008)
8. Embretson, S.E., Reise, S.P.: Item Response Theory. Psychology Press, New York (2013)
9. Verschaffel, L., Luwel, K., Torbeyns, J., Van Dooren, W.: Conceptualizing, investigating, and enhancing adaptive expertise in elementary mathematics education. Eur. J. Psychol. Educ. 24(3), 335 (2009)
10. Jones, V., Jo, J.H.: Ubiquitous learning environment: An adaptive teaching system using ubiquitous technology. In: Beyond the Comfort Zone: Proceedings of the 21st ASCILITE Conference. vol. 468, Perth, Western Australia, 474 p. (2004)
11. Wolf, C.: iweaver: towards 'learning style'-based e-learning in computer science education. In: Proceedings of the Fifth Australasian Conference on Computing Education, vol. 20. Australian Computer Society, Inc., pp. 273–279 (2003)
12. Paramythis, A., Loidl-Reisinger, S.: Adaptive learning environments and e-learning standards. In: Second European Conference on e-Learning, vol. 1, pp. 369–379 (2003)
13. Brusilovsky, P., Peylo, C.: Adaptive and intelligent web-based educational systems. Int. J. Artif. Intell. Educ. (IJAIED) 13, 159–172 (2003)
14. Klašnja-Milićević, A., Vesin, B., Ivanović, M., Budimac, Z.: E-learning personalization based on hybrid recommendation strategy and learning style identification. Comput. Educ. 56(3), 885–899 (2011)
15. Wainer, H., Dorans, N.J., Flaugher, R., Green, B.F., Mislevy, R.J.: Computerized Adaptive Testing: A Primer. Routledge, New York (2000)
16. Conejo, R., Guzmán, E., Millán, E., Trella, M., Pérez-De-La-Cruz, J.L., Ríos, A.: Siette: a web-based tool for adaptive testing. Int. J. Artif. Intell. Educ. 14(1), 29–61 (2004)
17. Weber, G., Brusilovsky, P.: Elm-art: an adaptive versatile system for web-based instruction. Int. J. Artif. Intell. Educ. (IJAIED) 12, 351–384 (2001)
18. Wainer, H., Bradlow, E.T., Du, Z.: Testlet response theory: an analog for the 3PL model useful in testlet-based adaptive testing. In: Computerized Adaptive Testing: Theory and Practice, pp. 245–269. Springer (2000)
19. Hinton, G., Deng, L., Yu, D., Dahl, G.E., Mohamed, A., Jaitly, N., Senior, A., Vanhoucke, V., Nguyen, P., Sainath, T.N.: Deep neural networks for acoustic modeling in speech recognition: the shared views of four research groups. IEEE Signal Process. Mag. 29(6), 82–97 (2012)

20. Wang, X., Zhang, Y., Yu, S., Liu, X., Wang, F.Y.: CAT based on Deep Learning (submitted). IEEE Trans. Learn. Technol. 2017)
21. Dolog, P., Henze, N., Nejdl, W., Sintek, M.: Personalization in distributed e-learning environments. In: Proceedings of the 13th International World Wide Web Conference on Alternate Track Papers & Posters, pp. 170–179. ACM (2004)
22. Quan, T.K., Fuyuki, I., Shinichi, H.: Improving accuracy of recommender system by clustering items based on stability of user similarity. In: International Conference on Computational Intelligence for Modelling Control and Automation, p. 61 (2006)
23. Nakagawa, A., Ito, T.: An implementation of a knowledge recommendation system based on similarity among users' profiles. In: Proceedings of the Sice Conference, Sice 2002, vol. 1, pp. 326–327 (2002)
24. Muñoz-Organero, M., Ramíez-Gonzlez, G.A., Muñoz-Merino, P.J., Kloos, C.D.: A collaborative recommender system based on space-time similarities **9**(3), 81–87 (2010)
25. Mustafa, Y.E.A., Sharif, S.M.: An approach to adaptive e-learning hypermedia system based on learning styles (AEHS-LS): implementation and evaluation. Int. J. Lib. Inf. Sci. **3**(1), 15–28 (2011)
26. Henze, N., Dolog, P., Nejdl, W., et al.: Reasoning and ontologies for personalized e-learning in the semantic web. Educ. Technol. Soc. **7**(4), 82–97 (2004)
27. Brown, E., Cristea, A., Stewart, C., Brailsford, T.: Patterns in authoring of adaptive educational hypermedia: a taxonomy of learning styles. Educ. Technol. Soc. **8**(3), 77–90 (2005)
28. Sarwar, B., Karypis, G., Konstan, J., Riedl, J.: Item-based collaborative filtering recommendation algorithms. In: Proceedings of the 10th International Conference on World Wide Web, pp. 285–295. ACM (2001)
29. Chorfi, H., Jemni, M.: Perso: towards an adaptive e-learning system. J. Interact. Learn. Res. **15**(4), 433 (2004)
30. Wang, G.: Survey of personalized recommendation system. Comput. Eng. Appl. (2012)
31. Albadvi, A., Shahbazi, M.: A hybrid recommendation technique based on product category attributes. Expert Syst. Appl. **36**(9), 11480–11488 (2009)
32. Linden, G., Smith, B., York, J.: Amazon.com recommendations: item-to-item collaborative filtering. IEEE Internet Comput. **7**(1), 76–80 (2003)
33. Hernandez, A.F.R., Garcia, N.Y.G.: Distributed processing using cosine similarity for mapping big data in hadoop. IEEE Latin Am. Trans. **14**(6), 2857–2861 (2016)
34. Min, S., Lee, B., Yoon, S.: Deep learning in bioinformatics. Briefings Bioinform. bbw068 (2016)
35. LeCun, Y., Bengio, Y., Hinton, G.: Deep learning. Nature **521**(7553), 436–444 (2015)
36. Schmidhuber, J.: Deep learning in neural networks: an overview. Neural Netw. **61**, 85–117 (2015)
37. Socher, R., Bengio, Y., Manning, C.: Deep learning for NLP. Tutorial at Association of Computational Logistics (ACL) (2012), and North American Chapter of the Association of Computational Linguistics (NAACL) (2013)
38. Manochehr, N.N., et al.: The influence of learning styles on learners in e-learning environments: an empirical study. Comput. High. Educ. Econ. Rev. **18**(1), 10–14 (2006)
39. Hinton, G.E., Osindero, S., Teh, Y.W.: A fast learning algorithm for deep belief nets. Neural Comput. **18**(7), 1527 (2006)
40. Hinton, G.E., Salakhutdinov, R.R.: Reducing the dimensionality of data with neural networks. Science **313**(5786), 504 (2006)

China-Finland EduCloud Platform Towards Innovative Education

Jiehan Zhou[1(✉)], Jukka Riekki[1], Mätti Hämäläinen[2], Pasi Mattila[3],
Xinguo Yu[4], Xiwei Liu[5], and Weishan Zhang[6]

[1] University of Oulu, Oulu, Finland
{jiehan.zhou, jukka.riekki}@oulu.fi
[2] DIMECC Oy, Tampere, Finland
matti.hamalainen@dimecc.com
[3] Finpeda Oy, Oulu, Finland
pasi.mattila@finpeda.fi
[4] Central China Normal University, Wuhan, China
xgyu@mail.ccnu.edu.cn
[5] Chinese Academy of Science, Beijing, China
xiwei.liu@ia.ac.cn
[6] China University of Petroleum, Beijing, China
zhangws@upc.edu.cn

Abstract. Education for innovation development is emphasized looking at the future of education. Cloud computing is regarded as the key trigger and enabling technology to advance innovative education. This paper specifies an intelligent Cloud-based platform for innovative education under the term of EduCloud. We give an overview and discuss the challenges facing future education, especially in the cases of China and Finland. We define innovative education and EduCloud-relevant concepts. We give an overview of Cloud computing and present EduCloud platform. We also describe current practices and initiatives in innovative education in the China-Finland arena.

Keywords: EduCloud · Education technology · Cloud-based education
Cloud computing · Innovation

1 Introduction

Education informatization (EI) is entering a new era with the gradual advancement and application of ICT into education. Activities and alliances around the world for advancing education informatization are growing. Unesco has organized the international education alliance and proposed the "Education 2030 framework" [1]. The Education 2030 framework aims to guide alliance members to apply Information and Communications Technology (ICT) to consolidating existing education systems, accelerating the spread of knowledge, broadening channels for retrieving information, strengthening the efficiency and quality of learning, and guaranteeing effective education services. As an example, Unesco held the 2017 international forum on ICT and Education 2030 in Qingdao, China with strong support from Chinese and local

© Springer International Publishing AG, part of Springer Nature 2018
S. Satoh (Ed.): PSIVT 2017, LNCS 10799, pp. 172–185, 2018.
https://doi.org/10.1007/978-3-319-92753-4_14

governments [2]. In 2010, China published middle and long-term plans for educational innovation and development for the first time and emphasized that ICT will play a significant role in the education revolution. Those plans marked a new era further deepening informatization of Chinese education [3]. Following this, the China thirteenth-five plan aims to build an education informatization system which promises to support education with the slogan "everyone learns, learning anywhere, learning anytime" [4].

Apart from alliances such as the association of China education technology [5], different levels of Chinese governments are advancing the EI development and deployment, focusing on the industrialization and commercialization of local education. For example, Jiangsu Education Bureau approved and established the provincial intelligent education industry alliance in 2015 [6]. The alliance aims to integrate related educational content, educational technology and education services in the education industry, and to provide a forum to exchange and share information, develop common enabling technology, foster application development and commercialization, and build policy consulting service, etc. The members include leading Chinese companies such as Xunfei [7] and Lenovo [8], etc.

In 2017 the Finnish Ministry of Education and Culture also approved and built the EduCloud Alliance (ECA) [9], which aims to build a state-level, internationally-oriented education ecosystem that brings together educational learners and buyers, service providers, technology developers, service providers, etc.

In the progress of education informatization, we can state that Cloud-based education is especially being regarded as a major enabler for its ability to deliver education resources such as Cloud services and transform traditional classes into Cloud-based online learning. Cloud-based education not only provides benefits through efficient course management, but also promotes education systems interactive learning, multiple channeled learning, and motivation-oriented learning in education systems. There are, also, many China-based companies which are developing Cloud-based education solutions. For example, in the 2017 Unesco Education 2030 expo, companies demonstrated their Cloud-based products and services, such as Lenovo Cloud [8], Ruijie Cloud class [10], Tsinghua Tongfang Cloud [11].

We will review Cloud computing and specify an intelligent Cloud-based platform for enabling innovative education in this paper. In practice, all practitioners emphasize that their Cloud-based services will create significant innovation in all areas of training and education. However, innovation is enhanced not only through book knowledge learning, but also through the acquisition of relevant experience and communication with relevant communities. This paper regards innovation as a collective concept built on a group of capabilities and skills as proposed by P21 Framework [12], including irreplaceable international experience. In addition, this paper will review the new features in innovative education and examine how our EduCloud accommodates them.

To accelerate and complement this reformation of education, China and Finland are planning to co-operate in exploring educational technology of the future, targeting an intelligent Cloud-based platform for innovative education. The paper is organized as the follows: Sect. 2 examines definitions of innovative education and education for innovation. Section 3 examines the characteristics of an innovative education ecosystem. Section 4 reviews some challenges facing education based on the experience of

Finland and China. Section 5 reviews the essentials of Cloud computing and proposes EduCloud platform as an innovative education solution. Section 6 examines EduCloud-driven education. Section 7 presents China-Finland initiatives on EduCloud cooperation. Section 8 draws a conclusion and presents future work in EduCloud.

2   Innovative Education

This section proposes to extend the current concept of innovation by examining both those characteristics of innovative capacity that may be called "people-centric" and those that may be called "collective". We also discuss how today's ICT facilitates both innovation focused on people and on the collectivity.

Based on the Merriam Webster Dictionary, innovation is the introduction of something new such as a "new idea, device or method"; innovation is the action or process of innovating. We all recognize that innovation is crucial to the continuing success of any organization. Innovation is also often viewed as the application of more effective products, processes, services, and technologies.

Further, this paper considers innovation to be a human capability. Human innovation is not only built on individual knowledge but also on collective intelligence, that is fostered by processes such as topic-based collaboration and communication. As mentioned, innovation is crucial to the continuing success of any organization and educating innovative individuals is crucial to the future of education.

Before we can define innovative education, we must first identify what is education for innovation and innovative education in the context of knowledge sharing, i.e., information and experience sharing.

Innovation is also constrained by space and time. To give just one example, ancient China had four great inventions: gunpowder, the compass, paper making and printing. The size of the country and its population and the need to communicate across distance and time doubtless recommended this innovation to ever wider use. But these innovations only became known slowly to the rest of the world. Based on Global Innovation Index 2016 [13], the small and relatively remote country, Finland, retains its place among the world's most innovative countries, although it has only 5.5 million population. Given modern communication, small countries like Finland can be aware of and build on innovation across the globe and people may come with an innovative idea in Finland, but implement it in China given an appropriate communication system. But today's innovation continues to be constrained by time, space, individual and collective intelligence.

We define innovation as a process of creating new things such as concepts, methods, processes, products and services. Innovativity is a new term that refers to the personal ability to generate innovation. In this paper, innovative education refers to educational systems intended to train innovative people. Education for innovation shares the same the goal as innovative education. Innovativity requires not only people's passion to observe and experience the environment and ability to trigger new ideas, but also requires rich individual knowledge and experience, collective knowledge and intelligence to implement new ideas.

Table 1 excerpts patents granted by the U.S. Patent and Trademark Office counted in pre-2002 and 2015 [14]. We can see the numbers of patents granted in USA and China in 2015 are much greater than the total pre-2002 numbers. Comparing with the slow pace of the past, innovation grows faster and faster nowadays. One significant reason is the rapid advancement of ICT, which is now triggering the 4th generation industrial revolution [15]. ICT is able to break the boundaries and constraints caused by time and space between individuals and collectives. As visualized in the video of "Finland defining the next 100 years" [16], people in a team do not need to travel to co-design a product. This can now be done virtually through 3D hologram technology. It is ICT that really accelerates human innovation through enriching and extending individual knowledge and bringing collective intelligence to bear easily and efficiently. Recently, 3D hologram technology is being studied for its application to virtual learning environments [17].

Table 1. Stats of patents in USA, China and Finland

	Pre-2002	2015
USA	2548916	325979
China	1140	9004
Finland	8048	1485

ICT is a principal driver of innovation today. We have witnessed how ICT has greatly changed the way people carry out activities around product development in recent decades. Telecommunication and instant messaging can keep people informed of the latest inventions, business opportunities, and information through virtually instant collaboration, using tools such as Skype [18], WeChat [19], Facebook [20], and QQ [21]. ICT drives online learning and Web-based media assist people to access information easily and freely through platforms like Youtube [22], Youku [23], Wikipedia [24], etc. Our proposed Cloud-based education platform fully accommodates emerging ICT communication and computing to realize innovation-oriented education.

3   Innovative Education Ecosystem

To obtain greatest benefits from ICT and to accelerate innovative education, we need to establish the characteristics of an education ecosystem and what role it can play in the overall education system, including what it requires and provides, especially from an international perspective. Innovation ecosystems in the education sector are typically the result of evolving collaborations between schools, organizations, and for-profit entities, among others, in which schools seek to procure particular technologies and/or technological services from their partners for the benefit of students [25]. We hence examine the educational ecosystem in the context of following education participants and emphasize that innovative education ecosystem is international in scope and even if built on cyber-physical environments:

- Student. The student is still the focus of the education of the future. Compared with traditional education, future education presents multiple choices for students to acquire knowledge, either from teachers in person in the class or online. Students also can choose to learn by watching publicly-available ready-made videos. These innovative educational practices allow learning and teaching in multiple forms that cross countries' borders, even the world. For example, with a public online MOOC, students could have a chance to listen to the course by Harvard University from anywhere in the world. Also students in a remote rural school have the opportunity to access recognized micro-courses collected by educational providers. The important thing is that the network space is not only providing a huge learning resource for students, but also presents them with online tutors, online FAQs and evaluation of learning. Furthermore, virtual learning space can provide students with immersive learning experience.
- Teacher. In innovative education, teachers are transformed from knowledge purveyors to organizers of learning activities. Their role changes from the transfer of knowledge to the guiding learning, from the curriculum implementers to the curriculum developers, from knowledge memorizers to lifelong learners. With the development of Artificial Intelligence (AI), an AI-based tutor can replace teachers to teach well-established courses, like math, physics, also in the support of online FAQs instead of real persons. Clearly the AI tutor and real teacher will co-exist in innovative education ecosystems.
- Service providers. These organizations provide schools and individual learners with computing, networking, Office Automation devices and after-sale maintenance services. Service providers guarantee that the service is up to date.
- Parents. The ecosystem must meet the needs of developing children as well as life-long learners. As far as children are concerned, it is well known that communication between school and home holds huge significance to a child's success in school. Innovative education provides parents a convenient platform to communicate with teachers. Parents need to know what their students are doing at any time and place. Parents also need to know student's attendance, exam results, academic reviews, school notices and other information through the platform. In addition, parents have the rights to express their views and suggestions to teachers, and give expectations to their students, encouraging them to study hard during school.
- Life-long learning. When students leave school, life-long learning on the educational ecosystem becomes the second classroom. Students can get knowledge they need in their work or life, especially those who have already graduated. In order to serve students properly, institutes can recommend social training for them in light of their study and living habits. All of us need to be learning all the time, and some, like certifications, will be recommended by employers or institutes. Others are found by the learner and the educational ecosystem should also allow

self-managed life-long learning as well as learning and training identified by institutes.

- Manufacturer. Manufacturers produce and provide learning products and equipment, and wish to prompt their products to existing and target users. There is a need of a platform for convenient education business and communication.
- ICT-built facilities include online systems, platforms, media services and computer, laptop, mobile phones, even smart desks. Nowadays they are indispensable for education and not only conventional tools for collecting information and presenting exercises, but also intelligent tools able to evaluate learning progress, correct learning mistakes, to notify signs of success, warning and failure.
- Administrator. Administrators are responsible for the rational allocation of educational resources. Future education needs an agile administration platform, which manages educational information, student enrollment and dormitory, teaching equipment, teachers, in a fine, flexible and efficient way.

4 Challenges for Innovative Education

Education facilitates learning and acquiring knowledge and skills. Learning can take place in formal or informal settings and from any experience. Learning is normally divided into stages such as preschool or kindergarten, primary school, secondary school and then college, university, or life-long learning. A right to education has been recognized by the United Nations. This section illustrates some of the challenges for innovative education based on the experience of China and Finland.

China is carrying out an educational revolution from exam-oriented education to what is viewed as quality education. Quality education [26] includes: learners who are healthy, well-nourished and ready to participate and learn. They are supported in learning by their families and communities. Outcomes in education encompass knowledge, skills and attitudes, and are linked to national goals for education and positive participation in society. We need to keep this definition in mind as we consider the nature of the education system. It is clear that the current Chinese education system pays too much attention to school ranking, which is based solely on student enrollment rates. This creates a biased ranking system that is completely at odds with the learner-centered and quality education. In China, the student entering school has too much homework to do; the teachers burn out attempting to increase students' scores.

Table 2 roughly lists challenges facing innovative education in China and Finland. Of the challenges facing Finland, Aulis Pitkälä, the Director of the Finnish Board of Education, states that a major future challenge will be in changing the culture of schools towards learning communities. A change from teaching centric to learning centric education means that the role of the teacher will be to act as a learning counsellor [27]. The Finnish new national core curriculum brings up to date the guidance regarding the use of digital technology in basic education and makes co-teaching and shared leadership an integral part of the organizational culture.

Table 2. Challenges emphasized in China and Finland for future education

	China	Finland
Access to education resource	Uneven	Relatively even
From learning school to learning communities	New	New
From teaching centric to learning centric	New	New
Digital technology in basic education	In progress	In progress
Equal opportunities	Difficult to meet all learners	Relatively equal
Highly educated teachers	Developing	Yes
Teacher training up to date	Developing	Yes
Organizational culture in school	Less attention	Attention
Making co-teaching and shared leadership	Less attention	Attention
Homework in school	High	Low
Education evaluation	Mainly by exams	Partly by exams
Inefficiency and irrelevant education	High	N/A
Talent pool and financial resources	Huge	Low
Social disparities	Growing	Not obvious
Regional development (migration & multiculturalism)	Accelerating	Growing slowly
Welfare and safe in school	Improving	High
Group size in basic education	Big	Small
Digital learning in school	Growing & unevenly	High and evenly
New skills & interests (computers, games, popular media)	Attention	Attention

5 EduCloud: Intelligent Cloud-Based Education Platform

To manage the challenges of education and develop an innovative education environment together between China and Finland, we believe that Cloud computing is the key trigger technology to meet the challenges since our proposed EduCloud intelligent platform presents all users with the opportunity to explore the nature of education.

5.1 Cloud Computing Overview

Cloud computing is transforming the conventional resource-dominated model of computing to a resource sharing model. Cloud computing is scalable in sharing computing resources such as CPU, memory, network, storage in the forms of Infrastructure as a Service (IaaS), Platform as a Service (PaaS), and Software as a Service (SaaS). Cloud computing allows the manipulation, configuration, and access of computing resources online. It offers data storage, infrastructure and applications. Those resources can be rapidly provided and released so that Cloud computing users can avoid up-front infrastructure costs (e.g., purchasing servers) and allow enterprises to get their applications up and running faster. Cloud computing enables the rapid realignment of computing resources to meet fluctuating and unpredictable business demand. In addition, Cloud computing allows users to avoid huge upfront costs, since Cloud computing providers typically use a "pay as you go" model.

5.2   EduCloud Computing

In this section we examine EduCloud, an intelligent Cloud-based Platform for inno-vative education. EduCloud that we propose is a child of Cloud computing, but includes specific applications and infrastructure appropriate to the innovative educa-tional arena. Figure 1 illustrates the EduCloud platform, which consists of ad-hoc three layers, IaaS, PaaS and SaaS, in addition to intElligence as a Service (EaaS).

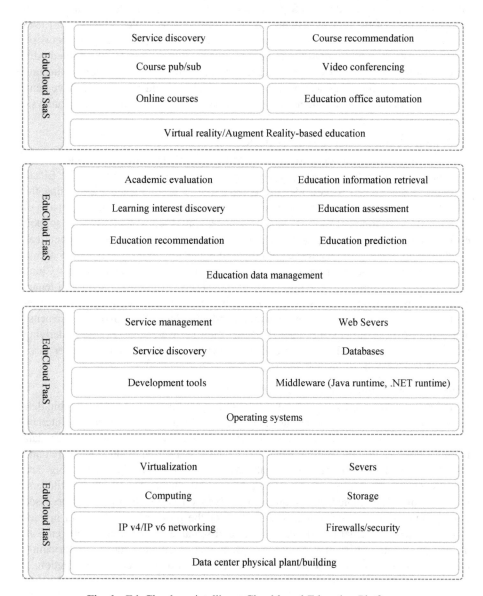

Fig. 1. EduCloud: an intelligent Cloud-based Education Platform

EduCloud Infrastructure as a Service (EIaaS)

EIaaS refers to online services that provide high-level APIs used to access various low-level details of underlying network infrastructure such as physical computing resources, location, data partitioning, scaling, security, networking etc. A hypervisor, such as Xen, Oracle VirtualBox, VMware ESX/ESXi, runs the virtual machines as guests. A networking resource is required, such as China education and research network (CERNET) [28], which is responsible for operation and management of CERNET backbone nationwide. EIaaS providers supply these resources on-demand from their large pool of equipment installed in physical data center plants/buildings. EIaaS infrastructure includes resources such as client devices, school servers, school network, national communication network, storage devices, etc. Common EIaaS-enabled education shares similar scenarios to [29] such that quick EduCloud education application development, hosting of educational websites, scalability and recovery management, web educational apps development, high-performance computing and big data analysis are all possible.

EduCloud Platform as a Service (EPaaS)

EPaaS provides an education application development platform as a Cloud service allowing developers to develop, run, and manage education applications. The EPaaS customer doesn't need to consider the complexity of building and maintaining the infrastructure for developing and launching an education application. EPaaS consists of middleware, development tools, database management systems, and more, to support education application development. EPaaS provides a framework that developers can build upon to develop or customize Cloud-based education applications. EPaaS allows developers create education applications using built-in software components. Cloud features such as simplicity, low up-front cost, scalability, availability, and multi-tenant capability are included. EPaaS enables the complete Web education application life-cycle: building, testing, deploying, managing, and updating. EPaaS avoids the expense and complexity of buying and managing education software licenses, the underlying education application infrastructure and middleware. The EduCloud developer manages education applications and services.

EduCloud Intelligence as a Service (EEaaS)

EEaaS refers to the application of collecting, storing and processing education big data as Web services to be accessed and consumed by multitenant through the Internet. EEaaS provides users with education intelligence services, such as education data mining, service recommendation, education analysis, education evaluation, search and discovery, course scheduling, etc. EEaaS enables the delivery of education big data process services that are sourced from the Cloud and constructed for the multitenant. EEaaS is often automated, and required by education administrators. It is accessed through Internet-based technologies dedicated for the processing of big data in education. EEaaS is Internet-based, on-demand, and scalable in providing intelligence in the education activities such as academic evaluation, on-demand education information retrieval, learning interest discovery, effective education assessment and prediction.

EduCloud Software as a Service (ESaaS)

ESaaS refers to education-related application accessible via the Internet. Software as a service (SaaS) refers to all applications accessible from various client devices, such as Web browsers and mobile phones. SaaS has become a common delivery model for business applications, including mail, office messaging, payroll processing, DBMS software, etc. ESaaS presents applications specific to participants in the education ecosystem, including online courses, office automation, course pub/sub, instant messaging, search, video conferencing, VR/AR-enhanced education, school monitoring, school-home communication, online maintenance, training organization recommendation, education device recommendation, employee management, course management. Those services are categorized and customized based on different learners in preschool education, k12, higher education, vocational education, corporate training, and life-long learning.

6   EduCloud-Enhanced Education

We regard Cloud computing as the core trigger to advance ICT into education revolution, in the form of the EduCloud that we propose. EduCloud customizes services to a set of users, including students, teachers, parents and others. EduCloud distributes services over the Internet. Multitenant can access a variety of education Cloud services, using whatever device (laptops, desktops, PDAs, etc.). EduCloud can scale services across dozens or even thousands of schools. EduCloud is building the specified education ecosystem by bringing person, resource, decision-making into cyber space across time and space. EduCloud drives innovative education and presents the following characteristics:

- Sharing excellent education resources over the Internet. Education participants from schools, communities, nations are able to access the entire world of knowledge through ESaaS, anytime, anywhere from any device.
- Promoting Individual education. EduCloud collects education data on the student's academic performance and learning progress, and enables the timely identification of weaknesses. ESaaS has the ability to present individualized educational paths based on the needs of the individual student.
- Online education. EduCloud advances innovative education by extending online education. Students learn anytime, anywhere, any disciplines with any schools in the cyber and physical world.
- Maker education. EduCloud supports STEM education and respects learners' interests. ESaaS provides rich services combining STEM approaches, Maker space, digital tools to support makers to hands-on and collaboratively prototype projects.
- Experience-enhanced education. Experience matters in a successful and innovative education. But physical experience usually costs money and time, and depends on opportunities. EduCloud with Virtual Reality and Augmented Reality services present learners with knowledge, experience, and a simulated environment. This improves learning and teaching efficiency and authenticity.

- Collective education. The time of teaching and doing things by oneself has passed. The school is moving towards learning communities, in which knowledge and experience are shared to promote the whole ecosystems. EduCloud enables the grouping of teams and collective intelligence to design, plan, and evaluate education through collaborations.
- Mobile education. Personal computing devices are booming and driving the growth of mobile learning, which focuses on the mobility of the learner. EPaaS and ESaaS provide a mobile user interface to access courses with portable technologies, such as MP3 players, notebooks, mobile phones and tablets.
- Multi-disciplinary education. EduCloud promotes the nature of education, quality education and human development through bringing together experts, learning materials, experiences and learners across disciplines and nations.

7   EduCloud Practices and Cooperation Initiatives

7.1   CCNU EduCloud Practices

Central China Normal University (CCNU) has developed many cloud products and applied them in teaching practice, including starC, which is used for daily teaching at CCNU. Concretely, starC presents the following ESaaS for online learning and teaching [30]. It provides: (1) quality education resources. This service provides curriculum resources that cover the K12 phase, and support personalized resource generation services. (2) an ubiquitous learning environment. This service provides teaching services covering the whole course before, during, and after class, including teaching preparation, classroom interaction, online personal space, network storage, cloud classroom, homework and exercises, education evaluation, teaching training, interaction between core applications. (3) Internet community service. This service supports the establishment of a teacher collaborative work community, research community, learning communication community, parents community which constitute the learning environment for the Internet community that supports teaching, learning, social participation and family-school interaction. (4) Education big data analysis. This service collects teaching and management data of cloud users and implements real-time big data analysis, then provides decision support for personalized teaching and management.

7.2   Finpeda Virtual Space

The Finnish education system is based on equality, high quality teachers and their training, special care and personalized learning. Finpeda is one of Finnish companies with a strong background in advancing innovative education and learning using emerging ICT. Its latest school innovation is a virtual learning environment that is called Finpeda Virtual Space (FVS) [31]. It is a web-based three-dimensional browsing platform for multi-user simultaneous online learning and training. The product is mainly used for education (virtual learning space) and the business sectors (virtual exhibition) to enrich experience in a multi-user interactive virtual environment, teaching simulation and games, multimedia space and virtual glasses.

7.3   China–Finland EduCloud Cooperation Initiatives

The remarkable initiative is to sign the agreement of China-Finnish Learning Garden between the Ministry of Education and Culture of Finland and the Ministry of Education of China in 2015. The agreement aims to promote the collaboration at all levels of education, bringing the academia, teachers, students, companies and policy makers all together to jointly co-create 21st century learning solutions. One of the promising leads of the collaborative concept is to joint work on EduCloud solutions that would enable scaling the joint development and testing of new learning solutions and utilizing big data approach to learning research and development in both countries.

Then China-Finnish EduCloud initiative forum was held to discuss the joint strategic initiative for scalable digital solutions in education and learning. The cooperation is significantly exploring the integration and application of EduCloud in education and learning of both countries. First, EduCloud promises to enhance and enrich the engagement and involvement of the learner in languages and culture exchange. This novel user experience will enhance the recognition, communication and cooperation between two countries. Two parties both have an excellent experience, skills, and expertise to research and develop the novel ideas. Second, EduCloud further promotes the construction of education informatization in both countries, and improves the development of the educational equality and personalized education. Third, EduCloud promotes Cloud-based education solutions of China and Finland, based on open standards, into the international market, and further makes the core technology of educational Cloud lower cost and more accessible for learning delivery. Fourth, EduCloud gives an opportunity for in-depth joint development and research to boost the educational cooperation between China and Finland, enhancing the ability to engage in educational cooperation and exchanges, and further developing more novel cooperative projects.

8   Conclusion and Future Work

Cloud computing presents a unified solution to wrap isolated applications as Cloud services and Web of Things accessible to everyone on the Internet. The EduCloud that we propose is a specific Cloud computing environment advancing education applications such as Web services realizing the vision that "anyone can learn anything anytime and anywhere". Innovative education recognizes that the education will respect human nature, move towards life-long learning, personalized learning, in learning communities, with a focus on quality education and the cultivation of creative thinking and innovation. Our proposed EduCloud platform extends general Cloud architecture, tackling challenges in advancing innovative education through accommodating new features, such as education intelligence as a service. Education technology cooperation is currently attracting the strategic attention of China and Finland as they move through the reformation of their education systems. While we are experienced in the research and development of Cloud services for education, there is much future work to be done to further advance the EduCloud platform, especially in the context of China-Finland co-operation and general consensus on challenges. To advance this work, we will research, develop and build the following Cloud services into the proposed EduCloud platform.

- Consolidating, enhancing and extending the existing artificial intelligence into EEaaS
- EPaaS for facilitating online and interactive education development
- ESaaS Virtual Reality and Augment Reality learning
- ESaaS education perception tools with the cooperation with Internet of education things
- AI tutor as ESaaS
- EEaaS in analytics and application based on education data
- EEaaS in learning analysis and assessment
- ESaaS in self-adaptive assistant learning for individual education.

References

1. Unesco: Education 2030 Framework. http://uis.unesco.org/sites/default/files/documents/education-2030-incheon-framework-for-action-implementation-of-sdg4-2016-en_2.pdf. Accessed 5 Sept 2017
2. Unesco: International forum on ICT and Education 2030. http://www.unesco.org/new/en/media-services/single-view/news/international_forum_on_ict_and_education_2030_opens_in_qingd/. Accessed 5 Sept 2017
3. Chinese State Council: China Middle-Long Term Education Reformation and Development Plan (2010–2020). http://pj.neusoft.edu.cn/pdf/wenjian/pjwj03.pdf. Accessed 5 Sept 2017
4. China e-learning white paper 2016: The Chinese Journal of ICT in Education, December 2016
5. Chinese education technology association. http://www.etr.com.cn/. Accessed 5 Sept 2017
6. Jiangsu Provincial Department of Education. Jiangsu Intelligence Education Industry Alliance (2015)
7. Xunfei, K., Wang, Z. http://www.zhixue.com/. Accessed 5 Sept 2017
8. Lenovo. http://www3.lenovo.com/ca/en/. Accessed 5 Sept 2017
9. Finnish EduCloud Alliance. https://eduCloudalliance.org/. Accessed 5 Sept 2017
10. Ruijie Networks Co., Ltd. http://www.ruijie.com.cn. Accessed 5 Sept 2017
11. Tsinghua Tongfang Co., Ltd. http://www.tongfangpc.com/index.html. Accessed 5 Sept 2017
12. Framework for 21st century learning. http://www.p21.org/our-work/p21-framework. Accessed 5 Sept 2017
13. Global Innovation Index | Innovation Feeding the World. https://www.globalinnovationindex.org/. Accessed 5 Sept 2017
14. United States patent and trademark office. https://www.uspto.gov/Web/offices/ac/ido/oeip/taf/cst_all.htm. Accessed 5 Sept 2017
15. Lasi, H., Kemper, H.-G., Fettke, P., Feld, T., Hoffmann, M.: Industry 4.0. Bus. Inf. Syst. Eng. 4(6), 239–242 (2014)
16. Tekes: Finland Defining the Next 100 Years. https://www.youtube.com/watch?v=lhSUjnX0qKY. Accessed 5 Sept 2017
17. Ghuloum, H.: 3D hologram technology in learning environment. In: Informing Science & IT Education Conference, pp. 693–704 (2010)
18. Microsoft: Skype. https://www.skype.com/. Accessed 5 Sept 2017

19. Tencent: Wechat. https://www.wechat.com/en/. Accessed 5 Sept 2017
20. Facebook. https://www.facebook.com/. Accessed 5 Sept 2017
21. Tencent Holdings Limited. https://en.mail.qq.com/. Accessed 5 Sept 2017
22. Youtube. https://www.youtube.com/. Accessed 5 Sept 2017
23. Youku. http://www.youku.com/. Accessed 5 Sept 2017
24. Wikipedia. https://en.wikipedia.org/wiki/Main_Page. Accessed 5 Sept 2017
25. Abdul-Jabbar, M., Kurshan, B.: Educational ecosystems: a trend in urban educational innovation. Penn GSE Perspect. Urban Educ. **12**(1), n1 (2015)
26. United Nations Children's Fund. Defining Quality in Education. The International Working Group on Education Florence, Italy, June 2000. https://www.unicef.org/education/files/QualityEducation.PDF. Accessed 5 Sept 2017
27. Education World Forum: Future Challenges to an Education System-Case Finland. http://www.fininst.uk/en/articles/1592-future-challenges-to-an-education-system-case-finland. Accessed 5 Sept 2017
28. Chinese Ministry of Education: China Education and Research Network. http://www.edu.cn/english/. Accessed 5 Sept 2017
29. Microsoft. Azure. https://azure.microsoft.com/en-us/. Accessed 5 Sept 2017
30. Central China Normal University: starC cloud teaching platform. http://nercel.ccnu.edu.cn/info/1024/3023.htm. Accessed 5 Sept 2017
31. Finpeda: Finpeda Virtual Space. http://finpeda.fi/portfolio/the-finpeda-virtual-space/. Accessed 5 Sept 2017

SPSE: A Smart Phone-Based Student Evaluation

Xiang Gao[1], Jiehan Zhou[2], Zhitao Yu[3], Jianli Zhao[1,4(✉)],
Zhengbin Fu[1], and Chunxiu Li[1]

[1] College of Computer Science and Engineering, Shandong University
of Science and Technology, Qingdao 266590, China
zhaojianli@gmail.com
[2] Faculty of Information Technology and Electrical Engineering,
University of Oulu, Helsinki, Finland
[3] College of Information Science and Engineering, Ocean University of China,
Qingdao, China
[4] Beijing Key Laboratory on Integration and Analysis of Large-Scale
Stream Data, Beijing 100144, China

Abstract. Data center in the university collects lots of students' achievement data. It is very important to improve the teaching performance through in-depth analyzing those students' data. However, traditional methods only pay attention to the analysis of static students' data such as mid-term and final scores, and ignore the analysis of students' daily behavior data. Data mining of students' daily behavior data becomes a key step to avoid students' failure and further improve students' performance. This paper proposes a smart phone-based method for evaluating students' performance (SPSE). First, a static student score is calculated using fuzzy-based method for evaluating student academic performance. Then, we use Affinity Propagation clustering algorithm to analyze WiFi data and time stamp collected by student smart phones in order to obtain student locations and learning status. Based on that we set dynamic students' behavior scores. Finally, we combine the two scores to comprehensively evaluate students' performance.

Keywords: Learning evaluation · Fuzzy-based evaluation · Affinity
propagation · Clustering · Fingerprint-based localization

1 Introduction

In recent years, computer-based learning analysis attracts attention from research and practices in order to evaluate students' performance. Learning evaluation refers to an assessment of students' learning performance based on their inherent needs and learning goals. With the wide usage of digital education technology, data center in universities usually stored lots of data on students. However, the existing education administration only focuses on the collection and storage of data on lectures and ignores the in-depth analysis of them. Student's performance is an important metric for assessing the quality of teaching and learning. Our research question is how to rationally evaluate students' performance and provide supporting services for the

© Springer International Publishing AG, part of Springer Nature 2018
S. Satoh (Ed.): PSIVT 2017, LNCS 10799, pp. 186–193, 2018.
https://doi.org/10.1007/978-3-319-92753-4_15

subsequent improvement. This paper proposes a smart phone based model for student evaluation. Firstly, we calculate the static student scores according to students' academic achievements. Then, we analyze students' behavior data collected by their smart phones and obtain the dynamic student scores. Combining these two scores, we calculate the comprehensive student scores so that we could provide students with appropriate suggestions on learning.

2   Related Works

Traditionally the student evaluation is generally based on the examination results which are divided into different grades. The advantage of this examination-based evaluation is that it is simple and easy to handle. But it cannot fully reflect the comprehensive student performance and it doesn't take the dynamic student context during the course into account to predict student performance.

Recently, data mining methods are being implemented at universities for analyzing available student data and extracting information to support the analysis of student achievements. Kabakchieva [1] selected data mining algorithms for classification on the university sample data in order to evaluate their potential usefulness and Anuradha [2] applied data mining to analyze available data and extract useful information to support decision making for university management. Chen [3] proposed an evaluation method based on k-means clustering algorithm for comprehensive student evaluation, excavating the general student characteristics and then classifying students according to them. Zhang [4] proposed a model based on fuzzy theory to establish a multi-objective fuzzy-based comprehensive evaluation system. Other researchers used the students' learning behavior to evaluate students comprehensively, Huang [5] proposed knowledge management methods to improve the learning process and optimize learning resources. Gupta [6] proposed a perceptual computing based algorithm for evaluating the student examination strategy through smart phone.

In this paper, we take into account of the student learning process in student evaluation. We collect the daily learning location of a student by smart phone, and then use AP clustering algorithm [7] and fuzzy-based evaluation [8] to determine the student performance. The traditional methods only considered the static student achievements. Our proposed method takes into account of the daily location of student learning. Our method would improve the student evaluation timely and effectively.

3   Smart Phone-Based Student Evaluation (SPSE)

3.1   SPSE Model

The SPSE model is illustrated in Fig. 1. In a sum, our model includes learning behavior analysis and learning achievement analysis. In behavior analysis, we collect the student WiFi data, analyze the student learning location and obtain the dynamic student scores by applying AP clustering. In achievement analysis, we extract the student examination results from educational system, make a fuzzy-based evaluation and obtain the static student scores. Combining both scores, we calculate the comprehensive student scores and evaluate student performance.

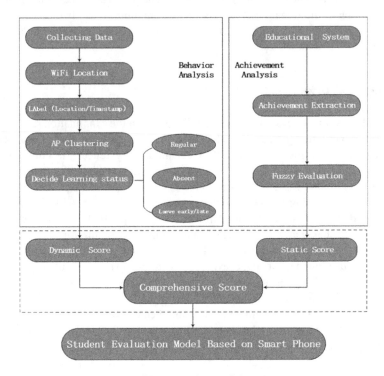

Fig. 1. SPSE model.

3.2   Dynamic Learning Behavior Analysis

In the learning behavior analysis, smart phone collects the student WiFi data including time stamp, Received Signal Strength (RSS) of a scanned access points, media access control (MAC) address of each access point, etc. In a certain time stamp range, we use the fingerprint-based localization method to calculate the current student location. Then we apply affinity propaganda clustering method to cluster all the WiFi data and divide students into different clusters. With student clusters and location labels, we can determine whether a student is in the classroom or other learning places at a given period. According to the student attendance and study time, we can predict a student learning status like regular attendance, late, early leave or absence so that we can set the student a dynamic score.

Fingerprint-Based Localization. Fingerprint-based indoor localization consists of two phases: training and localization. During the training phase, a number of reference points (RP) are set in a space, and the RSS is collected from the surrounding WiFi access points and the corresponding coordinates is calculated and form the original fingerprint radio map [9]. In the localization phase, the user sends location queries with the current RSS fingerprints to the positioning server. The server uses the KNN (K-Nearest Neighbor) method to retrieve the signal database and returns the matched locations [10]. Therefore we can calculate and label the student location according to the collected student WiFi data.

Affinity Propagation Clustering. Affinity Propagation (AP) clustering algorithm is proposed by Frey [7]. The principle of this algorithm is to calculate the similarity between data points. We have data set $D = \{x_1, x_2, \ldots, x_n\}$, where n is the number of data points, $x_i(i = 1, 2, \ldots, m)$ is a data point. The AP clustering algorithm is based on the similarity matrix between n data points. The similarity formula is as follows:

$$s(i, j) = -\left\| x_i - x_j \right\|^2, i, j = 1, 2, \ldots n; i \neq j \tag{1}$$

The AP algorithm passes two types of messages: the support degree r(i,k) represents the message sent from point i to the candidate cluster center k, reflecting the suitability of the k-point as the clustering center. The suitability a(i,k) is sent from the candidate cluster center k to i, reflecting the suitability of the i-point selecting k as its clustering center. The formulas of them are as follows:

$$r(i, k) = s(i, k) - \max\{a(i, j) + s(i, j)\}, j \in \{1, 2, \ldots, n, j \neq k\} \tag{2}$$

$$a(i, k) = \min\left\{0, r(k, k) + \sum_j \{\max(0, r(j, k))\}\right\}, j \in \{1, \ldots n, j \neq i, j \neq k\} \tag{3}$$

We cluster the student WiFi data at a given time using AP clustering and label the cluster each student belongs to. By computing the Euclidean distance between the student location and the labeled learning location, we determine whether a given student is in the learning location or not.

Dynamical Student Scoring. In a given time period, if a student's current position is located in the learning location clusters, we say that the student attends the class and we set a normal score to the student. If the current student position is not in the learning clusters on time, or not in the learning clusters before the course end time, we say that the student is late or leaves early. Therefore we set the student a lower score. If the student does not attend the class, we set the student a lowest score.

Application Analysis. Taking the graduate students' attendance as an example, we collected the data of all the students and got the location and AP clustering result in the class time from Monday to Friday. And analyze the attendance rate obtaining the dynamical score.

Data Preprocessing. According to the Access Point (AP) distribution in the teaching building, we selected 9 APs and set the phones' upload frequency as 5 min a time. The server took the WiFi data of all students during class time.

AP Clustering Analysis. Our sign in system application is shown in Fig. 2. Using the fingerprint-based WiFi localization method, the current coordinates of each student are obtained, the results are shown as follows:

Fig. 2. Sign in system application view.

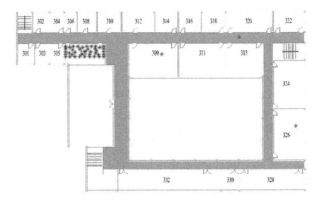

Fig. 3. Students' localization distribution.

Figure 3 shows the students' localization in the complete building floor plan and Fig. 4 shows the clustering result of students, a point is a student. The x axis is 1600 pixels converted to 9 m and y axis is 1280 pixels converted to 7.2 m respectively. According to Fig. 4, there are 3 clusters next to each other illustrating that the students are in the same classroom, and 3 other clusters are far more than 5 m to other clusters showing that the students in these clusters are not attend.

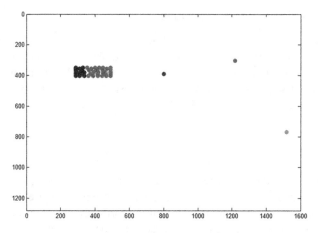

Fig. 4. AP clustering result.

Dynamical Score Calculation. Through the real-time calculation of the location and cluster labels of all the students, we can analyze the attendance rate of them. We only show an example of one class, by analyzing all the courses we can obtain the dynamical score of students according to the attendance rate.

3.3   Static Student Scoring

In the fuzzy-based evaluation, there are m factors $U = \{u_1, u_2, \ldots u_m\}$, the evaluation levels $V = \{v_1, v_2, \ldots v_m\}$. The fuzzy relation on the evaluation level is R. $R = (u_i, v_j) = r_{ij}$ represents the membership degree of u_i to v_j, and then we have the fuzzy weight vector A. The fuzzy weight vector A and fuzzy relation matrix R are combined to perform fuzzy comprehensive evaluation:

$$ANR = (a_1, a_2, \ldots, a_m) \begin{bmatrix} r_{11} & \cdots & r_{1n} \\ \cdots & \cdots & \cdots \\ r_{m1} & \cdots\cdots & r_{mn} \end{bmatrix} = (b_1, b_2, \ldots, b_n) = B \quad (4)$$

B is a fuzzy comprehensive evaluation vector, b_j represents the membership degree to the jth evaluation level. 'N' is a generalized fuzzy synthesis operator, which has different approaches depending on the actual situation. In this paper, we calculate the static student score according to the student examination results. In the experiment, we set the evaluation indices as all the courses, the evaluation level is $V = \{v_1, v_2, v_3, v_4\}$ including excellent, good, mediate and bad. We construct the membership function for each evaluation level. Then we use the membership function to obtain fuzzy matrix R. In addition, we give the course weight according to their credits, and get the fuzzy weight vector A. Using the above formulas, we can calculate student achievement degrees, that is, the static student score.

3.4   Comprehensive Student Evaluation

Integrating the dynamic student scores with the static student scores, we calculate the final student scores through the weighted average and obtain the student evaluation. By making student evaluation in real time, we can predict the student learning performance timely. If a student score is lower than a given threshold, we could provide the student appropriate learning suggestion or give the student a warning.

4   Conclusion

A rational, objective and comprehensive student evaluation promises to improve student learning performance. Traditional student evaluation systems only use the static student examination results to evaluate the student performance. This examination-based evaluation cannot fully reflect and predict the actual student learning performance in real time. This paper proposes a new method with the combination of the static student scores and the dynamic student scores based on analyzing student learning locations. Taking into account of student learning process, we propose the SPSE model - a smart phone-based student evaluation model. SPSE model makes a student evaluation by comprehensively considering the dynamic student scores and the static student scores. Through collecting and analyzing a student WiFi data collected by smart phone, we cluster the student location if it is located in learning spaces. Therefore we determine the dynamic student scores. We calculate the static student scores using fuzzy comprehensive evaluation. Finally, we evaluate and predict the student learning performance by the average of the two scores. Correspondingly we can provide the student with learning suggestions. In the future, we plan to extend our SPSE model with the use of other sensors equipped in smart phone and analyze the other student learning behaviors for improving student evaluation.

Acknowledgement. This work is supported by Open Research Fund Program of Beijing Key Laboratory on Integration and Analysis of Large-scale Stream Data.

References

1. Kabakchieva, D.: Predicting student performance by using data mining methods for classification. Cybern. Inf. Technol. **13**(1), 61–72 (2013)
2. Anuradha, C., Velmurugan, T.: A data mining based survey on student performance evaluation system. In: IEEE International Conference on Computational Intelligence and Computing Research. pp. 1–4 (2015)
3. Chen, Y., Huang, M.: Analysis of student comprehensive assessment based on k-means algorithm. Modern Computer, (2011)
4. Zhang, J.: Fuzzy comprehensive evaluation in college-student complex quality. J. Qingdao Technol. Univ. (2008)
5. Huang, F.F., Jiang, K.: High school students' study behavior analyze based on knowledge management. J. Guangxi Univ. (2005)

6. Gupta, P.K., Madan, M.: Per-C based student examination strategy evaluation in mobile evaluation system conducted through a smartphone. In: Uksim-Amss International Conference on Modelling and Simulation. IEEE, (2016)
7. Frey, B.J., Dueck, D.: Clustering by passing messages between data points. Science **315** (5814), 972–976 (2007)
8. Liu, Y., Hu, J.A.: Mathematical model and its parameters estimation for fuzzy evaluation. J. Beijing Polytech. Univ. **27**(1), 112–115 (2001)
9. He, S., Chan, S.H.G.: Wi-Fi Fingerprint-Based Indoor Positioning: Recent Advances and Comparisons. IEEE Commun. Surv. Tutor. **18**(1), 466–490 (2016)
10. Li, C., Qiu, Z., Liu, C.: An improved weighted k-nearest neighbor algorithm for indoor positioning. Wirel. Pers. Commun. **96**(2), 1–13 (2017)

Research on the Construction of Corpus for Automatic Solution of Elementary Mathematics Statistics Applications

Chuanyuan Lao, Qingtang Liu, Linjing Wu$^{(\boxtimes)}$, Jingxiu Huang, and Gang Zhao

Central China Normal University, Wuhan, Hubei, China
chuanyuan_lao@mails.ccnu.edu.cn,
{liuqtang, zhaogang}@mail.ccnu.edu.cn,
wlj_sz@126.com, jimsow@163.com

Abstract. The automatic solution of mathematical problems is one of the difficulties in the research of mathematics intelligent tutoring system. In recent years, the construction of corpus wins more and more attention, and is applied in various kinds of domains, especially in natural language processing. This paper is aimed at elementary mathematics statistics applications. We collected the university entrance exam questions, review questions and the relevant knowledge of 2008–2014, and then formed a corpus consists of the formalization of corpora in XML. The construction of the corpus is to make computer understand and then deal with the applications of elementary mathematical statistics, it's the foundation for automatic solution of the applications.

Keywords: The construction of corpus · Automatic solution of mathematical problem · Formalization in XML

1 Introduction

With the development of artificial intelligence technology, more and more researchers are concerning about the construction and application of intelligent tutoring system, and hope it to better assist teaching and learning. The automatic solution of mathematical problems is one of the difficulties in the research of mathematics intelligent tutoring system. Most of the existing mathematics intelligent tutoring systems realized the problem-solving function through the question bank in the system, and can't handle math problems described by natural language without the question bank. Thus, natural language processing is a key part of the automatic solution of mathematical problems.

In recent years, the construction of corpus and the effect of its application in natural language processing have attracted much attention. Corpus is a large database that uses computer technology to process and store massive natural language materials for automatic retrieving, indexing, and statistical analyzing [1]. The application of corpus can measure and improve the knowledge, even find out more knowledge through some methods. All in all, a perfect system is inseparable from the support of corpus while processing large-scale texts.

In this paper, we focus on the specific field of elementary mathematics statistics applications, and build a corpus based on related mathematics and knowledge, then the corpus can provide support for automatic solution of elementary mathematics statistics applications.

2   Related Research

2.1   The Construction of Corpus

Foreign research on corpus began in the 1960s, and ever since has undergone nearly 60 years [2]. As yet, the development of corpus has gone through three generations. Regardless of language, size, or processing methods, corpus have a certain development. For example, the Brown corpus [3], which is generally accepted as the first corpus, uses 500 English texts as the original corpus with a capacity of more than one million words. The Longman corpus [4] consists of three large sub-corpus, includes 50 million words. As one of the three famous corpus in the world, and the COBUILD English corpus [5] currently fixed in the scale of 450 million words.

Research on corpus in China started relatively late, and was marked by the JDEST developed by Professor Yang at Shanghai Jiao Tong University in the 1980s [6]. Thereafter, the trend is only expected to grow as the field progresses. The national modern Chinese corpus which is the largest modern Chinese corpus in the 20th century, has continuously improved its scale, and there are nearly 100 million words for now. The sharing resource of HIT-CIR includes HIT-CIR Chinese Dependency Treebank and HIT-CIR Tongyici Cilin(Extended), and its materials are about 100 thousand pairs of sentences and more than 70 thousand words, each pair of sentences includes one Chinese sentence and its corresponding English one.

Throughout the development of domestic and foreign corpus for decades, it can be found that the research of corpus is mainly focused on linguistic studies [7] such as Chinese and English, and there are still few studies in other fields, especially in the field of elementary mathematics.

2.2   The Automatic Solution of Mathematics Applications

The cognitive process involved in the solution of application is complex. To make computer to achieve this process, that is, to achieve the application of automatic solution, it's undoubtedly a more difficult task.

The first breakthrough in the automatic solution of mathematical problems is the fields of geometry and algebra. Wenjun academician established a characteristic set method to make made a major breakthrough in mechanical proving of geometrical theorem, and then summarized a well-ordering principle and zero structure from the solution of equations to offer some supports of algebraic machine solution [8]. Zhang academician proposed the elimination algorithm [9], and developed a number of mathematical education software with other researchers. Zhang's work make mechanical proving get further development. The development of mathematical intelligence tutoring system is not just that, it has yielded some results over the years.

For instance, Bobrow designed and developed a STUDENT system [10] which achieved the automatic solution of high school algebra applications described in English [11]. Dellarosa and others developed a ARITHPRO system [12] which can simulate human cognitive process to handle simple arithmetic applications. In addition, Z + Z intelligent education platform [13], which was managed the development by Zhang Jingzhong academician, also provided the function of intelligent solution of issues of secondary school mathematics. However, the researchers who studies on the automatic solution of elementary mathematics applications are still relatively few, and the theory and methods have not been shaped yet.

2.3   The Construction of Applications Corpus

The automatic solution of mathematical problems is one of the difficulties in the research of mathematics intelligent tutoring system [14]. The natural language processing of the text becomes a difficult technical problem in the automatic solution of mathematical problems. A high quality corpus is a big bottleneck for statistical-based methods used in natural language processing. At present, for the purpose of measurement, evaluation or else, the question bank of various subjects came into being. Given the trend of standardized examination, the construction of question banks is well under way [15], mathematics question bank is also included. However, the materials of the current mathematics question bank are mostly untagged, and can't play a good role in natural language processing. That is because computer only can understand and handle the manually segmented corpus which had noted all features needed.

At present, some colleges and universities, University of Electronic Science and Technology of China, Central China Normal University and Guangzhou University are all included, have built some mathematics corpus in particular fields under the need of sub-topic of 863 program to assist in the realization of automatic solution of elementary mathematical problem of mathematics applications. To meet the need of research subject, we construct a corpus for automatic solution of elementary mathematics statistics applications

3   The Construction of Corpus for Automatic Solution of Elementary Mathematics Statistics Applications

3.1   The Source of the Corpus

This paper is based on the university entrance exam questions, review questions of 2008−2014 from all provinces in China which are selected by the experienced high school mathematics teachers, and the relevant knowledge in not only mathematics examination paper but textbook, in allusion to elementary mathematics statistics applications. Beyond that, each corpus contains at least one knowledge point, and it also has detailed notes to meet the need of processing.

3.2   The Classification System of Elementary Mathematics Statistics

Based on the original corpus collected for a certain statistical classification, we selected some knowledge points and constructed a classification system of elementary mathematics statistics. The elementary mathematics statistics are mainly divided into four knowledge modules — random sampling, the estimation of population from samples, the correlation between variables and independence test. Random sampling consists of simple random sampling, systematic sampling and stratified sampling. The estimation of population from samples is also subdivided into two branches: using the frequency distribution of sample to estimate population distribution, including frequency distribution histogram, stem-and-leaf plot and others, and using the numerical feature of sample to estimate the overall digital features, including the median, average, standard deviation and variance. As shown in Fig. 1:

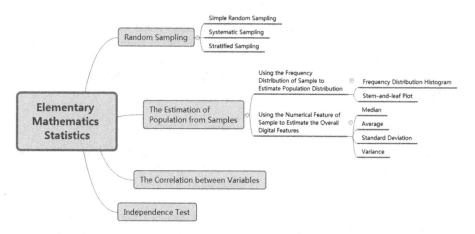

Fig. 1. The classification system of elementary mathematics statistics

3.3   The Metadata of Corpus Entry

Metadata is generally regarded as data about the data or information about the data, and is known as header information in the research of corpus. Information resource sharing is based on the standardization of metadata. Therefore, metadata is a problem should be attached importance to in the construction of corpus.

The materials of the corpus for automatic solution of elementary mathematics statistics applications is mainly collected from the university entrance exam questions and review questions of 2008–2014. According to the characteristics of mathematics application appeared in papers and the reference given by experienced mathematics teachers, we developed a set of metadata standards as show in Table 1.

Table 1. The metadata of elementary mathematics statistics applications

Metadata	Description
id	The number of storage
kids	The collection of knowledge
year	The year the application appeared
area	The province the application appeared
category	The category the application belongs
type	the type of question
qnumber	The number of question in exam
score	The score of question
haschart	Whether the question contains charts
qlink	The storage link of question

According to the specified metadata, users can know some related information of the corpus, such as year, area, category, type and others. In addition, researchers can form different sub-corpora through different metadata according to different research needs, and study and discover some factors that may affect the application and development of corpus.

3.4 Semantic Annotation and Representation of Corpus

The text of mathematical applications usually contains a number of clauses, and most of the clauses include the entity and its corresponding data, the relationship between entities and so on. Computer is unable to understand and deal with the "pure natural" elementary mathematics statistics applications. It's necessary to make the subject involved in entities, quantitative relations and mathematical knowledge characterized.

XML, that is, Extensive Markup Language, is a markup language used to mark electronic documents to make them well structured [12]. The special format of XML makes it easy to read and write in any program and system. In this paper, different XML representation frameworks are made for different knowledge points mathematical application because of the different solving processes. Although some knowledge belongs to the same knowledge chunk, their actual solutions are different from knowledge point not knowledge chunk, so are their XML representation frameworks.

Now, we would like to further present semantic annotation and representation of corpus by decoding the knowledge point of stratified sampling.

Stratified Sampling
In the case of stratified sampling, there are some important components in the text of applications, such as "total set", "the stratification of total set", "sample", "the stratification of sample", "the relation of entities", and "question". Some XML tags shown in Table 2 are defined to represent these components of stratified sampling. And each component always consists of "name","key name", "quantity" and "unit", these sub-components are directly related to solving problems.

Table 2. XML tags for the mathematics applications of stratified sampling

Tags	Description
TS	Total set
SOT	The stratification of total set
S	Sample
SOS	The stratification of sample
EQ	The relation of entities
QUE	Question

Here is a mathematics application of stratified sampling, entitled "某工厂生产甲、乙、丙三种不同型号的产品, 产品数量之比依次为 2:3:5, 现用分层抽样的方法抽出一个容量为 n 的样本, 样本中甲种型号的产品共有 16 件, 那么此样本的容量为多少?", and Fig. 2 shows a example for the use of XML characterization (Table 3).

4 The Implementation of Corpus

4.1 The Implementation of Corpus Indexing Tool

It is undoubtedly a more cumbersome project to mark the collected corpus according to the standards of characterization. In order to improve the efficiency of corpus annotation, we design and implement a corpus indexing tool.

Fig. 2. The labeling page of stratified sampling

Different knowledge points, mathematical knowledge have different forms of XML representation, and we designed different labeling page according to different representation. Once enter into home page, users can click on the button leads to the labeling page to index corresponding questions for actual needs. In the case of stratified sampling, the input of the labeling page can be divided into six parts — "TS", "SOT", "S",

"SOS", "EQ", "QUE". Each parts contains "name", "key name", "quantity", "unit" and other specific content, and they are all in blank. The labeling parts except "TS" and "S" are increased by selecting the number of content, this is because the number of them is at least one. In addition, "SOT" and "SOS" have the same amount, so if the number of either of the two parts are confirmed, the number of the other one will change accordingly to avoid repetitive operations. As shown in Fig. 3:

Table 3. The example for the use of XML characterization

```
<?xml version="1.0" encoding="UTF-8"?>
<Stratification>
 <TS><!--TotalSet 表示总体-->
  <name>产品</name><!--默认值是"总体"-->
  <keyName>TS</keyName><!--默认值是"null"-->
  <quantity>null</quantity><!--默认值是"null"-->
  <unit>件</unit>
 </TS>
 <SOT><!--Stratification of TotalSet 表示总体中的层-->
  <name>甲</name>
  <keyName>A</keyName>
  <quantity>null</quantity>
  <unit>件</unit>
 </SOT>
 <SOT>
  <name>乙</name>
  <keyName>B</keyName>
  <quantity>null</quantity>
  <unit>件</unit>
 </SOT>
 <SOT>
  <name>丙</name>
  <keyName>C</keyName>
  <quantity>null</quantity>
  <unit>件</unit>
 </SOT>
 <S>
  <name>样本</name><!--Sample 表示样本-->
  <keyName>S</keyName><!--默认值是"样本"-->
  <quantity>n</quantity>
  <unit>件</unit>
 </S>
 <SOS><!--Stratification of Sample 表示样本中的层-->
  <name>甲</name>
  <keyName>a</keyName>
  <quantity>16</quantity>
  <unit>件</unit>
 </SOS>
 <SOS>
```

```
    <name>乙</name>
    <keyName>b</keyName>
    <quantity>null</quantity>
    <unit>件</unit>
  </SOS>
  <SOS>
    <name>丙</name>
    <keyName>c</keyName>
    <quantity>null</quantity>
    <unit>件</unit>
  </SOS>
  <EQ>
    <entityName>A,B,C</entityName>
    <relation>比</relation>
    <value>2:3:5</value>
  </EQ>
  <QUE>
    <description>此样本的容量为</description>
    <keyName>S</keyName>
    <belong>null</belong>
    <name>样本</name>
    <unit>件</unit>
  </QUE>
</Stratification>
```

Select a mathematics application from the corpus, and then click on the "Generate XML file" button after filling in the various content modules in the page, finally an XML file generates and shows in the web page. At the same time, it will be named with the current timestamp, and automatically saved in the specified field of server. The Maple and the Drools engines can solve the problem automatically by the semantic information provided by the XML file.

4.2   Statistical Information of the Corpus

According to the established standardization of metadata, original corpora are all stored in database. As we have said before, researchers can extract different individual information or statistical information of the corpus according to different research needs.

Mathematics applications can be divided into three: single choice, completion and free-response question by type. There are 49 single choices, 46 completions and 81 free-response questions in the corpus. The knowledge of Statistic tested in free-response question is more.

Mathematics applications can be divided into two kinds: the one has charts and the one has no chart. According to statistics, the number of applications with charts are nearly a third of the total in corpus. It indicates that a lot of statistics applications need charts to help to understand them.

In the Sect. 3.2, the elementary mathematics statistics are mainly divided into four knowledge modules—random sampling, the estimation of population from samples, the correlation between variables and independence test. We also have calculated the distribution of these knowledge points collected in database as show in Fig. 4.

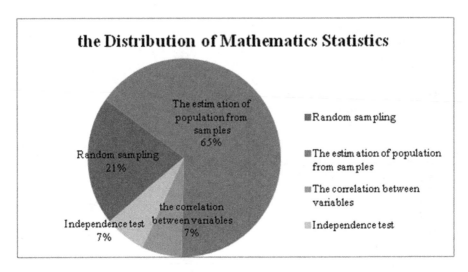

Fig. 3. The distribution of mathematics statistics

5   Conclusion

At present, there are few studies on corpus in elementary mathematics, and it's important construct a corpus for mathematical text processing. This paper is aimed at the specific fields of elementary mathematics statistics applications. We collect the university entrance exam questions, review questions and the relevant knowledge of 2008–2014, then classify them by the classification system of elementary mathematics statistics, make full use of the indexing tool to generate XML representation of applications, finally construct a corpus to make computer understand and handle the elementary mathematics statistics application.

The labeling work is mainly depended on manual labeling because of the diversity and detail of XML representation. There is a high accuracy, but the efficiency is still relatively low. Later, we will explore the semantic relations and characteristics of mathematical problems, then look for a more effective way to extract data under the premise of ensuring a certain accuracy, so as to achieve automatic extraction of information needed in XML representation and automatic generation of XML files.

Acknowledgements. This paper is supported by Chinese National Natural Science Foundation Project "Research on Machine Understanding Method for Math Word Problems"(No. 61772012), National High-tech Research and Development Program (No. 2015AA015408), Chinese National Natural Science Foundation Project "Research on Deep Aggregation and Personalized Service Mechanism of Web Learning Resources based on Semantic"(No. 71704062), National Science & Technology Supporting Program "Research on interactive virtual exhibition technology for Tujia Nationality's Brocade Culture" (No. 2015BAK27B02), Humanities and Social Science project of Chinese Ministry of Education "Research on Outdoor Experiential Learning Environment Construction Method Based on Scene Perception" (No. 17YJA880104).

References

1. He, T.: A study of corpus proper. Central China Normal University (2003)
2. Zhang, W.: Interpreting corpus and relevant researches in the last decade: present conditions and oncoming trends. J. Zhejiang Univ. (Humanit. Soc. Sci.) **2**, 193–205 (2012)
3. Charniak, E., Blaheta, D., Ge, N., Hall, K., Hale, J., Johnson, M.: BLLIP 1987–89 WSJ Corpus Release. Linguistic Data Consortium, Philadelphia (2000)
4. Chi, A.: A review of longman dictionary of contemporary english, (6th edition). Lexicography **2**(2), 179–186 (2016)
5. Sinclair, J.: Collins COBUILD Dictionary of English Language. Collins, London (1987)
6. Duan, H., Song, J., Guowei, X.U., et al.: The development of a large-scale tagged chinese corpus and its applications. Appl. Linguist. **2**, 016 (2000)
7. Huston, S.: Corpora in Applied Linguistics, p. 71. Cambridge University Press, Cambridge (2002)
8. Ji, Z.: Wu Wen-tsun and Mathematics Mechanization. J. Shanghai Jiaotong Univ. (Sci.) **03**, 13–18 (2001)
9. Zhang, J.-Z., Li, Y.-B.: Automatic theorem proving for three decades. J. Syst. Sci. Math. Sci. **09**, 1155–1168 (2009)
10. Bobrow, D.: Natural language input for a computer problem solving system. Report MAC-TR-1, Project MAC, MIT, Cambridge (1964)
11. Ma, Y., Tan, K., Shang, X., Guo, X.: A review of the method of semantic analysis in the automated problem solving of ITS. Mod. Educ. Technol. (08), 104–108+103 (2012)
12. Dellarosa, D.: A computer simulation of children's arithmetic word problem solving. Behav. Res. Methods Instrum. Comput. **18**(2), 147–154 (1986)
13. Tong, M., Zhang, J., Li, S.: Construction of resource management system in intelligent knowledge service platform. Appl. Res. Comput. (04), 71–73+82 (2007)
14. Li, Z.: Key technology and application of understanding elementary mathematical problem. University of Electronic Science and Technology of China (2016)
15. Li, G.: How to build an item bank: implications from UK and US examination institutions. China Exam. **12**, 3–8 (2011)
16. QU, Y., Zhang, J., Chen, Z., Wang, C.: A survey of XML and related technologies. Comput. Eng. (12), 4–6+30 (2000)

Constructing a Learning Map
with Lattice for a Programming Course

Xin Li[1], Han Lyu[1], Jiehan Zhou[2], Shuai Cao[1], and Xin Liu[1(⊠)]

[1] College of Computer and Communication Engineering,
China University of Petroleum (East China), Qingdao, China
18863987155@163.com, caoshuai594@gmail.com, lx@upc.edu.cn
[2] University of Oulu, Oulu, Finland
jiehan.zhou@oulu.fi

Abstract. Course management systems (CMSs) really promote the digital construction of an educational system. A Programming Course management system contains many questions prepared for students. The challenge is how to map data stored in CMSs to help students to structure a course knowledge. This paper proposes a visual knowledge analytic system, which can automatically extract features from the questions in a Programming Course management system, and construct a knowledge map based on lattice theory. According to the constructed knowledge map, students are able to better understand and grasp knowledge points in a programming course.

Keywords: Lattice · Knowledge map · Digital education
Meet-irreducible · Algorithm

1 Introduction

Course management systems (CMSs) are widely adopted in modern education systems because it can offer a great variety of channels and workspaces to facilitate information sharing and communication among participants in a course [15]. For example, a CMS called Moodle (modular object oriented developmental learning environment) has been adopted especially for programming courses by many universities and high schools. Using Moodle, students can submit codes online and receive results immediately. CMSs collect a large volume of data such as submitted codes. How to take advantage of those data to support and improve teaching and learning performance has been studied by many researchers.

CMS is important for programming course because programming course is a practical science. If students want to master this course, they must finish a lot of exercises. Finishing questions in programming CMSs is a better way to master programming skills. But questions in the CMSs for a programming course have logical complexity and they are hard to be classified. When students try to finish questions in programming CMSs during their course-learning or self-learning process, they always face some difficulties: What is the dependency

© Springer International Publishing AG, part of Springer Nature 2018
S. Satoh (Ed.): PSIVT 2017, LNCS 10799, pp. 204–213, 2018.
https://doi.org/10.1007/978-3-319-92753-4_17

relationship among those questions? Where should they start? What questions can be done next if they finish some questions?

To solve these problems, we combine concept lattice and visual analytic together to construct a knowledge map showed in Fig. 1. Firstly, we automatically extract features from all submitted source codes to build features for a specific problem. Then we regard problems in CMSs as objects and features as attributes to build a concept lattice. In the lattice, each concept can find their parents and children, therefore the dependency relationship among questions are built. Depending on the dependency relationship, the above questions can be solved easily. In addition, we also analyze the feature connection relationship to build a whole map for the course. Finally, we put those aspects together and build a visual analytic system to bridge pure theory and practical application.

The main contributions of this paper include:

- We construct the dependency relationship among knowledge points based on concept lattice.
- We analyze the connection relationship among features.
- We build a visual analytic system.

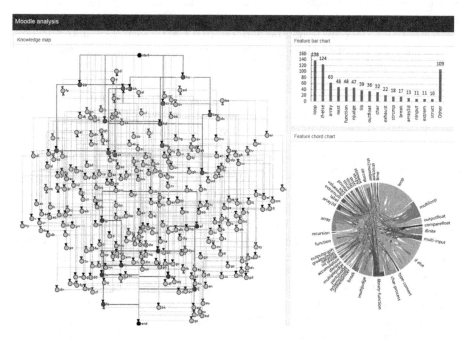

Fig. 1. The overview of knowledge map. The left part is the knowledge map of all concepts in the course. The bar chart on the top-right count up the usage frequency of each feature. The chord chart on the bottom-right shows the connection relationship among all the features.

2   Related Work

2.1   Algorithms for generating lattices

Formal concept analysis is a good theory framework to construct relationship between objects and attributes. The algorithms of obtaining a concept lattice have been proposed in [1,11,12,14,16]. The algorithms of generating lattices are mainly classified into two types: batch algorithms [6,9,10,13] and incremental algorithms [3,5,8,19]. Batch algorithms usually generate concepts in a top-down (or bottom-up) approach. Their efficiency is very high. They can generate all concepts quickly while ignoring the dependency between concepts. Incremental algorithms can generate concepts and lattices dynamically based on the dependency, which computes a new lattice or updates the existing lattice from a scratch. In this paper, we adopt incremental algorithms to construct the lattice because we mainly focus on the dependency relationship between concepts.

2.2   Online Learning System

In education, CMSs are widely used for online learning, storing course materials in database, assigning students to courses, tracking student performance, storing student submissions, and mediating communication between students and instructors [18]. Moodle is one of popular free CMSs with 23% market share [2]. Moodle can be customized by users meeting specific requirements. In programming course, Moodle provides an online submission module, which supports online submission and online judge. Using this module, students can learn programming by themselves. But as the development of the programming course construction, more and more data will be generated in the system. That causes difficulties for students to master the whole learning process.

2.3   Visual Analytics

In data analysis, visual analytic plays an important role for combining automatism and visual analytic algorithms through human-computer interaction [17]. Keim et al. [7] proposes a standard process for visual analysis, which transforms data into knowledge through data models and interactional visualization. Visual analytic system combines the high efficiency of computer and the intelligence of human being together, and is easy to be accepted by common individuals without professional knowledge. In this paper we collect and refine the data from a Moodle system first. Then we present the data in the forms of force-directed chart, bar chart and chord chart. Finally students achieve knowledge by the interaction with those charts.

3   Preliminaries

We define a formal context as a triplet $L = (G, A, I)$, where G is a non-empty finite set of objects and A is a non-empty finite set of attributes, and I is a relation between G and A. I is a subset of the Cartesian product $G \times A$, where $(g, a) \in I$ means that object g has attribute a. For a pair of elements $g \in G$ and $a \in A$, if $(g, a) \in I$, we write gIa and read it as "object g has attribute a", or "attribute a is possessed by object g".

Example 1. *Table 1 represents a formal context (G, A, I), where $G = \{x1, x2, x3, x4\}$, $A = \{a1, a2, a3, a4, a5\}$, and relation I is defined in Table 1.*

Let (G, A, I) be a formal context, with $X \subseteq G$ and $B \subseteq A$. The operator $\uparrow$ and $\downarrow$ are defined as:

$$X^{\uparrow} = \{a \in A | \forall x \in X, (x, a) \in I\},$$
$$B^{\downarrow} = \{x \in G | \forall a \in B, (x, a) \in I\}.$$

For simplicity, we denote $x^{\uparrow} = \{x\}^{\uparrow}$ and $a^{\downarrow} = \{a\}^{\downarrow}$ such that $x \in G$ and $a \in A$.

Table 1. A formal context (G, A, I)

	a1	a2	a3	a4	a5
x1	1	0	1	0	1
x2	0	0	1	0	0
x3	1	0	0	1	0
x4	0	1	1	0	1

A pair (X, B), $X \subseteq G$ and $B \subseteq A$ is called a formal concept of the context (G, A, I) if $X = B^{\downarrow}$ and $B = X^{\uparrow}$, where X is called the extent and B is the intent. Especially, for any $x \in G$ and $a \in A$, $(x^{\uparrow\downarrow}, x^{\uparrow})$ and $(a^{\downarrow}, a^{\downarrow\uparrow})$ are formal concepts, which are called object concept and attribute concept, respectively [4].

The concepts of a formal context (G, A, I) are ordered by $(X_1, B_1) < (X_2, B_2) \iff X_1 \subset X_2$ (which is equivalent to $B_2 \subset B_1$), where (X_1, B_1) is called the sub-concept of (X_2, B_2), and (X_2, B_2) is called the sup-concept of (X_1, B_1).

A set of formal concepts forms a complete lattice which denoted by $L(G, A, I)$.

4 Constructing Knowledge Map

4.1 Attribute Extraction

According to the lattice theory, we know that objects can be constructed by extracting attributes. In this paper, we extract knowledge points from source codes as attributes. A source code may contain syntax features such as condition and loop, architectural features such as float comparison and output asterisks, algorithmic features such as the method of exhaustion and the order of a method. We use regular expression to extract those above features from a source code.

In an online learning system, each question has some standard answers and submitted answers. The answers are source codes for the questions. We extract features from those source codes for one question, and regard the most used features as the question attributes. The extracted attributions may not be the best question attributes, but they are popularly approved for a given question by the users. Table 2 lists some question (i.e., objects) attributes.

After extracting attributes for each questions, we get a formal context (G, A, I), where G is a non-empty finite set of questions in the database, and A is a non-empty finite set of attributes for each question in G, and I is a relation between G and A, which is a subset of the Cartesian product $G \times A$, where $(x, a) \in I$ means that question x has attribute a.

4.2 Concept Construction

Depending on the question attributes, we can construct the concepts with the method proposed in [19] for the formal context (G, A, I). This method not only extracts all concepts and forms a complete lattice $L(G, A, I)$, but also obtains the parent nodes and child nodes directly. The concept lattice we constructed and subordinate relationship between them can clearly express the hierarchy degree of those exercises, which help learners to better clarify the learning route.

Concept attributes are different from each other. The intent of a concept is a unique knowledge point which can be used to solve problems. The extent of the concept contains those questions which can be solved at least with the knowledge points marked in the intent.

4.3 Knowledge Map Construction

To observe the relationship among concepts directly, we transform a complete lattice $L(G, A, I)$ into the Hasse diagram, in which each node is a concept.

Definition 1. *Let $(L, <)$ be a partial order set, $x, y \in L$ and $x < y$. x is called the lower close neighbor of y, if there does not exist $z \in L$ such that $x < z < y$, where, y is also called the upper close neighbor of x and is denoted by $x \prec y$ or $y \succ x$.*

Definition 2. *For $x, y \in L(G, A, I)$, if $x < y$, x is called the descendant of y and y is called the ancestor of x. Furthermore, if $x \prec y$, x is called the child of y and y is called the parent of x.*

In the Hasse diagram, each node only connects with its parents and children. All concepts are put together depending on their dependency. We introduce $start = (G, \phi)$ as the minimum concept and $end = (\phi, A)$ as the maximum concept. All concepts in the lattice must be nodes between *start* and *end*. To make a Hasse diagram serve as a knowledge map, we make the following changes

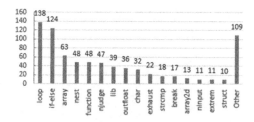

Fig. 2. The usage count of each feature.

for the diagram. For a node, if a question in its extent also appears in the extent of its children, we remove this question from its extents. Therefore the extent of one node only contains the questions which include the features in its intents. One question only appears in the knowledge map once.

If a student wants to learn the course, he/she first can start from the questions in the extent of a root. Second he or she can continue to finish the questions in the extent of its children. Repeating the process, the student can finish all the questions listed in the knowledge map. During this learning, the student is clear what he/she have done in the past and what he/she is going to do in the future.

5 Knowledge Map Application

We select 202 typical questions from an online learning system in a Chinese university. Based on these questions, we collect 20,000 source codes from 15,000 students. From those source codes, we extract 40 features including syntax features, architectural features and algorithmic features according to the actual teaching experience. We regard those features as the question attributes.

Table 2. A formal context (G, A, I)

question	if	loop	multiJudge	nest	prime	order	...
q1	1	0	1	0	1		
q2	0	0	1	0	0		
q3	1	0	0	1	0		
q4	0	1	1	0	1		
...							

5.1 Attribute Analysis

We use a bar chart to count the usage of a feature (Fig. 2). From Fig. 2, we can see that $if - else$ and $loop$ have been used greatly more than others.

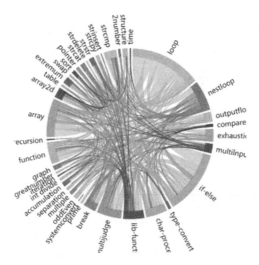

Fig. 3. The chord chart.

The reason is that they are the basic structural elements in a programming language. The usages of *array*, *nest*, *function* and *multi − judge* are also more than others.The reason is that they are the basic architectural features in a programming language. In contrast, the usage of algorithmic features is less. The reason is that they are only used for solving specific questions. With this kind of knowledge maps, a student will learn that he or she, as a programming beginner, should do more exercises about basic syntaxes features and architectural features than algorithmic ones.

5.2   Attribute Relationship

Next, we observe the relationship between different features (i.e., attributes). As shown in Fig. 3, two features will be connected if they appear in the same question. The chord length means the question count. The length for *loop*, *if − else* and *array* is longer, which tells us that they are used more frequently than others. When we move the mouse over a specific feature, other chords will be hide. Figure 4 represents the relationship between feature *if − else* and others. We can see that almost all the features are connected to feature *if − else*. Particularly the chord width between *if − else* and *loop* is thicker than others. That means they appear in many questions. In contrast, the feature *extremum*, as a algorithmic feature, is used less and only connected with some other features as shown in Fig. 5.

5.3   Knowledge Map

We construct a knowledge map base on the lattice theory. One node represents a concept in a lattice. The start node (G, ϕ) is put on the top and the end node

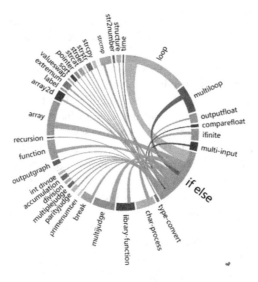

Fig. 4. The chord chart of feature *if*.

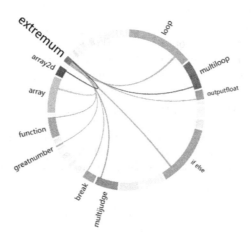

Fig. 5. The chord chart of feature *extremum*.

(ϕ, A) is put on the bottom. Other nodes are arranged according to the force-directed method. An arrow line pointers from parent node to children node. The most important thing is to draw the dependency relationship between different nodes. In lattice theory, the extent of a node contains all features in the extents of its children.

To give users learning suggestions, we append a new property called *question* to the nodes which remove all questions from the extent of a node if these questions also appear in the extent of its children nodes.

When we click one node called g, all connections with g are highlighted. The numbers (2, 24, 8) in the intent of g shows the indexes of features $loop$, $function$ and $if - else$, which means a user should master these three features if he or she wants to solve this type problem. The typical problem for g is No. 6. Users can jump to No. 6 through the hyperlink.

The red nodes are the parents or ancestors of g. The features of red nodes are less than the intent of g and only contain some of $loop$, $function$ and $if - else$. It suggests that students should finish those questions associated with red nodes before they finish g. In contrast, the blue nodes are the children or descendants of g. Their intents must contain all the features appeared in the intent of g and can have additional features. Students can finish those questions associated with blue nodes after they finish g. As a result, students will be clear what is prerequisite knowledge and propagating direction for questions associated with any concepts. The marked exercises at a node is the corresponding exercises needed to finish. Those nodes includes a large number of knowledge points a learner has mastered and less knowledge points he or she hasn't know about, which can help he or she to expand his or her knowledge reserve and at the same time they can review.

6   Conclusion

We introduce the lattice concept to build the dependency between knowledge points for a programming course. The knowledge map can automatically extract features from questions. The constructed knowledge map provides a learning guide to students when they learn programming with a CMS. We construct a learning map with a visual analytic system.

Acknowledgements. This work was supported by grants from the Shandong Provincial Natural Science Foundation (No. ZR2015FM022), National Natural Science Foundation of China (No. 61309024), the Key Research Program of Shandong Province (No. 2017GGX10140).

References

1. Aswani Kumar, C., Srinivas, S.: Concept lattice reduction using fuzzy K-means clustering, Exp. Syst. Appl. **37**(3), 2696–2704 (2010)
2. CampusComputing: The Compus computing project (2013)
3. Carpineto, C., Romano, G.: Concept Data Analysis: Theory and Applications, 1 edn., 3 September 2004. Wiley (2004)
4. Ganter, B., Wille, R.: Formal Concept Analysis: Mathematical Foundations (1999)
5. Godin, R., Missaoui, R., Alaoui, H.: Incremental concept formation algorithms based on galois (concept) lattices. Comput Intell. **11**(2), 246–267 (1995)
6. Grätzer, G., et al.: General Lattice Theory, 2 edn. Birkhäuser, Basel (2003)
7. Keim, D.A., Mansmann, F., Schneidewind, J., Thomas, J., Ziegler, H.: Visual analytics: scope and challenges. In: Simoff, S.J., Böhlen, M.H., Mazeika, A. (eds.) Visual Data Mining. LNCS, vol. 4404, pp. 76–90. Springer, Heidelberg (2008). https://doi.org/10.1007/978-3-540-71080-6_6

8. Kourie, D.G., Obiedkov, S., Watson, B.W., van der Merwe, D.: An incremental algorithm to construct a lattice of set intersections. Sci. Comput. Program. **74**(3), 128–142 (2009)

9. Kuznetsov, S.: A fast algorithm for computing all intersections of objects in a finite semilattice. Autom. Documentation Math. Linguist. **27**(5), 11–21 (1993)

10. Kuznetsov, S.O.: Learning of simple conceptual graphs from positive and negative examples. In: Żytkow, J.M., Rauch, J. (eds.) PKDD 1999. LNCS (LNAI), vol. 1704, pp. 384–391. Springer, Heidelberg (1999). https://doi.org/10.1007/978-3-540-48247-5_47

11. Li, K.W., Shao, M.W., Wu, W.Z.: A data reduction method in formal fuzzy contexts. Int. J. Mach. Learn. Cybern., 1–11 (2016)

12. Li, M.Z., Wang, G.Y.: Knowledge reduction in crisply generated fuzzy concept lattices. Fundamenta Informaticae **142**(1–4), 307–335 (2015)

13. Outrata, J., Vychodil, V.: Fast algorithm for computing fixpoints of Galois connections induced by object-attribute relational data. Inf. Sci. **185**(1), 114–127 (2012)

14. Singh, P.K., Cherukuri, A.K., Li, J.: Concepts reduction in formal concept analysis with fuzzy setting using Shannon entropy. Int. J. Mach. Learn. Cybern., 1–11 (2014)

15. Romero, C., Ventura, S., Garca, E.: Data mining in course management systems: moodle case study and tutorial. Comput. Educ. **51**(1), 368–384 (2008). https://doi.org/10.1016/j.compedu.2007.05.016. http://www.sciencedirect.com/science/article/pii/S0360131507000590

16. Dias, S.M., Vieira, N.J.: Concept lattices reduction: definition, analysis and classification. Expert Syst. Appl. **42**(20), 7084–7097 (2015)

17. Tominski, C.: Event-based visualization for user-centered visual analysis. Ph.D. thesis, Institute for Computer Science, University of Rostock (2006)

18. Wikipedia: LMS and CMS compared (2015)

19. Zou, L., Zhang, Z., Long, J.: A fast incremental algorithm for constructing concept lattices. Expert Syst. Appl. **42**(9), 4474–4481 (2015)

Data Mining as a Cloud Service
for Learning Artificial Intelligence

Weishan Zhang[1(✉)], Hao Lv[1], Liang Xu[1], Xin Liu[1], and Jiehan Zhou[2]

[1] China University of Petroleum, Qingdao, China
{zhangws,lx}@upc.edu.cn, lvhao.upc@gmail.com,
xuliang.upc.edu@gmail.com
[2] Faculty of Information Technology and Electrical Engineering,
University of Oulu, Oulu, Finland
jiehan.zhou@oulu.fi

Abstract. Education in artificial intelligence attracts increasing attention. Data mining is an important subject in artificial intelligence. Cloud Computing can help on providing resources for education, which motivates a data mining as a cloud service (DMCS) for facilitating the learning of data mining. However there exists few DMCS, where user-friendly and easy-to-use are critical for students to access the services. Therefore in this paper, we propose the concept of data mining as a cloud service as an answer to tackle this issue. The proposed DMCS consists of all necessary steps for data mining, including data fusion and preprocessing, a comprehensive machine learning library including common algorithms and deep learning algorithms, graphical presentation of the mining results. The whole mining process has a user-friendly graphical user interface for beginners to facilitate the learning process. The demo preliminarily analyzes the power used by the DMCS service and shows the DMCS service has an outstanding effect.

Keywords: Artificial intelligence · Data mining
Data mining as a cloud service · Deep learning

1 Introduction

Recently artificial intelligence is being rapidly developed. Particularly the news astonished the world when the AlphaGo developed by DeepMind defeated the human weiqi world champion in 2016. After that, China pays high attention to research and development on artificial intelligence. This July the State Council of China issued "Development Planning for a New Generation of Artificial Intelligence", and emphasized that primary and secondary schools need to start artificial intelligence related courses.

As we know that data mining is a key subject in artificial intelligence. There needs to develop a easy to use data mining service so that students from primary and secondary schools across the country could share the learning material in

© Springer International Publishing AG, part of Springer Nature 2018
S. Satoh (Ed.): PSIVT 2017, LNCS 10799, pp. 214–221, 2018.
https://doi.org/10.1007/978-3-319-92753-4_18

the cloud. There exist a few of well-developed machine learning libraries such as Apache Mahout [1] and Spark MLlib [2]. However, they are only applied into high-level application development, e.g., pattern recognition, by experts, not into primary and secondary education. Cloud computing delivers a new model of sharing computing facilities. We propose the concept of data mining as a cloud service (DMCS) for facilitating the learning of data mining in primary and secondary schools. In the design, the DMCS integrates the workflow of data mining, including data integration, data cleaning, data standardization, data mining and data visualization. In addition, the DMCS has a user-friendly GUI for students who don't have rich knowledge about programming, data mining and artificial intelligence.

Some work has been reported on developing a data mining service and its application to education. For example, Azure Machine Learning [3] provides a new way to construct and operate Machine Learning workflow on Azure. But it is not suitable for beginners. Cristobal,Romero introduced and reviewed key milestones and the current state of affairs in the field of EDM, together with specific applications, tools, and future insights. This inspired our work and we thought that a data mining service for student is needed. Villegas-Ch [4] applied data mining techniques into existing Learning Management Systems. The systems can customize learning services for individual students. Blikstein and Worsley [5] utilized computational technologies to measure complex learning tasks. Angeli et al. [6] presented two case studies. The first one presents how Education Data Mining can be used to advance education software evaluation. The second study presents how education technologists can use Education Data Mining for guiding and monitoring students' learning because have different learning environment and lots of factors affecting students' experience. However those work is not designed for beginners from primary and secondary schools. Bhise et al. [7] analysed how different factor affect a students learning behavior and performance using academic career using K-Means (Clustering) in an educational institute. It's a typical application of data mining in education with efficient results. But it's a work by researchers not students. Our target is to make students the protagonist of data mining and to stimulate their interest.

We design and develop a data mining as a cloud service, which is called DMCS. It has the following two main advantages. First it covers the whole steps of data mining, from the data integration to the result display. Second the service has a user-friendly GUI which provides an intuitive interface to easily operate for beginners from primary and secondary schools.

The remainder of the paper is organized as the follows: Sect. 2 presents the DMCS architecture. Section 3 presents the implementation of DMCS main components. Section 4 demonstrates and analyzes the power usage by using the DMCS in an apartment. Section 5 discusses the future work for the DMCS and concludes the paper.

2   DMCS Architecture

Based on our previously designed intelligent video processing platform [8], we
integrate the DMCS requirements into the platform. The DMCS architecture is
show as Fig. 1.

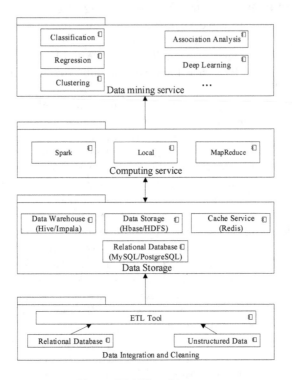

Fig. 1. DMCS architecture

As illustrated in Fig. 1, the DMCS architecture consists of four layers. The
bottom layer is for data integration and data cleaning. The second layer is for
the pre-processed data storage. The third layer is for the distributed computing
service, which supports the distributed computing for data mining algorithms.
The DMCS service will process big data based on Hadoop MapReduce [9] or
Spark [10] and small data in local servers. The top layer is the DMCS data mining
as a cloud service, which wraps data mining algorithms such as classification,
clustering and deep learning into cloud services. Each algorithm has a local and
spark version for different scenarios.

3   DMCS Implementation

In this section, we introduce the DMCS implementation which mainly consists
of three parts: the big data framework for DMCS, the comprehensive DMCS
library and the DMCS GUI.

3.1 Big Data Framework for DMCS

The DMCS cloud service is based on Hadoop framework. DMCS uses storage tools such as HDFS, HBase, MySQL and Redis for different scenarios. DMCS uses Hadoop MapReduce and Spark for the support of distributed computing and uses Yarn [11] to manage all computational resources.

3.2 DMCS Library for Machine Learning

The DMCS library for machine learning integrates plenty of machine learning algorithms. The DMCS library includes regression, classification, clustering and relation analysis, etc. The DMCS library adds deep learning algorithms into the library. It also contains other algorithms for supporting data integration, data cleaning and data standardization. The DMCS library allows students to adjust parameters in algorithms.

3.3 DMCS User-Friendly Interface

The DMCS user interface aims to ease students to use the cloud service. The DMCS user interface is based on Web browsers and has the following functions.

3.3.1 Resource Management

The resource management is divided into input data and computing resource management. The input data which needs to be processed can be visualized in the data management. And all the algorithms in DMCS are listed by types. Students can look for an algorithm and search a saved task flow. The computing resource management is to manage computing resource for lots of tasks running on the cluster efficiently. Before a data mining task starts to be executed, students can allocate appropriate computing resources for the task to maximize resource utilization. Students can also monitor the status of a cluster in real time. An example of DMCS GUI for data management is shown in Fig. 2. We can see that with the use of DMCS GUI, students can manage different databases by adding or removing data resources efficiently. There is also a SQL label management GUI as shown in Fig. 3.

Fig. 2. DMCS data management

Fig. 3. DMCS SQL management

3.3.2 Task Flow Customization

The task flow customization is indispensable in DMCS. We design a drag-and-drop module for this function. Students can select elements including data integration, data cleaning, data standardization, data mining algorithms and different data sources. After the selection, students can drag those selected elements to work panel and connect elements. Students can also adjust algorithms parameters based on a given problem. In the end, students save the task flow and execute it. Figure 4 illustrates the DMCS GUI for customizing a task flow.

Fig. 4. Task flow customization in DMCS

3.3.3 Task Monitoring

Students can monitor the status of a submitted task through Web. Students can execute a task manually, or in a given time or periodically in DMCS. With the use of task monitoring, students can check the start time, finish time and results for a submitted task. If the submitted task has errors, students can check the log to debug the program. When students find a problem in the submitted task, they can kill the task and resubmit it. Figure 5 illustrates the DMCS task monitoring GUI and Fig. 6 illustrates the DMCS task submitting GUI.

Fig. 5. DMCS task monitoring GUI

Fig. 6. DMCS task submitting GUI

4 DMCS Demonstration

To verify DMCS, we made a demo to analyze and predict the electricity usage in an apartment based on historical data. Figure 7 illustrates a sample DMCS workflow, which is also a standard data mining work flow.

```
 ○ → [data integration] → [data cleaning] → [data standardization]
 ◎ ← [results visualization] ← [data mining]
```

Fig. 7. A sample DMCS work flow

In the demo, first we collect and fuse the data on electricity usage from different databases. Then we build a table contains data on electricity usage. In the step of cleaning data, we delete the data which is beyond the given ranges. We distribute all data between 0 and 1. After pre-processing data, we train a model to predict efficiency based on the historical data. We select XGBoost [12] to analyze and predict the electricity usage. In the demo, we select ninety percent of the data as the training dataset and the remaining ten percent is used to test the prediction. The average root-mean-square error (RMSE) of the XGBoost model is 0.033 as show in Table 1. We can see that DMCS can obtain an outstanding performance on analyzing the electricity usage.

Table 1. RMSE of XGBoost

Experiment no.	1	2	3	4	5	Average
RMSE	0.03	0.02	0.03	0.06	0.03	0.033

5 Discussion

The advantages of the DMCS service can be summarized into the following two points.

- **The DMCS service is comprehensive.** First, DMCS has a comprehensive algorithm library. Second, DMCS contains several machine learning algorithms and deep learning algorithms. The task flow of data mining in DMCS is also complete from different data integration to mining result visualization. Third, DMCS supports not only big data mining but also functions such as cluster data management and task monitoring.
- **The DMCS GUI is user-friendly.** As we mentioned before, most of existing work doesn't provide a GUI. The DMCS provides a drag-and-drop-based GUI for beginners to customize data mining tasks. The DMCS enables students to monitor the status of a cluster, a task process, input data and visualize mining results through Web browsers. In addition, DMCS provides a GUI for students to adjust parameters used in data mining algorithms. The DMCS is quite suitable for those beginners who are not familiar with machine learning algorithms.

6   Conclusions and Future Work

This paper tackles the challenge of facilitating the learning of data mining for students from primary and secondary schools. We propose the concept of Data Mining as a Cloud Service - DMCS. We design and develop the DMCS architecture and make a preliminary demo to analyze the DMCS computing power usage in an apartment. The result shows DMCS has an outstanding effect. We state that the DMCS method is feasible, available and reliable for students from primary and secondary schools with the integration of most of data mining algorithms and a user-friendly interface. DMCS can help students to discover artificial intelligence and cultivate their interests in artificial intelligence.

In the future, we plan to develop a smart task scheduling module into DMCS for dispatching tasks in context of computing resource, space and task priorities. We will continuously optimize the DMCS GUI.

References

1. http://mahout.apache.org/
2. http://spark.apache.org/mllib/
3. Barga, R., Fontama, V., Tok, W.H.: Predictive Analytics with Microsoft Azure Machine Learning, pp. 21–42 (2014)
4. Villegas-Ch, W., Luján-Mora, S.: Analysis of data mining techniques applied to LMS for personalized education. In: IEEE World Engineering Education Conference (EDUNINE), pp. 85–89. IEEE (2017)
5. Blikstein, P., Worsley, M.: Multimodal learning analytics and education data mining: using computational technologies to measure complex learning tasks. J. Learn. Anal. **3**(2), 220–238 (2016)
6. Angeli, C., Howard, S., Ma, J., Yang, J., Kirschner, P.A.: Data mining in educational technology classroom research: can it make a contribution? Comput. Educ. **113**, 226–242 (2017)

7. Bhise, R., Thorat, S., Supekar, A.: Importance of data mining in higher education system. IOSR J. Hum. Soc. Sci. (IOSR-JHSS) **6**(6), 18–21 (2013). ISSN: 2279-0837

8. Zhang, W., Xu, L., Li, Z., Lu, Q., Liu, Y.: A deep-intelligence framework for online video processing. IEEE Softw. **33**(2), 44–51 (2016)

9. Dean, J., Ghemawat, S.: Mapreduce: simplified data processing on large clusters. Commun. ACM **51**(1), 107–113 (2008)

10. Zaharia, M., Chowdhury, M., Franklin, M.J., Shenker, S., Stoica, I.: Spark: cluster computing with working sets. HotCloud **10**(10), 95 (2010)

11. Vavilapalli, V.K., Murthy, A.C., Douglas, C., Agarwal, S., Konar, M., Evans, R., Graves, T., Lowe, J., Shah, H., Seth, S., et al.: Apache Hadoop Yarn: yet another resource negotiator. In: Proceedings of the 4th Annual Symposium on Cloud Computing, p. 5. ACM (2013)

12. Chen, T., Guestrin, C.: XGboost: a scalable tree boosting system. In: Proceedings of the 22nd ACM SIGKDD International Conference on Knowledge Discovery and Data Mining, pp. 785–794. ACM (2016)

Vision Meets Graphics

Workshop on Vision Meets Graphics (VG 2017)

The Second Workshop on Vision Meets Graphics (VG2017) was held in conjunction with the 8th Pacific-Rim Symposium on Video and Image Technology (PSIVT 2017), in Wuhan, China, on November 21, 2017.

Recent years have seen the convergence of computer graphics and computer vision. Image processing and computer vision techniques provide computer graphics with the means to create richer models and renderings than is practically possible when using purely synthetic models. Conversely, computer graphics can inform computer vision. For example, physical-based models can act as priors to computer vision algorithms. We believe graphics and vision can be mutually beneficial. Computer graphics/computer vision convergence has many possible applications, such as augmented environments, videoconferencing, post-production of films, computer games, interactive TV, education and training, video-based consumer electronics, and scientific imaging.

VG 2017 received 39 full-paper submissions, each of which was reviewed by three reviewers. This substantial increase in the number of submissions from the last workshop required us to substantially expand the Program Committee, and also enabled us to be very selective when deciding on the program. A total of 10 papers were selected for the workshop, and are collected in these proceedings.

We were fortunate to have four invited speakers at the workshop, who have worked extensively in the convergence area of computer graphics and computer vision: Reinhard Klette (Auckland University of Technology) and Dongwei Liu (Zhejiang University of Finance and Economics) whose talk was on "Stereo Vision for Artistic Photo Rendering," Shuaicheng Liu (University of Electronic Science and Technology of China) whose talk was on "MeshFlow for Application of Video Editing," and Ming-Ming Cheng (Nankai University) whose talk was on "Weakly Supervised Image Understanding with Graphics and Vision Applications." We would like to thank the invited speakers as well as all the members of the Program Committee for their help in organizing and running this event.

October 2017

Paul L. Rosin
Taehyun Rhee
Yu-Kun Lai
Fang-Lue Zhang

Organization

Workshop Organizers

Paul L. Rosin   Cardiff University, UK
Taehyun Rhee   Victoria University of Wellington, New Zealand
Yu-Kun Lai   Cardiff University, UK
Fang-Lue Zhang   Victoria University of Wellington, New Zealand

Program Committee

Ognjen Arandjelovic   University of St. Andrews, UK
Kyungim Baek   University of Hawaii, USA
Pierre Bénard   University of Bordeaux, France
Toby Breckon   Durham University, UK
Andrew Calway   University of Bristol, UK
Junjie Cao   Dalian University of Technology, China
Nathan Carr   Adobe Research, USA
Jian Chang   Bournemouth University, UK
Jongmoo Choi   University of Southern California, USA
Nicholas Costen   Manchester Metropolitan University, UK
Patrice Delmas   The University of Auckland, New Zealand
Bailin Deng   Cardiff University, UK
Neil Dodgson   Victoria University of Wellington, New Zealand
Hui Fang   Edge Hill University, UK
Bob Fisher   University of Edinburgh, UK
Wenyong Gong   Jinan University, China
Lewis Griffin   University College London, UK
Peter Hall   University of Bath, UK
Richard Harvey   University of East Anglia, UK
Junho Kim   Kookmin University, South Korea
Bo Li   Nanchang Hangkong University, China
Ik Soo Lim   Bangor University, UK
Chang Liu   Beihang University, China
Shao-Ping Lu   Vrije Universiteit Brussel, Belgium
Wei Ma   Beijing University of Technology, China
Brendan McCane   University of Otago, New Zealand
David Mould   Carleton University, Canada
Taijiang Mu   Tsinghua University, China
Yongwei Nie   China University of Technology, China
Zhibin Niu   Tianjin University, China

Crowd Counting from a Still Image Using Multi-scale Fully Convolutional Network with Adaptive Human-Shaped Kernel

Jinmeng Cao, Biao Yang$^{(\boxtimes)}$, Yuyu Zhang, and Ling Zou

Changzhou University, Changzhou, Jiangsu, China
yb6864171@cczu.edu.cn

Abstract. Crowd count estimation from a still crowd image with arbitrary perspective and density level is one of the challenges in crowd analysis. Techniques developed in the past performed poorly in highly congested scenes with several thousands of people. To resolve the problem, we propose a Multi-scale Fully Convolutional Network for robust crowd counting, that is achieved through estimating density map. Our approach consists of the following contributions: (1) an adaptive human-shaped kernel is proposed to generate the ground truth of the density map. (2) A deep, multi-scale, fully convolutional network is proposed to predict crowd counts. Per-scale loss is used to guarantee the effectiveness of multi-scale strategy. (3) Several attempts, e.g. de-convolutional and minimizing per-scale loss, are tried to improve the counting performance of the proposed approach. Our approach can adapt to not only sparse scenes, but also dense ones. In addition, it achieves the state-of-the-art counting performance in benchmarking datasets, including the World Expo'10, the UCF_CC_50, and the UCSD datasets.

Keywords: Adaptive human-shaped kernel · Crowd counting
Fully convolutional network · Multi-scale · Per-scale loss

1 Introduction

With the growth of the global population and the increase of urban population mobility, it is common that crowd disasters happened owing to a large number of intensive groups. For example, on New Year's Eve in 2015, 35 people were killed in a massive stampede in Shanghai, China. The incident investigation report shows that these events both lacked inadequate preparation for the prevention of mass activities, poor management of the site and improper handling caused by crowded trampling. As a result, it caused heavy casualties and serious consequences. If you can be prior to count up the number of people in the region and give rapid and reasonable guidance when the accident occurred, it will greatly reduce the number of casualties or even completely avoid the danger. So how to effectively manage the crowded places has attracted more and more attention

© Springer International Publishing AG, part of Springer Nature 2018
S. Satoh (Ed.): PSIVT 2017, LNCS 10799, pp. 227–240, 2018.
https://doi.org/10.1007/978-3-319-92753-4_19

from all over the world, and accurate estimation of the number of persons in public areas is extremely important information for safety control to prevent crowd disasters. Thus, many researchers have proposed strategies for automatic crowd counting based on computer vision.

Existing crowd counting methods are divided into three categories: counting by detection, counting by clustering, and counting by regression [1]. The former two methods perform well when the crowds appear sparse. However, errors may exist in detecting or clustering individuals when the crowds suffer from serious occlusions. Aiming to solve the problem, counting by regression method learns a direct mapping between crowd features and its count without detecting or clustering. Thus, it is more effective to count the crowd in the manner of regression in congested environments. Therefore, the main focus is how extract hand-crafted features and how to train a robust regression model. In spite of the widely researches on the above two issues, there are still shortages in them.

Recently, deep neural network provides a new solution to simultaneously extract features and learn a regression model. In our work, a Multi-scale fully convolutional network (MSFCN) is proposed for robust crowd counting. We also propose an adaptive human-shape kernel to generate the density map. Several attempts are tried to improve the performance of the proposed model. Finally, three benchmarking datasets are used to evaluate our approach, by comparing with the state-of-the-arts.

2   Related Work

Existing crowd counting techniques generally fall into three categories: counting by detection, clustering, and regression.

In counting by detection, crowd counts are always estimated by detecting the entire people in the scene. Some researchers also concentrated on the noteworthy parts of human body, such as heads and shoulders. For instance, Gao *et al.* detected heads by water filling algorithm and SVM [2]. The count of people was estimated by the number of detected heads. Unlike their approach, Luo *et al.* built a multi-view head-shoulder model to detect the number of head-shoulders [3]. Crowd counting through detecting local parts was more robust than detecting the entire body due to partial occlusion. However, almost all the detection approaches are time-consuming and sensitive to background noise.

In counting by clustering, Rao *et al.* proposed to estimate the crowd density using motion cues and hierarchical clustering [4]. It is easy to implement because it needs no prior information, such as object detectors or pre-defined features. However, motion patterns can only be extracted from image sequences. And it is also time-consuming.

Unlike the abovementioned approaches, the counting by regression method aims to learn a direct mapping between specific visual features and crowd counts. Thus, it is more practicable for counting the crowds under congested environments with reasonable time consumption. Mahdi *et al.* utilized the combination of key-point based and segment-based features, such as the size, density, and occlusion level of the crowd, to estimate its count [5]. Shafiee *et al.* proposed a novel low-complexity, scale-normalized feature called histogram of moving gradients [6]. It is a highly effective spatiotemporal representation of individuals and crowds within a video. Zhang *et al.* modeled the crowd as a flow and then a flow field texture representation was proposed to characterize the segmented crowd [7]. These approaches could achieve satisfactory performance under common conditions. However, they might fail when the crowds were heavily occluded or extremely dense.

Recently, convolutional neural network (CNN) has achieved remarkable success in pattern recognition, such as object detection, semantic segmentation, and so on. For the crowd counting problem, CNNs have been trained alternatively with two related learning objectives, namely, crowd density and crowd count. [8–10]. There are also some improvements of CNN based crowd counting. Panos *et al.* presented an efficient crowd counting approach by utilizing the responses of spatially context-aware CNN in the temporal domain [11]. Unlike the aforementioned researchers who focused on adding supplementary information into the model, some researchers focused on the structures of the network or the samples used for training. Zhang *et al.* designed a simple but effective Multi-column convolutional neural network to accurately estimate the crowd count on a still image with arbitrary crowd density and perspective [12]. Marsden *et al.* verified the superiority of fixed sampling to random sampling when collecting training samples for a fully convolutional crowd counting network [13]. Thus, we can conclude that deep neural network may provide a satisfactory solution for crowd counting in wild conditions.

3   Proposed Method

3.1   Generating the Ground Truth of Density Map

Most studies define the ground truth of the density map as a sum of Gaussian kernels, which are centered on object locations. A traditional Gaussian kernel is illustrated in Fig. 1(a). It is suitable for characterizing the density distribution of circle-like objects, such as cells and bacteria. To generate a more accurate density map, Zhang *et al.* [8] used a human-shaped Gaussian kernel. However, human shapes vary a lot in different crowds. For instance, both head and body of a pedestrian can be observed in a sparse crowd. The head is similar to a circle and the body is similar to an ellipse (Fig. 1(b)). However, bodies of different people may be severely occluded by others when the crowd is very dense. To resolve this problem, we improve the human-shaped kernel through adaptively adjusting the body part according to the crowd itself. Our adaptive human-shaped kernel is illustrated in Fig. 1(c). Compared with human-shaped kernel, our adaptive one looks like a head-shoulder model when the crowd is extremely dense. It is more close to the practical conditions than the human-shaped kernel.

The procedure of generating the ground truth of density map with adaptive human-shaped kernel is defined as follows. First, with the perspective map and

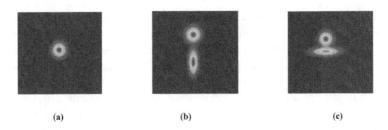

(a)   (b)   (c)

Fig. 1. Different kernels used to generate the ground truth of density map (a) Gaussian kernel; (b) Human-shaped kernel; and (c) Adaptive human-shaped kernel.

the center positions of pedestrian head P_h in the region of interest, the crowd density map can be calculated as

$$C_i(p) = \sum_{P \in P_i} \frac{1}{2\|Z\|} (N_h(p; P_h, \sigma_h) + N_b(p; P_b, \sigma_x, \sigma_y)), \tag{1}$$

where P_i is the list of labeled locations for a crowd image and Z is the actual number of people in that crowd. As shown in Eq. (1), the adaptive human-shaped kernel contains two terms, a normalized 2D Gaussian kernel N_h as a head part and a bivariate normal distribution N_b as a body part. Here P_b is the position of the body part. It is estimated based on two factors: (1) the head position P_h and (2) the density level of the crowd.

We use the average distance between the current point (represents a people) and ten nearest neighboring points to coarsely estimate the density level of the crowd. We define the average distance of the ith point as D_i, which can be represented as

$$D_i = \frac{1}{10} \sum_{j=1}^{10} d_{ij} \max_j \{d_{ij}\}, \tag{2}$$

where d_{ij} is the Euclidean distance of the i_{th} and j_{th} point. D_i is normalized to $(0,1)$ by the largest value of d_{ij}. A small D_i may indicate a dense crowd. Following Zhang et al. [8], we set the variance h = 0.2 Mp for the term Nh, where Mp is the pixel value in the perspective map. If no perspective map exists for a given scene, we roughly estimate Mp based on the vertical position of the pixel. Then, we identify the parameters of the bivariate normal distribution in consideration of the crowd density level. For the i_{th} point, its body position P_b is defined as $P_b = P_h + D_i \times M_p$ (taking top-left corner as the origin point of the image). Furthermore, we set the variance $\sigma_x = (0.6 - D_i/2)M_p$, $\sigma_y = (0.2 + D_i/2)M_p$ for the term N_b. The whole distribution is normalized by Z to ensure that the integration of all density values in a density map equals to the total crowd number in the original image.

3.2 Multi-scale Fully Convolutional Network for Crowd Counting

An overview of our MSFCN model is illustrated in Fig. 2. The input data are patches that are extracted from a still crowd image. Our model is similar to Multi-column CNN proposed by Zhang *et al.* [12]. There are three CNN channels in MSFCN. While considering the input data usually contain heads of different sizes due to perspective distortion, our Multi-scale strategy preprocesses the input data in three different scales (the original patch, $1/4_{th}$ of the patch and the $1/16_{th}$ of the patch). Per-scale loss is used and minimized to guarantee the effective of the multi-scale strategy. Furthermore, de-convolutional layers are added in each channels, not only to guarantee a same size ($W \times H$) for features to be merged, but also to account for the loss of details due to earlier pooling layers.

As illustrated in Fig. 2, filters of different sizes are labeled using different colors. Legend on the right-top corner indicates the colors and their corresponding sizes. The input data of each channel has different scales, thus, filters with different receptive fields are used to capture characteristics of crowd density. Generally speaking, filters with larger receptive fields are more effective for modeling the density maps corresponding to larger heads. We use less number of filters for CNN channels with larger receptive fields to reduce the computational complexity (the number of parameters to be optimized). The 2nd and 3rd layers in each channel are both followed by two 2×2 max-pooling layers. Thus, the spatial resolution is reduced by $1/4$ for each patch. Each convolution layer (except conv6) is followed by a dropout layer (with parameter 0.3), a parametric rectified linear unit activation function [14], and a local response normalization layer. We do not list them in Fig. 2 for simplification. For the 5th convolution layer in

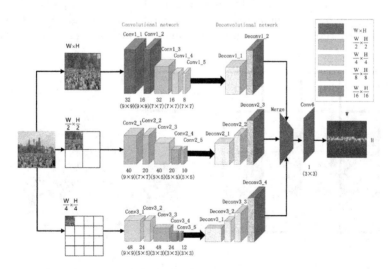

Fig. 2. Pipeline of the proposed MSFCN model. Dropout, PReLU, and LRN are not listed for simplification.

each channel, we adopt de-convolution operation for up-sampling. Times of de-convolution operation depend on the size of output features produced by the 5th convolution layer. For example, we adopt 4 de-convolution layers to enlarge the feature size from $\frac{W}{16} \times \frac{H}{16}$ to $W \times H$ in the 3rd channel. Furthermore, we improve traditional FCN model through using 3×3 filter in the 6th convolutional layer, instead of 1×1 filter, to map the fused feature into a one-output feature map. It is difficult to consider the local relationship between neighboring pixels if we use 1×1 filter. However, the network can capture contextual information if we use 3×3 filters [15]. Thus, it may have a sound ability to fit actual scenes.

3.3 Details

3.3.1 Details of Training and Testing

In the training stage, we adopt the non-overlapping sampling manner as proposed in [16]. Sindagi *et al.* argued that non-overlapping sampling is superior to overlapping sampling because too much redundant information exists in the overlapped patches. As illustrated in Fig. 3(a), the input image is divided into sixteen patches equally, and the density map of each patch is calculated as the ground truth for training the network. It is also classified that the generalization ability of MSFCN will go bad due to the similarity of the training patches if we adopt the overlapping sampling strategy.

In the testing stage, we do not consider the generalization ability of the network. Thus, we sample multiple overlapping patches from the input crowd image (as illustrated in Fig. 3(b)). For example, we initially sample the patch which is in the black box, and then sampled next patch in the red dotted box (the stride between two patches is set to be 10 pixels). The density map of the crowd image is then calculated by summing up the density map of each patch. Considering the overlapping among different patches, some regions of the whole density map are repeatedly accumulated. Thus, the cumulative frequency at each

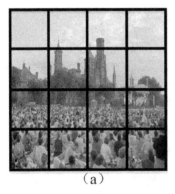 

(a)   (b)

Fig. 3. Different sampling manners. (a) Non-overlapping sampling strategy used in training stage, and (b) Overlapping sampling strategy used in testing stage. (Color figure online)

location of each patch is counted, then, it is used to be divided by the value of the density map at that location. After obtaining the density map of the whole image, the total crowd count is calculated through integration over the density map. Notably, the total number is a decimal, but not an integer.

3.3.2 Details of Loss Function

The MSFCN is intended to estimate the numbers of crowd by means of patch-based density map, and the Euclidean distance is used to measure the difference between the estimated density map and its ground truth. The Euclidean loss is defined as follows:

$$P(Y = y_i | x_i, \theta) = \frac{1}{2N} \sum_{i=1}^{N} \| f(x_i, \theta) - y_i \|_2^2 \tag{3}$$

where N is the number of training patches, θ is a set of network parameters, x_i is the input i^{th} patch, $f(x_i, \theta)$ stands for the estimated i^{th} density map and y represents the corresponding ground truth of the density map.

Inspired by the success of several works [17–19] about scale attention, we use per-scale loss that can make the learned features from multiple scales more discriminative, and thus improve the counting performance. The per-scale loss function P-L is defined as follows:

$$P - L = - \sum_{i=1}^{N} \log P(Y = y^i | x^i, \theta) + \sum_{j=1}^{M} -\alpha_i \times \left(\sum_{i=1}^{N} \log P(Y = y_i^j | x_i^j, \theta) \right), \tag{4}$$

where M represents the number of scales we use, α_i represents the weight for i^{th} scale. x^j, y^j represent the output and groundtruth, respectively. We initialize α_i to be larger in order to learn discriminative features for each scale. We then gradually decrease their values and focus on the training of the joint prediction.

Table 1. Parameter settings of the proposed MSFCN.

Parameters	Value
Learning rate	0.001
Learning policy	"inv"
Power	0.75
Gamma	0.001
Max iterations	2000000
Momentum	0.9
Weight decay	0.05
Optimization type	Adam

3.3.3   Implementing Details of MSFCN

Table 1 lists the parameter settings of the MSFCN in detail. The model is operated on NVIDIA GTX 1080 GPU (8G) using the Caffe framework. We set the batch size to 16 during training due to memory limitations. MSRA is used for initialization of each convolution layer.

4   Experimental Analysis

4.1   Evaluation Metrics

We evaluate different approaches by two indicators, the absolute error (MAE) and the mean squared error (MSE), which are defined as follows:

$$MAE = \frac{1}{N_t} \sum_{1}^{N_t} |z_i - \widehat{z_i}|, \tag{5}$$

$$MSE = \sqrt{\frac{1}{N_t} \sum_{1}^{N_t} (z_i - \widehat{z_i})^2}, \tag{6}$$

where N_t is the number of test images, z_i is the actual number of people in the ith image, and $\widehat{z_i}$ is the estimated number of people in the ith image. Generally speaking, MAE indicates the accuracy of the estimates, and MSE indicates the robustness of the estimates.

4.2   Evaluations of MSFCN

4.2.1   Evaluations of the Adaptive Human Shape Kernel

Table 2 shows the performance of different density maps that are generated using different kernels. A five-fold cross-validation is used to calculate MAE and MSE. It is obvious that our adaptive human-shaped kernel outperforms other two kernels, especially in the very crowded UCF_CC_50 dataset.

Table 2. Evaluations of different density maps in benchmarking datasets.

	Traditional Gaussian kernel		Human-shape kernel		Adaptive human-shape kernel	
	MAE	MSE	MAE	MSE	MAE	MSE
UCSD	2.41	3.96	2.23	3.52	**2.14**	**3.18**
UCF_CC_50	427	590	402	552	**395**	**510**
World Expo '10	11.2	N/A	10.8	N/A	**9.1**	N/A

4.3   Comparisons with State-of-the-art Approaches

We evaluate our approach with several state-of-the-art approaches in three benchmarking datasets, including the UCSD, the UCF_CC_50 and World Expo'10 datasets.

4.3.1   Comparisons in UCSD Dataset

This UCSD dataset contains 2,000 frames of size from the video sequence along with ground truth annotations of each pedestrian in every fifth frame in the UCSD campus [20]. The frame size is 158 × 238 and it is recoded at 10 fps. There are only about 25 individuals on average in each frame. The dataset contains a total of 49,885 pedestrian instances and it is split into the training set (frame 600 to 1,399) and the test set (the rest 1,200 frames). Generally speaking, this dataset consists of low density crowd images and there is no obvious variation in the scene perspective across images.

Table 3 shows the comparison results between our approach and several state-of-the-art approaches in UCSD dataset, which is relatively sparse. We train our model on training set (frame 600 to 1,399) and then evaluate it on test set (the rest 1,200 frames) according to the official segmentation of this dataset. For our approach, we repeat the training and evaluation procedures five times and then calculate the mean values of MAE and MSE. The results indicate that our approach outperforms the approaches used for comparison in terms of MAE and MSE. Meanwhile, some typical estimating results are illustrated in Fig. 4. It is obvious that the estimated crowd counts are very close to its ground truth.

Table 3. Comparisons with the state-of-the-art approaches in UCSD dataset

Method	MAE	MSE
Chan et al. [20]	2.24	7.97
An et al. [21]	2.16	7.45
Chen et al. [22]	2.25	7.82
Chen et al. [23]	2.07	6.86
Zhang et al. [8]	**1.6**	3.31
Our approach	2.14	**3.18**

4.3.2   Comparisons in UCF_CC_50 Dataset

The UCF_CC_50 dataset [24] is initially introduced by Idrees et al. This dataset contains 50 images created from publicly available web images, which includes scenes such as concerts, protests, stadiums and marathons. It is a very challenging dataset, because of not only limited number of images, but also the crowd count of the image changes dramatically. The head counts range between 94 and 4,543 with an average of 1,280 individuals per image. The authors provide 63,974 annotations in total for these fifty images.

Fig. 4. Ground truth and prediction of our approach in UCSD dataset.

Table 4. Comparisons with the state-of-the-art approaches in UCF_CC_50 dataset

Method	MAE	MSE
Idress *et al.* [24]	468.0	590.3
Rodriguez *et al.* [25]	655.7	697.8
Lempitsky *et al.* [26]	493.4	**487.1**
Zhang *et al.* [8]	467.0	498.5
Our approach	**395.0**	510.2

Table 4 shows the comparison results between our approach and several state-of-the-art approaches in UCF_CC_50 dataset. We employ this dataset for comparative evaluation because it is hard to predict a precise number of people in such extremely dense crowds. A five-fold cross-validation is used to evaluate this dataset. As shown in the table, our method achieves the best performance than other approaches in terms of MAE, while Lempitsky *et al.* achieves the best performance in terms of MSE. However, our MSE is just a little higher than that of Lempitsky *et al.* Some typical estimating results are illustrated in Fig. 5. It can be concluded from the figure that our approach can even estimate the counts of extremely dense crowds.

Fig. 5. Ground truth and prediction of our approach in UCF_CC_50 dataset.

4.3.3   Comparisons in World Expo'10 Dataset

This World Expo'10 dataset is first proposed by Zhang *et al.* [8]. To the best of our knowledge, this is the largest dataset focusing on cross-scene counting. This large-scale dataset contains 1,132 annotated video sequences, which are captured by 108 surveillance cameras, all from Shanghai 2010 World Expo event. It consists of a total of 3,980 frames of size 576 × 720 with 199,923 labeled pedestrians. The number of individuals varies from 1 to 253, with an average of 50 individuals per image.

Table 5 gives the comparison results in World Expo'10 dataset, which owns crowds of medium density level. This dataset is recently used to evaluate different

Table 5. Comparisons with the state-of-the-art approaches in World Expo'10 dataset

Method	MAE
Zhang *et al.* [8]	12.9
Rodriguez *et al.* [25]	11.6
Lempitsky *et al.* [26]	13.4
Zhang *et al.* [8]	9.4
Our approach	**9.2**

crowd counting approaches. It is officially split into training and test sets. We train our model on the training set and evaluated it on a test set. We repeat this procedure five times for the sake of fairness. Notably, we only calculate the MAE because only MAE are reported in original works that are used for comparison. As shown in Table 5, our approach achieves the best performance among several state-of-the-art counting approaches. Meanwhile, our approach almost estimates the identical crowd counts as the ground truth (Fig. 6). Both results indicate the superiority of our approach to the used state-of-the-art approaches.

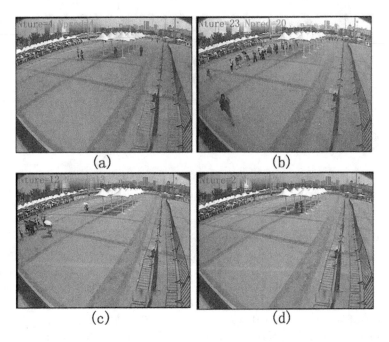

Fig. 6. Ground truth and prediction of our approach in World Expo'10 dataset.

5   Conclusion

In this work, we propose a crowd counting approach with MSFCN and adaptive human-shaped kernel. The kernel is used to generate the ground truth of density map. Comparisons with Gaussian kernel and human-shaped kernel indicate the effectiveness of our adaptive human-shape kernel, especially in extremely dense crowds. MSFCN is trained to predict the crowd counts due to its high performance in processing input of different scales. Several attempts are tried to improve the counting performance of the proposed approach. For instance, we extract features from different scales through minimizing per-scale loss. We up-sample feature maps in different CNN channels through de-convolution to compensate for the detail loss in the early pooling layers. We replace the final

1×1 convolutional kernel with a 3×3 convolutional kernel to capture contextual information. Finally, we compare our approach with several state-of-the-art crowd counting approaches in three benchmarking datasets. The results indicate that our approach can achieve the state-of-the-art performance. Our future work will focus on improving the generalization ability by employing transfer learning.

Acknowledgement. This work has been supported by the National Natural Science Foundation of China under Grant No. 61501060, the Natural Science Foundation of Jiangsu Province under Grant No. BK20150271, Key Laboratory for New Technology Application of Road Conveyance of Jiangsu Province under Grant BM20082061708.

References

1. Ryan, D., Denman, S., Sriharan, S., et al.: An evaluation of crowd counting methods, features and regression models. Comput. Vis. Image. Und. **130**, 1–17 (2015)
2. Gao, C.Q., Liu, J., Feng, Q., et al.: People-flow counting in complex environments by combining depth and color information. Multimedia Tools Appl. **75**(15), 9315–9331 (2016)
3. Luo, J., Wang, J., Xu, H., et al.: Real-time people counting for indoor scenes. Sig. Process. **124**, 27–35 (2016)
4. Rao, A.S., Gubbi, J., Marusic, S., et al.: Estimation of crowd density by clustering motion cues. Vis. Comput. **31**(11), 1533–1552 (2016)
5. Hashemzadeh, M., Farajzadeh, N.: Combining keypoint-based and segment-based features for counting people in crowded scenes. Inf. Sci. **345**, 199–216 (2016)
6. Siva, P., Shafiee, M.J., Jamieson, M., et al.: Scene Invariant Crowd Segmentation and Counting Using Scale-Normalized Histogram of Moving Gradients (HoMG). arXiv preprint arXiv:1602.00386 (2016)
7. Zhang, X., He, H., Cao, S., et al.: Flow field texture representation-based motion segmentation for crowd counting. Mach. Vis. Appl. **26**(7–8), 871–883 (2015)
8. Zhang, C., Li, H., Wang, X., et al.: Cross-scene crowd counting via deep convolutional neural networks. In: Proceedings of the IEEE Conference on Computer Vision and Pattern Recognition, pp. 833–841 (2015)
9. Oñoro-Rubio, D., López-Sastre, R.J.: Towards perspective-free object counting with deep learning. In: Leibe, B., Matas, J., Sebe, N., Welling, M. (eds.) ECCV 2016. LNCS, vol. 9911, pp. 615–629. Springer, Cham (2016). https://doi.org/10.1007/978-3-319-46478-7_38
10. Hu, Y., Chang, H., Nian, F., et al.: Dense crowd counting from still images with convolutional neural networks. J. Vis. Commun. Image Representation **38**, 530–539 (2016)
11. Sourtzinos, P., Velastin, S.A., Jara, M., Zegers, P., Makris, D.: People counting in videos by fusing temporal cues from spatial context-aware convolutional neural networks. In: Hua, G., Jégou, H. (eds.) ECCV 2016. LNCS, vol. 9914, pp. 655–667. Springer, Cham (2016). https://doi.org/10.1007/978-3-319-48881-3_46
12. Zhang, Y., Zhou, D., Chen, S., et al.: Single-image crowd counting via multi-column convolutional neural network. In: Proceedings of the IEEE Conference on Computer Vision and Pattern Recognition, pp. 589–597 (2016)
13. Marsden, M., McGuiness, K., Little, S., et al.: Fully Convolutional Crowd Counting On Highly Congested Scenes. arXiv preprint arXiv:1612.00220 (2016)

14. Zeiler, M.D., Ranzato, M., Monga, R.: On rectified linear units for speech processing. In: IEEE International Conference on Acoustics, Speech and Signal Processing (ICASSP), pp. 3517–3521 (2013)
15. Wang, T., Li, G., Lei, J., Li, S., Xu, S.: Crowd counting based on MMCNN in still images. In: Sharma, P., Bianchi, F.M. (eds.) SCIA 2017. LNCS, vol. 10269, pp. 468–479. Springer, Cham (2017). https://doi.org/10.1007/978-3-319-59126-1_39
16. Sindagi, V.A., Patel, V.M.: CNN-based cascaded multi-task learning of high-level prior and density estimation for crowd counting. arXiv preprint arXiv:1707.09605, pp. 833–841 (2017)
17. Liang, X., Wei, Y., Shen, X., et al.: Proposal-free network for instance-level object segmentation. arXiv preprint arXiv:1509.02636 (2015)
18. Chen, L.C., Yang, Y., Wang, J., et al.: Attention to scale: scale-aware semantic image segmentation. In: Proceedings of the IEEE Conference on Computer Vision and Pattern Recognition, pp. 3640–3649 (2016)
19. He, D., Yang, X., Liang, C., et al.: Multi-scale FCN with cascaded instance aware segmentation for arbitrary oriented word spotting in the wild. In: Proceedings of the IEEE Conference on Computer Vision and Pattern Recognition, pp. 3519–3528 (2017)
20. Chan, A.B., Liang, Z.S.J., Vasconcelos, N.: Privacy preserving crowd monitoring: counting people without people models or tracking. In: IEEE Conference on Computer Vision and Pattern Recognition, CVPR 2008, pp. 1–7 (2008)
21. An, S., Liu, W., Venkatesh, S.: Face recognition using kernel ridge regression. In: IEEE Conference on Computer Vision and Pattern Recognition, CVPR 2007, vol. 130, pp. 1–7 (2007)
22. Chen, K., Loy, C.C., Gong, S., et al.: Feature mining for localised crowd counting. In: BMVC, vol. 1, no. 2, p. 3 (2012)
23. Chen, K., Gong, S., Xiang, T., et al.: Cumulative attribute space for age and crowd density estimation. In: Proceedings of the IEEE Conference on Computer Vision and Pattern Recognition, vol. 124, pp. 2467–2474 (2013)
24. Idrees, H., Saleemi, I., Seibert, C., et al.: Multi-source multi-scale counting in extremely dense crowd images. In: CVPR, vol. 31, no. 11, pp. 2547–2554 (2013)
25. Rodriguez, M., Laptev, I., Sivic, J., et al: Density-aware person detection and tracking in crowds. In: IEEE International Conference on Computer Vision (ICCV), pp. 2423–2430 (2011)
26. Lempitsky, V., Zisserman, A.: Learning to count objects in images. In: Advances in Neural Information Processing Systems, pp. 1324–1332 (2010)

On Road Vehicle Detection Using an Improved Faster RCNN Framework with Small-Size Region Up-Scaling Strategy

Biao Yang[✉], Yuyu Zhang, Jinmeng Cao, and Ling Zou

Changzhou University, Changzhou, Jiangsu, China
yb6864171@cczu.edu.cn

Abstract. Vehicle active safety technology (VAST) is the precondition of intelligent vehicle. VAST is useful to reduce traffic accidents, as well as to guarantee the personal and property security of the drivers. Vehicle detection plays as the foundation of VAST, however, it suffers from many challenges, e.g. partial occlusion, severe weather conditions, and perspective distortion. We employ the faster region convolution neural network (Faster RCNN) model in this work. We specialize it to vehicle detection through fine-tuning the model with vehicle samples. Full convolution layers and region proposal network are improved to enhance the detection performance of small-size vehicles. A small region up-sampling strategy is proposed to further improve the detection performance if the image is captured by a camera mounted on a vehicle. The effectiveness of the proposed approach is demonstrated through experiments in our own dataset and two benchmarking ones. Comparisons with baseline Faster RCNN indicate the superiority of our approach.

Keywords: Faster RCNN · Vehicle detection
Densely connected layers · Region proposal network · Fine-tunning

1 Introduction

Rapid increase of vehicles has brought about many problems, e.g. environmental pollution, traffic congestion, and traffic accidents. Among them, traffic accidents may cause great damages to both life and property, thus lead to enormous negative effects to the society. The rear-end collision traffic accidents take more than 30% of all traffic accidents. These accidents can be avoided if early warnings are given to the drivers [1], based on the results of vehicle detection. Vehicles can be detected by different techniques, e.g. radar, infrared ray, and vision sensors. In general, vision based vehicle detection has many advantages, e.g. easy implementation, low cost, and high performance which depends on the vehicle detection algorithms. Despite its wonderful effects, vision based vehicle detection suffers from many challenges, e.g. partial occlusion, appearance differences

S. Satoh (Ed.): PSIVT 2017, LNCS 10799, pp. 241–253, 2018.
https://doi.org/10.1007/978-3-319-92753-4_20

among different vehicles, scale variations. In consideration of these challenges and the broad prospect, vision based vehicle detection has become an urgent need, which has led to an increasing focus in recent years.

So far, vision based vehicle detection has focused on designing hand-crafted features, such as Haar [2], Gabor filters [3], and histogram of oriented gradient (HOG) features [4]. Some researchers improved HOG and proposed local structured HOG [5] and PIHOG [6]. Other researchers tried to combine different features, for instance, Sun *et al.* [7] combined Haar and Gabor features together to robustly characterize the properties of a vehicle. These features have been commonly integrated along with object proposal methods, which can provide a set of potential regions where to look for the vehicles [8–11]. For instance, Haselhoff *et al.* proposed an adaptive sliding window based on prior information such as position of the camera, distance between the camera and target, and size of the target [8]. Further, Sudowe *et al.* added geometric constrains on adaptive sliding window to increase its robustness in vehicle detection [9]. Finally, different classifiers (e.g. Support vector machine (SVM) [12], extreme learning machine [13], and Adaboost [14]) are utilized to judge whether the proposal region belongs to a vehicle. Although these approaches achieve good performance under ideal conditions, they cannot perform satisfactory under the above mentioned challenges.

Recently, deep neural network (DNN) has been successfully applied to many visual tasks, such as object detection and location, human re-identification and face recognition. DNN can automatically extract task related features, which always outperform traditional hand-crafted features. A lot of efforts focus on object detection among enormous of deep learning based applications. Many state-of-the-art general object detection frameworks, e.g., region convolution neural network (RCNN) [15], Fast RCNN [16], Faster RCNN [17], YOLO [18], single shot multi-box detector (SSD) [19] are proposed to detect general objects. However, none of them are specialized to detect given targets, such as vehicles.

In this work, we try to perform vehicle detection using Faster RCNN due to its efficiency and robust performance in general object detection. We specialize it to on road vehicle detection and re-design its structure to improve its performance in detecting small-size vehicles. We term small-size vehicles as those vehicles that are far away from the camera, thus are appeared to be small due to perspective distortion. Pipeline of our approach is illustrated in Fig. 1. A traditional Faster RCNN framework is improved with special designs, which we will discuss in Sect. 2 in detail. Later, the improved Faster RCNN is initialized using a VGG16 model pre-trained on ImageNet. Then, we propose a small region up-sampling strategy if the image is captured by a camera mounted on a vehicle. Further, the improved network is fine-tuned with vehicle images selected from benchmarking datasets or our own dataset. Finally, robust vehicle detection can be achieved using the well trained model.

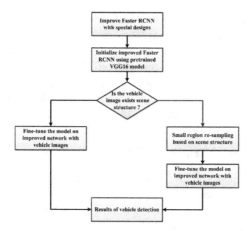

Fig. 1. Pipeline of the proposed on roan vehicle detection approach. A pre-trained VGG16 model was used for initializing the improved Faster RCNN. Small region up-sampling strategy was used if scene structure existed. Then the improved network was fine-tuned with vehicle images and vehicle detection was performed using the learned network.

2 Proposed Method

2.1 Introduction of Traditional Faster RCNN

Faster RCNN was proposed by Ren *et al.* for general object detection. It achieved a state-of-the-art 73.2 mean average precision (AP) in PASCAL VOC 2007 dataset. Evolved from RCNN and Fast RCNN, it improved the computational speed and proposal quality by introducing a Region Proposal Network (RPN). The pipeline of the traditional Faster RCNN is illustrated in Fig. 2.

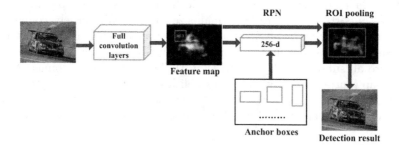

Fig. 2. Pipeline of a traditional Faster RCNN framework

As shown in above figure, Faster RCNN automatically extracts a feature map from the entire image with full convolution layers, which are constituted by a pre-trained VGG16 model without its full connection layers. A 33 convolution filter is used to slide through the whole feature map and outputs a 256-d vectors, which can be further used to infer both class/non-class classifications and bounding box proposals based on the suggestions of input anchor boxes. These proposals can be used as inputs to the region of interest (ROI) pooling, which also takes the feature map as input. Detection are achieved through adjusting the ROI pooling, with the aid of former class/non-class classifications. A thorough introduction to Faster RCNN is beyond the scope of this work, which can be referred to [17].

2.2 Improvements of Traditional Faster RCNN

Generally speaking, Faster RCNN fine-tuned with selected vehicle samples can detect vehicles appeared normal in size. However, it always fails when detecting small-size vehicles. Thus, we improve the RPN and Fast RCNN to make them more sensitive to small-size targets.

A small anchor box proposal is necessary for detecting small-size targets. Traditional RPN used 3 anchor boxes with areas 128, 256, and 512 (in pixels). We add another smaller anchor box, in consideration of the detecting ability and computational cost. Notably, our RPN use 4 anchor boxes with areas 64, 128, 256, and 512 (in pixels). We neglect those vehicles that occupy less than 64 pixels because they always suffer from lacking details and cannot be easily detected through adding a smaller anchor box (e.g. 32 in pixels). For each anchor box, we use 3 ratios ([1:2, 2:1, 1:1]).

Aside from adding a smaller anchor box, we also try to improve the full convolution layers to detect small targets. Gao *et al.* argued that current full convolution layers used in Faster RCNN may lead to a large receptive field, which means that the convolution feature map aggregates image information over a large area [20]. This large receptive field is harmful for detecting small-size targets due to the existence of too much background information. Thus, they re-designed the higher layers of Faster RCNN to extract information from different receptive fields. However, they neglected the effects of lower layers. Variations in higher layers cannot be effectively transmitted to lower layers, which are important for detecting small-size targets. We densely connect the full convolution layers to resolve the above mentioned problem. Feature maps of all preceding layers are used as inputs, and its own feature maps are used as inputs into all subsequent layers [21] (Fig. 3). Through densely connection, the feature map (output of Conv5_3) can establish a direct connection with outputs of lower layers, thus can better capture small-size targets. Parameters used in the full convolution layers are the same as the parameters used in VGG16 model.

2.3 Small Region Up-Sampling Strategy

We propose a small region up-sampling strategy to detect small-size vehicles in the images captured by a camera mounted on the vehicle. In general, they are always in the central part of the image. As shown in Fig. 4, we crop a patch from the input image (indicated by the red dotted box), and then up-sample this patch to the same size of the input image. We simply use the central patch after

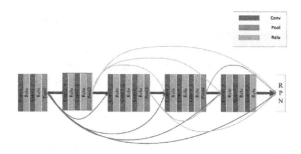

Fig. 3. Illustration of a densely connected full convolution layers. Red box represents the convolution layer, blue box represents the pooling layer, and green box represents the Relu layer. Parameters used in these layers are the same as the parameters used in VGG16 model. We do not list them for simplification (best viewed in color). (Color figure online)

Fig. 4. Illustration of the small region up-sampling approach. For vehicle images captured by a camera mounted on a vehicle, we crop the central patch from the original image and then re-size it to the size of input image. Vehicle detection is performed on both images and final results are obtained through fusion of detection results (best viewed in color). (Color figure online)

we segment the input image into 33 patches. After up-sampling, this patch is also detected using our improved Faster RCNN, together with the input image. Detection results on the cropped patch (indicated by yellow boxes) are mapped to the input image, and then are fused with detection results on the input image (indicated by yellow boxes). Mapping of detection results are achieved through shrinking the detected boxes of the cropped patch three times and then mark them in corresponding positions of the input image. Positions are calculated using their deviations corresponding to the central point, which is shared by the original image and cropped patch. Final detection results (indicated by blue boxes) are obtained using the union set (a simple fusion strategy) of former detection results.

3   Experimental Analysis

3.1   Implementation Details and Evaluation Indicators

The improved Faster RCNN framework, as well as the baseline network, is both initialized using a VGG16 model. Fast RCNN and RPN modules are fine-tuned end-to-end with vehicle images that are selected from different datasets. The threshold of the intersection-over-union is set to 0.7. Other network parameters of our approach are the same as those in traditional Faster RCNN. We employ an alternating training approach [17] to train Faster RCNN from one iteration to another. Primary parameters used in the training stage are shown in Table 1 in detail. All the evaluations are performed on a NVIDA Gefore Titan X GPU (12G).

Table 1. Parameters used in the training stage.

Parameters	Value
Base learning rate	0.001
Learning policy	"step"
Stepsize	40000
Gamma	0.1
Max iterations	80000
average loss	100
Momentum	0.9
Weight decay	0.05
Optimization type	SGD

We evaluate our approach in three datasets, including VOC2007, Kitti and our own datasets. Notably, small region up-sampling strategy is only used in Kitti and our own datasets. We use three terms, namely, precision (P), recall (R) and F1-score (F1), for evaluation. These terms are defined as follows.

$$P = \frac{T_P}{T_p + F_P} \tag{1}$$

$$R = \frac{T_p}{T_p + F_N} \tag{2}$$

$$F1 = \frac{2 * R * P}{R + P} \tag{3}$$

where T_P is the number of detected objects which are correctly marked as target, F_P is the number of detected objects which are not marked as target, F_N is the number of undetected objects which are correctly marked as target. T_P, F_P, and F_N are also known as true positive, false positive, and false negative, respectively. The precision and recall are highly related to the detection performance, and $F1$-score is their compromise.

3.2   Evaluations in VOC2007 Dataset

The VOC2007 dataset consists of 2,501 training images (6,301 objects) and 2,510 testing images (6,307 objects), respectively. There are totally 21 classes in the dataset, e.g. bicycle, bird, car, aeroplane and so on. We select 1,434 vehicle images and use a coarsely five-fold cross-validation for evaluation. More precisely, we randomly divide VOC2007 dataset into a training part (1,120 images) and a testing part (314 images). Average values of three terms are taken as the final results.

RPN loss of our approach in VOC2007 dataset is illustrated in Fig. 5. Weights for different losses are set to be the same as the traditional Faster RCNN. It is obvious that the training stage becomes convergent after 80,000 iterations.

The precision-recall and ROC curves in VOC2007 dataset are illustrated in Figs. 6 and 7, respectively. Curves of different approaches are labeled with different colors (red for the proposed approach and blue for the baseline). As indicated by these curves, both approaches perform well in detecting vehicles

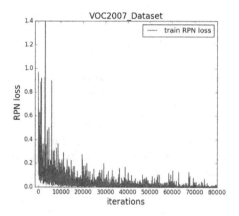

Fig. 5. RPN loss of our approach in VOC2007 dataset (80,000 iterations in the training stage).

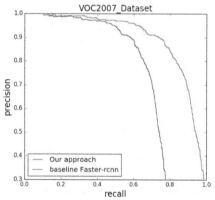

Fig. 6. Precision-recall curve of our approach and baseline Faster RCNN in VOC2007 dataset (best viewed in color). (Color figure online)

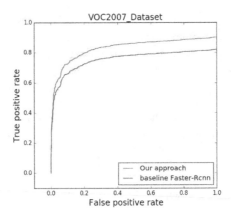

Fig. 7. ROC Curve of our approach and baseline Faster RCNN in VOC2007 dataset (best viewed in color). (Color figure online)

through fine-tuning strategy. Our approach is better than the baseline due to its special designs in detecting small-size vehicles.

Meanwhile, Table 2 shows the values of AP, average recall (AR), and average F1 score (AF1) of different approaches. Comparison results reveal the great improvements of our approach over the baseline. There are approximately 8%-9% increases in AP, AR, and AF1. The superiority of our approach is due to its improvements on traditional Faster RCNN. Meanwhile, fewer partial occlusion exists in vehicle images of VOC2007 dataset, comparing with vehicle images of other used datasets.

Table 2. Comparisons between our approach and baseline Faster RCNN in VOC2007 dataset

	AP	AR	AF
Baseline faster RCNN	79.6%	80.1%	79.8%
Our approach	88.5%	88.9%	88.7%

3.3   Evaluations in Kitti Dataset

The Kitti dataset consists of 7,481 images in total and we select 6,600 images containing vehicles. We use a six-fold cross-validation for evaluation and the average values of three terms are taken as the final results. The training stage also becomes convergent after 80,000 iterations (Fig. 8).

The precision-recall and ROC curves in Kitti dataset are illustrated in Figs. 9 and 10, respectively. Different approaches are labeled with different colors. Both figures indicate the superiority of our approach to the baseline. Table 3 shows the quantitative comparisons in terms of AP, AR, and AF1. There is an obvious

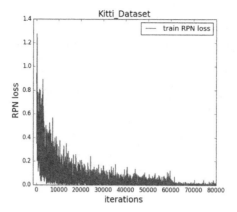

Fig. 8. RPN loss of our approach and baseline Faster RCNN in Kitti dataset (80,000 iterations in the training stage).

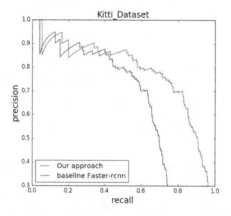

Fig. 9. Precision-recall curve of our approach and baseline Faster RCNN in Kitti dataset (best viewed in color). (Color figure online)

increase for each term, in a range of 5%–6% (the 2nd and 4th rows of Table 3). Meanwhile, the effectiveness of our small region up-sampling strategy can be verified by the 2%–5% increases in terms of AP, AR and AF1 (the 3rd and 4th rows of Table 3). Detection performance in Kitti dataset is not so well as that in VOC2007 dataset. We guess the reason may be that vehicle images of Kitti dataset are captured by cameras mounted on the cars. Thus, they may suffer from more challenges, e.g. perspective distortion, lacking details, partial occlusion, comparing with vehicle images of VOC2007 dataset. These negative factors may affect the detection performance of our approach in Kitti dataset despite of its improvements in detecting small-size vehicles.

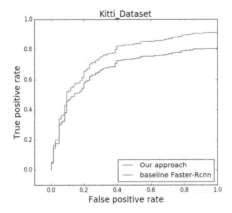

Fig. 10. ROC Curve of our approach and baseline Faster RCNN in Kitti dataset (best viewed in color). (Color figure online)

Table 3. Comparisons between our approach and baseline Faster RCNN in Kitti dataset

	AP	AR	AF
Baseline Faster RCNN	75.3%	76.9%	76.1%
Our approach without small region up-sampling	79.6%	80.8%	80.2%
Our approach	81.4%	85.2%	83.3%

3.4 Evaluations in Our Own Dataset

Our own dataset contains 63 video clips, which are captured using a camera mounted on a car. We choose totally 5,000 vehicle images and use a five-fold

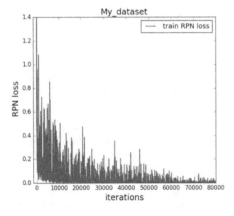

Fig. 11. RPN loss of our approach in our own dataset (80,000 iterations in the training stage).

cross-validation for evaluation. The final results are given by the average values of three terms. The training stage also becomes convergent after 80,000 iterations (Fig. 11).

The precision-recall and ROC curves in our own dataset are illustrated in Figs. 12 and 13, respectively. The red curves (our approach) are obviously better than the blue ones (baseline Faster RCNN). Quantitative detection results (Table 4) further verify our superiority. However, detection performance in this dataset is inferior to that in benchmarking datasets. We guess that vehicle images of our dataset may suffer from more severe challenges than images of benchmarking datasets. Our vehicle images may encounter with more complex road conditions (e.g. both vehicles and bicycles may exist in the images) and more nasty weather conditions (e.g. the fog) even comparing with images of Kitti dataset. However, obvious increase (in a range of 7%–8%) for each term can be still observed between our approach and the baseline (the 2nd and 4th rows of

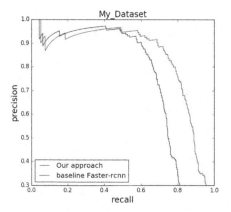

Fig. 12. Precision-recall curve of our approach and baseline Faster RCNN in our own dataset (best viewed in color). (Color figure online)

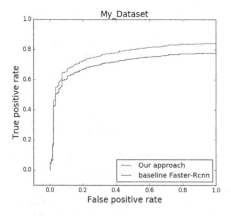

Fig. 13. ROC curve of our approach and baseline Faster RCNN in our own dataset (best viewed in color). (Color figure online)

Table 4). These increases indicate the superiority of our approach to the baseline Faster RCNN. Meanwhile, the effectiveness of our small region up-sampling strategy can be verified by the approximately 3% increases in terms of AP, AR and AF1 (the 3rd and 4th rows of Table 4).

Table 4. Comparisons between our approach and baseline Faster RCNN in our own dataset

	AP	AR	AF1
Baseline Faster RCNN	73.4%	72.9%	73.1%
Our approach without small region up-sampling	77.6%	77.2%	77.4%
Our approach	80.7%	80.1%	80.4%

4   Conclusions and Future Work

We specialize the state-of-the-art Faster RCNN for vehicle detection. We select vehicle images from benchmarking datasets and our own dataset to fine-tune the network. We re-design the full connection layers and RPN of traditional Faster RCNN to enhance its detection performance in small-size vehicles. We densely connect the full connection layers to allow more for lower layers that always have small receptive regions. We add a smaller anchor box in RPN to capture small-size targets. We further use a small region up-sampling strategy if special scene structure existed. Compared with a baseline Faster RCNN which is also fine-tuned with selected vehicle samples, our approach achieved 8.9%, 6.1%, and 7.3% increases in terms of AP, while executing in VOC2007, Kitti, and our own datasets, respectively.

Acknowledgment. This work has been supported by the National Natural Science Foundation of China under Grant No. 61501060, the Natural Science Foundation of Jiangsu Province under Grant No. BK20150271, Key Laboratory for New Technology Application of Road Conveyance of Jiangsu Province under Grant BM20082061708.

References

1. National Transportation Safety Board: Special investigation report-highway vehicle and infrastructure-based technology for the prevention of rear-end collisions. NTSB Number SIR-OI/(II) (2001)
2. Chang, W.C., Cho, C.W.: Online boosting for vehicle detection. IEEE Trans. Syst. Man Cybern. Part B (Cybernetics) **40**(3), 892–902 (2010)
3. Sun, Z., Bebis, G., Miller, R.: On-road vehicle detection using Gabor filters and support vector machines. In: 2002 14th International Conference on Digital Signal Processing (DSP 2002), vol. 2, pp. 1019–1022. IEEE (2002)

4. Yuan, Q., Thangali, A., Ablavsky, V., et al.: Learning a family of detectors via multiplicative kernels. IEEE Trans. Pattern Anal. Mach. Intell. **33**(3), 514–530 (2011)
5. Zhang, J., Huang, K., Yu, Y., et al.: Boosted local structured HOG-LBP for object localization. In: 2011 IEEE Conference on Computer Vision and Pattern Recognition (CVPR), pp. 1393–1400 (2011)
6. Kim, J., Baek, J., Kim, E.: A novel on-road vehicle detection method using π HOG. IEEE Trans. Intell. Transp. Syst. **16**(6), 3414–3429 (2015)
7. Sun, Z., Bebis, G., Miller, R.: Improving the performance of on-road vehicle detection by combining gabor and wavelet features. In: The IEEE 5th International Conference on Intelligent Transportation Systems, Proceedings, pp. 130–135 (2002)
8. Haselhoff, A., Kummert, A.: A vehicle detection system based on haar and triangle features. In: Intelligent Vehicles Symposium, pp. 261–266. IEEE (2009)
9. Sudowe, P., Leibe, B.: Efficient use of geometric constraints for sliding-window object detection in video. In: Crowley, J.L., Draper, B.A., Thonnat, M. (eds.) ICVS 2011. LNCS, vol. 6962, pp. 11–20. Springer, Heidelberg (2011). https://doi.org/10.1007/978-3-642-23968-7_2
10. Carreira, J., Sminchisescu, C.: CPMC: automatic object segmentation using constrained parametric min-cuts. IEEE Trans. Pattern Anal. Mach. Intell. **34**, 1312–1328 (2012)
11. Endres, I., Hoiem, D.: Category independent object proposals. In: Daniilidis, K., Maragos, P., Paragios, N. (eds.) ECCV 2010. LNCS, vol. 6315, pp. 575–588. Springer, Heidelberg (2010). https://doi.org/10.1007/978-3-642-15555-0_42
12. Wang, Y., Gao, X., Li, J.: A feature analysis approach to mass detection in mammography based on RF-SVM. In: IEEE International Conference on Image Processing, ICIP, pp. V-9–V-12 (2007)
13. Tang, J., Deng, C., Huang, G.B.: Extreme learning machine for multilayer perceptron. IEEE Trans. Neural Netw. Learn. Syst. **27**, 809–821 (2016)
14. Okuma, K., Taleghani, A., de Freitas, N., Little, J.J., Lowe, D.G.: A boosted particle filter: multitarget detection and tracking. In: Pajdla, T., Matas, J. (eds.) ECCV 2004. LNCS, vol. 3021, pp. 28–39. Springer, Heidelberg (2004). https://doi.org/10.1007/978-3-540-24670-1_3
15. Girshick, R., Donahue, J., Darrell, T., et al.: Rich feature hierarchies for accurate object detection and semantic segmentation. In: Proceedings of the IEEE Conference on Computer Vision and Pattern Recognition, pp. 580–587 (2014)
16. Girshick, R.: Fast R-CNN. In: Proceedings of the IEEE International Conference on Computer Vision, pp. 1440–1448 (1988)
17. Ren, S., He, K., Girshick, R., et al.: Faster R-CNN: towards real-time object detection with region proposal networks. In: Advances in Neural Information Processing Systems, pp. 91–99 (2015)
18. Redmon, J., Farhadi, A.: YOLO9000: better, faster, stronger. arXiv preprint arXiv:1612.08242 (to appear)
19. Liu, W., Anguelov, D., Erhan, D., Szegedy, C., Reed, S., Fu, C.-Y., Berg, A.C.: SSD: single shot multibox detector. In: Leibe, B., Matas, J., Sebe, N., Welling, M. (eds.) ECCV 2016. LNCS, vol. 9905, pp. 21–37. Springer, Cham (2016). https://doi.org/10.1007/978-3-319-46448-0_2
20. Gao, Y., Guo, S., Huang, K., et al.: Scale optimization for full-image-CNN vehicle detection. In: Intelligent Vehicles Symposium (IV), pp. 785–791 (2017)
21. Huang, G., Liu, Z., Weinberger, K.Q., et al.: Densely connected convolutional networks. arXiv preprint arXiv:1608.06993 (2016)

Fast Haze Removal of UAV Images Based on Dark Channel Prior

Siyu Zhang$^{(\boxtimes)}$, Congli Li, and Song Xue

Army Academy of Artillery and Air Defense, Hefei, Anhui, China
yusonzhang@foxmail.com, lcliqa@163.com, xs_xs6688@sina.com

Abstract. A fast haze removal algorithm based on dark channel prior is proposed to overcome the color distortion and inefficiency caused by the dark channel prior algorithm in the recovery of UAV images. The quad-tree subdivision of higher efficiency is used for solving the atmospheric light at the first, followed by down sampling and interpolation algorithm to optimize the solution process of the transmission, and fast guided filter is used for thinning transmission. Finally, the transmission can be got by correction of tolerance mechanism. We can get the restoration images by means of the atmospheric scattering model combined with above research. Experiments show that the algorithm can effectively improve the color restoration and distortion in the sky region image, and for the UAV images without the sky area, the dehazing result is also effective; at the same time, the running speed of the algorithm is greatly improved, which is about 34 times of the He method. It can satisfy the real-time requirement of the UAV images to dehaze.

Keywords: Dark channel prior · Haze removal · UAV
Fast guided filter

1 Introduction

UAVs are vulnerable to adverse weather conditions during reconnaissance and shooting, especially the haze. Haze will reduce the visibility and contrast of images, and blur the object information. The objective feature extraction and post-processing of image are affected. Therefore, the haze removal algorithm of UAV image is of great significance, especially in improving the efficiency of the algorithm.

At present, the image dehazing algorithm is divided into two main categories: method based on image enhancement and method based on image restoration [1]. Aiming at the low contrast characteristics of haze images, the first method use traditional image enhancement methods to process images. The main algorithms are histogram equalization algorithm and Retinex. Because the cause of image degradation is not considered, this method cannot achieve the real haze removal [2]. The second research the degradation reasons of haze images, and build the degradation model using prior knowledge or assumptions. The clear image can

© Springer International Publishing AG, part of Springer Nature 2018
S. Satoh (Ed.): PSIVT 2017, LNCS 10799, pp. 254–267, 2018.
https://doi.org/10.1007/978-3-319-92753-4_21

be obtained by inversion. In contrast, the haze removal effect of method based on image restoration is more authentic, and the image information is saved completely. It has become a hot spot in the field of image dehazing.

In recent years, experts and scholars have made a series of breakthroughs in the research of single image haze removal. Tan [3] observes that the contrast of haze images is lower than that in haze free images and he removes haze by maximizing the local contrast. A better visual effect is obtained but the color of restore image tend to oversaturated. Fattal [4] estimates the transmission by estimating the scene albedo and works better when dealing with mist. But for dense haze images and grayscale images, statistical errors will be caused by insufficient color information. The dark channel prior proposed by He et al. [5] are works very well for haze removal in most outdoor images. However, the transmission of bright regions such as the sky cannot be accurately estimated, resulting in color distortion of the restored image, and the algorithm has high time complexity because of the large sparse equations in calculate the transmittance of the soft matting. Therefore, it is not applicable to haze removal of UAV. He used guide image filtering [6] in place of soft matting in 2013, which increase the speed of operation, but also lead to the halo effect. Liu et al. [7] calculates the atmospheric light and transmission in the HSI color space and improves the haze removal effect by color adjustment, but the speed of haze removal is only two times of that of He method. It still cannot meet the requirement of haze removal speed of large size UAV images. Liao et al. [8] impose boundary constraints and local contrast for estimating accurate atmospheric veil. The method achieves better results when processing distant scenes where depth changes abruptly, but it may fail when the color of the object in the foggy image is close to the atmospheric light. Chen et al. [9] propose a new method to suppress visual artifacts in low quality inputs dehazing such as cellphone shots or compressed video clips. But it may overestimate the amount of haze for white objects that are close to the camera. The method is not very suitable for high resolution UAV images.

For the problems in the above algorithms, a fast haze removal algorithm based on dark channel priors is proposed in this paper. First, the quad-tree subdivision algorithm [10] with higher efficiency is used to solve the atmospheric light. Secondly, the sampling and interpolation algorithms is used to solve, the fast guided filter [11] is used to the refine transmission. Finally, a tolerance mechanism is introduced to correct the transmittance of the bright region, restoring images can be got with atmospheric scattering model. Experiments show that the algorithm can effectively remove haze and improve the color of restoration images, and has higher real-time performance.

2   Background

2.1   Atmospheric Scattering Model

The UAV image has the characteristics of stable tone of overall color and little change in depth of field [12,13]. Moreover, the imaging principle is consistent with that of ordinary images, so it is also applicable to the general atmospheric scattering model [14] widely used in haze removal [3–5,7].

$$I(x) = J(x)t(x) + A(1 - t(x)) \tag{1}$$

The formula consists of two parts, the first term is the direct attenuation, which represents the attenuation of the radiation of a scene in a medium; the second term is atmospheric light. $I(x)$ is a degraded image, $J(x)$ is the scene radiance (the clear image to be restored), $t(x)$ is the transmission, and A is global atmospheric light. The purpose of haze removal is to recover $J(x)$ from this ill conditioned equation by estimating the parameter A and $t(x)$.

2.2 Dark Channel Prior

He [5] proposed the definition of dark channel after studying nearly 5000 outdoor haze free images. For any image, the dark channel is defined as:

$$J^{dark}(x) = \min_{y \in \Omega(x)} (\min_{c \in \{r,g,b\}} J^c(y)) \tag{2}$$

Where J^c is a color channel for the image J and $\Omega(x)$ is a local area centered in pixel x. The dark channel prior means: For no-sky areas of most outdoor images, at least one color channel has some pixels whose brightness are very low and approach to zero:

$$J^{dark}(x) \to 0 \tag{3}$$

2.3 Dehazing Algorithm Using Dark Channel Prior

Estimating the Atmospheric Light A. He et al. [5] pick the top 0.1% brightest pixels in the dark channel at first. These pixels are usually the worst affected areas with the lowest transmission. Then, in the original haze image, the values of the brightest pixels corresponding to the positions of these pixels are found as global atmospheric light A.

Estimating the Transmission. It is assumed that the transmissivity is a constant at each local region, denoted as $\tilde{t}(x)$. (1) can be written as (4) with deformation and two minimum filtering processing:

$$\min_{c \in \{r,g,b\}} (\min_{y \in \Omega(x)} \frac{I^c(y)}{A^c}) = \tilde{t}(x) \min_{c \in \{r,g,b\}} (\min_{y \in \Omega(x)} \frac{J^c(y)}{A^c}) + 1 - \tilde{t}(x) \tag{4}$$

The dark channel image is close to zero by the prior knowledge of dark channel:

$$J^{dark}(x) = \min_{y \in \Omega(x)} (\min_{c \in \{r,g,b\}} J^c(y)) = 0 \tag{5}$$

Therefore, the transmittance is as follows:

$$\tilde{t}(x) = 1 - \min_{y \in \Omega(x)} (\min_{c \in \{r,g,b\}} \frac{I^c(y)}{A^c}) \tag{6}$$

Because of the influence of impurity particles in the atmosphere, it is not completely haze free even in clear images. So we use constant $\omega(0 < \omega \leq 1)$ to keep a certain amount of haze in the image.

$$\widetilde{t}(x) = 1 - \omega \min_{y \in \Omega(x)} (\min_{c \in \{r,g,b\}} \frac{I^c(y)}{A^c}) \tag{7}$$

Recovering Haze Free Images. After the estimation of atmospheric light and transmission, the haze image can be recovered by combining (1):

$$J(x) = \frac{I(x) - A}{\max(t(x), t_0)} + A \tag{8}$$

To prevent transmission approaching zero so that the restored image contains noise. We set a threshold to hold a certain of haze, with a typical value of 0.1.

The transmission obtained by (7) is inaccurate, He adopts the soft matting [5] to refine the transmission, and get the accurate transmission to recover the image. But the soft matting algorithm has a high spatial and temporal complexity, and the running rate is very slow. He suggested that the guide image filter [6] greatly accelerated the processing speed later, but also produced halo phenomenon, which could not satisfy the requirement of UAV to dehaze; at the same time, large areas of bright areas such as the sky do not meet the preconditions of dark channel, which will cause color distortion in the restored image, as shown in the red box area in Fig. 1. Therefore, only using the original atmospheric scattering model or image enhancement method cannot deal with haze images of UAV very well [15, 16]. The original model and method need to be improved to improve the robustness and real-time performance of the algorithm.

(a) Haze image   (b) He et al.'s result

Fig. 1. Effect of dark channel prior dealing with the sky area

3   Fast Haze Removal Algorithm Based on Dark Channel Prior

3.1   Estimates Atmospheric Light Using the Quad-Tree Subdivision

The conception of quad-tree subdivision in this paper is different from Ding et al.'s [17] method. We use quad-tree subdivision in the estimation of atmospheric light rather than acceleration. The acceleration in our method is achieved by fast guided filter introduced in the next section, which is more efficient than Ding et al.'s method. The atmospheric light estimation of Ding et al. is same as [5]. It may be more accurate when the images are not in the bright region such as sky. But the UAV will inevitably encounter bright areas such as sky region, large area of water bodies or white buildings in the shooting process, which will lead to inaccurate estimation results. In addition, threshold manual selection process in Ding et al.'s method will increase the operational complexity.

Kim observes that the brightness (variance) of pixels in the sky region is smaller overall. Based on this understanding, a more reliable and efficient algorithm called quad-tree hierarchical subdivision searching is proposed to estimate the atmospheric light. The effect is shown in Fig. 2. Specific practices are as follows:

Scoring Indicator. The images are divided into four rectangular regions at first. We then define the value of each region as the average pixel minus the standard deviation, and this value is used as a scoring indicator.

Iteration. Select the highest scoring area, repeat last step until the selected area size is smaller than the set threshold.

Fig. 2. Sketch of quad-tree subdivision

Estimate Atmospheric Light. In the smallest area selected, select the color vectors that minimize the distance $\|(I_r(p), I_g(p), I_b(p)) - (255, 255, 255)\|$ (including R, G, B, three channels) as atmospheric light intensity.

3.2   Improve Transmission Acquisition

Calculating Transmission Using Down Sampling and Interpolation Algorithm. The projection rate accuracy obtained by the dark channel algorithm is more precise than that of other algorithms, but the processing time is too long to satisfy the real time requirement of haze removal for UAV. To reduce the accuracy slightly in a certain extent, the haze removal effect in theory will not lead to much difference. Base on this acknowledge, we can improve the operation speed of the algorithm greatly. In this paper, we firstly estimate the transmission of the down Sampling image, then obtain the transmission of the original image by interpolation. Experimental results show that the proposed method greatly improves the real-time performance of the algorithm, but the haze removal effect is not visually different from the original method. Attention should be paid to the reasonable settings of sampling rate, such as using 1/2 times to reduce the original picture, the processing speed is not obvious; if the sampling rate is too large, it will seriously reduce the haze removal effect. It is proved by experiment that 1/9 scaling can not only satisfy the haze but also meet the real-time requirement.

Correction of Transmission Using Tolerance Mechanism. Through research (7), we find that when I closer to A, that is, the closer the bright region is to atmospheric light, the smaller the transmissivity is. Which will make transmission estimates in the sky and other bright regions are too small. In this paper, the transmission is corrected by Jiang's tolerance mechanism [18], and (8) will be rewritten as:

$$J(x) = \frac{I(x) - A}{\min(\max(K/|I(x) - A|, 1) \cdot \max(t(x), t_0), 1)} + A \qquad (9)$$

Where K is a tolerance. The area is considered to be the sky when $|I(x) - A| < K$ and increase the transmission of this region in this situation. At the same time, when $|I(x) - A| > K$, the region is considered to be a conforms to the dark channel prior, and the transmission is unchanged. The equation is equivalent to the original transmission formula when $K = 0$.

Refine Transmission Using Fast Guided Filter. The guided image filtering [6] and the bilateral filter are also having the property of edge preserving, and the former is better in detail. Because of its good visual effects, fast execution and easy implementation, it has been widely used in research and industry, and has been officially set up by Matlab and OpenCV. The fast guided filter [11] proposed by He in 2015 can further improve the speed of the algorithm. When the down sampling rate is s, the time complexity of the algorithm can be reduced from $O(n)$ to $O(n/s^2)$. In this paper, we use this achievement to accelerate the refining process of transmission.

4 Experimental Analysis and Comparison

The experiments in this paper are carried out under the MatlabR2016a environment of 64 bit Windows 10 operating system, 2.6 GHz Intel Core, i5 3230M CPU, and memory 8G notebook. The parameter settings are as follows: $\omega = 0.98$ in (7), in order to increase the dehazing effect; the dark channel window size is 15; the radius of fast guided filter is 60, the adjustment coefficient is 0.01. The sampling rate is 60/4, the other parameters have been set up in the above.

Taking into account the diversity of the perspective when UAV is shooting. We select four images that contain the sky region and four images of no-sky region to carry out the experimental analysis. The test images have an overhead shot and a side shot view, the natural landscapes and urban landscapes both included. In order to test the haze effect of the algorithm, five typical algorithms are compared: Multi-scale Retinex algorithm with color recovery(MSRCR), Tarel et al. [19], He et al. [5,6], Meng et al. [20], and Zhu et al. [21]. Considering the high efficiency of UAV image to work in haze, Meng's method adopts the algorithm to obtain the mode of atmospheric light automatically, rather than manually selecting the largest concentration of haze concentration. To avoid distortion and better dehazing effects, $\beta = 1.5$ in Zhu et al.'s method.

4.1 Subjective Analyses

Results Contrast Analysis of Sky Region Images. Figure 3 shows the haze removal comparisons of the images that have sky region. The sky area ratio of first image is less than 1/2, the second is greater than 1/2, and the third and fourth pictures are about 1/2.

As can be seen from Fig. 3(a), the MSRCR method can make this part darker for the darker areas of the original image, resulting in lower recognition and distortion and halo effect in the sky region. Tarel et al.'s work dealing with the first city image appear obvious oversaturated phenomenon, and the upper sky area of image appears halo effects. The second and fourth pictures of tall buildings are distorted, and the color in the third picture tends to yellow, as shown in Fig. 3(c). Because the Meng et al.'s method adds boundary constraints on the basis of the He method, it does not really solve the discomfort of the dark channel prior to the sky region, so the processing results are very similar to that of the He et al.'s method. The Zhu et al. handles the sky region slightly better than the previous algorithms, but the intensity of the haze is not enough, and there is a color distortion in the third picture, and also blurs some of the images. On the whole, the haze removal effect is the best in our algorithm, and the sky area did not appear color distortion and partial color phenomena. While other algorithms have emerged more or less partial color, color distortion or halo effects.

Results Contrast Analysis of No-Sky Region Images. Figure 4 shows the dehaze results of images without the sky region. The first and the second picture shows are side shot angle, and the third and the fourth picture shows the vertical Angle.

Through the observation of Fig. 4(a), MSRCR algorithm also present problems that aggravate dark regions and color distortions like previous processing of the sky region. Tarel et al.'s dehazing effect is not enough, and the second results blue, as shown in Fig. 4(b). The overall haze removal effect of the He et al.'s method is better, but the brightness of the tree area on the second coast image looks dim. Meng method result in color bias and the images remain misty when dealing with third and fourth images. The results of Zhu et al.'s method are generally dim, and the effect of haze removal was unstable; Compared Fig. 4(a)–(g), it can be seen that our algorithm has good performance for dehazing in image without sky area, not only has high color reproduction degree and is superior to He et al.'s method in brightness performance, but also more consistent with human visual.

In addition, 5 observers working on image processing are invited to rate the dehazing results of different algorithms. Scores are ranged from 0.1 to 1 and divided into ten grades at step of 0.1. The higher the visual quality of the image, the higher the score. The average subjective quality scores are given in Table 1. From the above analyses, we can see that the algorithm can get satisfactory haze removal effect for UAV images whether including sky region or not. Which proves that the algorithm has strong adaptability.

Table 1. Average subjective quality scores of different methods

Algorithms	Scores of Fig. 3	Scores of Fig. 4	The total score
MSRCR	0.34	0.38	0.72
Tarel et al.	0.53	0.45	0.98
He et al.	0.65	0.85	1.5
Meng et al.	0.72	0.76	1.48
Zhu et al.	0.77	0.81	1.58
Our method	0.88	0.93	1.81

4.2   Objective Evaluation

Quantitative Analysis of Haze Removal Effect. In this paper, we use contrast enhancement evaluation algorithm based on visible edges [22] and objective evaluation algorithm of haze removal algorithm [23] proposed by Li to evaluate the effect of haze removal.

Contrast enhancement evaluation algorithm based on visible edges was proposed by French scholar Hautière et al., which has become one of the most widely used algorithms in dehazing evaluation. The algorithm combines logarithmic image processing model for contrast, and take the new visible edges (e), normalized mean gradient of the visible edges ($\bar{r}$) and the percentage of saturated black or white pixels (σ) three indexes to evaluate haze removal effect. The larger the e and $\bar{r}$, and the smaller the σ, the result is better. The formula is as follows:

$$e = \frac{(n_r - n_0)}{n_0} \tag{10}$$

$$\bar{r} = \exp[\frac{1}{n_r} \sum_{P_i \in \Omega_r} \log r_i] \tag{11}$$

$$\sigma = \frac{n_s}{\dim_x \times \dim_y} \tag{12}$$

Where n_r and n_0 represent the number of visible edges in the restored image and the original image respectively; Ω_r represents the visible edge set of the restored image, P_i is the pixel of the visible edge of the restored image, and r_i represents the ratio of the gradient of the restored image at P_i and the original P_i; n_s is the number of saturated black or white pixels, $\dim_x$ and $\dim_y$ are the width and height of the image.

Objective evaluation algorithm proposed by Li et al. aggregate detail intensity, color reduction and structural information these three indicators as a final comprehensive index(Q). The bigger the Q, the better the dehaze effect.

Tables 1 and 2 are corresponding to the haze removal parameters of each of the image algorithms in Figs. 3 and 4 respectively. It can be seen that our algorithm has achieved better evaluation parameters. Especially the Q value is relatively high, and there are 5 of 8 images rank first. When the evaluation algorithm based on visible edges is applied, it should be ensured that a better algorithm can yield the same evaluation results for any parameter. Attention must also be paid to its limitations on high quality haze evaluation [24]. For example, in Fig. 3 of Table 2, Tarel et al.'s method achieves the best parameters, but it does not have a better visual effect, and even has partial color and false contours. In summary, this algorithm has better haze removal effect.

Algorithm Efficiency Comparison. A focal point of this algorithm is to speed up the haze removal efficiency. The typical resolution is selected from the above 8 experimental images, and test the speed of each algorithm. As shown in Table 3. It can be seen that the Tarel et al.'s method and the He et al.'s method have the most time consuming, and the time consuming increases greatly with the increase of the image size. However, our algorithm has the least time consumption and improves the efficiency of haze removal by about 34 times compared with the He et al.'s method (Table 4).

(a) Input images

(b) MSRCR

(c) Tarel et al.

(d) He et al.

(e) Meng et al.

(f) Zhu et al.

(g) Our results

Fig. 3. Dehazing effect comparisons of sky region images

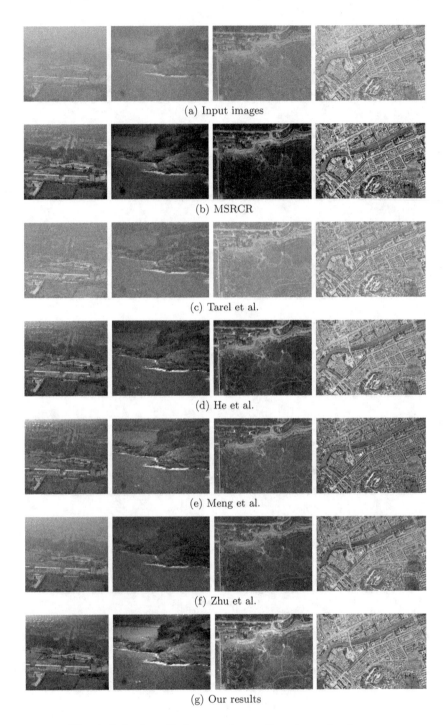

(a) Input images

(b) MSRCR

(c) Tarel et al.

(d) He et al.

(e) Meng et al.

(f) Zhu et al.

(g) Our results

Fig. 4. Dehazing effect comparisons of no-sky region images

Table 2. Dehazing result parameter comparisons of images in Fig. 3

Image number	Evaluating indicator	Algorithms					
		MSRCR	Tarel et al.	He et al.	Meng et al.	Zhu et al.	Our result
1 500 × 500	e	−0.0100	**0.1056**	0.0351	−0.0309	0.0089	−0.0073
	$\bar{r}$	1.1620	**1.5531**	1.4640	1.7022	1.2182	1.3702
	σ	0.0075	0.0001	0.0001	0.0002	0.0001	0.0001
	Q	0.1417	0.0882	0.1368	0.1410	0.1769	**0.2017**
2 684 × 512	e	0.2501	**0.2764**	0.0251	0.2713	0.0045	0.0969
	$\bar{r}$	1.2076	**2.0683**	0.9873	1.3775	0.9655	1.0870
	σ	0.0004	0.0000	0.0000	0.0000	0.0000	0.0000
	Q	0.2152	0.1861	0.2616	0.2701	0.3075	**0.4620**
3 680 × 509	e	**1.1116**	0.2753	0.4545	1.0649	0.1250	0.2553
	$\bar{r}$	2.3631	1.4497	1.5111	**2.3800**	1.0309	1.4175
	σ	0.0003	0.0000	0.0000	0.0000	0.0000	0.0000
	Q	0.1751	0.2972	0.2370	0.2179	0.2700	**0.3800**
4 592 × 443	e	0.2444	**0.3963**	0.1623	0.2795	0.2103	0.2410
	$\bar{r}$	0.5830	**2.2351**	0.9275	1.2504	0.9723	1.1881
	σ	0.0000	0.0000	0.0008	0.0000	0.0000	0.0014
	Q	0.1337	**0.4761**	0.3111	0.4471	0.3914	0.4666

Table 3. Dehazing result parameter comparisons of images in Fig. 4

Image number	Evaluating indicator	Algorithms					
		MSRCR	Tarel et al.	He et al.	Meng et al.	Zhu et al.	Our result
1 600 × 525	e	**4.3538**	1.8796	3.8944	3.9694	1.9064	4.0897
	$\bar{r}$	**4.2425**	2.5500	3.1090	3.7306	1.9717	3.2228
	σ	0.0000	0.0000	0.0000	0.0000	0.0000	0.0000
	Q	0.1547	0.1720	0.1782	0.1577	**0.2508**	0.1663
2 800 × 600	e	**14.0698**	4.3580	10.7986	8.9542	6.0579	12.7308
	$\bar{r}$	2.0348	2.3421	2.1457	2.7629	1.5459	**3.3460**
	σ	0.0000	0.0000	0.0002	0.0007	0.0000	0.0017
	Q	0.1501	**0.2483**	0.1743	0.1649	0.1649	0.1301
3 1200 × 900	e	**2.7703**	0.6052	2.6805	1.8694	2.2484	2.4804
	$\bar{r}$	1.4904	1.7769	2.1336	1.9607	1.7986	**3.2306**
	σ	0.0001	0.0000	0.0000	0.0000	0.0000	0.0001
	Q	0.0691	0.0907	0.1035	0.1084	**0.1161**	0.1070
4 800 × 534	e	−0.0717	**0.1252**	−0.0614	−0.1132	−0.0609	−0.0721
	$\bar{r}$	**1.6930**	1.3128	1.4165	1.5774	1.3225	1.3872
	σ	0.0008	0.0002	0.0007	0.0005	0.0002	0.0004
	Q	0.0636	0.1222	0.1495	0.1361	**0.1801**	0.1559

Table 4. Time comparison of algorithms/s

Image size/pixel	MSRCR	Tarel et al.	He et al.	Meng et al.	Zhu et al.	Our result
500 × 500	1.00	8.93	9.20	4.02	1.92	**0.28**
684 × 512	0.97	18.33	13.22	4.22	1.98	**0.38**
800 × 600	1.24	38.87	19.07	5.84	2.59	**0.58**
1200 × 900	3.20	192.19	42.21	12.44	5.33	**1.13**

5   Conclusion

This paper proposes an improved algorithm for the problem of color distortion and inefficiency in the processing of UAV images by the dark channel method. We use down sampling and interpolation algorithm to simplify, fast guided filter to accelerate, and tolerance mechanism to refine the solution process of transmission. Quad-tree subdivision algorithm is used for atmospheric light estimation. Experiments have proved that the algorithm can improve the color distortion and partial color phenomenon in the sky region, and greatly improve the speed of the algorithm on the premise of ensuring the dehaze effect. The next step is to further improve the algorithm's effect and adaptivity, and apply the algorithm to thin cloud removal and video haze removal.

References

1. Wu, D., Zhu, Q.: The latest research progress of image dehazing. Acta Automatica Sinica **41**(2), 221–239 (2015)
2. Nan, D., Bi, D., Xu, Y., S, Wang., Lu, X.: Image dehazing method based on dark channel prior. J. Cent. South Univ. (Sci. Technol.) **44**(10), 4101–4108 (2013)
3. Tan, R.T.: Visibility in bad weather from a single image. In: Proceedings of IEEE Conference on Computer Vision and Pattern Recognition, pp. 1–8. IEEE Computer Society, Washington, DC (2008)
4. Fattal, R.: Single image dehazing. ACM Trans. Graph. **27**(3), 1–9 (2008)
5. He, K., Sun, J., Tang, X.: Single image haze removal using dark channel prior. IEEE Trans. Pattern Anal. Mach. Intell. **33**(12), 2341–2353 (2011)
6. He, K., Sun, J., Tang, X.: Guided image filtering. IEEE Trans. Pattern Anal. Mach. Intell. **35**(6), 1397 (2013)
7. Liu, J., Huang, B., Wei, G.: A fast effective single image dehazing algorithm. Acta Automatica Sinica **45**(8), 1896–1901 (2017)
8. Liao, B., Yin, P., Xiao, C.: Efficient image dehazing using boundary conditions and local contrast. Comput. Graph. **70**, 242–250 (2017)
9. Chen, C., Do, M.N., Wang, J.: Robust image and video dehazing with visual artifact suppression via gradient residual minimization. In: Leibe, B., Matas, J., Sebe, N., Welling, M. (eds.) ECCV 2016. LNCS, vol. 9906, pp. 576–591. Springer, Cham (2016). https://doi.org/10.1007/978-3-319-46475-6_36
10. Kim, J.H., Jang, W.D., Sim, J.Y., Kim, C.S.: Optimized contrast enhancement for real-time image and video dehazing. J. Vis. Commun. Image Represent. **24**(3), 410–425 (2013)

11. He, K., Sun, J.: Fast guided filter. Technical report, Computer Vision and Pattern Recognition (cs.CV) arXiv:1505.00996v1 (2015)
12. Yang, J., Zhang, Y., Zou, X., Dong, G.: Using dark channel prior to quickly remove haze from a single image. Geomatics Inf. Sci. Wuhan Univ, **35**(11), 1292–1295 (2010)
13. Li, F., Wang, H., Mao, X., Sun, Y., Song, H.: Fast single image dehazing algorithm. Comput. Eng. Des. **32**(12), 4129–4132 (2011)
14. McCartney, E.J.: Optics of Atmosphere: Scattering by Molecules and Particles. Wiley, New York (1976)
15. Huang, Y., Ding, W., Li, H.: Haze removal method for UAV reconnaissance images based on image enhancement. J. Beijing Univ. Aeronaut. Astronaut. **43**(3), 592–601 (2017)
16. Yue, X., Wang, L., Lan, Y., Liu, Y., Ling, K., Gan, H.: Algorithm of dehazing UAVs aerial images based on DCP and OCE. Trans. Chin. Soc. Agric. Mach. **47**(s1), 419–425 (2016)
17. Ding, M., Tong, R.: Efficient dark channel based image dehazing using quadtrees. Sci. China Inf. Sci. **56**(9), 1–9 (2013)
18. Jiang, J., Hou, T., Qi, M.: Improved algorithm on image haze removal using dark channel prior. J. Circ. Syst. **16**(2), 7–12 (2011)
19. Tarel, J.P., Hautière, N.: Fast visibility restoration from a single color or gray level image. In: Proceedings of IEEE Conference on International Conference on Computer Vision, pp. 2201–2208. IEEE Press, Kyoto (2009)
20. Meng, G., Wang, Y., Duan, J., Xiang, S., Pan, C.: Efficient image dehazing with boundary constraint and contextual regularization. In: Proceedings of IEEE Conference on Computer Vision, pp. 617–624. IEEE Press, Sydney (2013)
21. Zhu, Q., Mai, J., Shao, L.: A fast single image haze removal algorithm using color attenuation prior. IEEE Trans. Image Process. **24**(11), 3522 (2015)
22. Hautière, N., Tarel, J.P., Aubert, D., Dumont, E.: Blind contrast enhancement assessment by gradient ratioing at visible edges. Image Anal. Stereol. **27**(2), 87–95 (2008)
23. Li, D., Yu, J., Xiao, C.: No-reference quality assessment method for dehazeged images. J. Image Graph. **16**(09), 1753–1757 (2011)
24. Guo, F., Cai, Z.: Objective assessment method for the clearness effect of image dehazing algorithm. Acta Automatica Sinica **38**(9), 1410–1419 (2012)

Watercolour Rendering of Portraits

Paul L. Rosin[✉] and Yu-Kun Lai

Cardiff University, Cardiff CF24 3AA, UK
Paul.Rosin@cs.cf.ac.uk, Yukun.Lai@cs.cardiff.ac.uk

Abstract. Applying non-photorealistic rendering techniques to stylise portraits needs to be done with care, as facial artifacts are particularly disagreeable. This paper describes a technique for watercolour rendering that uses a facial model to preserve distinctive facial characteristics and reduce unpleasing distortions of the face, while maintaining abstraction and stylisation of the overall image, employing stylistic elements of watercolour such as edge darkening, wobbling, glazing and diffusion.

Keywords: Non-photorealistic rendering · Watercolour · Portraits

1 Introduction

The goal of image-based non-photorealistic rendering (NPR) is to take an image and re-render it in an alternative style, generally for artistic effect. Target styles include natural media (oil painting, watercolour, pen and ink, etc.) and can also be categorised according to traditional artistic movements (impressionist, expressionist, pointillist, etc.). This paper describes an approach to NPR stylisation of portrait images using a watercolour effect. Watercolour provides an attractive abstraction, and has been used in several applications of NPR, such as the rendering of CAD models of interior decorating plans to provide a more aesthetic rendering [18] and for rendering 3D models for augmented reality [6], enabling a clear separation of original and inserted content.

Portraits are an important and long standing branch of art, which normally focuses on producing a representation of the sitter's face. However, good portrait paintings or photographs go beyond capturing just a realistic representation, but attempt to express or reveal aspects of the nature of the sitter that may not be otherwise directly visible in real life. Current NPR algorithms do not aim to automatically modify the stylisation according to the personality of the sitter. Nevertheless, there remain challenges for performing stylisation. For instance, if a substantial amount of abstraction is desired, then the identity of the sitter is liable to become obscured as discriminating features are removed. In addition, the human visual system is particularly sensitive to artefacts when viewing faces.

The contributions of this work are to provide a watercolour rendering method that is targeted at portraits. In order to preserve distinctive facial characteristics a facial model is used, while a salience map controls the degree of abstraction

ⓒ Springer International Publishing AG, part of Springer Nature 2018
S. Satoh (Ed.): PSIVT 2017, LNCS 10799, pp. 268–282, 2018.
https://doi.org/10.1007/978-3-319-92753-4_22

Fig. 1. An example of our watercolour portrait rendering. Important facial details have been preserved while other areas are more stylised.

elsewhere in the image. In addition, techniques for stylistic elements of watercolour such as wobbling, glazing and diffusion are introduced (Fig. 1). Results are shown on images from the NPRportrait benchmark [22].

2   Related Work

NPR Portraits: Given the importance of the portrait in art it is not surprising that there has been a substantial body of NPR work dealing specifically with portraits, and we describe some recent examples. Berger *et al.* [3] learned models of stroke parameters from training examples which consisted of line sketches at four abstraction levels that were provided by seven artists. The method by Rosin and Lai [21] first stylises the image with abstracted regions of flat colours plus black and white lines [15]. Facial features are localised in the input image. In the skin region of the face, shading is stylised, and reduced line rendering is applied to reduce visual clutter. In addition, the facial model is used to enhance the rendering of the eyes, lips, teeth and highlights. Zhang *et al.* [27] describe an approach to creating cartoon versions of faces. Facial components are detected in the input image, and are matched to a dictionary of cartoon stylised components. Support Vector Regression is used to train a composition model to ensure good layout of the selected components. Recent work [11] has applied style transfer to videos of faces, and uses a semantic segmentation guide to control the synthesis. In an attempt to analyse the performance of NPR portrait algorithms, Rosin *et al.* [22] recently introduced a benchmark data set of 40 images, split into two levels. The first level is constrained to contain frontal views of adult faces with neutral expressions, and uncluttered background. The second level is more challenging to algorithms, as it allows facial hair, a wider variety of facial expressions, more varied backgrounds, etc. They applied six stylisation algorithms, including three portrait-specific algorithms, to the benchmark, and demonstrated the benefits of using portrait-specific algorithms over general-purpose NPR algorithms. Namely, the former tended to use domain-specific information to preserve key details such as eyes and conversely to improve abstraction by removing semantically unnecessary details.

Watercolour Rendering: Watercolour painting allows for many effects that artists use to good effect, such as dry-brush, edge darkening, backruns, granulation, flow patterns and colour glazing. Several interactive painting tools have been developed for creating watercolour renderings [7,8] that attempt to capture these effects. They use stroke based rendering along with physical models of the painting process. Such particle based models can effectively describe the flow of water and pigment on the paper surface, taking into account many factors such as the water velocity, viscosity, drag, brush pressure, pigment concentration and paper saturation. Of more relevance to our work is the simple and efficient filter based approach of Bousseau et al. [5]. Dispensing with the physical model they use instead a series of image processing operations that can also mimic some of the watercolour effects. Wang et al. [25] extended the filter based approach in a number of ways, incorporating saliency to control level of detail, colour adjustment based on training examples, and extended the range of watercolour effects. Another approach to stylisation is to use general style transfer methods which can then be applied for the specific instance of watercolour. A pioneering example was Image Analogies [13], which effectively learns a mapping from a pair of training images containing one scene in two styles, and that style transform is then applied to an independent test image. In the last few years deep learning approaches to style transfer have become popular [12], and have the advantage that only a single style image is required rather than a corresponding pair (which is generally not convenient and may not be possible). Yan et al. [26] describe a method for automatic photo adjustment using CNNs, and apply it (amongst other things) to generate a watercolour style based on training examples provided by a professional photographer using Photoshop. However, the training and test images are not truly watercolour style. A recent work attempts to combine both the Image Analogies and deep learning approaches [17], but is computationally expensive. Such example based approaches have some limitations. First, errors can occur if local textures are not distinctive. Second, transfer is based on a combination of style and content, and this can lead to undesirable content from the style image being transferred to the content image.

3   Our Approach

We follow the basic elements of Bousseau et al.'s [5] filter based approach, although the details are not identical. Following Bousseau et al. [5] our approach is not to produce a physically accurate watercolour simulation, but rather capture the important stylistic elements. Abstraction is performed by the following set of filtering steps: 1/ apply a small amount of Gaussian smoothing, 2/ apply a larger amount of median filtering, 3/ apply morphological filtering (opening and closing), 4/ apply a small amount of Gaussian smoothing. We prefer to avoid relying on accurate segmentation, as this is potentially unreliable.

The edge darkening effect (in which pigment migrates towards edges of areas of paint) is simulated by extracting edges from the abstracted image using the Sobel operator. Although not detailed in [5], their technical report [4] specifies that the edge map is inverted and scaled, and then combined with the abstracted image using an overlay blend operation:

$$f(a, b) = \begin{cases} 2ab & \text{if } a < 0.5 \\ 1 - 2(1 - a)(1 - b) & \text{otherwise} \end{cases}$$

where a is the base layer value (the abstracted image) and b is the top layer value (the modified Sobel image). This combines the images so that the result is darkened where the base layer is dark and lightened where the base layer is light. The benefit of using the overlay blend rather than a multiply blend is that the former darkens the edges while preserving their colour, whereas the latter uniformly darkens the three colour channels, and so the darkening tends towards gray, which is less attractive.

Next, wobbling (distortion due to the paper's granularity) is added (see Sect. 3.2), and finally, paper and pigment textures are added using overlay blends.

3.1 Image Brightening

The image is brightened to make it more vibrant looking. This can go beyond scaling the intensities to fill the dynamic range, since blown out highlights are compatible with the watercolour style. However, this needs to be done in moderation, and therefore the scaling should be determined carefully. Moreover, for portraits the scaling should depend on the face rather than the background.

First, a morphological closing is performed on the image to remove small and medium sized bright spots from consideration. This stage controls the amount of blown out highlights that are created. A mask of the main facial area is created using the facial landmarks extracted from the image by OpenFace [2]. Content outside the face is removed according to the facial mask, and the maximum intensity $I_{\max}$ in this version of the image is determined.

Two brightening operations are considered. The first applies to each pixel a global scaling of $\min(1/I_{\max}, 1.5)$; the upper limit of 1.5 is set as we assume that images are taken under reasonably normal lighting conditions, and this avoids over-stretching that would otherwise occasionally occur due to dark skins. Clipping is applied to any overflowing values that may occur in the individual RGB colour channels; consequently, a colour shift may occur. The second operation reduces the scaling factor at each pixel, if necessary, so as to prevent any colour channel overflowing. While avoiding colour shift, the result shows a few blown out highlights, and moreover, can cause intensity variations to be removed, resulting in flat unattractive regions. We incorporate both approaches by taking a linear combination of the two colours c_1 and c_2, $\alpha c_1 + (1 - \alpha)c_2$ with the weight $\alpha = 0.75$, which achieves a good compromise in which a reasonable amount of blown out highlights are created while colour shift is reduced, and also faintly retains the original colours in blown out areas.

3.2 Wobbling

One of the watercolour effects is wobbling, which is the distortion due to the paper's granularity. Bousseau et al. [5] use the horizontal and vertical gradients of the paper to provide offsets in the rendered image, but do not describe their approach in detail. Doran and Hughes [10] found that a similar approach produced poor results, and therefore applied morphological smoothing to make the results more coherent. The jittering and smoothing was applied iteratively.

However, a limitation of the above approach is that it is difficult to control the wobble effect. Instead, to create wobbles we use spatially coherent noise. Given a 2D coherent noise function $n(\mathbf{x})$ producing a single noise value at location $\mathbf{x} = [x, y]$ we combine two instances to form an offset vector $\mathbf{t} = [n_1(\mathbf{x}), n_2(\mathbf{x})]$ which is used to produce the warped image W from the unwarped image U: $W[\mathbf{x}] = U[\mathbf{x} + \mathbf{t}]$.

This is a general approach that has two main benefits. First, there are a range of types of coherent noise that have been developed for generating procedural textures, for instance the well known Perlin noise [19] and also more recent examples such as Gabor noise [14]. Second, such noise functions can be easily controlled, with parameters for frequency, magnitude, orientation, etc. It is consequently straightforward to manipulate these values to provide more extreme effects that go beyond watercolour simulation in order to generate highly stylised renderings. Wang *et al.* [25] used the Perlin noise approach in their watercolour system, but applied it to simulate hand tremor rather than paper roughness. Bousseau *et al.* [5] incorporated Perlin noise into their 3D model rendering pipeline, but not their 2D image-based pipeline. Figure 2 shows examples of both Perlin and Gabor noise and their application to create offset vectors $\mathbf{t}$ and visualises their magnitude and phase.

Fig. 2. Noise functions: Perlin noise (left block), Gabor noise (right block). For each block, left: one of the 2D noise maps used to generate the offset vector; middle: magnitude of offset vector; right: phase of offset vector.

3.3   Glazing

Colour glazing is a watercolour technique of adding thin washes of colour. It creates semi-transparent layers, which are then blended. We propose a simple image processing approach to simulate this. We first obtain a set of regions from the image using segmentation. For robustness, we use a state-of-the-art superpixel generation method [1], although alternative segmentation methods can also be used. Superpixels naturally involve over segmentation, but with our method extra boundaries where regions on both sides have identical colour will remain unchanged during the process. For each region $R_i, i = 1, 2, \ldots, N_R$, where N_R is the number of regions, we obtain an expanded region $\tilde{R}_i$ using morphological dilation corresponding to the area affected by R_i, creating a layer with both solid and semi-transparent pixels. For each pixel $p_k \in \tilde{R}_i$, we work out its colour component value $\tilde{v}_{k,i}$ (corresponding to the R, G, B channels), and weight $\tilde{w}_{k,i}$ (where larger weight means more contribution in blending). $\tilde{v}_{k,i}$ is defined using membrane interpolation by minimizing the following harmonic energy:

$$\min_{\tilde{v}_{k,i}} \int_{p_k \in \tilde{R}_i} \|\nabla \tilde{v}_{k,i}\|^2 , \qquad s.t. \qquad \tilde{v}_{k,i} = v_k, \forall p_k \in R_i. \tag{1}$$

where v_k is the original pixel value for p_k. $\nabla \cdot$ is the gradient operator, and in the image setting is simply approximated using pixel differences. This can be easily solved by a sparse linear system. It keeps pixels in the region R_i unchanged, and propagates pixel values from the boundary of R_i to the pixels in the dilated region. To work out the weight $\tilde{w}_{k,i}$, denote by $d_{k,i}^F$ the shortest Euclidean distance between the pixel $p_k \in \tilde{R}_i$ and pixels in R_i (distance to "foreground"), and $d_{k,i}^B$ the shortest Euclidean distance between the pixel p_k and pixels outside of $\tilde{R}_i$ (distance to "background"), both of which are normalised to $[0,1]$ by linear scaling for pixels in $\tilde{R}_i$. The weight $\tilde{w}_{k,i}$ is then defined as:

$$\tilde{w}_{k,i} = 1 - d_{k,i}^F \Big/ \left(d_{k,i}^F + d_{k,i}^F + \varepsilon \right) \tag{2}$$

which ensures that pixels in R_i have weight 1, and pixels on the boundary of $\tilde{R}_i$ have weight 0. ε is a small value to avoid dividing by zero, and is set to 10^{-5} in our experiments. The pixel value $\bar{v}_k$ in the output image with glazing is simply obtained by the weighted sum of contributions of all the regions covering this pixel:

$$\bar{v}_k = \sum_{i, p_k \in \tilde{R}_i} \tilde{w}_{k,i} \tilde{v}_{k,i} \Big/ \sum_{i, p_k \in \tilde{R}_i} \tilde{w}_{k,i} \tag{3}$$

3.4   Pigment Diffusion

Diffusion of pigment tends to go from dark to light, and depending (amongst other factors) on the amount of water present,[1] a large amount of diffusion can be introduced for artistic effect. Many physically-based models and methods exist for simulating pigment diffusion [7]. Dong et al. [9] described a simple and efficient image-based approach for rendering Chinese ink paintings, which performed spattering (independent random movement of pixels) followed by median filtering. However, we did not find their approach effective for watercolour. Wang et al. [25] performed diffusion by first identifying regions that satisfy appropriate criteria on hue difference and intensity differences with their neighbouring regions; tighter thresholds are used for salient regions. Seeds are randomly scattered around each selected boundary on the light side only, and blurring is applied in the normal direction to the region boundary. A disadvantage is that

---

[1] For example, wet in wet is a watercolour technique in which paint is specifically applied to wet paper.

their approach requires accurate segmentation of both the image and saliency map. Also, their results consisting of blurred lines can look unnatural.

In this paper we only aim to generate small amounts of diffusion, and describe two simple methods for creating different effects. The first approach leverages the method for wobbling described in Sect. 3.2 and creates a "blobby" effect. Let W_1 be the watercolour image which has been stylised using the initial amount of wobbling, and W_2 be a version of the watercolour image that is created with more wobbling that is roughly simulating diffusion. Then $W_2' = \min(W_1, W_2)$ limits the diffusion to go from dark to light. To prevent the diffusion component $D = W_2' - W_1$ appearing too distracting we apply a gamma correction to it in order to reduce strong densities whilst preserving weak densities, and the final result is given by $W_1 + 0.5D^{0.7}$.

The second approach produces a more uniform diffusion effect by applying erosion to the image to diffuse dark pigment. To avoid isolated dark groups of pixels having an undue effect they are removed first by applying an opening. As before, the diffusion component is extracted, and then a uniform blur is appled: $D = \text{blur}(W_3 - W_1)$, where W_3 is the result after erosion. In order to limit the diffusion to go from dark to light, D is multiplied by the following weight map: $\max(W_1 - \text{blur}(W_1), 0)$. Before the diffusion D is added back to the watercolour image W_1 an overlay blend with a texture map can be optionally applied to D to make it less regular and more natural looking.

Both these diffusion methods are controlled using the level of detail scheme described in the next subsection to avoid distracting effects in foreground regions.

3.5   Level of Detail

When applying NPR to portraits, the desire for significant abstraction in order to obtain distinctive stylisation is potentially at odds with the requirement that the portrait should remain recognisable and the need to avoid unpleasant artifacts on the face. For instance, given the sensitivity of the human visual system to facial artifacts it is probably unacceptable to render an eye such that it appears mishapen.

A means to satisfying the above goal is to incorporate several levels of detail, so that important aspects of the face are preserved at high detail, while less important elements in the image can be more highly abstracted. Recently several state-of-the-art portrait-specific NPR algorithms were applied to a benchmark set of portraits [22], and it was notable that all of them ensured that the eyes were the most carefully rendered parts of the image. In addition to performing rendering at a higher resolution for the eyes, other elements in the processing can ensure accuracy. For instance, in [20] morphological cleaning of lines was uniformly applied to remove clutter and noise. However, the size threshold for cleaning was reduced for the eye regions to avoid the possibility of removing critical detail. Another example is given in [21] where an artificial highlight was added to the eye in case the real highlight was absent due to extremely low contrast in the input image. In the more general area of photo enhancement special attention is also paid to eyes [23].

In this work we also incorporate differential processing of different elements in the image. We use three levels of detail which are controlled by salience and face masks. The discriminative regional feature integration method (DRFI) [24] is used to provide the saliency map. DRFI segments the image into superpixels and uses a random forest regressor to map region features to salience values. Since DRFI provides crisp region based salience maps we also apply blurring so that the final rendering does not exhibit discontinuities between areas with different levels of detail. A sigmoid mapping is also applied to increase the separation in saliency values between foreground and background objects. For facial components we create our facial regions (eyes, eyebrows, nose, mouth) from the OpenFace landmarks. The regions are dilated to ensure that the regions are adequately covered (as the landmarks found by OpenFace may not be accurate), and blurred to provide soft masks.

In addition to rendering the eye area at higher resolution, they are further enhanced to ensure that they stand out. Contrast limited local histogram equalisation (CLLHE) is applied to the high resolution image before stylisation to enhance detail, increasing contrast in the eye regions. The original and equalised images are blended, with the weighting determined by the blurred eye mask.

A detailed description of the watercolour processing pipeline follows:

Brightening – Apply rescaling to the original input image (denoted by I_O).

Levels of detail – I_O is resized to double and half size versions (I_D and I_H).

Eye enhancement – Apply CLLHE to enhance detail in the eye regions of I_H.

Abstraction – The initial abstraction steps of the watercolour effect are applied at the three levels of resolution to produce A_O, A_D and A_H.

Edge darkening – Edge darkening is directly applied to A_O and A_D only, and A_D and A_H are then resized back to the input image size. Applying edge darkening with the above procedure to A_H resulted in the edge darkening appearing unnatural and unpleasant as the edges became too thick. Therefore, instead the edges from A_O were blended with A_H to perform edge darkening.[2]

Wobbling – Only a small amount of wobbling is applied to A_D in order to preserve the important details as much as possible. The magnitude and frequency of the spatially coherent noise are successively doubled and halved for A_O and A_H so as to make the stylisation of A_H more distinctive.

Pigment Diffusion – Compared to W_1, the increased amount of wobbling in W_2 is achieved by doubling the magnitude of the noise. In addition, multiple octave separated scales of noise are added to A_O and A_D, as listed in Table 1. Following that "blobby" diffusion, the uniform diffusion step is applied.

Granulation – For increased stylisation a strong pigment granulation or other effects can be applied to A_H using an overlay blend with an appropriate scanned texture map.

---

[2] Computing edges from A_H after it is resized to the original I_O size gives similar results, but the edges are still slightly thickened, and the additional more detailed mid-scale edges retained by the preferred method improve the watercolour effect.

Blending levels of detail – First the salience map S is used to blend the lower two resolution images $B_1 = S \cdot A_O + (1 - S) \cdot A_H$ and this blend is then further blended with the facial mask F to produce the final blend of the three levels of detail $B_2 = F \cdot A_D + (1 - F) \cdot B_1 = F \cdot A_D + S \cdot (1 - F) \cdot A_O + (1 - F) \cdot (1 - S) \cdot A_H$. This weighting ensures that the eye and eye brow regions are preserved at the highest resolution, salient features (apart from the eye and eye brows) are rendered at approximately mid resolution, while the remaining non-salient areas of the image are rendered towards the lowest level of detail.

Glazing – Glazing is applied on the single output image B_2 after the levels of detail have been combined to create B_3. In order to preserve the facial features these two renderings are combined using the facial mask to produce $B_4 = B_2 + F \cdot B_3$

Pigment and paper variations – Irregularities in appearance due to blotches caused by uneven pigment density and the paper texture are added as two overlay blends to B_4. When blending the pigment blotches, B_4 is set as the base layer so as to create variations in the colour density. Subsequently the paper blend sets the paper texture image as the base layer, which ensures that the texture is visible even in light and dark areas.

Table 1. Frequencies and magnitudes of coherent noise applied to make the standard wobble effect and the increased amount of wobbling used to produce the pigment diffusion effect.

Level of Detail	Standard Wobble	Increased Wobble
A_D	$\{f, m\}$	$\{f, 2m\}$
A_O	$\{\frac{f}{2}, 2m\}$	$\{f, 2m\}, \{\frac{f}{2}, 4m\}$
A_S	$\{\frac{f}{4}, 4m\}$	$\{f, 2m\}, \{\frac{f}{2}, 4m\}, \{\frac{f}{4}, 8m\}$

Figure 3 demonstrates some intermediate stages of the rendering pipeline. The top row shows that the combination of three levels of detail have ensured that while the hair has become significantly abstracted the eyes are only lightly stylised, and have retained their detail (see Fig. 3b). Likewise, diffusion is limited in the eye area (Fig. 3c). The second row shows how the input image (Fig. 3e) is brightened and the local contrast in the eye region enhanced (Fig. 3f). Although the difference between the abstracted results with (Fig. 3g) and without (Fig. 3h) eye enhancement is subtle, it is important to ensure that the eyes are rendered clearly. The third row shows how the two levels of wobbling (W_1 and W_2 in Fig. 3j and k) are combined to form blobby diffusion into the dark area only (Fig. 3l). Several texture overlays are added: strong pigment granulation in the background (Fig. 3n), pigment blotches (Fig. 3o), paper texture (Fig. 3p).

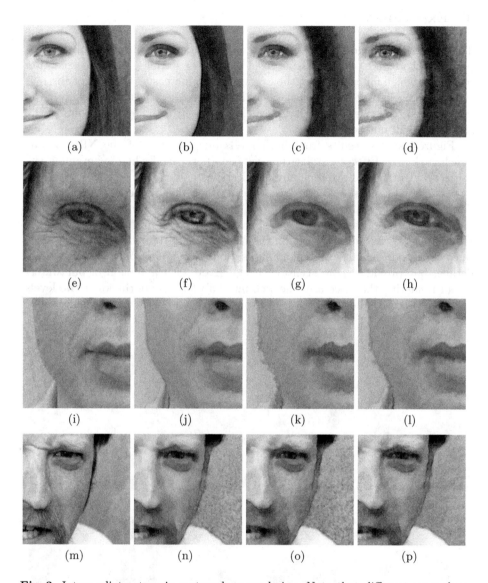

Fig. 3. Intermediate steps in watercolour rendering. Note that different rows show different steps. Top row: **overall process**, (a) section of original image, (b) basic Bousseau *et al.* [5] filtering, (c) wobbling and uniform diffusion effect, (d) addition of textures; Second row: **face and eye enhancement**, (e) section of original image, (f) contrast limited local histogram equalisation (CLLHE), (g) filtering applied to original image, (h) filtering applied to CLLHE image; Third row: **diffusion**, (i) section of original image, (j) standard amount of wobbling, (k) increased amount of wobbling, (l) combination to produce "blobby" diffusion effect; Bottom row: **texture overlays**, (m) section of original image, (n)-(p) addition of pigment granulation, blotches, paper texture.

4   Experiments

This section shows results of the watercolour rendering. All results of the proposed method were obtained using fixed parameter settings, with the exception of Fig. 5d, which for comparison shows the effect of increasing the level of abstraction of the background. Note that since the watercolour effect is quite subtle the images need to be viewed at a large scale, otherwise the different elements of the stylisation will not be apparent.

Figure 4 shows results from both levels one and two of the NPRportrait benchmark [22]. Effective stylisation has been performed while maintaining the subject's identity and avoiding any facial artifacts.

Additional results and comparisons with other image-based watercolour rendering methods are provided in Fig. 5. The output from our implementation of the method by Bousseau et al. [5] is shown in Fig. 5b. While the overall effect is reasonable, there is loss of detail on the face, particularly noticeable at the eyes. In contrast, our default watercolour stylisation (Fig. 5c) not only preserves these details, but provides more stylistic effects. Even with a version of our watercolour rendering that increases the amount of abstraction of the lower two levels of detail (Fig. 5d) the face is still well preserved, and artifacts avoided. Gabor

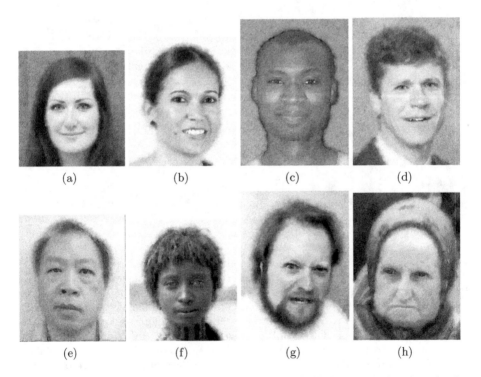

(a)   (b)   (c)   (d)

(e)   (f)   (g)   (h)

Fig. 4. Watercolour stylisation using the proposed method of images taken from levels one and two of the NPRportrait benchmark [22].

Fig. 5. Examples and comparison of watercolour rendering; inset images show the sources for style transfer. (a) target image, (b) Bousseau *et al.* [5], (c) our default watercolour stylisation, (d) our watercolour stylisation with Gabor noise and increased abstraction of background, (e) & (f) DeepArt [12], (g) CNNMRF [16], (h) Image Analogies [13], (i) Waterlogue, (j) BeCasso.

rather than Perlin noise has been used to perform the wobbling, which can be seen most clearly as the oriented streaking of the background. Two results from the commercial app "DeepArt", which is based on the deep learning approach to style transfer by Gatys et al. [12], are shown in Fig. 5e and f. Some elements of the source watercolour examples have been captured, but even though well matched source images are provided, Fig. 5e contains significant facial artifacts while the face in Fig. 5f appears washed out. Another deep learning style transfer approach is demonstrated in Fig. 5g. The CNNMRF [16] approach gives good results for some styles, but it can be hard to control. Again, some aspects of the watercolour style have been well captured, but mismatches and inappropriate transfer have caused undesirable artifacts in the face. Figure 5h shows the result of using the watercolour image pair from the original Image Analogies [13] paper. The colours in the face are overly flattened while the highlights in the original become an unnatural gray. Moreover there are many local discontinuities due to texture transfer from widely separated source locations. A result from the commercial app Waterlogue is shown in Fig. 5i. The overall effect is attractive, but the eyes would benefit from less abstraction, and the excessive diffusion of the lips into the mouth is unwanted. The effect of unpainted white patches can be effective, but in this example their dense occurrence in the background is overly distracting. Finally, Fig. 5j shows the watercolour result from the BeCasso commercial app, which incorporates the wet in wet technique from Wang et al. [25]. This appears attractive in some areas, but distracting in others such as the teeth and nose.

5   Conclusions

An image-based non-photorealistic rendering technique for producing a watercolour effect has been developed, incorporating several stylistic elements of watercolour, i.e. edge darkening, wobbling, glazing and diffusion. Multiple levels of detail are employed, and controlled by weight maps generated from a fitted facial model as well as a general purpose saliency model. This ensures that distinctive facial characteristics are preserved and facial artifacts are avoided. A consequence of this approach is that the stylisation of the face may be too conservative, which we will address in future work.

References

1. Achanta, R., Shaji, A., Smith, K., Lucchi, A., Fua, P., Susstrunk, S.: SLIC superpixels compared to state-of-the-art superpixel methods. IEEE Trans. PAMI **34**(11), 2274–2282 (2012)
2. Baltru, T., Robinson, P., Morency, L.P.: OpenFace: an open source facial behavior analysis toolkit. In: Winter Conference on Applications of Computer Vision, pp. 1–10 (2016)
3. Berger, I., Shamir, A., Mahler, M., Carter, E., Hodgins, J.: Style and abstraction in portrait sketching. ACM Trans. Graph. **32**(4), 55:1–55:12 (2013)

4. Bousseau, A.: Watercolor tutorial. Technical report, Grenoble University (2006). maverick.inria.fr/Membres/Adrien.Bousseau/watercolor_tutorial/tutorial1.pdf
5. Bousseau, A., Kaplan, M., Thollot, J., Sillion, F.X.: Interactive watercolor rendering with temporal coherence and abstraction. In: Symposium NPAR, pp. 141–149 (2006)
6. Chen, J., Turk, G., MacIntyre, B.: Watercolor inspired non-photorealistic rendering for augmented reality. In: ACM Symposium on Virtual Reality Software and Technology, pp. 231–234 (2008)
7. Curtis, C.J., Anderson, S.E., Seims, J.E., Fleischer, K.W., Salesin, D.H.: Computer-generated watercolor. In: ACM SIGGRAPH, pp. 421–430 (1997)
8. DiVerdi, S., Krishnaswamy, A., Mäch, R., Ito, D.: Painting with polygons: a procedural watercolor engine. IEEE Trans. TVCG 19(5), 723–735 (2013)
9. Dong, L., Lu, S., Jin, X.: Real-time image-based Chinese ink painting rendering. Multimedia Tools Appl. 69(3), 605–620 (2014)
10. Doran, P.J., Hughes, J.: Expressive rendering with watercolor. Master's thesis, Brown University (2013)
11. Fišer, J., Jamriška, O., Simons, D., Shechtman, E., Lu, J., Asente, P., Lukáč, M., Sýkora, D.: Example-based synthesis of stylized facial animations. ACM Trans. Graph. 36(4), 155 (2017)
12. Gatys, L.A., Ecker, A.S., Bethge, M.: Image style transfer using convolutional neural networks. In: Proceedings of CVPR, pp. 2414–2423 (2016)
13. Hertzmann, A., Jacobs, C.E., Oliver, N., Curless, B., Salesin, D.H.: Image analogies. In: ACM SIGGRAPH, pp. 327–340 (2001)
14. Lagae, A., Lefebvre, S., Drettakis, G., Dutré, P.: Procedural noise using sparse Gabor convolution. ACM Trans. Graph. 28(3), 54–64 (2009)
15. Lai, Y.K., Rosin, P.L.: Efficient circular thresholding. IEEE Trans. Image Process. 23(3), 992–1001 (2014)
16. Li, C., Wand, M.: Combining Markov random fields and convolutional neural networks for image synthesis. In: Proceedings of CVPR, pp. 2479–2486 (2016)
17. Liao, J., Yao, Y., Yuan, L., Hua, G., Kang, S.B.: Visual attribute transfer through deep image analogy. In: ACM SIGGRAPH, pp. 120:1–120:15 (2017)
18. Luft, T., Kobs, F., Zinser, W., Deussen, O.: Watercolor illustrations of CAD data. In: Eurographics, pp. 57–63 (2008)
19. Perlin, K.: An image synthesizer. ACM SIGGRAPH Comput. Graphics 19(3), 287–296 (1985)
20. Rosin, P.L., Lai, Y.K.: Artistic minimal rendering with lines and blocks. Graph. Models 75(4), 208–229 (2013)
21. Rosin, P.L., Lai, Y.K.: Non-photorealistic rendering of portraits. In: Proceedings of the Workshop on Computational Aesthetics, pp. 159–170 (2015)
22. Rosin, P.L., Mould, D., Berger, I., Collomosse, J., Lai, Y.K., Li, C., Li, H., Shamir, A., Wand, M., Wang, T., Winnemöller, H.: Benchmarking non-photorealistic rendering of portraits. In: Proceedings of Expressive, pp. 11:1–11:12 (2017)
23. Shu, Z., Shechtman, E., Samaras, D., Hadap, S.: EyeOpener: editing eyes in the wild. ACM Trans. Graph. 36(1), 1:11–1:13 (2017)
24. Wang, J., Jiang, H., Yuan, Z., Cheng, M.M., Hu, X., Zheng, N.: Salient object detection: a discriminative regional feature integration approach. Int. J. Comput. Vis. 123(2), 251–268 (2017)
25. Wang, M., Wang, B., Fei, Y., Qian, K., Wang, W., Chen, J., Yong, J.H.: Towards photo watercolorization with artistic verisimilitude. IEEE Trans. TVCG 20(10), 1451–1460 (2014)

26. Yan, Z., Zhang, H., Wang, B., Paris, S., Yu, Y.: Automatic photo adjustment using deep neural networks. ACM Trans. Graph. **35**(2), 11:1–11:15 (2016)
27. Zhang, Y., Dong, W., Ma, C., Mei, X., Li, K., Huang, F., Hu, B.G., Deussen, O.: Data-driven synthesis of cartoon faces using different styles. IEEE Trans. Image Process. **26**(1), 464–478 (2017)

Blind Image Deblurring via Salient Structure Detection and Sparse Representation

Yu Cai, Jinshan Pan, and Zhixun Su$^{(\boxtimes)}$

School of Mathematical Sciences, Dalian University of Technology, Dalian, China
zxsu@dlut.edu.cn

Abstract. Blind image deblurring algorithms have been improving steadily in the past years. However, most state-of-the-art algorithms still cannot perform perfectly in challenging cases, e.g., when the blurred image contains complex tiny structures or the blur kernel is large. This paper presents a new algorithm that combines salient image structure detection and sparse representation for blind image deblurring. Salient structures provide reliable edge information from the blurred image, while sparse representation provides data-authentic priors for both the blur kernel and the latent image. When estimating the kernel, the salient structures are extracted from an interim latent image solved by combining the predicted structure and spatial and sparsity priors, which help preserve more sharp edges than previous deconvolution methods do. We also aim at removing noise and preserving continuity in the kernel, thus obtaining a high-quality blur kernel. Then a sparse representation based ℓ_1-norm deconvolution model is proposed for suppressing noise robustly and solving for a high-quality latent image. Extensive experiments testify to the effectiveness of our method on various kinds of challenging examples.

Keywords: Blind image deblurring · Salient structure
Sparse representation · Kernel estimation · Image restoration

1 Introduction

Blind image deblurring has gained considerable attention from the image processing community in recent years. The formation process of image blur is usually modeled as:

$$B = I * k + \varepsilon, \tag{1}$$

where B, I, k and ε represent the blurred image, latent image, blur kernel (a.k.a. Point Spread Function (PSF)) and the additive noise, respectively, and $*$ denotes the convolution operator. It is a well-known ill-posed inverse problem, which requires regularization in order to obtain a high quality latent image.

© Springer International Publishing AG, part of Springer Nature 2018
S. Satoh (Ed.): PSIVT 2017, LNCS 10799, pp. 283–299, 2018.
https://doi.org/10.1007/978-3-319-92753-4_23

1.1 Related Work

In order to make blind deblurring more tractable, many literatures utilized some additional information,such as multiple images or specialized hardware. The works in [1–4] used images blurred in different directions to guide the kernel estimation and latent image restoration. Yuan et al. [5] used a pair of images, one blurry and one noisy, to facilitate capturing images in low light conditions. Zhuo et al. [6] used an image captured in a short exposure time to guide the latent image restoration. Although some of these methods yield good kernel estimates and deblurred results, they need additional hardware to capture the images or some extra operations performed by the users.

For single image deblurring, Chan and Wang [7] adopted the Total Variation (TV) regularizer to constrain both the kernel and the latent image. You and Kaveh [8] applied an anisotropic regularization technique to exploit the piecewise smoothness of the image and the motion blur kernel. Yitzhaky et al. [9] made an isotropy assumption to estimate a motion blur. Because of adopting parameterized forms of blur kernels, these methods cannot deal with complex motion blur.

In recent years, blind image deblurring methods have been greatly improved. Fergus et al. [10] adopted a zero-mean Mixture of Gaussian to fit the distribution of natural image gradients and employed a variational Bayesian method to deblur an image. Due to adopting the Richardson-Lucy method, the restored image contains some noise. Jia [13] proposed an alpha matte for kernel estimation, but this method largely depends on the quality of the input alpha matte. Shan et al. [12] used a certain parametric model to approximate the heavy-tailed natural image prior. Cho and Lee [11] used bilateral filtering together with shock filtering to predict sharp edges iteratively, and then selected the salient edges for kernel estimation. However, the Gaussian priors used in this method cannot keep the sparsity of the motion blur kernel and the latent image. As a result, the final deblurred results usually contain some noise and the estimated kernel is often dense. Levin et al. [14] illustrated the limitation of the simple MAP approach and further introduced an efficient marginal likelihood approximation [15].

It must be pointed out that the aforementioned works suffer a common problem: the kernel estimation result contains some noise. In order to remove noise in the estimated kernels, most current literatures [5,10–12] applied hard or hysteresis thresholding to the kernel estimates. However, this strategy will damage the inherent structure of a kernel. Figure 1 shows an example. Due to adopting hard or hysteresis thresholding to the kernel estimate, the structures of kernels estimated by Fergus et al. [10], Shan et al. [12], Cho and Lee [11] are all destroyed, especially the results of [10] and [12]. As a result, the corresponding deblurred results are still blurry.

To solve this problem, Xu and Jia [16] employed an Iterative Support Detection (ISD) method that can ensure the deblurring quality while removing noise. However, this method ignores the continuity of the motion blur kernel. Cho et al. [17] used the Radon transform to estimate the blur kernel and the continuity of blur kernel is preserved by employing the traditional gradient constraint.

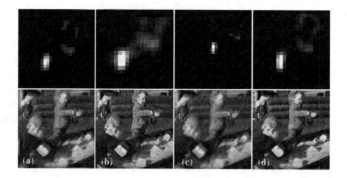

Fig. 1. Kernel estimation results. The top row is the estimated kernels and the bottom row is the corresponding deblurred images. (a)–(c) denote the results by Fergus et al. [10], Cho and Lee [11], and Shan et al. [12], respectively. (d) Our result. The kernel and the latent image are both estimated correctly. (**The images in this paper are best viewed on screen!**)

However, this constraint occasionally damages the shape of blur kernel [3,18]. Pan et al. [18] goes a further step. It combined reliable structures and an effective gradient constraint to estimate the kernel. However, the final deblurred results occasionally contain noise due to a less robust latent image restoration model.

Another group of methods [19–22] assume that the latent image patches can be sparsely represented by an over-complete dictionary and make use of this prior to guide the interim latent image restoration. However, the kernel estimation model that they used may not preserve the sparsity of the kernel. Cai et al. [23] tried to solve this problem by employing a sparsity model. They introduced a framelet and curvelet system to obtain the sparse representation for the kernel and the image. However, these special basis functions may not capture the properties of kernel and latent image well.

After obtaining the blur kernel, the blind debluring problem becomes a non-blind deconvolution. Many literatures used TV or statistical methods to model the distribution of natural image gradients. The main weakness of this type of methods is that the assumed probabilistic priors may not always hold true for general images. In order to overcome this issue, image deblurring based on sparse representation has been proposed by many literatures [20–22,24]. Dong et al. [24] adopted an adaptive sparse domain selection strategy and an adaptive regularization method to guide the latent image restoration. Zhang et al. [22] goes a further step. They combined the spatial information in the latent image restoration model to improve the robustness to noise. However, they assumed that the noise in the blurred image is Gaussian, which may not be true in real situations.

1.2 Our Contributions

We find that current state-of-the-art debluring methods may produce a noisy kernel. Some unreliable salient structures may mislead the kernel estimation. Even correct salient edges are chosen, the kernel estimate still contains some noise.

Thus, central to our method is to develop a robust kernel estimation model which combines sparse representation and reliable salient structures. This makes a high-quality kernel estimate and further yields an accurate deblurred result via a robust image restoration model.

According to this motivation, we develop several strategies which are significantly different from previous works in the following aspects.

1. First, to remove detrimental structures and obtain useful information for kernel estimation, reliable salient structures are selected. Furthermore, to preserve the sparsity and continuity of blur kernel, we propose a new kernel estimation method based on sparse representation together with a powerful spatial prior, which also helps remove the noise effectively.
2. Reliable structures and sparse representation method together with spatial priors are also used to guide the interim latent image restoration, whose sparsity and sharp edges can be preserved effectively.
3. To suppress severe noise, the final deblurred result is obtained by solving an ℓ^1-norm deconvolution model which combines sparsity and spatial priors. An efficient solver based on half-quadratic splitting is employed to solve our proposed models.
4. Finally, to provide a good initialization for our algorithm we develop a simplified version of our proposed algorithm which permits a closed-form solution.

The flowchart shown in Fig. 2 illustrates the framework of our deblurring process in detail.

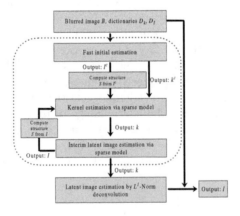

Fig. 2. The flowchart of our algorithm. The dotted line box encloses the process of kernel estimation.

We apply our method to some challenging examples, such as images with complex tiny structures or with large blur kernels, and verify that it is able to provide reliable kernel estimates which are noiseless and also satisfy the sparsity and continuity well. Moreover, high-quality final restored images can be obtained.

2 Kernel Estimation

In this section, we briefly introduce the basics of sparse representation and then employ it as a prior for kernel estimation.

2.1 A Brief Introduction to Sparse Representation

Sparse and redundant modeling of signals has been proven to be very effective for signal reconstruction. It approximates an input signal by a sparse linear combination of bases in an over-complete dictionary. Specifically, let Y be a set of N n-dimensional input signals and D is an over-complete dictionary that has K bases, i.e., $Y = [y_1, ..., y_N] \in R^{n \times N}$ and $D = [d_1, ..., d_K] \in R^{n \times K}$ (typically $n \leq K$). The sparse representation of Y from dictionary D can be accomplished by solving the following problem:

$$\min_{\alpha} \|Y - D\alpha\|_2^2, \quad s.t. \quad \|\alpha_i\|_0 \leq L, \tag{2}$$

where $\alpha = [\alpha_1, ..., \alpha_N] \in R^{K \times N}$ and L is a predefined threshold which controls the sparseness of the representation. The data Y can be prepared from clean images [25] or degraded ones [26], while D can be obtained by dictionary learning methods, e.g., K-SVD [26]. (2) can be solved by many methods, e.g., by solving

$$\min_{\alpha} \|Y - D\alpha\|_2^2 + \lambda\|\alpha\|_1 \tag{3}$$

instead [27], where λ is the Lagrange multiplier.

Sparsity plays an important or even crucial role in many fields, such as image restoration [24–26,28], compressive sensing, and face recognition. In this work, we regard it as a powerful prior to constrain the blur kernel and the latent image.

2.2 Interim Latent Image Estimation via Sparse Model

The salient structures have to be extracted from an interim latent image which is produced during the process of kernel estimation.

Although sparse representation has been successfully applied in many image processing problems, such as image denoising, inpainting, super-resolution and deblurring, as a new robust prior we do not follow the traditional model. To preserve more sharp edges for kernel estimation, we propose the following new robust model for interim latent image restoration:

$$\min_{I,\alpha_I} \|B - k * I\|_2^2 + \beta_I \|\nabla I - \nabla S\|_2^2 + \gamma_I \|I - D_I \alpha_I\|_2^2 + \eta_I \|\alpha_I\|_1 + \lambda_I \sum_{i=1}^{2} \|f_i * I\|_\kappa^\kappa, \tag{4}$$

where ∇I is the gradient of image (i.e. $\nabla I = (I_x, I_y)^T$), ∇S is the salient edges to be detailed in Sect. 2.3, D_I is the image dictionary, and α_I is the sparse coefficient for the image. We use the two first-order derivative filters $f_1 = [1, -1]$ and $f_2 = [1, -1]^T$ to denote ∂_x and ∂_y, respectively (a.k.a. $\partial_x I = f_1 * I$). Similar to the sparse coding-based deblurring methods [20–22], we use alternative minimization method to solve (4).

Different from [22], our image restoration model (4) incorporating the salient edges ∇S contains more sharp edges in the interim latent images. Figure 3 shows a comparison result which demonstrates the effectiveness of our model (4). One can see that our estimated result shown in Fig. 3(f) contains more sharp edges, which will provide more useful information for kernel estimation.

Fig. 3. Comparison of different deconvolution methods. (a) Blurred image. (b) Result of Xu and Jia [16]. (c) Result of Levin [15]. (c) Result of Zuo and Lin [29]. (d) Result of Krishnan and Fergus [30]. (e) Result of Zhang et al. [21]. (f) Our result. The result of our improved model (4) in (f) contains more sharp edges.

2.3 Image Structure Computation

How to get an accurate kernel is a challenging problem in blind image deblurring. To our knowledge, not all image details are useful for the kernel estimation. If we do not remove the detrimental details, we will obtain an unreliable deblurred result. Results shown in Fig. 4(b) illustrates such a possibility.

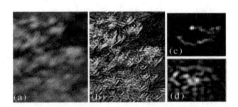

Fig. 4. Kernel estimation results using the raw input image. (a) Blurred image. (b) and (d) Results without eliminating details. (c) True blur kernel. Result in (b) is computed by using the deblurring framework in [11]. The kernel size is 35×35.

To obtain a good kernel estimate, we extract reliable salient structure, whose computation is as follows.

First, we adopt the following robust model to select the main structure of an image I:

$$\min_{I_s} \|\nabla I_s\|_1 + \frac{1}{2\theta\omega(x)}\|I_s - I\|_2^2, \tag{5}$$

where $\omega(x) = \exp(-(r(x))^{0.8})$ and $r(x)$ is defined as follows:

$$r(x) = \frac{\|\sum_{y\in N_h(x)} \nabla B(y)\|_2}{\sum_{y\in N_h(x)} \|\nabla B(y)\|_2 + \epsilon}, \tag{6}$$

in which B is the blurred image and $N_h(x)$ is an $h \times h$ window centered at pixel x. A small r implies that the area is flat, whereas a large r implies that there exist strong image structures in the local window. This equation is also employed by [16] to remove some narrow strips that may undermine the kernel estimation. We combine model (5) with the adaptive weight $\omega(x)$ to smooth such structures effectively. In our experiments, we set $\epsilon = 0.5$ and $h = 3$.

Second, we compute an image $\tilde{I}_s$ by a shock filter [31]:

$$\tilde{I}_s = -sgn(\triangle I_s)\|\nabla I_s\|_2, \tag{7}$$

where $\triangle I = I_x^2 I_{xx} + 2I_x I_y I_{xy} + I_y^2 I_{yy}$.

Finally, we compute salient edges ∇S which will be used to guide the kernel estimation:

$$\nabla S = \nabla \tilde{I}_s H(\mathbf{G}, t), \tag{8}$$

where $H(\mathbf{G}, t)$ is the unit binary mask function is defined as:

$$H(\mathbf{G}, t) = \begin{cases} 1, & G_i \geqslant t, \\ 0, & \text{otherwise}, \end{cases} \tag{9}$$

and $\mathbf{G} = (\|\nabla \tilde{I}_s\|_2, |\partial_x \tilde{I}_s|/5\sqrt{2}, |\partial_y \tilde{I}_s|/5\sqrt{2})$. The parameter t is a threshold of the gradient magnitude which is determined by the size of blur kernel. Figure 5(b) shows the salient edges ∇S.

(a)   (b)

Fig. 5. An illustration of salient edges. (a) Input blurred image. (b) Salient edges in (a).

To demonstrate the effect of salient edges ∇S, we use the deblurring algorithm by Cho et al. [11] to deblur with ∇S and image details[1], respectively.

---

[1] Image details is referred to as $I - I_s$.

Result in Fig. 6(d) shows that using salient edges only can improve the kernel estimation significantly, while using image details does not result in a satisfactory kernel estimate (e.g., Fig. 6(a)[2]). Figure 6(b) and (c) are computed using the image structure. They still contain some blur.

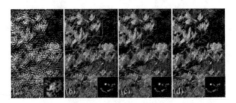

Fig. 6. Kernel estimation results with different image structures. (a) Result with image details. (b) Result of Cho and Lee [11]. (c) Result of Xu and Jia [16]. (d) Results with salient edges ∇S.

2.4 Kernel Estimation via Sparse Model

The motion blur kernel describes the path of camera shake during the exposure. Most literatures assume that distributions of blur kernels can be well modeled by a Hyper-Laplacian, based on which the corresponding model for kernel estimation is:

$$\min_k \|\nabla B - k * \nabla I\|_2^2 + \gamma \|k\|_\alpha^\alpha,$$
$$s.t. \quad k(x,y) \geq 0, \sum_{x,y} k(x,y) = 1, \tag{10}$$

where $0 < \alpha \leq 1$.

Although model (10) can preserve the sparsity of kernel effectively, it does not ensure the continuity of kernel and sometimes results in a noisy kernel estimate [3,18]. Another critical problem is that the imperfectly estimated image I used in model (10) also leads to a noisy kernel estimate.

To overcome these problems, first, we use the salient edges to replace the gradient ∇I in model (10); second, we constrain the gradients to preserve the continuity of kernel. Considering the speciality of kernel, we introduce a new spatial term $\mathcal{C}(k)$ which is proposed by [32] to remove tiny details. It is defined as follows:
$$\mathcal{C}(k) = \#\{(x,y)| \quad |\partial_x k(x,y)| + |\partial_y k(x,y)| \neq 0\}, \tag{11}$$

i.e., $\mathcal{C}(k)$ counts the number of pixels whose gradients are non-zeros. It can not only keep the structure of kernel effectively, but also remove some noise [18] (Fig. 7(d) shows the effectiveness of this metric). Finally, to preserve the sparsity well, we employ the sparse representation to constrain the blur kernel.

---

[2] We replace I_s with $I - I_s$ in (7), then result shown in (a) is obtained in the same way as (d).

Based on the above considerations, our novel model for kernel estimation is defined as:

$$\min_{k,\alpha_k} \|\nabla B - k * \nabla S\|_2^2 + \gamma_k \|k - D_k \alpha_k\|_2^2 + \eta_k \|\alpha_k\|_1 + \lambda_k \mathcal{C}(k),$$

$$s.t. \quad k(x,y) \geq 0, \sum_{x,y} k(x,y) = 1, \tag{12}$$

where ∇S is the reliable salient edges that are computed previously, D_k is the kernel dictionary and α_k is sparse coefficient of kernel. Model (12) is robust to noise and can preserve both sparsity and continuity of kernel because:

1. The salient edges in the first term provides reliable edge information;
2. The second and third terms use sparse representation to provide a data-authentic prior for the kernel;
3. The spatial term $\mathcal{C}(k)$ makes the kernel sparse and also discourages discontinuous points, hence promoting continuity.

We use the same optimization method proposed in [18] to solve (12).

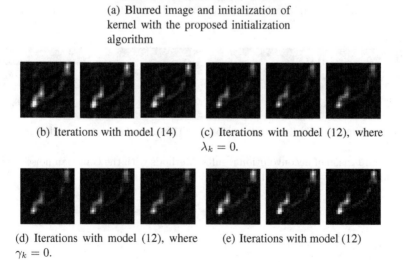

(a) Blurred image and initialization of kernel with the proposed initialization algorithm

(b) Iterations with model (14)

(c) Iterations with model (12), where $\lambda_k = 0$.

(d) Iterations with model (12), where $\gamma_k = 0$.

(e) Iterations with model (12)

Fig. 7. Effectiveness of the terms in our model (12). The result (e) of our model is the best.

Figure 7 shows the effectiveness of terms in our model (12). One can see that the estimated kernel k obtained from the proposed initialization algorithm contains severe noise, after several iterations with model (12), the noise in the kernel is removed effectively (Fig. 7(e)). Figure 7(b) shows that the Gaussian prior cannot keep the sparsity and remove the noise in the kernel. Compared with Fig. 7(c) and (d), the new spatial term $\mathcal{C}(k)$ and sparsity term are able to remove noise effectively. This example (i.e., comparison of Fig. 7(b) and (e)) further proves that applying a sparse model only to the latent image restoration [20–22] is not enough.

3   Latent Image Estimation by ℓ^1-Norm Deconvolution

Many works, including our interim latent image estimation model (4), have used $\|B - k * I\|_2^2$ in their deblurring model. This is equivalent to assuming that the noise in the blurred image is Gaussian. This is not always true in real situations. Many literatures have pointed out that this assumption possibly makes results vulnerable to large noise or outliers. To improve the robustness to outliers, we propose an ℓ^1-norm deconvolution model, which is written as,

$$\min_{I,\alpha} \|B - k * I\|_1 + \gamma\|I - D_I\alpha\|_2^2 + \eta\|\alpha\|_1 + \lambda\sum_{i=1}^{2}\|f_i * I\|_\kappa^\kappa. \tag{13}$$

This is an ℓ^1-norm deconvolution [16]. Similar to [16], we use the half-quadratic method to solve it.

Figure 8 shows an example which also appears in [33]. The blurred image contains impulse noise and many saturated pixels which increase the difficulty for deconvolution[3]. Our method performs better than methods presented in Fig. 8.

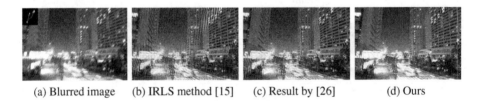

(a) Blurred image   (b) IRLS method [15]   (c) Result by [26]   (d) Ours

Fig. 8. Comparison of deconvolution results. Methods with the Gaussian noise assumption produce unconvincing results.

---

[3] In this paper, we regard noise and saturation pixels as outliers, and do not take any special strategy to deal with them. Thus, result of [33] performs better. However, our result is comparable with that of [33].

4   Initializing Our Algorithm

Our kernel estimation model (12) and latent image restoration model (4) are highly non-convex problems. Thus, a good initialization is critical. In this section, we introduce how to initialize them efficiently and effectively.

For kernel estimation, we use a simplified version of model (12) for computing the initial kernel estimate:

$$\min_{k^c} \|\nabla B - k^c * \nabla S\|_2^2 + \gamma_c \|k^c\|_2^2. \tag{14}$$

Note that model (14) is convex. By adopt a similar strategy as in [12,16], we can obtain a closed-form solution to (15):

$$k^c = F^{-1}\left(\frac{\overline{F(\partial_x S)}F(\partial_x B) + \overline{F(\partial_y S)}F(\partial_y B)}{\overline{F(\partial_x S)}F(\partial_x S) + \overline{F(\partial_y S)}F(\partial_y S) + \gamma_c} \right), \tag{15}$$

where $F(\cdot)$ and $F^{-1}(\cdot)$ denote the Fast Fourier Transform (FFT) and inverse FFT, respectively, and $\overline{F(\cdot)}$ is the complex conjugate operator.

In the interim latent image estimation, we also utilize a simplified version of model (4) for initialization:

$$\min_{I^c} \|B - k^c * I^c\|_2^2 + \lambda_c \|\nabla I^c\|_2^2. \tag{16}$$

Again, a closed-form solution of (16) exists and is given as:

$$I^c = F^{-1}\left(\frac{\overline{F(k^c)}F(B)}{\overline{F(k^c)}F(k^c) + \lambda_c F_g} \right), \tag{17}$$

where $F_g = \overline{F(\partial_x)}F(\partial_x) + \overline{F(\partial_y)}F(\partial_y)$.

Based on above considerations, we use the same framework by [18] to get the initializations for the proposed algorithm.

With the initialization algorithm, we can get rough estimates fast. Figure 9(b) shows the results with the proposed initialization algorithm.

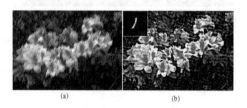

(a)   (b)

Fig. 9. Fast initialization results. (a) Blurred image. (b) Result with the proposed initialization algorithm. Both the kernel and latent image in (b) contain some noise.

Finally, we use the similar coarse-to-fine framework [18] to estimate blur kernel.

5   Experiments

5.1   Dictionary Learning

For the image dictionary D_I, there are many excellent algorithms for obtaining it. We randomly select raw patches from training images of similar statistical nature and use the K-SVD method proposed by [26] to compute the image dictionary. The patch size is 16×16 pixels and the number of bases is 256. So the size of image dictionary is 256×256.

For the blur kernel dictionary D_k, we collect some truth camera shake blur kernels as the training data. We set the patch size of data to 4×4 pixels and the number of bases 256. So the size of kernel dictionary is 16×256. Then we also use K-SVD [26] to learn the kernel dictionary.

5.2   Experimental Results and Evaluation

We first use a synthetic example to verify the effectiveness of our kernel estimation model. Figure 10 shows the kernel estimation results by state-of-the-art methods[4]. One can see that the continuity of kernel by [10] is destroyed and those by [11,12,15,16] still contain some noise. From Fig. 10(h) and (i) we can see that the proposed method results a sparse kernel. The Peak Signal to Noise Ratio (PSNR) values presented in Table 1 also show that our method has a higher PSNR value than the other state-of-the-art methods.

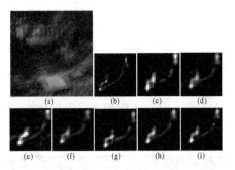

Fig. 10. Comparison of kernel estimation results with state-of-the-art methods. (a) Blurred image. (b) True kernel. (c) Result of Fergus et al. [10]. (d) Result of Shan et al. [12]. (e) Result of Cho and Lee [11]. (f) Result of Xu and Jia [16]. (g) Result of Levin et al. [15]. (h) Result of Pan et al. [18]. (i) Our result. Our method produces a better kernel estimate.

We then use another synthetic example to test the effectiveness of our method. Figure 11 shows an example that is presented in [21]. We compare our method with state-of-the-art methods [11,12,15,16,18,21,34]. Xu and Jia [16]

---

[4] The Matlab codes are available on authors' webpages.

Table 1. PSNR values of the deblurred results in Fig. 10

Methods	[10]	[12]	[11]	[16]	[15]	[18]	Our
PSNR (dB)	22.76	24.24	22.98	23.80	18.91	23.90	25.40

and Cho and Lee [11] fail to provide an accurate shape of the kernel and the deblurred results also have serious artifacts. The kernel by [15] looks perfect, but the quality of deblurred result is low. The kernel by Shan et al. [12] also looks perfect, but the deblurred result contains some visual artifacts due to the final hard thresholding operation (see the parts in the red boxes in Fig. 11(c)). The kernel by Zhang et al. [21] contains some noise, and the deblurred result has some visual artifacts (see the parts in the red boxes in Fig. 11(f)). The method in [34] cannot provide a correct kernel. So the deblurred result contains some blur. Result of [18] provides a better kernel estimate. However, the less robust deconvolution model leads to lower quality of the deblurred result. In contrast, the result of our method has the best visual quality and also the highest PSNR value.

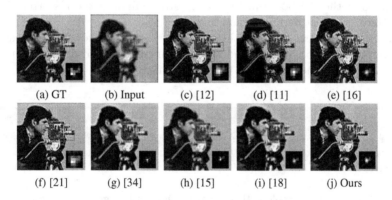

(a) GT   (b) Input   (c) [12]   (d) [11]   (e) [16]

(f) [21]   (g) [34]   (h) [15]   (i) [18]   (j) Ours

Fig. 11. Comparison with state-of-the-art methods on a synthetic example without noise. (c) PSNR: 22.48 dB. (d) PSNR: 19.50 dB. (e) PSNR: 19.32 dB. (f) PSNR: 22.66 dB. (g) PSNR: 21.25 dB. (h) PSNR: 19.25 dB. (i) PSNR: 19.44 dB. (j) PSNR: 23.41 dB. The red boxes in (c) and (f) indicate the serious artifacts. The result of our method has the highest quality.

Now we test our method with a real image with few outliers. We choose an image in [10] (Fig. 12(a)). It contains some outliers shown in the red boxes in Fig. 12(a). The result of [23], which is also a sparse representation based method, has many noise residuals and artifacts around edges in the deblurred images. Its kernel estimation and latent image restoration results show that the framelet and curvelet system cannot serve as good sparsity priors for kernel and latent image. The kernel estimate of Fergus et al. [10] contains some noise. The continuity of

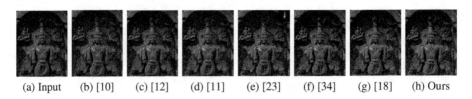

(a) Input   (b) [10]   (c) [12]   (d) [11]   (e) [23]   (f) [34]   (g) [18]   (h) Ours

Fig. 12. Results on an image with few outliers. Red boxes in (a) indicate outliers, and those in other sub-figures indicate outliers or artifacts. Our method removes the outliers in the red boxes of (a) effectively and its result does not contain detectable artifacts. (Color figure online)

kernel is also destroyed due to the hard thresholding operation. As a result, the corresponding deblurred result is not very sharp. Methods in [11,12] also use hard thresholding in the kernel estimation. So their kernels are sparse. However, their deblurred results contain some noise and the outliers in the red boxes in Fig. 12(c) and (d) still remain in the restored images. Method in [34] produces a noisy kernel and the restored image contains some noise and several visual artifacts. Pan et al.'s method [18] generates a perfect kernel estimate. However, the outliers in the red boxes in Fig. 12 (g) still remain in the restored results due to the less robust deconvolution model.

We test with a real image with large blur. Figure 13 shows a real example with large blur which can be found in [16]. Our method also performs the best in estimating both the kernel and the latent image.

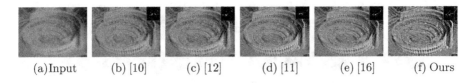

(a)Input   (b) [10]   (c) [12]   (d) [11]   (e) [16]   (f) Ours

Fig. 13. Another real example with large blur. Our method generates the best kernel and the restored image. The size of our estimated kernel is 45 × 45.

5.3 Evaluation on the Dataset of [14]

We perform quantitative evaluation of our method using the data set from [14]. For fair comparison, the kernel estimates of [10,11,15] are generated by using the authors' binary files. The final deblurred results are obtained by using the sparse deconvolution method of [15]. The parameters are assigned default values according to the suggestions in [15]. In Fig. 14, we plot the cumulative histogram of error ratios[5]. One can see that our method performs better than others.

---

[5] We only present the deblurred results with the error ratio (smaller than 3). Otherwise, We find that the results will be unreliable.

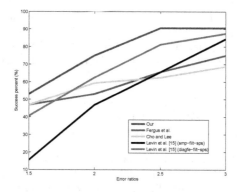

Fig. 14. Evaluation results: cumulative histogram of the deconvolution error ratio across tests.

6   Conclusions

For blind image deblurring, we have presented an effective method which combines salient structure detection and sparse representation. The salient structure provides reliable edge information, while sparse representation offers faithful priors for both the kernel and the latent image. Their combination greatly improves the quality of kernel estimation and latent image restoration. We also provide fast initialization methods for the optimization models and propose efficient alternative minimization based methods to solve our optimization problems. Extensive experiments testify to the superiority of our method over state-of-the-art methods, both qualitatively and quantitatively.

References

1. Chen, W.G., Nandhakumar, N., Martin, W.N.: Image motion estimation from motion smear-a new computational model. IEEE Trans. Pattern Anal. Mach. Intell. **18**(1), 234–778 (1996)
2. Rav-Acha, A., Peleg, S.: Two motion-blurred images are better than one. Pattern Recogn. Lett. **26**, 311–317 (2005)
3. Chen, J., Yuan, L., Tang, C.K., Quan, L.: Robust dual motion deblurring. In: CVPR, pp. 1–8 (2008)
4. Li, W., Zhang, J., Dai, Q.: Exploring aligned complementary image pair for blind motion deblurring. In: CVPR, pp. 273–280 (2011)
5. Yuan, L., Sun, J., Quan, L., Shum, H.Y.: Image deblurring with blurred/noisy image pairs. ACM Trans. Graph. **26**(3), 1–10 (2007)
6. Zhuo, S., Guo, D., Sim, T.: Robust flash deblurring. In: CVPR, pp. 2440–2447 (2010)
7. Chan, T., Wong, C.: Total variation blind deconvolution. IEEE Trans. Image Process. **7**(3), 370–375 (1998)
8. You, Y.L., Kaveh, M.: Blind image restoration by anisotropic regularization. IEEE Trans. Image Process. **8**(3), 396–407 (1999)

9. Yitzhaky, Y., Mor, I., Lantzman, A., Kopeika, N.S.: Direct method for restoration of motion-blurred images. J. Opt. Soc. Am. A **15**(6), 1512–1519 (1998)

10. Fergus, R., Singh, B., Hertzmann, A., Roweis, S.T., Freeman, W.T.: Removing camera shake from a single photograph. ACM Trans. Graph. **25**(3), 787–794 (2006)

11. Cho, S., Lee, S.: Fast motion deblurring. ACM Trans. Graph. **28**(5), 1–8 (2009). (SIGGRAPH Asia)

12. Shan, Q., Jia, J., Agarwala, A.: High-quality motion deblurring from a single image. ACM Trans. Graph. **27**(3), 1–10 (2008)

13. Jia, J.: Single image motion deblurring using transparency. In: CVPR, pp. 1–8 (2007)

14. Levin, A., Weiss, Y., Durand, F., Freeman, W.T.: Understanding and evaluating blind deconvolution algorithms. In: CVPR, pp. 1964–1971 (2009)

15. Levin, A., Weiss, Y., Durand, F., Freeman, W.T.: Efficient marginal likelihood optimization in blind deconvolution. In: CVPR, pp. 2657–2664 (2011)

16. Xu, L., Jia, J.: Two-phase kernel estimation for robust motion deblurring. In: Daniilidis, K., Maragos, P., Paragios, N. (eds.) ECCV 2010. LNCS, vol. 6311, pp. 157–170. Springer, Heidelberg (2010). https://doi.org/10.1007/978-3-642-15549-9_12

17. Cho, T.S., Paris, S., Horn, B.K.P., Freeman, W.T.: Blur kernel estimation using the Radon transform. In: CVPR, pp. 241–248 (2011)

18. Pan, J., Liu, R., Su, Z., Gu, X.: Kernel estimation from salient structure for robust motion deblurring. Signal Process. Image Commun. **28**(9), 1156–1170 (2013)

19. Lou, Y., Bertozzi, A.L., Soatto, S.: Direct sparse deblurring. J. Math. Imag. Vis. **39**(1), 1–12 (2011)

20. Hu, Z., Huang, J.B., Yang, M.H.: Single image deblurring with adaptive dictionary learning. In: ICIP, pp. 1169–1172 (2010)

21. Zhang, H., Yang, J., Zhang, Y., Huang, T.S.: Sparse representation based blind image deblurring. In: ICME, pp. 1–6 (2011)

22. Zhang, H., Yang, J., Zhang, Y., Huang, T.S.: Close the loop: joint blind image restoration and recognition with sparse representation prior. In: ICCV, pp. 770–777 (2011)

23. Cai, J.F., Ji, H., Liu, C., Shen, Z.: Blind motion deblurring from a single image using sparse approximation. In: CVPR, pp. 104–111 (2009)

24. Dong, W., Zhang, L., Shi, G., Wu, X.: Image deblurring and super-resolution by adaptive sparse domain selection and adaptive regularization. IEEE Trans. Image Process. **20**(7), 1838–1857 (2011)

25. Yang, J., Wright, J., Huang, T.S., Ma, Y.: Image super-resolution as sparse representation of raw image patches. In: CVPR, pp. 1–8 (2008)

26. Elad, M., Aharon, M.: Image denoising via sparse and redundant representations over learned dictionaries. IEEE Trans. Image Process. **15**(12), 3736–3745 (2006)

27. Donoho, D.L.: For most large underdetermined systems of linear equations the minimal ℓ^1-norm solution is also the sparsest solution. Comm. Pure Appl. Math. **59**, 797–829 (2004)

28. Turek, J., Yavneh, I., Protter, M., Elad, M.: On MMSE and MAP denoising under sparse representation modeling over a unitary dictionary. IEEE Trans. Signal Process. **59**(8), 3526–3535 (2011)

29. Zuo, W., Lin, Z.: A generalized accelerated proximal gradient approach for total variation-based image restoration. IEEE Trans. Image Process. **20**(10), 2748–2759 (2011)

30. Krishnan, D., Fergus, R.: Fast image deconvolution using Hyper-Laplacian priors. In: NIPS, pp. 1033–1041 (2009)

31. Osher, S., Rudin, L.I.: Feature-oriented image enhancement using shock filters. SIAM J. Numer. Anal. **27**(4), 919–940 (1990)
32. Xu, L., Lu, C., Xu, Y., Jia, J.: Image smoothing via l_0 gradient minimization. ACM Trans. Graph. **30**, Article No. 174 (2011). (SIGGRAPH Asia)
33. Cho, S., Wang, J., Lee, S.: Handling outliers in non-blind image deconvolution. In: ICCV, pp. 495–502 (2011)
34. Krishnan, D., Tay, T., Fergus, R.: Blind deconvolution using a normalized sparsity measure. In: CVPR, pp. 233–240 (2011)

Blur Estimation for Natural Edge Appearance in Computational Photography

Dongwei Liu[1(✉)] and Reinhard Klette[2]

[1] School of Information, Zhejiang University of Finance and Economic,
Hangzhou, China
dliu697@aucklanduni.ac.nz
[2] School of Engineering, Computer, and Mathematical Sciences,
Auckland University of Technology, Auckland, New Zealand

Abstract. Applying a labelling approach in computational photography (i.e. using a discrete set of labels for, e.g., image segmentation or stereo matching) typically leads to step edges in the output label map. Photorealistic editing requires to remove artificially looking step edges. This is especially true for varying photo effects that are guided by such a label map. The introduction of artificial object edges is commonly reverted by applying some kind of smoothing. This paper presents a specially designed strategy for achieving more natural-looking edges in photo effects by estimating the blur character of the original photograph, and by transferring this blur character onto the processed image. Our blur transfer strategy is tested in this paper for two photo effects, namely one based on image segmentation, and one based on stereo vision. Experiments show that our strategy is able to transfer the blur character from input to output images, and that it avoids the creation of artificial-looking step edges.

Keywords: Computational photography · Photo effects
Blur estimation · Natural-looking step edges

1 Introduction

Blur at object edges is an important feature of a photograph. Normally, an edge in a photograph cannot be "perfectly sharp" (i.e. an ideal step edge) for several reasons, such as limited optical quality of camera systems, or *diffraction* that occurs when light passes through the aperture of a camera.

A major factor that reduces sharpness is *defocus blur*. Theoretically, when an image is formed on a flat sensor by an optical lens, only surface points on a defined plane in the scene are mapped exactly into ideal points on the sensor; other visible surface points in the scene are mapped into small blurred disks. Defocus blur may be reduced by using a small aperture, but cannot be avoided completely. As a result, blur is a natural feature in digital photographs.

© Springer International Publishing AG, part of Springer Nature 2018
S. Satoh (Ed.): PSIVT 2017, LNCS 10799, pp. 300–310, 2018.
https://doi.org/10.1007/978-3-319-92753-4_24

In digital geometry [10], a *step edge* is defined by a polyline following grid edges of pixel locations. Such a step edge is usually seen as perfectly sharp in sharpness measurements [3]. A step edge looks artificial from the aspect of photo-realistic rendering, especially when zoomed in, because of a different sharpness character at edges in real-world photographs. See Fig. 1, left and middle, for an intuitive comparison.

Fig. 1. A step edge (*left*) in digital geometry is defined by a polyline in the pixel raster; it looks artificial from the aspect of photo-realistic rendering. An edge in a digital photograph (*middle*) is normally blurred a little, thus not as sharp as a step edge. By using a mask defined by a step edge (i.e. as shown on the left), a photo effect that changes color of a local object (*right*) introduces an artificial edge, around which the photo effect fails to fuse with the original photograph if no further action is taken.

Image analysis algorithms, such as image segmentation [1,15] or stereo matching [4,6,7], that label pixel locations by elements in discrete sets of labels generally output label maps with step edges around object silhouettes. Applying such a method, a pixel close to an object silhouette is labelled either as being foreground or background, ignoring the fact that the pixel might be actually a mix of foreground and background (because of the blur as discussed above). The edge blur character (possibly also described as fuzziness) of the original photograph is missing in such a label map.

Photo effects, rendered with the guidance of such a label map, may introduce artificial object edges. First, the rendered effects may include step edges that look artificial. Second, such effects may not fuse well with the original photograph in which edges are naturally blurred. See Fig. 1, right, for an illustration.

Image matting techniques [12] create object borders in a "soft" manner. Different to image segmentation, matting techniques assign an opacity value to any pixel near an object silhouette. Such a framework avoids artificial-looking step edges. The computational complexity of image matting is quite high, especially when applied to modern digital photographs with dozens of mega-pixels.

Blur strength estimation provides a possibility to transfer edge blur characters from an original photograph to a processed image with relatively low cost. Two traditional strategies are based on either gradient or frequency. Gradient based methods [2,3] measure the width of edges in pixel units; these methods lack precision regarding minor blur. Frequency based methods [17,18] assume that sharper image patches involve more high frequency components; these methods may be disturbed by image content, such as textures.

An interesting defocus blur-estimation method is presented in [16]. Considering a Gaussian blur model, this method is sensitive to defocus blur between $\sigma = 0.3$ and $\sigma = 2$. Such a range covers a large part of edges in common photographs.

In this paper, we explore the potential of using blur strength estimation on achieving more natural-looking edges in photo effects. We propose a blur transfer strategy such that rendered photo effects inherit edge blur characters from the original photograph. Thus, the rendered photo effects may fuse well with the original photograph, and thus appear natural.

In particular, we select the *just noticeable defocus blur estimation* method, presented in [16], for blur strength estimation. We apply the estimated blur strength for two photo effects, a meanshift filter, and a technique for naive depth-aware light control. The former is from the subject area of image segmentation, and the latter is based on stereo vision.

Both photo effects generate step edges if used in their original version. We modify these two photo effects by introducing blur strength estimation. This aims at achieving more natural-looking results by transferring the edge-blur character of an original photograph onto the processed image.

Note that a simple minor blur of edges may also remove step edges. Defocus blur is depth-aware, and thus spatially varying within a photograph. A uniform blur cannot ensure that a photo effect inherits the blur character of the original photograph.

The rest of the paper is structured as follows. Section 2 briefly recalls techniques related to our work. Section 3 provides implementation details when using our blur transfer strategy for two selected photo effects. Experimental results are shown and discussed in Sect. 4. Section 5 concludes.

2   Basics and Notations

This section provides notations and techniques used. An image I is defined on a rectangular set $\Omega \subset \mathbb{Z}^2$ of pixel locations, called the *carrier*. By default, I is a color image expressed in RGB color space.

2.1   Just Noticeable Defocus Blur Estimation

Just noticeable defocus blur estimation, proposed in [16], measures spatially varying blur by using external data. A set of 128 patch atoms is extracted from external images that are blurred by a Gaussian kernel defined by $\sigma = 2$. These atoms form a *blur dictionary* D. A patch y in the input image I is decomposed into a sparse representation using atoms in D satisfying

$$\min_x \|x\|_1 \text{ such that } \|y - Dx\|_2 < \varepsilon \tag{1}$$

where $\varepsilon = 0.07$ in [16].

It is observed that the stronger the blur, the less atoms are needed to represent the patch. Then a blur measure $b(y)$ of patch y,

$$b(y) = \|x\|_0 \tag{2}$$

is calculated (i.e. the number of non-zero elements of x).

Suppose the blur of an image is generated by a Gaussian model. The following relationship between the σ-parameter of the Gaussian blur and the blur measure b is estimated in [16] based on extensive experiments:

$$b = \frac{c_1}{1 + \exp(c_2\sigma + c_3)} + c_4 \tag{3}$$

where $c_1 = 39.49$, $c_2 = 4.535$, $c_3 = -3.538$, and $c_4 = 18.53$.

2.2 Image Segmentation and Meanshift Filter

Image segmentation [9] divides an image I into regions (i.e. connected sets of pixel locations), called *segments*. Mathematically, such a method partitions the carrier Ω of I into a finite number of segments $S_i \neq \emptyset$, for $i = 1, \ldots, n$, such that

$$\bigcup_{i=1}^{n} S_i = \Omega \quad \text{and} \quad S_i \cap S_j = \emptyset \tag{4}$$

for $i, j \in \{1, ..., n\}$ and $i \neq j$. Image segmentation is a labelling problem, defined by a discrete label set $L = \{S_0, S_1, S_2, ..., S_n\}$, and the goal to obtain a mapping $s : \Omega \to L$ optimising some defined constraints.

The border between two adjacent segments is a step edge in the resulting segmentation map where pixel values are from the set L. Segment borders in this map do not inherit the blur character of corresponding edges in the original photograph.

The *meanshift filter*, introduced in [1], is a discontinuity-preserving smoothing filter. It is a basic component for many photo effects. For example, a simple face-beautification effect can be formed by combining the meanshift filtered image with the original photograph using a linear combination of both. Such an effect reduces skin imperfections by reducing detailed texture.

The used *meanshift* algorithm, first presented in 1975 by Fukunaga and Hostetler [5], is an iterative steepest-ascent method for locating the maxima of a density function. As a clustering method, the points in the feature space, that move to the same local maxima, are clustered into a single class. The method is widely used in multi-dimensional data analysis, and not limited to the computer vision area.

For applying a meanshift filter, consider that we convert a given RGB image I first into the $L*u*v*$ color space. Pixel locations in Ω are clustered by running a meanshift algorithm on a 5-dimensional feature space formed by the three color channels $L*$, $u*$, $v*$, and the spatial coordinates x and y (using some normalization). Such a clustering forms an over-segmentation of Ω.

Let I_m be the filtered image. For a pixel location $p \in \Omega$, suppose that p is contained in a segment called S_p. Then we have that $I_m(p) = I(p_c)$ where $p_c \in S_p$ is the local peak in the 5-dimensional feature space that defines S_p.

Simply speaking, this filter smoothes the input image by firstly over-segmenting the image, and then assigning the same value to all the pixels in a segment. Step edges will thus occur on the borders of the created segments.

2.3 Stereo Vision

Scene depth is very useful for creating content-aware photo effects, such as the fog effect [13] or the bokeh effect [14]. Binocular stereo vision is a common sensor used for achieving depth information from image pairs.

A complete stereo vision process involves *camera calibration* (of all intrinsic and extrinsic camera parameters), *image rectification* (for mapping base and match image into a *canonical stereo geometry* where epipolar lines are identical image rows in both images), *stereo matching* for identifying corresponding pixels on *epipolar lines* (thus identifying disparities), and finally applying a triangulation for mapping disparities into depth values. See [9] for a detailed introduction.

Stereo matching techniques, such as belief-propagation [4] or semi-global matching [6,7], can be used for calculating a dense disparity map. These methods take a rectified stereo pair I_b and I_m (in canonical stereo geometry) as input. For each pixel p in I_b, a stereo matcher aims at identifying a corresponding pixel p_m in I_m; *correspondence* is here defined in the way that p and p_m are projections of the same point P in the scene.

Stereo matching solves a labeling task by assigning a label (i.e. a disparity mapping d) to each pixel location:

$$d : \Omega \to L \tag{5}$$
$$\text{for } L = \{0, 1, 2, ..., d_{\max}\} \text{ with } |L| = d_{\max} + 1$$

The set L of labels is discrete. The user parameter $d_{\max}$ is the maximum possible disparity. A pixel around object silhouettes is treated either as foreground or as background, thus leaving step edges on the estimated disparity map around object silhouettes. Postprocessing filters, such a *joint bilateral filter* [11], may blur the edges in a disparity map, and thus remove the step edges. Such a blur is not related to the blur character of the original image.

3 Method

This section describes the design and implementation details of our blur transfer strategy. Two photo effects, the meanshift filter and a naive light control, are selected for our experiments. The former is based on image segmentation, and the latter is based on stereo vision. Both effects generate step edges when using the effects in their original versions.

We modify these two photo effects by introducing blur-strength estimation. We expect achieving more natural-looking results by transferring the edge-blur character of an original photograph onto the processed image.

Fig. 2. Our modified meanshift filter. *Top row, left to right*: Original image I, standard meanshift filter result I_M, blur map σ shown in a color key, edge map e (purple for blur, yellow for sharp), and our final result $\hat{I}_M$. *Bottom row, left to right*: Local details of I, I_M, and $\hat{I}_M$. (Color figure online)

3.1   Meanshift Filter

A meanshift filter is defined as a discontinuity preserving smoothing [1]. It aims at protecting the spatial position of edges, but accepts losing some of the sharpness character. As described in Sect. 2.2, such a filter generates step edges around object silhouettes.

We denote by I the original input photograph, and by I_M the filtered image. In order to let I_M inherit the blur character of I, we calculate a blur map σ from I, for each $p \in \Omega$, by using just noticeable defocus blur estimation [16].

Note that a blur measure is only valid on edges. We thus calculate an edge map e from I using the Sobel operator (see, e.g., [9]) followed by a 3×3 dilation (i.e. local maximum). We blur those pixels p in I_M that have $e(p) > \tau$, where $\tau = 2$ is a threshold separating edge pixels from non-edge pixels. A Gaussian kernel with $\sigma(p)$ is used on an edge pixel at p. The blurred result is denoted as $\hat{I}_M$. See Fig. 2 for an illustration.

3.2   Simple Light Control Based on Stereo Vision

We define simple light control by darkening the foreground or background of the input photograph I according to a disparity map d provided by stereo vision. For the discussion of the method, assume that d is accurate and dense (i.e. there are defined disparities for all $p \in \Omega$). The results of darkening the foreground or background are denoted by I_F or I_B, respectively.

Without knowing the focal length or the base-line of the stereo vision system, a relative depth map D is calculated as follows:

$$D(p) = \frac{1}{d(p) + \delta} \tag{6}$$

where δ is a small positive number to avoid a division by zero.

The input photograph I is converted into the $L*a*b*$ color space. The darken-the-foreground effect is applied on the L channel by

$$L_F(p) = \max(0,\ L(p) - \Delta(p)) \tag{7}$$
$$\text{for } \Delta(p) = c \cdot \frac{D_{\max} - D(p)}{D_{\max} - D_{\min}}$$

where c is a parameter controlling the global strength of the darkening effect; $D_{\max}$ and $D_{\min}$ are the maximum and minimum depth value in D, respectively. The darken-the-background effect works in an analogous way. It can be seen that step edges in d transfer to L_F, and thus also to I_F.

In order to let I_F inherit the blur character of I, similar to the process described in Sect. 3.1, we calculate a blur map σ from I using just noticeable defocus blur estimation [16]. We nonuniformly blur L_F on those (edge) pixels at p where $e(p) > \tau$, where e is an edge map calculated from I using the Sobel operator followed by a 3×3 dilation (i.e. local maximum); $\tau = 2$ is again our threshold deciding about edge pixels. A Gaussian kernel with $\sigma(p)$ is used at edge pixel locations p. We denote the blurred versions by $\hat{L}_F$ and $\hat{I}_F$.

We do not apply blur onto the disparity map because a photo effect might be non-linear (e.g. when replacing the background by data from another photo); the simple light control effect considered in this paper is linear.

4   Experiments and Discussion

We demonstrate two successful contributions to photo effects, and illustrate also a limitation of the proposed method. In our experiments, we assume high-quality input photographs where noise is not visible. Obviously, our method cannot transfer incorrect sharpness, caused by strong noise, from an input to the output image.

4.1   Meanshift Filter

A comparison between the original meanshift filter [1] and our modified meanshift filter is illustrated in Fig. 3. The red and blue rectangles show in detail two local parts of the original photograph and the corresponding parts in the results when using either the original meanshift filter or our modified meanshift filter.

It can be seen that object edges are rendered as step edges by the original meanshift filter (see Fig. 3, middle), ignoring the blur character of the input photography. Our method (see Fig. 3, bottom) removes such step edges and leads to a more natural-looking result.

The original photograph in this example (see Fig. 3, top) shows a typical defocus blur varying across the carrier Ω. The camera was focused on the closest bead of the bracelet. As a result, the edge of the closest bead (shown in a red rectangle), which is very close to the focus point, is only blurred a little. The edge of the most far away bead (shown in a blue rectangle) is blurred relatively stronger. Our result (Fig. 3, bottom) successfully inherits the blur character of the original photograph.

Fig. 3. Comparison between original meanshift filter and our meanshift filter inheriting the blur character from the input image. *Top to bottom*: Original photograph, result of the original meanshift filter, and result of our modified meanshift filter that inherits the blur character from the input. Local parts in the left image, marked by the *red and blue rectangles*, are zoomed in and shown on the right. (Color figure online)

4.2 Depth-Related Darkening

Figure 4 shows an experiment of using our blur transfer strategy for two depth-aware light control effects, darkening the foreground or darkening the background. The used image and the disparity map is from the *Middlebury 2005 dataset* (vision.middlebury.edu/stereo/) [8]. Invalid disparity values, caused by occlusion, are simply filled by applying a joint bilateral filter. Similar to the above figure, two local parts of images are selected and shown in zoomed-in version.

In the darken-the-foreground effect (see Fig. 4, second row), the edge of the baby's head (see the red rectangle) is eroded by the darkening effect, leaving a dark frame around the silhouette. That is because the edge is blurred a little, and a part of the mixed region is treated as background in the disparity map. The darkening effect generates a significant step edge next to the blue toy (see the blue rectangle).

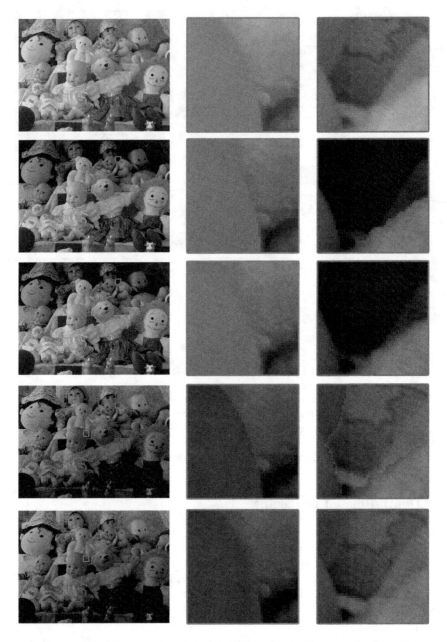

Fig. 4. Comparisons between depth-aware light control effects, with or without our blur-transfer strategy. *Top to bottom*: Original photograph, a darken-the-background effect, darkened background with our blur transfer strategy, a darken-the-foreground effect, and darkened foreground with our blur transfer strategy. Local parts in the left image, marked by *red and blue rectangles*, are zoomed in and shown on the right. (Color figure online)

By introducing our blur transfer strategy (see Fig. 4, third row), these issues are both resolved. For the darken-the-background effect (see Fig. 4, fourth row), dark frames can be seen in both the red and the blue rectangle. These issues are also resolved by our strategy (see Fig. 4, fifth row).

4.3   Defocus Blur

We used the just noticeable defocus blur estimation method [16], as specified above. This method is only sensitive to defocus blur between $\sigma = 0.3$ and $\sigma = 2$, considering a Gaussian blur model.

Strong defocus blur with $\sigma > 2$ cannot be effectively estimated. See Fig. 5 for an example of such a strong defocus blur. In this example, the fourth bar is in focus and thus very sharp. The third and the fifth bar are barely distinguishable from the background in the blur map. The blur strength of the other columns are not effectively estimated. Also, this blur estimation model is not fit for motion blur. In these cases, blur character cannot be successfully transferred using our strategy.

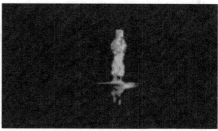

Fig. 5. Strong defocus blur with $\sigma > 2$ cannot be effectively estimated by using the just noticeable defocus blur estimation method [16]. *Left*: Input image with strong defocus blur. *Right*: Calculated blur map shown by using a color key (purple for blur, yellow for sharp). (Color figure online)

5   Conclusions

Image-labelling techniques using discrete sets of labels, such as image segmentation or stereo matching, generate step edges in output label maps. Spatially-varying photo effects that are guided by such a label map may introduce artificial object edges.

We present a strategy for achieving more natural-looking edges in photo effects by estimating the blur character of the original photograph, and by transferring the blur character onto the processed image.

Our blur transfer strategy is tested for two photo effects, the meanshift filter and a simple way of light control. The former is based on image segmentation, and the latter is based on stereo vision. Both effects would generate step edges when using the original versions of those techniques. Experiments shows that our strategy can transfer the blur character from input onto output image, and avoids that the output image contains artificial-looking step edges.

References

1. Comaniciu, D., Meer, P.: Mean shift: a robust approach toward feature space analysis. IEEE Trans. Pattern Anal. Mach. Intell. **24**, 603–619 (2002)
2. Elder, J.H., Zucker, S.W.: Local scale control for edge detection and blur estimation. IEEE Trans. Pattern Anal. Mach. Intell. **20**, 699–716 (1998)
3. Feichtenhofer, C., Fassold, H., Schallauer, P.: A perceptual image sharpness metric based on local edge gradient analysis. IEEE Sig. Process. Lett. **20**, 379–382 (2013)
4. Felzenszwalb, P.F., Huttenlocher, D.P.: Efficient belief propagation for early vision. Int. J. Comput. Vis. **70**, 41–54 (2006)
5. Fukunaga, K., Hostetler, L.: The estimation of the gradient of a density function, with applications in pattern recognition. IEEE Trans. Inf. Theory **21**, 32–40 (1975)
6. Hermann, S., Klette, R.: Iterative semi-global matching for robust driver assistance systems. In: Lee, K.M., Matsushita, Y., Rehg, J.M., Hu, Z. (eds.) ACCV 2012. LNCS, vol. 7726, pp. 465–478. Springer, Heidelberg (2013). https://doi.org/10.1007/978-3-642-37431-9_36
7. Hirschmuller, H.: Accurate and efficient stereo processing by semi-global matching and mutual information. In: Proceedings of CVPR, pp. 807–814 (2005)
8. Hirschmuller, H., Scharstein, D.: Evaluation of cost functions for stereo matching. In: Proceedings of CVPR, pp. 1–8 (2007)
9. Klette, R.: Concise Computer Vision: An Introduction into Theory and Algorithms. Springer, London (2014). https://doi.org/10.1007/978-1-4471-6320-6
10. Klette, R., Rosenfeld, A.: Digital Geometry: Geometric Methods for Digital Picture Analysis. Morgan Kaufmann, San Francisco (2004)
11. Kopf, J., Cohen, M.F., Lischinski, D., Uyttendaele, M.: Joint bilateral upsampling. ACM Trans. Graphics **26**(3), 96 (2007)
12. Levin, A., Lischinski, D., Weiss, Y.: A closed-form solution to natural image matting. IEEE Trans. Pattern Anal. Mach. Intell. **30**, 228–242 (2008)
13. Liu, D., Klette, R.: Fog effect for photography using stereo vision. Vis. Comput. **32**, 99–109 (2016)
14. Liu, D., Nicolescu, R., Klette, R.: Stereo-based bokeh effects for photography. Mach. Vis. Appl. **27**, 1325–1337 (2016)
15. Shi, J., Malik, J.: Normalized cuts and image segmentation. IEEE Trans. Pattern Anal. Mach. Intell. **22**, 888–905 (2000)
16. Shi, J., Xu, L., Jia, J.: Just noticeable defocus blur detection and estimation. In: Proceedings of CVPR, pp. 657–665 (2015)
17. Vu, P.V., Chandler, D.M.: A fast wavelet-based algorithm for global and local image sharpness estimation. IEEE Sig. Process. Lett. **19**, 423–426 (2012)
18. Zhu, X., Cohen, S., Schiller, S., Milanfar, P.: Estimating spatially varying defocus blur from a single image. IEEE Trans. Image Process. **22**, 4879–4891 (2013)

Structure-Preserving Texture Smoothing via Adaptive Patches

Hui Wang[1], Yue Wang[1], Junjie Cao[2], and Xiuping Liu[2(✉)]

[1] School of Information Science and Technology, Shijiazhuang Tiedao University,
Shijiazhuang, China
[2] School of Mathematical Sciences, Dalian University of Technology,
Dalian, China
xpliu@dlut.edu.cn

Abstract. Almost all of previous works on structure-preserving texture smoothing utilize statistical features of pixels within local *rectangular patch* to distinguish structures from textures. Since rectangular patches are not aligned to structural boundaries, inexact statistics are inevitable for patches containing both textures and structures. To overcome this problem, a novel structure-preserving texture smoothing approach is proposed via *structure-adaptive patches*, which conform to local structural boundaries and just contain textures. Specifically, structure adaptive-patches are first generated by several times of classical SLIC superpixel segmentations in the same scale. Secondly, superpixels among different SLIC segmentations are used for computing a guidance image that smooths the fine-scale textures while preserving main structures. Finally, guided bilateral filtering, which incorporates the guidance image into the range filter kernel, is utilized to smooth textures while preserving structural edges. Experimental results demonstrate that the proposed method achieves higher quality results compared to state-of-the-art works.

Keywords: Texture smoothing · Guided bilateral filtering
Structure-adaptive patches

1 Introduction

Many real-world natural scenes and human-created art pieces contain textures. Structure-preserving texture smoothing is a fundamental tool for many applications in computer vision and computer graphics, such as detail manipulation, tone mapping, visual abstraction, edge detection and image segmentation.

However, existing classical edge-preserving image smoothing methods cannot fully separate fine-scale textures from main structures [1–7]. Because these approaches distinguish edges from details based on color differences or gradients, where low-contrast details are smoothed and high-contrast edges are preserved. While textures usually contain strong enough contrast that is confused with main structural edges. Structure-preserving texture smoothing is still a challenging problem due to the difficulty of distinguishing fine-scale textures from main structures, and has received lots of attention recently [8–25].

© Springer International Publishing AG, part of Springer Nature 2018
S. Satoh (Ed.): PSIVT 2017, LNCS 10799, pp. 311–324, 2018.
https://doi.org/10.1007/978-3-319-92753-4_25

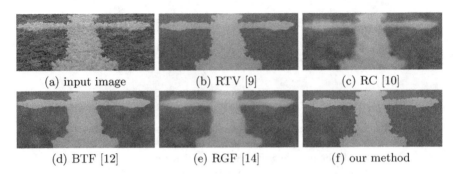

(a) input image   (b) RTV [9]   (c) RC [10]

(d) BTF [12]   (e) RGF [14]   (f) our method

Fig. 1. Comparisons with state-of-the-art methods. It is demonstrated that the proposed method can preserve sharp structural edges better than others. Parameters: (b) $\lambda = 0.03$, $\sigma = 2$. (c) Model 1, $\sigma = 0.5$, $k = 5$. (d) $k = 9$, $n_{iter} = 5$. (e) $\sigma_s = 10$, $\sigma_r = 0.1$. (f) $k = 9$, $\sigma' = 0.25$, $\sigma'_r = 0.05$, $n_{iter} = 5$.

Almost all of the previous methods of structure-preserving texture smoothing rely on statistical features within local *rectangular patches* to extract main structures from fine-scale textures. Xu et al. [9] propose the pixel-wise relative total variation, which is a statistical measure of color gradients within a rectangular patch centered at the pixel, to distinguish structures from textures. Karacan et al. [10] introduce a weighted-averaging method for structure-preserving texture smoothing, where the weights are computed from covariance matrices of image features within pixel-centered rectangular patches. These above pixel-centered rectangular patches based methods are prone to blur the structural edges illustrated in Figs. 1 and 3. Two neighboring patches centered at two adjacent pixels must have a larger overlap. Consequently, their local statistics should be similar even the two adjacent pixels on the opposite sides of a structural edge. The patch shift scheme and choosing local rectangles with adaptive radii [17,18] can alleviate the above problem but sill blurs some structural edges. This is because rectangular patches are not well adherent to small sharp structural edges.

In this paper, we propose a structure-preserving texture smoothing via adaptive patches. In our method, we first apply the state-of-the-art SLIC superpixel segmentation to generate structure-adaptive patches. Second, several times of superpixel segmentations in a fixed scale are used for weighting the guidance image via Gaussian weights. Finally, a guided bilateral filtering is used to extract main structures from textures.

2   Related Work

2.1   Edge-Preserving Image Smoothing

Local explicit filtering methods compute color intensity of each pixel as a linear combination of their neighbor pixels. The linear combination weights in the classical bilateral filter consider both spatial distance and range similarity between

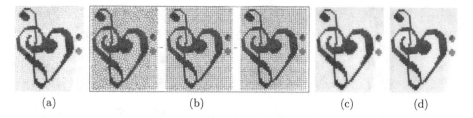

(a)   (b)   (c)   (d)

Fig. 2. Overall process and intermediate images of our structure-preserving texture smoothing approach with parameters $k = 11$, $\sigma' = 0.1$, $\sigma'_r = 0.05$ and $n_{iter} = 1$. (a) input image. (b) some used superpixel segmentations in a same scale. (c) the guidance image computed from superpixels. (d) the guided bilateral filtering result.

pixels [1]. If another image is used to calculate the range similarity, this filter becomes the guided bilateral filter [12]. Due to its simplicity and effectiveness, bilateral filter is widely used in many applications [26]. However, the implementation of bilateral filter is a bit slow. There are a number of accelerated versions [27]. Unlike using fixed kernels in the bilateral filter, moving windows is used to compute the average in the mean shift filter [28]. Based on a novel insight of a local linear relation between a guidance image and the final filtering result, an explicit and efficient guided filtering is introduced [7].

Global implicit optimization based approaches compute color intensities of all pixels together by minimizing some energy functions, which usually consists of a smoothing term and a data term. Smoothing terms of most optimization based methods are derived from gradients. Farbman et al. [2] minimize gradients in weighted L_2 norm with edge-ware weights. Gradients are also minimized in L_0 norm for edge-preserving image smoothing [3]. The well-known total variation method minimizes gradients in L_1 norm for edge-preserving image smoothing [29]. Compared with the local explicit filtering methods, the global implicit optimization based approaches avoid halos near weak edges at price of higher computational cost.

2.2 Structure-Preserving Texture Smoothing

Textures are usually referred to as small-scale surface patterns which have similar appearance and local statistics with respect to certain spatial scale [19]. Hence most of structure-preserving texture smoothing methods rely on statistical features of local rectangular patches to separate textures from structures. Subr et al. [8] define details as oscillations between local extrema envelopes in a certain spatial scale to smooth small-scale textures while preserve edges. Zang et al. [24] use a space-filling curve as the reduced domain to perform separation of edges and details. The smoothing effect is achieved by modulating local extrema after empirical mode decomposition. Xu et al. [9] introduce a pixel-wise relative total variation, which is a statistical measure of gradients within a rectangular patch. A global energy based on this relative total variation is minimized to extract main structures from textures. Zang et al. [25] regard psychological

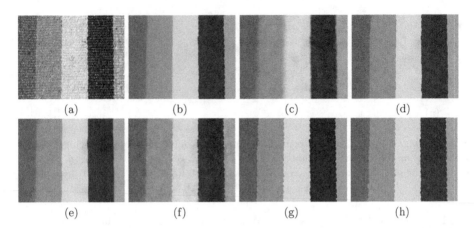

Fig. 3. Comparisons of our method with state-of-the-art previous works. From left to right: (a) input image, (b) RTV [9], (c) RC [10], (d) BTF [12], (e) RGF [14], (f) TF [13], (g) SGF [16] and (h) our method. It illustrates our approach achieves higher quality results. (Results of (f) and (g) are directly copied from reference [16]) Parameters: (b) $\lambda = 0.03$, $\sigma = 4$. (c) $\sigma = 0.75$, $k = 4$. (d) $k = 7$, $n_{iter} = 5$. (e) $\sigma_s = 10$, $\sigma_r = 0.1$. (h) $k = 15$, $\sigma' = 0.25$, $\sigma'_r = 0.025$, $n_{iter} = 3$.

perception as anisotropy, non-periodicity and local directionality, and use directional anisotropic structure measurement to distinguish texture and structure. A local averaging-weight approach is also proposed for structure-preserving texture smoothing, where the weights are based on a covariance matrix of images features within a rectangular patch [10]. The above approaches rely on statistical analysis of image features within rectangular patches centered at pixels. Two adjacent pixels on the opposite sides of a major edges would have patches sharing a larger overlap with similar local statistics, which would lead to salient structures blurring. Patch shift scheme relieves the above problem to some extent, where the texture representative patch of each pixel that excludes prominent structural edges is selected from rectangular patches with a fixed radius and containing this pixel [12]. Mean intensity of this selected patch is used to compute the guidance image in the guided bilateral filter. However, the patch shift using rectangular patches, which are not well adhered to sharp structural edges, also has the limitation of structure edges blurring. Rectangular patches with adaptive radii are also used for texture smoothing. Lin et al. [17] add a threshold to select rectangular patch with smaller radius for structure edges and larger one for texture regions. Jenon et al. [18] use collective flatness to find an optimal radius. In this paper, *structure-adaptive patches*, which just contain textures and conform to local structural boundaries, are used for statistical texture analysis.

Some other methods first smooth both textures and structures, various schemes are then used to recover the main structures. Su et al. [11] develop an iterative asymmetric sampling and a local linear model to suppress textures,

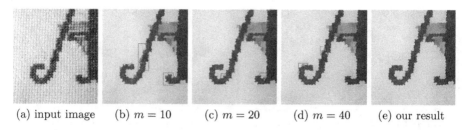

(a) input image   (b) $m = 10$ (c) $m = 20$ (d) $m = 40$ (e) our result

Fig. 4. Three iterations smoothing results of computing the guidance image from single vs multiple superpixel segmentations. None of result from single segmentation with $m = 10$, 20 or 40 obtains satisfactory results shown in blue rectangles, while our result via multiple segmentations is desirable. $k = 9$, $\sigma' = 0.25$ and $\sigma'_r = 0.05$ are fixed for all of the above results. (Color figure online)

and apply L_0 gradient minimization and joint filtering schemes for edge correction. Rolling guidance filter with fixed guidance image is used to refine edges that are blurred in the Gaussian filter for texture smoothing [14]. However, corner edges would be rounded in this process. Gaussian filter first smooths textures and structures, and joint bilateral filter recovers the blurred edges [15]. The other weighted-average methods are based on minimum spanning tree [13,16], where similarity of two pixels is measured via their shortest distances on the tree. To alleviate the leak problems in the global minimum spanning tree [13], a segment graph is used to compute the tree distances [16], where segment nodes in the graph are the SLIC superpixels [30].

2.3 SLIC Superpixel Segmentation

The state-of-the-art Simple Linear Iterative Clustering (SLIC) superpixel algorithm is faster, more memory efficient, and adheres to boundaries as well as or better than previous methods [30].

The SLIC is an adaptation of k-means for superpixel segmentation, which decomposes an input image I with N pixels into K non-overlapping superpixels $\{S_i, 1 \leq i \leq K\}$. Distance between two pixels p and q used in SLIC is a trade-off of the CIELab color distance d_c and spatial distance d_s as following

$$D_{pq} = \sqrt{d_c^2 + \left(\frac{d_s}{k}\right)^2 m^2},$$
(1)

where

$$d_c = \sqrt{(l_p - l_q)^2 + (a_p - a_q)^2 + (b_p - b_q)^2},$$
(2)

$$d_s = \sqrt{(x_p - x_q)^2 + (y_p - y_q)^2},$$
(3)

$k = \sqrt{N/K}$ is the sampling interval, and m is a parameter with range $[1, 40]$. For a gray image, the color distance is defined as $d_c = \sqrt{(l_p - l_q)^2}$.

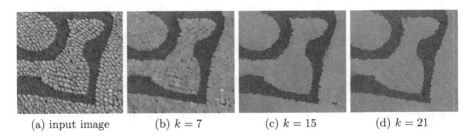

(a) input image   (b) $k = 7$ (c) $k = 15$ (d) $k = 21$

Fig. 5. Smoothing results with various sampling interval k. A bigger value of k would remove more textures. Parameters $\sigma' = 0.25$, $\sigma'_r = 0.05$ and $n_{iter} = 3$ are fixed for all of the above results.

The parameter k determines the scales of superpixels. The parameter m is used for the trade-off between color similarity and spatial proximity. When m is larger, the superpixels are more compact. Smaller m would lead to superpixels adhering more tightly to image boundaries, but having more irregular shapes.

3   The Proposed Method

The proposed structure-preserving texture smoothing approach mainly consists of two steps demonstrated in Fig. 2, i.e., the computation of Guidance Image (GI) via SLIC superpixel segmentations and the Guided Bilateral Filtering (GBF).

3.1   Guidance Image Computation via Superpixels

Unlike most of previous structure-preserving textures smoothing methods using rectangular patches for statistical texture analysis, *structure-adaptive* patches via SLIC superpixel segmentation, which just contain textures and conform to local structural boundaries, are utilized for computing the guidance image. However, not all of the superpixels are exactly coincided with structural boundaries. A small part of superpixels still cross structural edges, which lead to inexact statistical texture analysis. To relieve the above problem, several times of super-pixel segmentations with a fixed scale are used for computing the guidance image, which smooth the fine-scale textures while preserve the main structures.

Given an image I with N pixels, a fixed sampling interval k that determines the desired number of superpixels $K = N/k^2$, and n values for the parameter m as $\{m_j, j = 1, \cdots, n\}$, n times SLIC segmentations are first generated. The j-th segmentation is expressed as $\{S_{ij}, 1 \leq i \leq K_j\}$, where the actual number of superpixel K_j may not exactly equal to K. For each pixel p, superpixels $S_{i_1 1}, S_{i_2 2}, \cdots, S_{i_n n}$ containing p can be found from the above n different SLIC segmentations, where $S_{i_j j}$ is from the j-th segmentation. The intensity of guidance image G at p is a weight-average of intensities of pixels within the above n superpixels $S_{i_j j}, j = 1, \cdots, n$, i.e.,

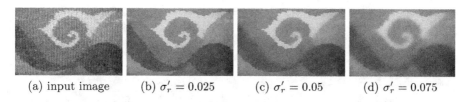

(a) input image   (b) $\sigma_r' = 0.025$ (c) $\sigma_r' = 0.05$ (d) $\sigma_r' = 0.075$

Fig. 6. Smoothing results of three iterations with various parameter σ_r', where $\sigma' = 0.25$ and $k = 7$ are fixed. A bigger value of σ_r' would lead to smoother results.

$$G_p = \frac{1}{w_p} \sum_{j=1}^{n} \sum_{q \in S_{i_j j}} w_{pq} I_q, \qquad (4)$$

where w_p is a normalization factor and w_{pq} is defined as follows

$$w_{pq} = exp(-\frac{\|I_p - I_q\|^2}{2\sigma^2}). \qquad (5)$$

The above Gaussian weight is used to alleviate the bad effect caused by a small portions of cross-edge superpixels, which will be analysed in Sect. 4.

3.2   Guided Bilateral Filtering

Given the guidance image G, the guided bilateral filter on the original image I is defined as following:

$$J_p = \frac{1}{k_p} \sum_{q \in N(p)} f(\|p - q\|)g(\|G_p - G_q\|)I_q, \qquad (6)$$

where J_p is the filtering result, k_p is a normalization term, $N(p)$ is the set of neighbor pixels in the $r \times r$ rectangular patch centered at pixel p. The spatial kernel f and range kernel g are two Gaussian functions with parameters σ_s and σ_r, i.e., $f(x) = exp(-\frac{x^2}{2\sigma_s^2})$ and $g(x) = exp(-\frac{x^2}{2\sigma_r^2})$.

For most images, a single iteration of the above two steps is insufficient. $3-5$ iterations are usually necessary to obtain a desired result.

4   Analysis

Multiple Superpixel Segmentations. The superpixel segmentation plays an important role in the proposed method. Unlike previous works using rectangular patches for statistical texture analysis, we use the fast and effective SLIC super-pixel segmentation for generating structure-adaptive patches, which just contain textures and conform to local structural boundaries.

(a) input image   (b) uniform   (c) Gaussian

Fig. 7. Five iterations smoothing results of using uniform vs Gaussian weights for computing the guidance image. The Gaussian weight achieves desirable result. $\sigma' = 0.1$ is used for Gaussian weighting; $k = 7$ and $\sigma'_r = 0.05$ are fixed for the two situations.

Even though the SLIC superpixels adhere well to image boundaries, a small portion of them still cross structural edges. Computing the guidance image from just single superpixel segmentation leads to different flaws demonstrated in Fig. 4(b), (c) and (d). However, using several superpixel segmentations with different values of parameter m and the same value of k for weighting guidance image in Eq. (4) would obtain the desirable result shown in Fig. 4(e). This is because if two pixels are from a region with same texture cues, they would have more times in the same superpixel generated using different values of m, and give more contributions to each other for the weighting in Eq. (4).

We use uniform sampling of the recommended range $[1, 40]$ of parameter m for generating n times superpixel segmentations. More sampling would get better results. In the consideration of computational cost, we use $\{5, 10, 15, 20, 25, 30, 35, 40\}$ as the sample values of parameter m for producing eights SLIC superpixel segmentations for guidance image computation in this paper.

Gaussian Weighting. The intuitive method of computing guidance image in Eq. (4) is using uniform weights $w_{pq} = 1.0$. However, using the above uniform weights may generate unsatisfactory results shown in Fig. 7(b), which is due to a small portion of unreliable superpixels. In this paper, we use Gaussian weights in Eq. (5) to relieve the above problem. This strategy means that texture smoothing would be weakened for unreliable superpixels. Combining multiple superpixel segmentations and Gaussian weighting, the proposed method obtains desirable results for most of images shown in Fig. 7(c).

Color Image. The guidance image of a color image is also in color. In this paper, CIELab mode images are used for the Gaussian weighting in Eq. (5) and the guided bilateral filtering in Eq. (6). Images in other color spaces can also be processed similarly.

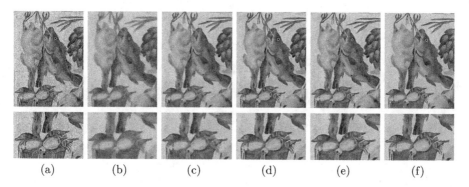

| (a) | (b) | (c) | (d) | (e) | (f) |

Fig. 8. Comparisons of our method with some state-of-the-art previous works. From left to right: (a) input image, (b) LE [8], (c) RC [10], (d) BTF [12], (e) RGF [14] and (f) our method. The proposed method preserves structural edges better than others. Parameters: LE: $k = 9$. RC: $k = 15$, $\sigma = 0.2$. BTF: $k = 5$, $n_{iter} = 3$. RGF: $\sigma_s = 3$, $\sigma_r = 0.1$. Our method: $k = 5$, $\sigma' = 0.25$, $\sigma'_r = 0.05$, $n_{iter} = 3$.

Parameters. Except the eight samples of parameter m are fixed, parameters σ_s and r are fixed as $\sigma_s = k - 1$ and $r = 2k + 1$ in the proposed method as in the bilateral texture filtering [12]. Hence, our algorithm has four parameters: n_{iter} (number of iterations), k (sample interval), σ and σ_r. We set $\sigma = \sigma' \times \sqrt{c}$ and $\sigma_r = \sigma'_r \times \sqrt{c}$, where c is the number of color channels of an image, σ' and σ'_r are both in the range $(0, 1]$.

The parameter k is determines by the scale of textures, where a larger value would remove more textures demonstrated in Fig. 5. $k \in \{5, 7, 9, 11\}$ can obtain desirable results for most images. The parameter σ' is used for computing the Gaussian weights between pixels within a same superpixel in Eq. (5). A larger value would lead to smoother results. $\sigma' = 0.25$ are used for most results in this paper. Like the classical bilateral filters [1], the parameter σ'_r is used to control the color range similarity. A bigger value would lead to smoother results and may blur some sharp edges illustrated in Fig. 6. We use $\sigma'_r = 0.05$ for almost all of the results in this paper.

Computational Times. All the experiments are conducted on a desktop using MATLAB with an Intel (R) Xeon (R) CPU E5-2620 v3 central processor. The computational time complexity is $O(Nk^2)$. The one iteration running times of some represented images are reported in Table 1.

5   Results and Comparisons

We compare the proposed method with the state-of-the-art structure-preserving texture smoothing methods, i.e., Local Extrema (LE) [8], Relative Total Variation (RTV) [9], Region Covariances (RC) [10], Bilateral Texture Filtering (BTF) [12], Tree Filtering (TF) [13], Rolling Guidance Filter (RGF) [14] and Segment

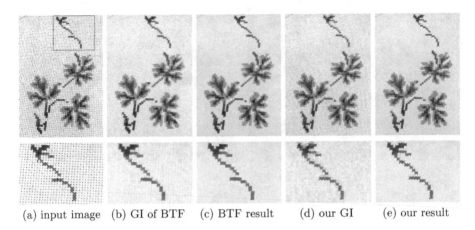

(a) input image   (b) GI of BTF   (c) BTF result   (d) our GI   (e) our result

Fig. 9. Comparisons of Guidance Image (GI) generation with BTF [12]. Our guidance image is more adhered to small sharp structural edges, and leads to better result. (c) and (e) are guided bilateral filtering from (b) and (d) with same parameter respectively. Parameters: (b) $k = 5$, $n_{iter} = 1$. (d) $k = 5$, $\sigma' = 0.5$, $\sigma'_r = 0.05$, $n_{iter} = 1$.

Table 1. The running times in second of our method with one iteration.

Figure	Pixels	k	SLIC	GI	GBF	Total
1	508 * 202	9	2.01	2.39	3.88	8.28
3	329 * 250	15	1.66	8.08	8.22	17.96
8	450 * 600	5	5.65	2.30	3.86	11.87

Graph Filtering (SGF) [16] in Figs. 1, 3 and 8. Experimental results demonstrate the proposed method achieves higher quality results compared with previous works. Most of the results are directly copied from previous papers or regenerated using the codes provided online with carefully tuning of parameters.

Bilateral Texture Filtering. The most similar work with ours is perhaps the Bilateral Texture Filtering (BTF) [12], where guided bilateral filters are used to smooth textures in the both two methods. The difference of the two methods is the computation of guidance images. The best representative texture patch clear of structural edges from the rectangular patches contained the considered pixel with fixed size is selected for computing the guidance image in the BTF. Since rectangular patches do not adhere well to sharp structural edges, the select representative patches may still contain both textures and structures, which lead to sharp structures blurring illustrated in Figs. 1(d), 3(d), and 10(b).

While in the proposed method, multiple adaptive SLIC superpixel segmentations, which adhere to structural edges, are used to compute the guidance image. The structure-adaptive patches lead to desirable results shown in Figs. 1(f), 3(h), and 10(c). The superiority of guidance image via adaptive patches comparing

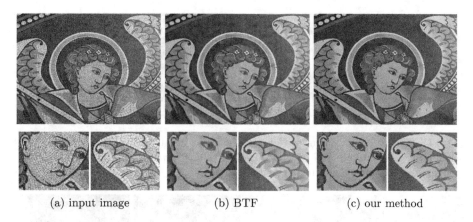

(a) input image   (b) BTF   (c) our method

Fig. 10. Comparison of our result with BTF [12]. The proposed method can better preserve sharp structure edges. (Results of (b) is directly copied from reference [12]) Parameters: (b) $k = 7$, $n_{iter} = 5$. (c) $k = 8$, $\sigma' = 0.1$, $\sigma'_r = 0.05$, $n_{iter} = 3$.

with patch shift from rectangular patches is illustrated in Fig. 9, where color guidance image are used for the both two methods.

Other Methods. Method of LE [8] often degrades structures shown in Fig. 8(b), because locating proper extrema in regions containing both textures and structures is difficult. The method based on relative total variation [9] can better smooth textures and preserve structures shown in Figs. 1(b) and 3(b). However, sharp structural edges are still a bit blurred compared with our method. This is because the relative total variation is a statistical measure of pixels within rectangular patches centered at each pixel. Patches of two adjacent neighbor pixels on the opposite sides of a major edge have a larger overlap and have the similar relative total variations. The region covariance based method [10] also uses the pixel-centered rectangular patches. Due to the above same reason, this method would blur structure edges illustrated in Figs. 1(c), 3(c), and 8(c). The sharp corner edges would be rounded in the rolling guidance filter [14] shown in Figs. 1(e), 3(e), and 8(e) compared with ours.

We also compare our work with the tree filtering methods, i.e., TF [13] in Fig. 3(f) and SGF [16] in Fig. 3(g). It can be shown that the proposed method can preserve sharp edges better than TF and as well as SGF. Both the methods of SGF and ours use SLIC superpixel segmentations. One superpixel segmentation with a random value of m is used to build the graph segment in SGF [16]. While multiple superpixel segmentations using different values of m are computed for generating the guidance image in our method.

6   Applications

Our texture smoothing results can be used in many applications, such as texture enhancement and edge detection.

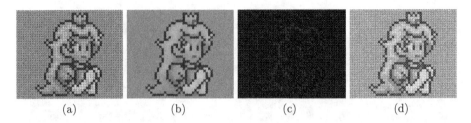

Fig. 11. Texture enhancement via our method. (a) input image. (b) our smoothing result with parameters $k = 7$, $\sigma' = 0.25$, $\sigma'_r = 0.05$ and $n_{iter} = 3$. (c) texture of the input image. (d) the enhancement result.

Fig. 12. Edge detection results without and with our proposed method. (a) input image. (b) our smoothing result with parameters $k = 9$, $\sigma' = 0.25$, $\sigma'_r = 0.05$ and $n_{iter} = 5$. (c) Canny edge detection of (a). (d) Canny edge detection of (b).

Given the input image I and our texture smoothing result J, the texture enhancement result J_D can be obtained as

$$J_D = J + \lambda(I - J), \tag{7}$$

where λ adjusts the scale of enhancement. Texture enhancement can produce clearer textures and get better visual effects shown in Fig. 11 with $\lambda = 3$.

Edge detection methods usually produce lots of noises which blurs the main structural edges. Operating the edge detection method on our texture smoothing result can remove the small noisy edges while maintain the main structure edges shown in Fig. 12.

7   Conclusions and Future Works

In this paper, a novel structure-adaptive patch based method is introduced. The well known SLIC superpixel segmentations are used for generating the structural-adaptive patches to compute the guidance image in the guided bilateral filter. Experimental results demonstrate the proposed method achieves high quality results compared with previous state-of-the-art works.

However, only color cue is used in the SLIC superpixel segmentation. If colors of textures and structures are extremely similar, the unfaithful SLIC segmentations would lead to undesirable smoothing results. The first logical next step would be adding texture cues for the current superpixel segmentations, which possibly extends our framework for a broader range of textures. The proposed method is a structure-adaptive patches based method in a single scale for textures smoothing. Structure-adaptive patches with adaptive scales would be another interesting and meaningful future work.

Acknowledgments. We thank the anonymous reviewers for their constructive comments. This work was supported in part by NSFC (No. 61402300, 61373160, 61363048, 61572099, 61772104, 61370143), Excellent Young Scholar Fund of Shijiazhuang Tiedao University, and Special Funds for Basic Scientific Research Business Fees in Central Universities (No. DUT16QY02).

References

1. Tomasi, C., Manduchi, R.: Bilateral filtering for gray and color images. In: IEEE International Conference on Computer Vision, pp. 839–846. IEEE (1998)
2. Farbman, Z., Fattal, R., Lischinski, D., Szeliski, R.: Edge-preserving decompositions for multi-scale tone and detail manipulation. ACM Trans. Graph. **27**(3) (2008). No. 67
3. Xu, L., Lu, C., Xu, Y., Jia, J.: Image smoothing via L_0 gradient minimization. ACM Trans. Graph. **30**(16) (2011). No. 174
4. Gastal, E.S.L., Oliveiral, M.M.: Domain transform for edge-aware image and video processing. ACM Trans. Graph. **30**(4) (2011). No. 69
5. Paris, S., Hasinoff, S.W., Kautz, J.: Local Laplacian filters: edge-aware image processing with a Laplacian pyramid. ACM Trans. Graph. **30**(4) (2011). No. 68
6. Farbman, Z., Fattal, R., Lischinski, D.: Diffusion maps for edge-aware image editing. ACM Trans. Graph. **29**(6) (2011). No. 145
7. He, K., Sun, J., Tang, X.: Guided image filtering. IEEE Trans. Patt. Anal. Mach. Intell. **35**(6), 1397–1409 (2013)
8. Subr, K., Soler, C., Durand, F.: Edge-preserving multiscale image decomposition based on local extrema. ACM Trans. Graph. **28**(5) (2009). No. 147
9. Xu, L., Yan, Q., Xia, Y., Jia, J.: Structure extraction from texture via relative total variation. ACM Trans. Graph. **31**(6) (2012). No. 139
10. Karacan, L., Erdemy, E., Erdemz, A.: Structure-preserving image smoothing via region covariances. ACM Trans. Graph. **32**(6) (2013). No. 176
11. Su, Z., Luo, X., Deng, Z., Liang, Y., Ji, Z.: Edge-preserving texture suppression filter based on joint filtering schemes. IEEE Trans. Multimedia **15**(3), 535–548 (2013)
12. Cho, H., Lee, H., Kang, H., Lee, S.: Bilateral texture filtering. ACM Trans. Graph. **33**(4) (2014). No. 128
13. Bao, L., Song, Y., Yang, Q., Yuan, H., Wang, G.: Tree filtering: efficient structure preserving smoothing with a minimum spanning tree. IEEE Trans. Image Process. **23**(2), 555–569 (2014)
14. Zhang, Q., Shen, X., Xu, L., Jia, J.: Rolling guidance filter. In: Fleet, D., Pajdla, T., Schiele, B., Tuytelaars, T. (eds.) ECCV 2014. LNCS, vol. 8691, pp. 815–830. Springer, Cham (2014). https://doi.org/10.1007/978-3-319-10578-9_53
15. Du, H., Jin, X., Willis, P.J.: Two-level joint local Laplacian texture filtering. Vis. Comput. **32**(12), 1537–1548 (2016)
16. Zhang, F., Dai, L., Xiang, S., Zhang, X.: Segment graph based image filtering: fast structure-preserving smoothing. In: IEEE International Conference on Computer Vision, pp. 361–369. IEEE (2015)

17. Lin, T., Way, D., Tai, Z., Chang, C.: An efficient structure-aware bilateral texture filtering for image smoothing. Comput. Graph. Forum **35**(7), 57–66 (2016)

18. Jeon, J., Lee, H., Kang, H., Lee, S.: Scale-aware structure-preserving texture filtering. Comput. Graph. Forum **35**(7), 77–86 (2016)

19. Wei, L.Y., Lefebvre, S., Kwatra, V., Turk, G.: State-of-the-art in example-based texture synthesis. In: Eurographics State of the Art Report. Eurographics Association (2009)

20. Yang, Q.: Semantic filtering. In: The IEEE Conference on Computer Vision and Pattern Recognition, pp. 4517–4526. IEEE (2016)

21. Zhu, L., Fu, C.W., Jin, Y., Wei, M., Qin, J., Heng, P.A.: Non-local sparse and low-rank regularization for structure-preserving image smoothing. Comput. Graph. Forum **35**(7), 217–226 (2016)

22. Eun, H., Kim, C.: Superpixel-guided adaptive image smoothing. IEEE Sig. Process. Lett. **23**(12), 1887–1891 (2016)

23. Su, Z., Zeng, B., Miao, J., Luo, X., Yin, B., Chen, Q.: Relative reductive structure-aware regression filter. J. Comput. Appl. Math. **329**, 244–255 (2018)

24. Zang, Y., Huang, H., Zhang, L.: Structure-aware image smoothing by local extrema on space-filling curve. IEEE Trans. Vis. Comput. Graph. **20**(9), 1253–1265 (2014)

25. Zang, Y., Huang, H., Zhang, L.: Guided adaptive image smoothing via directional anisotropic structure measurement. IEEE Trans. Vis. Comput. Graph. **21**(9), 1015–1027 (2015)

26. Paris, P., Kornprobst, J., Tumblin, J., Durand, F.: Bilateral filtering: theory and applications. Found. Trends Comput. Graph. Vis. **4**(1), 1–73 (2009)

27. Yang, Q., Tan, K.H., Ahuja, N.: Real-time O(1) bilateral filtering. In: IEEE Conference on Computer Vision and Pattern Recognition, pp. 557–564. IEEE (2009)

28. Comaniciu, D., Meer, P.: Mean shift: a robust approach toward feature space analysis. IEEE Trans. Patt. Anal. Mach. Intell. **24**(5), 603–619 (2002)

29. Rudin, L.I., Osher, S., Fatemi, E.: Nonlinear total variation based noise removal algorithms. Physica D **60**(1–4), 256–268 (1992)

30. Achanta, R., Shaji, A., Smith, K., Lucchi, A., Fua, P., Susstrunk, S.: SLIC superpixels compared to state-of-the-art superpixel methods. IEEE Trans. Patt. Anal. Mach. Intell. **34**(11), 2274–2282 (2012)

Robust Blind Deconvolution Using Relative Total Variation as a Regularization Penalty

Yunzhi Lin[1(✉)] and Wenze Shao[2,3]

[1] School of Automation, Southeast University, Nanjing 210096, China
linyunzhi1996@126.com
[2] College of Telecommunications and Information Engineering,
Nanjing University of Posts and Telecommunications, Nanjing 210003, China
shaowenze1010@163.com
[3] National Engineering Research Center of Communications and Networking,
Nanjing University of Posts and Telecommunications, Nanjing 210003, China

Abstract. Blind image deblurring or deconvolution is a very hot topic towards which numerous methods have been put forward in the past decade, demonstrating successful deblurring results on one or another benchmark natural image dataset. However, most of existing algorithms are found not robust enough as dealing with images in specific scenarios, such as images with text, saturated area or face. In this paper, a robust blind deblurring approach is presented using relative total variation as a regularization penalty. To the best of our knowledge, none of previous studies have followed this modeling principle. The underlying idea is to pursue more accurate intermediate image for more reliable kernel estimation by harnessing relative total variation which could extract salient structures from textures and suppress ringing artifacts and noise as well. An iterative estimating algorithm is finally deduced for alternatively update of sharp image and blur kernel by operator splitting and augmented Lagrangian. Extensive experiments on a challenging synthetic dataset and real-world images as well are conducted to validate the new method with comparison against the state-of-the-art approaches from 2006 to 2014. Based on both PSNR and SSIM and a non-reference evaluation metric, the results demonstrate that our approach is comparatively more effective to process blurred images in more challenging scenarios.

Keywords: Blind deblurring · Motion blur · Kernel estimation
Image restoration

1 Introduction

Motion blur is an artifact caused by the movement of the camera sensor during the exposure, which leads to significant information loss of the picture. This problem has been increasingly important since the widespread use of the hand-held cameras, particularly the smart phones.

© Springer International Publishing AG, part of Springer Nature 2018
S. Satoh (Ed.): PSIVT 2017, LNCS 10799, pp. 325–337, 2018.
https://doi.org/10.1007/978-3-319-92753-4_26

Generally, based on the assumption that the motion blur is shift-invariant, the blur process could be modeled as follows:

$$y = k * x + n \tag{1}$$

where x is the latent sharp image, k is the blur kernel, n is the image noise, $*$ denotes convolution and y is the observed blur image.

Thus, motion deblurring could be simplified to a blind deconvolution task, i.e., recovering both the latent image x and the kernel k from the observed blurry image y. It is apparent that the task is mathematically an ill-posed problem since different sharp images in combination with distinct blur kernels may produce the same blurry images. Nowadays, most existing methods are formulated in the Bayesian framework to solve this problem, specifically including two inference principles: Variational Bayes (VB) and Maximum a Posteriori (MAP). The proposed approach in this paper falls into the MAP considering its flexibility in both modeling and inference.

Recent years has witnessed much progress in blind image deblurring. One group of researchers [1, 2, 4, 7–11, 22, 24] concentrates on seeking appropriate sparse priors of x and k. Another group [12–14] combines the salient edge selection with simple Gaussian prior to speed up the computational process. Although many approaches seem to perform well on some particular dataset, e.g., provided by Fergus et al. [1], Levin et al. [2], they usually fail in getting satisfying results under more complex situations, such as images of text, face, natural environment, or dark scenes with light saturation. The recent comprehensive comparative study [5] has showed that the state-of-the-art approaches from 2006 to 2014 are not robust enough to suit all these cases.

In this paper, a robust blind deblurring approach is presented using relative total variation as a regularization penalty. Relative Total Variation (RTV) proposed by Xu et al. [3] is a tricky yet interesting method to extract salient structures from the image. To the best of our knowledge, none of previous studies have followed this modeling principle. The underlying idea is to pursue more accurate intermediate latent image x for reliable kernel estimation by harnessing RTV which may extract salient structures from textures and suppress ringing artifacts and noise as well. To be noted that, as in Cho et al. [12] and Xu and Jia [13] edge enhancing via shock filtering is also adopted during updating the latent image x. In the blur kernel estimation stage, an L0-L2 prior is imposed on the kernel just following one of our previous work [11] which is found adapt the proposed approach in this paper quite well. With above modeling processes, an iterative estimating algorithm is finally deduced for update of sharp image and blur kernel in an alternative manner by operator splitting and augmented Lagrangian. With estimated blur kernel, a non-blind deconvolution developed from the hyper-Laplacian prior [4] is adopted for the final restoration of the clear image. Extensive experiments on a comprehensive synthetic dataset including text, face and low illumination images and real-world images as well are conducted to validate the new method with comparison against the state-of-the-art approaches from 2006 to 2014. Based on both PSNR and SSIM and a non-reference evaluation metric [6] developed from the massive user study, the results demonstrate that our approach is comparatively more effective to process blurred images in more challenging scenarios.

2 Related Work

To solve the ill-posed problem of blind deconvolution, many previous methods employ multi-scale framework and impose constraints on not only the latent image but also blur kernel. For example, Fergus et al. [1] used a variational Bayesian method with a mixture of Gaussians and exponential prior on the image and kernel respectively. However, this statistical model is of great complexity and the resulting algorithm is vulnerable to noise. Shan et al. [7] proposed a piece-wise prior to satisfy the natural power-law of the image. Nevertheless, the deblurring results were much smooth and had many artifacts. Similarly, Krishnan et al. [8] introduced a normalized L1/L2 prior to distinguish the sharp image from the blurry one. However, the authors' claimed discrimination is questionable since L1/L2 is found fail in distinguishing many natural images. Lately, the L0 prior has proven to be the most efficient sparse prior. Xu et al. [9] first applied the L0 gradient prior to the estimation of latent image. Then Pan et al. [10] applied the L0 priors on both the gradient and intensity domains to the text image. Shao et al. [11] proposed an easy-to-implement and effective bi-L0-L2 prior on both the sharp image and blur kernel. While these algorithms obtain good results on one or another particular dataset, their performance is not robust enough to adapt diverse imaging scenarios. Recently, Pan et al. [18] further proposed to apply the L0 priors on both the gradient domain and the dark channel and achieved improved deblurring performance.

To avoid the negative influence of the textures or saturated areas on kernel estimation, another group of researchers employs smoothing/enhancing filters for salient edge selection. For example, Cho et al. [12] used bilateral filter and shocking filter; Xu and Jia [13] applied Gaussian filter and shocking filter, together with the Iterative Support Detection (ISD) to select salient edges. Recently, Pan et al. [14] proposed to remove the outliers in the saturated area to optimize the kernel estimation.

There are also studies making contributions to other aspects of motion deblurring. Whyte et al. [15] proposed a geometrically consistent model to take non-uniform blur into consideration. However, their performance is not satisfying within synthetic uniform dataset. Hu and Yang [16] selected a best region patch instead of the whole image for kernel estimation. Hu et al. [17] also used light streaks to predict the kernel in the dark scenario. While these novel algorithms expand the existing methods, none of them are competitive compared against other state-of-the-art approaches as surveyed in [5].

3 Robust Blind Kernel Estimation

In this section, we present a robust approach with RTV as the regularization term on the latent image x, combined with salient edge selection and L0-L2-norm regularized kernel estimation.

Following model (1), the basic cost function of our method is formulated as

$$\min_{x,k} \lambda \|k * x - y\|^2 + \alpha_x R_x(x) + \alpha_k R_k(k) \tag{2}$$

where $\lambda, \alpha_x, \alpha_k$, are the positive weights; $R_x(x), R_k(k)$ represent the regularization term on x and k respectively. Then, x and k can be solved alternatively by minimizing (2). Figure 1 shows the flowchart of final algorithm including an outer iteration and two inner iterations as well as additional salient edge selection step. Besides, a coarse-to-fine manner is adopted for the sake of avoiding the local minima, which is a common routine in the MAP-based blind deconvolution [2].

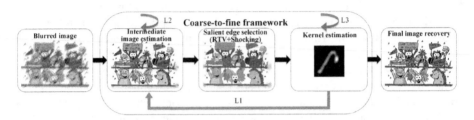

Fig. 1. Flowchart of the proposed method. L2 and L3 represent the inner iterations. L1 denotes the outer iterations and is implemented in a multi-scale (coarse-to-fine) framework.

3.1 Intermediate Latent Image Estimation

For the sake of clearness, the relative total variation is firstly introduced here which is proposed in [3], defined as

$$\sum_p \frac{D_{i,j}(p)}{L_{i,j}(p) + \varepsilon} = \sum_p \frac{\sum_{q(p)} g_{p,q} \left| (\partial_{i,j} x)_q \right|}{\left| \sum_{q \in R(p)} g_{p,q} (\partial_{i,j} x)_q \right| + \varepsilon} \tag{3}$$

$$g_{p,q} \propto \exp(-\frac{(x_p - x_q)^2 + (y_p - y_q)^2}{2\sigma^2}) \tag{4}$$

where i and j represent the horizontal and vertical direction respectively; q belongs to $R(p)$, the rectangle region centered at pixel p; ∂ denotes the partial derivative; $g_{p,q}$ is a correlation weighting function calculating the spatial affinity; ε specifies the maximum size of texture elements, we set it to 0.02 empirically; σ controls the spatial scale of the window.

Considering the MAP framework, we could obtain the intermediate image x by fixing the kernel k. By omitting the terms not involved in x, the intermediate image model is transformed to (5):

$$x_{i+1} = \arg\min_x \lambda \|k_i * x - y\|^2 + C_x^i \alpha_x \sum_p \frac{\sum_{q \in R(p)} g_{p,q} \left| (\partial_{i,j} x)_q \right|}{\left| \sum_{q \in R(p)} g_{p,q} (\partial_{i,j} x)_q \right| + \varepsilon} \tag{5}$$

where $0 \leq i \leq I - 1$, I is the outer iteration number; $C_x^i < 1$ is a positive continuation factor which is fixed as 2/3. In this way, the weight of RTV prior diminishes as the process goes on, resulting in the cost function less constrained.

To solve problem (5), we first rewrite it into a matrix-vector form:

$$x_{i+1} = \arg\min_x \lambda \left\| K_i * x - V_y \right\|^2 + C_x^i \alpha_x \sum_p \frac{\sum_{q \in R(p)} g_{p,q} \left| (\partial_{i,j} x)_q \right|}{\left| \sum_{q \in R(p)} g_{p,q} (\partial_{i,j} x)_q \right| + \varepsilon} \tag{6}$$

where $K \in R^{M \times M}$ is the BCCB (block circulant matrix with circulant blocks) blurring matrix, M is the number of image pixels, and V_y is the vector representation of y. We adopt the well-known OSAL (operator splitting and augmented Lagrangian) scheme [11] to solve (6). An auxiliary variable u is introduced to substitute x, thus (6) written as

$$(x_i^{l+1}, u_i^{l+1}) = \arg\min_{x,u} \lambda \left\| K_i * x - V_y \right\|^2 + C_x^i \alpha_x \sum_p \frac{\sum_{q \in R(p)} g_{p,q} \left| (\partial_{i,j} u)_q \right|}{\left| \sum_{q \in R(p)} g_{p,q} (\partial_{i,j} u)_q \right| + \varepsilon}$$
$$+ C_x^i \mu_x^l (x - u) + C_x^i \frac{\gamma_x}{2} x - u^2 \tag{7}$$

where $0 \leq l \leq P - 1$, P is the inner iteration number; γ_x is a fixed parameter ensuring the similarity between x and u which is set to 100 empirically; and μ_x is the augmented Lagrangian penalty parameter which is updated as

$$\mu_x^{l+1} = \mu_x^l + \gamma_x \left(x_i^{l+1} - u_i^{l+1} \right) \tag{8}$$

When x is fixed, u could be solved by minimizing (9)

$$u_i^{l+1} = \arg\min_u \alpha_x \sum_p \frac{\sum_{q \in R(p)} g_{p,q} \left| (\partial_{i,j} x)_q \right|}{\left| \sum_{q \in R(p)} g_{p,q} (\partial_{i,j} x)_q \right| + \varepsilon} + \frac{\gamma_x}{2} \left\| x + \frac{1}{\gamma_x} \mu_x^l - u \right\|^2 \tag{9}$$

Note that the form of (9) is similar to the cost function (10) in [3], i.e.,

$$\min_S \sum_p (S_p - O_p)^2 + \lambda \left(\frac{D_x(p)}{L_x(p) + \varepsilon} + \frac{D_y(p)}{L_y(p) + \varepsilon} \right) \tag{10}$$

We just set the parameters in (10) as $\lambda = \frac{2\alpha_x}{\gamma_x}$, $O = x + \frac{\mu_x^l}{\gamma_x}$, and (9) can be then solved exactly the same as in [3], i.e., in a plug-and-play manner.

Following (6), the intermediate image x can be solved with u provided,

$$\arg\min_x \frac{\lambda}{C_x^i} \left\| K_i * x - V_y \right\|^2 + \frac{\gamma_x}{2} \left\| x + \frac{1}{\gamma_x} \mu_x^l - u_i^l \right\|^2 \tag{11}$$

Due to the BCCB assumption over K_i, (11) can be efficiently solved by applying fast Fourier transform (FFT) based on the Paseval's theorem. The expression could be as follows:

$$x_i^{J+1} = F^{-1}\left(\frac{\overline{F(k_i)}_\circ F(y) + \frac{C_x^i \gamma_x}{2\lambda}F(u_i^l - \frac{1}{\gamma_x}\mu_x^l)}{F(k_i)_\circ \overline{F(k_i)} + \frac{C_x^i \gamma_x}{2\lambda}}\right) \tag{12}$$

where $F(\cdot)$ and $F^{-1}(\cdot)$ represent the FFT and the inverse FFT, respectively, $\overline{(\cdot)}$ denotes the conjugate operator and $\circ$ is an element-wise multiplication operator. Note that to reduce the ringing artifacts caused by implementation in the frequency domain, one way is to expand the image and taper discontinuities along image edges, which is a simple yet effective preconditioning step also mentioned in [1, 11].

3.2 Salient Edge Selection

Edge information is the key to estimate the kernel accurately. The principle has been validated by many papers [2, 12, 13], that a salient edge does not change much after the blur process. As Xu and Jia [13] pointed out, if the edge width is smaller than the kernel size, it may be weakened significantly, thus damaging the kernel estimation. However, previous edge selection methods have some drawbacks. The bilateral filter may weaken the salient edge and make them less robust. WLS filter [19] is too weak to remove the tiny small edges. Many of these edges still remain after the estimating process. Moreover, the approach of L0 gradient [20] could not effectively distinguish the small edges from the salient ones, thus removing too many edges. As a result, there are not enough salient edges for estimation.

We instead adopt the proposed Relative Total Variation (RTV) method [3] to finish the task. It is found that these small edges often exist in the form of texture in the image. Thus, RTV is the best method to remove them from the image since the method is primarily designed to differentiate the texture and structure signals. Note that this step plays a different role compared with our previous step, which utilizes RTV prior as a penalty term. The difference is illustrated in Fig. 1.

Cho et al. [12] suggested that the artifacts result from edge blurring. Therefore, we further employ the shocking filter to enhance the remaining edges after salient edges have been selected, which is to reduce the influence of the blur. Farbman et al. [19] suggested that sharpening also leads to halos and gradient reversals. Thus, we limit the degree of shocking to recover the authentic edge information at utmost.

The model of selecting the salient edge could be expressed as:

$$X = \phi(\arg\min_S \Sigma_p (S_p - I_p)^2 + \lambda_s \left(\frac{D_x(p)}{L_x(p) + \varepsilon} + \frac{D_y(p)}{L_y(p) + \varepsilon}\right)) \tag{13}$$

Where S denotes the salient edge image produced by applying additional RTV to the intermediate image x; $\phi(\cdot)$ represents the shocking filter; λ_s controls the degree of smooth; σ_s is the scale size of the window; and X is the final salient edge image.

3.3 Kernel Estimation

Many previous algorithms, including [9, 10, 12], employ a simple Gaussian prior to estimate the kernel. They believe that it is of great efficiency to do so based on the assumption that the latent image x estimation has guaranteed the accuracy of the model. However, it is a misunderstanding that the prediction step is enough to reduce the noise and ringing artifacts in the estimation process. Another group of people pointed out that many kernels are highly non-Gaussian, they instead try to seek a mixture of sparse priors to force the kernel to fit into the natural statistics, including [11, 13, 15, 21]. Among these algorithms, we find that the bi-L0-L2 method [11] is the most suitable one where the sparse L0 prior and the Gaussian prior is imposed together on the kernel, thus it can not only apply to the Gaussian kernel but also other circumstances. Moreover, the blur kernel is estimated in the derivative domain, which is found useful to suppress the noise.

Following [11], the blur kernel is estimated by solving

$$k_{i+1} = \arg\min_k \lambda \|k * x_i - y\|^2 + C_k^i \alpha_k (\|k\|_0 + \frac{\beta_k}{\alpha_k} \|k\|^2) \tag{14}$$

where $0 \le i \le Q - 1$, Q is the inner iteration number; β_k is a weight parameter; $\|\cdot\|_0$ denotes the L0-semi norm; and $C_k^i < 1$ is a positive continuation factor which is fixed as 4/5. Then k could be efficiently solved by OSAL in the same manner as x in (5)–(12).

To remove noise, we also impose a threshold on the kernel. Besides, we set negative elements to zero and normalize the kernel. In addition to this, we compute the connected components in the image to remove areas without enough components, following the idea in [17].

4 Image Recovery

Once the kennel is estimated at the finest scale, the blind deconvolution turns into a non-deconvolution. Numerious methods have been employed to address this classical scheme. However, early algorithms like Richardson-Lucy (RL) and mixture of Gaussians [1] are sensitive to kernel noise. We notice that the Hyper-Laplacian prior [4] strikes a balance between accuracy and speed. It relies on heavy-tailed natural image priors and look-up tables, which render it a comparative advantage over the other non-blind deconvolution methods. The prior has then be adopted by many papers [8–11, 21] afterwards. However, there is still some noise and artifacts left.

We employ a smoothness prior [22] developed from the Hyper-Laplacian prior [4]. The new prior makes use of the canny operator to locate the edges. Then it dilates the detected edges with a disk model. The objective function is defined as (15):

$$\min_x \lambda \|k_i * x - y\|^2 + \lambda_1 \|\nabla x\|^{0.5} \circ M + \lambda_2 \|\nabla x\|^2 \circ (J - M) \tag{15}$$

where $\nabla x = (\partial_x x, \partial_y x)^T$ is the gradient of the image x; λ_1 and λ_2 are the weights; J is an all-ones matrix and M is a mask. The parameter setting follows the idea in [4, 22].

5   Experimental Details and Results

In this section, we present the experimental evaluations of our proposed method on both synthetic and real image datasets [5] compared with the state-of-the-art approaches. All of our experiments are carried out on a laptop with an Intel i7-5500U processer and 8 GB RAM. A 255 * 255 image takes about 2 min to process on Matlab. In order to get better performance, we set the outer and inner iteration number to be 16 and 14 respectively at each scale. Moreover, $\lambda = 100$, $\alpha_x = 0.55$, $\gamma_x = 200$, $\sigma = 3$ in

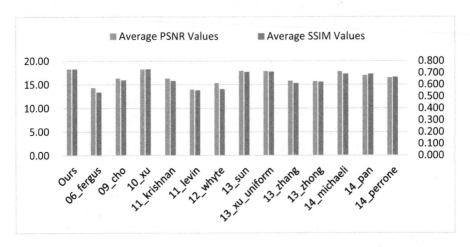

Fig. 2. Quantitative comparison on the synthetic dataset [5]. Our method and Xu and Jia [13] have a comparative advantage over the others on the SSIM and PSNR values.

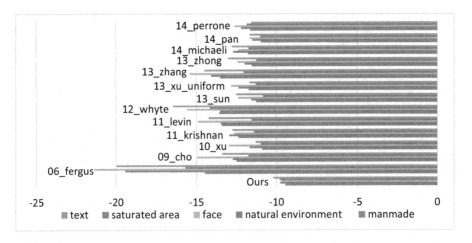

Fig. 3. Quantitative comparison on the synthetic dataset [5] measured by [6]. The larger value represents better performance. Our method outperforms in all five categories.

the intermittent image estimation. In the next stage of edge selection, the initial values of σ_s and λ_s are set to 1.5 and 0.02, respectively. We then gradually enhance the smooth effect by increasing them 1.1 times. Finally, we set $\alpha_k = 0.25$ in the kernel estimation empirically.

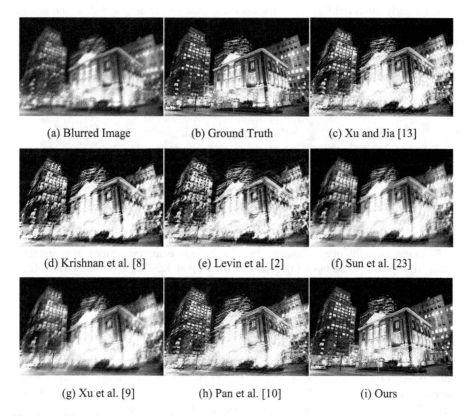

(a) Blurred Image	(b) Ground Truth	(c) Xu and Jia [13]
(d) Krishnan et al. [8]	(e) Levin et al. [2]	(f) Sun et al. [23]
(g) Xu et al. [9]	(h) Pan et al. [10]	(i) Ours

Fig. 4. Deblurred results of an image with saturated area. We showed the top 7 of all 14 methods. The metric's [6] scores of (c)–(i) are -11.84, -12.01, -12.50, -12.13, -12.38, -11.74 and -10.09, respectively. (d) and (g) fail to accurately restore the image because of the saturated area. (c), (e), (f) and (h) have varying degrees of ringing artifacts while ours gets superior result.

Synthetic Images. We run our algorithm on the synthetic dataset [5]. It contains 25 images, divided into 5 categories including some particular circumstances such as natural environment, text, face and saturation. We compare our SSIM and PSNR results with Fergus et al. [1], Cho et al. [12], Xu and Jia [13], Krishnan et al. [8], Levin et al. [2], Whyte et al. [15], Sun et al. [23], Xu et al. [9], Zhang et al. [24], Zhong et al. [25], Michaeli and Irani [26], Pan et al. [10], and Perrone et al. [27]. The average PSNR values are shown in Fig. 2.

Although SSIM and PSNR are the most popular metrics to measure a deblurring method, it cannot always faithfully reflect the performance of the methods since people's eyes may have different feelings not matched with the value. To be more specific, human visual system is influenced by many factors, for example, the surrounding area will affect people's evaluation on the target area. Thus, we adopt a no-reference metric [6], which is learned based on a massive user study. It can score image quality and artifacts consistently with human ratings. The results are illustrated in Fig. 3.

It is clearly observed that all of the previous state-of-the-art methods could not be considered as robust algorithms. There are always some scenarios where they perform badly or just completely fail. However, the proposed method has achieved universally better restoration performance across the five categories of images. Figures 4 and 5 demonstrate two examples, i.e., images with saturated area and text.

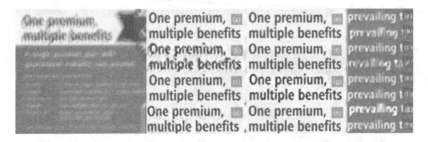

Fig. 5. Deblurred results of a text image. The left is the input blurry image; the middle and right are cropped regions from the input. (a)–(h) are Xu and Jia [13], Krishnan et al. [8], Sun et al. [23], Zhong et al. [25], Michaeli and Irani [26], Pan et al. [8], Perrone et al. [27], and Ours, respectively. We can see that our text results have less artifacts and are easy to recognize.

Real Images. Here we compare our method with the state-of-the-art algorithms on two real photographs [5]. Figure 6 shows the deblurring results on the real photograph fish for visual comparison. We can see that Fig. 6(d) and (h) have severe ringing artifacts. Figure 6(b), (c) and (e) have a sense of smoothness in which details are blurry. Comparatively, the results of Pan et al. [10] and our method are most visually pleasing. Figure 7 shows another group of results which also demonstrates the comparative performance of the proposed approach to other methods.

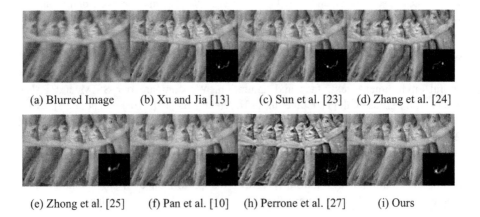

(a) Blurred Image   (b) Xu and Jia [13]   (c) Sun et al. [23]   (d) Zhang et al. [24]

(e) Zhong et al. [25]   (f) Pan et al. [10]   (h) Perrone et al. [27]   (i) Ours

Fig. 6. Deblurring results on the real photograph of fishes.

(a) Blurred Image   (b) Cho et al. [12]   (c) Xu and Jia [13]

(d) Levin et al. [2]   (e) Xu et al. [9]   (f) Ours

Fig. 7. Deblurring results on the real photograph statue. As we can see from the details and the estimated kernels, our algorithm has a superior performance over the state-of-the-art methods.

6 Conclusion

In this paper, we propose a robust blind deconvolution approach with RTV as a regularization penalty, which is easily solved by applying the OSAL (operator splitting and the augmented Lagrangian) scheme. Extensive experiments on a challenging synthetic dataset and real-world images as well are conducted to validate the new approach with comparison against the state-of-the-art approaches from 2006 to 2014. Based on both PSNR and SSIM and a non-reference evaluation metric, the results demonstrate that the new approach is comparatively more effective to process blurred images in more challenging cases including images with text, low illumination and face.

Acknowledgement. The research was supported in part by the Natural Science Foundation (NSF) of China (61771250, 61402239).

References

1. Fergus, R., Singh, B., Hertzmann, A., Roweis, S.T., Freeman, W.T.: Removing camera shake from a single photograph. ACM Trans. Graph. **25**(3), 787–794 (2006)
2. Levin, A., Weiss, Y., Durand, F., Freeman, W.T.: Understanding blind deconvolution algorithms. IEEE Trans. Pattern Anal. Mach. Intell. **33**(12), 2354 (2011)
3. Xu, L., Yan, Q., Xia, Y., Jia, J.: Structure extraction from texture via relative total variation. ACM Trans. Graph. **31**(6), 139 (2012)
4. Krishnan, D., Fergus, R.: Fast image deconvolution using hyper-Laplacian priors. In: International Conference on Neural Information Processing Systems, pp. 1033–1041. Curran Associates Inc. (2009)
5. Lai, W.S., Huang, J.B., Hu, Z., Ahuja, N., Yang, M.H.: A comparative study for single image blind deblurring. In: IEEE Conference on Computer Vision and Pattern Recognition, pp. 1701–1709. IEEE Computer Society (2016)
6. Liu, Y., Wang, J., Cho, S., Finkelstein, A., Rusinkiewicz, S.: A no-reference metric for evaluating the quality of motion deblurring. ACM Trans. Graph. **32**(6), 175 (2013)
7. Shan, Q., Jia, J., Agarwala, A.: High-quality motion deblurring from a single image. ACM Trans. Graph. **27**(3), 1–10 (2008)
8. Krishnan, D., Tay, T., Fergus, R.: Blind deconvolution using a normalized sparsity measure. Comput. Vis. Pattern Recogn. **42**, 233–240 (2011). IEEE
9. Xu, L., Zheng, S., Jia, J.: Unnatural L0 sparse representation for natural image deblurring. Comput. Vis. Pattern Recogn. **9**, 1107–1114 (2013). IEEE
10. Pan, J., Hu, Z., Su, Z., Yang, M.H.: Deblurring text images via L0-regularized intensity and gradient prior. In: IEEE Conference on Computer Vision and Pattern Recognition, pp. 2901–2908. IEEE Computer Society (2014)
11. Shao, W.-Z., Li, H.-B., Elad, M.: Bi-l0-l2-norm regularization for blind motion deblurring. J. Vis. Commun. Image Represent. **33**, 42–59 (2015)
12. Cho, S., Lee, S.: Fast motion deblurring. ACM Trans. Graph. **28**(5), 1–8 (2009)
13. Xu, L., Jia, J.: Two-phase kernel estimation for robust motion deblurring. In: Daniilidis, K., Maragos, P., Paragios, N. (eds.) ECCV 2010. LNCS, vol. 6311, pp. 157–170. Springer, Heidelberg (2010). https://doi.org/10.1007/978-3-642-15549-9_12
14. Pan, J., Lin, Z., Su, Z., Yang, M.H.: Robust kernel estimation with outliers handling for image deblurring. In: IEEE Conference on Computer Vision and Pattern Recognition, pp. 2800–2808. IEEE Computer Society (2016)
15. Whyte, O., Sivic, J., Zisserman, A., Ponce, J.: Non-uniform deblurring for shaken images. Int. J. Comput. Vis. **98**(2), 168–186 (2012)
16. Hu, Z., Yang, M.-H.: Good regions to deblur. In: Fitzgibbon, A., Lazebnik, S., Perona, P., Sato, Y., Schmid, C. (eds.) ECCV 2012. LNCS, vol. 7576, pp. 59–72. Springer, Heidelberg (2012). https://doi.org/10.1007/978-3-642-33715-4_5
17. Hu, Z., Cho, S., Wang, J., Yang, M.H.: Deblurring low-light images with light streaks. In: IEEE Conference on Computer Vision and Pattern Recognition, pp. 3382–3389. IEEE Computer Society (2014)
18. Pan, J., Sun, D., Pfister, H., Yang, M.H.: Blind image deblurring using dark channel prior. In: IEEE Conference on Computer Vision and Pattern Recognition, pp. 1628–1636. IEEE Computer Society (2016)
19. Farbman, Z., Fattal, R., Lischinski, D.: Edge-preserving decompositions for multi-scale tone and detail manipulation. ACM Trans. Graph. **27**(3), 1–10 (2008)
20. Xu, L., Lu, C., Xu, Y., Jia, J.: Image smoothing via L0, gradient minimization. In: SIGGRAPH Asia Conference, vol. 30, p. 174. ACM (2011)

21. Krishnan, D., Bruna, J., Fergus, R.: Blind deconvolution with non-local sparsity reweighting. In: Computer Science (2013)
22. Zhang, X., Wang, R., Tian, Y., Wang, W., Gao, W.: Image deblurring using robust sparsity priors. In: IEEE International Conference on Image Processing, pp. 138–142. IEEE (2015)
23. Sun, L., Cho, S., Wang, J., Hays, J.: Edge-based blur kernel estimation using patch priors. In: IEEE International Conference on Computational Photography, vol. 6, pp. 1–8. IEEE (2013)
24. Zhang, H., Wipf, D., Zhang, Y.: Multi-image blind deblurring using a coupled adaptive sparse prior. In: IEEE Conference on Computer Vision and Pattern Recognition, vol. 9, pp. 1051–1058. IEEE Computer Society (2013)
25. Zhong, L., Cho, S., Metaxas, D., Paris, S., Wang, J.: Handling noise in single image deblurring using directional filters. In: IEEE Conference on Computer Vision and Pattern Recognition, vol. 9, pp. 612–619. IEEE Computer Society (2013)
26. Michaeli, T., Irani, M.: Blind deblurring using internal patch recurrence. In: Fleet, D., Pajdla, T., Schiele, B., Tuytelaars, T. (eds.) ECCV 2014. LNCS, vol. 8691, pp. 783–798. Springer, Cham (2014). https://doi.org/10.1007/978-3-319-10578-9_51
27. Perrone, D., Favaro, P.: Total variation blind deconvolution: the devil is in the details. In: IEEE Conference on Computer Vision and Pattern Recognition, pp. 2909–2916. IEEE Computer Society (2014)

Passive and Active Electro-Optical Sensors for Areal and Space Imaging

Passive and Active Electro-Optical Sensors for Aerial and Space Imaging (EO4AS)

This volume presents the papers presented at the Workshop on Passive and Active Electro-Optical Sensors for Aerial and Space Imaging (EO4AS). These contributions were presented in conjunction with the 8th Pacific Rim Symposium on Video and Image Technology (PSIVT 2017), held in Wuhan, China, on November 21, 2017, and was supported by International Society of Photogrammetry and Remote Sensing (ISPRS) and the Deutsche Gesellschaft für Photogrammetrie, Fernerkundung und Geoinformation (DGPF). Each paper was assigned to three independent reviewers and carefully revised.

The topics of the workshop covered new and improved methods, techniques, and applications of (electro-optical) sensors on airborne and spaceborne platforms.

Over the past half century there has been a drastic development in air- and space-borne platforms as well as active/passive electro-optical sensors. New optical sensors for observations of the earth's surface, oceans, and the atmosphere provide a wide range of solutions for various applications. The aim is the acquisition of information about objects, structures, or phenomens on earth.

The huge amount of data, provided by these sensors, represents a new challenge regarding developments in processing, storage, and evaluation techniques.

The aim of this workshop was to bring together engineers and scientists from academia, industry, and government to exchange results and ideas for future applications of electro-optical remote sensing.

We would like to thank our authors for their efforts. We would like also to thank the Program Committee members for providing very useful and detailed comments. In addition, we thank the local organizers of PSIVT 2017 for their support.

November 2017

Ralf Reulke
Bin Luo

Organization

Workshop Organizers

Ralf Reulke   Humboldt-Universität zu Berlin, Germany

Local Chair

John Robertson   Auckland University of Technology, New Zealand

Program Committee

Andreas Brunn	Black Bridge AG, Germany
Byron, Smiley	Skybox, USA
Clive Fraser	University of Melbourne, Australia
Uwe Knauer	Fraunhofer IFF, Germany
Stephan Nebiker	FHNW Muttenz, Switzerland
Peter Reinartz	DLR, Oberpfaffenhofen, Germany
Tom Segert	Berlin Space Technology, Germany
Mark R. Shortis	RMIT Melbourne, Australia

An Aircraft Tracking Method in Simulated Infrared Image Sequences Based on Regional Distribution

Sijie Wu[1(✉)], Saisai Niu[2], Kai Zhang[1], and Jie Yan[1]

[1] School of Astronautics, Northwestern Polytechnical University,
Xi'an 710072, China
wusij@mail.nwpu.edu.cn
[2] Shanghai Institute of Spaceflight Control Technology, Shanghai, China

Abstract. Based on regional distribution, we propose an aircraft tracking method that exploits both gray-level value distribution and structural distribution. After analyzing aircraft characteristics, we form the region proposals by clustering the peak values in the equivalent topographic map. Based on the region proposals formed with clustering algorithm, we quantify the spatial distribution to describe the geometric structure of the target. Then we calculate the gray-level value distribution and structural distribution to obtain the regional distribution descriptor to be used for characterizing the structural and texture information on the target. Finally, we perform experiments on various trackers to quantitatively evaluate the performance of our aircraft tracking method. The experimental results demonstrate that our aircraft tracking method outperforms several other state-of-the-art tracking methods in simulated infrared image sequences.

Keywords: Aircraft tracking · Regional distribution
Simulated infrared image · Region proposal

1 Introduction

The detection and tracking of an airborne infrared target in a complex combat environment remain a challenging research field for infrared imaging guidance [1, 2]. Due to the extensive use of infrared decoy in battlefield, the information obtained from low-resolution infrared images is not enough to distinguish a target from the infrared decoy [3]. The infrared seeker needs to overcome inter-frame variations resulted from the rapid movement of an aircraft and the occlusion caused by the infrared decoy [4]. To effectively identify and track the target in the complex combat environment has become one of the most urgent problems to be solved for infrared imaging guidance.

Many approaches have been developed to solve the problem in infrared imagery [5–7]. Olson et al. [8] extracted the correlation value of the target image and the standard image based on the image library of the target and track a target according to the correlation value. Yilmaz et al. [9, 10] tracked the target in airborne forward-looking infrared (FLIR) imagery by computing the mean-shift vector that minimizes the distance between the kernel distribution of the target in the current frame and the model. Naidu

© Springer International Publishing AG, part of Springer Nature 2018
S. Satoh (Ed.): PSIVT 2017, LNCS 10799, pp. 343–355, 2018.
https://doi.org/10.1007/978-3-319-92753-4_27

et al. [11] processed the image of a target that exceeds the threshold signal within the search window and calculated the centric coordinates as the tracking point. Gao et al. [12] designed the edge operator to extract the target edge and track the selected edge. These algorithms work well in a simple combat environment with non-interference, but the performances of the algorithms degrade significantly in processing infrared decoys.

In order to prevent tracking failures caused by infrared decoys, inspired by [13, 14], we propose a regional distribution tracking algorithm and a clustering algorithm to generate region proposals and fuse structural information with the original distribution fields to enhance the description capability of the distribution field. The regional distribution is used to characterize the structural information and texture information of the target. With the features generated from the algorithms, the tracking performance in simulated infrared image sequences is more stable.

The rest of this paper is organized as follows. In Sect. 2, we introduce the distribution field. In Sect. 3, we propose region distribution tracking algorithm (RDT) in detail. Experiments in Sect. 4 show the performance of our proposed RDT in simulated infrared image sequences, and Sect. 5 concludes this paper.

2 Distribution Field

First of all, we will briefly introduce the distribution field proposed by Sevilla-Lara et al. [14]. Assuming the stratified number is m, the k-th layer image of the distribution field can be expressed as $d_m(i,j,k)$. The values of the distribution field are assigned using the Kronecker delta function, as shown in Eq. (1):

$$d(i,j,k) = \begin{cases} 1, & I(i,j) = k \\ 0, & I(i,j) \neq k \end{cases} \tag{1}$$

Because of the uncertainties of the spatial distribution of the target and the fluctuation of pixel values caused by fast movement, illumination change and occlusion, the Gaussian filtering is introduced into the space domain and feature domain of the target respectively.

$$d_s(k) = d(k) * h_{\sigma s} \tag{2}$$

$$d_{ss}(i,j) = d_s(i,j) * h_{\sigma f} \tag{3}$$

* represents the convolution operator, and $h_{\sigma s}$ is the two-dimensional Gaussian convolution kernel with the standard deviation σ_s. The distribution $d_s(k)$ after spatial filtering reflects the uncertainty of the location of the target. h_{σ_f} represents the one-dimensional Gaussian convolution kernel with the standard deviation σ_f. After applying the spatial domain and feature domain filters, the integrated feature value of each pixel across all layers remains to be 1. The characteristic value of each pixel means that its probability is the k-th feature layer; then the distribution field of the image can be considered as the probability distribution matrix. The gray-level

distribution of the image demonstrates the hierarchical distribution characteristic of the infrared target.

3 The Aircraft Tracking Algorithm

In the process of visual cognition, the object information is extracted stepwise to form high-level semantic information which can be used for recognition [15]. The shape structure and texture distribution are important feature descriptors. Based on the analysis of aerial target characteristics, and the concept of gray-level distribution field proposed by Sevilla-Lara et al. [14], the region distribution is introduced to extract the structure and texture distribution characteristics. Firstly, region proposals were generated with the clustering algorithm. Then we use the spatial distribution of the region proposals to reflect the structural information of the target. After that, we combine the structure with the gray-level distribution field to form a region distribution descriptor. Base on the robust representation of the descriptor, we verify the tracking performance in simulated infrared image sequences.

3.1 Region Proposal for Searching

The target and decoy are represented as high gray-value regions in a simulated infrared image, as shown in Fig. 1, forming visual salient regions. Firstly, we convert the gray-level values of the image into their equivalent topographic map. The gray-level values of a decoy region's distribution perform like the Gaussian distribution. The decoy region forms a peak that centers around the combustion and gradually descends to its surroundings. The target region shows multiple peaks according to the radiation characteristics of different regions.

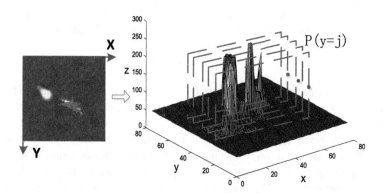

Fig. 1. Image's equivalent three-dimensional topographic map

The clustering centers and number of clusters are determined based on the analysis of the peak values of the topographic map, and the adjacent regions are aggregated according to the gray-level distribution characteristics to generate region proposals that have certain structural information. Assume the image's equivalent three-dimensional surface as $z(x, y)$, define the slice face as $p(y = j)$, as shown in Fig. 1. Then we use the slide window to extract the surface profile of the slide face of the three-dimensional surface. Each plot represents the gray-level value's variation with x coordinate, as shown in Figs. 2 and 3.

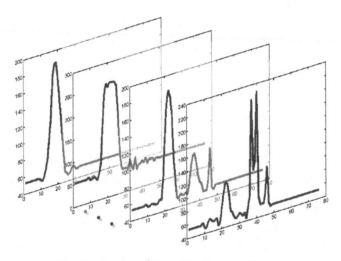

Fig. 2. Surface profiles of the topographic map

After we obtain each surface profile of the topographic map, as shown in Fig. 3, we use the first-order differential to find the peak values of the two-dimensional surface profile, as shown in Eq. (4), where z(x) stands for the gray-level value of the plot. Then we use p(x) to find its rising edge and falling edge. When p(x−1) is a positive number and p(x + 1) is a negative number, we record the p(x) as the peak value.

$$p(x) = z(x+1) - z(x) \tag{4}$$

Based the distance measure proposed by Achanta et al. [16], we define the pixel distance d_{ij} as Eq. (5), where G and R represent the gray-level value and spatial coordinates of the pixel respectively, i and j act as row and column indices of the input image, i_p and j_p stand for the row and column indices of each cluster center. To combine the gray-level proximity distance and the spatial distance into a single measure and keep the distance in same order of magnitude, we use σ_1 to weigh the relative importance between them. The weight of the spatial distance increases when σ_1 is increased [17]. As we discussed before, the gray-level values of a decoy region's distribution perform like the Gaussian distribution, so we add exponential distance corresponding to each cluster center. $1/\sigma_2$ acts as penalty factor to aggregate the pixels

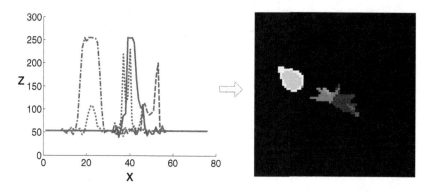

Fig. 3. Clustering by finding peak values of surface profiles

with similar gray-level value. In our experiment, we set $\sigma_1 = 5$ and $1/\sigma_2 = 0.05$ to maintain the balance between gray-level value similarity and spatial proximity.

Based on the defined distance measurement and the peak values acting as initial clustering center, we adapt k-means algorithm [18] to calculate the pixel distance from each cluster center and assign it to the nearest center. The final cluster result is shown in Fig. 3, the different pixel value in cluster result stands for different cluster center. Based on the pixel value of the cluster and the regional connectivity, we mark the same cluster center with red rectangle to obtain region proposals from the clustering results, as shown in Fig. 4.

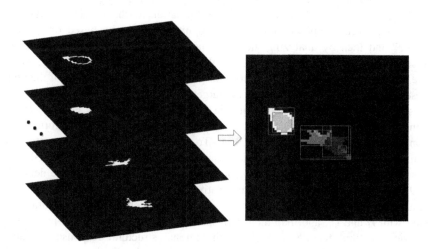

Fig. 4. Region proposals from the clustering results

$$d_{ij} = \frac{||G(i,j) - G(i_p,j_p)||_1 + \sigma_1 ||R(i,j) - R(i_p,j_p)||_2}{\sqrt{1 + \sigma_1^2}}$$
$$+ exp(-\frac{G(i,j) - G(i_p,j_p)}{\sigma_2}) \tag{5}$$

$$||X||_1 = ||(x_1, x_2, \ldots, x_n)||_1 = (\sum_{i=1}^{n} |x_i|) \tag{6}$$

$$||X||_2 = ||(x_1, x_2, \ldots, x_n)||_2 = (n \sum_{i=1}^{n} x_i|^2)^{1/2} \tag{7}$$

The peak value clustering algorithm based on the equivalent topographic map does not rely on the human manipulation of the clustering center and number of clusters, which, however, the traditional clustering algorithm relies on, thus effectively enhancing its efficiency and robustness.

3.2   Structural Feature Extraction

After obtaining region proposals, we improve the search strategy by replacing the local search area with global region proposals so as not to miss the target of an aircraft when the aircraft moves fast. The distribution matrix of the target is established by quantifying the gray-level value, and then the matrix is used as the feature descriptor for target tracking. The structural distribution descriptor is introduced on the basis of the target gray-level distribution to quantitatively analyze the target's geometrical structure.

The structure of an object is important information to characterize a target [19]. Fischler et al. [20] proposed that target recognition should be based on "pictorial structure" and then by analyzing the components of the target and measuring their geometric relations. Based on their regional topology formed by clustering, we calculate the structural response values from the relative spatial distribution of the region to describe the geometric structure of the target.

Assume that the region proposal obtained with clustering is $R = \{R_1, \ldots, R_n\}$; the regional centroids are $V_i(x_i, y_i), i \in (1, \ldots, n)$. C is the center of regions to form a set of regional connections for $\{CV_1, \ldots, CV_n\}$. To obtain a concise representation, we quantize structural information with the polar coordinate system. The conversion formulas from the pixel coordinate (x_i, y_i) to the polar coordinate (r_i, φ_i) are defined in Eq. (9), where r_i and φ_i represent the relative position and angle between the i-th region and the center of regions respectively. Then we encode the structural information with r_i and φ_i, and map their corresponding values to the region proposals to form the structural feature map. The i-th regional structural response w_i can be quantified with the definition in Eq. (10). The structural distribution s_i has been convolved with the Gaussian filter that has the standard deviation σ to introduce positional uncertainty into the response map, as shown in Eq. (11).

The structural feature map preserves the compact spatial information on regional distribution. Each region's response represents the geometric layout of the region, which embeds the magnitude and angle with respect to the center of regions. With the fusion between structural distribution and original distribution field, we obtain a more robust representation of the target, which encodes both structural information and gray-level value distribution. The schematic diagram for generating regional distribution is shown in Fig. 5.

$$x_c = (\sum_{i=1}^{n} x_i)/n \ , \quad y_c = (\sum_{i=1}^{n} y_i)/n \tag{8}$$

$$r_i = \sqrt{(x_i - x_c)^2 + (y_i - y_c)^2}, \quad \varphi_i = \arctan\frac{y_i - y_c}{x_i - x_c} \tag{9}$$

$$\theta_i = \varphi_{i+1} - \varphi_i, \quad w_i = r_i\theta_i \tag{10}$$

$$s_i = w_i * h_\sigma \tag{11}$$

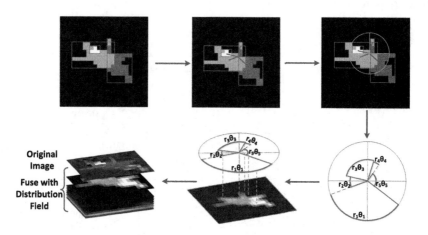

Fig. 5. The schematic diagram for generating regional distribution

3.3 Model Matching and Update

After modeling the distribution characteristics of the target, it is necessary to measure the similarity of regional distribution among region proposals and calculate the relative distance according to the L1 norm. For an m-dimensional vector D, the L1 norm is defined as Eq. (12). The similarity of distribution field can be calculated with Eq. (13), which calculates the distance of original distribution field $d(i,j,k)$ and the structural distribution $s(i,j)$ with α as the fusion coefficient. i and j represent the row and column indices of the input image's feature map respectively. In our experiments, α was related to the stratified number m in distribution field. For the distance in same order of magnitude, we set α approximate to $1/m$.

$$||D||_1 = ||(d_1, d_2, \ldots, d_m)||_1 = \sum_{i=1}^{m} |d_i| \tag{12}$$

$$L_1(d_1, d_2) = \sum_{i,j,k} \alpha||d_1(i,j,k) - d_2(i,j,k)||_1 + (1-\alpha)||s_1(i,j) - s_2(i,j)||_1 \tag{13}$$

3.4   Our Aircraft Tracking Algorithm

Region proposals formed by clustering are transferred to the tracker as initial search regions. Then we calculate the regional distribution formed by gray-level values and the spatial information on the regions. The region with the highest similarity is used as the tracking region. The aircraft tracking algorithm proposed by us is summarized as follows (Fig. 6):

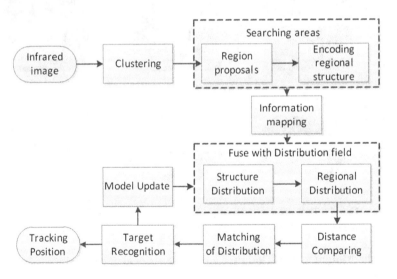

Fig. 6.   The flow chart of aircraft tracking process

Algorithm : The regional distribution tracker's tracking algorithm
Input: Simulated infrared image frame with initial target location
1: Region proposals clustered by finding peaks.
2: For i =1 to be equal to k (k is the count of regions);
3: Compute the gray-level value distribution field.
4: Calculate the spatial distribution of sub-regions, map the magnitude and angle information to raw image to form structure feature map.
6: Compare the distance between region and target's model
7: End form.
8: Select a region with the minimal distance as the tracking region
9: Update a target's model according to its distance
Output: Target location with bounding box.

4 Experiments

4.1 Analyzing Regional Distribution Tracker

We perform experiments on both gray-level distribution feature and regional distribution feature to validate the performance of our aircraft tracking algorithm. For convenience, we use the abbreviation RDT-Gd to represent the regional distribution tracker with original gray-level distribution features and RDT to represent the tracker with region distribution features, which includes gray-level value distribution feature and spatial distribution feature of a sub-region. DFT stands for the original distribution field tracker in accordance with the author's paper [14].

Then we evaluate the tracker with success plot and precision plot for quantitative analysis [21]. The metric of the success plot evaluates the tracker with bounding box overlap. Given the tracked bounding box B_t and the ground truth bounding box B_{gt}, the overlap score is defined as in Eq. (14).

$$S = \frac{|B_t \cap B_{gt}|}{|B_t \cup B_{gt}|} \tag{14}$$

The precision plot shows the percentage of image frames whose tracked location is within the given threshold distance of ground truth. As shown in Table 1, RDT shows the best tracking performance.

Table 1. Characteristics and tracking results of DFT, RDT-Gd and RDT

Trackers	Search space	Feature representations	Precision	Success
DFT	Local region	Gray-level value distribution	0.393	0.216
RDT-gd	Region proposal	Gray-level value distribution	0.984	0.867
RDT	Region proposal	Regional distribution	0.991	0.873

4.2   Evaluating Tracking Benchmark

To evaluate the performance of our aircraft tracking algorithm, we use the tracking benchmark code library [21] which includes 29 trackers and add five state of art trackers [22–26] to test the trackers in simulated infrared sequences with different attack angles. Figure 7 shows the success plot and precision plot of top 10 trackers in simulated infrared sequences. Compared with the trackers included in the tracking benchmark code library, the RDT has a much better tracking performance than the DFT and outperform most of other trackers.

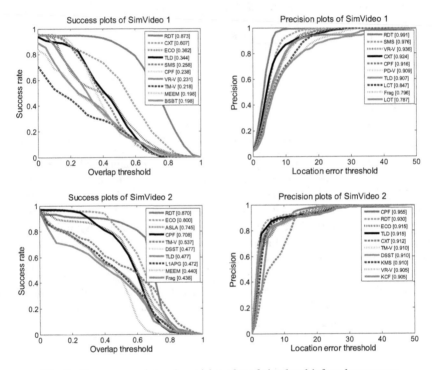

Fig. 7. The success plot and precision plot of simulated infrared sequences

Fig. 8. Tracking results of simulated infrared sequence 1 (Color figure online)

Fig. 9. Tracking results of simulated infrared sequence 2 (Color figure online)

Fig. 10. Failure case of tracking results

We show the tracking results of the trackers with differently colored bounding boxes, as shown in Figs. 8 and 9. To get a better view, we draw our tracker's results with red rectangle alone. As seen from the tracking results, most of the trackers can lock their target in a simple combat environment without interference, but when the target throws infrared decoys, the trackers drift significantly and begin to track the decoy instead of the aircraft. The clustering performance has an influence on our tracker, as shown in Fig. 10, the center image is the clustering result. At last, the tracker drifts to the decoy. Compared with others, our tracker can track aircraft more effectively.

5   Conclusion

In this paper, we propose a novel method for tracking aircraft in simulated infrared image sequences based on regional distribution. We exploit the characteristics of a target to generate region proposals in the equivalent topographic map generated with clustering algorithm. Based on the region proposals, we model the regional distribution descriptor for tracking aircraft under interference. Through the effective use of the texture and structural information formed by the region proposals, our aircraft tracking algorithm performs better than several other state-of-the-art trackers in simulated infrared image sequences in terms of accuracy and robustness.

Acknowledgments. This research was supported by the National Natural Science Foundation of China (61703337) and the Aerospace Science and Technology Innovation Fund of China (SAST2017-082).

References

1. Youpei, F., Jianping, Q.: Jamming technology research to the imaging IR guidance missile. Infrared Laser Eng. **29**(3), 7–14 (2000)
2. Zaveri, M.A., Merchant, S.N., Desai, U.B.: Air-borne approaching target detection and tracking in infrared image sequence. In: 2004 International Conference on Image Processing, ICIP 2004, vol. 2, pp. 1025–1028. IEEE (2004)
3. Lixiang, G., Qian, C., Weixian, Q.: Infrared aircraft-flare discrimination using improved JPDA algorithm. Infrared Laser Eng. **42**(2), 305–310 (2013)
4. Fan, G., Venkataraman, V., Fan, X., et al.: Appearance learning for infrared tracking with occlusion handling. In: Hammoud, R., Fan, G., McMillan, R.W., Ikeuchi, K. (eds.) Machine Vision Beyond Visible Spectrum, pp. 33–64. Springer, Heidelberg (2011). https://doi.org/10.1007/978-3-642-11568-4_2
5. Braga-Neto, U., Choudhary, M., Goutsias, J.: Automatic target detection and tracking in forward-looking infrared image sequences using morphological connected operators. J. Electron. Imaging **13**(4), 802–813 (2004)
6. Yoon, S.P., Song, T.L., Kim, T.H.: Automatic target recognition and tracking in forward-looking infrared image sequences with a complex background. Int. J. Control Autom. Syst. **11**(1), 21 (2013)
7. Berg, A., Felsberg, M., Häger, G., et al.: An overview of the thermal infrared visual object tracking VOT-TIR2015 challenge. In: Swedish Symposium on Image Analysis (2016)
8. Olson, T.L.P., Sanford, C.W.: Real-time multistage IR image-based tracker. In: AeroSense 1999. International Society for Optics and Photonics, pp. 226–233 (1999)
9. Yilmaz, A., Shafique, K., Lobo, N., et al.: Target-tracking in FLIR imagery using mean-shift and global motion compensation. In: IEEE Workshop on Computer Vision Beyond Visible Spectrum, pp. 54–58 (2001)
10. Yilmaz, A., Shafique, K., Shah, M.: Target tracking in airborne forward looking infrared imagery. Image Vis. Comput. **21**(7), 623–635 (2003)
11. Naidu, V.P.S., Girija, G., Raol, J.R.: Centroid Tracking and Target Identity Estimation using Image Sensor Data (2005)
12. Gao, G., Li, L., Song, J., et al.: Fast detecting and tracking algorithm of infrared target under complex background. In: 2011 International Conference on Electronics and Optoelectronics (ICEOE), vol. 2, pp. V2-430–V2-434. IEEE (2011)
13. Rodriguez, A., Laio, A.: Clustering by fast search and find of density peaks. Science **344**(6191), 1492–1496 (2014)
14. Sevilla-Lara, L., Learned-Miller, E.: Distribution fields for tracking. In: 2012 IEEE Conference on Computer Vision and Pattern Recognition (CVPR), pp. 1910–1917. IEEE (2012)
15. Ullman, S.: High-Level Vision: Object Recognition and Visual Cognition. MIT Press, Cambridge (1996)
16. Achanta, R., Shaji, A., Smith, K., et al.: SLIC superpixels compared to state-of-the-art superpixel methods. IEEE Trans. Pattern Anal. Mach. Intell. **34**(11), 2274–2282 (2012)
17. Chao, J., Huiying, L., Jingfeng, S., et al.: Calculating probability of objectness likelihood model based on superpixels. Infrared Laser Eng. **11**, 3156–3162 (2013)
18. Kanungo, T., Mount, D.M., Netanyahu, N.S., et al.: An efficient k-means clustering algorithm: analysis and implementation. IEEE Trans. Pattern Anal. Mach. Intell. **24**(7), 881–892 (2002)

19. Gong, J., Fan, G., Yu, L., et al.: Joint target tracking, recognition and segmentation for infrared imagery using a shape manifold-based level set. Sensors **14**(6), 10124–10145 (2014)
20. Fischler, M.A., Elschlager, R.A.: The representation and matching of pictorial structures. IEEE Trans. Comput. **100**(1), 67–92 (1973)
21. Wu, Y., Lim, J., Yang, M.H.: Object tracking benchmark. IEEE Trans. Pattern Anal. Mach. Intell. **37**(9), 1834–1848 (2015)
22. Zhang, J., Ma, S., Sclaroff, S.: MEEM: robust tracking via multiple experts using entropy minimization. In: Fleet, D., Pajdla, T., Schiele, B., Tuytelaars, T. (eds.) ECCV 2014. LNCS, vol. 8694, pp. 188–203. Springer, Cham (2014). https://doi.org/10.1007/978-3-319-10599-4_13
23. Henriques, J.F., Caseiro, R., Martins, P., et al.: High-speed tracking with kernelized correlation filters. IEEE Trans. Pattern Anal. Mach. Intell. **37**(3), 583–596 (2015)
24. Danelljan, M., Häger, G., Khan, F., et al.: Accurate scale estimation for robust visual tracking. In: British Machine Vision Conference, Nottingham, 1–5 September 2014. BMVA Press (2014)
25. Ma, C., Yang, X., Zhang, C., et al.: Long-term correlation tracking. In: Proceedings of the IEEE Conference on Computer Vision and Pattern Recognition, pp. 5388–5396 (2015)
26. Danelljan, M., Bhat, G., Khan, F.S., et al.: ECO: efficient convolution operators for tracking (2016). arXiv preprint arXiv:1611.09224

DESIS - DLR Earth Sensing Imaging Spectrometer

David Krutz[⊠], Holger Venus, Andreas Eckardt, Ingo Walter, Ilse Sebastian,
Ralf Reulke, Burghardt Günther, Bernd Zender, Simone Arloth,
Christian Williges, Matthias Lieder, Michael Neidhardt, Ute Grote,
Friedrich Schrandt, and Andreas Wojtkowiak

DLR, Institute of Optical Sensor Systems, Berlin, Germany
david.krutz@dlr.de

Abstract. The DLR Earth Sensing Imaging Spectrometer (DESIS) is
a new space-based hyperspectral sensor developed and operated by a
collaboration between the German Aerospace Center (DLR) and Tele-
dyne Brown Engineering (TBE). DESIS will provide hyperspectral data
in the visible to near-infrared range with high resolution and near-global
coverage. TBE provides the platform and infrastructure for the operation on the International Space Station (ISS), DLR is developing the
instrument. This paper gives an overview of the design of the DESIS
instrument together with first results from the optical calibration.

Keywords: DESIS · ISS · MUSES · Hyperspectral · Camera

1 Introduction

Space-based hyperspectral instruments are used in many applications requiring
identification of materials or helping to monitor the environment. Although there
are lots of useful applications, the amount of space born data is limited [1].
The development of the DESIS instrument arises from a collaboration between
DLR and TBE [2]. DLR is responsible for the instrument development, TBE
for the installation and operation of the Multi-User System for Earth Sensing
(MUSES) [3]. The MUSES platform was launched in June 2017 with SpaceX-11
and integrated to the ISS several days later. DESIS is the first instrument to
utilize the MUSES external payload accommodation. The launch of the DESIS
instrument is foreseen for early 2018. After robotic integration of the DESIS
instrument to the MUSES platform, a commissioning and validation phase will
be performed. In mid 2018 the operational phase will start. From specification
to delivery the instrument will has been developed in just three years.

The major parameters of the DESIS instrument are shown in Table 1. The
Signal-to-Noise Ratio (SNR) for maximum and minimum binning mode is shown
in Fig. 1. The daily download capacity is 225 GBit. These corresponds to 5 min
acquisition time under nominal conditions. With compression the acquisition
time is increased to 10 min.

© Springer International Publishing AG, part of Springer Nature 2018
S. Satoh (Ed.): PSIVT 2017, LNCS 10799, pp. 356–368, 2018.
https://doi.org/10.1007/978-3-319-92753-4_28

Table 1. DESIS parameters

	Parameter		Parameter
$F_\#$	2.8	focal length	320mm
FoV	4.1°	IFoV	0.004°
GSD	30m	Spatial Pixels	1024
Swath	30km		
Spec. range	400nm-1000nm	Spec. channels	235
Spect. sampling	2.55nm	Spec. Binning Modes	1, 2, 3, 4
SNR (albedo 0.3,	195 (no binning)		
550nm)	386 (binning 4)		
radio. Linearity	>95 (10%-90% FWC)	radio. resolution	12bit + 1 bit gain
MTF at Nyq.	>20%	FWHM	<3nm
Pixel Size	24μm x 24μm	max. frame rate	232Hz (Roll. Shutter)
pointing	±15°	pointing knowledge	<0.004°
mass	88kg		

Earth observation from the ISS is a trade-off. Using the ISS infrastructure (launch system, communication, power) reduces the effort and cost for the development of the earth observation mission and the operation in space. But there are also some disadvantages. The ISS orbit is not optimized for earth observation. With an inclination of 51.6° only 90% of the populated part of the earth will be scanned with an average cadence of 3 to 5 days. In comparison to sun-synchronous orbits of classical earth observation missions, ISS is using a non-sun synchronous orbit. The illumination conditions given by the sun incident angle are not reproducible. This implies the need of a very good atmospheric correction algorithm. This mission helps to validate the quality of the atmospheric correction algorithm. With the help of the pointing unit in front of the optics the line of sight could be changed with a high pointing accuracy, superior to the IFoV. This opens the field for new methods of atmospheric corrections, e.g. by applying Bidirectional Reflectance Distribution Function (BRDF).

Challenging is also the complex thermal environment of the instruments on board of the ISS. The variability in beta angle together with the flexibility of ISS structure elements (turning solar panels and radiators) complicates the thermal design and thermal analysis.

Following additional features are implemented in the DESIS instrument:

– The line of sight can be changed ±15° in flight direction independent of the MUSES orientation by the pointing unit. This function enables stereo imaging and BRDF imaging.
– The DESIS instrument has a calibration unit based on LEDs. The calibration unit will be used for in-orbit calibration of the detector. Dark and light conditions with a large variety of spectral features can be generated.
– The DESIS instrument has a GPS receiver, which will work as a calibration facility for the time information propagated over the ISS network from a ISS GPS receiver. The ISS GPS receiver is located on top of the ISS so that

the visibility to GPS satellites is excellent. But the offset and jitter error of the time information after propagation through the ISS network is unknown. The GPS receiver on-board of the DESIS instrument will help to measure the offset and the jitter error. With a location of the DESIS GPS antenna on the upper side of the ISS the line of sight coverage is not optimal. In only 15% of time at least four GPS satellites are visible and a high accuracy time information will be available. But this short time can be used for the measurement of jitter and offset errors.

- The DESIS instrument has a mass memory system of 64 GByte. This mass memory system is necessary, because the raw detector data rate of 1 Gbit/s is higher than the data rate to the MUSES server (<100 MBit/s).

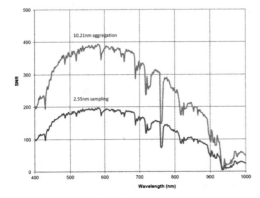

Fig. 1. The Signal-to-Noise Ratio (SNR) for spectral sampling without binning (2.55 nm) and binning mode 4 (10.21 nm). Simulation based on Modtran with standard mid-latitude summer atmosphere (Albedo 0.3)

Fig. 2. MUSES platform with the two small and two large slots for payloads. DESIS will be located in one of the large slots.

2   MUSES

MUSES is an Earth-pointing platform for remote sensing developed by TBE for the ISS. Up to four payloads/instruments can be accommodated on the platform (see Fig. 2). The platform is connected to the EXPRESS Logistics Carriers (ELC-4) and provides attitude, position, data downlink capability, power and the TC/TM interface. The communication interface between MUSES and the payloads is Gigabit-Ethernet. MUSES has a server system inside the ISS for massive data storage and for preparing the data for ground transfer. The gimbal system of the MUSES platform supports a two axis rotation: ±25° forward/backward view and 45° backboard view and 5° starboard view. The pointing knowledge is better than 0.008°, which corresponds to 60 m GSD. Together with the DESIS pointing unit a $\pm 40°$ forward/backward view is supported. The pointing knowledge will be calculated by star tracker and Miniature Inertial Measurement Unit. The filter algorithm provides a 10 Hz orientation solution.

3   DESIS Design

The DESIS instrument was especially designed for the MUSES platform. The optic parameters (e.g. aperture) were maximized under the constraint of the MUSES payload envelopment. The DESIS instrument consists of following subsystems: spectrometer optics with some auxiliary optical components (fix mirrors, baffle), focal plane array (FPA), instrument control unit (ICU) together with power supply (PCHU), a calibration unit, the pointing unit (POI) and the container (see Fig. 3).

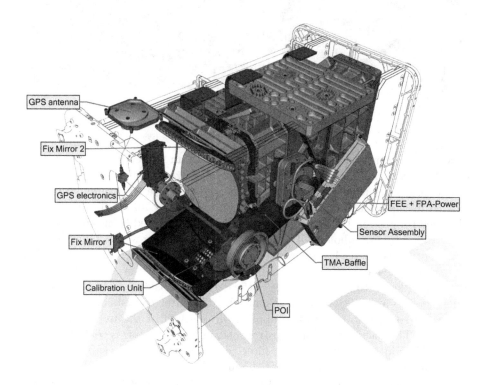

Fig. 3. DESIS instrument

3.1   Spectrometer Optic

The major component of the DESIS instrument is the optics together with the detector. The flight model spectrometer optic is shown in Fig. 4. It consists of a

Fig. 4. Spectrometer optics

Three-Mirror-Anastigmat (TMA) optic, a slit and an Offner spectrometer. The
DESIS spectrograph has a sophisticated mirror design: M1 and M2 are symmetrical identical free form mirrors. Both are located on the same base substrate and
grinded in one work stage. The design leads to a nearly aberration free image.
The spectral grating between both mirrors is manufactured by mechanical dia-
mond ruling by Fraunhofer IOF Jena. It is a plane grating with a binary groove
form. Optimized on its 1st order it suppresses any higher order light to less than
2%. To further reduce higher order light hitting the detector, DLR decided to
insert an order sorting filter in front of the detector. It is designed to reduce 2nd
order light to about 2 orders of magnitude. The filter consists of a substrate,
where the suppression coating is applied on one half of the front side of the
substrate. The back side of the substrate, facing the detector, is coated with an
Anti Reflection (AR) coating. The filter coating is designed to suppress wavelength smaller than 550 nm. The coated half of the substrate will be placed above
the part of the detector determined for the longer wavelength range. Applying
both measures, a 2nd order suppression to roughly 1/10000 is achieved. The
optical imaging is protected from stray light by a baffle-structure coated with
Actar Black. A detailed description of the optics is given in [4]. The mass of the
optics is 21 kg. The optics base on a single material: AlSi42 (CE13). This material matches very well to the Nickel plating Coefficient of Thermal Expansion
(CTE) of the mirrors and reduces the thermal gradients in the optics. With this
design the full performance range can be extended from 15 °C to 25 °C.

3.2   Focal Plane Assembly

The FPA comprises the detector and the detector near electronics. The detector is a CIS2001 back-illuminated CMOS detector array from BAE. It's sensitivity ranges from 400 nm to 1000 nm, which covers roughly the Visible Near Infrared (VNIR) sector. From the existing 256×1024 pixel only 235 are used by the instrument. The maximum number of spectral channels is defined by the maximum frame rate of the detector. A typical orbit of 400 km and a GSD of 30 m requires a frame rate of 240 Hz. This can only by achieved in a rolling shutter mode. In this mode each spectral channel is integrated over the same time period, but the time when the integration starts and ends slightly varies for each spectral channel. The result is that the spectral channels integrate over slightly different surface areas. By using the rolling shutter mode (in contrast to the global shutter mode) the frame period can be increased by a factor of two. Another positive side-effect of this mode is a reduced noise.

3.3   Instrument Control and Power Supply

The instrument control unit (ICU) controls all subsystems of DESIS. It contains also the telecommand/telemetry interface (GigEthernet) to the MUSES platform. The ICU consists of a processor board, a network interface board and a FPGA board (see Fig. 5). All power management functionality (generation of secondary powers, power control of subsystems and heater power management) are located in the power supply unit (PCHU). The processor board is a radiation qualified P2020 processor from Freescale. The operating system is Linux. The processor board communicates over the GigEthernet network board with the MUSES platform. The architecture supports network speeds up to 1 GBit/s. To handle all the subsystems in the instrument a FPGA board with a Xilinx Virtex-4 is attached to the processor board. The communication between processor board and FPGA board works over PCI. The major challenge of the ICU design is the implementation of the mass memory functionality. The ICU receives the image data from the FPA with a throughput of 1 GBit/s. These data has to be written to an internal 64 GByte NAND-flash based mass memory system. A detail description of the mass memory system of DESIS can be found in [5].

3.4   Calibration Unit

The calibration unit is responsible for the in-flight calibration of the DESIS instrument. With the pointing unit the line of sight can be changed to the Calibration unit. The calibration unit consists of two identical LED bank arrays (see Fig. 6). Each bank has 9 different types of LED (see Fig. 7 for the spectral coverage of the LED types). In front of each LED an Integrated Micro Optical Systems (IMOS) lens is used for collimating the light to a cone of $\pm 16°$. The LED banks are temperature stabilized. The calibration unit will be used for PRNU cross-calibration and for DSNU calibration.

Fig. 5. ICU FPGA board   **Fig. 6.** CalibrationUnit

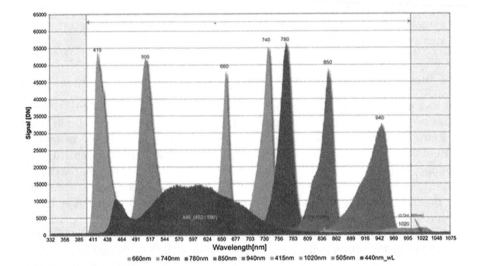

Fig. 7. Spectrum of DESIS calibration unit

The LED types used in the calibration unit were tested for Displacement Damage (DD) using proton radiation at 30 MeV and for Total Ionization Dose (TID) effects using Co60 gamma radiation source. The TID effects are negligible below the tested range up to 3.2 kRad(Si). All LEDs are stable in peak and dominant wavelength as well as in their spectral bandwidth after proton radiation. However, the maximum peak intensity changed as a result of DD. For most of the LED types the intensity increased by 1% after $3.2 \cdot 10^{10} \frac{proton}{cm^2}$, though, for two types the intensity decreased by 4% under the same radiation. This effect can be used to compensate LED degradation in flight. The IMOS lens shows a degradation of 0.6% under this radiation.

3.5 Pointing Unit

The function of the pointing unit is to change the line of sight of the instrument (see Fig. 8). The pointing mirror on top of the pointing unit will be controlled by a stepper motor. Two modes of operation are supported: earth observation mode and forward motion compensation mode. In the earth observation mode the nominal image strip acquisition will be performed. The Line of Sight is programmable between $\pm 15°$ with an repeatability accuracy of $0.001°$ ($\frac{1}{4}$ of pixel). During image acquisition the pointing angle is constant. The forward motion compensation mode will be used for improving the SNR by increasing the integration time. In this mode a constant speed of the line of sight vs. the earth surface reduces the relative speed of the pixel on ground. The speed is programmable from $0.3°/s$ to $0.75°/s$ with an accuracy of $0.001°/s$. The stepper motor will be operated in half-step mode (earth observation mode) or 8-fold micro stepping mode (forward motion compensation mode). Between stepper motor and pointing mirror axle a gear with a ratio of 1:288 is set. The high ratio helps to improve the accuracy. The mirror inertia will be compensated by a counter balance mass. The back-lash of the system is reduced by a permanent return spring operation. Dedicated positions of the mirror will be detected by magnetic sensors. These position sensors will also be used for auto-calibration of the stepper motor (homing).

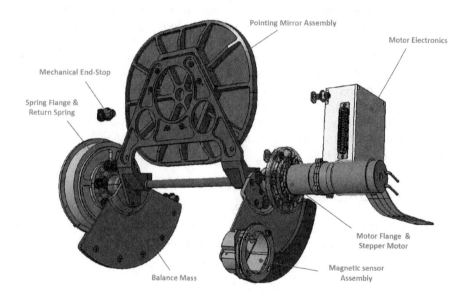

Fig. 8. Pointing unit

3.6 Container and Thermal Design

The container of the instrument is the mechanical interface of the instrument to the MUSES platform and the Extra Vehicular Robotics (EVR). The container is also responsible for the thermal insulation of the DESIS instrument to the MUSES platform and other instruments on MUSES. The material of the optical instrument has to have high conductive values and a CTE that is compatible with the rest of the DESIS design. In addition the TMA and Offner have a highly polished, highly planar mechanical interface with high linear conductive values to each other. The optical instrument is connected to the container at one location. Due to this an insertion of temperature gradient is prevented. The fix mirrors, the Pointing Unit and the instrument have to stay in the same distances to each other to maintain the pointing knowledge and prevent a focus drift. This is established by using Honeycomb material for the crosspanels, which has a very low coefficient of thermal expansion. The electronic boxes ICU, PCHU and FEE are attached outside of the instrument compartment to minimize thermal interaction with the optical instrument and are partly thermally insulated from the crosspanels. The main conductive path goes along thermal links to the radiators. The full performance range of the optical instrument is defined between $+15\,^{\circ}\mathrm{C}$ and $+25\,^{\circ}\mathrm{C}$. Maintenance heater system, dynamic heater system and DESIS container design have to keep the optical instrument temperature within the full performance ranges for the hot environment with heavy duty cycle as well as the cold environment with no duty cycle over the full beta angle range. This is also true for all other units of DESIS, however the temperature ranges are less stringent there. Since the radiator sizes are maximized the thermal design can influence the choice of coatings and the thermal conductor values between the units and parts of the DESIS container. Also the locations of the heaters and the amount of heater power can be selected, as well as the temperature set on and off times of the thermal switches. With the exception of the maintenance and dynamic heater systems, the thermal control system shall work as a passive thermal control system. No Multi-Layer Insulation (MLI) will be used at the outsides of the DESIS container.

4 First Calibration Results

In early 2017 the first calibration measurement on detector level has been performed. In this section, some measurements and results are presented.

4.1 MTF

The MTF measurement on DESIS detector at sub-system level has been done at DLR laboratory before full-system integration. The detector MTF in later spectral and spatial imaging direction has been measured at three different wavelengths, in rolling and global shutter mode and for two different gain factors for comparison. The MTF has been measured using monochromatic "Single Pixel Illumination" by slit sampling (see Fig. 9). "Single Pixel Illumination" on DESIS

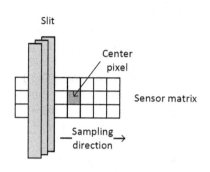

Fig. 9. MTF measurement principle

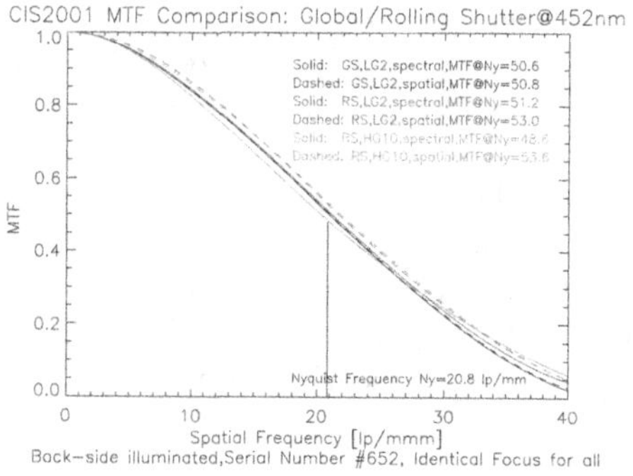

Fig. 10. Detector MTF for different modes and gains

detector has been applied by slit image perpendicularly oriented to spatial and spectral direction. The slit image at infinity has been moved over one pixel by step motor in about 1/10 sub-pixel steps while the pixel signal has been stored for each step.

The extracted pixel signal vs. stepping has been used as baseline for later Discrete Fourier Transformation and set-up correction to derive detector MTF. Auxiliary lens optics Flektogon 2.8/20 has been used in front of the detector for support of imaging. Figure 10 illustrates the measured detector MTF curves vs. spatial frequency at the wavelength of 452 nm. The detector MTF is presented for rolling/global shutter mode, in spectral/spatial direction and for low gain 2/high gain 10 each with identical spot position and with identical focus. As result the MTF value at Nyquist frequency of 20.8 lp/mm has been found to be roughly about $(50 \pm 3)\%$ for all. No significant discrepancy between them has been detected. It appears a small difference between spectral MTF direction and slightly better spatial MTF direction of about 2%–5% using rolling shutter mode. Different wavelength measurements show approximately the identical performance.

4.2 Linearity

The linearity measurement were made by varying the intensity of the integrating sphere and by changing integration time. The principle of the measurement is to increase the incident exposure by changing either the integration time or the irradiance. Integration time can be measured with high accuracy. To test the entire measurement set-up the change of irradiance should also be taken into account. In this case the spectral behaviour of the radiation source should not change. The straight line fit to the data can be found by a least squares fit. Below saturation (i.e. on the straight line part of the linearity plot), it can normally be arranged that the fit is over a range of data points such that the correlation coefficient between the data and the fitted line should normally be greater than 0.995 (see Fig. 11).

The camera is operated under its nominal operating conditions with nominal frame rate, operational temperature and parameter settings. The illumination source is uniform and exposure change was realized by integration time. The integration time changed in between 0 ms and the nominal integration time. On 10 different places on the chip, a linearity investigation was performed by changing integration time. Dynamic range is from 8000DN to 16000DN. The saturation begins above 14000DN. Below this range the linearity was evaluated. In Fig. 12 the residual error of the linearity measurement is shown. This result shows that the linearity requirement of the DESIS instrument is fulfilled.

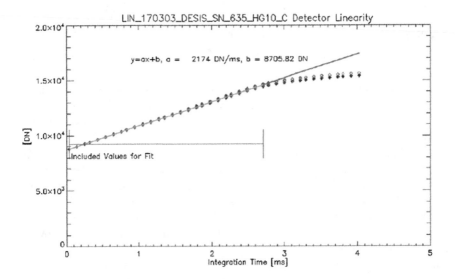

Fig. 11. Linearity and slope

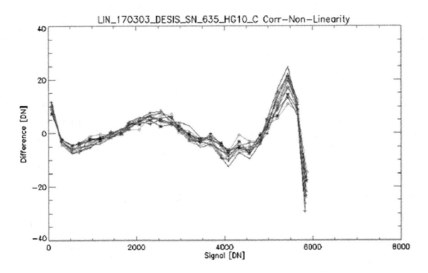

Fig. 12. Linearity error

4.3   Photo Transfer Curve and Conversion Gain

The measurement concept is based on an analysis of detector signal and the corresponding noise by variation of input exposure. As described in [6] the conversion gain can be derived from the slope between noise variance and signal. Figure 13 shows an example for a single pixel. The histogram of the gains of all active pixels is shown in Fig. 14.

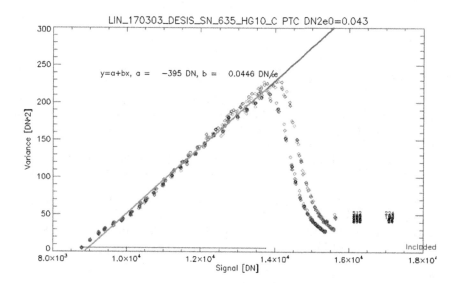

Fig. 13. Slope between noise variance and signal

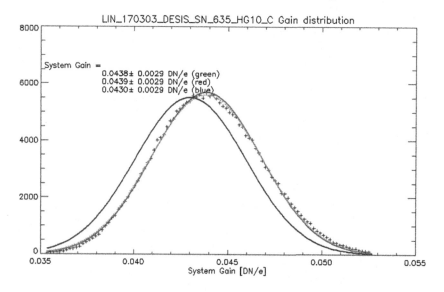

Fig. 14. Histogram of conversion gain of all active pixels

5   Conclusion and Outlook

In this paper the design of the DESIS instrument was presented. Also first results of the optical performance of the detector were shown. All actual test results imply that the instrument requirements will be fulfilled. The next steps will be the integration of the instrument, the environmental testing and the final characterization of the optical parameters. The process will be finalized in the end of 2017.

References

1. Guanter, L., et al.: The EnMAP spaceborn imaging spectroscopy mission for earth observation. Rem. Sens. **7**(7), 8830–8857 (2015)
2. Müller, R., et al.: The new hyperspectral sensor DESIS on the multi-payload platform MUSES installed on the ISS. In: The International Archives of the Photogrammetry, Remote Sensing and Spatial Information Sciences, XXIII ISPRS CONGRESS, Prague, Czech Republic (2016)
3. Perkins, R., et al.: Teledynes Multi-User System for Earth Sensing (MUSES), JACIE (Joint Agency Commercial Imagery Evaluation) Workshop, Fort Worth, Texas, USA (2016)
4. Peschel, T., et al.: Design of an imaging spectrometer for earth observation using freeform mirrors. In: ISCO 2016, Biarritz, France (2016)
5. Krutz, D., et al.: The DESIS Mass Memory System, BiDS (Big Data From Space), Toulouse, France (2017)
6. Janesick, J.R.: Scientific Charge-Coupled Devices. SPIE Press Book, Bellingham (2001)

FireBIRD Mission Data for Gas Flaring Analysis

Agnieszka Soszyńska[✉]

Institute of Optical Sensor Systems, German Aerospace Center,
Rutherfordstr. 2, 12489 Berlin, Germany
agnieszka.soszynska@dlr.de

Abstract. German Aerospace Center (DLR) initiated the FireBIRD mission for the purpose of fire analysis. Twin satellites, TET-1 and BIROS, provide data specialized in this field. This data can be used in gas flaring analysis. Gas flaring is a process of burning the associated gas obtained during crude-oil extraction. During this process, great amounts of greenhouse gases are emitted into the atmosphere. In order to enable monitoring this process, reliable data is necessary. The paper provides an overview on existing thermal sensors which can be used in researching the subject of gas flares. The comparison discusses sensor features important to gas flaring studies. The FireBIRD mission is described and assessed for the purpose of this application. The data is compared to the existing database from the World Bank. FireBIRD proves to have potential for this application, and in some cases significant advantages over other sensors. Research in this direction will be continued in the project.

Keywords: FireBIRD · Fire analysis · Remote sensing · Gas flares
Thermal remote sensing

1 Introduction

The development of modern optical space sensors gives us possibilities to ensure better protection of people and of the environment by providing more exact data for analysis and for warning systems. With respect to global warming, satellite data can be of use in safety applications. Climate changes, by increasing the frequency of hurricanes, heavy storms, and other extreme weather events, result in serious hazards for the safety of people. Global warming is intensified by human activities, such as greenhouse gas emissions to the atmosphere. We are able to monitor some of those activities using satellite imagery. Constant monitoring of the Earth by satellite systems enables us to observe global climate changes and their causations.

One of the factors contributing to significant greenhouse gas emissions to the atmosphere is gas flaring: the process of burning natural gas released as a side-product during crude oil extraction. Even though it is natural gas, which could be used in multiple ways such as providing warm water or electricity, the small quantities in question usually lead to flaring: alternative solutions would require investments in additional infrastructure. Although new, sustainable energy sources are getting

© Springer International Publishing AG, part of Springer Nature 2018
S. Satoh (Ed.): PSIVT 2017, LNCS 10799, pp. 369–381, 2018.
https://doi.org/10.1007/978-3-319-92753-4_29

increasingly more popular, oil production, and therefore greenhouse gas emissions to the atmosphere, do not regress (Fig. 1).

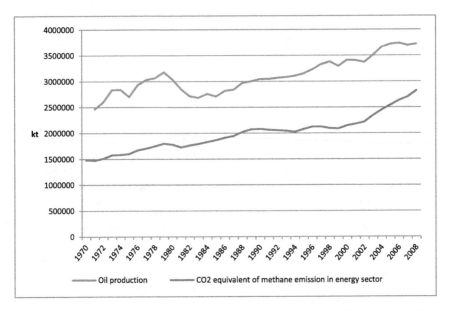

Fig. 1. Global oil production and methane emission to the atmosphere. Source: World Bank.

Natural gas consists mostly of methane (up to 99%), but often contains some other hydrocarbons (e.g. ethane) and other chemical compounds, such as hydrogen sulphide. Its combustion temperature is very high and differs from station to station. Literature provides different information on flaring temperature – most probably between 1300 K and 1800 K [1, 2], but it would be safer to assume that the gas burns at the flares between 1000 K and 2000 K due to the broad variety of stations and the technology used. The burning process is also not complete – the average efficiency of the flares reaches around 68% [3], hence, combustion products as well as unburned compounds are emitted into the atmosphere.

The process of gas flaring is increasingly capturing attention of different international agencies, governments and scientific institutes. In 2002, the World Bank initiated the Global Gas Flaring Reduction (GGFR) partnership, bringing together governments, organisations and oil companies all over the World, in order to monitor and encourage a decrease in flaring. As the official description says, "GGFR works to increase use of natural gas associated with oil production by helping remove technical and regulatory barriers to flaring reduction, conducting research, disseminating best practices, and developing country-specific gas flaring reduction programs" [18]. The World Bank introduced also the "Zero Routine Flaring by 2030" initiative, in which the partners cooperate to eliminate routine flaring by 2030 [19]. Within the framework of the GGFR partnership, a global gas flaring database was created, to provide daily information on the location of gas flares and some fire parameters on global scale. The input data for the database comes from the VIIRS sensor (see below).

2 Remote Sensing of Gas Flaring

Observation of gas flares on satellite imagery has been first done in 1978 [4]. Ever since, new attempts have been made to study gas flares from space with four main purposes:

1. To provide the exact location of the flaring stations [1, 5–8]
2. To estimate the temperature or other fire parameters of the flares [1, 2, 5, 6, 9–12]
3. To calculate the flared volumes [2, 6, 8, 9]
4. To assess the environmental consequences of the flaring process [13–15].

The above mentioned studies provide a good overview of the possible development and needs for future research. The main problems and conclusions, which are drawn in the listed reports are:

- Some flares are being omitted by algorithms due to the too coarse spatial resolution of the sensors.
- Sensors tend to saturate the pixels containing gas flares.
- Big amounts of data are hard to obtain due to long revisit time of the satellites.
- Sensors do not have spectral bands in the range where Planck curve of the flares has its maximum.
- Algorithms tend to mix gas flares with city lights.
- Targets are often covered with clouds, in some regions for the greater part of the year.
- Reference data (i.e. information on flaring temperature, volume, etc.) is very hard to access.

There is a group of thermal sensors, which can be used for studying gas flares, such as VIIRS, which is already providing data for the World Bank gas flaring database. Some other sensors have already been used for gas flare research, or their very promising optical characteristics suggest usage in this field. A comparison of sensors well-suited for gas flare analysis, based on a literature review is presented below.

Until now, the most common method for estimation of flare characteristics is the Planck curve fitting. This method assumes that a gas flare is a black-body source covering a small part of the pixel. Therefore, a proper estimation of the background temperature and gas flare size are crucial factors for the accuracy of the final product. Hence, the most important spectral bands suitable for the gas flare analysis are those in three spectral ranges: around 1.6 μm (for the hottest flares), around 4.0 μm (for the colder flares), and around 9.0 μm (for background temperature estimation) (Fig. 2).

Spatial resolution is another important feature of the sensors. Due to the fact that the gas flares are almost point sources, they can be omitted in case of coarse spatial resolution. It would be advisable to use the data with higher spatial resolution, but one also has to take into account the inverse proportion of radiometric and spatial resolutions in the thermal sensors. With higher spatial resolution, the radiometric contrast in

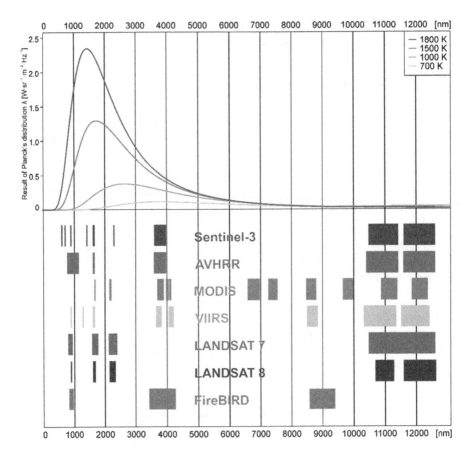

Fig. 2. Comparison of the IR-bands of selected sensors with Planck curves for different gas flare temperatures

the data decreases. This is the cause, why modern thermal sensors do not achieve as good spatial resolution as the optical sensors. A visualisation of the pixel size in selected thermal sensors, suitable for gas flare analysis, is presented below (Fig. 3).

Typically, spatial resolution is also nearly inversely proportional to the temporal resolution of the sensors. Low revisit time can also be a very important factor – especially for mapping large regions or for change analysis, which in case of gas flares is desirable for monitoring the changes in the process and for more exact parameter estimation. An overview of the revisit patterns of the above mentioned satellite sensors is presented below (Fig. 4).

If we consider all the previously discussed characteristics, we can say that a suitable sensor for gas flare studies should have spectral bands in short-wave (around 1,6 μm), mid-wave (around 4,0 μm) and long-wave (around 9,0 μm) infrared, possibly high spatial resolution and low revisit time.

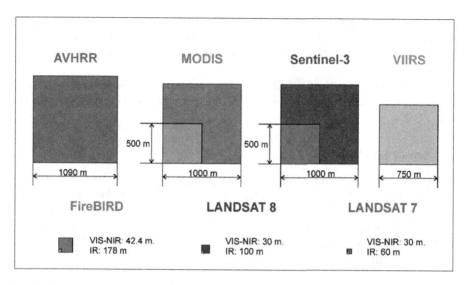

Fig. 3. Representation of the pixel sizes from channels useful for the gas flaring analysis of the above mentioned sensors.

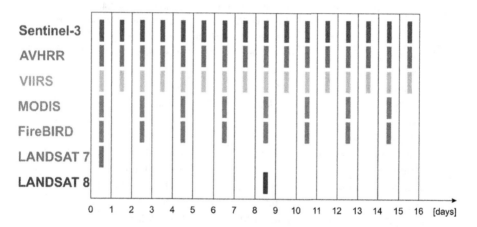

Fig. 4. Illustration of an average revisit pattern of the sensors in 16 days.

3 FireBIRD Mission

The German Aerospace Center (Deutsches Zentrum für Luft- und Raumfahrt, DLR) initiated the FireBIRD mission for high-temperature event analysis. The project comprises twin-satellites providing data with the same optical features and configuration. The first satellite, TET-1 (Technologieerprobungs-Träger-1) was launched in 2012, and is providing data ever since; the second, BIROS (Berlin Infrared Optical System) – in 2016, and is currently undergoing an in-orbit validation phase of the project.

The main objective of the FireBIRD mission is the examination of high-temperature events, which have significant influence on global climate. This way research in the subject "Gas flares" meets perfectly the scientific purposes of the mission.

The image data from the FireBIRD satellites is open for the science community and can also be ordered within the framework of different projects in cooperation with the DLR.

3.1   Sensor Specifications

The optical systems of both satellites are an heritage of the BIRD satellite mission (2001–2014) of the DLR. The optics were specially designed to be able to provide good quality data of high-temperature events, e.g. by avoiding saturation of the pixels [17]. Channels imaging in visual and near-IR spectral ranges have been added (while the BIRD sensor system had only two). The spatial resolution of the VIS/NIR camera is higher than in IR cameras (Table 1).

Table 1. Characteristics of the sensor system

Spectral range	VIS/NIR camera	IR cameras
	Green: 460–560 nm Red: 565–725 nm Near IR: 790–930 nm	Mid-wave IR: 3.4–4.2 μm Long-wave IR: 8.5–9.3 μm
Focal length	90.90 mm	46.39 mm
F-number	3.8	2.0
Field-of-View	19.6°	19.0°
Swath width	211 km	178 km
Detector type	CCD	CdHgTe
Number of pixels	3×5164	2×512
Ground sampling distance	42.4 m	178.0 m
Pixel size	7×7 μm	30×30 μm
Detector cooling	Passive. 293 K	Stirling. 80–100 K
Quantisation	14 bit[a]	14 bit
Data rate	Max. 44 Mbit/s nom. 11.2 Mbit/s	0.35 Mbit/s

[a]The quantisation in the VIS data of TET is decreased to 8 bit due to computer processing.

The two IR cameras have been pre-flight calibrated, but they also maintain in-flight calibration routines basing on the two external blackbodies located in front of each camera. Therefore, the temperature span for accurate radiometry can be broadened. Another important feature of the sensor is a specially designed hot-area mode, which insures lack of saturation in hotspot pixels. Thus, cold regions containing high-temperature events can be accurately pictured.

The data, which is provided by the DLR is not directly georeferenced, but each dataset includes information required for georeferencing of the imagery. Since in some cases the geolocation accuracy of the satellite can be impaired (e.g. when one or both of the star cameras are blinded by the Sun), a key was introduced, describing the quality of the geolocation, averaged for the whole image – 4.0 for the best result, with reliable data from both star cameras and inertial measurement unit and 1.0 for the worst case, where both star cameras are blinded.

3.2 Fire Products

In order to fulfil the mission purpose, some additional products are included to the end-product data package apart from the imagery. Each image is processed with the fire processor, which analyses the hotspots in the image and provides the fire characteristics basing on the bi-spectral method of Zhukov et al. [16, 17]. As a result, the user gets a map of hotspots and a corresponding table with fire parameters (Fig. 5).

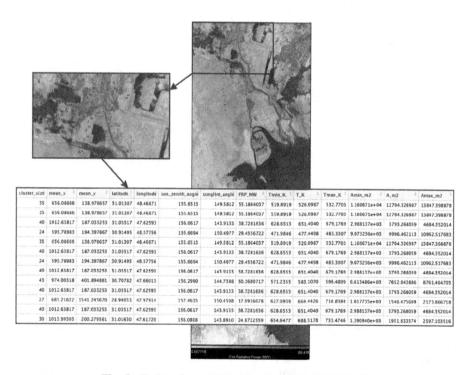

Fig. 5. End-products delivered with the FireBIRD data.

The fire processor was initially designed and optimized for fires which have far larger areas than gas flares. Subsequently, as the preliminary examination suggests, the temperature estimation is often underestimated, in comparison with other models (e.g. the World Bank gas flaring database from VIIRS data). The probable cause for this situation is the fact that in the algorithm, the temperature strongly depends on the effective fire area, which is estimated significantly bigger than a point source [16].

Even though the FireBIRD data does not have spectral bands in short-wave infrared (SWIR), the high spatial resolution, high Signal-to-Noise Ratio, and the specially designed hot-area mode ensuring lack of saturation, results in recording around six times more energy than for example in VIIRS sensor, which can record in the SWIR spectral range (Fig. 6). Therefore, the lack of absolute measurement in this spectral range can be compensated by careful modelling and specialized algorithms.

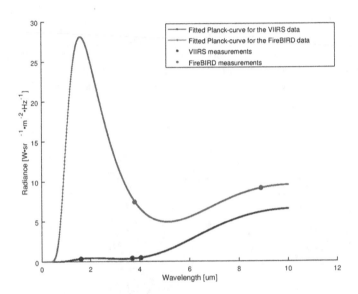

Fig. 6. Measurements of FireBIRD and VIIRS for the same gas flare.

3.3   Fire Processor Validation for the Case of Gas Flares

In order to get the first impression of the data, a comparison study has been undertaken. The data from the FireBIRD fire processor has been compared with the World Bank Gas Flares database based on the VIIRS data. To this end, 19 cloud-free datasets were chosen, where datasets have been available for FireBIRD and for VIIRS from the same day. To reliably compare the two datasets, some preparation steps were necessary (Fig. 7).

Due to the fact that the World Bank database provides data in the form of a table containing geocoordinates of hotspots and corresponding fire characteristics, the datasets have been transformed to GIS layers to make the comparison of individual flares more exact. In the next step, both datasets have been photo-interpreted with the aim of identifying the same flares in both cases and avoiding miscalculations due to georeferencing errors. In the World Bank dataset as well as in the FireBIRD product-data, each gas flare is marked as a group of pixels or points, containing information on the same flare. In the FireBIRD data, all the hotspot pixels are grouped

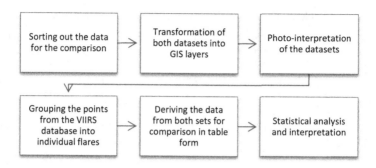

Fig. 7. Data-processing steps.

into clusters, and for each cluster a set of parameters is provided. The VIIRS database contains points and for each point a set of parameters is written in the data base as an individual database entry. This situation is misleading, because each point (as pictured in Fig. 8) is treated as an individual hot event, but there is only one actual flare located in the centre of the group of VIIRS points. Therefore, the points have been grouped during the photo-interpretation into individual flares. On this basis a comparable set of tables from both datasets has been derived and extracted for statistical analysis. The results are presented below.

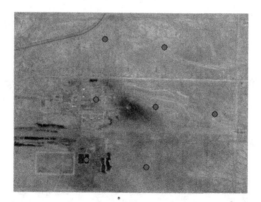

Fig. 8. Points representing centres of pixels in VIIRS database. Source: Imagery: Esri, Digital Globe, GeoEye, Earthstar Geographics, CNES/Airbus DS, USDA, USGS, AeroGRID, IGN, and the GIS User Community; Points: Data originally downloaded from VIIRS Database and further processed: www.ngdc.noaa.gov/eog/viirs/download_viirs_fire.html.

Table 2 presents the comparison of both datasets. It is worth pointing out that within the VIIRS datasets only part of the recognized number of flares is provided with temperature estimation (for each dataset this number is represented in the column "VIIRS points with temperature estimation"). Generally, the VIIRS sensor recognized a bigger number of flares than FireBIRD. Nevertheless, FireBIRD also recognized some

Table 2. Comparison between FireBIRD and VIIRS data

	Data-take	Points recognized by VIIRS	VIIRS points with temperature estimation	FireBIRD clusters	Flares recognized by			FireBIRD detection rate
					Both sensors	FireBIRD only	VIIRS only	
1	17.01.2016	234	(75) 32%	67	52	15	24	74%
2	04.02.2016	357	(170) 48%	69	50	19	27	72%
3	20.02.2016	289	(94) 33%	75	66	9	11	87%
4	01.03.2016	207	(89) 43%	75	62	13	5	94%
5	25.03.2016	310	(43) 15%	32	27	5	4	89%
6	09.04.2016	295	(81) 27%	22	18	4	10	69%
7	19.04.2016	356	(175) 49%	45	39	6	12	79%
8	12.05.2016	404	(82) 20%	49	44	5	11	82%
9	03.06.2016	194	(62) 32%	65	51	14	7	90%
10	10.06.2016	565	(131) 23%	89	75	14	16	85%
11	20.06.2016	538	(123) 23%	94	82	12	8	92%
12	16.07.2016	72	(37) 51%	35	24	11	10	78%
13	05.08.2016	92	(72) 78%	69	39	30	1	99%
14	29.08.2016	279	(69) 25%	78	61	17	7	92%
15	12.09.2016	344	(108) 31%	71	61	10	12	86%
16	04.10.2016	455	(100) 22%	73	63	10	13	85%
17	20.10.2016	432	(92) 21%	65	63	2	22	75%
18	13.11.2016	572	(190) 33%	71	57	14	10	88%
19	10.12.2016	269	(119) 44%	24	23	1	20	55%

flares in each dataset, which were omitted by VIIRS. The column "FireBIRD detection rate" is calculated as follows:

$$FireBIRD\ detection\ rate = \frac{FireBIRD\ clusters}{FireBIRD\ clusters + VIIRS\ only} \qquad (1)$$

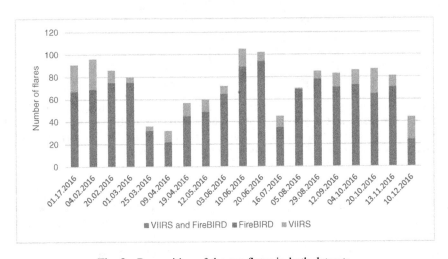

Fig. 9. Recognition of the gas flares in both datasets.

The FireBIRD processor has been designed to analyze fires of relatively big areas – such as forest fires. Consequently, the analysis of gas flares, which are almost point sources, can be only done after adjustments of the algorithm. Nevertheless, gas flares are mostly well-identified and the hot pixels do not saturate, despite extreme temperatures of the flares. In some cases, the FireBIRD data recognized smaller flares, which were not identified in VIIRS data.

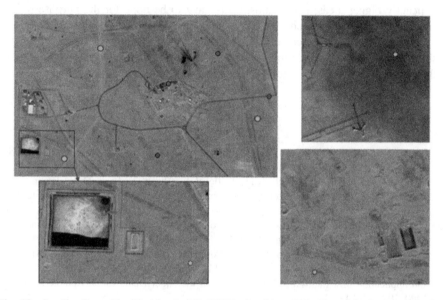

Fig. 10. Smaller flares identified by the FireBIRD algorithm (light-blue points) and omitted in VIIRS data (magenta points). Source: Imagery: Esri, Digital Globe, GeoEye, Earthstar Geographics, CNES/Airbus DS, USDA, USGS, AeroGRID, IGN, and the GIS User Community; Points: Data originally downloaded from VIIRS Database and further processed: www.ngdc.noaa.gov/eog/viirs/download_viirs_fire.html and FireBIRD data.

4   Summary and Outlook

Gas flaring is a very important subject for monitoring of global climate changes and greenhouse gas emissions. The subject has been capturing attention of international agencies and institutions, and actions, aimed at reducing the flaring process, have been initiated. One of the most important tasks, and the first step to be done, is gathering information on the process: how much gas is being flared, where are the flaring stations, how many are there, and with how much power do they flare. Answering these question is not trivial and requires objective and trustworthy data, regularly delivered for monitoring. The use of remote sensing data is a perfect way to meet those requirements.

With the development of thermal remote sensing, new sensors have appeared, which can fulfil the requirements of gas flaring research. These instruments should be characterized by high spatial resolution, high temporal resolution, high radiometric contrast, lack of saturation in hotspot areas, and the ability to record in SWIR, MWIR and LWIR spectral ranges. Fire- BIRD sensors, TET-1 and BIROS, fulfil these requirements.

The FireBIRD mission of the German Aerospace Agency provides data open to scientific research, specialized in fire analysis. The data was compared with already existing data on gas flaring and proved to have potential for gas flaring studies.

Due to the fact that the existing fire processor has been designed for fires of significantly bigger areas, some adjustments have to be done for the purpose of gas flaring research. It would be advisable to examine the sensor system characteristics, i.e. the sensor type and the procedure of signal recording, in order to propose a sensor design specialized for gas flaring analysis. Research in this area will be continued within the framework of the FireBIRD project.

References

1. Casadio, S., Arino, O., Serpe, D.: Gas flaring monitoring from space using the ATSR instrument series. Remote Sens. Environ. **116**, 239–249 (2012)
2. Elvidge, C.D., Ziskin, D., Baugh, K.E., Tuttle, B.T., Ghosh, T., Pack, D.W., Erwin, E.H., Zhizhin, M.: A fifteen year record of global natural gas flaring derived from satellite data. Energies **2**, 595–622 (2009)
3. Leahey, D.M., Preston, K., Strosher, M.: Theoretical and observational assessments of flare efficiencies. J. Air Waste Manag. Assoc. **51**, 1610–1616 (2001)
4. Croft, T.A.: Nighttime images of the earth from space. Sci. Am. **239**, 86–98 (1978)
5. Anejionu, O.C.D., Blackburn, G.A., Whyatt, J.D.: Satellite survey of gas flares: development and application of a Landsat-based technique in the Niger Delta. Int. J. Remote Sens. **35**, 1900–1925 (2014)
6. Anejionu, O.C.D., Blackburn, G.A., Whyatt, J.D.: Detecting gas flares and estimating flaring volumes at individual flow stations using MODIS data. Remote Sens. Environ. **158**, 81–94 (2015)
7. Chowdhury, S., Shipman, T., Chao, D., Elvidge, C.D., Zhizhin, M., Hsu, F.-C.: Daytime gas flare detection using Landsat-8 multispectral data. In: 2014 IEEE International Geoscience and Remote Sensing Symposium (IGARSS), pp. 258–261. IEEE (2014)
8. Peterson, K.N.: Monitoring of gas flares with MSG active fire data - A new application of the Land SAF FRP PIXEL product. In: LSA SAF 4th User Workshop, Toulouse (2010)
9. Elvidge, C.D., Baugh, K.E., Anderson, S., Ghosh, T., Ziskin, D.: Estimation of gas flaring volumes using NASA MODIS fire detection products. NOAA National Geophysical Data Center (NGDC), Annual report 8 (2011)
10. Elvidge, C.D., Zhizhin, M., Hsu, F.-C., Baugh, K.E.: VIIRS nightfire: satellite pyrometry at night. Remote Sens. **5**, 4423–4449 (2013)
11. Elvidge, C.D., Zhizhin, M., Baugh, K., Hsu, F.-C., Ghosh, T.: Methods for global survey of natural gas flaring from visible infrared imaging radiometer suite data. Energies **9**, 14 (2015)
12. Casadio, S., Arino, O., Minchella, A.: Use of ATSR and SAR measurements for the monitoring and characterisation of night-time gas flaring from off-shore platforms: the North Sea test case. Remote Sens. Environ. **123**, 175–186 (2012)
13. Anejionu, O.C., Whyatt, J.D., Blackburn, G.A., Price, C.S.: Contributions of gas flaring to a global air pollution hotspot: spatial and temporal variations, impacts and alleviation. Atmos. Environ. **118**, 184–193 (2015)

14. Haus, R., Wilkinson, R., Heland, J., Schäfer, K.: Remote sensing of gas emissions on natural gas flares. Pure Appl. Opt. J. Eur. Opt. Soc. Part A **7**, 853 (1998)
15. Allen, D.T., Torres, V.M.: TCEQ 2010 Flare Study Final Report. The University of Texas at Austin (2011)
16. Zhukov, B., Lorenz, E., Oertel, D., Wooster, M., Roberts, G.: Experience of Detection and Quantitative Characterization of Fires During the Experimental Small Satellite Mission BIRD. Dt. Zentrum für Luft-und Raumfahrt, Bibliotheks-und Informationswesen (2005)
17. Skrbek, W., Briess, K., Oertel, D., Lorenz, E., Walter, I., Zhukov, B.: Sensor system for fire detection on-board the small satellite BIRD. In: International Symposium on Optical Science and Technology, pp. 23–36. International Society for Optics and Photonics (2002)
18. GGFR Homepage. http://www.worldbank.org/en/programs/gasflaringreduction#1. Accessed 05 Sept 2017
19. Zero Routine Flaring by 2030 homepage. http://www.worldbank.org/en/programs/zero-routine-flaring-by-2030. Accessed 05 Sept 2017

Automatic Ship Detection on Multispectral and Thermal Infrared Aerial Images Using MACS-Mar Remote Sensing Platform

Jörg Brauchle[✉], Steven Bayer, and Ralf Berger

Institute of Optical Sensor Systems, German Aerospace Center (DLR),
Berlin, Germany
{Joerg.Brauchle,Steven.Bayer,Ralf.Berger}@DLR.de

Abstract. The Modular Aerial Camera System (MACS) is a development platform for optical remote sensing concepts, algorithms and special environments. For Real-Time Services for Maritime Security (EMSec joint project) a new multi-sensor configuration MACS-Mar was realized. It consists of 4 co-aligned sensor heads in the visible RGB, near infrared (NIR, 700–950 nm), hyperspectral (HS, 450–900 nm) and thermal infrared (TIR, 7.5…14 µm) spectral range, a mid-cost GNSS/INS system, a processing unit and two data links. On-board image projection, cropping of redundant data and compression enable the instant generation of direct-georeferenced high resolution image mosaics, automatic object detection, vectorization and annotation of floating objects on the water surface. The results were transmitted over a distance up to 50 km in real-time via narrow and broadband data links and were visualized in a maritime situation awareness system.

For the automatic onboard detection of objects a segmentation and classification workflow based on RGB, NIR and TIR information was developed and tested in September 2016. The completeness of the object detection in the experiment resulted in 95%, the correctness in 53%. Mostly bright backwash of ships led to overdetection of the number of objects, further refinement using water homogeneity in the TIR, as implemented in the workflow, couldn't be carried out due to problems with the TIR sensor. To analyze the influence of high resolution TIR imagery and to reach the expected detection quality a further experiment was conducted in August 2017. Adding TIR images the completeness was increased to 98% and the correctness to 74%.

Keywords: Maritime security · Ship detection · MACS · Real-time
Aerial camera

1 Introduction

Remote sensing methods have been used in maritime scenarios for many years with different scopes that can be attributed to maritime security and safety [1]. Passive optical sensors in multi-spectral or hyper-spectral configurations are widely used for the monitoring of large-scale ecological issues like algal blooms, coral reef studies, or the analysis of sediment transport in estuaries [2, 3]. The inclusion of thermal infrared

© Springer International Publishing AG, part of Springer Nature 2018
S. Satoh (Ed.): PSIVT 2017, LNCS 10799, pp. 382–395, 2018.
https://doi.org/10.1007/978-3-319-92753-4_30

allows for additional applications like monitoring thermal plumes of warm water discharges caused by power plants [4, 5]. With the constant improvement of spatial resolution, also ship detection is now possible from satellite based passive optical systems [6, 7]. Radar and especially synthetic aperture radar (SAR) have been studied for sea state monitoring [8, 9], oil spill [10] and ship detection [11, 12], especially exploiting the benefits of a satellite platform regarding the vast area of interest. Also satellite based receivers for 'Automatic Identification System' (AIS) are under study and in experimental use [13, 14].

All those sensors and methods have been tested or applied also on airborne platforms [14]. Especially security related applications benefit from the feasible higher spatial resolutions, combinations of sensors [15] and the merging with information from ground-based sensors or sensor networks [16]. Therefore an extensive suite of instruments and methods is available for gathering information about the maritime environment.

Several of these remotes sensing methods are applied today in a regular manner. German Navy operates a pollution control aircraft mainly for oil spill detection [17], several national search-and-rescue operations use helicopters equipped with multi-sensor reconnaissance payloads [18]. Also, in Germany the main agencies with maritime security tasks have created a joint 'Maritime Safety and Security Center of the Federal Government and the Coastal States' in which information gathered by the contributing partners are shared [19].

Nonetheless, remote sensing is only scarcely and sporadically applied for maritime security challenges. Patrolling extended areas with a plane or assigning singular missions to sensor-equipped helicopters does not amount to constant, multi-scale situation awareness. Relatively high effort is necessary to sustain the aforementioned solutions especially given the comparatively low risk of incidents. This is a limiting factor for the establishment of persistent and comprehensive maritime monitoring system. Also ship- and ground-based installations like AIS and Radar are often seen to be generally adequate.

Information in maritime environment is shared predominantly by direct voice communication between stakeholders. A unified view on the situation for every participant is all but impossible. With a rising number from about 1,300 marine incidents and casualties reported to the European Maritime Security Agency in 2011 to about 3,300 in 2016 [20], a combination of diverse methods to enable a robust maritime situation awareness over an extended time-frame is deemed necessary at least for regions of particular interest.

Our objective in the joint project 'Echtzeitdienste für die Maritime Sicherheit – EMSec' ('Real-Time Services for Maritime Security – EMSec') was the development of a special airborne camera system including processing and data deployment, which had to meet several user-defined requirements. The main products were to deliver a high-resolution true-color overview of a confined area (georeferenced image mosaic) as well as automatically detected and annotated objects on the water surface. Every product had to be provided in real-time to an existing ground-based central situation awareness system and its human-machine-interface.

2   Methodology

2.1   Automatic Object Detection

One goal of the experiment is the detection of small floating objects in water. For a generally applicable method it is very important to develop universal algorithms which are working in different environments, recording times and under changing weather and water conditions; that is a big challenge.

Besides extraction algorithms input data has a big influence on extraction results. In order to have a functional algorithm it is necessary to use the special characteristics of each sensor. One useful sensor for object detection in a maritime environment is a thermal IR imager. Because of almost homogeneous water temperature and the missing effect of sun glint a thermal image is suitable to detect objects of a certain minimum size on water with a very high accuracy. Due to the ground sampling distance (GSD) of thermal IR images (1.22 m GSD at 2,500 m altitude) small objects like sea marks or persons in water cannot be extracted reliably. Common RGB and NIR sensors can provide sufficient resolution. At an altitude for our surveillance flights of 2,500 m the used RGB sensor has a GSD of 0.37 m and the NIR sensor of 0.49 m (Table 2).

For the development of the algorithm a flight altitude of 2,500 m was assumed. So in our case the thermal IR images are used for the detection of objects with a size of more than 1.5 m × 2.5 m. Offshore most objects have a larger size than 1.5 m × 2.5 m. Therefore by using thermal IR images a bulk of objects can be detected. However, the existence of smaller objects cannot be excluded. Due to this reason the RGB and NIR images are additionally necessary to improve the completeness of object extraction. On the one hand the main advantage of RGB and NIR images is the higher GSD in comparison to the thermal IR images. On the other hand maritime RGB and NIR images are mainly influenced by sun glint [21]. Sun glint is the specular reflection of sunlight from water surface into the sensor [22]. This is an enormous source of irritation and leads to incorrect object detections. For successful object detection the effect of sun glint has to be reduced significantly.

In order to discover water pollution NIR and hyperspectral sensors are helpful. An overview of airborne sensors for water quality assessment is given in a review [23]. The proposed method to detect water quality [24] was developed by the team Optical Remote Sensing of Water at the DLR.

Based on the specific characteristics of all but hyperspectral sensors an automatic object detection algorithm in maritime environments was developed. The algorithm is divided into five parts (Fig. 1).

   I.   Preprocessing to identify regions of interest and the reduction of sun glint in RGB and NIR images as well as noise in thermal IR images.
  II.   Image segmentation.
 III.   Classification and object detection.
 IV.   Improvement of object border (reshaping).
  V.   Object catagorization (object catalog).

Test flights with the DLR-developed aerial camera MACS (Sect. 3.1) showed that sun glint has a negative influence on automatic object detection. Due to the reflection and

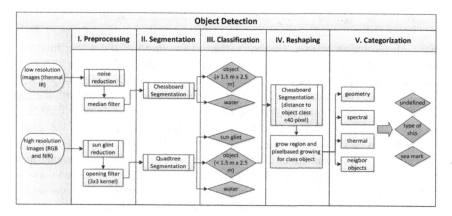

Fig. 1. Object detection algorithm flow chart

refraction of sun light on waves many incorrect objects were detected. Because of this effect a very fast preprocessing of the images became necessary. Because of the realtime preprocessing on the camera system the complex existing algorithms for sun glint reduction were not suitable. Therefore we used a software-based opening filter [25]. to reduce the impact of sun glint (Fig. 2). The opening filter was used with a 3x3 kernel. By using this kernel all objects were preserved and the sun glint was reduced partly but not completely. A 5x5 kernel reduced the sun glint but very small objects as well. As Fig. 2b shows the used 3x3 opening filter can not remove the whole sun glint. Because of that fact sun glint still had an influence on object extraction results.

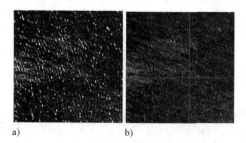

a)   b)

Fig. 2. Reduce of sun glint; (a) RGB image, (b) image after opening filter

The thermal IR images have a small noise. Therefore a median filter was used to reduce the noise.

The filtered aerial images were used for image segmentation (part II). For high resolution images a quadtree segmentation (Fig. 3a) was implemented due to almost homogeneous water surface and short processing time. Chessboard segmentation was used for the thermal IR images which are more homogeneous and have a lower resolution.

Based on the segments a very simple and transferable local thresholding classification algorithm was executed to distinguish between water, sun glint and objects
within high resolution images. For every channel the mean of the whole image was
calculated (image mean) and added with a value of 8,000 which was determined
empirically. This value depends on light conditions and was changeable by operator
during the flight. The classification is based on comparing image mean with the mean
of the segments. For the object class the blue and the red channels were used. If the
mean of the segment in the blue or red channel was less than image mean the segment
was classified as an object. Following the object segments were merged. For sun glint
classification it was assumed that the brightness of sun glint segment is higher than a
water segment and that sun glint affects only small areas. If the image mean was less
than the segment mean of the red, green, blue and NIR channel as well as the segment
was smaller than 2 m^2 the segment was classified as sun glint. The other segments were
classified as water (part III).

To distinguish between water and objects within low resolution thermal IR images
in part III a standard deviation was calculated. Therefore the 49 neighbour pixels of
each pixel (three rows around center) were considered to find pixels with high contrast.
It was assumed that water has homogeneous temperature and objects on the water have
clear temperature difference. If the standard deviation was more than 0.5 the pixel was
classified as an object pixel. All object pixels were merged to filled polygons. Small
objects of less than 1.5 m × 2.5 m were removed.

In part IV the border of detected objects was improved applying a region- and pixel
based growing algorithm. This step was necessary for the following object
identification.

Object identification was implemented in the final (part V) step to distinguish
between different ship types (red objects), sea marks (small green object) and undefined
objects (Fig. 3d). Therefore geometric (size and shape) and spectral properties as well
as relations to neighbour objects were used. For example, a ship is an elongated object
which is longer than wide and surrounded by water. The type of ship was distinguished
by size (Table 1).

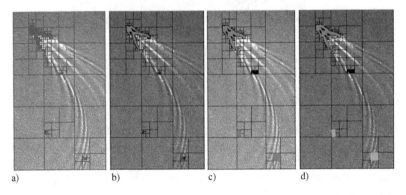

Fig. 3. Steps of automatic object detection with (a) segmentation, (b) classification, (c) border
improvement, (d) object identification (Color figure online)

Table 1. Ship size categories

Type of ship	Size [m × m]
Yacht	<20 × 5
Ferry/small cargo ship	<150 × 25
Container ship/huge cargo ship	>400 × 60

2.2 Accuracy Assessment

An accuracy analysis is executed to evaluate the automatic object detection accuracy. Due to the fact that outlines of an object cannot be extracted exactly in many cases the evaluation of the accuracy for every object is a challenge. The automatically extracted objects may be too small, too big or just a sub-part of another extracted object. Hence for every object it is necessary to decide whether extraction is correct or false. According to Egenhofer [26] eight theoretical relations between two objects are possible, divided into correct, false, and unclear cases. In the latter cases it has to be distinguished between correct and false extracted objects. This can be estimated by the overlapping factor [27]:

$$OF = \frac{|\mathcal{A}^\circ \cap \mathcal{B}^\circ|}{min(|\mathcal{A}^\circ|, |\mathcal{B}^\circ|)} \tag{1}$$

with OF = overlapping factor
  A° = extent of object A
  B° = extent of object B.

The object is extracted as false if the overlapping factor in our case is equal or smaller than 0.3. This value was determined empirically during previous campaigns. An object is correctly extracted if the overlapping factor is greater than 0.3. The determination as false, correct and missed objects is executed with the overlapping factor. During the EMSec test campaigns which are described in Sects. 3.2 and 3.3, all recorded objects were identified and automatic object detection algorithm was applied to aerial imagery. After the identification of correct, false and missed objects the determination of the overall accuracy is possible. To determine the accuracy the completeness (producers accuracy) and the correctness (users accuracy) according to Straub [28] is calculated. The completeness (com) of the results is calculated as:

$$com\ (\%) = \frac{ceo}{ceo + neo} * 100 \tag{2}$$

The correctness (corr) of the results is calculated as:

$$corr\ (\%) = \frac{ceo}{ceo + weo} * 100 \tag{3}$$

with ceo = correctly extracted objects, neo = not extracted objects, weo = wrong extracted objects.

3   Experiment

3.1   MACS – Modular Aerial Camera System

The MACS camera system enables the fast and easy development of novel aerial camera concepts for special applications [29, 30]. Multiple passive optical sensors can be combined to acquire the relevant information (Fig. 4). The sensors and their field of vision can be adjusted to specific use-cases. All sensors and their optics are calibrated geometrically and for radiometric correction. The mechanical design must be rigid to allow for a precise co-registration of images taken by all sensors of the respective configuration. To efficiently evaluate such a configuration, an approach for combined photogrammetric processing of multiple sensor heads had been developed [31].

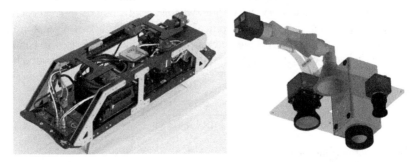

Fig. 4. MACS-Mar configuration with RGB, NIR, thermal IR, hyperspectral

Image processing and recording is done by a desktop class embedded computer. This computational power is necessary to allow for simultaneous recording of various sensor data, online georeferencing, map projection of those data and implementation of suitable real-time image classification algorithms. In this way, various higher level geoinformation can be generated automatically during operation. The automatic objects of interest detection is based on co-registered image map and executed in real-time. As any pixel of the maps created has a reliable coordinate and time designation, the same applies to any detected object. By sending only detected objects to a ground station, the amount of data to be transmitted can be reduced and the amount of information to be examined by an human operator decreases.

The sensor system is controlled via ground-based mission control center through a 9,600 Bit per second narrowband radio link. The operator is able to monitor system healthiness, to change the configuration and to receive classification results. The current position of the aircraft and the footprints of the images taken are shown continuously on a scalable moving map. Enabling a more powerful air-to-ground link providing a data rate of 5–10 Megabit per second, seamless cropped images are transmitted in full geometric and radiometric resolution (Fig. 5).

The visual information can be directly interpreted by humans. In addition, object detection algorithms are applicable. Different sensors and lenses can be used which allow task-specific footprints and ground resolutions. A ground sampling distance of up

Fig. 5. Real-time map with full geometric and radiometric resolution

to 3 cm is achievable depending on the flight altitude and optical configuration. Within the map, distances and areas can be determined, e.g. the length of a vessel or the extent of oil contamination areas.

3.2 Joint EMSec Experiment

During a verification experiment, stretching over several days, a set of scenarios was carried out. One scenario simulated the hijacking of a ferry ship and subsequent deactivation of AIS for a covert change of the course [32]. MACS-Mar was used to deliver information about objects on the water surface and to deliver detailed optical imagery for interpretation assistance for human operators.

Carried by the autopilot-controlled DLR research aircraft Dornier 228 (D-CODE) [33], MACS-Mar operated largely automatically. Data products were delivered continuously via radio link. All geo-referencing, mosaicking and image interpretation tasks were designed to operate on board automatically, so the derived information could be directly put into distribution system and human-machine interface.

To match the specific requirements of the EMSec project and following the investigation of preliminary work [34], four optical sensor heads acquiring wavelengths from 400 nm to 14 μm were chosen (Table 2). Figure 4 shows the MACS-Mar remote sensing system including both narrowband and broadband data links.

From 5th to 9th September 2016 the EMSec experiment was conducted over the North Sea off Cuxhaven. Different sub-experiments were performed with more than 9 h of image acquisition including dusk operation at solar altitude down to 2.5°.

3.3 Thermal Imagery Experiment

During the joint EMSec experiment unfortunately the thermal IR sensor did not work properly. Insufficient amount of data was acquired to perform the intended object detection analysis. In August 2017 a second experiment was conducted over the same area like the 2016 flights using the camera system again. Now all four sensors worked as they should (Fig. 6). To catch as many objects as possible the flight altitude was increased to 2,500 m ASL reducing the GSD by factor 3 compared to the 820 m ASL altitude in the first experiment.

Table 2. MACS-Mar Sensor Set-up

	RGB (Bayer color pattern)	Near Infrared	Thermal Infrared	Hyperspectral
Spectral bands (nm)	400–520 (blue) 500–590 (green) 590–680 (red)	700–950	7,500–14,000	450– 950 (105 channels)
Resolution (pixels)	4,864 × 3,232	3,296 × 2,472	1,024 × 768	80 × 80
GSD @ 820 m above sea level (cm)	12	16	40	400
GSD @ 2,500 m above sea level (cm)	37	49	122	1220
Field of view across track (deg)	40	36	32	22

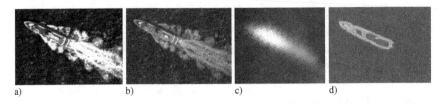

a)   b)   c)   d)

Fig. 6. Same scene on all sensors: (a) RGB 37 cm GSD, (b) NIR 49 cm, (c) Hyperspectral@570 nm 12.20 m, (d) TIR 1.22 m

4   Results

During the 2016 five days experiment approx. 12 GB of image data were radio-transmitted reliably in full geometric and radiometric resolution at a distance up to 50 km. Remote control worked stable at a distance more than 80 km.

Visual identification of ships has been investigated during low light flights. The ship names were not identifiable in the images due to near vertical perspectives. Position, heading, shape and extend were determined within a single image. Dynamic parameters like course and speed were measured by including adjacent images or images of a later fly-over. In the realtime map the ship's length was repeatedly determined between 65.7 and 66.1 m while the ship's actual length is 65.9 m. This results in a deviation of 20 cm resp. 1.5 pixels (Fig. 7).

Image-based detected occurrences (without thermal IR) were indicated real-time on the maritime management system and corresponding images were displayed.

Despite of acquiring more than 9 h data recording no real water pollution could be observed. The popcorn was originally used to evaluate drift forecast. On the other hand the spectral signature is untypical for water pollution. Due to the high visibility in RGB and NIR imagery the popcorn was automatically extracted as an object.

Fig. 7. Coast guard ship BP25 at solar altitude 5.5° (cutout)

The 2017 campaign added the missing thermal imagery to the data set. Object detection algorithm was activated to process this data source.

During the 2016 campaign 77 objects were observed without thermal IR Images. Due to the missing thermal IR images the object extraction on the high resolution RGB and NIR images was carried out without an object size limit of 1.5 m × 2.5 m. 73 objects were extracted correctly and four objects were not extracted.

The completeness of the automatic object extraction algorithm was 95%. The four missing ships were not extracted because of the object extraction size threshold. The minimum size for object detection was 25 m^2. Because of the missing thermal IR images a smaller object size was not applicable. Too much sun glint resulted in false positives when the object size was smaller than 25 m^2.

Automatic object extraction extracted 65 objects false. According to this result the correctness was by 53%. The low correctness is explainable by the missing thermal IR information. By incorporating just RGB and NIR aerial images the backwash of the ships was very often identified as a single object (Fig. 8). The backwash of the ships was not observable in thermal IR images and increased the correctness.

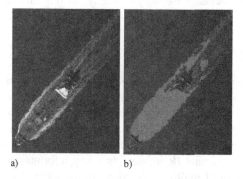

a)   b)

Fig. 8. Object detection *without* thermal IR, (a) original RGB image, (b) multiple objects detected

Adding thermal IR images the detection quality was expected to significantly increase as shown in preliminary work [34]. The second flight campaign with thermal IR images resulted in 40 objects observed. 39 objects were correctly extracted and one object was not extracted. The acquired objects were ships and sailing boats as well as windmills (Fig. 9). The completeness of the automatic object extraction algorithm including thermal IR was 98%. Due to the use of this source the completeness of the automatic object detection was increased. The missing object was a small water sign.

Beside the completeness the correctness of the automatic object detection was gained. 14 objects were extracted false. According to this result the correctness raised from 53% to 74% by adding thermal IR images. All wrong extracted objects were image errors in the thermal images, which led to a peak in the according image. These peaks were detected as small objects. The results of the object detection are summarized in Table 3.

Table 3. Results of object detection

	Thermal IR images	No. of objects	Completeness (%)	Correctness (%)
September 2016	No	77	95	53
August 2017	Yes	40	98	74

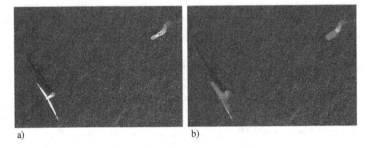

a)   b)

Fig. 9. Object detection *including* thermal IR imagery, (a) original RGB image, (b) correctly detected objects

5 Discussion

In general the objectives of the presented sub-project – situation map and automatic object extraction – have been successfully realized and demonstrated. As shown in the results for automatic object extraction a combination of passive optical sensors is essential to achieve high rates of completeness and correctness. Because of the homogeneous water temperature and temperature differences between floating objects and surrounding water thermal IR imagery is a key information for this application. Particularly the problem of multiple detections in the RGB due to backwash can be drastically reduced by thermal IR which is directly distinguishable in the different imagery.

True-color RGB and NIR imagery are necessary to categorize objects and tag semantic information. Furthermore, high resolution RGB image data is highly beneficial for the manual interpretation by human operators. Bigger objects like ships can be characterized by measuring the size and visual interpretation. Identification of ships by name would require high resolution oblique view.

A real-time supply of object information as well as high-resolution image mosaic is a novel approach in maritime security applications. In conjunction with other information provided within the scope of the EMSec project it provides detailed information about the offshore situation in a manageable form.

6 Future Work

Next steps should be acquiring a greater database to make the algorithm more robust against image errors and thus avoiding detection of seemingly very small objects. Additionally this database can be used to feed deep learning approaches. The influence of ground pixel resolution on detection accuracy has to be examined because realtime processing on a satellite cannot be feeded with high resolution imagery as given here. By sensor data fusion the results should be improved further which will be evaluated in near future.

Acknowledgments. This work was funded by the Federal Ministry of Research and Education (FKZ 13N12746). The research was supported by the Program Coordination Defence & Security Research at DLR.

References

1. Jha, M.N., Levy, J., Gao, Y.: Advances in remote sensing for oil spill disaster management: state-of-the-art sensors technology for oil spill surveillance. Sensors **8**(1), 236–255 (2008). https://doi.org/10.3390/s8010236
2. Zimmermann, G., Badaev, W.W., Malkevich, M.S., Piesik, B.: The MKS-M remote-sensing experiment for determination of ocean and atmospheric parameters from SALYUT-7. Acta Astronautica **12**(7–8), 475–483 (1985). https://doi.org/10.1016/0094-5765(85)90118-3
3. Keith, D.J., Schaeffer, B.A., Lunetta, R.S., Gould Jr., R.W., Rocha, K., Cobb, D.J.: Remote sensing of selected water-quality indicators with the hyperspectral imager for the coastal ocean (HICO) sensor. Int. J. Remote Sensing **35**(9), 2927–2962 (2014). https://doi.org/10.1080/01431161.2014.894663
4. Sobrino, J.A., Jiménez-Muñoz, J.C., Zarco-Tejada, P.J., Sepulcre-Cantó G., de Miguel, E., Sòria, G., Romaguera, M., Julien, Y., Cuenca, J., Hidalgo, V., Franch, B., Mattar, C., Morales, L., Gillespie, A., Sabol, D., Balick, L., Su, Z., Jia, L., Gieske, A., Timmermans, W., Olioso A., Nerry, F., Guanter, L., Moreno, J., Shen, Q.: Thermal remote sensing from airborne hyperspectral scanner data in the framework of the SPARC and SEN2FLEX projects: an overview. Hydrol. Earth Syst. Sci. **13**(11), 2031–2037 (2009). https://doi.org/10.5194/hess-13-2031-2009
5. Legeckis, R.: A survey of worldwide sea surface temperature fronts detected by environmental satellites. J. Geophys. Res. **83**(C9), 4501–4522 (1978). https://doi.org/10.1029/JC083iC09p04501
6. Corbane, Ch., Najman, L., Pecoul, E., Demagistri, L., Petit, M.: A complete processing chain for ship detection using optical satellite imagery. Int. J. Remote Sensing **31**(22), 5837–5854 (2010). https://doi.org/10.1080/01431161.2010.512310

7. Müller, R., Berg, M., Casey, S., Ellis, G., Flingelli, C., Kiefl, R., Kornhoff, A., Lechner, K., Reize, T., Máttyus, G.S., Schwarz, E., Simon, E., Twele, A.: Optical satellite service for EMSA (OPSSERVE)–near real-time detection of vessels and activities with optical satellite imagery. In: ESA Living Planet Symposium, pp. 2–12. ESA, Edinburgh (2012)
8. Barrick, D.: Remote sensing of sea state by radar. In: Ocean 72 - IEEE International Conference on Engineering in the Ocean Environment, Newport pp. 186–192 (1972). https://doi.org/10.1109/oceans.1972.1161190
9. Daedelow, H., Schwarz, E., Voinov, S.: Near Real Time Applications to retrieve Wind Products for Maritime Situational Awareness. DLRK 2016, 13–15 September 2016, Braunschweig (2016)
10. Pavlakis, P., Sieber, A., Alexandry, S.: Monitoring oil-spill pollution in the Mediterranean with ERS SAR. ESA Earth Obs. Q. **52**, 13 (1996)
11. Eldhuset, K.: An automatic ship and ship wake detection system for spaceborne SAR images in coastal regions. IEEE Trans. Geosci. Remote Sensing **34**(4), 1010–1019 (1996). https://doi.org/10.1109/36.508418
12. Brusch, S., Lehner, S.: Near real time ship detection experiments. In: Proceedings of SeaSAR, pp. 1–5. Frascati/Rome (2010)
13. Høye, G.K., Eriksen, T., Meland, B.J., Narheim, B.T.: Space-based AIS for global maritime traffic monitoring. Acta Astronautica **62**(2–3), 240–245 (2008). https://doi.org/10.1016/j.actaastro.2007.07.001
14. Clazzer, F., Lázaro Blasco, F., Plass, S.: Enhanced AIS receiver design for satellite reception. CEAS Space J. **8**(4), 257–268 (2016). https://doi.org/10.1007/s12567-016-0122-8
15. Optimare Systems GmbH, Octopod - The All-in-One Airborne Surveillance Pod, Product Flyer. http://www.optimare.de/cms/fileadmin/PDF/GB_FEK/Flyer-DINA3-OctoPod-28-02-2017-ENGL_klein.pdf. Accessed 12 Oct 2017
16. Fischer, Y., Bauer, A.: Object-oriented sensor data fusion for wide maritime surveillance. In: International WaterSide Security Conference, Carrara, pp. 1–6 (2010). https://doi.org/10.1109/wssc.2010.5730244
17. Gruener, K.: The three-frequency microwave radiometer of a 2nd generation airborne surveillance system for remote sensing of maritime oil pollution. In: Proceedings of IEEE Workshop RF and Microwave Noise, Ilmenau, pp. 66–69 (1996)
18. L3-WESCAM, MX-25 Technical Data Sheet. http://www.wescam.com/wp-content/uploads/PDS-MX-25-25D-January-2017.pdf. Accessed 12 Oct 2017
19. The Maritime Safety and Security Center. http://www.msz-cuxhaven.de/EN/Home/home_node.html. Accessed 12 Oct 2017
20. European Maritime Safety Agency, Annual Overview of Marine Casualties and Incidents. http://www.emsa.europa.eu/news-a-press-centre/external-news/item/2903-annual-overview-of-marine-casualties-and-incidents-2016.html. Accessed 12 Oct 2017
21. Kay, S., Hedley, J.D., Lavender, S.: Sun glint correction of high and low spatial resolution images of aquatic scenes: a review of methods for visible and near-infrared wavelengths. Remote Sensing **1**(4), 697–730 (2009). https://doi.org/10.3390/rs1040697
22. Streher, A.S., Goodman, J.A., Soares Galvao, L., Faria Barbosa, C.C., Freire Silva, T.S., Leao de Moraes Novo, E.M.: Sunglint removal in high spatial resolution hyperspectral images under different viewing geometries. In: Anais XVI Simpósio Brasileiro de Sensoriamento Remoto, Brasil, pp. 7958–7965 (2013)
23. Gholizadeh, M.H., Melesse, A.M., Reddi, L.: A comprehensive review on water quality parameters estimation using remote sensing techniques. Sensors (Basel, Switzerland), **16**(8), 1298 (2016). http://doi.org/10.3390/s16081298

24. Krawczyk, H., Neumann, A., Riha, S.: Multivariate interpretation algorithm for water quality in the Baltic Sea. In: Proceedings of SPIE 7473, Remote Sensing of the Ocean, Sea Ice, and Large Water Regions 7473, Berlin. https://doi.org/10.1117/12.830400
25. Dougherty, E.: Introduction to Morphological Image Processing. SPIE Press, Michigan (1992)
26. Egenhofer, M.J.: A model for detailed binary topological relationships. Geomatica **47**(3&4), 261–273 (1993)
27. Winter, S.: Beobachtungsunsicherheit und topologische Relationen. In: Workshop Daten-qualität und Metainformation in Geo-Informationssystemen, Rostock, pp. 141–154 (1996)
28. Straub, B.-M.: Automatische Extraktion von Bäumen aus Fernerkundungsdaten, Hannover (2003)
29. Lehmann, F., Berger, R., Brauchle, J., Hein, D., Meißner, H., Pless, S., Strackenbrock, B., Wieden, A.: MACS – modular airborne camera system for generating photogrammetric high-resolution products. In: Deutsche Gesellschaft für Geowissenschaften, vol. 6, pp. 435–446 (2011)
30. Brauchle, J., Hein, D., Berger, R.: Detailed and highly accurate 3D models of high mountain areas by the MACS-Himalaya aerial camera platform. In: International Archives of the Photogrammetry, Remote Sensing and Spatial Information Science, vol. sXL-7/W3, pp. 1129–1131 (2015). https://doi.org/10.5194/isprsarchives-xl-7-w3-1129-2015
31. Wieden, A., Stebner, K.: Referenzorientierung für Bilddaten aus Mehrkopfkamerasystemen. In: DGPF Tagungsband, vol. 22, pp. 518–525 (2013)
32. Suhr, B., Lange, A.-Th., Mohrs, R.: Automatische Detektion von AIS Auffälligkeiten in naher Echtzeit. In. Deutscher Luft- und Raumfahrtkongress (DLRK), Braunschweig (2016)
33. Kreienfeld, M., Giese, K.: Development of a RPV-demonstrator for maritime security applications. In: Deutscher Luft- und Raumfahrt Kongress, Rostock (2015)
34. Scherbaum, P., Brauchle, J., Kraft, Th., Pless, S.: MACS-Mar – a real-time capable multisensor remote sensing system for maritime applications. In: IEEE International Conference on Aerospace Electronics and Remote Sensing Technology (ICARES). Curan Associates, Inc. ICARES, Kuta, Bali, Indonesien (2015). https://doi.org/10.1109/icares.2015.7429839

Extracting Plücker Line and Their Relations for 3D Reconstruction of Indoor Scene

Huihui Sun[1,2(✉)], Xinguo Yu[1], and Chao Sun[1]

[1] National Engineering Research Center for E-Learning,
Central China Normal University, Wuhan, China
`sunhh-nercel@mails.ccnu.edu.cn`
[2] Computer Science School, Huaibei Normal University, Huaibei, China

Abstract. The structure line is an important clue for understanding indoor space. Unfortunately, in the context of indoor scene, very little structural data is available due to occlusion. To address this issue, this paper proposes to extract structural lines and analyze their relations to obtain the structure lines, which are continuous, anti-occlusion, able to reconstruct indoor space. In this paper, Plücker line is used to express the lines in 3D indoor scene. And then it studies the properties and the benefits of using Plücker line. For the first time, a new strategy is suggested to maintain the integrity of indoor space, which uses the extracted high confidence lines to infer the properties of other lines. Experimental results show that our methods have many advantages in obtaining a complete 3D interior structure line, which resists most occlusion in near ground.

Keywords: Structural line analysis · 3D indoor reconstruction
Plücker line

1 Introduction

Recently, the vast majority of land-based mobile robotic systems in use today rely on indoor reconstruction. Due to various changes of environment, occlusions and overlapping, 3D reconstruction of indoor scene is still an open challenging problem. Its main research purpose is to recur and analyze the structure, objects and semantic of indoor scene. Accordingly, vision sensor, with its rich environment information and low cost, becomes potentially the most powerful scanned devices used on robots to date for reconstruction. The main difficulty of this problem lies in the complexity and variability of the environment. Targeting at this challenge, researchers perform the task by extracting visual features, instead of directly employing tremendous amount of vision information. From this point of view, there is still a strong view that good feature candidates are key issues in reconstruction. Thus many classic algorithms have been developed by carefully

© Springer International Publishing AG, part of Springer Nature 2018
S. Satoh (Ed.): PSIVT 2017, LNCS 10799, pp. 396–409, 2018.
https://doi.org/10.1007/978-3-319-92753-4_31

choosing geometric shapes features, such as lines, corners, rectangles and so on. And they have made encouraging achievements in the field.

Here it is noteworthy that the recent theoretical efforts directed toward the development of feature designed. And the main flaw of direct feature-based methods is that it is difficulty in finding and preserving the structure integrity of the indoor space. As a result, a number of the structure information is hidden or remains largely unknown. The reasons for this limitation are as follows:

(1) On most smooth indoor surfaces, there are barely having sufficient and stationary features to distinct similar views. Besides, they are usually local characteristics, which are not conducive to overall reconstruction.
(2) The presence of obstacle often blocks a continuous structure line, which is impossible for local feature to break through.
(3) The loss of structural integrity is difficult to repair, caused by neglecting the symmetry of the ceiling and interior space, leaving only discrete information.

Now, it is needed to clarify the primary research basis of this area. In man-made indoor scene, it always has continuous geometric properties of spatial structure, which is the best to none for the reconstruction task. Consequently, our eyes focus on analyzing the structural line, which is continuous and can be used as natural feature for 3D reconstruction of indoor scene. Here we propose to consider it as the basic element for describing space. In that case, when vehicles freely move around the room, the key continuous feature would be the structural lines of room, apart from various overlap or changing features. Moreover, it is noticed that most floor line is blocked by sundry furniture, while ceiling structure is almost entirely captured. So we design to utilize the symmetry of the floor and ceiling to fill the missing part by comparison from up to down. During the process of above analysis, it requires repeated computation the geometric relations between various structural lines. Accordingly, in order to simplify the calculation, Plücker coordinate is adopted in reconstruction work for its simplicity in expression and properties for spatial screw motion, discussed in Sect. 4. To summarize, we propose analyzing the relations of spatial line from ceiling to floor in Plücker coordinate for 3D reconstruction indoor scene.

The main contribution of this work includes as follows. First, we propose using indoor structural line and their relations for 3D reconstruction. Second, for the first time, a new strategy from ceiling to floor is applied to overcome the occlusion on the floor. Third, Plücker coordinate is used to represent indoor structural line and reason the relations of spatial lines to simplify the calculation processes.

The rest of this paper has been organized in 6 sections. In Sect. 2, it reviews the main development of solutions in indoor 3D reconstruction. The reconstruction strategy and the algorithms of extension and filling-gap of structural line are given in Sect. 3. And then it provides a related introduction to Plücker coordinate, explains its properties and usage. In Sect. 5, experiment results and analysis for the approach are presented. Lastly, conclusion and future work are given in Sect. 6.

2   Related Work

Indoor scene can provide requisite environmental information data for kinds of location-based services [1]. As an important research field of robot vision, 3D indoor reconstruction has received considerable attention and many techniques have been suggested.

The main process of 3D reconstruction is to describe the variation of two variables with respect to time, which is the movement of sensor and the data captured by the sensor. More precisely, the first variable is estimated by sensor data. And based on this, the latter is used to gradually reconstruct the global scene in the world coordinate system.

At present, different features detection methods are well developed to solve this problem. The evolution methods of 2D features in computer vision, such as SIFT [2], ORB [3], Harris corners [4], have dominate intensive 3D reconstruction. These feature points can be distinguished from others by analysis the pixel comparing with its neighbor. However, local feature descriptor has weak constraints for maintaining the integrity of indoor scene structure. Due to the number of interest points in indoor space is limited, the above methods are suitable for interior space with rich texture information.

As is known to all, common indoor space has the following characteristics: orthogonality, connectivity and mainly demonstrated by large plane structure [5]. Relatively, structure line has better robustness for its continuous in global reconstruction. Nowadays, the mainstream structural line reconstruction methods can be divided into the following categories: prior-knowledge based method, decomposition method and new distance measuring of structural line method.

(1) Prior-knowledge Based Method
By using interior structure features as a priori knowledge and formulate as maximum a posteriori estimation, Kofuji et al. [5] exploit the global structure of artificial objects to estimate 3D surfaces of the shapes. To fulfill the reconstruction with clutter and occlusion, the study in [6] argues that the shapes of common furniture provide considerable knowledge for incomplete view scene. After recognizing the wall parts of the occluded region, they also design an gap filling algorithm to reconstruct the full wall. Generally, basic elements are a combination in building, especially with respect of the position attributes. Along this lines, the algorithm [7] interpreters indoor scene by analyzing the layout relations between main panel and reasons their semantic label.

(2) Decomposition Method
Recently, Turner et al. [8] concludes from their study of the effects of decomposing the whole environment into common things and then filling the space up with different elements, the primary indoor components are identified, and the occluded areas are restored according to a particular shape. Further, a general case with an algorithm has been designed to handle this by separately recognition main panels, including floor, ceiling, walls and openings, then assess them in building [9]. Similar strategy of recognition reconstruction after decomposition

was adopted in [10]. In their paper on object boundary detection and hierarchical segmentation, they suggest extract super pixels in order to classify dominant object categories.

(3) New Distance Measuring of Structural Line Method

For efficiently solve the scene reconstruction problem, a new approach [11] was applied the geometric constraint of weak epipolar established the relations between straight segments in various views. Different from directly changing the measurement approach, Zhou et al. [12] suggested to represent structural line by a point on a parameter plane and an associated principal direction. On this basis, they obtained the similarity of lines and formulated position estimation using the structure regularity of man-made environment.

In view of the fact that most location service is oriented from path planning, as the prior knowledge, indoor environment is reconstructed by registration continuous characteristics of the floor structure line [13]. By contrast and analysis the current literature studies, it is believed that the structural line is very important elements for 3D reconstruction. So far, however, the method of recovering the integrity of structural lines has not been proposed. Analyzed the layout of indoor, most occlusion and changes appear in near floor. To overcome this dilemma, this paper proposes to obtain missing structural lines by comparison them with their corresponding lines in 3-space. Therefore, the reconstruction strategy from ceiling to ground is put forward.

In this paper, we investigate efficient solutions to this problem. The novel aspect of this platform is that it represents structural line and their relations in a fairly simple way. Plücker Coordinate has largely been used in kinematics [14] and has been proved to be the simplest and effective way in spiral movement. We study the problem by analyzing relations of Plücker line and then apply them for 3D reconstruction.

3   Overview of the Proposed Method

Assuming that any indoor scene can be completely generated and represented by basic structural lines and their relations. So the purpose of this paper is to study of structural lines and their relations for 3D reconstruction. And the relations here are refereed to parallel, intersecting, coplanar and opposite planes. Generally, horizontal and vertical lines are more detectable and widely existing in the typical indoor room, such as walls, doors and so on. Taking into account the structural property of interior space, these lines can be used to construct large structural surfaces, even in less textured rooms. By comparing the existing methods and our new findings, it is defined a new reconstruction strategy, which is from ceiling to floor.

The structural line of ceiling and its corresponding of floor has special geometric relation in room, including coplanar, parallel and maintaining a certain vertical distance. However, it becomes quite different scenes in the view of vision sensor. For example, it may observed completely different segments, even they are the same straight line in the world coordinate. As shown in Fig. 1, the line

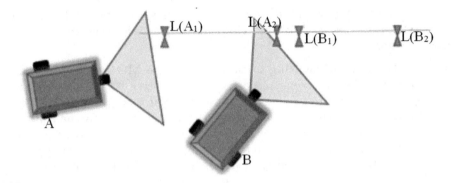

Fig. 1. Different views observed two different segments from the same line.

L is described as a segment $L(A)$ from $L(A_1)$ to $L(A_2)$ at location A, while at B, it becomes $L(B)$ from $L(B_1)$ to $L(B_2)$.

To solve the above issues, this paper addresses structural line features and their relations for modeling indoor scene. A geometric systematic constraints condition is well designed to provide necessary information for matching line features.

The overview of our approach as shown in Fig. 2, a structural line reconstruction approach is developed. From raw RGB and depth image scans of cluttered indoor scene, parameters of robot is estimated after data alignment. And then through the estimated camera parameters, the image coordinate is transform into the camera coordinate system. In the meanwhile, we detect lines from RGB images by Hough transform [15]. After that, we represent these segments in the Plücker coordinate. The trajectory of robot is estimated from registration of lines, according to the geometry of Plücker line correspondence, registration is done by contrasting their neighbor frames. After iterating and repeating the above steps, it will obtain the relation between robot motion, its relative pose in time, and the line descriptors in each frame. Next step is matching the lines with robot pose estimation. So it is need to map all lines to the world coordinate

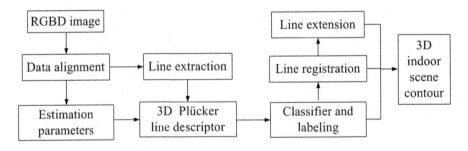

Fig. 2. The overview of our structural line reconstruction approach.

system, according to the motion equation. And then the most important step, shown in next subsection, is to classify Plücker line into four classes according to their location, whereas the chiefly concerned classes are the ceiling and the floor. Then extension step will execute when homonymous lines are determined within class. And when finding corresponding lines between classes, it will accordingly fill the residual structure line. Finally, 3D reconstruction of indoor scene contour is done by complete structure lines.

In the framework of our design, 3D reconstruction is carried out by deriving the relations between spatial structure lines. The corresponding key algorithm is given as follows.

The algorithm is designed to divide all segments into four classes and label with floor line, ceiling line, wall line and others. It explores the geometric relations that exist between these lines. we extend the structural lines through the geometric constraint characteristics of man-made buildings, thus reducing the basic structural line information lost due to occlusion. Moreover, we complete registration with relative label, and fix the gap of blocked line by the relations.

The algorithm of extension and filling structural line

```
Given: a series of line descriptor L of scene RGB-D images I and
some thresholds
Return: full view structural lines with labels
{
1 Line representation:
  representing all extracted lines using line descriptor, as shown
  in Fig.2,
2 Line registration:
  matching each line to the ones of its neighbor frame, estimate
  the pose and registration each line in world coordinate, repre
  -senting the floor plane by lowest height of lines in world
  coordinate P_floor.
3 Computing the geometric relations and then classify lines into
    four classes
  (a) if L is coplanar with P_floor
    then label L_floor
  (b) if L.u // P_floor && mean(L.height)>=T_height
    then label L_ceiling
  (c) if L.v // P_floor && L.length<=T_length
    then label L_wall
  (d) else label L_others and neglect them
4 Repeat checking in the ceiling and floor segment class, for
  each line L_mi of each image sample m, the index of the line is
  i, and frame n is neighbor frame of m.
  (a) if L_ceiling(mi) // L_ceiling(nj)
      && D(L_ceiling(mi),L_ceiling(nj))=T_min
```

then Lceiling(mi) is homonymous line with Lceling(nj),
    do extension process.
  (b) if L_ceiling(mi) // L _floor(nj)
    && D(L_ceiling(mi), L_floor (nj))T_length,
    then the two lines are corresponding pairs,
      do filling-gap process to floor.
}
end.

---

4   The Related Properties of Plücker Line

Since the importance of structure line is considered on the basis of the above, it needs to find an efficient and concise way to represent these data governed by motion variables and some other derivation. In order to make full use of the structural characteristics of lines, the research is deployed in Plücker coordinate for analyzing the relations of lines, which is widely used in computational geometry [16].

Equality up to a non-null scale factor is denoted by $\sim$, transposition and transposed inverse by $[\,]^T$, and is used to designate the L^2-norm of vector. The skew-symmetric 3 * 3 matrix is noted as the cross product by $[\cdot]^\times$.

4.1   Introduction of Plücker Coordinate

A line in 3-space has four degree of freedom, and can be defined by its pairs of arbitrary 3D points, $P = (P_x, P_y, P_z)^T$ and $Q = (Q_x, Q_y, Q_z)^T$. Here refers six parameters to represent the line L in classic Euclidean coordinate. 3-space line can be represented in parametric equations.

$$L = (1 - t)P + tQ, t \in R \tag{1}$$

Straight line can be easily given by listing the coordinates of six numbers in two distinct points. Obviously, the disadvantage of this situation is that arbitrary point is involved, which makes the line representation entirely depend on the choice of points. Besides, it has no corresponding geometric meaning. Plücker coordinate, with simple properties of dot products and cross products, takes the same number of parameters to represent a line in homogeneous geometry. Assuming the scale factor is set to 1, and P is not the original point, then $P = (P_x, P_y, P_z, 1)^T$ and $Q = (Q_x, Q_y, Q_z, 1)^T$. Vectors from the origin, the Plücker coordinate for the line is essentially

$$\begin{cases} U = P - Q \\ V = P \times Q \end{cases} \tag{2}$$

U gives the direction of the line, which passes P and Q, and V is perpendicular to the plane through P, Q and the origin. Here, since P is a distinct point from Q, so at least one component of U is non-zero. We usually normalize the two vectors by U, into a and b, L is noted as $[a, b]$, shown in Fig. 3. Because a and b are perpendicular, thus the dot product of the two vectors is 0, which expresses that a line intersects itself.

$$a^T \cdot b = 0 \tag{3}$$

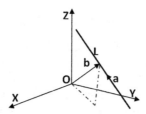

Fig. 3. The Plücker coordinate of a 3D line.

Plücker coordinate is concise and efficient for numerous chores. Moreover, U and V do not depend on the specific P and Q. Noted L_{ab} is line L in Plücker line, and a, b are the two key vectors. In Plücker coordinate, points, lines, planes and flats in spaces can be manage uniformly and these relationship can be determined by simple equations [17]. It makes whole scene description task easier. In the algorithm, there is the constant need for the quickest way to know the relations.

An equation to test if L_1 is equal to L_2, S is a scaling factor.

$$[u_1, v_1] = S \cdot [u_2, v_2] \tag{4}$$

The minimum squared distance of L from the origin is in (5),

$$D = (v \cdot v)/(u \cdot u) \tag{5}$$

The Eq. (6) is used for testing whether L_1 coincident with L_2,

$$u_1 \cdot v_2 + u_2 \cdot v_1 = 0 \tag{6}$$

If the lines L_1 is parallel with L_2, it holds the equation

$$u_1 \times u_2 = 0 \tag{7}$$

Let x_1, x_2, x_3 be unit vectors along the coordinate axes, with $u.x_1$ is non-zero. The common plane P for non-parallel lines can be presented as follow:

$$P = [u_1 \times u_1 : v_1 \cdot v_2] \tag{8}$$

In the mean while, for parallel distinct lines, their common plane is :

$$P = [(u_1 \cdot x_1)v_2 - (u_2 \cdot x_1)v_1 : (v_1 \times v_2) \cdot x_1] \tag{9}$$

The distance Eq. (10) of two lines L_1 and L_2,

$$
D = \begin{cases}
\dfrac{|(u_1, v_1) \cdot (u_2, v_2)|}{\|u_1 \times u_2\|} & : \quad if \ u_1 \times u_2 = 0 \\[3mm]
\dfrac{|u \cdot (v_1 - v_2)|}{\|u^2\|} & : \quad else \ u_1 = u_2 = u
\end{cases}
\tag{10}
$$

The above equations brings us many benefits for computation and some helpful properties.

4.2   The Presentation of Spatial Screw Motion of Robot

As is known that, the image of indoor space scene is obtained from different pose condition. The procedure of global map reconstruction requires calculating the changes relations between different pose of robots vision sensor.

From Fig. 4, it is easy to refer that transform of the line is complex, caused by robots screw motion. The essence of the transform is the combination of rotation and translation motion with rigid body movement. Plücker coordinate treats the two unified consideration as the space motion expression transform rigid space line. Established on this basis, the Plücker linear geometric algebra is more stable and effective in spiral movement. Therefore, Plückers linear equation is the most effective way to represent screw motion of line.

The 3D line motion homography matrix is introduced and proofed in [18], then line in WGS-84 L_g can be represent by its homogeneous line L in reference frame with a rotation matrix R and a translation vector T.

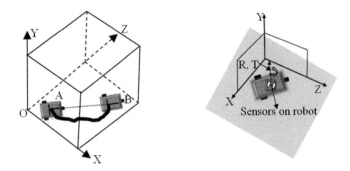

Fig. 4. (a) The moving robot from A to B, the bold line shows its real trajectory by time, and the dotted line is its result, (b) The vision sensor scans the scene accompanied with rotation R and transform T.

$$
L_g = \begin{bmatrix} R & [T]_\times R \\ 0 & R \end{bmatrix} \cdot L_r
\tag{11}
$$

It is a convenient way to represent the transformation between Plücker line by means of the matrix (11), so that the angle and distance between lines can be handily discovered. Therefore, we can analyze and determine the relations between Plücker line according to the above formulas.

5   Experiments and Results

To validate the capabilities and effectiveness of the proposed method, we conduct our evaluation on a public challenging TUM database in this community [19]. We choose the freiburg2 360 hemisphere validation as experimental dataset, which has a hall as indoor scene. It contains floor, ceiling, doors and many other objects, such as high-foot cameras, gas exhaust pipes and so on. The whole scanning process was rotating the device horizontally around 360°. The chosen database consists of 2670 color images, related depth images, captured by a Kinect camera, pointing to the ceiling, and moving trajectory groundtruth, which is obtained from a high power motion capture device. The length of floor-truth trajectory is 14.773 m.

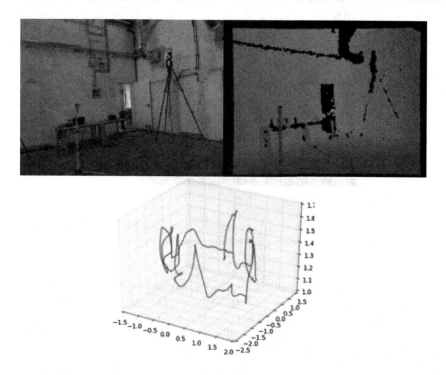

Fig. 5. A pair of RGB-D image sample and ground truth in TUM

As depth images were obtained faster than RGB images in the database, it is needed to find a pairs of RGB-D image for the same scene, see Fig. 5. Then after aligned the images of dataset, the Hough line detection algorithm is used in extraction line tasks, while recording the corresponding depth value. In order to emphasize the importance of structural line in 3D reconstruction, the extracted line segments are screened by their slope, see Fig. 6, and the filtering results are shown in the below figure.

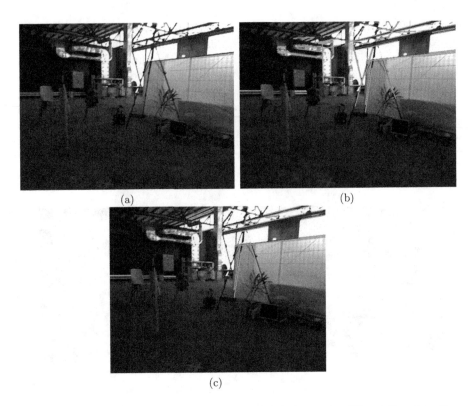

(a)   (b)

(c)

Fig. 6. Structural line extraction. (a) raw image, (b) the result of Hough line detection, (c) is limitation with slope and spacing between lines from (b)

As for mutual occlusion caused by overlapping objects and the limitation of sensor, it is difficult to get full line. In Fig. 7(a), the right part of floor line is completely blocked by objects, and left part is detected as two separate segments, see Fig. 7(b). It has two segments with gap and missing part of floor line. By applying the extension and filling line algorithm to fix the integrity of structural line, the results is shown in Fig. 7(c). After extension and filling step, the separate floor segments is linked and the missing part, corresponding to its above ceiling line is filled up, shown with blue lines. In this way, our approach promises a high quantity of structural lines for reconstruction. From Fig. 7, it is obvious that our method can fix the structural line occlusion by objects. To evaluate the influence of the extension and filling method, it is tested by comparing with directly use structural line ones. As a special roof structure line of the experiment room is a triangle, it brings more difficulties for us to obtain ceiling line. However, our

(a)   (b)

Fig. 7. The results of our algorithm (a) classified lines with partial label proceed from Fig. 6(a) and (b) is after extension and filling structural line.

method still effective. Furthermore, we use these relations for 3D reconstruction of indoor scene, as shown in Fig. 8. As we can see, it improves the integrity of structural lines.

Additionally, we show our method in real 3D reconstruction scene in Fig. 8, separately correspond to the effect of the Fig. 7.

To attain a high level confidence of indoor structural lines, the process of 3D reconstruction could be done by following continuous instructors of analysed lines. The goal of this study is therefore to explore the importance of structural lines for 3D reconstruction, we test this in experimental 3D indoor scene according the guide of Plücker line. From Fig. 9, the left picture shows 3D reconstruction results with occlusion structural lines. While the right one is obtained from Fig. 8(b), which has continuous structural lines. So we can conclude that the new approach is helpful for maintaining the integrity of structural lines. To sum up, our approach is effective in maintaining the integrity of structural lines, by analyzing the relations of Plücker line. Therefore, it gives a new perspective for 3D reconstruction in abstracting its full structural lines.

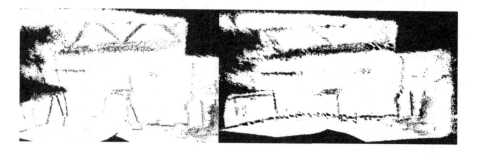

Fig. 8. The structural line abstract results with or without analyzing relations.

Fig. 9. The 3D reconstruction of indoor scene, left image directly use structural line and right is applied the relations of lines.

6   Conclusion and Future Work

Regarding the significant role of spatial structure lines for interior space description, this paper has presented a new method for extracting Plücker line, analyzing the relations of Plücker line, and inferring the properties of lines from high-confidence lines to obtain the structural lines in good properties for 3D reconstruction of indoor scene. This work has devoted its efforts in creating a consistent reconstruction of indoor spaces by enhancing consistence of structural lines. Through proposing and using these methods this paper has three contributions in technique. First, this paper proposed Plücker line for indoor structure in 3D reconstruction. In other word, it is the first to use Plücker coordinate to express lines in 3D indoor space. Second, it presented the method to analyze the relation of structure lines. It further showed that the proposed analysis method is better than directly extracted methods. Third, this paper studied a strategy to infer properties of lines from high-confidence extracted Plucker lines.

Based on the panorama obtained, this work also points out future directions. The first is to further and systematically study the properties of Plücker line in expressing structural lines. The second one is to study the effect that Plucker lines in 3D reconstruction of indoor scene. Last one is to develop an efficient solution of 3D reconstruction.

Acknowledgements. This work has been supported by "Fundamental Research Funds for the Central Universities" (No. 20205170442).

References

1. Armesto, J., Sánchez-Villanueva, C., Patiño-Cambeiro, F., et al.: Indoor multi-sensor acquisition system for projects on energy renovation of buildings. Sensors **16**(6), 785 (2016)
2. Lin S., Wen C.: Preproessing and modeling for visual-based 3D indoor scene reconstruction. In: The 8th International Conference on Computer Science Education, pp. 1324–1328 (2013)

3. Mahmoud, N., Cirauqui, I., Hostettler, A., Doignon, C., Soler, L., Marescaux, J., Montiel, J.M.M.: ORBSLAM-based endoscope tracking and 3D reconstruction. In: Peters, T., Yang, G.-Z., Navab, N., Mori, K., Luo, X., Reichl, T., McLeod, J. (eds.) CARE 2016. LNCS, vol. 10170, pp. 72–83. Springer, Cham (2017). https://doi.org/10.1007/978-3-319-54057-3_7

4. Torr, P.H.S., Zisserman, A.: Feature based methods for structure and motion estimation. In: Triggs, B., Zisserman, A., Szeliski, R. (eds.) IWVA 1999. LNCS, vol. 1883, pp. 278–294. Springer, Heidelberg (2000). https://doi.org/10.1007/3-540-44480-7_19

5. Kofuji, K., Watanabe, Y., Komuro, T., et al.: Stereo 3D reconstruction using prior knowledge of indoor scenes, vol. 19, no. 6, pp. 5198–5203 (2011)

6. Adán, A., Huber, D.: Reconstruction of wall surfaces under occlusion and clutter in 3D indoor environments. Technical report CMU-RI-TR-10-12, Robotics Institute, Pittsburgh (2010)

7. Nüchter, A., Hertzberg, J.: Towards semantic maps for mobile robots. Robot. Auton. Syst. 56(11), 915–926 (2008)

8. Turner, E., Zakhor, A.: Automatic indoor 3D surface reconstruction with segmented building and object elements. In: IEEE International Conference on 3D Vision, pp. 362–370 (2015)

9. Arnaud, A., Christophe, J., Ammi, M.: 3D reconstruction of indoor building environments with new generation of tablets. In: ACM Conference on Virtual Reality Software and Technology, pp. 187–190 (2016)

10. Gupta, S., Arbeláez, P., Girshick, R., et al.: Indoor scene understanding with RGB-D images: bottom-up segmentation, object detection and semantic segmentation. Int. J. Comput. Vis. 112(2), 133–149 (2015)

11. Hofer, M., Maurer, M., Bischof, H.: Efficient 3D scene abstraction using line segments. Comput. Vis. Image Underst. 157, 167–178 (2017)

12. Zhou, H., Zou, D., Ling, P., et al.: StructSLAM: visual SLAM with building structure lines. IEEE Trans. Veh. Technol. 64(99), 1364–1375 (2015)

13. Gao, R., Zhao, M., Ye, T., et al.: Multi-story indoor floor plan reconstruction via mobile crowd sensing. IEEE Trans. Mobile Comput. 15(6), 1427–1442 (2016)

14. Andreff, N., Espiau, B.: Revisiting Plücker Coordinates in Vision-Based Control. In: Lenarčič, J., Thomas, F. (eds.) Advances in Robot Kinematics. Springer, Dordrecht (2002). https://doi.org/10.1007/978-94-017-0657-5_28

15. Sewisy, A., Leberl, F.: Detection ellipses by finding lines of symmetry in the images via an hough transform applied to straight lines. Image Vis. Comput. 19(12), 857–866 (2001)

16. Skala V.: Plücker coordinates and extended cross product for robust and fast intersection computation. In: Computer Graphics International, pp. 57–60. ACM (2016)

17. Dorst, L., Fontijne, D., Mann, S.: Geometric Algebra for Computer Science: An Object-Oriented Approach to Geometry, pp. 328–342. Morgan Kaufmann Publishers, San Francisco (2007)

18. Bartoli, A., Sturm, P.: The 3D line motion matrix and alignment of line reconstructions. Int. J. Comput. Vis. 57, 159–178 (2004)

19. Computer Vision Group. http://vision.cs.tum.edu/data/datasets

Computer Vision and Modern Vehicles

Workshop on Computer Vision and Modern Vehicles (CVMV 2017)

The Second Workshop on Computer Vision and Modern Vehicles (CVMV 2017) was held in conjunction with the 8th Pacific Rim Symposium on Video and Image Technology (PSIVT 2017), in Wuhan, China, on November 21, 2017.

Computer vision for modern vehicles has provided researchers with access to camera technology for wide-ranging applications in the automotive industry. Computer vision-based driver assistance is an emerging technology, in both the automotive industry and academia. Despite the existence of some commercial safety systems such as night vision, adaptive cruise control, and lane-departure warning systems, we are at the beginning of a long research path toward a future generation of intelligent vehicles. Modern vehicles learned to see in recent years. Vision-based driver assistance moves toward autonomous driving. Controlled environments, especially with a mild climate or indoor environment, are the cases where autonomous driving is expected to become a standard first, within the next 4–7 years. Modern camera and vision technology supports a wide-range of applications in the traditional and emerging automotive industry. Initial solutions for night vision, adaptive cruise control, or lane- departure warning paved the way for future generations of intelligent vehicles, using already existing or novel sensor and vision technologies.

CVMV 2017 received 12 full-paper submissions that underwent a double-blind review, with five reviewers per paper. A total of five papers were selected for the workshop, and are collected in these proceedings. We were fortunate to have one invited speaker at the workshop, who has worked extensively in the area of computer vision and modern vehicles: Jian Yao (Computer Vision and Remote Sensing Group, School of Remote Sensing and Information Engineering, Wuhan University) whose talk was on "Computer Vision in Modern Remote Sensing." We would like to thank the invited speaker as well as all the members of the Program Committee for their help in organizing and running this event.

November 2017

Jinsheng Xiao
Atsushi Imiya

Organization

Workshop Organizers

Jinsheng Xiao   Wuhan University, China
Atsushi Imiya   Chiba University, Japan

Program Committee

Hui Chen	Sandong University, China
Junli Tao	Auckland University of Technology, New Zealand
Reinhard Klette	Auckland University of Technology, New Zealand
Yanyan Xu	Massachusetts Institute of Technology, Boston, USA
Mutsuhiro Terauchi	Osaka, Japan
Bijun Li	Wuhan University, Wuhan, China
Ching-Hsien(Robert) Hsu	Chung Hua University, Taiwan
Asaad Hakeem	JDX Silicon Valley Research Center, USA
Yuan-Fang Wang	University of California, Santa Barbara, USA
Mahdi Rezaei	QIAU, Iran
Sandino Morales	Terrabotics, UK
Yanqiang Li	Institute Automation Shandong Academy of Science, China
Waqar Khan	WelTec, New Zealand
A. B. M. Shawkat Ali	The University of Fiji, Fiji
John Barron	University of Western Ontario, Canada
Changxin Gao	Huazhong University of Science and Technology, China
Wang Han	Nanyang Technological University, Singapore
Konstantin Schauwecker	Nerian Vision Technologies, Germany
Ales Prochazka	UCT and CTU, Czech Republic
George Azzopardi	University of Malta, Malta
Eduardo Destefanis	UTN National University of Technology, Argentina
Anko Boerner	German Aerospace Center, Germany
Alfred M. Bruckstein	Technion, Israel

Context-Awareness Based Adaptive Gaussian Mixture Background Modeling

HongGang Xie[1]([✉]), JinSheng Xiao[2], and JunFeng Lei[2]

[1] School of Electrical and Electronic Engineering, Hubei University
of Technology, Wuhan 430068, China
honggang.xie@gmail.com
[2] School of Electronic Information, Wuhan University, Wuhan 430072, China

Abstract. Classical Gaussian mixture model (GMM) can represent the multi-states of a single pixel. GMM is robust when dealing with complex scenes with gradual-changed illumination. However, it still leads to false detection because of the change of pixel values in the same position when the background scenes get revealed after being covered. In this paper, a Context-Awareness based Gaussian mixture model (CAGMM) is proposed to tag the Gaussian model which used to be background. Experimental results show that the proposed CAGMM can remember scenes and adapt to the change of scenes more quickly, thus the false detection rate is reduced.

Keywords: Background modeling · Gaussian mixture model (GMM)
Context-Awareness · Background subtraction

1 Introduction

Background subtraction is one of the key techniques for automatic video analysis. It has a wide range of applications especially in video surveillance. Background subtraction consists of modeling and storing the background, so it can be later compared to newly observed images. In this way, background subtraction is commonly used to segment out moving foreground objects from their backgrounds [1, 2]. Despite the simplicity of this concept, in real world, temporal and spatial changes in pixel values such as due to shadows, gradual/sudden changes in illumination make modeling backgrounds a quite difficult task [3–5]. In recent years, many methods have been proposed to set up background models. For dynamic scenes containing textures, a new fuzzy color histogram was used to weaken the color change caused by motion background [6]. Some built a four-layer feed forward neural network to model background [7]. And others combined color, gradient, Harr feature to build a background model and used support vector machine to do the background classification [8]. To represent the repetitive background changes, [3] used multiple eigen subspaces to handle such changes.

Gaussian model is a widely used technique developed in recent years. In 1999, Stauffer et al. [4] used Gaussian mixture model to build background model. The background model composed of a plurality of Gaussian distributions for each pixel in each frame was established. Since then, this method has been widely used for its

© Springer International Publishing AG, part of Springer Nature 2018
S. Satoh (Ed.): PSIVT 2017, LNCS 10799, pp. 415–425, 2018.
https://doi.org/10.1007/978-3-319-92753-4_32

efficiency in more robustly describing multimodal distribution background, but it still has problems in processing speed and cannot cope with the mutant backgrounds [9]. After that, many experiments have been conducted to improve the results of Gaussian mixture background modeling. Zivkovic [10] presented a simple adaptive method to constantly update the parameters of a Gaussian mixture model and to simultaneously select the number of components for each pixel. [11] proposed an illumination-sensitive background modeling approach to analyze the illumination change and detect moving objects. Some used the entropy image to select Gaussian function number for each pixel and used membership to indicate the possibility of pixels belonging to the background. This approach made classification results more reliable [12]. In order to handle the variation of the scene, [13] proposed a foreground detection algorithm based on memory (Memory-based GMM, MGMM). In this algorithm, each pixel will be processed in three spaces, namely, immediate memory, short-term memory and long-term memory.

The above methods of Gaussian mixture model are mainly focused on process efficiency and the convergence rate of the model. However, when applying the traditional GMM to practical use, if the repetitive background scenes occurred, eg, being covered and uncovered repeatedly, the sudden change of the scene cannot be immediately learnt into the background model due to the model learning speed. And it will produce a large number of false detections.

In this paper, the Context-Awareness based Gaussian mixture model (CAGMM) is proposed. This approach can memory the repetitive background in the process of model learning; when background appears again background and foreground can be separated. So the background pixel which is wrongly detected as the foreground can fuse into the background quickly. This article is organized as follows: Sect. 2 makes an introduction of Gaussian mixture model; Sect. 3 explains the proposed method in detail. Section 4 compares the experimental results of CAGMM with those of GMM and MGMM in [13]; finally, conclusions are presented in Sect. 5.

2   Gaussian Mixture Model

In classical Gaussian mixture model [4], K states are defined for each pixel to represent its value. The value of K is generally taken between 3 and 5. If the pixel value is denoted as X_t, the corresponding probability density function can be represented with K Gaussian functions:

$$f(X_t = x) = \sum_{i=1}^{K} \omega_{i,t} \cdot \eta(X_t, \mu_{i,t}, \Sigma_{i,t}) \tag{1}$$

$\eta(X_t, \mu_{i,t}, \Sigma_{i,t})$ is the i-th Gaussian model of time t, $\omega_{i,t}$ is the weight for the i-th Gaussian model of time t, and

$$\sum_{i=1}^{K} w_{i,t} = 1 \tag{2}$$

In order to reduce the amount of computation, it is assumed that the pixel values of each point in R, G, B channels are mutually independent and have the same variance [14]. So the covariance matrix is:

$$\Sigma_{i,t} = \sigma_{i,t}^2 \cdot I \tag{3}$$

Among them, $\sigma_{i,t}$ is the standard deviation, I is the unit matrix. All K Gaussian models are sorted according to the descending order of $\omega_{i,t}$. And the first B Gaussian models are selected as the background model:

$$B = \arg \min_{b} (\sum_{k=1}^{b} \omega_{i,t} > T) \tag{4}$$

Wherein, T is the weight threshold given in advance, usually ranging from 0.7 to 0.9.

Formula (5) is used to judge whether a new pixel point matches one of the existing K Gaussian models.

$$\left| (X_{t+1} - \mu_{i,t}) \right| < \delta \sigma_{i,t} \tag{5}$$

If this new point and some Gaussian model satisfy Formula (5) (δ is usually set within the range of $3 \sim 5$), it is considered to match the Gaussian model.

Online K-means approximation algorithm [9] is used in updating the Gaussian distribution parameters. For the first matched Gaussian model, all parameters are updated. And for the other K-1 Gaussian models, only weights are updated.

1. Weight update

$$\omega_{i,t+1} = (1 - \alpha) \cdot \omega_{i,t} + \alpha \cdot O_{i,t+1} \tag{6}$$

Where $O_{i,t+1}$ equals 1 for the first matched model and 0 for the others. α is the learning rate which is related to the update speed of the background. When α is too large, it may lead to incompleteness of foreground. When it is too small, the algorithm may not adapt to the change of the scenes in time. Usually, α will be set between 0.002 and 0.005. $\omega_{i,t}$ and $\omega_{i,t+1}$ respectively stand for the weight before and after updating.

2. Mean and variance update

$$\mu_{i,t+1} = (1 - \alpha) \cdot \mu_{i,t} + \alpha \cdot X_{i,t+1} \tag{7}$$

$$\sigma_{i,t+1}^2 = (1 - \alpha) \cdot \sigma_{i,t}^2 + \alpha \cdot (X_{t+1} - \mu_{i,t+1})^T \cdot (X_{t+1} - \mu_{i,t+1}) \tag{8}$$

Wherein α is the same meaning as in the formula (6). $\mu_{i,t}$ and $\mu_{i,t+1}$ separately stand for the mean before and after updating, $\sigma_{i,t}^2$ and $\sigma_{i,t+1}^2$ separately stand for the variance before and after updating.

If the current pixel cannot be matched with all models, a new Gaussian model with mean of X_{t+1}, high variance and low weight will be generated to substitute the tail of the Gaussian distributions.

When using traditional Gaussian models in complex environment, its computational complexity is proportional to the number of the Gaussian models. And it is very difficult to adjust the parameters of models. When the repetitive background scene occurs, the background point may be wrongly detected as foreground point because of the sudden change of the pixel values.

An ideal background subtraction system should have the adaptive ability to maintain and update background according to the changes of the scene. Normal Gaussian mixture model has no special treatment for those had been adjudged as the background models. When the background repeatedly appears at the same position, it will be judged as foreground because of the change of pixel values.

If the marks of background model were introduced in the updating of the Gaussian mixture model, the historical background model would update in time based on marks. Thus it is possible to memory background. When the same background repeatedly occurs, the detection error rate is reduced.

3   Context-Awareness Based Gaussian Mixture Models

To solve the problem of classic GMM, a model that used to be background is marked as historical model in the modeling process. The match numbers of historical models are recorded after updating parameters. If the match number exceeds a user-set threshold in a single cycle, an additional weight (T times α) will be added for this model. After sorting all the models by the descending weight order, the historical model will be in the front of the queue and fall into the background range. So the point will be judged as background rather than foreground. Therefore, the aforementioned problem is solved to some extent.

Improvements of classic Gaussian model algorithm are shown as follows:

1. First, a historical background is marked. Then match numbers of the historical backgrounds in a cycle are recorded. The cycle period is set to N in advance. If the match number exceeds a user-set threshold, an extra weight (T times α) will be added for the model. The weight update formula is modified as follows.

$$\omega_{i,t+1} = (1 - \alpha) \cdot \omega_{i,t} + \alpha \cdot O_{i,t+1} + \alpha c_{i+1} \tag{9}$$

Among them, α, $\omega_{i,t}$, $\omega_{i,t+1}$ and $O_{i,t+1}$ are the same meaning with Formula (6). c_{i+1} equals 2 for the model which satisfies historical condition and 0 for the others. The historical condition means: the model is matched, the current model weight is in the foreground range, and match number is more than N in the period T (in this paper, T is 10 and N is 5). If this condition is satisfied, an extra weight αc_{i+1} will be added for the model. Experimental results show that any c_{i+1} which is more than 4 will result in the incompleteness of the foreground. If c_{i+1} is set less than 3, there is no effect dealing with the repetitive scenes. According to the above analysis, c_{i+1} is set to 3.

2. If the model weight is less than a certain threshold, the historical and non-historical models will be treated in different ways. Non-historical model will be deleted and historical model's weight will be reset to 0. It will not be deleted.

The detailed description of the algorithm is as follows:

Step 1:

Initialize the memory space in the first frame, and create a Gaussian model for each pixel point with pixel (R_i, G_i, B_i) in the current frame image. The model weight is assigned to 1. Assign an initial variance for it.

Step 2:

For each new frame, the K models of each pixel need to be sorted by the descending weight order. According to the formula (4), B Gaussian distribution is selected from the first end as candidate background models. T is the user-defined threshold.

Step 3:

The new sampled value $X_{t+1}(R, G, B)$ will be matched with the original K Gaussian models sequentially. The distance between means of the model (R, G, B) and the current point (R, G, B) will be calculated according to formula (5). If the distance satisfies formula (5) on the condition of $\delta = 3$, the point is considered to match the current model. If the model falls in the B models from step 2, the pixel is judged as the background, while the current model is marked as a historical model. Otherwise, the pixel point is judged as the foreground. If a certain match is found, it will no longer be looking for other matching model and turn to step 4. Otherwise this point is considered not to match any model and go to step 5.

Step 4:

If a matching model is found, the weight, mean and variance of the matching model need to be updated in accordance with formulas (6), (7), (8) and (9). match numbers of historical models should be memorized. If the match number is more than N in a fixed period (such as 10 frame), the weight should be added up T times α. Only weights of other models need updating. Then, all models are sorted by the descending weights.

After updating model weight, if some model weight is less than pre-set αC_T and this model has not been marked as a historical model, it should be removed; otherwise, only its weight will be reset to 0 and the model itself will not be deleted.

Step 5:

If the current point is not matched with any model, in accordance with the formula (9), all the model weights need to be updated. If the model number is less than the user set limit, a new model will be added into the model queue; otherwise, the new model is used to replace the model with the smallest right. At last, all models are sorted by the descending weight order with their weights being normalized.

Based on the above analysis, the historical background-based Gaussian mixture modeling algorithm is shown in Fig. 1.

In the update process of traditional Gaussian mixture model, a mark of the background model is introduced. And in accordance with this mark, the historical

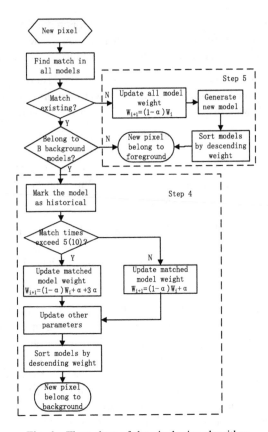

Fig. 1. Flow chart of the pixel-wise algorithm

background model is treated with different update processing. It is possible to memorize the background and avoid false detection when the background repeatedly appears.

4 Experimental Results and Discussion

To verify the validity of the historical model algorithm, it is tested on a 2.8 GHz Core i5 dual core processor and VS2012 platform with three real shot sequences and is compared with the traditional GMM method and MGMM method in [13] respectively. Those three sequences will be treated differently to test the algorithms both in quantity and quality ways.

In order to ensure the validity of the comparison, the parameter values of the three methods are basically the same. Table 1 shows the value of the parameters that are used by the three modeling methods.

The first sequence "fast move" is a piece of surveillance video on the highway where vehicles frequently keep driving and slight shaking leaves also appear. In order to test repeatable background issues, a color patch is added into the original video for every 400 frames to simulate a repetitive moving target. The initial 50 frames are used

Table 1. Parameters used by the three background modeling methods

Model	Parameters
GMM	K = 5; σ = 20; T = 0.75; α = 1/2T; w = α;
MGMM	K = 4; N = 1; σ = 25; T = 0.75; α = 1/2T; w = α;
Proposed algorithm	K = 5; σ = 20; T = 0.75; α = 1/2T; w = α;

for the model learning and it will not be superimposed with color patches. After the disappearance of color blocks, the original position will be wrongly detected as foreground. The more frames which the false foreground point uses to disappear, the worse the modeling algorithm can be in handling the repetitive scenes. The specific number of frames of the color patches is as shown in Table 2.

Table 2. Frame number comparison of the three background modeling methods

Block appearing frames	51–200	601–999
GMM	51–81	601–612
MGMM	51–200	201–700
Proposed algorithm	51–81	601–608

Figure 2(a) shows the original image in the test video and Fig. 2(b) shows the effect of superimposing the color patch to the original video. Figure 3 shows the detection results of moving object with frame 608, 609, 611, 612 of the sequence respectively using classic GMM, MGMM in [14] and CAGMM of this paper.

(a) Original video   (b) original video with color block

Fig. 2. Background changes in "Fast move"

Table 2 displays the number of frames for the color blocks detected as the foreground respectively using the three methods to the test frames. Thus the effect of three modeling algorithms can be analyzed in detail.

Integrating Fig. 3 and Table 2, the colored box appears in frame 600 for the second time. The traditional GMM wastes 12 frames before its absorption into the background. And the proposed algorithm used only 8 frames. When repetitive background appears, the proposed method need less frames to ablate wrongly detected foreground into background. Thus the repeated scenes will not last as foreground for a long time.

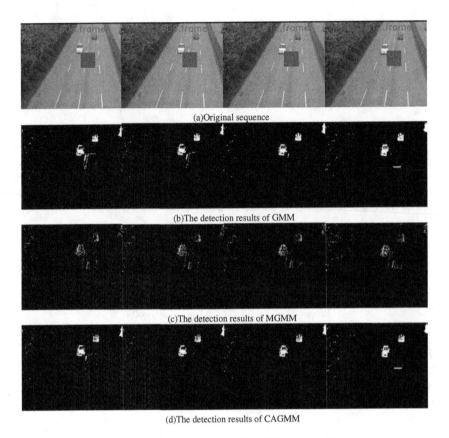

(a)Original sequence

(b)The detection results of GMM

(c)The detection results of MGMM

(d)The detection results of CAGMM

Fig. 3. The detection results of "Fast move"

In order to test the background modeling algorithms more accurately, we compare the segmented foreground of three different algorithms with the ground truth of every video sequence. For quantitative evaluation, F1 score is introduced to represent how much the segmented foreground resembles the real moving object in videos. The F1 score can be calculated by

$$F_1 = 2 \times \frac{precision \times recall}{precision + recall} \tag{10}$$

Where precision is defined as $\frac{n(B_T \cap B_{BGS})}{n(B_T)}$ and recall is defined as $\frac{n(F_T \cap F_{BGS})}{n(F_T)}$, F_T and B_T stand for the ground truth of foreground and background respectively. And F_{BGS} and B_{BGS} represent foreground and background obtained by modeling algorithms [8]. The higher F_1 score gets the better modeling algorithms are at extracting foreground from background.

The second sequence "Office" records indoor scene [15]. One person walks in, stays for a while and then leaves. We choose two frames, 1999, 2004 from this video to compute F1 score. Those frames show a person walks away from where he stands and the wall behind him reveals again. The reappearing wall should be detected as background according to the ground truth because it is not a moving object indeed. So the modeling effect can be judged by how much the detection results of these three modeling algorithms are similar to the ground truth set using F1 score.

From Fig. 4, we can see when historical background happens again, CAGMM can absorb it into background more quickly than GMM and MGMM. And the F_1 score calculated between the detected foreground and ground truth is shown in Table 3. Those scores show that CAGMM gains the highest F_1 score with all the two frames. It is superior to the other two algorithms at handling repetitive scenes.

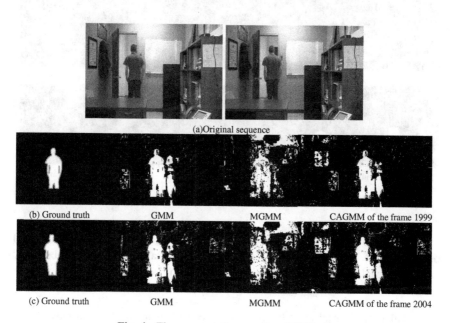

(a)Original sequence

(b) Ground truth   GMM   MGMM   CAGMM of the frame 1999

(c) Ground truth   GMM   MGMM   CAGMM of the frame 2004

Fig. 4. The segmentation results of "Office"

To further test the effect of CAGMM, we use another video "Sofa". It is also a surveillance video of indoor scene [15]. People come into the lobby and drop their baggage on the chair. The two frames we select from the original video represent a person lift a box onto the chair. The revealing ground underneath the box should be detected as background. Figure 5 shows the segmentation results of three modeling algorithms and Table 4 represents the F1 score computed for "Sofa".

Table 3. Comparison of F_1 score with three background modeling methods

Frame	1999	2004
GMM	0.5628	0.5231
MGMM	0.4300	0.4238
CAGMM	0.5764	0.5446

(a)Original sequence

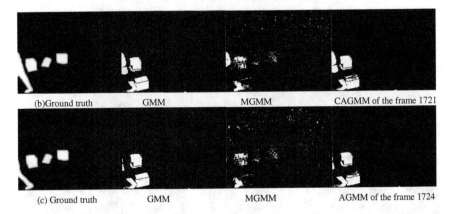

(b)Ground truth   GMM   MGMM   CAGMM of the frame 1721

(c) Ground truth   GMM   MGMM   AGMM of the frame 1724

Fig. 5. The detection results of "Sofa"

From the above figure and table, we can see, CAGMM still obtains the highest F1 score among the three algorithms. Its detection results also show that it absorbs the wrongly detected foreground of repetitive scenes into background more quickly.

Table 4. Comparison of F_1 score with three background modeling methods

Frame	1721	1724
GMM	0.4650	0.4717
MGMM	0.4222	0.4355
CAGMM	0.4838	0.4923

5   Conclusions

The mark of background model is introduced in the updating process of traditional Gaussian mixture model. In accordance with this mark, different historical background models have different update processing. Repetitive contrast experiments using traditional GMM, MGMM and CAGMM are conduct. Experimental results show that this method realized recording repeat background and is suitable for the presence of repetitive motion scene modeling.

Acknowledgment. This paper was partially funded by the Natural Science Foundation of Hubei Province (Grant No. 2014CFB585), and the Natural Science Foundation of China (Grant No. 61573002).

References

1. Gamboa-Aispuro, J.M., Aguilar-Ponce, R.M., Tecpanecatl-Xihuitl, J.L.: Background subtraction based on mutual information. In: IEEE International Autumn Meeting on Power, Electronics and Computing. Institute of Electrical and Electronics Engineers Inc., Mexico (2016)
2. Ge, W., et al.: Dynamic background estimation and complementary learning for pixel-wise foreground/background segmentation. Pattern Recogn. **59**, 112–125 (2016)
3. Dong, Y., Desouza, G.N.: Adaptive learning of multi-subspace for foreground detection under illumination changes. Comput. Vis. Image Underst. **115**, 31–49 (2011)
4. Stauffer C., Grimson, W.E.L.: Adaptive background mixture models for real-time tracking. In: IEEE Conference on Computer Vision and Pattern Recognition, Fort Collins, CO (1999)
5. Wang, K., Liang, Y., Xing, X., Zhang, R.: Target detection algorithm based on gaussian mixture background subtraction model. In: Deng, Z., Li, H. (eds.) Proceedings of the 2015 Chinese Intelligent Automation Conference. LNEE, vol. 336, pp. 439–447. Springer, Heidelberg (2015). https://doi.org/10.1007/978-3-662-46469-4_47
6. Kim, W., Kim, C.: Background subtraction for dynamic texture scenes using fuzzy color histograms. IEEE Sig. Process. Lett. **19**(3), 127–130 (2012)
7. Wang, Z., Zhang, L., Bao, H.: Adaptive background model based on hybrid structure neural network. Acta Electronica Sinica **39**(5), 1053–1058 (2011)
8. Han, B., Davis, L.S.: Density-based multifeature background subtraction with support vector machine. IEEE Trans. Pattern Anal. Mach. Intell. **34**(5), 1017–1023 (2012)
9. Lin, H.-H., Chuang, J.-H., Liu, T.-L.: Regularized background adaptation: a novel learning rate control scheme for gaussian mixture modeling. IEEE Trans. Image Process. **20**(3), 822–836 (2011)
10. Zivkovic, Z.: Improved adaptive Gaussian mixture model for background subtraction. In: IEEE International Conference on Pattern Recognition, pp. 28–31. IEEE (2004)
11. Cheng, F.-C., Huang, S.-C., Ruan, S.-J.: Illumination-sensitive background modeling approach for accurate moving object detection. IEEE Trans. Broadcast. **57**(4), 794–801 (2011)
12. Zuo, J., Liang, Y., Zhao, C., et al.: Gaussian mixture background model based on entropy image and membership-degree-image. J. Electron. Inf. Technol. **30**(8), 1918–1922 (2008)
13. Qi, Y.-J., Wang, Y.-J., Li, Y.-P.: Memory-based Gaussian mixture background modeling. Acta Automatica Sinica **36**(11), 1520–1526 (2010)
14. Xiao, J., et al.: Hierarchical tone mapping based on image colour appearance model. IET Comput. Vis. **8**(4), 358–364 (2014)
15. Wang, Y., Jodoin, P.-M., Porikli, F., et al.: CDnet 2014: an expanded change detection benchmark dataset. In: Proceedings of the IEEE Workshop on Change Detection (CDW-2014) at CVPR-2014, pp. 387–394 (2014)

Robust Expression Recognition Using ResNet with a Biologically-Plausible Activation Function

Yunhua Chen[1]([⊠]), Jin Du[1], Qian Liu[2], and Bi Zeng[1]

[1] School of Computers, Guangdong University of Technology,
Guangzhou, China
yhchen@gdut.edu.cn
[2] School of Computer Science,
The University of Manchester, Manchester, UK

Abstract. The recently developed deep artificial neural networks (ANNs) have outperformed the traditional methods in the field of facial expression recognition with multiple head poses, and varied illuminations. However they still face a degradation problem when they become extremely deep. Although the deep residual networks (ResNets) architecture has been proposed to solve this problem, and obtained promising results, they are still rate-based neural networks, which need to be implemented on traditional CPUs with strong numerical processing capabilities and enormous energy cost. The newly emerging brain-like neuromorphic hardwares provide a prospective way of solving these problems. However, training spiking neural networks (SNNs) and programming those brain-like neuromorphic hardware to be competent as AI applications in the market is still an open question. Therefore, a novel activation function named Noisy Softplus (NSP) was proposed to model the response function of a spiking neuron, so that we can train the SNNs exactly the same way as ANNs. Besides, We found NSP can improve the anti-noise ability of a deep ANN. Aims at gaining a robust facial expression recognition deep ANN, which latter can be transformed into energy efficient deep SNNs, we build an 18-layered ResNet using NSP to perform facial expression recognition across datasets KDEF and GENKI-4K. We demonstrate that the resulting facial expression recognition method is able to achieve better anti-noise ability on CPUs/GPUs and lower power consumption on a neuromorphic hardware.

Keywords: Noisy Softplus · Convolutional neural networks
Spiking neural networks · Residual learning
Facial expression recognition

1 Introduction

Facial expression recognition has been widely studied due to its potential usage in human-computer interaction and intelligent driving. The key problem of it is

© Springer International Publishing AG, part of Springer Nature 2018
S. Satoh (Ed.): PSIVT 2017, LNCS 10799, pp. 426–438, 2018.
https://doi.org/10.1007/978-3-319-92753-4_33

to find effective features for the recognition [3]. The most frequently used traditional methods include Local Binary Pattern (LBP) [29], Histogram of Oriented Gradients (HOG) [11], and Scale Invariant Feature Transform (SIFT) [34] etc. But they all have the same flaw that they often need to impose some restrictions on head poses or illumination, thus making them not so robust under the natural scene [37].

In the past few years, thanks for the improvement in deep learning algorithms and [10] the computer hardware, deep Artificial Neural Networks (ANNs) has achieved many remarkable results in cognitive tasks including facial expression recognition [15,16,19]. Some studies have showed that [30,32,33] the recognition accuracy will increase as the network grows deeper, but they also found that the training of the very deep neural network will become extremely difficult. Srivastava et al. [31] pointed out that optimization of a very deep neural network has proven to be considerable more difficult. He et al. [8] discovered the degradation problem, and proposed a solution — adding residual learning in very deep neural networks, and build the deep residual networks (ResNets) architecture. As a result, a 152 layered ResNet training on ImageNet [7], the top-5 error rate is only 5.71%, which is much lower than the error rate of a *plain* Convolutional Neural Network (CNN) with the same depth which simply stack layers.

Although CNNs has gained more and more remarkable results in cognitive tasks, the sizes of the networks keep growing and the learning algorithms become more and more complex, thus require more and more dedicated high performance computing platforms, which has restrained their applications on platforms with insufficient computing resources such as portable devices and wearable devices etc. The key point is that CNNs are rate-based neural networks, which means that they need to be implemented on traditional CPUs/GPUs with strong numerical processing capability and enormous energy cost. The newly emerging brain-like neuromorphic hardwares provide a prospective way of solving this problem. The communication mechanism between the neurons of Spiking Neuronal Networks (SNNs) [12,13] is a series of spikes formed by voltage fluctuations, rather than numerical values of CNNs. Therefore, compared with CNNs, SNNs can perform cognitive tasks with lower power consumption [25]. However, training SNNs and programming these brain-like neuromorphic hardware to be competent as AI applications in the market is still an open question. Masquelier and Thorpe [23] firstly use Spike Timing Dependent Plasticity (STDP) to learn pre-classification features, then they send these feature to a non-spiking classifier. Unfortunately, the recognition accuracy is far less than those CNNs. Perez-Carrasco et al. [26] Proposed a frameless spike-based convolution neural network, which employs kernel projection to implement convolution operations. Although this approach has achieved rapid input-to-output response time, it requires massive amount of digital hardware resources.

In our previous work, we studied the characteristics of Leaky Integrate and Fire (LIF) neurons, proposed Noisy Softplus (NSP) to model the response function of a spiking neuron to a novel activation function used in conventional ANNs, so that the SNNs can be trained exactly the same way as ANNs [20].

A 5-layer CNN trained using NSP as an activation function can achieve 98.85% recognition rate on MNIST [17], but the result on facial expression recognition is unclear. As facial expression recognition is a more complex task than the handwritten digital recognition, a few layers of networks is insufficient to achieve robust results. Aims at gaining a robust facial expression recognition deep ANN, which latter can be transformed into energy efficient deep SNNs, we build an 18-layered ResNet using NSP to perform facial expression recognition across the datasets KDEF and GENKI-4K. We found that compared with ReLU, NSP is more biologically plausible and performs better when the data contains noises. We demonstrate that the resulting facial expression recognition method is able to achieve better anti-noise ability when running on CPUs/GPUs, and consumes much lower power on a neuromorphic hardware [4].

2   Background

2.1   Response Function

CNNs has shown its strong learning ability and has surpassed the human brain in more and more cognitive fields, but the high power consumption also indicates its limitations. Compared with artificial neurons, the communication mechanism between biological neurons is the pulse of membrane potential elevation, which has a unique advantage in power consumption. The commonly used models of biological neurons include hodg-kin-huxley (HH) model [6], Izhikevich model [14], Adaptive Exponential Integrate and Fire (AdEx IF) model [1], Leaky Integrate and Fire (LIF) model [21], etc. LIF model is the most widely used model because of its comprehensive performance in biological accuracy and computational complexity. LIF neuronal membrane potential follows the following dynamics formula:

$$\tau_m \frac{dV}{dt} = V_{rest} - V + R_m I(t) \tag{1}$$

The membrane potential V changes in response to the input current I, starting at the resting membrane potential V_{rest}, where the membrane time constant is $\tau_m = R_m C_m$, R_m is the membrane resistance and C_m is the membrane capacitance. Given a constant current injection I, the response function, i.e. firing rate, of the LIF neuron is:

$$\lambda_{out} = [t_{ref} - \tau_m \log(1 - \frac{V_{th} - V_{rest}}{IR_m})]^{-1} \tag{2}$$

When $IR_m > V_{th} - V_{rest}$, a spike will be triggered, otherwise the membrane potential can not reach the threshold V_{th} and the output firing rate is zero. However, in practice, a noisy current generated by the random arrival of spikes, rather than a constant current, flows into the neurons. The response function of the LIF neuron to a noisy current is as follows, where μ and σ are the mean and variance of the current:

$$\lambda_{out} = [t_{ref} + \tau_m \int_{\frac{V_{rest} - u\tau_m}{\sigma\sqrt{\tau_m}}}^{\frac{V_{th} - u\tau_m}{\sigma\sqrt{\tau_m}}} \sqrt{\pi} \exp(u^2)(1 + erf(u))du]^{-1} \tag{3}$$

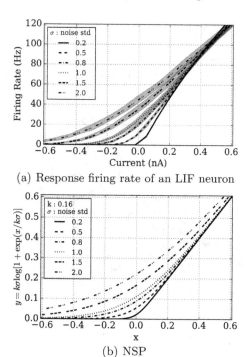

(a) Response firing rate of an LIF neuron

(b) NSP

Fig. 1. NSP models the LIF response function. (a) Firing rates measured by simulations of a LIF neuron driven by different input currents and discrete noise levels. Bold lines show the average and the grey colour fills the range between the minimum and the maximum. (b) NSP activates the input x according to different noise levels where $k = 0.16$.

2.2 Noisy Softplus (NSP)

Consequently to model the practical LIF response function (see Fig. 1(a)) whose output firing rates are determined by both the mean and variance of the noisy input currents, the NSP was proposed as follows:

$$y = f_{ns}(x, \sigma) = k\sigma \log[1 + \exp(\frac{x}{k\sigma})] \ , \tag{4}$$

where x and σ refer to the mean and standard deviation of the input current, y indicates the intensity of the output firing rate, and k, determined by the biological configurations on the LIF neurons [20], controls the shape of the curves. Note that the novel activation function we proposed contains two parameters, the mean current and its noise, which can be estimated by Eq. 5:

$$x = \tau_{syn} \sum_i w_i \lambda_i \ , \quad \sigma^2 = \frac{1}{2}\tau_{syn} \sum_i w_i^2 \lambda_i \ , \tag{5}$$

where λ_i indicates the firing rate of an input spike train.

Figure 1(b) shows the activation function in curve sets corresponding to different discrete noise levels which mimics the responding activities of practical simulations of LIF neurons, shown in Fig. 1(a). Since the NSP takes two variables as inputs, the activation function can be plotted in 3D, see Fig. 2.

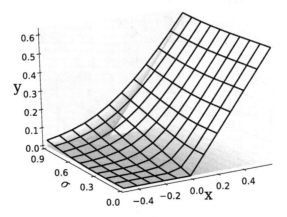

Fig. 2. Noisy Softplus in 3D.

The derivative of the NSP is the logistic function scaled by $k\sigma$:

$$\frac{\partial f_{ns}(x, \sigma)}{\partial x} = \frac{1}{1 + exp(-\frac{x}{k\sigma})}, \tag{6}$$

which could be applied easily to back propagation in any ANN training.

3   Methods

3.1   Residual Learning

There are some studies [8] showed that the degradation problem is not caused by over-fitting, but by the intensive parameters caused by a large number of layers and neurons, that is why residual learning can help us to solve this problem. In a ResNet, two or more stacked layers are used as one unit, and a short-cut is added between each neighbouring unit, which is called identity mapping. Therefore, the unit and the short-cut together form a residual unit. Suppose, the output of a residual unit is expressed as $H(x)$, where x is the input, then $F(x) = H(x) - x$ represents a residual mapping. Compared with direct fitting $H(x)$, the fitting of $F(x)$ makes the output change more sensitively, and the amount of adjustment for the parameters is larger, which speeds up the learning speed and thus improve the network performance.

The forward propagation of a residual unit can be defined as shown in Fig. 3,

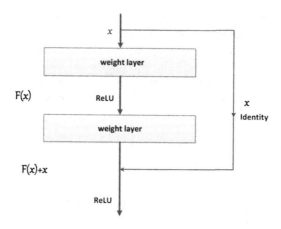

Fig. 3. The structure of a residual unit

$$y = F(x, \{W_i\}) + x \qquad (7)$$

In Eq. (7), x and y represent the input and output vectors of the residual unit respectively. The function $F(x, \{W_i\})$ represents the residual mapping that needs to be learned. Figure 3 shows two stacked layers as a unit, where f represents the ReLU function. The operation $F + x$ is performed by a shortcut connection, followed by a ReLU activation, that is $f(y)$. The quick connection in Eq. (7) does not introduce any additional parameters, neither does it increase any computation, thus ResNets will achieve better performance than plain CNNs with the same number of parameters, depth, width and computation cost.

The dimension of x and F must be equal in Eq. (7). If this is not the case (e.g., when changing the input/output channels), we can perform a linear projection W_s by the short-cut to match the dimension:

$$y = F(x, \{W_i\}) + W_s x \qquad (8)$$

3.2 Network Architecture

Since residual learning can be used to solve the problem of network degradation, the network depth of ResNet can increase further, and the most deepest ResNet has 1001 layers [9]. To validate and estimate the performance of NSP in more complex visual tasks, we built a 19-layered ResNet by adding residual units to VGG-19 [30], and performed facial expression recognition on several public expression datasets.

VGG–19 consists of sixteen convolutional layers and three fully connected layers. Each convolutional layer has different number of convolution kernels, from 64 to 512. But all the convolution kernel has the same size of 3×3. The convolutional layer is activated using the ReLU function after the convolution operation. Based on VGG–19, we remove two full connection layers and add two convolutional layers, meanwhile we add seven short-cuts to construct residual units, then we can construct a 19-layered residual network, which we called ResNet-19. Compared with VGG-19, ResNet-19 has only one fully connected layer and two more convolutional layers, which leads to less parameters and less complexity. The activation function ReLU used in the VGG-19 is replaced by NSP in ResNet-19.

4   Experiments

4.1   Datasets

We select Karolinska Directed Emotional Faces (KDEF) [22] and GENKI-4K [36] as our experimental datasets to evaluate NSP.

The KDEF dataset contains seven kinds of basic expressions of 70 people, each person is shot twice from five different angles, so KDEF contains a total of 4900 images. Figure 4(b) shows the expression images of one person. The dataset is divided into seven categories according to the basic expression, we randomly select one image from each person to form the testing set, and the rest of the images form the training set, then the ratio of the image number in two sets is just4:1.

GENKI-4K contains 4000 images with different faces, head poses and illumination. It has two categories of facial expression, one is happy and the other is neutral, each category has 2000 images. Figure 4(c) shows some sample images of happy expression. Similarly, the two categories are divided into a training set and a testing set according to the ratio of 4:1 respectively. Note that the input data must be normalized to $[0, 1]$.

4.2   Results and Analysis

To evaluate the performance of ResNet–19, we carried out several groups of experiments on the above two datasets.

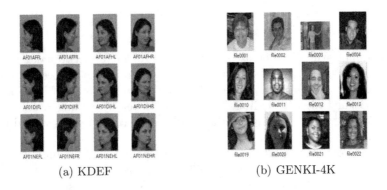

(a) KDEF   (b) GENKI-4K

Fig. 4. Sample images of the datasets

Firstly, we compare our proposed ResNet–19 with some traditional methods, as can be seen from Table 1, ResNet–19 outperforms the state-of-the-art traditional methods on all the two datasets. The accuracy is 0.7% higher on the KDEF dataset, and 0.66% higher than PwDV+ELM [5] on the GENKI-4K dataset.

Table 1. The recognition accuracy of ResNet-19 compared with traditional methods

KDEF		GENKI-4K	
Method	Accuracy (%)	Method	Accuracy (%)
AdaBoost [18]	87.20	AdaBoost [5]	79.22
LDBP+SVM [28]	92.15	LBP+FAP [38]	92.00
SCAE [27]	92.52	PwDV+ELM [5]	93.42
ResNet-19 (proposed)	92.85	ResNet-19 (proposed)	94.08

Secondly, we compared the recognition accuracy of VGG–19 and ResNet–19 with different activation functions. We can see from Table 2 that the best recognition rate is obtained by ResNet–19 with ReLU which is 93.72% on KDEF and 94.67% on GENKI-4K. ResNet–19 with NSP achieved the second high rates which is 92.85% on KDEF and 94.08% on GENKI-4K, just slightly lower than ResNet–19 with ReLU.

Table 2. Recognition accuracy of different network structures (%).

Dataset	Network	Activation	Afraid	Angry	Disgusted	Happy	Neutral	Sad	Surprised	Average
KDEF	VGG-19	ReLU	92.80	89.72	95.15	96.55	87.32	88.55	90.80	**91.55**
	ResNet-19	ReLU	95.71	90.71	98.57	99.58	87.14	92.86	91.43	**93.72**
	ResNet-19	NSP	95.71	92.86	94.29	97.14	87.14	88.57	94.29	**92.85**
genki-4k	VGG-19	ReLU	-	-	-	91.32	93.55	-	-	**92.43**
	ResNet-19	ReLU	-	-	-	93.70	95.65	-	-	**94.67**
	ResNet-19	NSP	-	-	-	93.15	95.00	-	-	**94.08**

Thirdly, we tested the anti-noise ability of different activation functions by adding different level of noises to the testing images in GENKI-4K. We set the values of σ to 0, 0.01, 0.05, 0.15, 0.2 respectively. We can see from Table 3 that ReLU gets the highest accuracy when we set $\sigma = 0$, and NSP became to surpass ReLu when we set $\sigma = 0.01$, and as the value of σ increases, the accuracy of ReLU decreases much quickly than NSP. From Table 3, we can see that in terms of anti-noise ability, NSP is better than ReLU.

Because the computational complexity of NSP is still higer than ReLU, we tried a less complex solution of combined activation functions by adding fine-tune process. As can be seen from Table 3, we use NSP to do just one epoch of fine-tune after pre-trained the data by ReLU for 30 epochs, and then we get a solution of higher anti-noise ability with slightly decreased accuracy and largely improved computing efficiency.

Table 3. Recognition accuracy on GENKI-4K with different level of testing noise (%).

Activation function			Testing noise (σ)					
Pretrain (epoch)	Finetune (epoch)	Testing	0	0.01	0.05	0.1	0.15	0.2
ReLU (30)	-	ReLU	94.5	93.0	92.0	90.4	85.6	71.0
NSP (30)	-	NSP	94.0	93.5	93.4	91.9	88.5	77.3
ReLU (30)	NSP (1)	ReLU	93.5	92.3	92.1	91.2	86.9	76.9

Finally, we tested the accuracy of different approaches in different epochs, see in Fig. 5. From which we can see that ResNet-19-NSP performs next only to ResNet-19-ReLU in terms of recognition accuracy, but surpasses VGG19-ReLU, which is mainly due to the second dimension of input noise involved in the computation. Moreover, regarding to the anti-noise ability, ResNet-19-NSP performs much better than ResNet-19-ReLu.

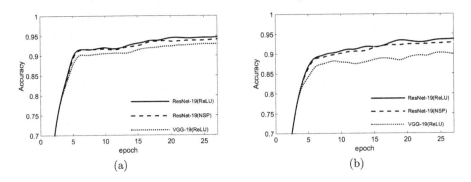

Fig. 5. Recognition accuracy in different epochs (a) KDEF (b) GENKI-4K.

4.3   Power Consumption Evaluation

Since the weights obtained by training CNNs using NSP can be directly used as the weights of SNNs of the similar structure. When SNNs are running on the neuromorphic hardware DARPA SyNAPSE [4, 24], the synapses consume about 0.37 pJ of energy per spike, and the number of connections in resnet-19 is about 1.15×10^8. Suppose the firing rate of spike is 100 HZ, when we run SNNs with the same structure as resnet-19 on SyNAPSE, the power consumption in each second will be:

$$0.37 \times 10^{-12} \times 1.15 \times 10^8 \times 100 \approx 0.0043 \, \text{J} \tag{9}$$

The power consumption will be about 5 J/s [2] when we run a CNN with 4.35×10^8 connections on the Field-Programmable Gate Array (FPGA) [35]. In this paper, the number of connections in ResNet–19 is about 1.15×10^8, so we can infer that when it runs on the FPGA-based hardware, the power consumption in per second is about:

$$5 \times \frac{1.15 \times 10^8}{4.35 \times 10^8} \approx 1.32 \, \text{J} \tag{10}$$

Therefore, the network weights obtained by our method training are directly used in SNN with the same structure. When the SNN running on SyNAPSE, The recognition accuracy is similar to that of ResNet-19, but it is $1.32/0.0043 \approx 307$ times lower than ResNet-19 running on FPGA-based hardware.

5 Conclusions

In this paper, we built a 19-layered ResNets by adding short-cuts between network layers in VGG-19, and use NSP as the activation function. ResNet-19-NSP performs next only to ResNet-19-ReLU in terms of recognition accuracy, but surpasses its origin, ResNet-19-Softplus, which is mainly due to the second dimension of input noise involved in the computation. Moreover, regarding to the anti-noise ability, ResNet-19-NSP performs the best among these networks. Considering the biological background, it counts in the noise of the current influx generated by Poissonian arriving spikes, therefore works robust to noise in natural scene. Although, the computational complexity of NSP is relatively low comparing to biological LIF response function Siegert, it is still the highest among these abstract activation functions. Thus, we propose the fine-tuning method to reduce the use of NSP in training procedure, and keep using ReLU in the inference stage. This method hugely reduces the computation of NSP, actually running only 1 extra epoch of NSP, but remains the recognition accuracy with clean testing data and greatly improved robustness when inference in noisy data.

In the future work, we will gain insight into practical side of NSP training especially in designing hyper parameters for deep and challenging tasks. We will also take the advantage of the effortless transformation from NSP trained networks to SNNs, thus running the facial expression recognition on neuromorphic hardware in an energy-efficient way.

Acknowledgments. The research leading to these results has received funding from the Natural Science Foundation of Guangdong Province, China (No: 2016A030313713) and also from the Natural Science Foundation of Guangdong Province, China (No: 2014A030310169), Production and Research Cooperation Special Project of Guangdong Province, China (No: 2014B090904080), and Science and Technology Projects of Guangdong Provincial Transportation Department, China (Science and technology-2016-02-030).

References

1. Brette, R., Gerstner, W.: Adaptive exponential integrate-and-fire model as an effective description of neuronal activity. J. Neurophysiol. **94**(5), 3637–3642 (2005)
2. Cao, Y., Chen, Y., Khosla, D.: Spiking deep convolutional neural networks for energy-efficient object recognition. Int. J. Comput. Vision **113**(1), 54–66 (2015)
3. Chen, Y., Liu, W., Zhang, L., Yan, M., Zeng, Y.: Hybrid facial image feature extraction and recognition for non-invasive chronic fatigue syndrome diagnosis. Comput. Biol. Med. **64**, 30–39 (2015)
4. Cruz-Albrecht, J.M., Yung, M.W., Srinivasa, N.: Energy-efficient neuron, synapse and stdp integrated circuits. IEEE Trans. Biomed. Circuits Syst. **6**(3), 246–256 (2012)
5. Cui, D., Huang, G.B., Liu, T.: Smile detection using pair-wise distance vector and extreme learning machine. In: 2016 International Joint Conference on Neural Networks (IJCNN), pp. 2298–2305. IEEE (2016)
6. Dayan, P., Abbott, L.F.: Theoretical Neuroscience, vol. 806. MIT Press, Cambridge (2001)
7. Deng, J., Dong, W., Socher, R., Li, L.J.: Imagenet: a large-scale hierarchical image database. In: Proceedings of the IEEE Conference on Computer Vision and Pattern Recognition, pp. 248–255 (2009)
8. He, K., Zhang, X., Ren, S., Sun, J.: Deep residual learning for image recognition. In: Proceedings of the IEEE Conference on Computer Vision and Pattern Recognition, pp. 770–778 (2016)
9. He, K., Zhang, X., Ren, S., Sun, J.: Identity mappings in deep residual networks. In: Leibe, B., Matas, J., Sebe, N., Welling, M. (eds.) ECCV 2016. LNCS, vol. 9908, pp. 630–645. Springer, Cham (2016). https://doi.org/10.1007/978-3-319-46493-0_38
10. Hinton, G.E., Osindero, S., Teh, Y.W.: A fast learning algorithm for deep belief nets. Neural Comput. **18**(7), 1527–1554 (2006)
11. Hu, Y., Zeng, Z., Yin, L., Wei, X.: Multi-view facial expression recognition. In: IEEE International Conference on Automatic Face & Gesture Recognition, pp. 1–6 (2008)
12. Hunsberger, E., Eliasmith, C.: Spiking deep networks with lif neurons. arXiv preprint arXiv:1510.08829 (2015)
13. Izhikevich, E.M.: Simple model of spiking neurons. IEEE Trans. Neural Networks **14**(6), 1569–1572 (2003)
14. Izhikevich, E.M.: Which model to use for cortical spiking neurons? IEEE Trans. Neural Networks **15**(5), 1063–1070 (2004)
15. Kahou, S.E., Pal, C., Bouthillier, X., Froumenty, P., Memisevic, R., Vincent, P., Courville, A., Bengio, Y., Ferrari, R.C., Mirza, M.: Combining modality specific deep neural networks for emotion recognition in video. In: ACM on International Conference on Multimodal Interaction, pp. 543–550 (2013)
16. Kim, B.K., Lee, H., Roh, J., Lee, S.Y.: Hierarchical committee of deep CNNs with exponentially-weighted decision fusion for static facial expression recognition. In: ACM on International Conference on Multimodal Interaction, pp. 427–434 (2015)
17. LeCun, Y., Cortes, C., Burges, C.J.: MNIST handwritten digit database. AT&T Labs, vol. 2 (2010). http://yann.lecun.com/exdb/mnist
18. Liew, C.F., Yairi, T.: A comparison study of feature spaces and classification methods for facial expression recognition. In: 2013 IEEE International Conference on Robotics and Biomimetics (ROBIO), pp. 1294–1299. IEEE (2013)

19. Liu, M., Li, S., Shan, S., Wang, R., Chen, X.: Deeply learning deformable facial action parts model for dynamic expression analysis. In: Cremers, D., Reid, I., Saito, H., Yang, M.-H. (eds.) ACCV 2014. LNCS, vol. 9006, pp. 143–157. Springer, Cham (2015). https://doi.org/10.1007/978-3-319-16817-3_10

20. Liu, Q., Furber, S.: Noisy softplus: a biology inspired activation function. In: Hirose, A., Ozawa, S., Doya, K., Ikeda, K., Lee, M., Liu, D. (eds.) ICONIP 2016. LNCS, vol. 9950, pp. 405–412. Springer, Cham (2016). https://doi.org/10.1007/978-3-319-46681-1_49

21. Liu, Y.H., Wang, X.J.: Spike-frequency adaptation of a generalized leaky integrate-and-fire model neuron. J. Comput. Neurosci. **10**(1), 25–45 (2001)

22. Lundqvist, D., Flykt, A., Öhman, A.: The karolinska directed emotional faces (kdef). CD ROM from Department of Clinical Neuroscience, Psychology section, Karolinska Institutet (1998)

23. Masquelier, T., Thorpe, S.J.: Unsupervised learning of visual features through spike timing dependent plasticity. PLoS Comput. Biol. **3**(2), e31 (2007)

24. Merolla, P., Arthur, J., Akopyan, F., Imam, N., Manohar, R., Modha, D.S.: A digital neurosynaptic core using embedded crossbar memory with 45pj per spike in 45nm. In: 2011 IEEE Custom Integrated Circuits Conference (CICC), pp. 1–4. IEEE (2011)

25. Paugam-Moisy, H., Bohte, S.: Computing with spiking neuron networks. In: Rozenberg, G., Back, T., Kok, J.N. (eds.) Handbook of Natural Computing, pp. 335–376. Springer, Heidelberg (2012). https://doi.org/10.1007/978-3-540-92910-9_10

26. Perez-Carrasco, J.A., Serrano, C., Acha, B., Serrano-Gotarredona, T., Linares-Barranco, B.: Spike-based convolutional network for real-time processing. In: 2010 20th International Conference on Pattern Recognition (ICPR), pp. 3085–3088. IEEE (2010)

27. Ruiz-Garcia, A., Elshaw, M., Altahhan, A., Palade, V.: Stacked deep convolutional auto-encoders for emotion recognition from facial expressions. In: 2017 International Joint Conference on Neural Networks (IJCNN), pp. 1586–1593. IEEE (2017)

28. Santra, B., Mukherjee, D.P.: Local dominant binary patterns for recognition of multi-view facial expressions. In: Proceedings of the Tenth Indian Conference on Computer Vision, Graphics and Image Processing, p. 25. ACM (2016)

29. Shan, C., Gong, S., Mcowan, P.W.: Facial expression recognition based on local binary patterns: a comprehensive study. Image Vis. Comput. **27**(6), 803–816 (2009)

30. Simonyan, K., Zisserman, A.: Very deep convolutional networks for large-scale image recognition. arXiv preprint arXiv:1409.1556 (2014)

31. Srivastava, R.K., Greff, K., Schmidhuber, J.: Highway networks. arXiv preprint arXiv:1505.00387 (2015)

32. Sun, S., Chen, W., Wang, L., Liu, X., Liu, T.Y.: On the depth of deep neural networks: a theoretical view. In: AAAI, pp. 2066–2072 (2016)

33. Szegedy, C., Liu, W., Jia, Y., Sermanet, P., Reed, S., Anguelov, D., Erhan, D., Vanhoucke, V., Rabinovich, A.: Going deeper with convolutions. In: Proceedings of the IEEE Conference on Computer Vision and Pattern Recognition, pp. 1–9 (2015)

34. Tariq, U., Lin, K.H., Li, Z., Zhou, X.: Emotion recognition from an ensemble of features. In: IEEE International Conference on Automatic Face & Gesture Recognition and Workshops, pp. 872–877 (2011)

35. Trimberger, S.M.: Field-Programmable Gate Array Technology. Springer Science & Business Media, New York (2012). https://doi.org/10.1007/978-1-4615-2742-8

36. Whitehill, J., Movellan, J.R.: A discriminative approach to frame-by-frame head pose tracking. In: Proceedings of 8th IEEE International Conference on Automatic Face & Gesture Recognition. FG 2008, pp. 1–7. IEEE (2008)

37. Xiao, J., Liu, T., Zhang, Y., Zou, B., Lei, J., Li, Q.: Multi-focus image fusion based on depth extraction with inhomogeneous diffusion equation. Sig. Process. **125**, 171–186 (2016)

38. Zhang, L., Tjondronegoro, D., Chandran, V., Eggink, J.: Towards robust automatic affective classification of images using facial expressions for practical applications. Multimedia Tools Appl. **75**(8), 4669–4695 (2016)

Local Fast R-CNN Flow
for Object-Centric Event Recognition
in Complex Traffic Scenes

Qin Gu[1,2(✉)], Jianyu Yang[1], Wei Qi Yan[2], Yanqiang Li[3], and Reinhard Klette[2]

[1] University of Electronic Science and Technology of China,
Chengdu 611731, Sichuan, People's Republic of China
guqin.uestc@outlook.com
[2] Auckland University of Technology, Auckland 1010, New Zealand
[3] Shandong Provincial Key Laboratory of Automotive Electronics and Technology,
Jinan 250000, People's Republic of China

Abstract. This paper presents a solution for an integrated object-centric event recognition problem for intelligent traffic supervision. We propose a novel event-recognition framework using deep local flow in a fast region-based convolutional neural network (R-CNN). First, we use a fine-tuned fast R-CNN to accurately extract multi-scale targets in the open environment. Each detected object corresponds to an event candidate. Second, a deep belief propagation method is proposed for the calculation of local fast R-CNN flow (LFRCF) between local convolutional feature matrices of two non-adjacent frames in a sequence. Third, by using the LFRCF features, we can easily identify the moving pattern of each extracted object and formulate a conclusive description of each event candidate. The contribution of this paper is to propose an optimized framework for accurate event recognition. We verify the accuracy of multi-scale object detection and behavior recognition in extensive experiments on real complex road-intersection surveillance videos.

Keywords: Deep learning · Event recognition
Convolutional neural network · Belief propagation

1 Introduction

Object-centric event recognition is pivotal for traffic violation recording, traffic monitoring, and traffic control [9]. Vision-based intelligent transportation surveillance systems have been an active research area in past decades due to high credibility and low costs of those systems.

There are various definitions for an *event*. In general, an event in video content refers to an object of interest with a certain behavior in the given scenes. Here, we focus on traffic scenes at road intersections; our object-centric events include object detection, object recognition, and object behavior recognition in an interval of time.

© Springer International Publishing AG, part of Springer Nature 2018
S. Satoh (Ed.): PSIVT 2017, LNCS 10799, pp. 439–452, 2018.
https://doi.org/10.1007/978-3-319-92753-4_34

Representing different object-centric events usually leads to high computational costs because a single event requires (in general) object motion detection, object tracking, and object behavior understanding.

Following those three steps, robust object detection is the key step for event modeling. Low-level feature-based methods such as Gabor wavelets, histogram of gradients (HOG), or optical flow have been used in pioneering research in this field. Recently, deep learning [14] achieves remarkable advances in solving the given problems. Deep learning defines the state-of-the-art approach for object detection or human activity recognition. However, deep learning is also run-time consuming when detecting, tracking, and understanding objects, class by class. Taking the need for real-time traffic monitoring and analysis into consideration, we concluded that traditional scanning of all potential patches is impractical.

In this paper, we combine moving object detection as well as tracking and event recognition with a *convolutional neural network* (CNN) using a *local fast region-based CNN flow* (LFRCF) descriptor. For this purpose, the already well-studied *fast region-based CNN* (fast R-CNN) architecture is fine-tuned for fast event candidate generation. Next, spatio-temporal motion information is compressed into local region flow in the deep convolutional space for event representation, called *deep local flow*. Finally, the LFRCF is used for further event recognition and identification. The contributions in this paper are as follows:

1. A novel LFRCF descriptor is proposed using deep belief propagation.
2. We propose a fine-tuned fast R-CNN architecture for automatically generating a group of regions of interest for real-time traffic event recognition.
3. We investigate a particular framework of deep CNNs, trained for integrated object detection and behavior recognition in video data.

The remainder of this paper is organized as follows. Section 2 presents related work. Section 3 details the proposed event recognition method using our LFRCF descriptor. Section 4 shows experimental results for verifying the proposed method. Section 5 concludes.

2   Related Work

In general, object-centric event recognition algorithms follow three steps, briefly outlined below.

First, selective object detection and motion estimation can be beneficial for both speed-up and accuracy. A Gaussian mixture model (GMM) is used in [26] for vehicle detection in complex urban traffic scenes.

A diversity of feature-vector representation schemes has been proposed for object detection in complex scenes. The active basis model [24] has been widely employed for vehicle detection [11,16] in traffic surveillance. With the assistance of a shared skeleton method, it can be easily trained with a considerable detection performance. However, it can only be used for one object with a fixed pose. An AND-OR graph [15] has been proposed for vehicle detection in congested traffic conditions. A deformable part-based model for object detection was introduced in [5]. These two methods still need multi-models for various targets and multiple viewing points, which is rather time-consuming.

Deep learning methods improved dramatically the state-of-the-art in visual object detection and recognition. The CNN [13] powered the performance of object detection and recognition. Recently, a focus in this area [6, 20] is on process acceleration with a fundamental algorithm for region search [22]. However, it is still a challenge to detect, track, and analyse the behavior for moving targets in continuous frames, even with GPU-enabled computing.

Second, object tracking algorithms are proposed for trajectory reconstruction. Region-based tracking algorithms [8], feature-based tracking algorithms [25], and model-based tracking algorithms [19] have all been widely applied for various outputs.

Third, for the tracking of moving objects in adjacent frames of a video sequence, the problem of understanding object behaviors from image sequences arises naturally. Subsequently, methods such as hidden Markov models (HMM) [2], Bayesian approaches [3], or 3-dimensional (3D) models [10] are used to understand the trajectory of moving targets.

There is also work [17, 21] that aims at a more focused anomaly detection, but so far in a global sense only, not for individually acting objects. Global anomalies (involving multiple objects) are, for example, a traffic jam, an accident, or changes of global motion in scenes of crowds. Global anomaly detection also requires further research.

Different to existing work, our contribution in this paper is an integrated framework for multi-class event recognition in complex road scenes. Event localization and recognition are conducted in a deep CNN using the proposed LFRCF (i.e. local fast R-CNN flow) descriptor.

3   Methodology

This section presents our event recognition method using a fast R-CNN [6] architecture and the proposed LFRCF descriptor. We divide this section into three parts. First, we provide an overview of the event recognition framework. Then we present the fundamental method of fast R-CNN. Finally, we detail the calculation of the LFRCF descriptor with deep belief propagation for behavior recognition and event identification.

3.1   Overview

As illustrated in Fig. 1, the proposed framework recognizes a multi-scale and object-centric event by using two non-adjacent frames, denoted as Frame `input1` and Frame `input2`. First, fast R-CNN is implemented for convolutional feature extraction, object detection, and bounding box regression. Hence, by using the extracted location of each bounding box, we use a new spatial-temporal pooling algorithm to extract the local convolutional feature (i.e. a local Conv feature map) in the 4th convolutional layer, for two non-adjacent frames. Finally, the

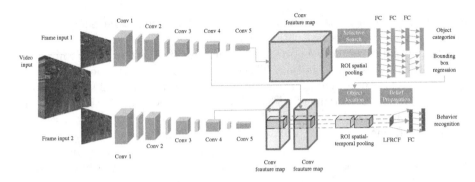

Fig. 1. Framework of the proposed method

LFRCF descriptor is calculated between the obtained two local Conv feature maps, which refers to the moving patterns of candidate events; this descriptor is the applied for the final behavior recognition and event identification.

3.2   Region-Based Convolutional Neural Network

In this paper, we use convolutional layers, max pooling layers, rectified linear units (ReLUs), and fully connected (FC) layers to construct our traffic-event recognition network.

Input data pass through all the organized layers to generate the final recognition outputs. In the convolution layers, a group of kernels is used to filter the input such as to produce feature maps for deeper feature extraction. The function of the pooling layer is to calculate the overall response of a neighborhood area in a feature map, which is one of the outputs of the convolution layer. Being aware of the problem of over-fitting, dropout layers are proposed for training towards optimization. Finally, by using the softmax optimization method, a multi-class identification result is given with an FC layer.

One of the most effective approaches for solving a multi-scale object detection task is the family of R-CNNs. By using the selective search algorithm, a group of regions is extracted for further scale normalization (i.e. resized to 227×227 in our case). Then, a traditional CNN is used for feature extraction and object recognition. This method achieves high accuracy, however, it is very time consuming because of redundant feature extraction in a deep ConvNet.

In this paper, we use a fast R-CNN framework for multi-scale object detection and event hypothesis generation. This framework solves the previous problems by computing the feature map only once per image. The corresponding region-based deep convolutional feature map is extracted in form of a new ROI-pooling map. We also propose a multi-task loss function for bounding-box regression.

The ConvNet is regarded as a feature descriptor of specific video frames. In this paper, we use the *VGG-16* deep ConvNet for our fast R-CNN, which is pre-trained on a large *Pascal Voc 2007* dataset, as Table 1 shows.

Table 1. Details of all selected layers of the pre-trained fast R-CNN

Layer	conv1	pool1	conv2	pool2	conv3	pool3	conv4	pool4	conv5
Input	600	600	300	300	150	150	75	75	38
	×975	×975	×488	×488	×244	×244	×122	×122	×61
	×3	×64	×64	×128	×128	×256	×256	×512	×512
Output	600	300	300	150	150	75	75	38	38
	×975	×488	×488	×244	×244	×122	7×122	×61	×61
	×64	×64	×128	×128	×256	×256	×512	×512	×512
Channel	64	64	128	128	256	256	512	512	512

Categories and bounding box locations of 20 classes of objects are used to finish the training stage.

By using a multi-task loss-function training algorithm, the loss (or error) function during the fine-tuning work of the initial VGG-16 neural network is represented as follows:

$$E(\mathcal{X}, \mathcal{C}, \mathcal{L}) = E_{cls}(f(\mathcal{X}), \mathcal{C}) + \zeta \cdot E_{loc}(\mathcal{X}, \mathcal{L}) \tag{1}$$

where, $\mathcal{X}$ is the location of the considered region of interest (ROI) defined by (r_1, r_2, c_1, c_2). $\mathcal{C}$ and $\mathcal{L}$ are the ground truth for object category and location, respectively. $E_{cls}(f(\mathcal{X}), \mathcal{C})$ is the loss function regarding the recognition of an object in $\mathcal{X}$ as being in the correct class $\mathcal{C}$. The second term E_{loc} is the loss function of bounding box regression; ζ is a parameter to control the balance between these two terms. In this paper, we simply use $\zeta = 1$.

3.3 Local Fast R-CNN Flow

Accurate object detection and recognition results define already an important step towards accurate event analysis. However, in order to give a detailed description of an object-centric event for recognition, we still need to analyze the motion pattern of any detected and recognized object of interest.

Flow is an effective approach for moving pattern description. However, pixel-wise flow matching in a large-scaled spatial image is time-consuming and inaccurate. Therefore, we directly analyze the flow in the local region of interest as fast R-CNN flow, or *deep flow* for short.

Feature Reorganization. For extracting flow features in the extracted bounding box by using fast R-CNN, we reorganize convolution features in extended bounding boxes in two non-adjacent frames.

The convolutional feature map in the k-th layer is taken into account, formally expressed by

$$f_c(V(t), k) = C_k^t \in \mathbb{R}^{h_k \times w_k \times d_k}, \text{ for } k = 1, \ldots, 5 \tag{2}$$

Here, $V(t)$ is the t-th frame in video V, and C_k^t is the feature map in the k-th convolutional layer of the t-th frame.

By implementing this method of feature description for two selected non-adjacent frames (e.g. $t - a$ and $t + b$), we obtain two convolutional feature maps C_k^{t-a} and C_k^{t+b}; k is the index of the convolutional layers. These two maps indicate the motion patterns within the interval of $a + b + 1$ frames.

The location of recognized Object n in Frame $t - a$ is expressed by

$$\mathcal{X}_f(n) = [r_1(n), r_2(n), c_1(n), c_2(n)] \tag{3}$$

where r_1, r_2, c_1, c_2 are the row and column coordinates of the object's bounding box in this frame. Considering that an object may easily move out of its current bounding box in a short period of time, we construct a spatial extended bounding box for each object. Let the standard extending scale s_t be defined as follows:

$$s_t(n) = \eta \cdot \max\left(\left\lfloor \frac{r_2(n) - r_1(n)}{2} \right\rfloor, \left\lfloor \frac{c_2(n) - c_1(n)}{2} \right\rfloor\right) \tag{4}$$

where η is a parameter to change the scale. Thus, the nth extended region is represented as

$$\mathcal{X}_e(n) = [\max(1, r_1(n) - s_t(n)), \min(M, r_2(n) + s_t(n)),$$
$$\max(1, c_1(n) - s_t(n)), \min(N, c_2(n) + s_t(n))] \tag{5}$$

M and N are the row and column numbers of the whole image.

By using the spatial extended bounding box region, we further reorganize the kth convolutional feature matrix for object-centric behavior recognition. The reorganized features, for considered object n in two non-adjacent frames, are further written as two local feature matrices $L_k^{t-a,n}$ and $L_k^{t+b,n}$. $L_k^{t-a,n}$ and $L_k^{t+b,n}$ consist of all pixels in the tensor $C_k^{t-a}(x, y, z)$ and $C_k^{t+b}(x, y, z)$, with

$$\lceil \chi_1 \cdot \mathcal{X}_e(1,1) \rceil \le x \le \lfloor \chi_1 \cdot \mathcal{X}_1(1,2) \rfloor \tag{6}$$
$$\lceil \chi_2 \cdot \mathcal{X}_e(1,3) \rceil \le y \le \lfloor \chi_2 \cdot \mathcal{X}_e(1,4) \rfloor \tag{7}$$

for $1 \le z \le d_k$. $\lceil \cdot \rceil$ and $\lfloor \cdot \rfloor$ are the ceiling and floor function, respectively. χ_1 and χ_2 are the layer's scale factors, with

$$\chi_1 = \frac{h_k}{M}, \quad \chi_2 = \frac{w_k}{N} \tag{8}$$

After feature reorganization, we extract the local convolution feature matrix $L_k^{t-a,n}$ and $L_k^{t+b,n}$ for each object which has already been recognized by the fast R-CNN framework. These matrices are used for recognizing events occurring between the selected two non-adjacent frames.

LFRCF Matching. Following related work [7], we transfer the behavior recognition problem into a label parsing problem using probabilistic graphical model. Two local convolution feature matrices $L_k^{t-a,n}$ and $L_k^{t+b,n}$ are used to analyze the behavior of the nth object which is detected in Frame $t - a$. For convenience, we directly set the value of a and b as 0 and 5, respectively, in this paper.

Let $w(p) = [u(p), v(p)]$ be the LFRCF at a pixel location $p \in \Omega$, where Ω is the set of all pixel locations of a map $L_k^{t-a,n}$. To calculate the LFRCF w from $L_k^{t-a,n}$ to $L_k^{t+b,n}$, we introduce a unary *cost function* $E(w)$ as follows:

$$E(w) = \sum_{p \in \Omega} \min(\left\|L_k^{t+b}(p)\right\|_1 - \left\|L_k^{t-a}(p + w(p))\right\|_1, d)$$
$$+ \sum_{q \in A(p)} \{\min(\alpha \left|u(p) - u(q)\right|, e)$$
$$+ \min(\alpha \left|v(p) - v(q)\right|, e)\} \tag{9}$$

Here, $A(p)$ is the set of pixel locations being 4-adjacent with p; d and e are two thresholds for truncating the L_1 norms.

We have two terms in the cost function, namely the data and the smoothness term. By using the data term, the convolutional event descriptor is constrained to be matched; the smoothness term is employed to constrain adjacent pixels to having similar LFRCFs.

For minimizing the cost function $E(w)$ and obtaining the most accurate directional LFRCF vector w, we use belief propagation (BP) [18]. Compared with the method in [18], the proposed cost function ignores the small-displacement term, as the object may move obviously between non-adjacent frames.

By using an improved loopy belief propagation algorithm, the cost function is minimized after 40 iterations for each object. In this paper, due to the next two reasons, instead of using the calculated LFRCF in the area $\mathcal{X}_e(n)$, we retrospect the location $\mathcal{X}_f(n)$ and extract the central LFRCF for further behavior representation.

First, we only focus on the moving pattern of an object which has already been located in the area $\mathcal{X}_f(n)$, which corresponds to the central area of $\mathcal{X}_e(n)$. Second, by considering the convolutional processing in the neural network we may influence the boundary of on object in an image.

Let $m_l(n)$, $n_l(n)$ be the height and width of map $L_k^{t-a,n}$, respectively. Thus, the central LFRCF area for further behavior representation is given by

$$[\eta \cdot \max(m_l, n_l), m_{l-\eta} \cdot \max(m_l, n_l), \eta \cdot \max(m_l, n_l), n_{l-\eta} \cdot \max(m_l, n_l)] \tag{10}$$

The behavior recognition result is denoted by $w(x_l, y_l)$, with $\eta \cdot \max(m_l, n_l) \le x_l \le m_{l-\eta} \cdot \max(m_l, n_l)$, and $\eta \cdot \max(m_l, n_l) \le y_l \le n_{l-\eta} \cdot \max(m_l, n_l)$.

Motion Visualization. The parsing result, which corresponds to dynamic local motion, is represented as shown in Fig. 2 by using a color-key. Then, based on the visualization results of the proposed LFRCF descriptor, the behavior can be easily distinguished. In order to further clarify an object-centric event in complex on-road scenes, we further provide a motion-representation method for events.

A behavior vector is calculated as follows:

$$u_m = \frac{1}{Z} \sum_{x,y} u(x,y), \quad v_m = \frac{1}{Z} \sum_{x,y} v(x,y)$$

$$x \in [\eta \cdot \max(m_l, n_l), m_{l-\eta} \cdot \max(m_l, n_l)]$$

$$y \in [\eta \cdot \max(m_l, n_l), n_{l-\eta} \cdot \max(m_l, n_l)] \tag{11}$$

Calculated u_m and v_m are the mean horizontal and vertical flow of the calculated LFRCF, u and v are the horizontal and vertical LFRCF flow components, respectively. Z is the area of the current region. See Fig. 3 for examples of event representation.

In Fig. 4, the green rectangular lines are regression results of object detection and event location. The directed red bar in the blue circle represents the central mean flow $w_m = [u_m, v_m]$. It accurately represents the behavior of the detected object, and even provides a coarse information of the current speed of the object.

4   Experiments

The experimental report is divided into three segments. Detailed information of the dataset is given at the beginning. Then, we compare the performance of event localization for different methods. Finally, we present the performance of event recognition for extensive data recorded at a real traffic intersection using the proposed method.

Datasets. It is always a challenging problem to detect and track vehicles and pedestrians in outdoor scenes for traffic event recognition. In this paper, focusing on various scenes, we use three groups of datasets which are selected from the publicly available *HIGHWAY* dataset and the *UA-DETRAC* dataset. These video datasets are captured under various lighting conditions, viewing angles, and for different road scenes.

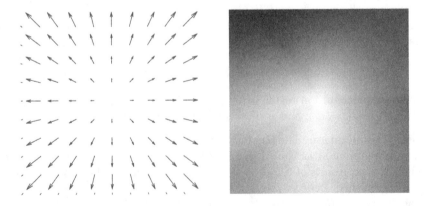

Fig. 2. Visualization of deep convolution flow. *Left*: Flow directions and magnitudes for selected pixels. *Right*: Color-key-based representation of optical flow for all pixels

Fig. 3. LFRCF visualization for multi-scale events

Fig. 4. Event localization and recognition examples. (Color figure online)

To evaluate the proposed method, we also collected an extensive data-set, called the *JINAN* data-set, at inner-city road intersections with a camera located about 8 m over the road surface. Our videos record top or rear views of vehicles moving below the camera level. It is possible to observe in the recorded data vehicles and pedestrians in a distance such as on the other side of the intersection. These videos were recorded at a frequency of 25 frames per second.

Summarizing ground truth for event localization, brief event descriptions (for three selected time intervals of traffic videos) are listed in Table 2.

Event Localization. Normally, robust object detection and tracking are necessary for event localization. In order to identify object movements, we compare the performance of vehicle localization of the *active basis model* of [11],

Table 2. Used datasets for object detection and tracking, and event characterisation

	Resolution	Frames	Frames showing vehicle events	Frames showing pedestrian events
HIGHWAY	640 × 480	1,652	742	0
UA-DETRAC	720 × 960	1,466	426	0
JINAN	2,592 × 2,048	1,304	179	97

Table 3. Comparisons of event localization on the *HIGHWAY* data-set

	Active basis model [11]	V-J cascade detector [23]	Deformable part model [4]	Proposed method
Recall	83.2%	94.5%	46.1%	92.7%
Precise	56.1%	45.3%	91.5%	98.4%

Table 4. Comparisons of event localization on the *UA-DETRAC* data-set

	Active basis model [11]	V-J cascade detector [23]	Deformable part model [4]	Proposed method
Recall	77.3%	84.8%	90.3%	88.7%
Precise	84.2%	50.6%	91.9%	97.1%

Table 5. Comparisons of event localization on the *JINAN* data-set

	Active basis model [11]	V-J cascade detector [23]	Deformable part model [4]	Proposed method
Recall	-	-	74.8%	81.8%
Precise	-	-	97.8%	94.3%

the *Viola-Jones cascade detector* of [23], the *deformable part model* of [4], and our proposed method (Tables 3, 4 and 5).

The active basis model and the V-J cascade detector perform well for rear-view vehicles, but it is difficult to train them for accurate vehicle event localization in cases of other viewing-angles (see the *JINAN* data-set results). The deformable part-based model is very accurate for detecting objects with a rigid structure, but it costs too much time to process one frame for one kind of targets even when using a cascading speed-up technology. Besides, we even need to cope with whole frames several times to extract different objects. The method proposed by us shows competitive results but proves to be much more time-efficient for extracting multiple moving objects of interest. A further validation of recognition accuracy is given in the next section.

Event Recognition. In this paper, multi-class object-centric (i.e. vehicle and pedestrian) events are taken into consideration. For an event sample, we selected

Table 6. Comparison of comprehensive event recognition results

	Accuracy	Computational cost
Optic flow [1]	63.1%	0.9 s (CPU)
Dense SIFT flow [18]	98.9%	10.9 s (CPU)
Proposed method	98.7%	0.4 s (CPU)

Fig. 5. Event recognition performance. *Top to bottom*: Results for the *HIGHWAY*, *UA-DETRAC*, and *JINAN* data-sets

five subsequent frames. The manually labeled 1,347 vehicle-centric and 97 pedestrian-centric events are studied for recognition by the proposed method.

According to the calculated behavior vector $[u_m, v_m]$, we generally define nine directions of motion (i.e. bottom-up, up-bottom, right-left, left-right, bottomright-topleft, bottomleft-upright, upright-bottomleft, topleft-bottomright, and remaining static). Based on manually labeled results, accurate event recognition is defined by matching flow direction and flow magnitude (Fig. 5).

The accuracy A is defined as follows:

$$A = \frac{P_p + P_v}{N_p + N_v} \tag{12}$$

where P_p and P_v are the number of accurately recognized events for pedestrians and vehicles, respectively. N_p and N_v are the number of all manually labeled events for pedestrians and vehicles.

We also use optic flow and dense SIFT flow for comparison on behavior recognition; see Table 6. Here, the 1st and the 5th frame are used for deep flow calculation.

Fig. 6. Examples of false event recognition

By using the proposed event recognition framework, each moving object of interest is detected, frame by frame. The entire algorithm is implemented in Matlab 2016a with *MatConvNet* in OS Windows 10, using 16 GB RAM and an i5 CPU processor. Processing is on average at 0.2 fps on a CPU-only mode. Some false event recognition examples (i.e. false-positive detection and false-flow calculation) are given in Fig. 6 illustrating a need for further refinements.

5   Conclusions

This paper presents a novel traffic-event recognition method using a descriptor defined by local fast R-CNN flow (LFRCF). Specifically, we use a fine-tuned fast R-CNN for multi-scaled object (i.e. vehicles or pedestrians) detection in complex traffic scenes. Then, by using a new spatial-temporal pooling algorithm, we extract the proposed LFRCF descriptor in the 4th convolutional layer for each object. Local convolutional features of two non-adjacent frames are used for event recognition with an improved loopy belief propagation algorithm.

By using the identified three datasets (i.e. data collected under various lighting, viewing angles, and for different road scenes), we evaluate the robustness and accuracy of traffic-event recognition and the computing cost of the proposed method.

It might be of interest to extend DCF analysis to the recognition of more generalized events. A high-level understanding (e.g. by linking multiple traffic events of the same vehicle together) is also worth considering.

Acknowledgement. The experimental work was partially supported by Shandong Provincial Key Laboratory of Automotive Electronics and Technology, Institute of Automation, Shandong Academy of Sciences.

References

1. Baker, S., Scharstein, D., Lewis, J.P., Szeliski, R.: A database and evaluation methodology for optical flow. Int. J. Comput. Vis. **92**(1), 1–31 (2011)
2. Bashir, F.I., Khokhar, A.A., Schonfeld, D.: Object trajectory-based activity classification and recognition using hidden Markov models. IEEE Trans. Image Process. **16**(7), 1912–1919 (2007)
3. Dore, A., Regazzoni, C.: Interaction analysis with a Bayesian trajectory model. IEEE Trans. Intell. Syst. **16**(7), 1912–1919 (2007)
4. Felzenszwalb, P.F., Girshick, R.B., McAllester, D.: Cascade object detection with deformable part models. In: Proceedings IEEE Conference on Computer Vision, Pattern Recognition, pp. 2241–2248 (2010)
5. Felzenszwalb, P.F., Girshick, R.B., McAllester, D., Ramanan, D.: Object detection with discriminatively trained part-based models. IEEE Trans. Patt. Anal. Mach. Intell. **32**(9), 1627–1645 (2010)
6. Girshick, R.: Fast R-CNN. In: Proceedings of IEEE International Conference on Computer Vision, pp. 1440–1448 (2015)
7. Gu, Q., Yang, J., Cui, G., Ling, K., Hua, Z., Klette, R.: Multi-scale vehicle logo recognition by directional dense SIFT flow parsing. In: Proceedings of IEEE International Conference on Image Processing, pp. 3827–3831 (2016)
8. Gupte, S.O., Masoud, O., Martin, R.F.K., Papanikolopoulos, N.P.: Detection and classification of vehicles. IEEE Trans. Intell. Transp. Syst. **3**(1), 37–47 (2002)
9. Hu, W., Tan, T., Wang, L., Maybank, S.: A survey on visual surveillance of object motion and behaviors. IEEE Trans. Syst. Man Cybern. Part C **34**(3), 334–352 (2004)
10. Hu, W., Xiao, X., Xie, D., Tan, T., Maybank, S.: Traffic accident prediction using 3D model-based vehicle tracking. IEEE Trans. Veh. Technol. **53**(3), 677–694 (2004)
11. Kamkar, S., Safabakhsh, R.: Vehicle detection, counting and classification in various conditions. IET Intell. Transport Syst. **10**(6), 406–413 (2016)
12. Klette, R.: Concise Computer Vision. Springer, London (2014). https://doi.org/10.1007/978-1-4471-6320-6
13. Krizhevsky, A., Sutskever, I., Hinton, G.E.: ImageNet classification with deep convolutional neural networks. In: Proceedings of Advances Neural Information Processing Systems, pp. 1097–1105 (2012)
14. LeCun, Y., Bengio, Y., Hinton, G.: Deep learning. Nature **521**(7553), 436–444 (2015)

15. Li, Y., Li, B., Tian, B., Yao, Q.: Vehicle detection based on the and-or graph for congested traffic conditions. IEEE Trans. Intell. Transp. Syst. **14**(2), 984–993 (2013)

16. Li, Y., Li, B., Tian, B., Yao, Q.: Vehicle detection based on the deformable hybrid image template. In: Proceedings of IEEE International Conference on Vehicular Electronics Safety, pp. 114–118 (2013)

17. Li, Y., Liu, W., Huang, Q.: Traffic anomaly detection based on image descriptor in videos. Multimedia Tools Appl. **75**(5), 2487–2505 (2016)

18. Liu, C., Yuen, J., Torralba, A.: SIFT flow: dense correspondence across scenes and its applications. IEEE Trans. Patt. Anal. Mach. Intell. **33**(5), 978–994 (2011)

19. Niknejad, H.T., Takeuchi, A., Mita, S., McAllester, D.: On-road multivehicle tracking using deformable object model and particle filter with improved likelihood estimation. IEEE Trans. Intell. Transp. Syst. **12**(2), 748–758 (2012)

20. Ren, S., He, K., Girshick, R., Sun, J.: Faster R-CNN: towards real-time object detection with region proposal networks. In: Proceedings of Advances Neural Information Processing Systems, pp. 91–99 (2015)

21. Sabokrou, M., Fayyaz, M., Fathy, M., Klette, R.: Deep-cascade: cascading 3D deep neural networks for fast anomaly detection and localization in crowded scenes. IEEE Trans. Image Process. (2017). ieeexplore.ieee.org/document/7858798/

22. Uijlings, J.R.R., Van De Sande, K.E.A., Gevers, T., Smeulders, A.W.M.: Selective search for object recognition. Int. J. Comput. Vis. **104**(2), 154–171 (2013)

23. Viola, P., Jones, M.: Robust real-time face detection. Int. J. Comput. Vis. **57**, 137–154 (2004)

24. Wu, Y.N., Si, Z., Gong, H., Zhu, S.-C.: Learning active basis model for object detection and recognition. Int. J. Comput. Vis. **90**(2), 198–235 (2010)

25. Xu, Y., Yu, G., Wu, X., Wang, Y., Ma, Y.: An enhanced Viola-Jones vehicle detection method from unmanned aerial vehicles imagery. IEEE Trans. Intell. Transp. Syst. (2016). ieeexplore.ieee.org/document/7726065/

26. Zhang, Y., et al.: Vehicles detection in complex urban traffic scenes using Gaussian mixture model with confidence measurement. IET Intell. Transport Syst. **10**(6), 445–452 (2016)

Mixed-Noise Removal in Images
Based on a Convolutional Neural Network

Ling Ding[1,2], Huyin Zhang[1(✉)], Bijun Li[3], Jian Zhou[3], and Wenhao Gu[4]

[1] School of Computer Science, Wuhan University, Wuhan, China
zhy2536@whu.edu.cn
[2] College of Computer Science and Technology,
Hubei University of Science and Technology, Xianning, China
[3] State Key Laboratory of Information Engineering in Surveying,
Mapping and Remote Sensing, Wuhan University, Wuhan, China
[4] Faculty of Resources and Environmental Science, Hubei University, Wuhan, China

Abstract. Aiming at limiting drawbacks of denoising algorithms that can only remove one or two specific types of noise (and which are inefficient for other types), we propose a combined neural-network model for mixed-noise removal in images. Nine convolutional layers are adapted, and noisy images are trained through feature extraction, shrinking, nonlinear mapping, expanding, and reconstruction. Experimental results show that the algorithm achieves better denoising results and is more suitable than other algorithms for dealing with different types of mixed noise in images. Subjective visual effects and an objective evaluation demonstrate the achieved improvements.

Keywords: Image denoising · Mixed noise
Convolutional neural network

1 Introduction

Image denoising is a critical task in image processing. Images are destroyed by noise under some conditions such as malfunctions in the camera sensor, hardware memory errors, disturbance of transmission channel noise, and so on. Results are described as "salt-and-pepper" noise", Poisson noise, Gaussian noise, or speckle noise. An image may be polluted by a variety of noise types. In recent years, image denoising remains to be a very popular in the field of computer vision and image processing [1].

For Gaussian noise, the total variation method is one of the traditional denoising algorithms. However, it has a tendency to produce over-smoothed results [2]. Aiming at improvements, the K-SVD method (a generalization of the k-means

This work is supported by the National Natural Science Foundation of China (61540059, 41671441, 91120002); Plan Project of Guangdong Provincial Science and technology(2015B010131007); Hubei Provincial Department of Education Guiding Project (B2016187).

© Springer International Publishing AG, part of Springer Nature 2018
S. Satoh (Ed.): PSIVT 2017, LNCS 10799, pp. 453–464, 2018.
https://doi.org/10.1007/978-3-319-92753-4_35

clustering method) provided remarkable achievements. A dictionary is used to learn the relevant knowledge, and the sample information is sparsely encoded [3]. But this method cannot be applied if the level of image noise is unknown. Non-local block matching and DCT coefficient thresholding are combined in BM3D; see [4]. DDID [5] achieves better denoising results, but the algorithm is more complex. 3-dimensional (3D) block-matching video denoising algorithms based on dual-domain filtering [6] has a better effect on Gaussian noise removal.

However, all of the above algorithms can only re-move the Gaussian noise of an image. For "salt-and-pepper" noise, adaptive median filter [7] (AMF), central weighted median filter [8], multi-level median filter [9], and other methods are applicable. The idea of these filters is to assign the value of surrounding pixels to the noisy pixels. But these filtering methods are only effective for the removal of "salt-and-pepper" noise, and not applicable to mixed noise.

For mixed noise, an time-expensive denoising algorithm is to remove first the "salt-and-pepper" noise by median filtering, and then remove the Gaussian noise by the corresponding method [10]. Besides a computing time issue, this method may also remove details in an image. The robust Bayesian algorithm of [11] has a slightly better denoising effect, but it cannot be applied to all scenes.

Based on K-SVD, the WK-SVD algorithm makes some improvements in which a mixed Gaussian model was added to image denoising. But this method is very sensitive for the type of the median filter; sometimes the denoised image would be over-smoothed [12]. The *spatio-spectral total variation* (SSTV) algorithm is better to restore a mixed-noise spectrum image [13].

Currently, machine learning and *convolutional neural networks* (CNNs) are also applied in image processing, and the use of CNNs for denoising is at an exploring stage. The achievement of removing Gaussian noise based on a CNN in [14] and Multi-focus image fusion based on depth extraction with inhomogeneous diffusion equation [15] won widespread attention.

This paper proposes a denoising algorithm based on a CNN by drawing lessons from convolutional network structure of the FSRCNN image super-resolution algorithm in [16]. An improved network is put forward which is applied for mixed noise removal; it provides significant results. This article recalls at first the FSRCNN neural network structure in some detail in Sect. 2. The improved network structure of our algorithm is explained in the third section. Next, the fourth section will show results for making objective and subjective comparisons with other denoising methods. Section 5 concludes.

2   Image Super-Resolution Algorithm

We refer to the network structures of the FSRCNN and SRCNN image super-resolution algorithms. Before introduce the FSRCNN algorithm, we need to introduce the SRCNN algorithm of [17].

2.1   Super-Resolution Convolutional Neural Network

The *super-resolution convolutional neural network* (SRCNN) algorithm is put forward by Dong et al. at the Chinese University of Hong Kong. The algorithm is

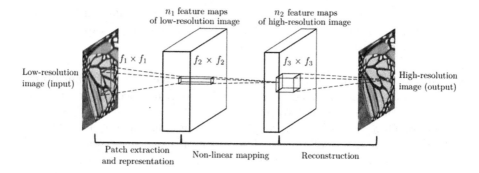

n_1 feature maps
of low-resolution image

n_2 feature maps
of high-resolution image

Low-resolution
image (input)

$f_1 \times f_1$ $f_2 \times f_2$ $f_3 \times f_3$

High-resolution
image (output)

Patch extraction
and representation   Non-linear mapping   Reconstruction

Fig. 1. Structure of the SRCNN [17]

defined by three convolutional layers; this ideas coincides with a CNN's structure. This article is based on this convolutional layers algorithm; we provide further optimization and improvement. The outline of the algorithm is shown in Fig. 1.

The learning process of the entire mapping relation F consists of three parts: feature extraction, nonlinear mapping, and high-resolution image reconstruction. Suppose that Y represents the initial high-resolution image, X represents a real high-resolution image, to be approximated by $F(Y)$ by means of the image super-resolution algorithm (based on a convolutional neural network). Deep learning aims at studying the formation of F, prompting $F(Y)$ to be as much as possible close to X, formally expressed by $F(Y) \approx X$.

Feature Extraction. In this layer, the image blocks are extracted from the initial image. Each block represents a high-dimensional vector. In this way, we can obtain the feature graph of the input image. According to certain sizes, the initial high-resolution image Y is divided into subblocks. The feature information of the image is extracted by convolution with multiple convolution kernels. The process of feature extraction is expressed by the following formula:

$$F_1(Y) = Max\{0, W_1 \star Y + B_1\} \tag{1}$$

where $\star$ represents the convolution symbol, W_i is the convolution kernel, B_i is the bias vector of neurons, and f_i is the filter size in the current layer.

The characteristic graph of convolution is processed by the ReLU activation function $Max\{0, x\}$. Under normal conditions, c is the number of channels that enter the image. Here we only consider the Y channel of image brightness.

If the number of convolution kernels equals n_1, the size of W_i equals

$$c \times f_1 \times f_1 \times n_1 \tag{2}$$

The activation function can also be considered as part of the second step of a nonlinear mapping. The derivative and computation of ReLU is easier than the sigmoid function [18], and the number of neurons in the network equals 0. While implementing network sparsity, the coupling degree of the parameters is reduced, and the fitting phenomenon can be suppressed. Considering network training, ReLU converges faster.

Non-linear Mapping. By nonlinear mapping we map each high-dimensional vector onto another high-dimensional vector, and each mapped vector represents a high-resolution block. Part 1 to get the characteristics of the figure, the input to the second layer convolution, through a nonlinear mapping, the characteristics of the figure from low resolution to high resolution space space transformation, to generate the characteristics of the high resolution block diagram.

$$F_2(Y) = Max(0, W_2 \star F_1(Y) + B_2) \tag{3}$$

Similarly, W_2 is the convolution kernel, and B_2 is the bias vector of the neuron. If it has n_2 convolution kernel, it has n_2 characteristic graph of a dimension after convolution. W_2 size is $n_1 \times f_2 \times f_2 \times n_2$. After the nonlinear operation, the output n_2 dimension vector is the high-resolution block feature expression.

Reconstruction. The high-resolution image reconstruction process can also be considered as a convolution process, with the aim of generating the final high-resolution image using the previously obtained block output feature graph. In the traditional method, the predicted overlapping high-resolution blocks are obtained by means of means. The mean operation can also be viewed as a filter for the feature graph.

$$F(Y) = W_3 \star F_2(Y) + B_3) \tag{4}$$

W_3 Contains 3 (channel number) convolution kernels, so W_3 size is $n_2 \times f_3 \times f_3 \times c$. In the image domain, W_3 is considered to be a mean filter, the whole reconstruction process is a linear operation. Although the purpose of these three steps is very different, it can be used as a convolution layer to form a convolutional neural network.

2.2   FSRCNN

The network has these layers [15]: feature extraction, shrinking, non-linear mapping, expanding and de-convolution. The whole network structure can be seen as a left and right sides that is symmetrical, both ends of convolution kernels is bigger, convolution kernels is smaller structure in the middle (Fig. 2).

Feature Extraction. This layer aims to extract blocks from the original image and get the characteristics of the input image. Actually, each block represents a high dimensional vector. The input image Y is divided into blocks with a certain size, and then image feature information is extracted from blocks by multiple convolution kernels. The formula of feature extraction is shown as

$$F_1(Y) = W_1 \star Y + B_1 \tag{5}$$

Here $\star$ represents convolution symbol, W_1 is convolution kernels, B_1 is the bias vector of neurons.

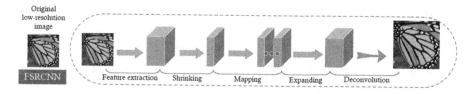

Fig. 2. Structure of FSRCNN

Shrinking. The formula of the other layers is defined as

$$F_i(Y) = W_i \star F_{i-1}(Y) + B_i \qquad (6)$$

Here $\star$ represents convolution symbol, i represents the current layer, W_i, B_i and f_i are convolution kernels, biases and the filter size in the current layer respectively. If convolution kernels number is n_i, W_i size is $n_{i-1} \times f_i \times f_i \times n_i$. In shrinking layer, the size and number of convolution kernels are 1×1 and 12 respectively. It is also the second layer, we set $n_1 > n_2$ aiming to reduce the dimensions of the feature.

Non-linear Mapping. This layer means mapping each feature vector onto another vector. And the number of convolution kernel layers is closely related to the precision and complexity of denoising effect. The greater size of kernels is, the better effect of output may have. But meanwhile the larger amount of calculation will be. Therefore, considering the computational complexity and the experimental effect, the size and number of convolution kernels are 3×3 and 12 respectively. In addition, using more layers mean better denoising results, much more training time and calculation. Layers, the more features to obtain the fine, · the higher the effect, but also increase amount of calculation, time-consuming.

Expanding. The purpose of shrinking is to reduce the dimension of extracted feature and reduce calculation. However, to restore output images, simply base reduced characteristics will lead to lower the quality of the images. Therefore, the purpose of expanding layer is to restore the more image details. the size and number of convolution kernels are 1×1 and 56 respectively.

Deconvolution. For convolution layer, when the step length is set as k, the size of convolution result is $\frac{1}{k}$ of input. On the contrary, for deconvolution layer, when the step length is set as k, the size of convolution result is k times of input. Therefore, in the FSRCNN image super-resolution algorithm, step $k = n$, e set will, n is the desired upscaling factor.

Activation Function. Activation function is used after each convolution layer, aiming to retain the feature and delete the redundant data. FSRCNN takes PReLU(parametric rectified linear unit) as activation function, $f_P(x_i)$ is shown as

$$f_P(x_i) = \max\{x_i, 0\} + a_i \cdot \min\{0, x_i\} \tag{7}$$

Here x_i is the input feature of i_{th} channel, a_i is the coefficient of the negative part. PReLU as an activation function can avoid the occurrence of nerve death, and can make full use of all parameters to test the maximum capacity of different network structures.

3   Improved CNN-Based Denoising Algorithm

The purpose of FSRCNN algorithm is to achieve image super-resolution, simply speaking is to enlarge the image, so the deconvolution layer is used, and the magnification coefficient is the deconvolution step. While in this paper, we are aiming to achieve image noise removal.

The Replacement of Deconvolution. The effect of magnification on deconvolution layer cannot be appeared. So deconvolution is replaced by convolution layer. On the one hand, in order to maintain the depth of convolution network, the replacement is keep to the accuracy of feature extraction; On the other hand, the improved network is more suitable for the requirement of image denoising rather than image super-resolution.

This layer can be expressed by Eq. (6). Convolution kernel size is 5×5. The experimental results show that the deconvolution layer has little effect on the image denoising, and the convolution layer has better results.

The Selection of Training Input Image Channels. Working on image super-resolution, FSRCNN algorithm chooses Y channel of YC_bC_r to extract feature while training $c = 1$. However, for image denoising, only extracting single channel of image cannot remove noise. Because of the presence of noise on all RGB channels, the input of the feature extraction layer and the output of the last layer are all set as 3. It can be explained that the improved network in training input and output are cubes. length and width are the number of features respectively, and height are the number of image 3 channels.

The Network Structure of Improve the Denoising Algorithm. In accordance with the above improvements, convolution network is shown in Fig. 3.

On the whole, the network structure of this article has 9 convolution layers, and is symmetrical on both ends. The first part is feature extraction, which is a convolution layer with 3 input channels, 5×5 kernel size and 56 convolution kernels. The second convolution layer in order to shrinking have 12 convolution kernels with 1×1 size. The next step is non-linear mapping, here we adapt 5 convolution layers, and the size and number of convolution kernels on each layer are 3×3 and 12, respectively. Expanding is used after non-linear mapping, in

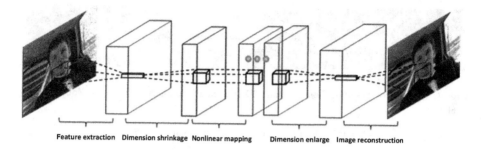

Feature extraction   Dimension shrinkage   Nonlinear mapping   Dimension enlarge   Image reconstruction

Fig. 3. Convolution network structure

which the size of 56 convolution kernels are 1×1. And the final part aiming to image reconstruction is the convolution layer as well, the amount of convolution kernels is 3, which is the same as the output image channels, and the size is set as 5×5.

4 Experimental Results and Analysis

This section mainly introduces a series of experiments and tests, and puts forward the corresponding test plan. The comparisons of different algorithms are used to get the corresponding subjective effect and objective indicators.

4.1 Data and Testbed

This section only considers a network model generated training off-line; the results are compared with traditional algorithms. Training set is collected from 11 standard test videos. We take first 50 frames from each video respectively, next, noise level 10 for the Gaussian noise and 10% of "salt-and-pepper" noise are aided in all of these 550 frames with 352×288 pixels.

The experimental environment includes both hardware and software: Tests are operated on Intel Core i7-5820K CPU 3.30 GHz x12 with NVIDIA GeForce TITAN X and 16 GB RAM; the operating system is 64-bit Ubuntu 14.04 LTS; MATLAB R2014a, CUDA Toolkit 7.0 and OpenCV 3.0 are all used while conducting experiments.

4.2 Comparing with DDID, AMF and SSTV

DDID algorithm [6], AMF algorithm [8] and SSTV algorithm [14] are compared with the proposed algorithm. DDID is the excellent denoising method for Gaussian noise, AMF algorithm is the classical method to remove "salt-and-pepper" noise which is widely used. SSTV is the latest algorithm to remove mixing noise. To ensure reasonable objective test results, this paper chose six representative images to test and makes comparison. Test images are shown in Fig. 4, and image resolutions are presented in Table 1. While training, the maximum number of iterations of our algorithm were 1,710k (Fig. 5).

Fig. 4. Images for testing. *Left to right*: Akiyo, Bus, Carphone, Foreman, Mobile, and Mother

Table 1. The resolution of the test images

	Akiyo	Bus	Carphone	Foreman	Mobile	Mother
Resolution	352×288	352×288	176×144	352×288	352×288	352×288

Fig. 5. Akiyo. Gaussian mixture of "salt-and-pepper" noise denoising subjective effect comparison. *Upper row, left to right*: No noise, mixed noise, DDID. *Lower row, left to right*: AMF, SSTV, and proposed algorithm

4.3 Subjective Results

In this paper, a Gaussian noise level (i.e. standard deviation) of 10 was chosen together with 10% of "salt-and-pepper" noise, both mixed in the test images. We made comparisons with the DDID, AMF, and SSTV algorithms. Due to length limitation, this article only shows a few experimental results, but for commonly used test images. Results are as follows (Figs. 6, 7 and 8).

Fig. 6. Bus. Gaussian mixture of "salt-and-pepper" noise denoising subjective effect comparison. *Upper row, left to right*: No noise, mixed noise, DDID. *Lower row, left to right*: AMF, SSTV, and proposed algorithm

Fig. 7. Mobile. Gaussian mixture of "salt-and-pepper" noise denoising subjective effect comparison. *Upper row, left to right*: No noise, mixed noise, DDID. *Lower row, left to right*: AMF, SSTV, and proposed algorithm

Fig. 8. Mother. Gaussian mixture of "salt-and-pepper" noise denoising subjective effect comparison. *Upper row, left to right*: No noise, mixed noise, DDID. *Lower row, left to right*: AMF, SSTV, and proposed algorithm

It can easily be seen that the DDID algorithm cannot remove "salt-and-pepper" noise; the AMF algorithm can remove "salt-and-pepper" noise, but Gaussian noise still exists; SSTV can remove "salt-and-pepper" noise completely, but images still show some Gaussian noise. The proposed algorithm effectively removes mixed noise, and the subjective-evaluation rates results clearly higher than the results for the other three algorithms.

4.4   Objective Results

The *peak signal to noise ratio* (PSNR) and *structural similarity* (SSIM) are used as the objective evaluation measures. The higher the PSNR value means that the distortion is smaller. If the SSIM values is closer to 1, the processed image is more similar with the original image.

It can be seen from the objective indicators that the proposed algorithm for removing Gaussian noise mixed with "salt-and-pepper" noise has obvious advantages. The SSTV algorithm performs better than the DDID or AMF algorithm, but is still far below the performance of our algorithm. See Table 2.

Table 2. Objective index comparison

Image	Index	DDID	AMF	SSTV	Proposed
Akiyo	PSNR	24.5427	30.0805	31.0245	34.57
	SSIM	0.75877	0.83637	29.858	0.94465
Bus	PSNR	24.1313	28.0554	31.0245	29.555
	SSIM	0.85331	0.90638	0.90533	0.86106
Carphone	PSNR	24.4216	29.179	29.985	29.8847
	SSIM	0.81479	0.8913	0.86902	0.93286
Foreman	PSNR	24.5496	28.9935	30.6801	31.1452
	SSIM	0.77577	0.85722	0.8303	0.91334
Mobile	PSNR	23.9533	26.3506	24.3829	28.4837
	SSIM	0.87847	0.91337	0.89242	0.92859
Mother	PSNR	25.2392	28.6133	31.8036	34.3763
	SSIM	0.75259	0.83353	0.78481	0.93823

5   Conclusions

This article presents a novel CNN-based algorithm for mixed-noise removal in images. The article also presents denoising experiments on images impacted by mixed Gaussian noise and "salt-and-pepper" noise. In a series of tests, we compared the proposed algorithm with the traditional DDID algorithm, AMF algorithm, and the SSTV algorithm. Experiments show in subjective and objective indexes that the proposed method has better results in general, removing noise more clearly. Furthermore, applying the PSNR and SSIM measures, which are commonly used as image-evaluation standards for noise-removal algorithms, the paper shows that the proposed method can produce better noise-removal effects.

Acknowledgement. I would like to extend my heartfelt thanks to a host of people without whose assistance the accomplishment of this paper would have been impossible. They are Bijun Li, Jian Zhou and my supervisor Huyin Zhang. I am also grateful to Reinhard Klette (Auckland), whose valuable instruction has benefited me a great deal. Authors thank Reinhard Klette (Auckland University of Technology, New Zealand) for comments on the paper.

References

1. Jiang, J., Zhang, L., Yang, J.: Mixed noise removal by weighted encoding with sparse nonlocal regularization. IEEE Trans. Image Process. **23**, 2651–2662 (2014)
2. Rudin, L.I., Osher, S., Fatemi, E.: Nonlinear total variation based noise removal algorithms. Physica D **60**(1–4), 259–268 (1992)
3. Aharon, M., Elad, M., Bruckstein, A.: K-SVD: an algorithm for designing over complete dictionaries for sparse representation. IEEE Trans. Signal Process. **54**(11), 4311–4322 (2006)

4. Dabov, K., Foi, A., Katkovnik, V., et al.: Image denoising by sparse 3-D transform-domain collaborative filtering. IEEE Trans. Image Process. **16**(8), 2080–2095 (2007)
5. Knaus, C., Zwicker, M.: Dual-domain image denoising. In Proceedings of IEEE International Conference Image Processing, pp. 440–444 (2013)
6. Xiao, J., Li, W., Jiang, H., Peng, H., Zhu, S.: Three dimensional block-matching video denoising algorithm based on dual-domain filtering. J. Commun. **9**, 91–97 (2015)
7. Hwang, H., Haddad, R.A.: Adaptive median filters: new algorithms and results. IEEE Trans. Image Process. **4**(4), 499–502 (1995)
8. Ko, S.J., Lee, Y.H.: Center weighted median filters and their applications to image enhancement. IEEE Trans. Circ. Syst. **38**(9), 984–993 (1991)
9. Chen, T., Wu, H.R.: Space variant median filters for the restoration of impulse noise corrupt-ed images. IEEE Trans. Circ. Syst. II Analog Digital Signal Process. **48**(8), 784–789 (2001)
10. Cai, J.F., Chan, R.H., Nikolova, M.: Fast two-phase image deblurring under impulse noise. J. Math. Imaging Vis. **36**(1), 46–53 (2010)
11. Mitra, K., Veeraraghavan, A., Chellappa, R.: Robust RVM regression using sparse outlier model. In: 2010 IEEE Conference on Computer Vision and Pattern Recognition (CVPR), pp. 1887–1894. IEEE (2010)
12. Liu, J., Tai, X.C., Huang, H., et al.: A weighted dictionary learning model for denoising images corrupted by mixed noise. IEEE Trans. Image Process. **22**(3), 1108–1120 (2013)
13. Aggarwal, H.K., Majumdar, A.: Hyperspectral image denoising using spatio-spectral total variation. IEEE Geosci. Remote Sens. Lett. **13**(3), 442–446 (2016)
14. Burger, H.C., Schuler, C.J., Harmeling, S.: Image denoising: can plain neural networks compete with BM3D? In: 2012 IEEE Conference on Computer Vision and Pattern Recognition (CVPR), pp. 2392–2399. IEEE (2012)
15. Xiao, J., Liu, T., Zhang, Y., et al.: Multi-focus image fusion based on depth extraction with inhomogeneous diffusion equation. Signal Process. **125**(C), 171–186 (2016)
16. Dong, C., Loy, C.C., Tang, X.: Accelerating the super-resolution convolutional neural network. In: Leibe, B., Matas, J., Sebe, N., Welling, M. (eds.) ECCV 2016. LNCS, vol. 9906, pp. 391–407. Springer, Cham (2016). https://doi.org/10.1007/978-3-319-46475-6_25
17. Dong, C., Chen, C.L., He, K., et al.: Image super-resolution using deep convolutional networks. IEEE Trans. Pattern Anal. Mach. Intell. **38**(2), 295 (2016)
18. Krizhevsky, A., Sutskever, I., Hinton, G.E.: ImageNet classification with deep convolutional neural networks. In: Advances in Neural Information Processing Systems, pp. 1097–1105 (2012)

A Systematic Scheme for Automatic Airplane Detection from High-Resolution Remote Sensing Images

Jiao Zhao[1,2], Jing Han[2], Chen Feng[2], and Jian Yao[2(✉)]

[1] Department of Sociology, Wuhan University,
Wuhan, People's Republic of China
[2] School of Remote Sensing and Information Engineering, Wuhan University,
Wuhan, People's Republic of China
jian.yao@whu.edu.cn

Abstract. Airport and airplane are typical objects in remote sensing research field. However, there are rare methods to detect airport and airplane in a unit system. In this paper, we propose a systematic scheme for airport detection and airplane detection from high-resolution remote sensing images. The airport detection part is mainly based on the parallel line features of runway, containing six main stages: down-sampling, Frequency-Tuned (FT) saliency detection, Line Segment Detector (LSD) line detection, line growing, parallel lines detection and line clustering. The airplane detection part is mainly based on Circle Frequency Filter (CF-filter) and a Fast R-CNN deep learning model. Experimental results on 500 high-resolution remote sensing images acquired more than 95% accuracy, and the average detection time was about 14 s, which proved that the proposed system was effective and efficient.

Keywords: Airplane detection · High-resolution remote sensing images
Circle Frequency Filter · Deep learning

1 Introduction

Airplane detection is one of the hot and important application in the processing of high-resolution remote sensing images and many methods have been proposed.

In the early research, Circle Frequency Filter (CF-filter) and template matching had been the principal methods. Cai et al. [1] presented the approach to detect airplanes by constructing a CF-filter. Liu et al. [2] proposed a coarse-to-fine method by integrating shape priors. Li et al. [3] proposed detecting aircrafts using a contour-based spatial model. With the exploring of generic framework, more robust methods for object detection were proposed [4–10].

Current object detection algorithms mainly contain two parts: proposals extraction and object identifying. Li et al. [11] first used CF-filter to locate the airplane candidates, then accomplished precise airplane detection by combining HOG and AdaBoost algorithms. For the aircraft target, the CF-filter is an effective method to highlight the airplane center points from the background. However, some points of background objects like terminals and runways also meet the conditions of CF-filter. So, to detect

© Springer International Publishing AG, part of Springer Nature 2018
S. Satoh (Ed.): PSIVT 2017, LNCS 10799, pp. 465–478, 2018.
https://doi.org/10.1007/978-3-319-92753-4_36

airplane in large images more efficiently, we should first locate airport area that indicate the candidate locations of airplanes. Some airport detection methods have been proposed in recent years and can be classified into two groups: one is based on image segmentation [12–14] and the other is built on edge detection [15–19].

In this paper, we propose a systematic airplane detection algorithm. We firstly propose a new airport detection method that is based on FT saliency detection and LSD line detection algorithm. Then a new airplane detection algorithm is proposed by combining CF-filter and Convolutional Neural Networks (CNNs).

The paper is organized as follows: In Sect. 2, airport detection is discussed. In Sect. 3, airplane detection algorithm is introduced. In Sect. 4, experiments on our own built dataset are discussed. In Sect. 5, the paper closes with conclusion.

2   Airport Detection

In this section, we will introduce the airport detection algorithm. FT saliency detection is first applied to down-sampled image, and then, LSD line detection is applied. Next, the final line segments is obtained through line connection, short line removal and parallel line selection. Finally, we accumulate adjacent parallel line segments and the area with minimum circumscribed rectangle is the obtained airport region.

2.1   Down-Sample and FT Saliency Detection

Dataset. Our own built dataset Computer Vision and Remote Sensing Dataset for Airports (CVRS-Airports) contains 534 remote sensing images from airports around the world. The image resolution is either 4 or 8 m, and average image size is almost 1 G. Examples of the dataset are shown in Fig. 1.

(a)   (b)   (c)   (d)

Fig. 1. CVRS-Airports.

Down-Sample. As the original remote sensing images are too large, we down-sample images to 4000 × 4000 as exemplified in Fig. 2. In such scale, we can reduce the amount of data as much as possible without hurting image quality.

FT Saliency Detection. We take advantage of Frequency-tuned saliency detection to remove background and increasing the accuracy of LSD line segments. FT saliency

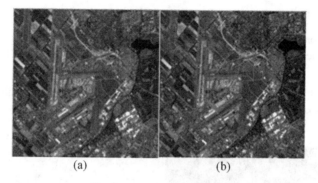

Fig. 2. Down-sample the image: (a) Original image; (b) Down-sampled image.

detection algorithm is applied to the down-sampled image, and generate full resolution saliency image as illustrated in Fig. 3.

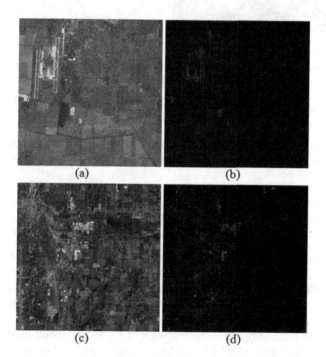

Fig. 3. The original high-resolution remote sensing image and FT saliency detection result: (a) and (c) are the original images; (b) and (d) are the FT saliency detection result of (a) and (c).

As we can see, FT saliency detection algorithm removes most of the background, and we can see the runways of airport clearly.

2.2   Airport Region Locating Based on LSD

The process for airport detection includes four major parts: Application of LSD, line segment connection, parallel line segment extraction and parallel line segment accumulation.

Application of LSD. We apply LSD line segment algorithm to the FT saliency image, obtaining line segments as shown in Fig. 4.

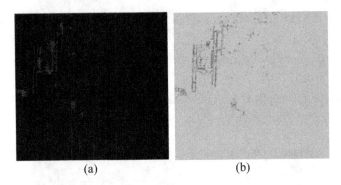

(a)   (b)

Fig. 4. LSD detection result: (a) is the FT saliency image; (b) is the LSD detection result of (a).

As illustrated in Fig. 4. LSD has successfully detected the line segments. The line segments of runway are much more outstanding compared with those in other areas.

Line Segment Connection. Line segment connection aims at making line segments of runway continuous. Three conditions should be satisfied simultaneously. They are listed as follows:

(1) The line segments are nearly parallel.
(2) The line segments are close to each other.
(3) The line to be connected is on the extension line of another straight line.

Firstly, according to strategy 1, we calculate the angles of all the line segments detected by the LSD, and sort by the degree. Then the line segments that have similar degrees will be calculated to determine whether to be connect. As shown in Fig. 5, α, δ, β, γ represent the angles of AB, CD, EF and GH respectively. If we take AB as our reference, then GH is excluded for which degree of γ is different from that of α. EF is excluded for the distance between the midpoint of EF and midpoint of AB. However, the distance of the midpoint of CD is close to the extension line of AB, so CD is preserved, and should be connected to the line segment AB.

To connect AB and CD, the length of AC, AD, BC and BD are all calculated firstly. Then the two points having the longest distance will be connected. As shown in Fig. 5, the new line AD will be generated and may be connected with other line segments. However, the AB and CD lines will not be used again.

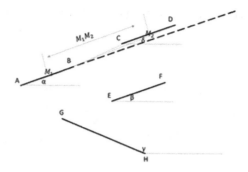

Fig. 5. Line segment connecting.

With the proposed strategies, we could implement the line segment connecting process. Obviously, the line segments are effectively connected and this will be helpful for the subsequent detection process.

Parallel Line Segment Extraction. The airport runway is usually expressed as a pair or pairs of parallel lines in the remote sensing image. Thus, we extract long straight lines in the next stage. Line segments in the airport regions are characterized by following factors:

(1) Line segments in the airport area are parallel.
(2) Line segments in the airport area have a certain length.
(3) The distance between two straight lines is much smaller than the length of two straight lines.

So, we find parallel lines firstly according to their angles of slope, and then calculating the distance between the two midpoints of parallel line segments to determine whether it is a pair of parallel lines. As shown in Fig. 6, AB, CD and EF are parallel. Due to the distance between M1 and M2 is less than a certain threshold, AB and CD will be marked as a pair of parallel lines, and EF will be excluded.

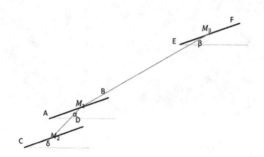

Fig. 6. Parallel line segment extraction.

Parallel Line Segment Accumulation. We can observe that there will be some error detection lines due to the interference of some non-airport areas in the image. So, we propose a new linear clustering algorithm to get more accurate location of the airport as illustrated in Fig. 7.

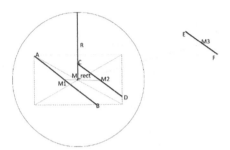

Fig. 7. Parallel line segment accumulation.

As can be seen from Fig. 7, AB, CD and EF are the parallel straight lines. Firstly, we take the longest straight line AB as our reference, taking the length as the radius, and using the AB midpoint as the center of the circle to search straight lines. Then, as the CD line is included in the range of the circle, we add the CD line to the first class as S1. The range of S1 is denoted by the minimum enclosing rectangle of the straight line AB and CD. Then, we take the center of the rectangle S1 as the center, rectangular diagonal as the radius to update the searching circle. When the S1 class no longer have straight line to be added, stop the S1 update, search the remaining lines, find the longest line in the remaining lines, set the S2 class, iterate over the above steps until all the lines are added to a category. After the set of S = {S1, S2, ..., Sn} is obtained, the smallest rectangular area included in the outermost boundary point is taken as the airport area. Example of the extraction results is shown in Fig. 8.

(a)   (b)

Fig. 8. Airport area extraction results.

As shown in the Fig. 8, the airports in remote sensing image are extracted and the detection boxes are very accurate. Moreover, the average detection time is 14 s.

3   Airplane Detection

After obtaining the airport regions in remote sensing image, we focus on airplane detection. Firstly, we quickly locate airplane candidate regions by CF-filter. Then, the well trained CNNs model is used to validate airplanes.

3.1   Candidate Location Extraction by CF-Filter

Airplane Features Analysis. The region of candidate airplane is extracted based on two common features. Firstly, airplanes have different pixel values from background. Secondly, airplanes generally contain four main bulges: head, tail, and two symmetrical wings. As shown in Fig. 9, the intensities along the circle will change regularly from darkness to brightness and will repeat four peaks and valleys. Clearly, the periodicity only happens when the proper circle is chosen. Then we could calculate the Fourier transform amplitude of the array, and the regions with the amplitude with the higher values are the candidate plane regions.

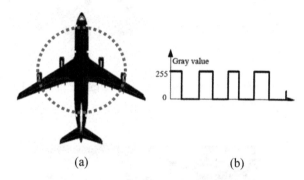

(a)   (b)

Fig. 9. Airplane feature analysis: (a) is the airplane image; (b) is the intensities periodicity of (a) along the circle.

CF-Filter. Assume a pixel $p(x,y)$ in the image, and $f_i (i = 0, 1, \ldots, N-1)$ are the pixel values array along the circle with radius R, where N represents the length of the array, and R is smaller than half length of wingspan and larger than half width of fuselage. Then we can obtain the expression of CF-filter by using Eq. (1):

$$F(x,y) = (\sum_{k=0}^{N-1} f_k \cos(8\pi \frac{k}{N}))^2 + (\sum_{k=0}^{N-1} f_k \sin(8\pi \frac{k}{N}))^2 \tag{1}$$

as illustrate in the Fig. 10, we can find that the amplitudes of airplane center areas are much greater than other regions after filtering by CF-filter.

Proposals Generation. We obtain maximum response M of CF-filter, and choose threshold scale factor α $(0 < \alpha < 1)$. Points with response values greater than αM are described as candidate points. Then, using the BLOB detection algorithm, the center point of BLOB is obtained as center of the candidate aircraft target as illustrated in Fig. 11.

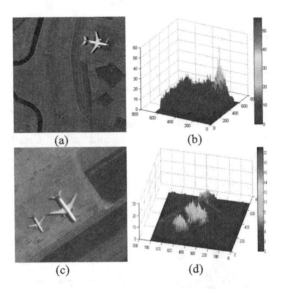

Fig. 10. The response of CF-filter: (a) and (c) are the airplane images; (b) and (d) are the CF-filter responses of (a) and (c).

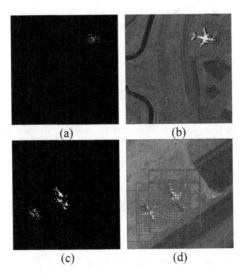

Fig. 11. The candidate regions of airplanes: (a) and (c) are the CF-filter response images; (b) and (d) are the extracted candidate regions of (a) and (c).

From Fig. 11, we can see that the extracted candidate box accurately selects the location of the aircraft.

3.2   Identify Airplanes by CNNs Model

Different from traditional target detection method using the manual set of features, deep learning method extracts target features through independent learning.

Fast R-CNN. We use the deep learning method of Fast R-CNN to identify airplanes. The architecture is illustrated in Fig. 12. An input image and multiple regions of interest (RoI) are put into the network. Each RoI is pooled into a fixed-size vector and then mapped to a feature vector by fully-connected layers. The network has two output vectors per RoI: softmax probabilities and per-class bounding-box regression offsets.

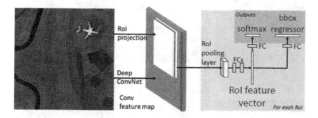

Fig. 12. Fast R-CNN architecture.

Dataset. Our own built dataset Computer Vision and Remote Sensing Dataset for Airplanes (CVRS-Airplanes) are downloaded from Google Earth with a resolution of 0.3 m. It contains 16596 airplane samples, and each sample size is between 800×800 and 1300×1300. Samples of the dataset are shown in Fig. 13.

Fig. 13. CVRS-Airplane samples.

CNNs Model Training and Airplane Detection. From the CVRS-Airplanes dataset, we randomly select 8479 training samples, 4239 validation samples and 4238 test samples. We send the candidate airplane regions generated by CF-filter into Fast R-CNN model and set the candidate box with a score higher than 0.5 for the correct detection of aircraft. Samples of the detection results are shown in Fig. 14.

Fig. 14. Airplanes detection results.

The results in Fig. 14 show that the algorithm can accurately extract aircrafts, and is able to extract aircraft targets with various sizes and directions. The 4000 samples in the test set show that the detection accuracy is more than 95%.

4　Experiment and Analysis

The proposed system is implemented on 438 remote sensing images obtained from Google Earth which have 0.12 m resolution. The system is run under C/C++ program, and the computer has Intel Core i5 with 3.2 GHz, 8 GB memory.

In the first experiment, airport detection module is tested. Figure 15 shows several results. The detection accuracy is 92%, which proves the effectiveness of our method. It is worth noting that average detection time for each airport is less than 14 s.

In the second experiment, we make a comparison between the method that uses the FT saliency method with the method that not utilizes the FT saliency method in terms of airport detection accuracy as exemplified in Fig. 16.

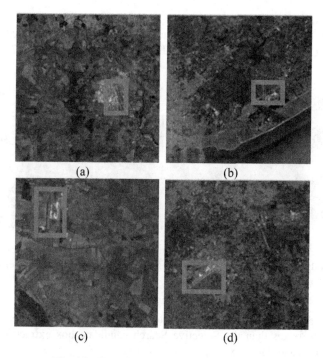

Fig. 15. Samples of airport detection results.

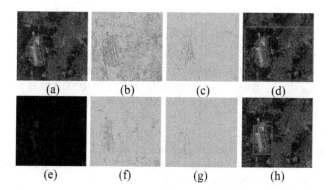

Fig. 16. Austin international airport detection result: (a) The source remote sensing image; (b) LSD detection result on the original image; (c) Parallel line test results on (b); (d) The final airport area detection results on the (c) map; (e) FT saliency detection result; (f) LSD detection result on the saliency detection map; (g) Parallel line test results on (f); (h) The final airport area detection results on the (g) map.

Observing the final extraction area of several results, we can find that the results of the use of FT are significantly more concentrated in the real airport area. The area of the airport area that does not use this FT saliency algorithm is very large.

In the third experiment, we compare CF-filter candidate extraction method and Selective Search method in detection accuracy and the number of candidate regions to be generated. Examples of the experimental results are shown in Fig. 17.

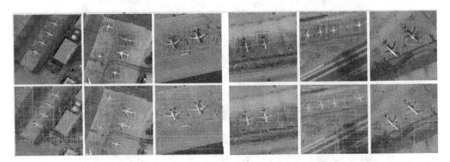

Fig. 17. CF-filter VS. Selective Search. The first row: candidate region extraction results using CF-filter method; the second row: candidate region extraction results using Selective Search algorithm.

As can be seen from Fig. 17, the CF-filter candidate region extraction method has fewer candidate boxes than the Selective Search candidate box extraction algorithm, and its resulting candidate boxes are more accurate.

In the fourth experiment, we compared the CNNs model with the HOG+SVM model (Table 1).

Table 1. CNNs method precision-recall statistics.

Score	0.5	0.6	0.7	0.8	0.9	**0.9450**
Precision	0.9486	0.9663	0.9702	0.9798	0.9884	**0.9978**
Recall	0.9521	0.9497	0.9477	0.9412	0.9333	**0.9222**
F-Measure	0.9503	0.957	0.9588	0.9601	0.9600	**0.9584**

Experiments show that the generalized ability of the CNNs model is much higher than that of the HOG+SVM method. The results of the CNNs method are more accurate than that of the HOG+SVM method (Table 2).

Table 2. HOG+SVM method precision-recall statistics.

Score	0.5	0.6	0.7	0.8	0.9	**0.9450**
Precision	0.8489	0.8663	0.8864	0.9098	0.9384	**0.9578**
Recall	0.9102	0.9062	0.8988	0.8875	0.8652	**0.8432**
F-Measure	0.8784	0.8858	0.8925	0.8985	0.9003	**0.8968**

5 Conclusion and Future Works

In this paper, we proposed a coarse-to-fine method to detect airplane in the high-resolution remote sensing images. CF-filter is used to remove most background and extract the candidate regions of airplanes in coarse stage. In the fine stage, we applied CF-filter algorithm to extract objects in candidate regions. And then, CNNs model is used to identify the airplanes. We have built a unit system based on this method and experimental results on 500 high-resolution remote sensing images and 16000 samples containing more than 60000 airplanes acquired more than 95% accuracy, with an average detection time of about 14 s, which proved the good performance of this proposed method.

Although our algorithm was implemented for the detection of airport and airplane in a remote sensing image, the idea can be generalized and applied to other fields such as car detection in air bone images, where we can similarly first detect the candidate regions and then further detect cars in the regions. In the future, we will explore more application domains of our proposed method.

References

1. Cai, H., Su, Y.: Airplane detection in remote-sensing image with a circle-frequency filter. In: International Conference on Space Information Technology, Proceedings of SPIE, Wuhan, China, vol. 5985, November 2005
2. Liu, G., Sun, X., Fu, K., Wang, H.: Aircraft recognition in high-resolution satellite images using coarse-to-fine shape prior. IEEE Geosci. Remote Sens. Lett. 10(3), 573–577 (2013)
3. Li, Y., Sun, X., Wang, H., Sun, H., Li, X.: Automatic target detection in high-resolution remote sensing images using a contour-based spatial model. IEEE Geosci. Remote Sens. Lett. 9(5), 886–890 (2012)
4. Yao, J., Zhang, Z.F.: Semi-supervised learning based object detection in aerial imagery. In: IEEE Conference on Computer Vision and Pattern Recognition (CVPR), pp. 1011–1016 (2005)
5. Zheng, H., Hu, X.M., Si, X.S., Yang, W.B.: A novel object detection approach for satellite imagery based on danger theory. In: International Conference on Intelligent Networks and Intelligent Systems, pp. 445–448 (2008)
6. Inglada, J.: Automatic recognition of man-made objects in high resolution optical remote sensing images by SVM classification of geometric image features. ISPRS J. Photogrammetry Remote Sens. 62(3), 236–248 (2007)
7. Renard, N., Bourennane, S.: Improvement of target detection methods by multiway filtering. IEEE Trans. Geosci. Remote Sens. 46(8), 2407–2417 (2008)
8. Bourennane, S., Fossati, C., Cailly, A.: Improvement of target-detection algorithms based on adaptive three-dimensional filtering. IEEE Trans. Geosci. Remote Sens. 49(4), 1383–1395 (2011)
9. Sun, H., Sun, X., Wang, H., Li, Y., Li, X.: Automatic target detection in high-resolution remote sensing images using spatial sparse coding bag-of-words model. IEEE Geosci. Remote Sens. Lett. 9(1), 109–113 (2012)
10. Zhang, W., Sun, X., Fu, K., Wang, C., Wang, H.: Object detection in high-resolution remote sensing images using rotation invariant parts based model. IEEE Geosci. Remote Sens. Lett. 11, 74–78 (2013)

11. Li, W., Xiang, S.M., Wang, H.B., Pan, C.H.: Robust airplane detection in satellite images. In: 2011 18th IEEE International Conference on Image Processing (ICIP), pp. 2821–2824 (2011)
12. Radhakrishna, A., Appu, S.: SLIC superpixels compared to state-of-the-art superpixel methods. IEEE Trans. Pattern Anal. Mach. Intell. **34**, 2274–2281 (2012)
13. Felzenszwalb, P., Huttenlocher, D.: Efficient graph-based image segmentation. Int. J. Comput. Vis. **59**(2), 167–181 (2004)
14. Akcay, H.G., Aksoy, S.: Automatic detection of geospatial objects using multiple hierarchical segmentations. IEEE Trans. Geosci. Remote Sens. **46**(7), 2097–2111 (2008)
15. He, L.H., Carin, L.: Airport detection in large aerial optical imagery. In: IEEE International Conference on Acoustics, Speech, and Signal Processing, Proceedings (ICASSP 2004), pp. 761–764 (2004)
16. Lei, Z., Fang, T., Huo, H., Li, D.R.: Rotation-invariant object detection of remotely sensed images based on texton forest and hough voting. IEEE Trans. Geosci. Remote Sens. **50**, 1206–1217 (2012)
17. Tao, C., Tan, Y.H., Cai, H.J., Tian, J.W.: Airport detection from large IKONOS images using clustered SIFT key points and region information. IEEE Geosci. Remote Sens. Lett. **8**, 128–132 (2011)
18. Atteia, G.E., Collins, M.J.: On the use of compact polarimetry SAR for ship detection. ISPRS J. Photogrammetry Remote Sens. **80**(6), 1–9 (2013)
19. Alonso, M.T., Lopez-Martinez, C., Mallorqui, J.J., Salembier, P.: Edge enhancement algorithm based on the wavelet transform for automatic edge detection in SAR images. IEEE Trans. Geosci. Remote Sens. **49**(1), 222–235 (2011)

Author Index

Printed in the United States
By Bookmasters